Palgrave Studies in Classical Liberalism

This series offers a forum to writers concerned that the central presuppositions of the liberal tradition have been severely corroded, neglected, or misappropriated by overly rationalistic and constructivist approaches.

The hardest-won achievement of the liberal tradition has been the wrestling of epistemic independence from overwhelming concentrations of power, monopolies and capricious zealotries. The very precondition of knowledge is the exploitation of the epistemic virtues accorded by society's situated and distributed manifold of spontaneous orders, the DNA of the modern civil condition.

With the confluence of interest in situated and distributed liberalism emanating from the Scottish tradition, Austrian and behavioral economics, non-Cartesian philosophy and moral psychology, the editors are soliciting proposals that speak to this multidisciplinary constituency. Sole or joint authorship submissions are welcome as are edited collections, broadly theoretical or topical in nature.

More information about this series at
http://www.palgrave.com/gp/series/15722

Walter E. Block • Roy Whitehead

Philosophy of Law

The Supreme Court's Need for Libertarian Law

palgrave
macmillan

Walter E. Block
Loyola University
CARROLLTON, LA, USA

Roy Whitehead
University of Central Arkansas
Conway, AR, USA

ISSN 2662-6470 ISSN 2662-6489 (electronic)
Palgrave Studies in Classical Liberalism
ISBN 978-3-030-28359-9 ISBN 978-3-030-28360-5 (eBook)
https://doi.org/10.1007/978-3-030-28360-5

This Palgrave Macmillan imprint is published by the registered company Springer Nature Switzerland AG.
The registered company address is: Gewerbestrasse 11, 6330 Cham, Switzerland

Contents

Introduction

The libertarian philosophy of law is based on the premise that no one may threaten or initiate violence against other people or their legitimately owned property. The source of licit ownership is broadly based upon Lockean homesteading principles and self-ownership.

As such, libertarianism is not very controversial. Who, after all, advocates murder, rape, or theft, quintessential violations of this code? However, when this perspective is applied to a whole host of legal issues, the fireworks begin. For the mainstream view on these issues is very much in the direction of *violating* these supposedly acceptable to all principles.

This book will lay out the libertarian philosophy in all of its dimensions and apply it to several very fascinating issues, including the following: sexual, religious and racial discrimination, environmentalism, markets in human body parts, drug legalization, the Boy Scouts and anti-gay discrimination, sexual harassment, and criminology.

A person could be forgiven for thinking that this collaboration is one between "strange bedfellows." Block, best described as a New York City Jew, hails from Brooklyn. Whitehead is a "good old boy" from the backwoods of Arkansas.

We both crossed paths while professors at the business school at the University of Central Arkansas (UCA), in Conway, AR. Roy taught business ethics and business law, and Walter was the chair of the economics and finance department.

What was the occasion of our first meeting? It was in 1998, when our business school was faced with the accreditation process from the Association to Advance Collegiate Schools of Business (AACSB). This was very important to us, since without it we would not be accredited and suffer all sorts of grievous penalties. One of the dimensions upon which we would be rated was the quantity and also the quality of the publications authored by the UCA professors. Hard copies of these journal articles (published in the previous five years) were duly collected and perused by the entire professoriate.

It turned out that by far the most voluminous publishers were the two of us. We were head and shoulders above all our colleagues in this regard, pretty much tied with each other at about 40 articles each (our third best colleagues registered only in the low teens). Not unexpectedly, the two of us expressed interest in each other's writings, began to have lunch together, formed a friendship, and then began to collaborate with each other in future publications. The first of these appeared in print in 1999, and appears as Chap. 1 in the present book. Our co-authorships continued for many years (Whitehead has retired from UCA, and Block took up a professoriate with Loyola University New Orleans in 2001), and our last one saw the light of day in 2017, and appears as Chap. 16 below.

We have had some interesting experiences in having these article of ours published, mainly, in law reviews. Typically, Whitehead would write the first half of our essays, and Block the last half. Whitehead, a lawyer, would typically discuss, describe, analyze, and pontificate upon extant law and court decisions. The contribution of Block, an economist and libertarian theoretician, was very different. Instead of looking at the state of law, he would opine about what the law should be, a rather different undertaking.

When academics publish in the field of economics, they are allowed to submit their papers only to one journal at a time. If their first foray was rejected, they would typically try a second scholarly publication, and so on, seriatim. The process for law reviews is quite different. Here, one could submit an essay to dozens, even hundreds of them at a time. Naturally, in the latter case, we would receive dozens of responses for each submission. Many rejected our feeble efforts outright, and, as you can see, below, some few accepted them (as it happens, every piece we co-authored appeared in a law review; this book compiles them).

The most interesting of these letters fit into neither of these categories, neither accepting our submissions outright nor rejecting them entirely. In this category, editors might say something along the following lines: "The first half of this essay is splendid. It constitutes a sober, measured, information-packed analysis of the xyz subject. But the second part was written by a madman, an ignoramus, a moron, and idiot, someone who should be incarcerated in a mental institution. If you break up this article into two parts, we will gladly publish the first, brilliant, half of it. But the second part should be confined to the dustbin." Very, very rarely, did the opposite occur. Here is a paraphrase of the second type of editorial response: "The first half of this essay is dull, boring, repetitive of other work, and singularly unhelpful. But the second part is magnificent, brilliant, creative. We will accept this otherwise wonderful essay for publication, if you deep-six the opening section." We presume that none of these editors knew which author was primarily responsible (we each helped the other with our contributions) for which section of these papers.

Needless to say, we stuck together through thick and thin. We never broke ranks. We rejected all offers of publication which praised only one section of these papers, some from very prestigious law reviews.

You now have fair warning about the chapters you are about to read. We expect that most people who pick up this book will like it in its entirety. But, there may well be some who are edified by one part of each chapter, and horrified, or bored, by the other. Happy reading.

Walter E. Block
Roy Whitehead

Part I

Discrimination

1

Gender Equity in Athletics

Background

For years intercollegiate athletics has offered interested and able students opportunities to experience the lessons of competition, develop physical and leadership skills, be a part of a team, and perhaps most important, enjoy themselves. Good intercollegiate athletics programs require competitive parity, universal and consistently applied rules, and an opportunity to participate according to one's interest and ability. The majority of National Collegiate Athletic Association (NCAA) members have sought to assure the foregoing conditions, but there is considerable evidence that they have not fully succeeded with regard to women.

Because there was no assurance of equal opportunity in the range of components of education, Congress enacted Title IX of the Educational Amendments of 1972.[1] The federal law stipulates that:

> [n]o person in the United States shall, on the basis of sex, be excluded from participation in, be denied the benefits of, or be subjected to discrimination

[1] 20 U.S.C. §1681 *et seq*. (1972).

W. E. Block, R. Whitehead, *Philosophy of Law*, Palgrave Studies in Classical Liberalism,
https://doi.org/10.1007/978-3-030-28360-5_1

> under any education program or activity receiving federal financial assistance.[2]

Interestingly, an often ignored subsection of the statute, often quoted by football coaches, provides:

> [N]othing contained in subsection (a) … shall be interpreted to require any educational institution to grant preferential or disparate treatment to the members of one sex on account of an imbalance that may exist with respect to the total number or percentage of persons of that sex participating in or receiving the benefits of any federally supported program or activity, in comparison with the total number or percentage of persons of that sex in any community, State, section or other area.... (20 U.S.C. §1681(b))

In 1991, the NCAA surveyed its member's expenditures for women's and men's athletics programs. The survey revealed that undergraduate enrollment was roughly equally divided by sex, but men constituted 69.5% of the participants in intercollegiate athletics, and their programs received approximately 70% of the athletics scholarship funds, 77% of operating budgets, and 83% of recruiting money.[3]

In response to the study, the NCAA appointed a Gender Equity Task Force that submitted its report during July 1993. The Task Force, in its report, defined gender equity as follows:

> An athletics program can be gender equitable when the participants in both men's and women's sports programs would accept as fair and equitable the overall program of the other gender.[4]

The report defined the ultimate goal of gender equity as:

> The ultimate goal of each institution should be that the numbers of male and female athletes are substantially proportionate to their numbers in the institution's undergraduate population.[5]

---

[2] 20 U.S.C. §1681(a) (1972).

[3] Final report of the NCAA Gender-Equity Task Force, page 1, 1993, hereinafter referred to as The Report.

[4] The Report, page 2.

[5] The Report, page 3.

In January 1994, the NCAA members gave a lukewarm endorsement of gender equity by voting to encourage member institutions to follow the "law" concerning gender equity.[6] One purpose of this article is to review the guiding regulations and cases that interpret the "law" for the benefit of those who are interested in effectively accommodating the interest and abilities of women athletes. We are concerned that the Federal court decisions which have dealt specifically with Title IX and "gender equity" have generally failed to focus on the real meaning of Title IX, "fully and effectively accommodating the interests and abilities of women athletes." This is due to a misguided focus almost solely on proportionality in numbers rather than on a real accommodation of athletic abilities.

Another goal of this article is to philosophically and legally examine the underlying principles of gender equity in athletics. To this end, we will criticize this "law" from a perspective based on property rights and economic freedom.

What Are the Requirements?

Part I

The primary sources of gender equity responsibilities are found in Title IX, the implementing regulations,[7] and, perhaps more important, the Title IX Athletics Investigators Manual used by the Department of Education, Office of Civil Rights (OCR).[8] Judges who are involved in Title IX cases frequently cite the Office of Civil Rights Manual as authority. The OCR takes several major factors into account in determining whether intercollegiate athletic programs are gender equitable. The program components are[9]:

1. Accommodation of athletic interests and abilities;
2. Equipment and supplies;
3. Scheduling of games and practice times;

[6] Amendment No. 2-1, Principle of Gender Equity, NCAA Convention, January 1994.

[7] 34 C.F.R. Part 106, effective July 21, 1975, see also 34 C.F.R. §106.41 and §106.37 (1992).

[8] Title IX Athletics Investigators Manual, Office of Civil Rights, Department of Education, 1990, hereinafter referred to as the Manual.

[9] 34 C.F.R. §106.41 and 34 C.F.R. §106.37 (1992).

4. Travel per diem allowance;
5. Opportunity to receive coaching and academic tutoring;
6. Assignment and compensation of coaches and tutors;
7. Locker rooms, practice, and competitive facilities;
8. Medical and training facilities and services;
9. Housing and dining facilities and services;
10. Publicity; and,
11. Athletic scholarships.

Although all the program components are considered important, perhaps the most relevant issue is whether or not the university is providing an effective accommodation of students' interests and abilities. The regulations require institutions that offer athletics programs to accommodate effectively the interests and abilities of students of both genders to the extent necessary to provide equal opportunity in selection of sports and levels of competition. The Office of Civil Rights uses three factors to assess the opportunity for individuals of both genders to compete in intercollegiate programs:

1. Whether intercollegiate level participation opportunities for male and female students are provided in numbers substantially proportionate to the respective enrollments;
2. Where members of one sex have been and are underrepresented among intercollegiate athletics, whether the institution can show a history and continuing practice of program expansion which is demonstrably responsive to the developing interests and abilities to that sex; and
3. Where members of one sex are underrepresented among intercollegiate athletics, and the institution cannot show a continuing practice of program expansion such as that cited above, where it can show that the interests and abilities of the members of that sex have been fully and effectively accommodated by the present program.[10]

Unfortunately, very few institutions, especially those with football programs, are able to meet the first test, proportionality. Additionally, a

[10] 34 C.F.R. §106.41(c)(1) (1992).

training session with an author of the OCR Investigators Manual reveals that no institution, to his knowledge, has ever met the second test consisting of a history and practice of program expansion responsive to the interests and abilities of women.[11]

Given that few institutions can meet parts one and two of the test, we must focus on whether the institution is effectively accommodating the interests and abilities of the underrepresented sex.

Recall that the NCAA Gender Equity Task Force defined gender equity as having the same proportion of female and male athletes as in the undergraduate student body. Much to the dismay of some interest groups, OCR has ruled that the third part of the test may be satisfied by the institution showing it has accommodated the interest and abilities of its female students, although there may be a substantial disproportionality of numbers between male and female athletes. According to the OCR, this may be demonstrated by showing that the opportunity to participate in intercollegiate athletics is consistent with the interests of enrolled women undergraduates who have the ability to play college sports, which can be determined by an external survey of the university's recruiting area, including high school and junior college competition, summer league competition, and sanctioned state sports. The university need only accommodate women who have the ability to play at the intercollegiate level.[12]

The Office of Civil Rights does not generally interview undergraduates who cannot play at the intercollegiate skill level. It is clear, however, that if the undergraduate survey, or external survey of the recruiting area, suggests that potential female students who possess the required interest and ability are present, and there is a reasonable availability of competition for a team, they must be accommodated. If the conference, for example, has women's softball, and softball interests and abilities are discovered in the undergraduate population and the recruiting area, the university must accommodate this by inaugurating a woman's softball team.

---

[11] Remarks of Lamar Daniel, Office of Civil Rights, Gulf South Conference Meeting, Birmingham, Alabama, January 26, 1994.

[12] The Manual, Effective Accommodation of Students Interests and Abilities, pp. 21–28, see also 34 C.F.R. §106.41(c)(1) (1992).

Secondly, there is perhaps the most misunderstood area of gender equity compliance, athletic financial assistance. OCR regulations provide that:

> [Institutions must provide reasonable opportunities for athletic scholarships awards for members of each sex in proportion to the number of students of each sex participating in … intercollegiate athletics.[13]

OCR will determine compliance with this provision of the regulation primarily by means of a financial comparison. The requirement is that proportionately equal amounts of financial assistance (scholarship aid) are available to men's and women's athletics programs. This rule is often misinterpreted as mandating that the amount of financial assistance to male and female athletes be proportionate to their undergraduate enrollments. For example, if a university has 60% female and 40% male, 60% of the financial assistance would have to go to female athletes. Fortunately, or unfortunately, depending on one's point of view, the foregoing is not the test for compliance.

OCR measures compliance with the athletic financial assistance standard by dividing the amounts of aid available for members of each sex by the numbers of male or female participants in the athletic program and tabulating the results. Institutions may be found in compliance if this comparison results in substantially equal amounts (plus or minus 2 to 4%) or if a resulting disparity can be explained by adjustments that take into account a legitimate, nondiscriminatory factor.[14] Because of this interpretation, the institution described above with an undergraduate enrollment of 60% female and 40% male may be in compliance if it spends equal amounts on each male and female athlete even if there are more male than female athletes. For example, if it has an athletic financial assistance budget of $1 million and spends $700,000 of that on 70 male athletes and $300,000 on 30 female athletes. Note that if 60% of the participants in athletics programs are men, then male athletes should receive about 60% of the available athletic financial assistance even if the

[13] 34 C.F.R. §106.37 (1992).

[14] The Manual, pp. 14–20.

undergraduate female enrollment exceeds the male undergraduate enrollment.

If the financial assistance provided is not substantially equal, the Office of Civil Rights will determine whether there is a legitimate nondiscriminatory factor to explain the difference.[15] For example, the institution can justify the differences in awards by noting the higher costs of tuition for students from out of state that in some years may be unevenly distributed between men's and women's programs. These differences are nondiscriminatory if they are not the result of policies or practices which limit the availability of out of state scholarships to either men or women. Further, an institution may decide the awards most appropriate for program development. Often this may initially require the spreading of scholarships over as much as four years for developing programs. This may result in the award of fewer scholarships in the first few years than would be necessary to create equality between male and female athletes. The OCR Investigators Manual, however, directs investigators to investigate carefully "reasonable professional decisions" when there is a negative effect on the underrepresented sex.

The regulations require "equitable" treatment for female athletes in the provision of equipment and supplies.[16] The OCR defines equipment and supplies as uniforms, other apparel, sports-specific equipment and supplies, instructional devices, and conditioning and weight training equipment. In assessing compliance, the OCR takes a careful look at the quality, amount, suitability, maintenance and replacement, and availability of equipment and supplies to both male and female athletes. If there is a disparity, the university is in violation. The OCR permits nondiscriminatory differences based on the unique aspects of particular sports, and the regulations do not require equal expenditures for each program. For example, the equipment for the (male) football team may be more expensive than the equipment for the women's volleyball team.[17]

[15] The Manual, p. 19.

[16] 34 C.F.R. §106.41(c)(2) (1992).

[17] The Manual, page 29.

The regulations also require equality in the scheduling of games and practice time.[18] OCR assesses five factors in determining compliance. They are[19]:

1. Number of competitive events per sport;
2. Number and length of practice opportunities;
3. Time of day competitive events are scheduled;
4. Time of day practice opportunities are scheduled; and
5. Opportunities to engage in preseason and postseason competition.

Considerable emphasis is placed on practice and game time. It is usual for women's practice to be scheduled immediately before or immediately after men's. As a result, female athletes may have to skip lunch or dinner or eat a very light lunch or dinner to effectively participate. Additionally, it is common to schedule women's games before men's games and start them at about 5:30 p.m. This results in denying female athletes the opportunity to have their parents, friends, and acquaintances present at the event unless they live nearby or can get off work early. To be in compliance, some programs have adopted a rotating schedule for practice and/or games. For example, every other women's game would start at 7:30 rather than 5:30. The men's team would alternate, correspondingly.

The regulations require an assessment to decide whether the athletic program meets the travel and per diem allowances requirement.[20] OCR assesses the following factors to decide compliance[21]:

1. Modes of transportation;
2. Housing furnished during travel;
3. Length of the stay before and after competitive events;
4. Per diem allowance; and
5. Dining arrangements.

---

[18] 34 C.F.R. §106.41(c)(3) (1992).

[19] The Manual, pp. 35–42.

[20] 34 C.F.R. §106.41(c)(4) (1992).

[21] The Manual, pp. 43–48.

The easy way for an athletic program to ensure compliance is to treat male and female teams alike. If male athletes stay two to a room, they should house female athletes in the same manner. If the male team travels by airplane, the comparable female team should do so also. If they provide the male team a catered meal before the event, this should apply to the female team as well.

The regulations also require equality in the opportunity to receive academic tutoring, and assignment and compensation of tutors.[22] OCR looks for the academic qualifications, training, experience, and compensation of tutors. If there is any disparity in the opportunity to receive academic tutoring and assignment and compensation of tutors, the university is violating Title IX.[23]

The regulations require equality in the opportunity to receive coaching and assignment and compensation of coaches.[24] The OCR looks at three factors in this regard. They are:

1. Relative availability of full-time coaches;
2. Relative availability of part-time and assistant coaches; and
3. Relative availability of graduate assistants.

The OCR lists two factors to be assessed in determining compliance in assignment of coaches:

1. Training, experience, and other professional qualifications; and
2. Professional standing.

The policy interpretation lists seven factors in determining compliance in compensation of coaches. They are:

1. Rate of compensation;
2. Duration of contract;
3. Conditions relating to contract renewal;
4. Experience;

---

[22] 34 C.F.R. §106.41(c)(5) (1992).

[23] The Manual, pp. 49–54.

[24] 34 C.F.R. §106.41(c)(5) & (6) (1991).

5. Nature of coaching duties performed;
6. Working conditions; and
7. Other terms and conditions of employment.

Whether opportunity to receive coaching assignments and compensation of coaches is "equitable" has been difficult to determine. This is because of the subjectivity involved in assessing the training, experience, and professional qualifications of coaches assigned to men's and women's programs. Although the OCR seems to limit its investigation to the experience and qualifications of the coaches, at least one case seems to suggest that another factor, the size of the crowds and the ability to attract boosters, may be a factor in compensation.[25] The intent of the regulation is that equal athletic opportunity be provided to participants, not coaches. When a coach's compensation is based on seniority or longevity, a recognized method of paying employees, alleging that a female team coach with five years of experience is somehow being discriminated against because he or she receives less than a coach with 15 years of experience is difficult to prove. This brings up an interesting point because it is possible for a male coach of a female team to be protected under this provision because the intent of the Act is to provide effective coaching to females.

Perhaps the most important regulation from the health and safety aspect of athletics is the regulation that requires equal medical and training facilities and services.[26] In the recent past, and perhaps in some institutions today, female athletes only have access to trainers after male athletes or, sometimes, not to anyone but assistant trainers or graduate assistants. It is not too unusual for the head trainer to travel with the men's teams and a graduate assistant or an assistant trainer to travel with the women's teams. One can be assured that the discovery of such information during the compliance review will result in a finding of discrimi-

[25] In the case of *Stanley v. University of Southern California*, 13 F.3d 1313 (9th Cir. 1994), the court found that evidence of the male coach's greater responsibility in raising funds and level of responsibility justified the disparity in salary The court said that the men's team "generated greater attendance, more media interest, and larger donations" and that the men's coach, George Raveling, has fund-raising duties not required of the women's coach. The court found that the university was not responsible for "societal discrimination in preferring to witness men's sports in greater numbers."

[26] 34 C.F.R. §106.41(8) (1992).

nation in violation of Title IX. To assess compliance and provision of medical training facilities, OCR investigates five areas.[27] They are:

1. Availability of medical personnel and assistants;
2. Health, accident, and injury insurance coverage;
3. Availability and quality of weight and training facilities;
4. Availability and quality of conditioning facilities; and
5. Availability and qualification of athletic trainers.

The regulations specifically require gynecological care coverage where such health problems are a result of participation in the athletics program.[28] Schools must either hire a trainer for the women's programs who possesses the same qualifications as the counterpart for the men's programs, or have the travel with the teams on a rotating basis. There can also be other considerations; for example, some women's team coaches prefer a female trainer because she can room with the female players and reduce expenses.

To achieve substantial proportionality in accommodating interests and abilities of both male and female athletes, it is clear that OCR will carefully review the recruitment of student athletes.[29] OCR looks at three factors in assessing compliance. They are:

1. Whether coaches or other professional athletic personnel in the program serving male and female athletes are provided with substantially equal opportunities to recruit;
2. Whether financial and other resources made available for recruitment in male and female athletic programs are equivalently adequate to meet the needs of each program; and
3. Whether differences in benefits, opportunities, and treatment afforded prospective student athletes of each sex have a disproportionately limiting effect on the recruitment of students.

---

[27] The Manual, pp. 72–80.

[28] 34 C.F.R. §106.39 (1992).

[29] 34 C.F.R. §106.41 (1992) and the Manual, pp. 97–101.

OCR carefully checks the recruitment funds allotted to each team and compares the proportionate recruitment funds with the proportion of male and female athletes in the athletics program. In judging whether or not the resources are equivalently adequate to meet the needs of each program, the OCR determines the availability of recruitment resources to both men's and women's programs, including access to telephones, recruitment brochures, mailing costs, and travel.

They allow nondiscriminatory differences in some cases. For example, the recruiting of budget for a particular team either male, or female, may be increased because of a disproportionate number of student athletes either graduated or dropped out of the program in a particular year, thereby requiring extra effort to replace them.

What Is Compliance?

The federal courts, in at least three instances, have appeared to impose a more stringent accommodation test than the Office of Civil Rights.[30] Recall that the regulations state that an institution is in compliance if it can show that it "fully and effectively accommodates the interests and abilities of female students who have the ability to participate in intercollegiate sports." Most federal court cases stress that the percentage of female athletes accommodated has to be proportionate to the total female undergraduate enrollment rather than relate solely to those women who have the interests and abilities to participate.

For example, in a case involving Colorado State University, the court found that there was a 10.5% disparity in the percentage of women athletes and undergraduate women students. If determined that the female participation in intercollegiate sports was not substantially proportionate to female enrollment and ordered the university to reinstate a woman's softball team, hire a coach, and maintain a competitive schedule.[31]

---

[30] *Cohen v. Brown University*, 991 F.2d 888 (1st Cir. 1993) and *Cohen v. Brown University*, 879 F.Supp. 185 (D.RI. 1995); *Roberts v. Colorado State Board of Agriculture*, 998 F.2d 824 (10th Cir. 1993), and *Favia v. Indiana University of Pennsylvania*, 812 F.Supp. 578 (W.D. PA 1993) Aff'd 7 F.3d 322 (3d Cir. 1993).

[31] *Roberts v. Colorado State Board of Agriculture*, 998 F.2d 824 (10th Cir. 1993).

In an ongoing case involving Brown University, the court ordered reinstatement of female teams when there was about a 13% disparity between the percentage of female athletes and the percentage of females in undergraduate enrollment.[32] The Colorado State University case is difficult to square with Title IX because the opinion appears to rely solely on the proportionality test and to de-emphasize the "interest and abilities test." This strong reliance on proportionality is contrary to the OCR regulations that tend to treat the prongs of the three-part test equally.[33]

The statute also prohibits reliance solely on proportionality by providing "Nothing contained in subsection (a) … shall be interpreted to require any educational institution to grant preferential or disparate treatment to the members of one sex on account of an imbalance which may exist with respect to the total number or percentage of persons of that sex participating in or receiving the benefits of any federally supported program or activity, in comparison with the total number or percentage of persons of that sex in any community, State, section or other area…."[34]

The question posed is whether the strong emphasis on proportionality in the Colorado State and Brown cases is, or should be, the trend in the law. Unfortunately for this determination, the U.S. Supreme Court denied certiorari in both cases.[35] To provide appropriate guidance, the question we must answer is: How will other Circuit Courts of Appeals deal with the regulatory three-prong test and ultimately, what will the U.S. Supreme Court do when they eventually grant certiorari?

To answer the question, the remainder of Part I of this chapter will deal with the decisions on the merits and appeals in the four separate decisions involving *Cohen v. Brown University*,[36] the District Court deci-

---

[32] *Cohen v. Brown University*, 809 F.Supp. 978 D.RI. 1992, Aff'd. 991 F.2d 888 (1st Cir. 1993).

[33] 34 C.F.R. §106.41(c)(1) (1992).

[34] 20 U.S.C. §1681(b) (1972).

[35] Roberts v. Colorado State Board of Agriculture, 998 F.20 824 (10th Cir. 1993), cert. denied U.S.___(1994).

[36] Prior to trial on the merits of the Brown cases, the district court granted the plaintiffs a preliminary injunction, ordering the women's volleyball and gymnastics teams be restored from club to university funded status, Cohen v, Brown, 809 F.Supp. 978 (D.RI. 1992) ("Brown I"). The first circuit upheld the district court's decision after reviewing the district court's analysis of Title IX and the implementing regulations. Cohen v. Brown, 991 F.2d 888 (1st Cir. 1993) ("Brown II"). On

sion in *Peterson v. Louisiana State University*,[37] and the recent "Clarification of Intercollegiate Athletics Policy Guidance: the Three Part Test"[38] (The Clarification) distributed by the U.S. Department of Education, Office of Civil Rights.

Brown I and II: The District Court, in Brown I, while assessing this University's compliance with Title IX, specifically addressed whether it accommodated effectively "the interest and abilities of students to the extent necessary to provide equal opportunity in the selection of sports and levels of competition available to members of both sexes."[39] The Court commenced by stating that it may not find a violation solely because there is a disparity between the gender composition of the educational institution and student constituency, on the one hand, and its athletic programs, on the other.[40] The Court, however, stated that Subsection (b) also provides that it "shall not be construed to prevent the consideration in any proceedings … of statistical evidence tending to show that such an imbalance exists with the respect to the participation in, or the receipt of benefits of, any such program or activity by the members of one sex."[41]

The judges concluded that an institution satisfied prong one (proportionality) if the gender balance of its intercollegiate athletic program substantially *mirrors* the gender balance of its student enrollment.[42] Taking the view that the phrase "substantially proportionate" must be a standard stringent enough to effectuate the purposes of the statute,[43] the Court said that Title IX established an illegal presumption that discrimination exists if the university does not provide participation opportunities to

---

remand, the district court found that Brown's intercollegiate program violated Title IX and the supporting regulations. Cohen v. Brown 879 F.Supp. 185 (D.RI. 1995) ("Brown III"). Brown appealed and on November 21, 1996, the First Circuit affirmed. Cohn v. Brown, No. 95-2205 (1st Cir. 1996) ("Brown IV").

[37] No. 94-247, Slip. Op. (Md. La. Jan. 22, 1996).

[38] Letter from Norma Cantu, Assistant Secretary for Civil Rights, U.S. Department of Education, to Colleges and Universities (Jan. 16, 1996).

[39] 991 F.2d 888 (1st Cir. 1993).

[40] Id. at 18.

[41] Id. at 19.

[42] Id. at 33.

[43] Id. at 36.

men and women in substantial proportionality to their respective student enrollments.[44] It found that the numerical disparity between male and female athletes in Brown's program, approximately 13%, was not "substantially proportionate" and was certainly not a mirror image of the gender of the respective male and female enrollments.[45] The Court concluded that Brown University did not meet the requirements of prong one of the three-part test.[46]

With regard to prong two, the issue was whether the institution can show a history and continuing practice of program expansion which is demonstrably responsive to the developing interest and abilities of the members of the underrepresented sex.[47] Prong two illustrates that Title IX does not require the University to leap to complete gender parity in a single bound. It does, however, require an institution to show that it has continued to increase the number of underrepresented athletes participating in intercollegiate athletics.[48] The Court stated that schools may not twist the ordinary meaning of the word "expansion" to find compliance under prong two when schools have increased their relative percentage of women participating in athletics by making cuts in both men's and women's sports.[49] Because Brown had attempted to comply with prong two by reducing both men and women's sports to equalize proportionality, the Court found it had failed the prong two test.

The Court said that prong three (interests and abilities) requires a relatively simple assessment of whether there is unmet need in the underrepresented gender that rises to a level sufficient to form a new team or require the upgrading of an existing one.[50] Thus, if athletes of the underrepresented gender have both the ability and interest to compete at the intercollegiate level, they must be fully and effectively accommodated.[51] Institutions need not upgrade or create a team where the interest and

---

[44] Id. at 45.
[45] Id. at 47.
[46] Id. at 50.
[47] Id. at 50.
[48] Id. at 51.
[49] Id. at 51.
[50] Id. at 52.
[51] Id. at 52.

ability of the students are not sufficiently developed to field a varsity team.[52]

Brown declared that "to the extent students interests in athletics are disproportionate by gender, colleges should be allowed to meet those interests incompletely as long as the schools response is in direct proportion to the comparative level of interests."[53] In other words, Brown argued that it may accommodate *fewer* than all of the interested and able women if, on a proportionate basis, it accommodates *fewer* than all the interested and able men.

The Court took considerable pains to address why this reading of Title IX was flawed. Brown argued that they could read the third prong, providing for accommodation of interests and abilities, separately from prong one, requiring substantial proportionality. This view was rejected because the policy interpretation, which requires full accommodation of the underrepresented gender, draws its essence from the statute and requires an evaluation of the athletic program as a whole.[54]

Secondly, the Court stated that any argument that prong three somehow countervails the meaning of prong one is wrong. Such a position overlooks the accommodation test's general purpose: to decide whether a student has been "excluded from participation in, or denied the benefits of," an athletic program on the basis of sex. The test is whether or not the athletic program as a "whole" is reasonably constructed to carry out the statute.[55] Brown's proposal would be contrary to the purpose of the statute. It would determine athletic interest and abilities of students in such a way as to take into account the nationally increasing levels of women's interest and abilities as related to their population in the student body. The Court clearly did not agree that full and effective accommodation can satisfy the statute when prong one proportionality is not found.

Brown's reliance on student surveys of interest and abilities was also found at fault. The Athletic Investigators Manual (The Manual) stated that the intent of its provisions was to use surveys of interest and abilities

---

[52] Id. at 52.

[53] Id. at 53.

[54] Id. at 53.

[55] Id. at 54.

to follow a determination that an institution does not satisfy prong three: they could not use it to make that determination in the first instance.[56] The Court was also concerned that a survey of interests and abilities of the students at Brown would not be a true measure of their interest and abilities because the school's recruiting methods could predetermine such interests and abilities in the first place.[57] The judges noted that the test was full and effective accommodation, in the whole program, not solely an accommodation of interests and abilities at the expense of disregarding proportionality.[58] Prong three would excuse Brown's failure to provide substantial proportionate participation and opportunities only if this University fully and effectively accommodate the underrepresented sex. But Brown did not comply with prong three because it failed to increase the number of intercollegiate participation and opportunities available to the underrepresented sex and also failed to maintain and support women's donor-funded teams at Brown's highest level, thus preventing athletes on those teams from developing fully their competitive abilities and skills.[59]

Finally, the Court found that far more male athletes were being supported at the University-funded varsity level than female athletes, and thus, women receive less benefit from their intercollegiate varsity programs as a whole than do men.[60]

Louisiana State: In *Peterson v. Louisiana State*,[61] the District Court examined prongs one, two, and three, of the three-part test in the context of whether the University had fully and effectively accommodated the interests and abilities of its female students. The plaintiffs argued that Louisiana State University (LSU) failed to accommodate its female athletes by providing greater athletic opportunities to its male students at a time when the sufficient interest and ability existed in its female student population to justify

[56] Id. at 56.
[57] Id. at 56.
[58] Id. at 60.
[59] Id. at 61.
[60] Id. at 65.
[61] No. 94-247(MD. La. Jan. 22, 1996).

increasing women's sports opportunities.[62] The specific complaint concerned a perceived failure to provide a woman's fast pitch softball team.

Relying on *Colorado State* and *Brown*, both plaintiffs and defendants asked the Court to find that, so long as males and females are represented in athletics in the same proportion as found in the general student population and are given numerically proportionate opportunity to participate in advanced competition, the university should be in compliance with Title IX. Further, if numerical proportionality is not found, the university should be deemed in violation of Title IX.[63] The Court rejected this proposition and specifically stated that it disagreed with the rationale of the *Brown* and *Colorado State* opinions. "Title IX does not mandate equal numbers of participants. Rather, it prohibits exclusion based on sex and requires equal opportunity to participate for both sexes."[64] Therefore, ending the inquiry at the point of numerical proportionality does not comport with the mandate of the statute. Title IX specifically does not require preferential disparate treatment based on proportionality. Rather, those percentages should be considered as evidence "tending to show that such an imbalance exists with the respect to the participation in, or receipt of benefits of, any such program or activity by members of one sex." Consequently, the clear language of the statute prohibits the requirement of numerical proportionality and regarded the Brown case as a "safe harbor" for a university. Clearly, the pivotal element of the LSU analysis is the question of effective accommodation of interests and abilities. Given the foregoing, it was imperative that LSU be acquainted with the interests and abilities of its female students.

Because this University had not conducted a survey of its female students, the Court found that there was no creditable evidence to establish their actual interests and abilities. LSU simply had no method, discriminatory or otherwise, by which a determination could be made. This school was, and had been, ignorant of the interests and abilities of its student population for some time.[65]

---

[62] Id. at 10.

[63] Id. at 14.

[64] Id. at 15.

[65] Id. at 16.

The trial evidence found that LSU's student population during the relevant period was approximately 51% male and 49% female, and its athletic participation for the same period was about 71% male and 29% female.[66] Throughout the relevant period, LSU fielded a man's baseball team. The Court accepted evidence that women's fast pitch softball was the closest approximation to this sport.[67]

The plaintiffs established that there was sufficient interest and ability at LSU to fill a successful Division I varsity fast pitch softball team since 1979 and that for some unknown reason, in 1983, LSU disbanded that program. The plaintiffs also were able to establish that the interest in fast pitch softball increased since 1979.[68] They presented credible evidence that they themselves had an interest in playing intercollegiate varsity fast pitch softball plus the requisite ability. Finally, and critically, the plaintiffs established that intercollegiate play is provided for male students with similar interests and abilities by way of the varsity baseball team.[69] At the same time, LSU provided absolutely no opportunity for women to compete in fast pitch softball at any level.

By not fielding a women's fast pitch softball team, LSU was not accommodating the interests and abilities of the plaintiffs individually and at least one segment of its total female student population. The Court's findings suggested that sex discrimination accounted for the discrepancy.[70]

The Court then examined the history of expanding opportunities for women athletes at LSU and concluded that the University has demonstrated a practice not to expand women's athletics at the University before it became absolutely necessary to do so.[71] It could find no evidence of a workable plan of action by the University to address the failure to accommodate interests and abilities of women students and concluded that LSU was violation of Title IX. The Court noted that LSU was a national leader in resisting gender equity.[72]

---

[66] Id. at 17.

[67] Id. at 17.

[68] Id. at 17.

[69] Id. at 17.

[70] Id. at 17.

[71] Id. at 18.

[72] Id. at 18.

The Court, in a harsh assessment of the athletic department, wrote that its director's one-dimensional assessment of programs created an atmosphere of arrogance by management that had continued to be undaunted by the facts, up to the date of the trial.[73] LSU's action was seen as a direct result of the director's belief that his "women's athletics" program was "wonderful."[74] He equated winning teams, rather than participation, as accommodating interest and abilities. The judge interpreted the violations as a result of an arrogant ignorance, and confusion regarding the practical requirements of the law, and a remarkable outdated view of women athletes which created the resistance to change.[75]

A comparison of *LSU* with *Brown* and *Colorado State* clearly shows a potential split in the circuits concerning the proportionality requirement. According to *LSU,* the theory that numerical proportionality is a "safe harbor" is contrary to the prescriptions of Title IX because it treats women as a class rather than as individuals. This decision appears to support the use of surveys to determine the unmet interests and abilities of the student body. In contrast, *Brown* shows surveys are inherently unreliable because they only reflect the predetermined interest of the student body.

Policy Guidance: On January 16, 1996, the Office of Civil Rights released its long overdue "Clarification of Intercollegiate Athletics Policy Guidance: Three Part Test." It starts off by focusing on the athletics programs as a whole. This is interesting because the same language is used in *Brown*, *Louisiana State*, and the Clarification.[76] The latter states that an institution's failure to provide nondiscriminatory participation opportunities for the whole student body usually amounts to a denial of equal athletic opportunity.

The clarification appears to follow past policy interpretation concerning prong one of the three-part test. It states, "where an institution provides intercollegiate level athletic participation opportunities for male and female students in numbers substantially proportionate to the respective full-time undergraduate enrollments, OCR will find that the institu-

[73] Id. at 20.

[74] Id. at 20.

[75] Id. at 20.

[76] Letter from Norma Cantu, Assistant Secretary for Civil Rights, U.S. Department of Education (Jan. 16, 1996).

tion is providing nondiscriminatory participation opportunities for individuals of both sexes."[77] The so-called safe harbor test is still safe as far as the OCR is concerned despite the reluctance of the court in the LSU case.

The test for part two remains essentially the same. Under part three, OCR says that the institution must provide equal athletic opportunity to its admitted and enrolled students. Accordingly, the policy interpretation does not require an institution to accommodate the interests and abilities of merely potential students. This would appear to mean an institution need not accommodate the interests and abilities of potential female athletes in its recruiting area. How does that advance the interest of the underrepresented sex? This question is left unanswered by the policy.

Among the factors OCR uses to determine whether female interests and abilities are being accommodated are[78]:

1. Requests by students and admitted students that a particular sport be added;
2. Requests that an existing club sport be elevated to intercollegiate team status;
3. Participation rates in particular or intramural club sports;
4. Interviews with students, admitted students, coaches, administrators, and others regarding interest in particular sports;
5. Results of questionnaires of students and admitted students regarding interest in sports;
6. Participation in particular interscholastic sports by admitted students.

Finally, the clarification suggests that schools have flexibility in choosing a nondiscriminatory method of determining athletic interests and abilities provided they meet the appropriate requirements.[79]

Brown IV, The Appeal: Brown appealed the district court's order to effect changes (Brown III) and challenged the analysis of the three-part test employed by the district court in Brown I which was approved by the

[77] Id. at 5.

[78] Id. at 6.

[79] Id. at 6.

First Circuit in Brown II. The Appeals court stunned Brown by announcing it had squarely rejected Brown's reading of the three-part test and that under the "law of the case" doctrine the Court was precluded from relitigating the issues previously decided. It affirmed the district court's finding concerning Brown's obligation to fully and effectively accommodate the interests and abilities of women athletes. The appellate court did, however, again take strong issue with Brown's argument that it could meet prong three of the three-part test by incompletely meeting the interests and abilities of women to the same extent that it incompletely meets the interests and abilities of men. If there are sufficient unmet interests and ability among the underrepresented sex, the institution necessarily failed the test, said the Court: "Brown reads the 'full' out of the duty to accommodate fully and effectively. Prong three demands not partial, but full and effective accommodation." Brown's interpretation of full and effective accommodation is not the law because it cannot withstand scrutiny on legal or policy grounds.

The Appellate Court again stressed the importance of the proportionality "mirror" image test by observing that a school creates a presumption it is in compliance when it has achieved a statistical balance. Further, in its view, when a statistical balance is not present, the school must fully and effectively accommodate women's interests and abilities even when that requires a larger slice of the athletic department pie go to women's programs.

Finally, the Court viewed with distaste Brown's argument that there is a gender-based difference in the level of interest in sports participation that should be considered to allow fewer participation opportunities for women. They viewed such a position as an attempt to ignore the purpose of Title IX and to rely on an outdated stereotyping of women's interests. In its view, the perceived lack of interest evolves directly from the historical lack of opportunity for women to participate in sports; precisely what Title IX is designed to remedy. Several times the Court pointed out that Title IX implementation deserves some credit for the showing of American women athletes in the Olympic summer games.

The Dissent: Schools with football programs may find some comfort in the dissent because for the first time a judge advocated that contact sports, like football, should be eliminated from the calculus. The judge cited 34 C.F.R. section 106.41 (b) which says that a school may have separate teams for members of each sex "when selection is based on ... activity involving a contact sport." In counting participation opportunities for comparison of proportionality, it does not make sense to compare athletes who participate in contact sports that include only men's teams, said the judge. He believed that not all sports are the same and the school should be able to choose those most beneficial.

Discussion

Given the law, the Brown case was properly decided because the university failed all three parts of the test, not just the one mandating proportionality. But there are several problems with both the courts' and the OCRs' strong emphasis on a "substantially proportionate to female enrollment test." First, failure to achieve strict proportionality need not be evidence of discrimination and therefore cannot be used as a shortcut to determine whether an institution is unlawfully discriminating based on sex.[80] Congress explicitly held that proportionality alone was not relevant when it stated that the statute should not be interpreted to require preferential disparate treatment to members of one sex on account of an imbalance which may exist with respect to the total number of percentages of persons of that sex participating in institutional programs.[81]

Secondly, the courts have no authority to impose liability under a Federal antidiscrimination law unless a defendant has unlawfully discriminated.[82] Title IX simply provided that no individual may be excluded from a federally funded program on "the basis of sex." A holding, as in

[80] The Supreme Court has strongly cautioned lower courts against comparisons to the general population when special interests or qualifications are required. *Hazelwood School District v. U.S.*, 433 U.S. 299, 308 N.13 (1977). In a recent voting rights case, the Supreme Court held that proportionality cannot serve as a shortcut to determine whether a set of districts unlawfully dilutes minority voting strength, *United States v. Florida*, No. 92-512 (1994).

[81] 20 U.S.C. §1681(b) (1972).

[82] St. Mary's Honor Center v. Hicks, 113 S. Ct. 2742, 2751 (1993); see also *Cannon v. University of Chicago*, 648 F.2d 1104, 1109 (7th Cir.), cert. denied 454 U.S. 1128 (1981) where the 7th Circuit states that "a violation of Title IX requires an intentional discriminatory act and that disparate impact alone is not sufficient to establish a violation."

the Colorado State case, that the lack of proportionality creates a disparate impact, without considering the impact on accommodating interest and ability, runs contrary to cases that indicate that "a violation of Title IX requires an intentional discriminatory act and that disparate impact alone is not sufficient to establish a violation."[83] For a violation to occur there must be a failure to accommodate interests and abilities. Because Title IX provisions are virtually identical to Title VI of the Civil Rights Act of 1964, the Court should look to Title VI cases which hold that the act only "reaches instances of intentional discrimination."[84]

Colorado State and to some extent *Brown* disregard the plain meaning of the statute concerning proportionality. These decisions are not in the best interest of the institutions subject to the law nor to the intended beneficiaries, female students. *Colorado State* holds conduct discriminatory which the statute does not prohibit and appears to specifically permit without regard to the actual interest of female students.[85] Educational (and other) institutions should be able to rely on reasonable implementing regulations promulgated by the responsible government agency. That agency has published regulations that contain the three-part test including accommodation of interest and abilities of members of both sexes. The OCR regulations explicitly provide that a sports team is required when there is (1) interest; (2) ability to play the sport; (3) a likelihood that the team can be sustained for a number of years; and (4) a reasonable expectation of competition within the institution's normal competitive region.[86] Admittedly, it may be difficult in some instances to fashion an

---

[83] *Cannon v. University of Chicago*, 648 F.2d 1104, 1109 (7th Cir.), cert. Denied 454 U.S. 1128 (1981).

[84] Alexander v. Choate, 469 U.S. 287, 293 (1985). Additionally, Title IX is patterned after Title VI. *Grove City v. Bell*, 465 U.S. 555, 566 (1984). By setting up the same administrative structure and using virtually the same language, Congress intended that the interpretation of Title IX was to be the same as Title VI. See Hearing before the House subcommittee on Post Secondary Education of the Committee on Education and Labor, 94th Cong., 1st Sess. 16, 150 (1971).

[85] The *Roberts* Court was apparently relying on *Guardians Association v. Civil Service Commission of New York*, 463 U.S. 582 (1982) to justify a holding that a federal agency, or in this case a court, may proscribe, as discriminatory, conduct which the statute itself does not prohibit. The courts reliance is misplaced because the court in Guardians found that the authority was delegated to the agency by statute. Unlike the Guardians case, the Congress in Title IX specifically withheld authority to take action on account of a statistical imbalance between the sexes, see 20 U.S.C. 1981(b).

[86] C.F.R. §106.41(c)(1) (1992).

instrument to achieve a good measure of the interest and abilities in the particular area. However, a properly designed and conducted study of the institution's drawing and recruiting area can be used to accurately determine whether the interest and abilities of female athletes are being fully accommodated. Such a survey is a much better, and more intellectually honest, measure of compliance with the intent of the Title IX than an unreasoning reliance on numbers.

The analysis should focus on the athlete's interest and ability to participate in college sports. One cannot seriously argue that all students have the same ability to participate at the university level. Data collected must focus on the disparity between male and female athletes who have the interest in and ability to compete rather than on the number of males and females in the entire educational community. A simplistic percentage comparison without considering competitive qualifications for varsity athletics lacks real meaning.[87] The rationale of *Colorado State* and *Brown*, insofar as they are based solely on statistical disparity, does not allow the university reasonably to present possible interest and ability justifications.

Finally, a reasonable fact finder should be able to listen to evidence and decide if a college is making a good faith effort to meet the "interests and abilities" test. In an article appearing in the *Arkansas Democrat-Gazette* regarding the lack of junior women golfers in the state of Arkansas, Arkansas State University's women's golf coach, Neil Able, stated, "I would love to recruit girls from Arkansas, but they are not here. There is not a lot of emphasis on girls golf, nobody seems to be pushing it. It is really a shame because if a girl can shoot between 78 and 82, she can get her education mostly paid for."[88]

Clearly, this kind of information would be relevant evidence of whether there is sufficient female interest and ability to justify a team in the sport of golf in Arkansas. The bottom line is that when a college or university is honestly accommodating the interests and abilities of its female undergraduates, and potential participants in its recruiting area, the intent of the Title IX and the OCR guidelines have been met.

---

[87] *City of Richmond v. J.A. Crosen Co.*, 488 U.S. 469, 501 (1989) and *Mayor v. Educational Equity League*, 415 U.S.605, 620 (1974).

[88] *The Arkansas Democrat-Gazette*, July 31, 1994, at C 10, Col. 2.

What Does It All Mean?

Some athletic administrators, particularly at football-playing institutions with a majority female enrollment, have placed considerable faith, or maybe hope, in their ability to comply with Title IX by accommodating the interests and abilities of female athletics who have the ability to participate at the collegiate level. This faith, or hope, has been shattered by several courts' perceived reliance solely on proportionality, the first of the three factors used by OCR to assess the equality of opportunity for individuals of both sexes to participate in intercollegiate programs. In *Favia*, *Cohen*, and *Roberts*, the court found that the participation rates for male and female students were not proportionate to their respective enrollments. Most commentators in analyzing these decisions have focused solely on the first prong and concluded that effective accommodation always requires substantial proportionality of numbers. There has been an unquestioned acceptance that only the first part of the test is relevant.

But this analysis is factually incorrect and even disingenuous. These decisions were compatible with the law: the three involved universities failed to meet any of the three requirements, including the interests and abilities test. Because the three universities failed all three parts of the test, their cases offer no precedent relevant to a school which meets the interest and abilities test.

A compelling argument can be made that a college which meets the third part of the test (i.e., accommodates the interests and abilities of its male and female students) is in compliance with Title IX. The purpose of the statute is to provide equality of opportunity. The Louisiana State case clearly supports that view. Use of the first step, the proportionality test, without considering the interests and abilities of female students, would have little value in providing equal opportunity to the actual students with ability to play at the college level. What is the logical extension of the proportionality argument which does not include interests and abilities? It would demand female teams even if there were no interests on the part of the women students. Substantial proportionality erroneously presumes that men and women in the general student body will have the same interest and ability to participate at the same rates in intercollegiate athletics. There is no valid statistical or any other kind of evidence to support that presumption. Additionally, a strict proportionality approach violates the Supreme Court's holdings concerning the use of statistical analyses to support discrimination claims. Finally, the purpose of the statute and the implementing regulations is to accommodate the interests and abilities of both male and female students who have the ability to participate in intercollegiate sports, not to establish some mechanical numerical quota based on the ratio of student population. A mechanical application of proportionality does violence to the purpose of the statute. The slavish and unreasoned reliance on numbers has already created an unfavorable backlash harmful to gender "equity."

There is another factor that should reduce administrators' comfortable reliance on the current investigator's manual and the three-part test. This is the stated goal of the NCAA Gender Equity Task Force report that the numbers of male and female athletes should be substantially proportionate to their numbers in the institution's undergraduate population.[89] It is reasonable to expect that this report language will soon start appearing in future decisions, given the perceived rationale of *Favia*, *Cohen*, and *Roberts*.

Summary

Obviously, athletic administrators and boards of trustees are presently in an untenable position because of the dramatic conflict between the provisions of Title IX, its implementing regulations promulgated by the Office of Civil Rights, and the outcome of Federal court cases, particularly *Colorado State* and *Brown*. Certainly the safe harbor approach is to ensure a strict proportionality of percentages of female athletes compared with the number of females in the total university enrollment. The recent OCR clarification clearly underscores this.

[89] The Report, page 3, states that it should be ultimate goal of each institution that the numbers of male and female athletes are substantially proportionate to their undergraduate population. The Report also stresses that maintaining current revenue-enhancing programs like football is essential to enhancing opportunities for women athletes.

The strict proportionality approach, while attractive on its face, is in fact counterproductive to athletes who have the ability to participate at the collegiate level, and is contrary to the meaning of the statute and its implementing regulations. Many contend that female athletes have been subjected to discrimination in the past and in many cases are still being victimized in this way by institutions of higher learning. Even so, an unthinking reliance on proportionality at the expense of accommodating the interest of women who have the ability to participate at the collegiate level is not only contrary to the law, it is not even in the best interests of such female athletes.

When the Federal Courts are persuaded to carefully read the statute, its implementing regulations, and properly evaluate the intent of the statute, and its impact on female athletes, as the court did in *Louisiana State*, they will conclude that a university may comply with the statute by effectively and fully accommodating the interest and abilities of female athletes.

Part II

The goal of this section of the chapter is to cast aspersions on the Office of Civil Rights and to criticize the legislation against discrimination it has promulgated. The basic premise from which all such government "equity" laws proceed is that absent discrimination, all groups, whether based on race, ethnicity, or, in the present case, gender, would be exactly alike in all major regards[90]; that if virtually exact proportional representation of all categories of people in all activities and accomplishments has not been achieved, this is "inequitable"; that under these conditions, the results represent an exploitation of the "victims" by the "privileged."

This politically correct perspective is so well entrenched in legal thinking that to even question it is to call forth the charge of irrational and "outdated stereotyping."[91] It is so inviolable, that to question it is to open the critic to charges of "racism" or "sexism," which are fighting words in any man's lexicon. The view that all groups are equally endowed with all

---

[90] The conventional wisdom does make one set of exceptions in the case of sex: it "concedes" that men and women have different sets of internal plumbing, and that only females can become pregnant and give birth.

[91] See *Brown*.

sorts of interests and abilities is so impregnable that to even mention evidence for the opposite contention is widely seen as rude, unseemly, dirty, or in some other way improper; such claims are refuted not by providing evidence, but through ad hominem attacks. The findings of Sowell and Williams[92] to this end, for example, are dismissed not due to errors which have been found in the logic or empirical evidence they offer, but because they are "uncle Toms."

And yet, as in the case of the Emperor and his new clothes, the evidence against any such contention is legion and undeniable. This understanding has been subjected to withering intellectual refutation by the findings of Sowell and Williams. Sowell, for example, points to the following facts about which "it is virtually impossible to claim that the statistical differences in question are due to discrimination"[93]:

American men are struck by lightning six times as often as American women
Cognac consumption in Estonia was more than seven fold, per capita, than in Uzbekistan
In the 1960s, members of the Chinese minority in Malaysia received over 400 degrees in engineering, compared to only 4 for the majority Malays.
Afrikaners in South Africa in 1946 earned less than half the income of the less politically powerful British

---

[92] Sowell, Thomas, *Race and Economics*, New York: Longman, 1975; Sowell, Thomas, *Pink and Brown People*, San Francisco: The Hoover Institution Press, 1981; Sowell, Thomas, *Ethnic America*, New York: Basic Books, 1981; Sowell, Thomas, "*Weber* and *Bakke* and the presuppositions of 'Affirmative Action,'" *Discrimination, Affirmative Action and Equal Opportunity*, Walter Block and Michael Walker, eds., Vancouver: The Fraser Institute, 1982; Sowell, Thomas, *The Economics and Politics of Race: An International Perspective*, New York, Morrow, 1983; Sowell, Thomas, *Civil Rights: Rhetoric or Reality*, New York: William Morrow, 1984; Sowell, Thomas, *A Conflict of Visions: Ideological Origins of Political Struggles*, New York: William Morrow, 1987; Sowell, Thomas, "Preferential Policies," in *Thinking About America: The United States in the 1990s*, Annelise Anderson and Dennis L. Bark, eds., San Francisco: The Hoover Institution Press, 1988; Sowell, Thomas, *Race and Culture: A World View*, New York: Basic Books, 1994; Sowell, Thomas, *The Vision of the Anointed*, New York: Basic Books, 1995; Williams, Walter, E., *The State Against Blacks*, New York, McGraw-Hill, 1982; Williams, Walter E., *South Africa's War Against Capitalism*, New York: Praeger, 1989; Williams, Walter, "On Discrimination, Prejudice, Racial Income Differentials, and Affirmative Action," *Discrimination, Affirmative Action and Equal Opportunity*, Walter Block and Michael Walker, eds., Vancouver: The Fraser Institute, 1982.

[93] Sowell, "The Vision of the Anointed," pp. 35–37.

Orientals in the United States in 1985 scored over 700 on the mathematics SAT at twice the rate of whites
Germans were only 1% of the population of czarist Russia but accounted for some 40% of that army's high command
Japanese immigrants accounted for more than 66% of potato and 90% of tomato production in the Brazilian state of Sao Paulo
In the 1850s, over 50% of Melbourne's clothing stores were owned by Jews, who were less than 1% of the Australian population

All of these facts are simply incompatible with the "vision of the anointed" that absent anything untoward, there would be homogeneity of all groups of people over all activities. Sometimes, this basic premise has annoying and perhaps even infuriating results, but mostly on an intellectual plane. An example might be its influence in the United States at the close of the twentieth century in general, and the debate over female participation in college athletics, in particular. Whatever the demerits of this perspective, it cannot reasonably be claimed that anyone was murdered as a result of them. At other times, however, this flawed philosophy has had far more serious repercussions. For example, the Nazi attempt to exterminate the Jews was, at bottom, due to Hitler's resentment that this minority was more than proportionately represented among German bankers, professors, university students, playwrights, businessmen, doctors, and lawyers, and was far more wealthy than the average citizen.[94] But it is crucial to realize that it is the same animus and analysis that underlies both cases.[95]

It is a matter of no little interest that failure to register statistical homogeneity should be interpreted as discrimination in some cases, but not others. To return to our focus on athletics, consider this statement by Sowell,[96] "No one regards the gross disparity in 'representation' between

[94] On this see Steven Farron, "Naziism and the Holocaust," undated manuscript.

[95] One might expect Jews to be among the most vociferous opponents of affirmative action, given their historical experiences with this phenomenon. Why this is not the case is explored by Friedman, Milton, "Capitalism and the Jews," in *Morality of the Market: Religious and Economic Perspectives*, Walter Block, Geoffrey Brennan and Kenneth Elzinga, eds., Vancouver: The Fraser Institute: 1985, pp. 429–442 and Block, Walter, "The Mishnah and Jewish Dirigisme," *International Journal of Social Economics*, Vol. 23, No. 2, 1996, pp. 35–44.

[96] Sowell, "The Vision of the Anointed," op. cit., p. 35.

blacks and whites in professional basketball as proving discrimination against whites in that sport." Were it not for the miasma of political correctness which wafts over the entire subject, this statistical disparity would occasion as much wailing and gnashing of teeth as any other. After all, if blacks are to be proportionately represented in every other profession and calling, there simply would not be enough of them left to dominate the National Basketball Association to the degree they presently do. That this situation is not widely resented is thus more than passing curious.

What are the facts of the case? Let us consider both professional basketball and football:

Racial and ethnic composition of professional athletic employment (in %)

	White	Black	Hispanic	Other
Total population	73	12	11	4
NBA				
Players	20	79	0	0
General Managers	72	28	0	0
Coaches	67	33	0	0
Staff	77	17	2	3
NFL				
Players	31	66	1	0
General Managers	83	17	0	0
Coaches	75	24	1	0
Staff	80	15	3	2

Source: Michael Lynch and Rick Henderson, "Team Colors," *Reason*, July 1998, p. 21

As can be seen from the table, the roster of professional athletes includes far fewer whites than would occur were they distributed to this employment slot from a random sampling of the population; and, obversely, we must also reject the null hypothesis that blacks are randomly distributed as well. Yet there is not one in a million people who thinks that the owners of these sports leagues (100% white) engage in anti-white, pro-black prejudice; that they turn away better scoring, higher jumping, stronger whites to make room on their rosters for weaker, smaller, less athletic blacks. No, the thought never occurs that black success in this field is due to anything but the fact that they bring to the table a great amount of athleticism, power, strength, and grace.[97]

Having introduced our topic with a discussion of the fallacious homogeneity hypothesis, and applied it to male sports, let us now consider how it applies to females vis a vis males.

First of all, if we are to take seriously the nondiscrimination ethic, there should be no division between female and male sports programs. Given the feminist contention[98] that the genders are alike (apart from unimportant matters of internal plumbing), it is an egregious matter of segregation to separate the sexes into two different categories. Gender integration is now commonly practiced for children's soccer leagues,[99] and based on the premises of the anointed, there is no reason not to follow this practice at university level.

The problem, here, is that while seven-year-old girls are reasonably competitive with boys of that age, the same does not at all apply to adult men and women. A perusal of any of the male and female world's records in swimming, running, throwing, jumping, rowing, skiing, skating, bicycling, and so on suggests that were there no segregation by sex, there would be virtually no females with the requisite strength, speed, or other physical attributes to even earn a berth on a university team.[100] In order to be competitive, males and females of very different vintages must confront one another (e.g., the famous tennis match between Billie Jean King, then at the apex of her tennis game, and Bobby Riggs, who was

---

[97] It is often charged that while blacks are hired as players in professional sports leagues, there is in effect a "glass ceiling" which prevents them from rising to management, coaching, and other staff positions after they retire as athletes. This contention cannot be supported by the reported facts.

[98] For an antidote, see Levin, Michael, *Feminism and Freedom*, New York: Transaction Books, 1987; Epstein, Richard A., *Forbidden Grounds: The Case Against Employment Discrimination Laws*, Cambridge: Harvard University Press, 1992.

[99] This is perhaps due to the "soccer moms'" thralldom to feminist dogma.

[100] Golf may well be an exception; if so, and to that extent, its pedigree as an athletic event in the first place comes into question. In other words, we may perhaps distinguish between "real" sporting activities and mere "play" on the basis of whether adult males and females are competitive with each other. True, female Olympic athletes of 1998 can swim rings around males of an earlier era (e.g., Buster Crabbe, Johnny Weismuller), but records have been significantly improving over the intervening decades. These two swimmers who later played the role of Tarzan in the movies could best their female contemporaries of the day by similar margins as men now out distance women in the pool.

long past his prime, and never had attained King's stature among men even at the apex of his abilities). Surely, it is inequitable in at least some reasonable senses of that word to have special categories for female athletes at all. Were there not any such, and universities wished to field as many athletes as they now do, there would be a large number of relatively mediocre male athletes who could instead enjoy this experience. On this basis, then, women "athletes" ought to be glad universities spend *any* money on these pursuits, for in a purely "fair" world, where slots on teams were awarded strictly in accordance with ability, hardly any of them would be able to break through the "sports ceiling."

Clearly, this state of affairs is not due to the early conditioning of "culture." Or of females by male misogynist fathers. Mothers do most of the early childhood rearing, of both boys and girls. Nor, yet, is it due to "self hating" mothers, who conspiratorially undermine athletic abilities on the distaff side. No, there are good and sufficient sociobiological reasons why females should be weaker and slower, on average, than males, and therefore make poorer athletes. According to scholars of sociobiology and evolutionary psychology, we are the way we are now in large part because of what it took to survive and leave progeny hundreds of thousands of years ago. In those days, and at present as well, for that matter, women were the genetic bottleneck. Or, to put this the other way around, most males were genetically superfluous. That is, one man could fertilize hundreds of women; the others were, biologically speaking, in effect, drones. In contrast, each female was precious in terms of preserving the human race, in that she could leave progeny with the genetic contribution of a single male. Suppose, a long time ago, there were two tribes of (pre) humans: one of which sent the women out hunting (which sharply penalized non-athleticism) and accorded the men the role of staying in the relatively safer caves with the children while the other group inverted this process. Which of them would survive and leave descendants? To ask this question is to answer it. In fact, we have a name for the first (presumably imaginary) tribe: "extinct."[101] Thus, the reason men are now far better

[101] On this see Dawkins, Richard, *The Selfish Gene*, New York: Oxford University Press, 1976/1989; Dawkins, Richard, *River Out of Eden: A Darwinian View of Life*, New York: Basic Books, 1995; Frank, R. H., *Passion within Reason: The Strategic Role of the Emotions*, New York: Norton, 1988; Wilson, E. O., *Sociobiology*, Cambridge, MA: Harvard University Press, 1975; Symons, D., *The*

athletes than women is that males without such attributes were weeded out of the genetic stock to a far greater extent than females. Or, to put this the other way around, male but not female athleticism contributed to evolutionary success.

With success, of course, comes interest. That is, there tends to be a positive correlation between what we do well in, and what we are interested in. Nerds and geeks tend to be interested in computers and mathematics, because they succeed in mastering their intricacies. (And, of course, there is a positive feedback loop between them, where interest breeds success which in turn leads to yet greater involvement.) Likewise, those who achieve in athletic arenas tend to focus on them, and are positively reinforced for doing so. This being the case, it should not occasion any surprise that boys are not only better at sports, but also more occupied with them as well.

But sociobiology is merely an explanation of the human (and other species') condition. We can transcend our "selfish genes"[102] if we wish. That is, this academic discipline can only account for the fact that girl students would have less interest and ability to pursue intercollegiate competition than boys. However, it is not at all *pre*scriptive. Just because female athletes are vastly inferior to their male counterparts does not mean that their desires to indulge in such activities, lesser though they be, should not be accommodated in modern society. On the other hand, given these sociobiological insights, it is difficult to credit the findings of various Courts that lesser support for female athletic programs is evidence of sexist discrimination on the part of university administrations. Girl children are more interested in dolls, and cloths, boys in guns and trucks. College age males are more interested in sports, females in other

Evolution of Human Sexuality, New York: Oxford University Press, 1979; Buss, D. M., "Evolutionary Psychology: A new paradigm for psychological science," *Psychological Inquiry*, 6, 1–30; Buss, D. M., *The Evolution of Desire*, New York: Basic Books, 1994; Tooby and Cosmides, "On the Universality of Human Nature," *J. of Personality*, 1990b, 58, 17–67; Tooby and Cosmides, "The past explains the present: Emotional adaptations and the structure of ancestral environments," *Ethnology and Sociobiology*, 11, 375–424; Wright, R, "Feminists, meet Mr. Darwin," *New Republic*, November 28, 1994a; Wright, R, *The Moral Animal*, New York: Pantheon, 1994b; Trivers, R., *Social Evolution*, Reading, MA: Benjamin/Cummings, 1985; Axelrod, R.: The Evolution of Cooperation, New York: Basic Books, 1984; Axelrod R., and Hamilton, W.D., "The Evolution of Cooperation," Science 1981, 211, 1390–1396.

[102] See Dawkins, op. cit., "The Selfish Gene."

pursuits. Anyone who sees in this a plot, or sexism, or discrimination, indicates only how much he has been taken in by politically correct feminism.

How, then, would the more limited interests of females in athletic pursuits be accommodated, absent the Office of Civil Rights, Title IX of the Education Amendments of 1972, the Civil Rights Law of 1964, Gender "Equity" Task Forces, and all the rest of the panoply of government intervention into private arrangements? Simple. Through the free enterprise system.

Men, apart from a few transvestites, have very little interest in wearing women's clothes. Yet, this has not prevented a gigantic industry from arising, dedicated to satisfying women's desires in this regard, stores and other institutions of public accommodation. Then, too, industries which provide makeup, hair styling, nail polish, hair removal, and weight loss services are all "biased" in the direction of females: they disproportionately service this gender as opposed to the other. These phenomena would be very difficult to understand on the feminist model that female wants are ignored, or deprecated in favor of those of the male.

How does this work? Why is it that the market is led by "an invisible hand"[103] to provide goods and services for women, who are not "dominant," or "aggressive," and are thought by the ignorant to be victims of discrimination? It is based on profit and loss. The market provides goods and services proportional to the dollars which are "voted" in their behalf.[104] If, for example, females have 55% of the spending power, then

[103] Smith, Adam, *An Inquiry into the Nature and Causes of the Wealth of Nations*, New York: Modern Library, 1776/1965.

[104] But doesn't this just put back the real question? The claim might be made that women have fewer dollar votes in the first place because of male discrimination in the labor market. Even if, then, goods and services are provided according to spending power, females still get the short end of the stick due to this prior injustice.

This may well be the popular view, but it is erroneous. Wages tend to be proportional to productivity, and male and female productivity is roughly equal. Why, then, do women earn less in the market? This is not because of favoritism toward males; rather, it is due to the fact that females have less attachment to the labor force, and have invested in less work-specific human capital. And the explanation for this state of affairs, in turn, is the unequal sharing of child rearing and household tasks in marriages. Again there are good and sufficient sociobiological reasons why this should be the case, but whether or not this explanation for unequal household duties is true, it is a bit of a stretch to blame this state of affairs on the market, or capitalism, or employers, or discrimination, or any other of the feminist whipping boys. For an economic account of male–female earnings'

this proportion of the GDP will tend to be allotted to their demands, and 45% to that of males. This can be proven by the following considerations. Suppose that, given this division of income, the market has somehow produced 70% of its wares according to males' tastes, and only 30% in the direction of female wants. This would imply relative satiety for things such as golf clubs, baseball bats, power boats, and beer, but an under supply relative to demand of makeup, high-heeled shoes, and jewelry. Profits would rise in the latter industries and fall in the former ones. Entrepreneurs would be led by Adam Smith's invisible hand into producing more female-oriented products, and fewer male ones. If they failed to do so, there would continue to be more bankruptcies among firms serving preponderantly male needs.

A similar analysis applies to the arena of male and female sports programs at the university level. Assume that such spending for each gender was on a 50–50 basis. Suppose, for argument's sake, that the optimal proportion of expenditure for women's and men's teams is 25:75 in terms of actual demand. Then, on the assumption of private schools which by assumption are subjected to the market forces of profit and loss, educational "firms" (e.g., universities) would be led to conform their practices to this proportion. The same principle applies no matter what the statistical assumption. If tastes somehow change, and women athletes now want, say, 70% of the sports dollar, and men only 30%, then a similar shift would again occur, this time in the direction of more money for female teams.

The assumption of private universities is crucial for the case that government intervention is not needed if women are to be accommodated regarding their demand for intercollegiate sports teams, at whatever level. To the extent that there are public institutions of higher learning, we can no longer rely on market forces to bring about any such result. Thus, feminists, did they but have any conception of economics, would advo-

differentials in terms of unequal sharing of family, household, and child rearing tasks, see Block, Walter and Walker, Michael, eds., *Discrimination, Affirmative Action and Equal Opportunity*, Vancouver: The Fraser Institute, 1982; Block, Walter, and Williams, Walter, "Male-Female Earnings Differentials: A Critical Reappraisal," *The Journal of Labor Research*, Vol. II, No. 2, Fall 1981, pp. 385–388; Block, Walter and Walker, Michael, *Focus on Employment Equity: A Critique of the Abella Royal Commission on Equality in Employment*, Vancouver: The Fraser Institute, 1985.

cate the privatization of education.[105] In public universities, there is no economic profit and loss oversight to counteract any tendencies toward antifemale discrimination.

So far, we have been discussing sexual discrimination from a positive or scientific perspective. Let us now conclude with a normative analysis. Setting aside the causes and effects of gender discrimination, and the issue of whether it exists on college campuses (or is due to lesser female interest in sports teams), let us ask the question of whether individuals have a right to discriminate in this regard. At first blush, only a Neanderthal or Nazi would even raise such a question, let alone consider a positive answer to it. But upon further consideration, the subject is by no means so crystal clear.

First of all, there is matter of the limitation of the application of this doctrine. For example, it applies to "public" accommodations,[106] such as stores, hotels, and movie theaters, but not in private life. That is, it is illegal for the owner of a firm to discriminate on the basis of sex,[107] race, ethnicity, and so on, but this may be done, and commonly is done, in dating, friendship patterns, and marriage. But if discrimination is such an utter evil, why should it be countenanced in *any* realm of human endeavor?

Secondly, even within the area of commerce, there is a curious lack of symmetry. Customers are allowed to discriminate between, say, restaurants selling Chinese, Italian, Indian, and Mexican food, while none of these establishments would be allowed by law to reciprocate in a similar

[105] This is on the assumption that the feminist agenda is actually one of promoting the welfare and best interests of women. An alternative hypothesis emanates from the Public Choice School of economics, according to which there may be in addition, or possibly instead, a hidden agenda. The disparate treatment accorded President Bill Clinton, and Supreme Court Justice Clarence Thomas suggests that it is to promote Democrats, or socialists, at the expense of Republicans, or conservatives, and not at all to help females.

[106] This is a bit of a misnomer, since enterprises of this sort are *privately* owned. Nor are they necessarily "open to the public." On the contrary, this is precisely the point at issue.

[107] Both hetero- and homosexuals discriminate in their choice of bed partner on the basis of gender. Of all groups, only bisexuals are completely without sexual bias. The law, if logically consistent, would thus impose this practice upon us all. But even bisexuals discriminate on the basis of other characteristics: beauty (they are guilty of "lookism"), talent, sense of humor, intelligence, and so on. It would appear that there are no people innocent of prejudice in this regard. Perhaps all of humanity ought to be incarcerated on this ground.

manner. That is, none of them could legally restrict their clientele to any one ethnic group, or, indeed, exclude any of them.

So the philosophical premise upon which gender equity is built, far from being impregnable, is itself intellectually incoherent. Perhaps, then, an alternative may one day come to take its place: the right of free association. According to this doctrine, people should be free to associate with whomever they wish, on whatever basis they choose; there should be no law compelling them to deal with those they wish to avoid. Although such a perspective falls upon deaf ears in some quarters, strong historical and moral precedent for it exists: this is the philosophy upon which the antislavery movement is built. For the kidnapping of innocent people is the paradigm case of the violation of the law of voluntary association. The point is that forcing individuals to interact with one another when it is not on a mutually agreeable basis is a form of slavery, and this must still resonate widely, even in this benighted age of gender "equity."

2

Should the Government be Allowed to Discriminate?

Introduction

This chapter attempts to address the question of whether the government should be allowed to engage in racial, sexual, or other acts of discrimination. It does so, in section "I. The Law", by analyzing extant law, to determine whether such acts are or are not compatible with the U.S. Constitution. It takes as an initial point of departure the case of governmental discrimination against blacks in the field of education, using Arkansas as a case study.[1] In section "II. Political Philosophy", the chapter analyzes this issue from the libertarian perspective and considers generalized government discrimination in fields other than education, and on numerous criteria other than race.

[1] See Hicks, et al., v. Arkansas Department of Higher Education, No. Civ-00672, E.D. Ark. (September 5, 2000).

W. E. Block, R. Whitehead, *Philosophy of Law*, Palgrave Studies in Classical Liberalism,
https://doi.org/10.1007/978-3-030-28360-5_2

I. The Law

The State of Arkansas provides a full academic scholarship to a state-approved public or private Arkansas Institution of Higher Education to graduates of Arkansas secondary schools who demonstrate "extraordinary academic ability."[2] The sole measure of the graduate's "extraordinary ability" is demonstrated by scoring 32 or above on the American College Test (ACT), 1410 or above on the Scholastic Aptitude Test (SAT), or selection as a finalist in the National Merit Scholarship competition.[3] The purpose of the Governor's Scholarship Program, according to the enabling legislation, is "that outstanding students are an essential ingredient for the economic and social benefit of the State of Arkansas. Benefits accrue to the state when a majority of National Merit Scholars and superior students attend Arkansas institutions of higher learning and remain in the state."[4] The scholarship award dollar amount equals the tuition, room and board, and mandatory fees charged for a regular full-time course load student by the approved institution of higher education in which the student is enrolled.[5] There are eight public and seven private, church-related, approved institutions participating in the program.[6]

The dollar value of the scholarship award varies considerably between public and private institutions. It is estimated, for example, that a scholarship recipient enrolled in Hendrix, a private church-related institution, costs the state about $15,474 per year. In contrast, a distinguished scholar enrolled at Southern Arkansas University, a public institution, will cost the state only about $5088 per year.[7] It is critical to understand that the scholarship funds are dispersed from the state *directly* to the approved public and private, church-related institutions.[8] No funds are sent to the

[2] Ark. Stat. Ann. § 6-82-305.

[3] Ark. Stat. Ann. § 6-82-305(b).

[4] Ark. Stat. Ann. § 6-82-301.

[5] Ark. Stat. Ann. § 6-82-312(b).

[6] Arkansas Department of Higher Education, Student enrollments, Table III, State Appropriations Per Student for Arkansas Governor's Distinguished Scholars for 1999–2000 Fiscal Year, May 2000.

[7] Id.

[8] Arkansas Department of Higher Education, Program Rules and Procedures, Rule 5, hereinafter DHE.

parents or recipients.[9] The responsibility for selecting the scholarship recipients rests with the Director of the Arkansas Department of Higher Education (DHE).[10]

As a condition of participation in the program, each institution of higher education, public or church-related, has to agree to provide to the state the same level of administrative services in administering the program. Among these services are appointing an institution representative to act as administrator of the program for that campus, to receive all disbursements, complete all forms and rosters, verify all data, and ensure compliance with all DHE program rules and regulations.[11] In addition, the institution, public or private, must maintain disbursement records, prepare an annual Institutional Financial Information Sheet for all programs administered by DHE, prepare a list of program drop outs, certify full-time enrollment, provide DHE with an institutional verification of compliance at least twice yearly, and finally, from time to time, submit to a DHE review of the institution's records to demonstrate its due diligence as a *steward of state funds* (Emphasis added).

The program has been much used. The state awarded a total of 808 Distinguished Governor's Scholarships for the 1997–1998, 1998–1999, and 1999–2000 academic years.[12] Of those, 425 (52.6%) chose to attend a public institution, and 383 (47.4%) chose to attend a private, church-related institution. The approximate expenditure of state funds for the scholarship program has resulted in disbursements of $6,149,087 to the private, church-related, institutions and $3,666,371 to their public counterparts.[13] As a result, 62.6% of the total state-distinguished scholarship funds were forwarded directly to the former and 37.4% to the latter.[14] Of the scholarship recipients, 4 (0.4%) were African-American, 19 (2.0%)

[9] Id.

[10] Ark. Stat. Ann. § 6-82-304 (3).

[11] DHE Rules and Procedures, Rule 5.

[12] Arkansas Department of Higher Education, Student Enrollments, Table 1, Comparison of The Number of Arkansas Governor's Distinguished Scholarship Awards by Institution for the 1997–1998 Through 1999–2000 Academic Years.

[13] Arkansas Department of Higher Education, Table II, Amount of Arkansas Governor's Distinguished Scholarship Awards by Institution.

[14] Id.

Asian, 5 (0.5%) Native American, 885 (94.6%) Caucasian, 3 (0.3%) Hispanic, and 20 (2.1%) other or unknown. Finally, 532 (56.8%) of the scholars were male, and 404 (43.2%) female.[15]

Federal Government Jurisdiction over State Discrimination?

Does the federal government have jurisdiction over states, when and if they engage in racial discrimination against their citizens? Some argue that state courts lack jurisdiction over plaintiff's federal damage claims under Section 1983 and because they are not persons amenable to suit under Section 1983. However, it is well-settled in the judicial circuit which includes Arkansas that to survive a motion to dismiss, all the plaintiffs must do is plead a facially neutral practice's adverse effects fall disproportionally on a group protected by Title VI. As the Court of Appeals for the 8th Circuit explained in the Fair Housing Act discrimination case of *Ring v. First Interstate Mortgage*,[16] "the prima facie case under disparate impact analysis is an evidentiary standard–it defines the quantum of proof plaintiff must present to create a rebuttable presumption of discrimination…." Under the Federal Rules of Civil Procedure, an evidentiary standard is not a proper measure of whether a complaint fails to state a claim.[17] Additionally, the Supreme Court has stated, "when a federal court reviews the sufficiency of a complaint … the issue is not whether the plaintiff will ultimately prevail but whether the claimant is entitled to offer evidence to support such claims."[18]

Given that the state of Arkansas has promulgated a program which clearly has disparate impact on black students, in that they are underrepresented among the scholarship winners, a clear implication is that they are at the very least entitled, under *Ring*, to offer evidence to support their claims.

---

[15] Id.

[16] 984 F.2nd 924 (8th Cir. 1993).

[17] Id. at 926.

[18] *Scheuer v. Rhodes*, 416 U.S. 232, 236 (1974).

Under certain circumstances, the Congress can pass laws that give individual citizens a right of action in federal court against an unconsenting state. The circumstances require, first, that "Congress has 'unequivocally expressed its intent to abrogate the immunity,'" which "must be clear and obvious from a clear legislative statement," and, second, that Congress has acted "pursuant to a valid exercise of power."[19] The High Court has held that Congress can abrogate state immunity when it acts pursuant to section 5, the enforcement provision of the Fourteenth Amendment, which provides "the Congress shall have the power to enforce, by appropriate legislation, the provisions of this article."

A plaintiff's cause of action in such a case fits squarely within the circumstances where private citizens have a right of action in federal court. Section 601 of Title VI of the Civil Rights Act of 1964 provides:

> No person in the United States shall, on the grounds of race, color, or national origin, be excluded from participation in, be denied the benefits of, or be subjected to discrimination under any program or activity receiving federal financial assistance.

Moreover, section 602 of Title VI "authorizes and directs federal departments and agencies that extend federal financial assistance to particular program or activities to effectuate the provision of 2000d [Section 601] … by issuing rules, regulations, or orders of general applicability."[20]

The Department of Education, in exercising statutory authority under Section 602, promulgated such a regulation codified at 34 C.F.R. Section 100.3(b)(2) which prohibits a funding recipient from "utilizing criteria or methods of administration which have the effect of subjecting individuals to discrimination because of their race, color, or national origin, or have the effect of defeating or substantially impairing accomplishment of the program as respects an individual of a particular race, color, or national origin." Any such complaint, then, would be fairly based on the foregoing statutes and regulations prohibiting discriminatory effects in

[19] *Seminole Tribe of Florida v. Florida*, 517 U.S. 44 (1996).

[20] 42 U.S.C. Section 2000d.

educational programs such as the Arkansas Distinguished Scholarship Program (Program).

Congress, through the legislation that established Title VI, abrogated the state's immunity in order to effectuate the provisions of the Fourteenth Amendment of the U.S. Constitution.[21] A private right of action under a federal statute requires analysis of the factors set forth in *Cort v. Ash*.[22] The *Cort* factors ask:

> First, is the plaintiff one of the class for who special benefit the statute was enacted –that is, does the statute create a federal right in favor of the plaintiff? Second, is there any indication of legislative intent, explicit or implicit, either to create such a remedy or to deny one? Third, is it consistent with the underlying purposes of the legislative scheme to imply such a remedy for the plaintiff? And finally, is the cause of action one traditionally relegated to state law, in an area basically concerns of the states so that it would be inappropriate to infer a cause of action based solely on federal law?

Plaintiffs fit squarely under the *Cort* rationale. Furthermore, The 3rd Circuit Court of Appeals has applied a three-prong test in deciding whether to approve a private of action from an agency rule such as Section 602. First, a court must ascertain whether a private of action exists under the statute from which the rule was promulgated. If under *Cort v. Ash* a court finds that Congress did not intend the statute to be enforced by private actions, then the inquiry is concluded. Otherwise, two further inquiries must be made: "Whether the agency rule is properly within the scope of the enabling statute and whether implying a private right of action will further the purpose of the enabling statute."[23]

Citing *Chester Residents v. SEIF*,[24] the *Powell* court determined that the agency rule (Section 602) is properly within the scope of Title VI because of the Supreme Court's unanimous opinion in *Alexander*,[25] that "actions having a unjustifiable disparate impact on minorities can be redressed

[21] *Atascadeo State Hospital v. Scanlon*, 105 S.Ct. 3142 (1985).

[22] 422 U.S. 66, 78 (1975).

[23] *Powell v. Ridge*, 189 F.3d 388, 398 (1996).

[24] 132 Fed. 3rd at 933.

[25] 468 U.S. at 293.

through agency regulations designed to implement the purposes of Title VI."

The court also concluded that the third prong, whether implying a private cause of action under the disparate impact regulation will further the purposes of Title VI, was also satisfied. Title VI purposes are to (1) combat discrimination by entities who receive federal funds; and (2) provide citizens with effective protection against discrimination.[26] The court concluded that a private right of action will increase enforcement and increased enforcement will further Title VI's purposes, compensating for the agencies' lack of sufficient resources to adequately enforce the regulation itself. The court in *Powell v. Ridge* cited *Chester*,[27] for the proposition that:

> Procedural requirements in Section 602 provide a fund recipient with a formal notice that the agency has begun an investigation which may cumulate in determination of funding. We note that a private lawsuit also affords a fund recipient similar notice.

Finally, and most importantly for our purposes, the question of whether this was an area basically of the concern of the states was deemed "irrelevant" because Title VI is a federal law.[28]

Continuing now to whether the plaintiffs would have a claim under 42 U.S.C. Section 1983, we begin with the regulation. Section 1983 states:

> Every person who, under cover of any statute, ordinance, regulation, custom, or usage, of any state or territory or the District of Columbia, subjects or causes to be subjected, any citizen of the United States or other person within the jurisdiction thereof to the deprivation of any rights, privileges, or immunities secured by the Constitution and laws shall be liable to the parties injured in the proper proceeding for redress.

A 1983 action has two essential elements: (1) that the conduct complained of was committed by a person acting under cover of state law;

---

[26] *Cannon v. University of Chicago*, 441 U.S. 677, 704 (1979).

[27] 132 F.3d at 936.

[28] *Ridge v. Powell*, 189 F.3d at 398.

and (2) that this conduct deprived a citizen or other person of rights, privileges, or immunities secured by the Constitution or the laws of the United States.[29]

When a 1983 plaintiff seeks damages against state officials in their official or personal capacities, it may be maintained even though they acted in their official capacities in the mattered issue.[30] A government official in the role of personal capacity … fits comfortably within the statutory term "person."[31] The Supreme Court has held that a state official sued for injunctive relief is a person under Section 1983 because the action of perspective relief is not treated as a suit against the state.[32] A state official in his official capacity when sued for injunctive relief would be a person under Section 1983 because official capacity actions for perspective relief are not treated as actions against the state.[33]

Once a plaintiff has identified a federal right that has allegedly been violated, there arises a "rebuttable presumption that the right is enforceable under Section 1983."[34] The presumption is rebutted "if Congress specifically foreclosed a remedy under Section 1983 … either expressly, or forbidding the recourse to Section 1983 and the statute itself, or impliedly by creating comprehensive enforcement scheme that is incompatible with the individual enforcement under Section 1983."[35]

Neither Title VI nor the regulation promulgated there restricts the availability of relief under Section 1983. Defendants thus must make the difficult showing that allowing a Section 1983 action to go forward in these circumstances would be inconsistent with Congress' carefully tailored scheme.[36] Neither Title VI nor the Department of Education regulations establish an elaborate procedural mechanism to protect the rights of plaintiffs.[37] The plaintiffs in such a case would have identified and pled

---

[29] *Powell*, 189 F.3d at 400.

[30] *Chafer v. Melo*, 502 U.S. 21, 27 (1991).

[31] Id.

[32] See *Will*, 491 U.S. at 71n10.

[33] Id.

[34] *Blessing v. Freestone*, 520 U.S. 329 (1997).

[35] Id.

[36] *Blessing v. Freestone*, 520 U.S. 329, 341 (1997).

[37] Id.

disparate impact discrimination, the Fourteenth Amendment "evil" or wrong that Congress intended to remedy by Title VI.[38] It is thus clear that the propriety of the Section 5, Fourteenth Amendment legislation, must be judged with reference to the historical reference of racial discrimination it reflects.[39] Consequently, given the historical record of racial discrimination in violation of the Fourteenth Amendment's Equal Protection Clause, as reflected by the State of Arkansas' Program, the plaintiffs would be entitled to maintain their 1983 action against the individual defendants pursuant to the enforcement provisions of the Fourteenth Amendment.

Ripeness

The doctrine of ripeness poses the query of whether the harm asserted has matured sufficiently to warrant judicial intervention.[40] The Supreme Court has held that the ripeness doctrine's purpose is "to prevent the courts, through avoidance of premature adjudication, from entangling themselves in abstract disagreements over administrative policies and also to protect the agencies from judicial interference until an administrative decision has been formalized and its effects have been felt in a concrete way by the challenging parties," *Abbot Lab v. Garner*, 387 U.S. 136, 148–149 (1967).

In *Columbia Broadcasting System v. United States*, 314 U.S. 407 (1942), the Court held ripe for review a Federal Communication Commission regulation that pronounced that the Agency would not license local stations that maintained certain contracts with chain broadcasting networks. The Court stated although the rule was only a statement of intentions and that no license had yet been denied or revoked, that type of regulation had the effect of law both before and after its sanctions were enforced. The regulation could be challenged because the *expected conformity* to the rule caused an injury that a court could recognize.

---

[38] *See College Savings Bank*, 119 S.Ct. 2207.

[39] Id.

[40] *Sierra Club v. Marita*, 46 F.3d 606, 611 (7th Cir. 1995) (quoting Gene R. Nichol, "Ripeness in the Constitution," 54 *University of Chicago Law Review* 153, 155, 172–73 (1987)).

In *Frozen Food Express v. United States*, 351 U.S. 40, 44–45 (1956), an order of the Interstate Commerce Commission exempting vehicles that carried certain commodities from licensing regulations was held reviewable. The Court held that the order was a final agency action under the A.P.A. *Frozen Foods* holds that "where there has been formal action, as the adoption of a regulation … presumptively the action is reviewable."

In *Abbot Laboratories v. Garner*, the Supreme Court observed that "the cases dealing with judicial review of administrative action have interpreted the 'finality' element in a pragmatic way, and concluded that there was no reason to deviate from those precedents." In that case, regulations published by the Commissioner of Food and Drug were found to be a final agency action and thus subject to judicial review under the A.P.A. and the Declaratory Judgment Act.

Fitness of Issues for Judicial Review

The issues raised by this lawsuit are fit for judicial decision because the State had enacted the Governor's Distinguished Scholarship program into law. This law and the connected implementing regulations have been in effect for a period of over three years. The critical and concrete factor dispositive of this issue is that there has been formal action on the part of the General Assembly, the Governor, and the Department of Higher Education.[41] The law and DHE regulations have a concrete and lasting effect on the citizens of Arkansas. It is entirely appropriate that the state's formal action be reviewed by a Court, particularly in light of the seriousness of the continuing disparate impact on minority citizens of that state.

Hardships to the Parties

The plaintiffs, in this case, have suffered a hardship because, as stated in *Columbia Broadcasting System v. United States*,[42] the "expected conformity" to the rule causes an injury that a court can recognize. The authors

[41] See *Frozen Foods*, Supra.

[42] Cite to be supplied.

of *Griggs v. Duke Power Company*,[43] and *Connecticut v. Teal*,[44] would be astonished to learn that the continuing disparate impact on African-Americans resulting from conformity to the present regulations of this program causes them no actionable harm.

An even stronger argument that harm has occurred to African-American students in Arkansas because of disparate impact is found in a Pennsylvania school funding case. The Third Circuit, in *Powell v. Ridge*,[45] decided that in order to go to trial, all the plaintiff must do is plead that a facially neutral practice's adverse effects fall disproportionally on the group protected by Title VI and its implementing regulations. The court cited *Guardians Association v. Civil Service Commission of New York*[46] for the proposition that administrative regulation incorporating disparate impact standard (like the regulations of the Department of Higher Education) is actionable. Because the law and regulations are final and because the plaintiffs have suffered the egregious harm of disparate impact, the matters raised in the complaint are ripe for judicial review. In a recent case, the Supreme Court held that a school official's deliberate indifference to discrimination amounts to an intentional violation of Title IX.[47]

Plaintiff's Complaint Clearly States a Claim for Relief

The First Amendment to the U.S. Constitution says that "Congress shall, make no law respecting the establishment of a religion, or prohibiting the free exercise thereof."[48] It is settled that "the Fourteenth Amendment has rendered the legislatures of the states as incompetent as the Congress to

[43] U.S. 424 (1971).
[44] 457 U.S. 440 (1982).
[45] 189 F.3d 387 (3rd Cir. 1999).
[46] 463 U.S. at 582 (1982).
[47] *Davis v. Monroe County Board of Education*, 119 S.Ct. 1661 (1999).
[48] Amendment I, Constitution of the United States.

enact such laws."[49] Consequently, the Arkansas General Assembly is constitutionally prohibited from enacting laws respecting an establishment of a religion. But what sort of state action offends the Establishment Clause? Does the distinguished scholarship program that provides for direct payment of state funds to private, church-related institutions of higher education offend the prohibitions of the First Amendment? The answer lies in the intent of the founders and the relevant cases.

First, let us visit James Madison. Thomas Jefferson's famous letter about a separation of church and state to the Danbury Baptist Association is often cited as the primary authority about the intent of the Establishment Clause. However, two Madison veto messages and a letter to the Baptist Churches of Neal's Creek and Black Creek, North Carolina, arguably are more revealing of the intent of the writers of the Constitution and the First Amendment. Jefferson's letter reflected his concern over the establishment of a state religion. Madison's veto messages and letter deal with situations like the Arkansas scholarship program and reveal his notion that religious societies should remain pure, for example, apart from government influence. In 1811, Congress passed a bill giving certain powers to an Episcopal Church in Virginia.[50] Among them was the authority to provide for the support of the poor, and the education of poor children.[51] On February 11, 1811, President Madison returned the bill to Congress with a veto message. Madison argued that the government had no authority over the affairs of the church because of the Establishment Clause. He said the bill violated the Constitution because it "would be a precedent for giving religious societies, as such, a legal agency in carrying into effect a legal and public duty."[52] Again, in February, 1811, Madison vetoed another bill that, in part, reserved a parcel of government land in the Mississippi Territory for the Baptist Church at Salem Meeting House. He

[49] *Cantwell v. Connecticut*, 314 U.S. 296, 303 (1940).

[50] *See*, The Debates and Proceedings of the Congress of the United States with an Appendix containing Important State papers and The Public Documents, and all the Laws of a Public Nature; with a Copious Index; Eleventh Congress—Third Session. Comprising the Period from December 3, 1810, to March 3, 1811, Inclusive, Compiled from Authentic Materials, Washington: Printed and published by Gales and Seaton, (1853), pp. 982–985.

[51] Id.

[52] Id.

maintained that the bill violates the principle of the Establishment Clause prohibiting the use of government money to support religious societies.[53] Shortly thereafter, Madison received a letter from two Baptist churches in North Carolina approving his veto of the Bill to provide support to the Mississippi Baptist church.[54] In his response, Madison wrote "having regarded the practical distinction between Religion and Civil Government as essential to the purity of both and as guaranteed by the Constitution of the United States, I could not have otherwise discharged my duty… .[55]" It is clear that Madison believed that government possesses no authority to impose a duty or responsibility on a religious body. Nor, as evidenced in the Baptist Church at Salem Meeting House matter, to use government funds to directly support a religious society. Madison believed that the Constitution granted the government absolutely no power over religion. Religion was to be entirely removed from government influence. And the best way to separate them is to forbid the government from imposing any responsibilities or duties on religious societies. To maintain this "purity," government was given no Constitutional authority or cause to directly support religious societies. This attitude arose not from hostility to religion but from a desire to protect it from the heavy hand of government regulation. Why? Because we know that government regulation follows government funds. What better witness than Madison himself?

How has the Supreme Court dealt with this issue? In *Lemon v. Kurtzman*,[56] the Supreme Court announced a three-pronged test to determine whether the Establishment Clause had been violated. According to *Lemon*, a statute does not violate the Establishment Clause when (1) it has a secular legislative purpose, (2) its primary effect neither advances nor inhibits religion, and (3) it does not excessively entangle government with religion. In *Lemon,* the high court considered a Pennsylvania state statute that authorized the state to "purchase certain secular educational services from nonpublic schools, directly reimbursing those schools solely for teacher's salaries, textbooks, and instructional

---

[53] Id.

[54] Id.

[55] Id.

[56] 403 U.S. 602, 612–613, (1971).

materials."[57] Most of the schools were affiliated with the Roman Catholic Church.[58] These schools were subject to state audit and had to "identify the separate cost of the secular educational service" to receive reimbursement.[59]

Here, the high court decided that the state statute violated the Establishment Clause because "schools seeking reimbursement must maintain accounting procedures that require the State to establish the cost of the secular as distinguished from the religious instruction."[60] The court then warned of the dangers of providing state financial aid directly to a church-related school citing *Waltz v. Tax Commission* for the proposition that:

> Obviously, a direct money subsidy would be a relationship pregnant with involvement and, as with most government grant programs, could encompass sustained and detailed administrative relationships for enforcement of statutory or administrative standards....[61]

According to the court, the history of government grants reveals that they typically result in various measures of government control and surveillance.[62] Here, the state's power to audit, inspect, and evaluate a church-related school's expenditures creates an intimate and continuing relationship between church and state.[63] The Pennsylvania arrangement violated the First Amendment because the intent of the Establishment Clause is to protect religion from government interference or supervision.[64] Direct payments and state supervision would certainly violate Mr. Madison's expressed "purity" view of the proper relationship between church-related schools and the state.

---

[57] Id. at 602–603.

[58] Id. at 602–603.

[59] Id. at 602–603.

[60] Id. at 620.

[61] 397 U.S. 664, 668 (1970).

[62] *Lemon*, 403 U.S. at 621.

[63] Id. at 622.

[64] Id. at 623.

In *Committee for Public Education & Religious Liberty v. Nyquist*,[65] the High Court dealt with a program that provided direct money grants to certain nonpublic schools for repair and maintenance, reimbursed low-income parents for a portion of the cost of private school tuition, including sectarian school tuition, and granted other parents certain tax benefits.[66] The judges decided that the maintenance and repair provisions of the New York statute violated the Establishment Clause because its effect was to subsidize and advance the religious mission of sectarian schools.[67] The court also held that the tuition reimbursement plans, if given directly to sectarian schools, would similarly violate the Establishment Clause.[68] This was notwithstanding the fact that the grants were delivered to the parents rather than the schools, as the effect of the aid is unmistakably to provide financial support for nonpublic sectarian institutions.[69]

The *Nyquist* holding concerning payments to parents was substantially weakened with respect to vouchers by *Agostini v. Felton*.[70] Here, the High Court stated, "we have departed from the rule … that all government aid that directly aids the educational function of religious schools is invalid."[71] The high court rejected the argument that government and religion are too closely linked merely because a school voucher program transfers money from the government to sectarian schools. It stated, "we reject the argument, primarily because funds cannot reach a sectarian school unless the parents or student decide independently of the government, to send their child to a sectarian school."[72] Consequently, *Agostini* supports the proposition that when parents or students choose to use funds provided to them by the state to attend a church-related school, the Establishment Clause is not offended. This is so because the state funds are paid to the student or parent rather than directly to the church-related school. The

[65] 413 U.S. 756 (1973).

[66] Id. at 757.

[67] Id. at 774–780.

[68] Id. at 780–789.

[69] Id. at 780.

[70] 521 U.S. 203 (1997).

[71] Id. at 223.

[72] Id. at 230.

state, then, has no call to compel a church-related school to perform administrative tasks for it or submit to its audit. This benefit to the parent approach (it allows a tax deduction for parents for certain educational expenses whether they were incurred in private, church-related, or public schools) is also seen in *Mueller v. Allen*.[73] The court stressed that all the decisions invalidating aid to parochial schools have involved direct transmission of assistance from the states to the schools themselves.[74] But, the decision left the *Nyquist* prohibition of aid "directly" paid to a church-related school unaffected.

In *School District of The City of Grand Rapids v. Ball*,[75] the Supreme Court dealt with a district that adopted a shared time and community education program with nonpublic schools. The program was conducted for nonpublic school children at state expense in classrooms located in and leased from the private schools. It offered state-funded classes during the regular school day that were intended to supplement, for the private school students, the "core curriculum" courses required by the state.[76] The shared-time teachers were full-time employees of public schools.[77] Of the 41 private schools involved in the program, 40 were church-related.[78] The High Court decided that this initiative had the "primary or principal" effect of advancement of religion, and, therefore, violated the Establishment Clause.[79] According to the judges, "even the praiseworthy secular purpose of providing for the education of school children cannot validate government aid to parochial schools when the aid has the effect in promoting a single religion or religion generally or when the aid unduly untangles the government in matters religious."[80] They held that "the symbolic union of church and state inherent in the provision of secular state-provided public instruction in the religious school buildings threatens to convey a message of state support for religion to students in the

[73] 463 U.S. 338 (1983).
[74] 463 U.S. at 399.
[75] 473 U.S. 373 (1984).
[76] Id. at 375.
[77] Id. at 376.
[78] Id. at 379.
[79] Id. at 397.
[80] Id.

general public."[81] Further, "the programs in effect subsidize the religious functions of parochial schools by taking over a substantial portion of their responsibility…."[82] The court also said that the Establishment Clause "rests on the belief a union of government and religion tends to destroy government and degrade religion."[83]

Clearly, the most instructive case for our purposes is *Whitters v. Washington Department Of Services For The Blind.*[84] In *Whitters*, the court ruled on an objection to the state of Washington's vocational rehabilitation program for the visually handicapped that financed petitioner's training at a Christian college. The record shows that assistance to Mr. Whitters College was provided under a Washington state program that paid money directly to the student, who then transmitted it to the educational institution of his choice.[85] The Washington statute authorized the state to "provide for special education and/or training in the professions, business or trades so as to assist visually handicapped persons to overcome vocational handicaps and to obtain the maximum degree of self-support and self-care."[86] Mr. Whitters, who suffered from a progressive eye disease, was eligible for vocational rehabilitation assistance under the terms of the statute. He attended Inland Empire School of the Bible, a private Christian College in Spokane, Washington.[87] He was studying the Bible, ethics, speech, and Church administration in order to equip himself for a career as a pastor, missionary, or youth director.[88]

The Washington court ruled that the "principal or primary effect" of the state financial assistance to Whitters was to train him become a pastor, missionary, or church youth director.[89] In the view of the court, the state aid clearly had the primary effect of advancing religion and violated

[81] Id.

[82] Id.

[83] 473 U.S. at 398.

[84] 374 U.S. 481 (1986).

[85] Id. at 483.

[86] Id.

[87] Id.

[88] Id.

[89] Id. at 485.

the Establishment Clause.[90] On appeal, the High Court reversed this decision. It said, "it is well-settled that the Establishment Clause is not violated every time money previously in the possession of the state is conveyed to a religious institution.[91] For example, a state may issue a pay check to one of its employees, who may then donate all or part of that pay check to a religious institution, all without constitutional barrier; and the state may do so even knowing that the employee so intends to dispose of his salary."[92] The court continued, "it is equally well settled, on the other hand, the state may not grant aid to a religious school, whether cash or in kind, where the effect of the aid is that of a 'direct subsidy' to the religious school from the state."[93] The issue "is whether, on the facts, the extension of aid to petitioner and the use of that aid by petitioner to support religious education is a permissible transfer similar to the hypothetical salary donation, described above or is an impermissible *direct* (emphasis added) subsidy."[94]

In the opinion of the Supreme Court, the facts central to the inquiry in the *Whitters* case were whether (1) "any aid provided under Washington's program that flows to religious institution does so only as a result as a genuine independent private choice of the aid recipient;" (2) it is not one of the "ingenious plans for channeling state aid to sectarian schools that periodically reach the court;" (3) it creates no financial incentive for students to undertake sectarian education; (4) "it does not tend to provide greater or broader benefits for recipients for recipients who apply their aid to religious education;" and (5) "in this case, the fact that aid goes to individuals means that the decision to support religious education is made by the individual, not the State."[95]

And, importantly, nothing in the record indicated that any significant portion of the aid spent on the Washington program as a whole will end up flowing to religious education. The court stated, "respondent is correct in pointing out that aid to a religious institution, unrestricted in its

[90] Id. at 484.

[91] Id. at 486.

[92] Id.

[93] Id.

[94] Id.

[95] Id. at 488.

potential usage, if properly attributable to the state, is clearly prohibited under the Establishment Clause."[96] But the respondent's argument does not apply in this case because there was no *direct aid* to the religious school.[97] The court decided that, on the facts present, the Washington program did not constitute sufficiently direct support of religion so as to violate the Establishment Clause.[98] Justice Powell, concurring, said that the Washington scheme was constitutionally permitted because the student or parent directly received the state payments, citing *Mueller v. Allen*,[99] for the proposition that payments directly to parents are constitutional because any benefit to religion results from "numerous private choices of individual parents of school-age children."

Before we turn to the Arkansas Scholarship program, it will be helpful to review the common threads woven through these cases that bind them together. First, requiring church-related schools to maintain administrative and accounting procedures for review by the state offends the Establishment Clause.[100] Second, payment of financial aid directly to a church-related school offends the Establishment Clause.[101] Third, when there is a disparity in the amount of state funds spent on public and church-related students, the establishment clause is offended.[102] Fourth, the establishment Clause is offended if the scholarship program creates a financial incentive for the student to attend a church-related school.[103] And finally, and perhaps most troubling, is this program an ingenious scheme designed to channel state aid directly to church-related schools condemned by the decisions in *Committee For Public Education And Religious Liberty v. Nyquist*?[104]

---

[96] Id. at 489.

[97] Id.

[98] Id.

[99] 463 U.S. 388, 399 (1983).

[100] *Lemon v. Kurtzman*, 403 U.S. 602 (1971), and *Agostini v. Felton*, 521 U.S. 203 (1997).

[101] *Lemon v. Kurtzman*, 403 U.S. 602, *Waltz v. Tax Commission*, 397 U.S. 664 (1970), *Committee For Public Education And Religious Liberty v. Nyquist*, 413 U.S. 756 (1973), *Grand Rapids School District v. Ball, Mueller v. Allen*, 473 U.S. 373 (1984), and *Whitters v. Washington Department Of Services For The Blind*, 474 U.S. 481 (1986).

[102] *Whitters v. Washington*, Id.

[103] *Whitters. v. Washington*, Id.

[104] See, 413 U.S. 756 (1973), and *Whitters v. Washington*, See, 474 U.S. 481 (1986).

The State of Arkansas attempts to cloak itself in the recent case of *Mitchell v. Helms.*[105] Unfortunately, for the State of Arkansas, the cloak does not fit. It does not fit because the *Mitchell* case concerned Chapter II of the Education Consolidation and Improvement Act of 1981.[106] Chapter II channels federal funds to the local educational agencies, which are usually public school districts, by state educational agencies, to implement programs to assist children in elementary and secondary schools. Among other things, Chapter II provides aid for "the acquisition and use of instructional and educational materials, including library services and materials (including media materials), assessments, reference materials, computer software and hardware for instructional use, and other curricular materials."[107] In effect, the Chapter II program was a neutral, per capita aid program. In sharp contrast, however, the Arkansas program is clearly not a per capita aid program.

Secondly, as Justice O'Connor highlights in her concurring opinion, Justice Thomas writing for the *Mitchell* plurality did not even consider the important and decisive issues raised by these plaintiffs in their complaint. The issues in this case are whether (1) any aid provided under Arkansas' program that ultimately flows to a religious institution does so only as a result of the genuinely independent private choices of scholarship recipients, (2) the program is not one of the ingenious plans for channeling state aid to sectarian schools that periodically occur, (3) it creates no financial incentive for students to undertake sectarian education, (4) it does not intend to provide greater or broader benefits for recipients who apply their aid to religious institutions, and (5) that any aid that ultimately flows to a church-related institution does so only as a result of the genuinely independent and private choice of aid recipients.

As Justice O'Connor says in concurring with the plurality in *Mitchell*, "specifically, we decided *Whitters and Zobrest* on the understanding that the aid was provided directly to the individual student who, in turn, made the choice of where to put that aid to use," and "accordingly, our

[105] 120 S.Ct. 2330 (2000).

[106] 20 U.S.C. Section 7301–7373.

[107] 20 U.S.C. Section 7351(b)(2).

approval of the aid in both cases rely to a significant extent on the fact that any aid that ultimately flows to a religious institution does so only as a result of genuinely independent and private choices of aid recipients."[108]

Justice O'Connor continued by saying she believed the distinction between a per capita school aid program and a true private choice program is significant for the purposes of endorsement. In terms of public perception, a government program of direct aid to religion based on the number of students attending each school differs meaningfully from the government distributing aid directly to individual students, who, in turn, decide to use the aid at the very same religious schools.

Finally, she writes that the distinction between a per capita aid program and a true private choice program is important when considering aid that consists of direct monetary subsidies. The Supreme Court has recognized special Establishment Clause dangers when the government makes direct money payments to sectarian institutions. Consequently, there are important distinctions between the issue dealt with in the *Mitchell* case and the line of cases that we cite that make direct payments of state monies to church-related institutions offensive to the Establishment Clause.

A reasonable interpretation will conclude the Arkansas Distinguished Scholarship Program violates the Establishment Clause for a wide variety of reasons. First, the program requires church-related institutions to agree to perform administrative tasks and ensure compliance with state regulations. The institution must submit to a review of its records and demonstrate its due diligence as a *steward of state funds*.[109] One would reasonably believe that the administrators of church schools would strongly object to the grubby hands of State officials thumbing through their private school files. Does this mean they agree to having the Legislative Audit look at their books? Apparently, yes! In any case, the regulations clearly offend the Establishment Clause holdings[110] that the state may not compel religious societies to perform state administrative tasks.

---

[108] Roy, please supply something here.

[109] DHE Rule 6.H.

[110] Under *Lemon*, 403 U.S. 602 (1971), and *Agostini*, 521 U.S. 203 (1997).

Second, the state funds are paid directly to church-related institutions. This direct aid offends the Establishment Clause.[111] If there is one thing certain under all these cases, it is that state money paid directly to a church-related school is unconstitutional. This is so because the scholarship funds are a direct subsidy condemned in all the cases cited. This issue was not even raised in *Mitchell.*

Third, there is a considerable disparity between the amount of state funds per distinguished scholarship provided by church-related institutions and public institutions under the program. Recall that, for example, Hendrix will typically receive $15,000 and Southern Arkansas $4730 per scholarship student.[112] There is also a disparity in the total funds sent to private and public schools. Church-related schools received $2,182,000 and public institutions $1,334,000 in the years 1998–1999.[113] This disparity in treatment of public and church-related institutions offends the Establishment Clause.[114]

Fourth, the program clearly creates a financial incentive for the distinguished scholarship student to attend a church-related school. This is so because the program is open-ended. The state pays whatever the church-related institution considers a reasonable level of tuition and fees.[115] The state-sponsored creation of a considerable financial incentive to attend a church-related school is offensive to the Establishment Clause.[116]

Finally and most disturbing, the distinguished scholarship program, if newspaper reports are accurate, may be a scheme to channel state aid directly to church-related schools that offends the Establishment Clause under *Whitters.*[117] According to Doug Smith,[118] the impetus for the

---

[111] Under *Lemon*, 403 U.S. 602, *Waltz*, 397 U.S. 664, *Nyquist*, 413 U.S. 756, and *Whitters*, 474 U.S. 481.

[112] Arkansas Department of Higher Education, Supra, footnote 5.

[113] Id.

[114] *Whitters*, 474 U.S. 481.

[115] Ark. Stat. Ann. 6-82-312(b).

[116] *Whitters*, 474 U.S. 481.

[117] Id.

[118] Doug Smith, "Pushing And Shoving For The State's Top Scholars," *Arkansas Times*, Aug 27, 1999, p. 13, Col. 3–4.

distinguished scholars program did not emanate from the Department of Higher Education. Rather, it was proposed by state senators. The legislation that came back was not that proposed to the General Assembly by the DHE. The DHE had little choice because 35 senators sponsored the enabling legislation. One of its sponsors is quoted as stating that the bill was brought to him by the President of the Independent Colleges and Universities Association and by the Association's lobbyist.[119] This certainly raises the issue of a scheme to support religious schools. It will be interesting to see why the association would want the state rummaging around in their private, church-related educational programs to determine stewardship of state funds. The North Carolina Baptists who wrote to Mr. Madison would surely be offended.[120]

Mr. Madison would be saddened by the abuse of his Amendment on the part of the DHE of the state of Arkansas. His two veto messages and letter to the Baptist Churches of Neal's Creek and Black Creek, North Carolina, in 1811, sent a powerful message that government has no (none at all) business regulating a religious society, giving a religious society legal agency to carry into effect a public duty, nor giving direct aid to a religious society. The Arkansas Distinguished Scholars Scholarship Program has the unique and dubious distinction of offending *all* of Madison's notions of separation of religion from influence and regulation by the government. This was not so because of hostility toward religion but rather to protect religion from the government. He believed that the Constitution granted government no power over religion. And it surely follows, as in the Arkansas example, that when a religious society accepts government funds in this manner, the heavy hand of government regulation is sure to follow.[121] It makes no constitutional difference that church-related schools volunteer for regulation. It still offends the Constitution!

---

[119] Doug Smith, "Pushing and Shoving For The State's Top Scholars, *Arkansas Times*, Aug. 27, 1999, at 13, Col. 4.

[120] See, The Debates and Proceeding of the Congress of the United State, Supra.

[121] Id.

II. Political Philosophy

In this section, we will review the issue of discrimination from a libertarian point of view. We will utilize that perspective in order to focus on the issue of whether the government should be allowed to discriminate between its citizens, and if so, on what basis. In this section, we take a much broader perspective than that of the constitution as it applies to racial discrimination by the government in the field of education in one state, Arkansas. We apply this theory, generally, to all discrimination, federal, state, or local government, in any field, on any basis.

Libertarianism

Since we shall be applying libertarianism to this thorny terrain, it behooves us to begin with a review of that philosophy. Libertarianism is the political philosophy which maintains that justice can only be attained by an adherence to the nonaggression axiom: all acts are legitimate, except those that transgress against a person or his legitimately owned property. That is, murder, kidnaping, rape, theft, trespass, fraud, assault and battery, and so on, and all such other invasive acts should be illegal, but no other deeds should be prohibited by law. Included in the latter category are victimless crimes such as pornography, prostitution, gambling, drug taking, homosexuality, and so on.[122]

What is the proper role of government in this system? For most libertarians,[123] it consists solely of the duty to protect persons and property

[122] See on this Block, Walter, *Defending the Undefendable*, New York: Fox and Wilkes, 1985; Block, Walter, "Libertarianism vs. Libertinism," *The Journal of Libertarian Studies: An Interdisciplinary Review*, Vol. 11, No. 1, 1994, pp. 117–128.

[123] For some, there is no legitimate role for the government at all. On this see Anderson, Terry and Hill, P.J., "An American Experiment in Anarcho-Capitalism: the *not* so Wild, Wild West," *Journal of Libertarian Studies* Vol. 3, No. 1, 1979, pp. 9–29; Barnett, Randy E., *The Structure of Liberty: Justice and the Rule of Law*, Oxford: Clarendon Press, 1998; Benson, Bruce L., 1989, Enforcement of Private Property Rights in Primitive Societies: Law Without Government," *The Journal of Libertarian Studies*, Vol. IX, No. 1, Winter, pp. 1–26; Benson, Bruce L., "The Impetus for Recognizing Private Property and Adopting Ethical Behavior in a Market Economy: Natural Law, Government Law, or Evolving Self-Interest," 6 Rev. Austrian Econ. 43 (1993); Benson, Bruce, *To Serve and Protect*, New York: New York University Press, 1998; Benson, Bruce L., "The Spontaneous

from invasion. Given that government should exist at all, there are three but only three legitimate state institutions: armies to keep foreign aggressors from attacking us, police to quell crimes emanating from local evil doers, and courts to distinguish between victims and criminals.[124]

Evolution of Commercial Law," *Southern Economic Journal*, 55: 644–661, 1989; Benson, Bruce L., *The Enterprise of Law: Justice Without the State*, San Francisco: Pacific Research Institute for Public Policy, 1990; Cuzán, Alfred G., "Do We Ever Really Get Out of Anarchy?," *Journal of Libertarian Studies*, Vol. 3, No. 2 (Summer, 1979); De Jasay, Anthony, *The State*, Oxford: Basil Blackwell, 1985; De Jasay, Anthony, *Against Politics: On Government, Anarchy, and Order*, London, Routledge, 1997; Friedman, David, *The Machinery of Freedom: Guide to a Radical Capitalism*, La Salle, IL: Open Court, 2nd ed., 1989; Friedman, David, "Private Creation and Enforcement of Law: A Historical Case," *Journal of Legal Studies*, 8: 399–415, 1979; Hoppe, Hans-Hermann, *A Theory of Socialism and Capitalism: Economics, Politics and Ethics*, Boston: Kluwer, 1989; Hoppe, Hans-Hermann, *The Economics and Ethics of Private Property: Studies in Political Economy and Philosophy*, Boston: Kluwer, 1993; Hoppe, Hans-Hermann, "The Private Production of Defense," *Journal of Libertarian Studies*, Vol. 14, No. 1, Winter 1998–1999, pp. 27–52; Hummel, Jeffrey Rogers, National Goods Versus Public Goods: Defense, Disarmament, and Free Riders, 4 *Rev. Austrian Econ.* 88 (1990); Martin, James J., *Men Against the State: The Expositors of Individualist Anarchism in America*, 1827–1908 (1970); Morriss, Andrew P., "Miners, Vigilantes and Cattlemen: Overcoming Free Rider Problems in the Private Provision of Law," *Land and Water Law Review*, Vol. XXXIII, No, 2, 1998, pp. 581–696; Oppenheimer, Franz, *The State*, New York: Free Life Editions, (1914), 1975; Peden, Joseph R., 1977, "Property rights in Celtic Irish law," *The Journal of Libertarian Studies*, Vol. 1, No. 2, Spring, pp. 81–96; Rothbard, Murray N., *For a New Liberty*, Macmillan, New York, 1978; Rothbard, Murray N., *The Ethics of Liberty*, Humanities Press, Atlantic Highlands, N.J., 1982; Rothbard, Murray N., "Society Without a State." J. R. Pennock and J. W. Chapman (eds.), *Anarchism: Nomos XIX*. New York: New York University Press, 1978, pp. 191–207; Rothbard, Murray N., *Man, Economy and State*, Auburn AL: Mises Institute, 1993; Skoble, Aeon J. "The Anarchism Controversy," in *Liberty for the 21stCentury: Essays in Contemporary Libertarian Thought*, eds. Tibor Machan and Douglas Rasmussen, Lanham MD: Rowman and Littlefield, 1995, pp. 77–96; Sechrest, Larry J., "Rand, Anarchy, and Taxes," *The Journal of Ayn Rand Studies*, Vol. I, No. 1, Fall 1999, pp. 87–105; Spooner, Lysander, *No Treason*, Larkspur, Colorado, (1870) 1966; Stringham, Edward, "Justice Without Government," *Journal of Libertarian Studies*, Vol. 14, No. 1, Winter 1998–1999, pp. 53–77; Tinsley, Patrick, "With Liberty and Justice for All: A Case for Private Police," *Journal of Libertarian Studies*, Vol. 14, No. 1, Winter 1998–1999, pp. 95–100; Tannehill, Morris and Linda, *The Market for Liberty*, New York: Laissez Faire Books, 1984; Woolridge, William C., *Uncle Sam the Monopoly Man*, New Rochelle, N.Y.: Arlington House, 1970.

[124] On limited government libertarianism as defined above, see Machan, Tibor, 1978, "Against non-libertarian natural rights," *The Journal of Libertarian Studies*, Vol. 2, No. 3, Fall, pp. 233–238; Machan, Tibor, *Capitalism and Individualism*, New York: St. Martin's Press, 1990; Machan, Tibor, ed., *The Libertarian Reader*, Totowa, N.J.: Rowman and Littlefield, 1982; Murray, Charles, *What It Means to be a Libertarian*, New York: Broadway Books, 1997; Nozick, Robert, *Anarchy, State and Utopia*, New York: Basic Books, 1974; Read, Leonard, E. *Awake for Freedom's Sake*, Irvington-on-Hudson, N.Y.: Foundation for Economic Education, 1977; Read, Leonard, E. *Anything That's Peaceful*, Irvington-on-Hudson, N.Y.: Foundation for Economic Education, 1964; Mises, Ludwig von, *Theory and History*, New Haven: Yale University Press, 1957; Mises, Ludwig von, *Human action*, Chicago: Regnery, 1966; Mises, Ludwig von, *Socialism*, Indianapolis: Liberty Fund, 1981

Discrimination

Whichever of the two versions of this philosophy is under discussion, both are united on the proposition of free association: all interaction between people shall be voluntary; no one should be forced to deal with another person against his will. Thus, discrimination against certain individuals or groups or segments of society would also be considered a "victimless crime." Since no one has a right to force anyone to interact with him against the will of the latter, it would be no crime, under libertarian law, to refuse to buy from, sell to, employ, marry, befriend, join, or in any other way whether commercial or personal, interact with people on the basis of race, religion, sex, or, indeed, any other criteria. This implies that all laws which seek to compel people to engage with one another, such as the so-called Civil Rights Act of 1964, would be invalid under libertarian law.[125] If the authors of the present chapter believe that left handers are

(1969); Mises, Ludvig von, *Bureaucracy*, New Rochelle, N.Y.: Arlington House, 1969; Mises, Ludwig von, *Omnipotent Government*, New Rochelle, N.Y.: Arlington House, 1969; Mises, Ludwig von, *The Anti-Capitalist Mentality*, South Holland, IL: Libertarian Press, 1972.

There are still other writers who characterize themselves as libertarians but allow greater scope for government than courts, armies, and police. For such self-styled libertarians, see Bethell, Tom, *The Noblest Triumph: Property and Prosperity Through the Ages*, New York: St. Martin's Press, 1998; Boaz, David and Crane, Edward H., 1985, *Beyond the Status Quo*, Washington D.C.: Cato Institute; Boaz, David, *Libertarianism: A Primer*, New York: Free Press, 1997; Epstein, Richard A., *Simple Rules for a Complex World*, 1995; Friedman, Milton, *Capitalism and Freedom*, Chicago: University of Chicago Press, 1962; Friedman, Milton, *Money Mischief: Episodes in Monetary History*, New York: Harcourt Brace Jovanovich, 1992; Friedman, Milton, "Alleviation of Poverty," *The Economics of Poverty: An American Paradox*, Burton A. Weisbrod, ed., Englewood Cliffs, N.J.: Prentice-Hall, 1965; Friedman, Milton & Rose, *Tyranny of the Status Quo*, Harcourt Brace Jovanovich, San Diego/New York/London, 1983; Friedman, Milton & Rose, *Free to Choose*, New York, Harcourt, Brace, Jovanovich, 1980; Friedman, Milton, *There's No Such Thing As a Free Lunch*, Open Court Publishing Co., LaSalle, Illinois, 1975; Gwartney, James D., and Richard L. Stroup, *What Everyone Should Know about Economics and Prosperity*, Vancouver, B.C.: The Fraser Institute, 1993; Pipes, Richard, *Property and Freedom: The story of how through the centuries private ownership has promoted liberty and the rule of law*, New York: Knopf, 2000.

[125] For the libertarian case in opposed to the criminalization of discrimination, see Block, Walter, "Discrimination: An Interdisciplinary Analysis," *The Journal of Business Ethics*, Vol. 11, 1992, pp. 241–254; Block, Walter, "Compromising the Uncompromisable: Discrimination," *American Journal of Economics and Sociology*, Vol. 57, No. 2, April, 1998, pp. 223–237; Epstein, Richard, *Forbidden Grounds*, New York: Cambridge University Press, 1992; Gottfredson, Linda, "Reconsidering Fairness: A Matter of Social and Ethical Priorities," *Journal of Vocational Behavior*, 1988, Vol. 33, pp. 292–319; Gottfredson, Linda, "The Practical Significance of Black-White Differences in Intelligence," *The Behavioral and Brain Sciences*, 1987, Vol. 10, pp. 510–512;

the spawn of the devil, and place a sign on front door of their hotel,[126] "No dogs or left handed people allowed on the premises," we would not be subjected to any legal penalty under the libertarian code of law.[127]

Private discrimination, however, must be sharply differentiated from public variety. *Individual citizens*, in this view, have the right to freedom of association. This is so important it deserves to be underlined. To say that they do not have the freedom to associate with whomever they wish is actually to claim the legitimacy of outright slavery. For the only thing wrong with that "curious institution" was that it violated the rights of freedom of association of the slaves. Forget about the whips and the chains. There is nothing unique about these to slavery; sado masochists engage in their use every day. The problem with slavery was that its victims had no right to quit; that is, to dis*associate* themselves from their masters. If they but had a right to free association, this would render slavery innocuous. It would reduce it to no worse than the status of voluntary sado masochism.

But government is not an individual person, with rights to associate with those it wishes to, and to avoid those with whom it wishes to have no interaction. Very much to the contrary, the state has responsibilities, not rights. If the limited government and anarchist wings of libertarianism are united on the claim that private individuals or groups have a complete and total right to discriminate on any basis they choose, and

---

Hernstein, Richard, and Murray Charles, *The Bell Curve*, New York: The Free Press, 1994; Levin, Michael, 1996, "Why Race Matters: A Preview," *The Journal of Libertarian Studies*, Vol. 12, No. 2, Fall, pp. 287–312; Levin, Michael, September 1984, "Comparable Worth: The Feminist Road to Socialism," *Commentary*; Levin, Michael, 1987, *Feminism and Freedom*, New York: Transaction Books; Levin, Michael, *Why Race Matters*, Westport, CT: Praeger, 1997; Murray, Charles, "Affirmative Racism," December 1984, *The New Republic*, 31: 18–23; Murray, Charles, *What It Means to be a Libertarian*, New York: Broadway Books, 1997; Narveson, Jan, "Have we a right to non-discrimination?," *Business Ethics in Canada*, Deborah Poff and Wilfrid Waluchow, eds., Scarborough, ON: Prentice-Hall Canada, 1987, pp. 183–198; Nozick, Robert, 1974, *Anarchy, State, and Utopia*, Basic Books Inc., New York; Rothbard, Murray N., *For a New Liberty*, Macmillan, New York, 1973, pp. 206–207; Rushton, J.P., "Race Differences in Behavior: A Review and Evolutionary Analysis," *Personality and Individual Differences*, 1988, Vol. 9, pp. 1009–1024; Seligman, Daniel, *A Question of Intelligence*, New York: Birch Lane, 1992.

[126] Our critics might think that a good name for this hotel, in view of our last names, would be "Chez Blockhead."

[127] And the same goes for Jews, blacks, homosexuals, females, old people, young people, or any other supposedly "victimized" groups.

against any group or individual they wish, both would also agree that government, if it is justified at all, should *not* be allowed to do so.[128] The point here is that the purpose of the state is to protect the lives, liberties, and fortunes of all of its citizens, and on a basis that does not distinguish between them. Government, in this philosophy, is not only to be blind to the race, color, natural or ethnic origin, religion, sex, disability, age, sexual orientation, or veteran status, the usual suspects, but is to totally ignore *all* other criteria as well.[129] For example, the state must not discriminate on the basis of intelligence, athletic ability, eye color, business acumen, initiative, and ambition, unless these characteristics are somehow related to conducting its business of protecting person or property rights.

Let us consider a few examples. First, as mentioned above,[130] the State of Arkansas provides a full academic scholarship to a state-approved public or private Arkansas Institution of Higher Education to graduates of Arkansas secondary schools who demonstrate "extraordinary academic ability."[131] Previously, we criticized this policy on the ground that a disproportionately high number of the members of one racial group wins these scholarships, whites, and a disproportionately low number of another, blacks, fails to do so. We are now in a position to criticize this scholarship plan on a much more radical basis: even if the *same* proportion of white and blacks won these scholarships, the program would *still* be contrary to libertarian law since it would continue to make invidious comparisons between inept and brilliant students, awarding tax money to virtually all of the latter and none of the former.[132] That is to say, even if

[128] We shall henceforth consider the views of the minarchists, or limited government advocates alone, so as to obviate for argument's sake the point made by the anarchist libertarians, that government should not exist at all.

[129] There is only one exception to this general rule. If the legitimate function of the government pertains to any of these distinctions, then that may be taken into account. For example, if the police must infiltrate the Mafia, it cannot ask a black cop to do so; for the Blood or the Crips, a Jewish officer simply will not do; if the police must send someone in to spy on a gang of criminals composed of females, or lesbians, a male is counter indicated.

[130] Text accompanying footnote 1, Supra.

[131] See footnote 1, Supra.

[132] We abstract from the question of whether or not the testing instrument accurately distinguishes the one group from the other, assuming for the sake of argument that it does.

the program were not problematic on racial grounds, it would be so on the basis of intelligence. For the scholarships would be awarded to smart students of either race, while ignorant students of both races would be victimized by state discrimination. But where is the warrant for governments to divide the population on the basis of intelligence, supporting those who exhibit this characteristic to a great degree, and ignoring those who do not[133]? There is no such justification. If it is illegitimate for the government to discriminate on the basis of IQ, then they may not give out scholarships on this basis. If they wish to award scholarships to students, they must do so in an actuarily "fair" way, for example, by lottery.

And the same goes for entrance requirements for public universities. They, too, are part of the apparatus of government. If the state is prohibited by libertarian law from awarding scholarships on the basis of perspicaciousness, then, too, colleges which are part of government cannot do this either, nor can they pick and choose among applicants for admission on this basis. It cannot be denied that the University of California at Berkeley,[134] for example, would lose its reputation for prestige under these conditions, but it is no part of libertarian law to preserve or enhance the renown of institutions such as these which are illegitimate in the first place. Short of complete privatization of state colleges, reducing their level of excellence would be entirely acceptable from the perspective of this political philosophy.

The point is, if something is illegitimate to its core, as public education is for the libertarian perspective, but somehow, we stipulate, that it *must* exist, then it is a positive benefit that it be run as *in*efficiently as possible. Yes, it would be the death knell for prestigious public institutions of higher learning to be forced not to discriminate in favor of the highly

[133]Robert B. Reich criticizes analogous policies (elite universities accepting only very sharp-witted students) because they increase income inequality. This reason should be sharply distinguished from our own: that awarding scholarships to the "best and the brightest" is an instance of statist discrimination. In our view, private citizens, in sharp contrast to governmental agencies, are entirely justified in acting in ways which increase income inequality. See on this Reich, Robert B., "How Selective Colleges Heighten Income Inequality," *Chronicle of Higher Education Review*, September 15, 2000; see also www.prospect.org/reich.

[134]What about ostensibly "private" institutions of higher learning such as Harvard, Yale, Columbia, and so on. These, too, would be considered public in that an inordinate percentage of their budgets emanate from coercive tax levies.

intelligent. But this is precisely what is required by considerations of justice. If an institution should not exist at all, but somehow persists, then equity entails that it be *in*effective.[135]

Let us now consider the characteristic of athletic ability. It is a well-known fact[136] that with the exception of a few sports such as swimming and diving, yachting, hockey, and handball, blacks exceed whites in terms of athleticism.[137] Certainly, major league football and basketball, whether at the college or professional level, are vastly over represented by blacks.[138] Therefore, the logic of our case against the Governor's Scholarship Program of Arkansas based on intelligence mitigates against any and all athletic scholarship awards on the part of all state institutions. If the academic scholarships favor whites at the expense of blacks, and must therefore be rescinded, then athletic scholarships elevate blacks to the detriment of whites, and must be repealed on the same ground. But more. Just as we were able to offer a more radical critique of the Governor's Scholarship Program in that it disadvantaged the ignorant, so can we criticize all athletic scholarships in that they discriminate against those who are inept in sports. That is, even were it the case that blacks and whites won athletic scholarships in exact proportion to their overall numbers, these awards would *still* be unjustified in that athletic whites and blacks would be treated better than their more awkward counterparts in both racial groups. The authors of the present chapter realize full well that if athletic scholarships were bestowed in a manner unrelated to athleticism, this would spell the death knell for competitiveness. Yet, promoting competitiveness is not part of the mandate of limited government, certainly not from a libertarian perspective. If institutions wish to field excellent teams,

---

[135] For the application of this argument to Nazi concentration camps, and the voluntary army employed to support an unjust war, see Block, Walter, "Against the Volunteer Military," *The Libertarian Forum*, August 15, 1969, p. 4.

[136] Sowell, Thomas, *The Vision of the Anointed*, New York: Basic Books, 1995, p. 35, states: "No one regards the gross disparity in 'representation' between blacks and whites in professional basketball as proving discrimination against whites in that sport."

[137] See on this the movie *White Men Can't Jump*. Also, "white man's disease" is now common parlance in basketball circles, and refers to the inability of white men to jump high for rebounds, or blocks.

[138] See Appendix, below.

they would have the option of privatizing; otherwise, mediocrity would be their (deserved) fate.[139]

Objections

Let us conclude by considering several objections to the foregoing.

1. Typically, advocates of free enterprise and economic freedom, such as ourselves,[140] oppose affirmative action, quotas, equal proportionality. In the present case, the very opposite is true. Namely, we are on record herein as *supporting* these programs. We consider in some detail scholarships based on intelligence and athletic ability as cases in point, but would generalize to cover any other such criteria. Why the difference?

This is because while we oppose the imposition of quotas and so on, for private individuals or firms, this certainly does not hold true with regard to

---

[139] See on this footnote 135, Supra.

[140] Block, Walter, and Roy Whitehead, "Human Organ Transplantation: Economic and Legal Issues," (with Clint Johnson, Mana Davidson, Alan White and Stacy Chandler), *Quinnipiac College School of Law Health Journal*, Vol. 3, 1999–2000, pp. 87–110; Block, Walter, and Roy Whitehead, "Environmental Justice Risks in the Petroleum Industry," *William and Mary Environmental Law and Policy Review*, Vol. 24, No. 1, Winter 2000, pp. 67–88; Block, Walter, and Roy Whitehead, "Direct Payment of State Scholarship Funds to Church-Related Colleges Offends the Constitution and Title VI," *Brigham Young University Journal of Public Law*, Vol. 14, No. 2, 2000, pp. 191–207; Block, Walter, and Roy Whitehead, "Gender Equity in Athletics: Should We Adopt a Non-Discriminatory Model?," (with Lu Hardin), *The University of Toledo Law Review*, Vol. 30, No. 2, Winter 1999, pp. 223–249; Block, Walter, and Roy Whitehead, "Mandatory Student Fees: Forcing Some to Pay for the Free Speech of Others," *Whittier Law Review*, Vol. 20, No. 4, 1999, pp. 759–781; Block, Walter, and Roy Whitehead, "The Unintended Consequences of Environmental Justice," *Forensic Science International*, Vol. 100, Nos. 1 and 2, March 1999, pp. 57–67; Whitehead, Roy and Walter E. Block. 2004. "The Boy Scouts, Freedom of Association and the Right to Discriminate: A Legal, Philosophical and Economic Analysis," Oklahoma City Law Review, Vol. 29, No. 3, Fall, pp. 851–882; Whitehead, Roy, Walter E. Block and Patrick Tinsley. 2008. "Christian Landlords and the Free Exercise Clause: Sinners Need Not Apply," Oklahoma City University Law Review; Vol. 33, No. 1, Spring, pp. 115–150; Whitehead, Roy and Walter E. Block. 2002. "Sexual Harassment in the Workplace: A Property Rights Perspective," University of Utah Journal of Law and Family Studies, Vol. 4, pp. 226–263; Block, Walter E., Katherine Wingfield and Roy Whitehead. 2003. "Re-Evaluating America's Failing Drug Control Laws: A Legal, Philosophical, and Economic Proposal," Oklahoma City Law Review, Vol. 28, No. 1, Spring, pp. 119–159.

the minions of the state. Very much to the contrary, anything to rein in the unjustified use of government power is all to the good, in this philosophy. Not only schools, but libraries, museums, art galleries, opera, symphony orchestras, and so on discriminate against blacks, vis a vis whites, since the latter make greater proportional use of them. Moreover, and just as important, expenditures in these directions vitiate against the stupid and those who are and wish to remain ignorant. That is, even if blacks and whites availed themselves of these services strictly according to their proportion to the overall population, this would still be an unwarranted discrimination on the part of the government against various elements of the population. That is, as long as smart people use libraries, museums, and so on to a greater degree than their ignorant counterparts, this is an illegitimate incursion of government into the economy. Therefore, government is unjustified in offering these goods and services no matter what the relative utilization of them by blacks and whites.

2. But if government purchases from the private sector the land, labor, and capital necessary to provide those "intellectual" services, so does this hold true for things like desks, pencils, paper, computers, jet planes, pistols, bazookas, battle ships, police and soldiers' uniforms, paper clips, rubber bands, envelopes, and so on. These, too, discriminate against those on the low end of the bell curve.[141] Thus, if government is prevented from financing the former, this holds for the latter as well.

This is obviously an attempt at a reductio ad absurdum of the libertarian position in that were the state not allowed to purchase these latter set of items, it could not fulfill its obligations under minarchism.

The reply is that the provisions of armies, courts, and police are part and parcel of the proper scope of government, according to limited government libertarianism, while competing with industries which provide these other services is not. And this applies, as well, for the myriad of other services supplied by government, for example, in health and welfare,

[141] That is, whites, and males, are likely to be over represented in the provision of these goods and services to the government. See on this footnote 125, Supra, particularly, Hernstein, Richard, and Murray Charles, op. cit.

which have nothing to do with upholding the rights to personal safety and property mandated by the libertarian vision. It must be conceded that it would be possible for the public sector to provide all sorts of goods and services on a nondiscriminatory basis, not only in terms of race, sex, ethnicity, and so on, but also intelligence and other abilities. They could all be supplied on a "fair" basis, through lottery. However, this will still be inappropriate in the libertarian view, since these are not within the proper scope of a limited government.

Conclusion

A word on federal state relations. Ordinarily, writers such as ourselves who favor markets, private property, and the freedom of association also approve of subsidiarity for government.[142] That is, when there is a conflict between different levels, we advance the cause of the most local: cities vis a vis states, and the latter when in conflict with the federal government.[143] However, in the present case, we are taking the side of the federal government vis a vis the state of Arkansas.

There are three possible theories on this matter; together they are seemingly exhaustive:

1. the federal always has jurisdiction over the states;
2. the states are supreme vis a vis the federal government; therefore, the federal government never has jurisdiction over the states;
3. subsidiarity; whenever there is a conflict between the two levels of government, the presumption is in favor of the least centralized; thus, the nod must go to the state when in conflict with the federal, but also to the town or county when in conflict with the state. It is our contention, however, that there is a fourth alternative, superior to any of these three. It is:

---

[142] For a debate on this issue between two libertarians, see Healy, Gene, "Liberty, States' Rights, and the Most Dangerous Amendment," *Liberty*, August 1999, pp. 13–16; Pilon, Roger, "In Defense of the Fourteenth Amendment," *Liberty*, February 2000, pp. 39–45; Healy, Gene, "Roger & Me," *Liberty*, February 2000, pp. 46–49; Pilon, Roger, "I'll Take the 14th," *Liberty*, March 2000, pp. 15–16.

[143] This is option #3, listed below.

4. Ignore the level of government which is taking any given position on the ground that it is irrelevant to libertarianism; instead, take the correct position, regardless of from which level of government it is emanating.

In the present circumstance, this is our story, and we are sticking with it. That is, it cannot be denied that in the present case, the state of Arkansas, with its Governor's Scholarship Program, not only vitiates against black people, but against those on the left side of the bell curve of intelligence as measured by IQ as well. Therefore, it is an unwarranted discrimination on the part of this state government.

Appendix

Racial and ethnic composition of professional athletic employment (in %)

	White	Black	Hispanic	Other
Total population	73	12	11	4
NBA				
Players	20	79	0	0
General Managers	72	28	0	0
Coaches	67	33	0	0
Staff	77	17	2	3
NFL				
Players	31	66	1	0
General Managers	83	17	0	0
Coaches	75	24	1	0
Staff	80	15	3	2

Source: Michael Lynch and Rick Henderson, "Team Colors," *Reason*, July 1998, p. 21; cited in Whitehead, Roy, Walter Block and Lu Hardin, "Gender Equity in Athletics: Should We Adopt a Non-Discriminatory Model?," *The University of Toledo Law Review*, Vol. 30, No. 2, Winter 1999, p. 244

3

Christian Landlords: Sinners Need Not Apply

I. Sinners Need Not Apply: Background to the *Thomas* Controversy

Kevin Thomas and Joyce Baker are owners of residential rental properties who do not discriminate against the vast majority of potential tenants. They willingly rent their properties to women and men of all races and ethnic backgrounds, whether they are single, separated, or widowed. But as practicing Christians, Thomas and Baker refuse to rent to unmarried cohabitants on the grounds that premarital sex offends their religious beliefs. Despite their broad commitment to discrimination-free rental practices, Thomas and Baker face possible imprisonment under an Alaskan statute that makes it unlawful to "refuse to sell, lease, or rent … real property to a person because of … marital status."[1] Alaskan courts

[1] § 18.80.240. §18.80.270 makes violation of that prohibition on discrimination a misdemeanor punishable by fine or imprisonment. Thomas and Baker could also face punishment under Anchorage Ordinance, Section 5.30.070, which makes it a misdemeanor to "willfully resist the Equal Rights Commission or its representatives." Our analysis can safely overlook the Anchorage Ordinance, however, because it is virtually identical to the Alaskan state statute in every material respect.

W. E. Block, R. Whitehead, *Philosophy of Law*, Palgrave Studies in Classical Liberalism,
https://doi.org/10.1007/978-3-030-28360-5_3

have interpreted this statute to prohibit discrimination against unmarried couples.[2]

Knowing that their rental practices violate Alaska's marital-status discrimination laws, Thomas and Baker filed suit in Federal District Court against Paula Haley, the Executive Director of the Alaska State Commission on Human Rights, the Anchorage Equal Rights Commission ("AERC"), and the municipality of Anchorage seeking declaratory and injunctive relief pursuant to 42 U.S.C. § 1983 and 28 U.S.C. § 2201.[3] The District Court found that application of the antidiscrimination laws to Thomas and Baker would violate their rights under Free Exercise Clause and permanently enjoined the state of Alaska from enforcing its laws against the landlords.[4] The Ninth Circuit Court of Appeals affirmed this result.[5] This article critically reassesses the rationale underlying the Court of Appeals' decision.[6] Our analysis consists of two main steps.

First, using the *Thomas* case as a point of departure, we situate marital-status discrimination within a broader legal landscape defined by both procedural issues, such as ripeness and justiciability, and a suite of substantive issues arising out of the complex interaction between various provisions of the U.S. Constitution, including the taking clause of the Fifth Amendment and the free speech, free exercise, and establishment clauses of the First Amendment.

---

[2] See *Foreman v. Anchorage Equal Rights Commission*, 779 P. 2d 1199, 1202 (Alaska 1989).

[3] *Thomas and Baker v. Anchorage Equal Rights Commission*, No. 95-0275-HRH (D. Alaska 1996).

[4] Id.

[5] *Thomas v. Anchorage Equal Rights Comm'n*, 165 F.3d 692 (9th Cir. 1999).

[6] Although the parties brought numerous appeals, in both state and federal courts, we analyze the first decision by the Ninth Circuit Court of Appeals, cited at id. We restrict our analysis to this decision because it offers the most thorough and nuanced consideration of the merits of the case. Readers interested in the case's subsequent history, however, will find that the Court of Appeals later withdrew its initial decision and granted a rehearing en banc. *Thomas v. Anchorage Equal Rights Comm'n*, 192 F.3d 1208 (9th Cir. 1999). Upon rehearing, the Court of Appeals dismissed the landlords' complaint on the grounds that it was not ripe for adjudication, a decision the Supreme Court of the United States declined to review. *Thomas v. Anchorage Equal Rights Comm'n*, 220 F.3d 1134 (9th Cir. 2000) (en banc), *cert. denied*, 531 U.S. 1143 (2001). The landlords subsequently litigated their claim in Alaskan state courts, which ultimately ruled against them, with the Supreme Court of the United States again declining review. *Thomas v. Anchorage Equal Rights Comm'n*, 102 P.3d 937 (Alaska 2004), *cert. denied, Bubna v. Anchorage Equal Rights Comm'n*, NEED CITE.

Second, we argue that the decision in *Thomas*, although correct insofar as it vindicates a landlord's right to exclude unwanted tenants, appears to accept propositions of "civil rights" law that are philosophically unsatisfying, economically unsound, and morally unjustified. In order to correct these deficiencies, we propose an alternative legal arrangement that retains the goal of diminishing discrimination while offering a more robust respect for the religious and economic liberties of individual property owners.

II. Marital Discrimination: A Sketch of the Legal Landscape

In order to assess the Ninth Circuit's decision in *Thomas*, we must first get the "lay of the land" by following the court's path through preliminary issues of ripeness and justiciability as well as substantive questions of Constitutional law.

A. Ripeness

The Court of Appeals first focused on whether Thomas and Baker's claims were ripe for review.[7] In the absence of any active effort to enforce Alaska's marital discrimination statute against Thomas and Baker, the Court had to satisfy itself that "there is a substantial controversy … of sufficient immediacy and reality to warrant the issuance of the declaratory judgment."[8] The ripeness inquiry "focuses on whether there is sufficient injury, or threat of injury, and thus it is closely tied to the standing requirement."[9] Under the standing doctrine, because Thomas and Baker are not presently subject to prosecution, they must demonstrate a "reasonable threat of prosecution for conduct allegedly protected by the Constitution."[10]

---

[7] *Thomas v. Anchorage Equal Rights Comm'n*, 220 F.3d 1134 (9th Cir. 2000).

[8] *Lake Carriers Association v. MacMullen*, 406 U.S. 498, 506 (1972).

[9] *Portland v. County of Santa Clara*, 995 F. 2d 898, 902–03 (9th Cir. 1993).

[10] *Ohio Civil Rights Commission v. Dayton Christian Schools, Inc.*, 477 U.S. 619, 625 & n.1 (1986).

Courts look to several factors to decide whether a "reasonable threat" of prosecution exists. The Ninth Circuit has deemed it significant that the plaintiffs have articulated "concrete plans to violate" the Acts they challenge.[11] Given that Thomas and Baker admitted that they have refused in the past, and will continue in the future, to rent to unmarried cohabitants in violation of Alaska housing laws, it was clear that they had concrete plans. The next question is whether or not there was a reasonable threat of prosecution. Here, the laws at issue were enforced in the recent past against similarly situated landlords.[12] Moreover, the statute has been interpreted by the Alaska Supreme Court as mandating affirmative action on the part of the Human Rights Commission to discover and root out all vestiges of such housing discrimination.[13] The legislature intended the Commission to be more than a simple complaint-taking bureau; the statutory scheme constitutes a mandate to the Commission to seek out and eradicate discrimination "in … the sale, lease, or rental of real property."[14]

B. Justiciability

The court also looked into the justiciability of Thomas and Baker's claim by considering whether the laws in question have fallen into disuse or should be considered dead letter. The Circuit had previously held that claims may be justiciable, notwithstanding a record of nonenforcement of the laws in question, if the record does not show that the laws in question are dead letter or have been "commonly and notoriously" violated.[15]

[11] See *San Diego County Gun Rights Commission v. Reno*, 98 F. 3d 1121, 1126–27 (9th Cir. 1996), *aff'd*, 926 F.Supp. 14155 (S.D. Cal. 1995).

[12] On rehearing, however, the Ninth Circuit Court of Appeals opened its en banc opinion by calling Thomas and Baker's complaint a "case in search of a controversy" and describing the dispute as "purely hypothetical" and the claimed injury "speculative." *Thomas v. Anchorage Equal Rights Comm'n*, 220 F.3d 1134, 1134 (9th Cir. 2000). The dissent ably contests that characterization.

[13] See *Swanner v. Anchorage Civil Rights Commission*, 874 P. 2d 274 (Alaska 1994), *cert denied*, 513 U.S. 979 (1994).

[14] *Hotel, Motel, Restaurant, Construction Camp Employees & Bartenders Union Local 879 v. Thomas*, 551 P. 2d 942, 945 (Alaska 1976).

[15] *San Francisco County Democratic Central Committee v. Eu*, 826 F. 2d 814, 821–22 (9th Cir. 1987), *aff'd*, 489 U.S. 214.

Here, the recent enforcement of the antidiscrimination laws[16] demonstrates that these laws are not dead letter, nor is there any indication on the record that these laws are so "commonly and notoriously" violated by landlords as to render them dead letter.

The Supreme Court has held that when plaintiffs wish to engage in conduct proscribed by statutes, they may challenge those laws prior to enforcement where their fear of enforcement or alleged enforcement is not "imaginary or wholly speculative."[17] A simple imaginary or speculative fear of prosecution is not enough. Thomas and Baker's fears of enforcement were not imaginary or wholly speculative in view of the facts (1) that Thomas and Baker continue to violate the antidiscrimination laws; (2) that the laws have been, and presently are being, enforced against similarly situated landlords; (3) that Alaska and Anchorage authorities are aware of Thomas and Baker's persistent refusals to rent to unmarried couples; and (4) that the state human rights commission labors under an ongoing and affirmative duty to seek out any offending conduct. As a consequence, their claims are justiciable.

C. The Free Exercise Clause

Having decided this point, the Ninth Circuit then turned to the question of a potential for the violation of the Free Exercise Clause of the Constitution. In *Employment Division v. Smith*,[18] the Supreme Court reviewed the constitutionality of an Oregon law that criminalized the ingestion of peyote as applied to two individuals who claimed to use this drug as part of a Native American religious ceremony. In upholding the law against a Free Exercise Clause challenge, the court held that "the right of free exercise does not relieve the individual of the obligation to comply with a valid and neutral law of general applicability on the ground that

[16] See, for example, *Swanner*, 874 P.2d 274. At the very same time that Thomas and Baker's litigation was underway in the Ninth Circuit, the Alaska Commission on Human Rights was engaged in antimarital-status discrimination proceedings against Alaska Pacific University. See ASCHR No. C-96-010 (complaint served February 3, 1997).

[17] *Babbit v. United Farm Workers Nat'l Union*, 442 U.S. 289, 302–03 (1979), *vacated*, 442 U.S. 936 (1979).

[18] 494 U.S. 872 (1990), *rehig. denied*, 496 U.S. 913 (1990).

the law proscribes (or prescribes) conduct that his religion prescribed (or proscribed)."[19] In *Smith*, the Supreme Court made clear, however, that a law failing to satisfy the requirement of neutrality and general applicability must be justified by a compelling governmental interest and must be narrowly tailored to advance that interest.[20]

Citing *Church of Lukumi Babalu Aye v. City of Hialeah*,[21] Thomas and Baker contend that the statute and ordinance are not applicable to them because they fail to satisfy *Smith*'s requirements that the laws be of general applicability and thus subject to First Amendment scrutiny. Thomas and Baker in effect claim that the laws target them. The *Lukumi* decision involved ordinances that targeted certain religious practices, specifically ritual and animal sacrifice of the Santeria religion. The Court concluded that, because the ordinances were carefully drafted to forbid few killings other than those occasioned by religious sacrifice, the ordinances were neither neutral nor generally applicable.[22] The *Lukumi* Court subjected the ordinances to a most rigorous scrutiny because they targeted the Santeria religion and ultimately the Court voided them as violation of the Free Exercise Clause.[23]

The underinclusiveness of the laws in *Lukumi*, however, was altogether different from the underinclusiveness in *Thomas*. In *Lukumi*, the ordinances were "drafted with care to forbid few killings but those occasioned by religious sacrifice."[24] By contrast, Thomas and Baker challenged laws that apply essentially to all landlords.

There was no hint that the Alaska laws were drafted with care to forbid all instances of marital-status discrimination. There is, in sum, no indication that Alaska lawmakers were driven by the desire to target or suppress religious exercise. Here, the housing laws are aimed at preventing discrimination on the basis of marital status; any burden on religiously motivated conduct, even if substantial, is incidental. Consequently,

---

[19] See id. at 879 (quoting *United States v. Lee*, 455 U.S. 252, 263 & n.3 (1982)).

[20] See, for example, Church of Lukumi Babalu Aye v. City of Hialeah, 508 U.S. 520, 531 (1993).

[21] 508 U.S. 520 (1993).

[22] Id. at 545.

[23] Id.

[24] Id. at 543.

absent some other exception, *Smith*, not *Lukumi*, governs the landlord's claims.[25]

But this does not end the inquiry. Thomas and Baker insist that the laws at issue here fall within the scope of a second exception to *Smith*, the so-called hybrid-rights exception. They point to the court's language in *Smith*:

> The only decisions which we have held that the first amendment bars application in a neutral, generally applicable law to religiously motivated action have involved not the Free Exercise Clause alone, but the Free Exercise Clause in conjunction with other constitutional protections, such as freedom of speech and the press, see *Cantwell v. Connecticut*, 310 U.S. at 304–307 (invalidating a licensing system for religious and charitable solicitations under which the administrator had discretion to deny a license to any cause he deemed non-religious).[26]

Thomas and Baker insisted that the Alaska discrimination laws implicate not only their rights to free exercise, but other constitutional rights secured by the Takings Clause and the First Amendment. Consequently, they argue that their claims fall within the hybrid-rights exception to *Smith* and Alaska's marital-status discrimination laws should receive strict scrutiny. Thomas and Baker first maintained that the laws' prohibition against "refusing to sell, lease, or rent"[27] to unmarried cohabitants infringes their rights, grounded in the Fifth Amendment, to exclude others from their property. They also alleged that the housing laws burden their free speech rights, pointing to the provision to the law makes it unlawful for the landlord to "make a written or oral inquiry"[28] of the marital status of the prospective lessee, or to represent that real property is not available for inspection, sale, rental, or lease on basis of the lessee's marital status.[29]

---

[25] *Thomas v. Anchorage Equal Rights Comm'n*, 165 F.3d 692, 702 (9th Cir. 1999).

[26] *Employment Division v. Smith*, 494 U.S. 872,881 (1990).

[27] ALASKA STAT. § 18.80.240 (1).

[28] § 18.80 240 (3).

[29] § 18.80. 240 (1).

D. Hybrid-Rights

The Court commenced an analysis of the hybrid-rights argument by referring to the District Court's findings. The District Court had concluded that:

> These prohibitions … impact plaintiff's freedom of speech and bring this case within the purview of those hybrid cases acknowledged by the Supreme Court in *Smith*. Plaintiffs assert a colorable claim under the First Amendment and a compelling interest test should be applied.[30]

In a footnote, the District Court clarified its understanding of the hybrid-rights exception's scope:

> Plaintiffs do not contend that they could 'carry the day' with these First Amendment arguments, nor does the *Smith* decision imply any such requirements. Plaintiffs simply assert that their free speech rights are implicated in this case along with their free exercise rights, and therefore the compelling interest test should be used. The court agrees.[31]

Thomas and Baker contend it is sufficient to trigger strict scrutiny that their free speech and property rights were "burdened." The appellants, in contrast, maintain that the "companion" right (the nonfree exercise half of the hybrid) must itself be constitutionally protected; that is, it must be independently viable.[32]

The Circuit Court considered the nature of "hybrid" rights. It stated that, "we believe that the best understanding of *Smith* actually suggests an approach to a hybrid-rights claim that falls somewhere between two extremes." That is to say, an individual claiming to be within the hybrid-rights exception may not rest upon a bald assertion that the companion right exists or the companion right is somehow "implicated" by a government policy. Nor, however, is he required to show that the law challenged is invalid under the companion provision alone, without regard to the

[30] See *Thomas*, 165 F.3d at 703.

[31] Id.

[32] Id.

Free Exercise Clause. The Circuit Court, like the District Court, concluded that a plaintiff invoking *Smith*'s hybrid exception must make a "colorable claim" that the companion right (free speech and takings clause) has been infringed.[33] The problem is how to measure a "colorable" claim?

The "colorable claim" standard is difficult to articulate because it does not provide the exactitude of an allegation-only standard or of an independently viable- rights standard: it will require courts reviewing the free exercise claims to make difficult, qualitative, case-by-case judgments regarding the strength of the companion-claim arguments.[34] The term "colorable" is certainly not meaningless, however. Webster's defines it to mean "seemingly valid and genuine."[35] Here, the court indicated that the colorable claim standard it adopted for evaluating hybrid-rights claim is not that different from the traditional "lack of success on the merits" test that governs the issue of some preliminary injunction relief. The court indicated that in order to trigger strict scrutiny, a hybrid-rights plaintiff must show a "fair probability ... a likelihood" of success on the merits of his companion claim.[36]

The court then announced a rule requiring a free exercise plaintiff to make out a "colorable claim" that a companion right has been violated, and that is, a "fair probability" or a "likelihood," but not a certitude, of success on the merits. The court noted (somewhat smugly) that its colorable claim standard is neither too lax nor too strict, but "just right."[37]

The first question under the hybrid-rights claim is whether or not Thomas and Baker have demonstrated a "colorable claim of infringement with respect to their so-called companion rights." Recall that they complained the nondiscrimination laws infringed their Fifth Amendment "right to exclude" as well as their First Amendment "right to free speech." Because of the landlord's principal complaint that the Alaska laws purport

[33] *Swanson v. Guthrie Indep. Sch. Dist. No. 1*, 135 F.3d 694, 700 (10th Cir. 1998).

[34] Id.

[35] Webster's Third New International Dictionary 449 (1986).

[36] *Kuhlmann v. Wilson*, 477 U.S. 436, 454 (1986); *Coalition for Economic Equality v. Wilson*, 110 F.3d 1431,1338 (9th Cir. 1997), *cert. denied* 118 S. Ct. 397 (1997).

[37] Thomas, 165 F.3d at 705.

to require them to rent to unmarried cohabitants, the court considered the Fifth Amendment "takings" claim first.

Thomas and Baker contend that the Takings Clause of the Fifth Amendment, "provides that a property owner's constitutional protection to exclude others from the owner's property," is protected. The Supreme Court has repeatedly held that the right to exclude others is one of the most essential sticks in the bundle of rights commonly characterized as property.[38] The Takings Clause, however, does not "provide" the right to exclude; it merely protects against the right being taken without "just compensation."[39] The relevant inquiry, therefore, is not whether Thomas and Baker possess a right to exclude others from their rental properties. They do! The question is whether, by forbidding them from refusing them to sell, lease, or rent the real property to a person because of marital status, the state has "taken" that right.[40]

The question whether a law gives rise to an unconstitutional taking depends upon the nature of the challenged governmental action. The Takings Clause cases generally fall into one of two categories:

> Where the government authorizes a physical occupation of property (or actually takes title), the Takings Clause generally requires compensation. But where the government merely regulates the use of property, compensation is required only if considerations such as the purpose of the regulation or the extent to which it deprives the owner of the economic use of the property suggests that the regulation has unfairly singled out the property owner to bear a burden that should be borne by the public as a whole. The first category of cases requires courts to apply a clear rule; the second necessarily entails complex factual assessments of the purposes and economical effects of the governmental actions.[41]

In judging whether a governmental regulation promptly constitutes a "regulatory taking," a reviewing court must undertake an essentially ad

---

[38] *Nollan v. California Costal Comm'n*, 483 U.S. 825, 831 (1987).

[39] The Takings Clause provides, "…nor shall private property be taken for public use, without just compensation."

[40] See *Thomas*, 165 F.3d at 707.

[41] Id. (citing *Yee v. City of Escondido*, 503 U.S. 519, 522–23 (1992)).

hoc, factual inquiry.[42] The Supreme Court has recognized three factors of particular importance to the regulatory taking calculus:

1. The economic impact of the regulation on the claimant,
2. The extent to which the regulation has interfered with the distinct investment-backed expectations, and
3. The character of the governmental action.[43]

Thomas and Baker have not alleged that the laws interfere with their investment-backed expectations or otherwise adversely impact their economic interest. Nor could they, absent a showing, that, by renting to unmarried couples in accordance with a challenged laws, their net number of units rented would be decreased. The Alaska rule may very well enlarge the pool of effective renters, and thus, perhaps increase, but certainly not decrease, T & B's bottom line by reducing the likelihood that any given apartment will remain vacant.

The Supreme Court has acknowledged, however, that the "bottom line" is not the sole measure of a successful Takings Clause claim. The court has concluded, for instance, that a property right has been "taken" notwithstanding the fact that the claimed infringement, a requirement that apartment owners permit the installation of cable television boxes and wires in their buildings, in all likelihood increased the value of the owner's property.[44] The court has reaffirmed its long-standing commitment to the proposition that "property is more than economic value; is also consists of the group of rights that the so-called owner exercises in his dominion of the physical thing, such as the right to possess, use and dispose of it."[45] The court concluded that the Alaska laws may not reduce the monetary value of Thomas and Baker's properties; however, there can be no doubt that the laws interfere with the landlord's "dominion" and "possession" of that property.[46]

---

[42] Id. at 708 (citing *Kaiser Aetna v. United States*, 444 U.S. 164, 175 (1979)).

[43] Id. (citing *Eastern Enterprises v. Apfel*, 118 S. Ct. 2131, 2135 (1998)).

[44] *Loretto v. Teleprompter Manhattan CATV Corp.*, 458 U.S. 419, 426 (1982).

[45] Id. at 426.

[46] See *Thomas*, 165 F.3d at ???

Stating that a taking may be more readily found when the interference with property can be characterized as a physical invasion by the government then when it arises from some public program adjusting the benefits and burdens of economic life to promote the social good,[47] the court determined that although the Alaska housing laws do not rise to the level of permanent physical occupation sufficient to trigger a per se right to compensation, they clearly constitute a "physical invasion" of the landlord's property just the same. The court concluded that Thomas and Baker had made out a substantial argument that the Alaskan laws "go too far," and thus, a colorable claim that their rights under the Takings Clause of the Fifth Amendment have been infringed.[48] Hence, the Fifth Amendment serves to "hybridize" their Free Exercise Clause challenge to the Alaska laws and legitimatizes their claim.

E. First Amendment Free Speech

Alaska contends that the landlord's expression at issue is "constitutionally unprotected" commercial speech. Although so-called commercial speech is not outside the scope of the First Amendment, the Supreme Court has made clear that "the Constitution … affords a lesser protection to commercial speech than to other constitutionally guaranteed expression."[49] The first question is whether Thomas and Baker's speech could properly be characterized as commercial speech? The Supreme Court has acknowledged that the "precise bounds" of commercial speech are "subject to doubt."[50] A long line of Supreme Court decisions indicates that reviewing courts have to carefully analyze restrictions on commercial speech to ensure that speech deserving of greater constitutional protection is not inadvertently suppressed. As a guide, the Supreme Court in *Bolger*[51] set out three indicia of noncore commercial speech:

---

[47] *Penn Central Transportation Company v. New York*, 438 U.S. 104, 124 (1978).

[48] See *Thomas*, 165 F.3d at ???

[49] *United States v. Edge Broadcasting Co.*, 509 U.S. 418, 426 (1993). The First Amendment provides, "Congress shall make no law respecting an establishment of religion, or prohibiting the free exercise thereof…."

[50] U.S. CONST. amend I. *Zauderer v. Office of Disciplinary Counsel of the Supreme Court of Ohio*, 471 U.S. 626, 637 (1985).

[51] *Bolger v. Youngs Drug Products Corp.*, 463 U.S. 60, 66–67 (1983).

1. An advertising format;
2. A reference to a specific product; and
3. An underlying economic motive of the speaker.[52]

Here, the court stated it was clear enough that the speech restrictions at issue are not aimed solely at proscribing expression that does "no more than propose a commercial transaction." Rather, the restrictions go much further, and make it unlawful for a landlord to:

1. To "make a written or oral inquiry on the record; of the marital status of a perspective lessee,"
2. To "represent to a person that real property is not available for inspection, sale, rental, or lease" on the basis of the lessee's marital status, or
3. To "make, print or publish" any communication or statement indicating any preference or discrimination based upon marital status.[53]

Here, this simply is not a case of "I will sell you X at Y price," contemplated by the commercial speech rules. That factor alone suffices to classify the landlord's expression in opposition to renting to nonmarried roommates as noncommercial in nature.

The court concluded that the expression prohibited (I prefer not to rent to unmarried couples) by the Alaska laws is not mere commercial speech but protected religious speech because none of the three noncore commercial speech factors outlined in *Bolger* were applicable. It concluded, reasonably enough, that although a landlord seeking to rent an apartment would, almost by definition, possess an underlying "economic motive," it is religious conviction, not economics that would cause Thomas and Baker (or any other similarly situated landlord) to make the inquiries, records, representations, or communications forbidden by the Alaska laws. Indeed, far from emanating from any pecuniary motive, a landlord's statement, "I prefer not to rent to unmarried couples," runs directly counter to his economic interest. A Christian landlord in Thomas and Baker's position has a distinct economic disincentive to speak up about his opposition to nonmarital cohabitation. For one thing, he can

[52] Id. at 67.

[53] Id.

escape notice by the "Human Rights" authorities. For another, by expressing his beliefs, he runs the risk of losing a perspective tenant and leaving a vacant apartment unrented. When he speaks up anyway, he does so, not for economic reasons, but out of strong religious conviction. The court concluded that the expression targeted by the Alaska housing laws cannot be considered mere commercial speech. The simple fact that not all speech takes place in the context of a commercial transaction (like renting an apartment) shows that T & B's utterances and actions far exceed the scope of "commercial speech."[54]

Here, the expression forbidden by the Alaska antidiscrimination laws is, at its essence, religious speech, which enjoys plenary First Amendment protection.[55] And, there can be no doubt that both the Alaska statute and the Anchorage ordinance purport to regulate speech based on its content. "It is axiomatic that the government may not regulate speech based on its substantive content or the message it conveys." Further, content-based regulations of expressions are presumed invalid under the First Amendment. Consequently, the court held that Thomas and Baker made a colorable claim that the Alaska housing laws infringe on their rights of free speech. The First Amendment thus serves to "hybridize" their free exercise challenge to the Alaska laws.[56]

F. Does a Compelling Government Interest Justify the Burden on Religion?

Because the court concluded Thomas and Baker successfully demonstrated a hybrid-rights claim under both the Takings and Free Speech clause, it must then determine (1) "whether government has placed a substantial burden on the observation of a central religious belief or

[54] *Riley v. National Federation of the Blind*, 487 U.S.781, 796 (1988). Commercial speech does not "retain its Commercial Character when it is inextricably intertwined with otherwise fully protected speech." Id.

[55] See, for example, *Lamb's Chapel v. Center Morihes Union Free School District*, 508 U.S. 384, 393–4 (1993).

[56] *Thomas*, 165 F.3d at 711 (citing *Rosenberger v. Rector & Visitors of the Univ. of Virginia*, 515 U.S. 819 (1995)).

practice and, if so, (2) whether a compelling governmental interest justifies the burden?"[57]

With regard to the burden issue, Thomas and Baker are faced with a choice between (1) violating their religious beliefs by renting to unmarried couples, (2) serving punishment for refusing to rent to unmarrieds, or (3) forsaking their livelihood as apartment owners altogether. That choice, they argue, renders the burden on their religious beliefs "substantial." Director Haley counters their argument on two fronts. As initial matter, she points out that "the landlord's religion does not require them to rent housing;" rather they do so "as a matter of choice for personal profit." She insists that "the fact that the landlord's religious obligation arises from regulation of their voluntary commercial activities renders any burden insubstantial." In support of her proposed prophylactic "commercial activity" exception to this substantial burden rule, Haley relies on *United States v. Lee*[58] and *Tony and Susan Alamo Foundation v. Secretary of Labor*.[59] Most prominently, Haley points to the Lee Court's statement that:

> when followers of a particular sect enter into commercial activity as a matter of choice, the limits they accept on their own conduct as a matter of conscience and faith are not to be superimposed on the statutory schemes which are binding on others in the activity.[60]

Contrary to Haley's suggestion, however, *Lee* never even intimated that the fact that a free exercise dispute arises in a "commercial" context might in and of itself affect the substantiality of the claimed burden. On the contrary, the *Lee* decision expressly concluded that the government regulation at issue, compulsory participation in social security system, did "interfere" with the petitioner's free exercises rights. The *Lee* court then decided that the government could save the law by demonstrating a *compelling* state interest in maintenance of the challenged social security

---

[57] *Hernandez v. Comm'r of Internal Revenue*, 490 U.S. 680, 699 (1989), *reh'g denied*, *Graham v. C.I.V.*, 492 U.S. 933 (1989).

[58] 455 U.S. 252 (1982).

[59] 471 U.S. 290 (1985).

[60] See *United States v. Lee*, 455 U.S. at 261.

program. Concluding that it could, the court rejected Lee's free exercise claim.[61] The mere fact that the court in *Lee* reached the compelling-interest issue (which is logically subsequent to the burden issue) confirms that it found a substantial burden on religion.

Reliance upon *Alamo* is similarly misplaced. Haley cites *Alamo* to support the proposition that regulations which "apply only to commercial activities undertaken with a business purpose do not constitute a constitutionally substantial burden on free exercise."[62] The language she recites, however, is taken, not from the portion of the opinion addressing the substantial burden issue, but rather from a passage disposing of Establishment Cause challenges.[63] Consequently, neither *Lee* nor *Alamo* supports a per se rule that burdens on religion levied in a commercial context are not constitutionally substantial. The fact that the defendants' free exercise of religion claim arises in commercial context, although relevant in engaging in the balancing of various interests, does not mean that their constitutional rights are not substantially burdened.[64]

The Director's second argument regarding the burden issue is even more preposterous in a free society. She says that Thomas and Baker may avoid having either to compromise their religious beliefs or to face criminal penalties by simply "cashing out," and selling their apartments or redeploying their capital in another investment. Because the landlords retained that option (choice), she says, any burden on their religious rights is constitutionally insubstantial. In response, the court looked to the degree that the government's requirement will, directly or indirectly, render a believer's religious duties more difficult or costly.[65] The court stated that a minimum, the interference with religious beliefs "must be more than an inconvenience."[66] Haley, of course, attempted to show that the burden on T & B's religious exercise was nothing more than a simple inconvenience that is not constitutionally protected.

[61] Id. at 260.

[62] 471 U.S. at 305.

[63] 471 U.S. at 306.

[64] See, for example, *Attorney General v. Desilets*, 636 N.E. 231, 233, 238 (Mass. 1994).

[65] See LAURENCE TRIBE, AMERICAN CONSTITUTIONAL LAW 1247 (2d ed. 1988).

[66] *Graham v. Comm'r*, 822 F. 2d 844, 851 (9th Cir. 1987).

It cannot be denied that a government regulation that merely "operates so as to make the practice of an individual's religious beliefs more expensive" does not per se impose a sufficiently substantial burden to trigger a free exercise scrutiny.[67] Expense, however, is not the sole consideration involved in determining whether a burden is constitutionally substantial or merely inconvenient.[68] The burden imposed upon Thomas and Baker (putting them out of business) is different and severe. The housing laws (when enforced) de facto banish both Thomas and Baker from the Alaska rental market and force them to altogether forsake their livelihoods as apartment owners and lessors. The laws do not affect a mere marginal reduction in business; they put Thomas and Baker out of business entirely! In unemployment compensation cases, the Supreme Court did not entertain, much less credit, the argument that a believer could simply leave his job and find an occupation that better suited his religious beliefs and practices. Rather, the court's cases have centered on one simple principle:

> where the state conditions receipt of an important benefit upon conduct proscribed by a religious faith, or where it denies such benefit because of conduct mandated by religious belief, thereby putting substantial pressure on an adherent to modify his behavior and violate his beliefs, a burden on religion exists. While the compulsion may be indirect, the infringement upon free exercise is nonetheless substantial.[69]

The same "substantial pressure" to modify behavior and to violate religious beliefs is at work here. The landlords are faced with the same Hobson's choice that confronted the prevailing plaintiffs in the workman compensation cases, either renounce their well-founded religious beliefs or forego government largesse.

Director Haley insists that the employment compensation cases are "inapplicable, because engaging in a rental business is not a government benefit," as is receiving welfare. In this instance, the court acknowledged a distinction between losing employment "benefits" and being deprived

---

[67] *Braunfield v. Brown*, 366 U.S. 599 (1961).

[68] Id. at 605.

[69] *Hobbie v. Unemployment Appeals Comm'n of Florida*, 480 U.S. 136, 141 (1987) (quoting *Thomas v. Review Bd. of Indiana Employment Div.*, 450 U.S. 707, 717–18 (1981)).

of one's chosen occupation. It is difficult to imagine, however, why there is a constitutional difference. Surely, one's statutory entitlement to government largesse owns no compelling significance over and above one's interest in exercising his professional skills in his own way, such that the denial of the former triggers the First Amendment scrutiny but denial of the latter does not.[70] The Fourteenth Amendment liberty interest recognizes the right of an individual to engage in any of the common occupations in life.[71] Renting property is surely one of those common occupations. The court concluded that the Alaska laws and the limit they present do "substantially burden" Thomas and Baker.

However, all burdens on religion are not unconstitutional.[72] Sometimes even substantial burdens on religious exercise may be justified by showing that a regulation's restrictions are necessary to achieve some *compelling* state interest. The next question confronting the court was whether a compelling governmental interest justifies the enforcement of Alaska's marital-status discrimination laws. In order to restrict the landlord's religious exercise, the state must advance some overriding "paramount interest."[73] Director Haley contends that the marital-status laws pass constitutional muster even under strict scrutiny because "Alaska has compelling interests in eradicating discrimination in housing on the basis of marital status." The court disagreed. It maintained that Alaska's purported interest in preventing marital-status discrimination is simply not sufficiently "paramount" to satisfy strict scrutiny.

The court pointed out that only twice in history has the Supreme Court recognized prevention of discrimination as an interest compelling enough to justify restrictions on other constitutional rights. In *Bob Jones University v. United States*,[74] the Supreme Court concluded that there is

---

[70] See, for example, *Meyer v. State of Nebraska*, 262 U.S. 390, 399 (1923).

[71] Id. at 399.

[72] *Bowen v. Roy*, 476 U.S. 693, 701 (1986).

[73] *Church of the Lukumi Babalu Aye, Inc. v. City of Hialeah*, 508 U.S. 520, 546 (1993). "The compelling interest standard that we apply once a law fails to meet the Smith requirements is not watered down, but really means what it says." Id. (quoting *Employment Div. Dept. of Human Resources of Ore. v. Smith*, 494 U.S. 484, 488 (1990)). "Courts will defer only to interests of the highest order." *Wisconsin v. Yoder*, 406 U.S. 205, 215 (1972).

[74] 461 U.S. 574 (1983).

an "overriding interest" in eradicating racial discrimination.[75] Shortly thereafter, in *Roberts v. United States Jaycees*,[76] the court acknowledged a compelling government interest in preventing discrimination based on gender. The high court in *Bob Jones* was explicit: it based its decision upon on what it deemed a "firm national policy" against racial discrimination.[77] As evidence of this national policy, the court referred to several examples of antirace-discrimination measures taken by all three branches of the federal government. It cited, in the judiciary *Brown v. Board of Education,*[78] in Congress the Civil Rights Act of 1964[79] and the Voting Rights Act of 1965,[80] and in the executive branch, executive orders issued by Presidents Truman, Eisenhower, and Kennedy preventing racial discrimination in various sectors of the government. The *Bob Jones* court might have further elaborated and cited for its support for a "firm national policy" the Civil War and the Thirteenth, Fourteenth, and Fifteenth Amendments that followed on its heels. The postreconstruction history of this country leaves little room for argument about the existence of a national commitment to the elimination of racial discrimination.

Here, the court found it is beyond cavil that there is no similar "firm national policy" against marital-status discrimination. The Supreme Court has never accorded marital status any heightened scrutiny under the equal protection clause, as it has in both race, see *Adarand Constructors, Inc. v. Pena*,[81] and gender, see *United States v. Virginia*.[82] Nor has any court of appeals taken such a step.[83] The Supreme Court has recognized a substantive due process right to live with relatives (such as spouses), but it has expressly declined to extend such a right to "unrelated" individuals (like unmarried cohabitants).[84]

---

[75] Id. at 604.

[76] 648 U.S. 609 (1984).

[77] 461 U.S. at 593.

[78] 347 U.S. 483 (1954).

[79] Pul. L. No. 88-352, § 1 (codified as amended at 42 U.S.C. § 2000a (1999)).

[80] Pul L. No. 89-110, § 2 (codified as amended at 42 U.S.C. § 1973 (1994)).

[81] 515 U.S. 200 (1995).

[82] 518 U.S. 515 (1996).

[83] For that matter, see *Smith v. Shalala*, 5 F.3rd 235, 239 (7th Cir. 1993), *cert. denied*, 510 U.S 1198 (1994).

[84] *Moore v. City of East Cleveland*, 431 U.S. 494, 498 (1977).

Because a classification based on marital status does not involve a suspect class and does not impact a declared "fundamental" national interest, the court examined it under a rational basis text. In other words, there is no compelling interest in preventing some forms of marital-status discrimination. The fact that courts have not given unmarried couples any special consideration under the equal protection clause constitutes potent circumstantial evidence that there is no compelling governmental interest in eradication of discrimination based on marital-status.

Supreme Court precedents establish a recognized substantive due process right to live with relatives (such as spouses) but has expressly declined to extend such a right to "unrelated" individuals (such as unmarried cohabitants).[85] Therefore, far from articulating any constitutional marital-status discrimination protections, the Supreme Court has itself approved regulations containing distinctions between married and unmarried couples, bestowing upon the former rights it withholds in the latter. Indeed, the Fair Housing Act makes no mention whatsoever of "marital status" among its catalog of six protected categories. The Act prohibits refusing to "sell or rent … a dwelling to any person because of race, color, religion, sex, familiar status, or national origin."[86] The absence of any mention of marital status is strikingly obvious.

Is there a governmental interest in eradicating marital-status discrimination? One law certainly cannot alone suffice to demonstrate a "firm national policy." Nor can a *single* state's law evidence, under any standard, a compelling governmental interest for federal constitutional purposes. The fact that Alaska has granted to citizens a "civil right" to obtain housing accommodation without discrimination because of marital status is irrelevant to the purposes of the First Amendment.[87]

Finally, even if one state alone could create a compelling governmental interest in preventing discrimination against unmarried couples, Alaska's legislation would not meet this constitutional test. For example, the very enactments under review contain an exception for "married-only hous-

[85] Id. at 498.

[86] 42 U.S.C. §§ 3601–3631 make no mention whatsoever of "marital-status."

[87] Pub.L. No. 105-220 (1998). The court said that other states are "less enthusiastic."

ing, and for space rented in the home of a landlord."[88] Moreover, Alaska expressly discriminates against unmarried couples in a number of contexts like intestate succession,[89] worker's compensation death benefits,[90] no marital communication privilege between unmarried couples,[91] and no insurance coverage for an unmarried partner under a family accident insurance policy.[92] Alaska's underenforcement of its purported interest in eradicating marital-status discrimination is critical, because "it is established in … strict scrutiny jurisprudence that a law cannot be regarded as protecting an interest of the highest order when it leaves appreciable damage to that supposedly vital interest unprohibited."[93] The circuit court concluded there was no support for recognizing a compelling governmental interest in eradicating marital-status discrimination that would excuse what would otherwise be a violation of the Free Exercise Clause. Not all discrimination is created equal!

G. The Establishment Clause

Finally, after holding that T & B had successfully demonstrated the hybrid-rights claims that the Alaska housing laws substantially burden their free exercise rights, and that the laws were not justified by any compelling government interest, the court dealt with Haley's last argument. The Director said that any exceptions to the marital-status laws granted under the Free Exercise Clause will actually violate the Establishment Clause "where the conducts sought to be protected by the Free Exercise Clause would result in direct injury to other identifiable persons."[94] She argued that allowing Thomas and Baker relief under the Free Exercise Clause would "establish" or otherwise endorse Christianity as an official state religion. The Supreme Court has "long recognized that the govern-

---

[88] See ALASKA STAT. § 18.80.240 (containing exceptions for "married only" housing).

[89] Id.

[90] ALASKA STAT. § 23.30.215 (a).

[91] See *Serradell v. Handford Accident and Indemnity Co.*, 843 P. 2d 639, 641 (Alaska 1992).

[92] Id. at 288–89.

[93] *Florida Star v. B.J.F.*, 49 U.S. 524, 541–42 (1989).

[94] *Thomas*, 165 F.3d at ???

ment may (and sometimes must) accommodate religious practices and that it may do so without violating the Establishment Clause."[95] Here, the court applied the three-prong standard of *Lemon v. Kurtzman*[96] that government action violates the establishment clause only if: (1) it does not have a "secular legislative purpose," or (2) its "principal or primary effect" is to advance or inhibit religion, or (3) it fosters an "excessive government entanglement" with religion.[97] And, under the so-called endorsement test whether the challenged governmental practice has the purpose or effect of endorsing religion.[98]

The court held that even if the exception from the Alaska laws granted to Thomas and Baker might result in harm to some third parties (like unmarried cohabitants), this still does not materially affect the Establishment Clause calculus. Establishment Clause cases concern only one kind of "harm," the stigmatization of religious minorities.[99] It sends a message to nonadherents that they are outsiders, not full members of the political community.[100] In the present case, the only injury suffered by an unmarried tenant turned away by a Christian landlord for religious reasons is a marginal reduction of the number of apartment units available for rent. The "harm" to the rejected lessee, if any, is economic, *not religious*; as such, it is beyond the reach of the establishment clause.

The court decided that by exempting Thomas and Baker from the scope of the Alaska antimarital discrimination laws, it did not "establish" or otherwise endorse Christianity as an official state religion. Rather, the opinion "reflects nothing more than the governmental obligation of neutrality in the face of religious differences."[101] The Establishment Clause does not forbid what the Free Exercise Clause requires. The Ninth Circuit concluded, "noble as their purpose may be, neither the Alaska statue nor the Anchorage ordinance may be enforced against landlords, like Thomas

---

[95] See *Hobbie v. Unemployment Appeals Comm'n of Florida*, 480 U.S. 136, 144–45 (1987).

[96] 403 U.S. 602 (1971), *reh'q denied*, 404 U.S. 876 (1971).

[97] Id. at 612–13.

[98] *County of Allegheny v. ACLU Greater Pittsburgh Chapter*, 492 U.S. 573, 592 (1989).

[99] See *Lynch v. Donnelly*, 465 U.S. 668, 688 (1994).

[100] Id. at 688.

[101] *Sherbert v. Verner*, 374 U.S. 398, 409 (1963).

and Baker, who prefer for religious reasons to refuse to rent to unmarried couples."

The Court of Appeals properly disposed of this narrow freedom of religion issue, but its analysis relies on legal concepts and precedents that are not suited to a full-blooded respect for private property rights and individual autonomy. Accordingly, we offer below a solution to these vexing problems surrounding marital-status discrimination that reaches the same end, but does so without regard to government regulators, human rights commissions, and the unending governmental meddling in private beliefs.

III. Libertarian Alternatives to Discrimination Laws

So far, we have limited our purview to the law as it stands, based on the Constitution, the laws of the land, and Supreme Court interpretations thereof. That is, we have in effect accepted as legitimate these institutions, at least for argument's sake. It is now time to broaden our analysis, and to criticize not merely proscriptions against discrimination by the single state of Alaska, and on one ground, marital status, but rather the entire iceberg, of which this is only one tip. Accordingly, we now consider laws prohibiting discrimination anywhere in the United States, for any reason at all, with any target group in mind, specifically including those based on race, gender, national origin, sexual preference, and all other such criteria. In particular, we cast a jaundiced eye at the much beloved (in many quarters) but seriously misnamed Civil Rights Act of 1964.

The philosophy underlying all such initiatives is that some people have a right such that others may with impunity be forced to interact with them whether they wish to do so or not. In other contexts, it would be clear that to compel A to become involved with B against his will was a basic violation of the A's rights. At this level of generality, forcing one party to associate with another could describe not only antidiscrimination laws, but also acts of rape, kidnapping, and slavery. For what does the rapist do to his victim other than force her to "associate" with him in a way contrary to her own preferences? The contention, here, is that the kidnapper does nothing to the kidnapee, or the slave master to the slave—apart, perhaps, from a matter of degree—fundamentally different than what the supposed "victim" perpetrates upon the discriminator; namely, to force his presence upon a person without permission. That is, in discrimination cases, the real perpetrator of the crime is he who would force his presence on another individual through force of law, and not the discriminator, the one who *peacefully* goes about his business, but refuses to deal with persons of a certain category or categories. The true crime in all such cases is a violation of the basic libertarian premise of the freedom of association.

Murray argues:

> In a free society freedom of association cannot be abridged. Implicit in this freedom is also the freedom *not* to associate. Individuals and private groups may accept, reject, embrace, ignore, hire for, fire from, lease to, evict from, anyone for any reason. In other words, free people must be free to make judgments about their fellows and to act upon them. This kind of discrimination plays the same role in a flourishing civil society that market prices play in a flourishing economy.[102]

What, then, is this "freedom of association"? It is the natural right of all human beings not to be forced to associate with others against their will (such as blacks, women, unmarried renters, gays, etc.). In this philosophy, all (all!) human interactions should be strictly voluntary. Rights, in this perspective, are totally *negative*[103]; we all have a right *not* to be murdered; *not* to be raped, *not* to be kidnaped, *not* to be enslaved, *not* to have our physical property subjected to arson or to theft or to trespassing. In very sharp contrast, *all* laws which prohibit discrimination, on *whatever* basis, are attempts to enshrine so-called positive rights; for example, the "right" to use other people, or their property, as means for one's own ends, even contrary to the specific and vociferous objections of the vic-

[102] Murray, Charles, *What It Means to be a Libertarian*, New York: Broadway Books, 1997, p. 81.

[103] Rothbard, Murray N., "Isaiah Berlin on Negative Freedom," in *The Ethics of Liberty*, New York: New York University Press, 1998 (1982), pp. 215–218; Selick, Karen, "Too Many 'Rights' Make a Wrong," *Canadian Lawyer*, September 1991, p. 56.

tims of such invasions. Were this philosophy of freedom of association to once again become entrenched in our legal system, as it should be, then the so-called Civil Rights Act of 1964 would be repealed root and branch as an unwarranted attack on the rights of innocent human beings.[104] Thus, we do not at all confine ourselves to the far less controversial claim that Christian landlords should not have thrust down their throats, so to speak, people whose acts they perceive as immoral; we logically extend this reasoning to all cases where some are forced to associate with others involuntarily.

Blacks, women, gays, and members of national minorities have a right against all of the rest of us that we not commit murder or mayhem against them; that we not violate their (negative) rights of person and property. Do they also have the (positive) right against us that we marry them, employ them, buy from them, sell to them, rent to them, rent from them? Not a bit of it, for such coercion would be in conflict with our right to free association.

But is it not enough to articulate a vision[105] that competes with the prevailing one in support of positive "civil liberties" to nondiscrimination. This may be necessary, but it is hardly sufficient. Also, required, if this pernicious "civil rights" vision is to be undermined, is a demonstration that these laws (1) are not required to do the good they are presumably set up to do, and (2) are logically incoherent, internally self-contradictory, and thus incapable of consistent interpretation and operation. It is to these tasks that we now turn.

---

[104] Why do we take this position? For two reasons. First, justice demands no less. Second, there is an economic way: the market can attain all of the legitimate goals of the advocates of this legislation. See below.

[105] On this see Epstein, Richard A., *Forbidden Grounds: The Case Against Employment Discrimination Laws*, Cambridge: Harvard University Press, 1992; Levin, Michael, *Feminism and Freedom*, New York: Transaction Books, 1987; Levin, Michael, *Why Race Matters: Race Differences and What They Mean*, New York: Praeger, 1997; Levin, Michael, 1996, "Why Race Matters: A Preview," *The Journal of Libertarian Studies*, Vol. 12, No. 2, Fall, pp. 287–312; Selick, Karen, "The Ramp to Hell," *Canadian Lawyer*, September 1995, p. 46; Selick, Karen, "Brave New Work: Fair New World," *Canadian Lawyer*, March, 1995, p. 46; Block, Walter, "Discrimination: An Interdisciplinary Analysis," *The Journal of Business Ethics*, Vol. 11, 1992, pp. 241–254; Block, Walter, "Compromising the Uncompromisable: Discrimination," *American Journal of Economics and Sociology*, Vol 57, No. 2, April, 1998, pp. 223–237; Block, Walter, "Economic Intervention, Discrimination, and Unforeseen Consequences," *Discrimination, Affirmative Action and Equal Opportunity*, Walter Block and Michael A. Walker, eds., Vancouver: The Fraser Institute, 1982, pp. 101–125.

What is the goal articulated by those who advocate using the majesty of the law to prohibit discrimination? It is mainly to be "inclusive": to integrate racial, national, gender, sexual preference, and other such minorities into civil society; to eradicate, or at least reduce, the incidence of negative social indicators, such as high crime rates, infant mortality, single female headed households, low educational attainments; it is, essentially, an attempt at social alleviation: to bring these groups into the social and economic mainstream.

To the extent these considerations are the motivating force behind the outlawry of discrimination, they are misguided. For the Civil Rights Law was a product of 1964. Before that time, of course, and hence without its dubious "benefits," more than a score of national groups successfully became parts of the American culture and economy: Germans, Irish, Swedes, Norwegians, Finns, Icelanders, Portuguese, Polish, Welsh, Jews, Scots, Spaniards, Dutch, French, Greeks, Italians, Swiss, Armenians, Albanians, Russians, Belgians, Chinese, Japanese, Koreans, the list goes on and on. After this epoch, the main groups still not to have partaken fully in this American dream were the blacks and the Hispanics. Despite the presence of this legislation of 1964, missing in the earlier period, no one would contend that these latter two have become as successfully engaged with the mainstream as their predecessors.[106]

If discrimination were a major (let alone an important) explanation of failure to join the melting pot, then, how to account for the experience of the Jews and Orientals? They were subjected to a far more extreme and explicit form of discrimination prior to 1964 than experienced by blacks and Hispanics since that year, particularly in the last decade or two. Certainly, the exclusionary policies visited upon the latter two groups in 1999 are as nothing compared to that inflicted upon the former two, in,

[106] Sowell, Thomas, *Race and Economics*, New York: Longman, 1975; Sowell, Thomas, *Ethnic America*, New York: Basic Books, 1981; Sowell, Thomas, *The Economics and Politics of Race: An International Perspective*, New York, Morrow, 1983; Sowell, Thomas, *Civil Rights: Rhetoric or Reality*, New York: William Morrow, 1984; Sowell, Thomas, *A Conflict of Visions: Ideological Origins of Political Struggles*, New York: William Morrow, 1987; Sowell, Thomas, "Preferential Policies," in *Thinking About America: The United States in the 1990s*, Annelise Anderson and Dennis L. Bark, eds., San Francisco: The Hoover Institution Press, 1988; Sowell, Thomas, *Race and Culture: A World View*, New York: Basic Books, 1994; Sowell, Thomas, *The Vision of the Anointed*, New York: Basic Books, 1995.

say, 1895, or 1912, or 1939 or even 1958. Yet Jews and Orientals have for many years attained higher than average incomes, intact families, educational success, and so on, things which at least so far have eluded many blacks and Hispanics. If one is seriously looking for an explanation of this failure, one will have to look elsewhere.

Why is it that discrimination is so impotent a weapon with which to subjugate a minority population? It is because contained within such acts are the seeds of their own undoing. In the ancient Greek story,[107] a god named Antaeus often fought other higher beings. He, however, was the son of the earth goddess, Ge, or Gaia. Whenever his opponent threw, kicked, or punched the giant Antaeus down to the ground, the latter would rise up, even stronger, thanks to the little push imparted to him by his mother on all such occasions. There is no mystery as to who would win such combat. Antaeus' opponent's efforts contained within them the seeds of their own undoing. Their every *success* brought about, ultimately, their own failure, as it strengthened their enemy Antaeus, the very one they had just "successfully" smitten.

In like manner, a similar phenomenon applies to the present situation. Suppose that the majority Ws engage in economic discrimination against the minority Bs. Let us assume that the former refuse to hire (or pay as much to) or sell goods to the latter. Then, and to the extent that these discriminators carry out this policy, the wages of the latter will tend to fall, and the prices they must pay rise. But if Bs' wages decrease, then Ws with only a slight taste[108] for discrimination, or none at all,[109] will have a competitive advantage over their fellows. In particular, these lesser or not at all discriminating employers can hire a labor force on the cheap. Hypothesize that absent discrimination the wage of the typical B would have been $100. In the presence of this act, pay falls to, say, $75. The productivity of the Bs has of course not changed by one iota. As a result,

[107] See on this Morford, Mark, P.O., and Lenardon, Robert J., *Classical Mythology*, New York: David McKay, 1971, p. 327. (We owe this cite to our UCA English department colleague Wayne Stengel). To finish this story, the god Antaeus was finally killed by Hercules, who held him aloft away from the beneficial effects of his mother.

[108] Becker, Gary, *The Economics of Discrimination*, Chicago: The University of Chicago Press, 1957.

[109] We assume that Ws are not homogeneous in this regard, or that, if so, there are third or fourth communities which differ from the Ws.

those economically wise enough not to indulge in discrimination will earn profits of \$100 – \$75 = \$25. In contrast, employers who do engage in such acts will garner returns of zero in equilibrium: \$100 (in marginal revenue product) – \$100 (wages paid to fellow members of the W community by W employers who refuse to deal with Bs) = \$0. Thus, the free enterprise system will tend to "weed out"[110] those who exhibit racist or nationalistic or sexist tendencies. It is not a very powerful weapon which blows up in the face of those who attempt to use it. No, if the Ws want to bring about the ruination of the Bs, it would be irrational for them to rely on discrimination. To do this is only to bring about their own bankruptcy. Like the god ababab, they would be well advised to seek other means toward their ends.

A similar analysis[111] applies to the case where Ws refuse to sell to Bs (or do so only at artificially higher than market prices). Again, we have two subsets of Ws, those who are serious about their discrimination (and end up, as before, to anticipate, by shooting themselves in the foot), and those who are not.[112] When the Ws snub the Bs, it translates into a leftward shifting supply curve, in economics parlance. With fewer offerings, the Bs will, temporarily, pay more for their purchases. This, in turn, will enrich those Ws willing to "barter and truck"[113] with the Bs as compared to those Ws not less willing, or not willing at all. Why? Because when the Bs pay higher prices, this means more profits for the Ws who take advantage of this situation, for example, the ones willing to deal with them. By definition, the Ws who totally cold-shoulder the Bs cannot profit from them in this way. And the Ws who are willing to deal with them, but only at higher prices than they would charge their fellow Ws, will tend to be shunned by the Bs in favor of lower charging Ws.[114]

[110] Hazlitt, Henry, *Economics in One Lesson*, Arlington House Publishers, New York, 1979.

[111] We are dealing here, and in the previous example, only with discriminatory tastes on the part of employers or merchants, not with that of employees, other customers, and so on. To bring in the latter cases would complicate the analysis without changing its underlying premises.

[112] More realistically, as in the previous case, there will be many subgroups defined by the differing intensity of their desire to avoid the Bs, or, even, a continuum in this regard.

[113] Smith, Adam, *An Inquiry into the Nature and Causes of the Wealth of Nations*, New York: Modern Library, 1776/1965.

[114] This entire analysis is predicated on the supposition that it costs no more to service a B than a W. But if the costs of doing business in a B neighborhood are higher than in a W one due, say, to

Thus, at any given time there will be forces mitigating against the discriminating merchants. They are, due to their tastes, avoiding high profit opportunities. They refuse to "exploit" the Bs, the only behavior consistent with profit maximization. Other things equal, they will earn lower returns on investment than other sellers, who "discriminate" only in favor of the color green, as in money. In the push and shove of the marketplace, the latter will be able to expand their base of operations, the former, at least relatively speaking, will have to contract, or, in the extreme, be forced into bankruptcy. All throughout the market process, the nondiscriminators will increase market share, the discriminators will suffer decreases. At any given time, the extant vendors are the ones who have survived and even prospered under just this sort of competitive struggle. Thus, the implication is that, under the free enterprise system, discrimination on the basis of race, or sex, or national origin, is likely to be minimal or even mythical.

Why, then, does it appear that blacks, or females, or Hispanics get the "short end of the stick" compared to white male Anglo Saxons?[115] There are several possible departures from the model we are implicitly assuming. First of all, we by no means have yet attained the fully laissez faire economic system depicted above, the one which would tend to end the effects of discriminatory behavior. On the contrary, there are unions, there is employment in the public sector, there are minimum wage laws, and we still have vestiges of the medieval guild system,[116] all of which interfere with or even completely negate the market's tendency to penalize such actions. Why? This is because to the extent these things exist, the ordinary profit and loss considerations of the market become attenuated. That is, in the public sector, bureaucrats who eschew discrimination do not earn more profits than their colleagues who engage in it. Secondly, it is possible that the levels of human capital or skills or productivity are not

---

higher crime rates, then this factor has to be incorporated. Again, such a factor might change the example quantitatively, but the underlying critique would remain unchanged.

[115] We must not forget the even greater success of Jews and Orientals, which casts doubt on all discrimination explanations. On this see Seligman, Daniel, "Of Japanese and Jews," in *A Question of Intelligence: the IQ Debate in America*, New York: Citadel, Carol Press, 1994, pp. 118–135.

[116] On this see Rothbard, Murray N., *For a New Liberty*, Macmillan, New York, 1973.

identical between all of these groups.[117] In such cases, disparities in results would be properly attributed not to discrimination, but to these phenomena. Third, at least historically, there were Jim Crow laws in effect,[118] mainly in the south, which short circuited the market's reward and penalty situation. If blacks are forced by law to ride in the back of the bus, then no white bus owner, or even black one for that matter, would be able to do anything to alleviate the situation. In contrast, if this institution were solely a function of discrimination on the market, other entrepreneurs would surely come along with an obvious solution, and be handsomely rewarded for their efforts.[119]

Let us now consider some of the many anomalies that are part and parcel of laws prohibiting discrimination. After all, if the law is internally contradictory, it cannot be justified in and of its own sake, and this provides further evidence against the idea that it could be credited for alleviating any problems or doing any good.

---

[117] Levin, Michael, "Comparable Worth: The Feminist Road to Socialism," *Commentary*, September 1984; Levin, Michael, *Why Race Matters: Race Differences and What They Mean*, New York: Praeger, 1997; Levin, Michael, 1996, "Why Race Matters: A Preview," *The Journal of Libertarian Studies*, Vol. 12, No. 2, Fall, pp. 287–312; Seligman, op. cit., "Of Japanese and Jews"; Murray, Charles and Herrnstein, Richard J., *The Bell Curve: Intelligence and Class Structure in American Life*, New York: The Free Press, 1994; Jensen, Arthur R., "How Much Can We Boost IQ and Scholastic Achievement?" *Harvard Educational Review*, 39 (1969), No. 1, pp. 1–123; Jensen, Arthur R., *Genetics and Education*, New York: Harper and Row, 1972; Rushton, J. Philippe, "Brain size and cognitive ability: Correlations with age, sex, social class and race," *Psychonomic Bulletin and Review*, 1996, 3 (1), pp. 21–36; Rushton, J. Philippe, and Osborne, R.T., 1995, "Genetic and environmental contributions to cranial capacity estimated in Black and White adolescents." *Intelligence*, 20, pp. 1–13; Rushton, J. Philippe, "Reply to Wilerman on Mongoloid-Caucasoid Differences in Brain Size," *Intelligence*, 15 (1991), pp. 365–367; Rushton, J. Philippe, "The reality of racial differences: A rejoinder with new evidence," *Personality and Individual Differences*, 9, pp. 1035–1040.

[118] Williams, Walter, E., *The State Against Blacks*, New York, McGraw-Hill, 1982; see also Williams, Walter E., *South Africa's War Against Capitalism*, New York: Praeger, 1989.

[119] For the argument that the so-called pay gap between males and females is due not to discrimination but to unequal productivity, mainly due, in turn, to marital and child rearing asymmetries, see Williams, Walter, "On Discrimination, Prejudice, Racial Income Differentials, and Affirmative Action," *Discrimination, Affirmative Action and Equal Opportunity*, Walter Block and Michael Walker, eds., Vancouver: The Fraser Institute, 1982; Block, Walter, "Discrimination: An Interdisciplinary Analysis," *The Journal of Business Ethics*, Vol. 11, 1992, pp. 241–254; Block, Walter and Williams, Walter E., "Male-Female Earnings Differentials: A Critical Reappraisal," *The Journal of Labor Research*, Vol. II, No. 2, Fall 1981, pp. 385–388; Block, Walter, "Compromising the Uncompromisable: Discrimination," *American Journal of Economics and Sociology*, Vol 57, No. 2, April, 1998, pp. 223–237; Block, Walter, "Economic Intervention, Discrimination, and Unforeseen Consequences," *Discrimination, Affirmative Action and Equal Opportunity*, Walter Block and Michael A. Walker, eds., Vancouver: The Fraser Institute, 1982, pp. 101–125.

One difficulty is that while the law of free association is violated, this is done in a haphazard manner. For example, discrimination on the basis of race, sex, national origin, and so on is prohibited in the area of commerce, but not in personal life. But if the former really is a rights violation, why is not the latter, also? That is, if a Christian merchant is unwilling to sell to a Jew, why is this different, in any relevant way, from the case where a Christian is unwilling to date, or to befriend, or to marry a Jew? (Or vice versa, of course.) Surely, if the former is rights violating, then so is the latter, despite the fact that the law of the land only enjoins the one, not the other. The problem, here, is that the law is either not consistently, fully, and vigilantly pursuing "improper" behavior, that is, chasing it down where ever it exists, even unto the personal sphere; or, that in proscribing it in the commercial arena, it is infringing upon the human right to pick and choose business associates. It is clear that the civil rights law does too much, not too little.

Even within the realm of business, there are discordances. If a law firm of 100 partners does not promote a black associate to this status, the courts will entertain a lawsuit to the effect that this failure is due to unwarranted discrimination.[120] But if two lawyers hook up to found a dual person firm, there is no third party (e.g., a black or a woman) who will be adjudicated to have enough standing to complain he was not included.

Further, the requirement not to discriminate in many circumstances rests with buyers, not sellers. If a man refuses to patronize a Chinese, or a Jewish or an Italian restaurant due to aversion to the members of these national origins he is likely to find at such establishments,[121] the law will count this as a matter of right. On the other hand, were a restaurant to post a sign stating that Chinese, Jews, or Italians will not be served there, he would be summarily hauled off to the Equal Employment Opportunity Commission (EEOC). Why, if to discriminate is to violate rights, would our society punish discriminators in the former case, but not the latter?

On the other hand, it is possible to specify circumstances where it is incumbent upon *buyers* not to discriminate. Were General Motors or

[120] See *Price Waterhouse v. Hopkins*, 104 L. Ed. 2d 268 (1989).

[121] This is itself another violation of the antidiscrimination laws that is virtually never enjoined.

Microsoft to let out a subcontract for tires or keyboards, and to specify in its offering that no firms owned by, or employing, Irish or Portuguese need apply, it would quickly be found guilty of an offense under these enactments. But if a purveyor of tires or keyboards or tires refused to make a bid for this business on the ground that these larger firms were owned by people against whom they held prejudices, a similar fate would not await them. The statement that "the law is an ass"[122] was never more true than in these cases.

Then, too, the law is applied differently depending upon the identity of the specific group involved, whether in the business or personal sphere. For example, were an athletic club to institute a "whites only" policy and ban blacks from membership or other forms of participation, there would be a great hue and cry, and large attendant legal risks.[123] On the other hand, were an analogous black or Puerto Rican organization to adopt a similar program vis a vis whites, its legal status would be very different.[124] Similarly, no Shabazz[125] operation, such as a grocery store, dry cleaners, or restaurant ever need fear that the forces of law and order would swoop down on it and compel openness toward whites, something that does not apply, for example, to Denny's Restaurant or Texaco.[126]

Perhaps the lagniappe of this phenomenon is the flap about the "n" word. For many years, it has been a legal offense for a white to call or characterize a black with this appellation. Yet, were one black to use it on another, this would be legally acceptable, de facto if not de jure. However

[122] Charles Dickens, *Oliver Twist*, ch. 2: "'If the law supposes that,' said Mr. Bumble, 'the law is an ass, an idiot.'"

[123] Because, as a place of public accommodation, the club's action violates the Civil Rights Act of 1964. See 42 U.S.C., Sections 2000c-2000e-17. See also Heart of Atlanta Motel v. United States, 379 U.S. 241 (1964), "Congress has power under the Commerce Clause to regulate places of public accommodation."

[124] Murray, Charles, *What It Means to be a Libertarian*, pp. 81–82 points to another idiosyncracy: "People are free to call other people 'racist' or 'sexist' on the slightest pretext. But when it comes to anything else, being judgmental is bad." Certainly, to publicly call a black, or a Jew, or a woman by a racial or sexual epithet would be a matter for the constable, whereas name calling in the opposite direction would call forth no such response from that quarter. But this is no less than a direct threat to the concept of equal rights for all.

[125] These are enterprises run by the Black Muslim organization.

[126] Ditto, op cit.

conventional, this practice flies in the face of the rule of law.[127] Either an act is licit or illicit. If it is legal for one group to engage in it, but illegal for another, this violates our most basic premises of jurisprudence: that all should be equal before the bar of justice. Suppose an enactment specified it were lawful for a white to break the speed limit, but not for a black; or that it was mandated that men could not litter, but women could; or that Jews were prohibited from jay walking, but this practice was allowed to Christians. There would be no doubt in any of these examples that the impartiality of the law had been breached. But no less is true in the present case.

But things get worse. In Washington D.C., a white government official used the word "niggardly" in describing budgetary matters.[128] This created a furor in the local black community. So much so that the official felt he had to hand in a letter of resignation. This was *accepted* by the duly constituted mayor of this major American city.[129]

IV. Conclusion

We began this chapter with a narrow consideration of antidiscrimination law, and found it very much wanting. That is, we saw no defense for the Alaskan enactment which compels Christian landlords to rent to unmarried couples, neither as an aspect of natural law nor as being compatible with the fundamental constitutional law of the land. We then broadened our purview to include, also, a consideration of the law of free association, and laws which prohibit discrimination on the basis of race, sex, national origin, or any other such characteristics. We found these, too, very much less than persuasive, both on grounds of natural liberties and economics. This spate of legislation, stemming from the Civil Rights Act

[127] Hayek, Friedrich A., *The Constitution of Liberty*, Henry Regnery Company, Chicago, 1960, pp. 397–411.

[128] Yardley, Jonathan, "Use the right word for 'the Times,'" *The Washington Post*, February 1, 1999, p. 2, col. 1; Dooling, Richard, "What a Niggling Offense! Oops, We Mean … " *Wall Street Journal*, January 29, 1999.

[129] The official was later rehired by the municipality, but that is another matter.

of 1964, was also seen as problematic in that it has led to several legal anomalies, inconsistencies, and philosophical embarrassments. For all these reasons, we conclude that the justice system ought to be turned back in time to its pre-1964 situation and these more recent accretions repealed, since they are evil, pernicious, and rights violating.

4

The Boy Scouts' Right to Discriminate

I. Introduction

In *Boy Scouts of America v. Dale*,[1] the Supreme Court was squarely faced with one of the most contentious questions facing today's society. That is whether an organization like the Boy Scouts can determine with whom it associates or is there some overriding public interest in compelling associational acceptance of, as in this case, an avowed homosexual. Are the Boy Scouts to be regarded by some as heroic defenders of James Madison's treasured idea of freedom of association? Or are they to be seen, as they are in many quarters, as evil discriminators against individuals who have a privacy right to their sexual orientation? This controversy commenced when the complainant James Dale became a Scout in 1981 at the age of eight.[2] He remained one until he turned 18.[3] Dale was a good Scout and

The authors would like to thank Sackitey Mate Kole for the calculations that undergird our statistical tables.

[1] 530 U.S. 640 (2000).

[2] Id. at 644.

[3] Id.

W. E. Block, R. Whitehead, *Philosophy of Law*, Palgrave Studies in Classical Liberalism,
https://doi.org/10.1007/978-3-030-28360-5_4

achieved its highest honor, the rank of Eagle Scout.[4] About the time he left home to attend Rutgers University, the Scouts approved his application for the adult position of assistant scout master in Troop 73.[5] When Dale arrived at Rutgers University, he acknowledged that he was gay and quickly became involved in, and eventually became the co-president of, the Rutgers Lesbian/Gay Alliance.[6] Later, Dale was interviewed by a newspaper reporter writing of the psychological and health needs of lesbian and gay teenagers. The newspaper published the interview and Dale's photograph over a caption identifying him as the co-president of the Lesbian/Gay Alliance.[7]

Not surprisingly, Dale then received a letter from the Monmouth counsel executive revoking his adult membership. In response to Dale's inquiry about his revocation, the executive responded by letter indicating that the Boy Scouts "specifically forbid membership to homosexuals."[8]

Thereafter, Dale responded by filing a complaint against the Boy Scouts in New Jersey Superior Court. He alleged that the Boy Scouts had violated New Jersey's Public Accommodation statute and its common law by revoking his membership based solely on his sexual orientation.[9] New Jersey's Public Accommodation statute prohibits, among many things, discrimination on the basis of sexual orientation in a laundry list of places considered to be places of public accommodation.[10] Some of these appear not to be physical "places" in the traditional meaning of the word.

---

[4] Id.

[5] Id.

[6] Id. at 645.

[7] Id.

[8] Id.

[9] Id.

[10] *See* N.J. Stat. Ann. section 10:-4 (West Supp. 2000), that provides, "l. A place of public accommodation shall include, but not be limited to: any tavern, roadhouse, hotel, motel, trailer camp, summer camp, day camp, or resort camp, whether for entertainment or transient guest or accommodation of those seeking health, recreation or rest; any producer, manufacturer, wholesaler, distributor, retail shop, store, establishment, or concession dealing with goods or services of any kind; any restaurant, eating house, or place where food is sold for consumption on the premises; any place maintained for the sale of ice cream, and food preparations or their derivatives, soda water or confections, or where any beverage of any kind for consumption on the premises; any garage, any public conveyance operated on land or water, or in the air, any stations or terminals thereof; any bath house, boardwalk, or seashore accommodations, any auditorium, meeting place, or hall; any theater, motion picture house, music hall, roof garden, skating rink, swimming pool and amuse-

The New Jersey Superior Court Chancery division granted summary judgment in favor of the Boy Scouts.[11] The Superior Court decided that the Boy Scouts was not a place of public accommodation and was a distinct private group exempted from coverage under New Jersey's accommodation law.[12] The Court also decided that the Boy Scout's beliefs about homosexuality were unmistakable and decided that the First Amendment freedom of expressive association prevented the state from compelling the Boy Scouts to associate with Mr. Dale as an adult leader.[13]

On appeal, the New Jersey Superior Court, Appellant Division, reversed and remanded, holding that the State's Public Accommodations law applied to the Boy Scouts and rejecting the Boy Scouts' federal constitutional claims of freedom of association.[14]

On appeal to the New Jersey Supreme Court, the Scouts argued that the application of New Jersey's Public Accommodation law violated their constitutional rights "to enter into and maintain … intimate and private relationships … and to associate for the purposes of engaging in protected speech."[15] The New Jersey Supreme Court, however, concluded that the Boy Scouts' "large size, non-selectivity, inclusive rather than exclusive purpose, and practice of inviting or allowing non-members to attend meetings, establish that the organization is not sufficiently personal or private to warrant constitutional protection under the freedom of intimate association."[16] In regard to the Scouts' claimed right of expressive

---

ment and recreation park, fair, bowling alley, gymnasium, shooting gallery, pool parlor, or other places of amusement; any comfort station; any dispensary, clinic, or hospital; any public library; any kindergarten, primary or secondary school, trade or business school, high school, academy, college and university, or any educational institution under the supervision of the State Board of Education, or the Commissioner of Education for the State of New Jersey. Nothing herein contained shall be construed to include or to apply to any institution, bona fide club, a place of accommodation, which is in its nature distinctive private; or shall anything herein contained apply to any educational facility operated or maintained by a bona fide religious or sectarian institution, and the right of a natural parent or one in loco prentice to direct the education and up-bringing of a child under his control is hereby affirmed; nor shall anything herein contain or be constructed to bar any private, secondary or post-secondary school from using in good faith criteria other than race, creed, color, national origin, ancestry, or affectional, or sexual orientation in the admission of students."

[11] 530 U.S. at 645.

[12] Id.

[13] Id. at 646.

[14] Id.

[15] See, James Dale v. Boy Scouts of America, 160 N.J. 562, 605, 734 A.2d 1196, 1219 (1999).

[16] 160 N.J.608–609, 734 A.2d at 1221.

association, the New Jersey Supreme Court "agreed that Boy Scouts expresses a belief in moral values and uses its activities to encourage moral development of its members."[17] The Court said, however, that it was "not persuaded … that a shared goal of Boy Scout members is to associate in order to preserve the view that homosexuality is immoral."[18] Therefore, the Court held that "Dale's membership does not violate the Boy Scouts' right of expressive association because his inclusion would not affect in any significant way the Boy Scouts existing member's ability to carry out their various purposes."[19] The New Jersey Court also determined that the State had a compelling interest in eliminating "the destructive consequences of discrimination from our society,"[20] and that the State's Public Accommodation law does no more than necessary to accomplish its purpose of stamping out such "destructive discrimination."

The Scouts relied on *Hurley v. Irish-American Gay, Lesbian and Bi-Sexual Group of Boston*[21] to support its First Amendment right to exclude Dale from the organization. The New Jersey Court decided that *Hurley* was not definitive. This was so because in the Court's view, unlike the situation in *Hurley*, the "the reinstatement of Dale does not compel the Boy Scouts to express any message."[22]

The Scouts then took their association issue to the Supreme Court. In *Boy Scouts of American v. Dale*,[23] Chief Justice Rehnquist commenced his analysis of the issue by citing *Roberts v. United States Jaycees*[24] for the

17 160 N.J. at 613, 734 A.2d at 1223.

18 Id., 734 A.2d at 1223–1224.

19 Id. at 615, 734 A.2d at 1225.

20 160 N.J. at 619–620, 734 A.2d at 1227–1228.

21 515 U.S. 557 (1995). Here, as we will explore in greater detail later, the Supreme Court held that a gay group did not have a First Amendment right to march in a St. Patrick's Day parade. The High Court decided that inclusion of the gay group would interfere with the parade organization's First Amendment rights by giving the impression that they sponsored the views of the gay group. Id. 572–573. The Court said that the parade… "is an inherently expressive undertaking." Id. at 568–570.

22 160 N.J., at 634, 734 A.2d, at 1229.

23 530 U.S. 640, 647 (2000).

24 468 U.S. 609 (1984). Here, the Jaycees brought an action contending that the application of Minnesota's public accommodations law requiring them to admit women violated the male members' intimate association rights. The Supreme Court concluded that "Jaycees chapters lacked the distinctive characteristics that might afford constitutional protection to the decision to exclude women." Id. at 621. The court emphasized that the local chapters are neither small nor selective,

proposition that "implicit in the right to engage in activities protected by the First Amendment" is "a corresponding right to associate with others in pursuit of a wide variety of political, social, economic, educational, religious, and cultural ends."[25] He pointed out that government actions may constitutionally burden this freedom in many ways, including "intrusion into the internal structure or affairs of an association,"[26] for example, imposing a "regulation that forces the group to accept members it does not desire."[27] Obviously, forcing a group to accept members it does not desire may impair the ability of the group to express the views it wants to articulate. Still relying on *Roberts*, he explained, "freedom of association plainly pre-supposes a freedom not to associate."[28] Consequently, he said that the forced inclusion of an unwanted person in a group infringes the group's freedom of expressive association when his presence has an effect on the group's ability to advocate their views.[29]

The freedom of expressive association, however, is not always absolute. The Supreme Court has ruled that this freedom may be impacted "by regulations adopted to serve compelling state interests, unrelated to the expression of ideas, that cannot be achieved through means significantly less restrictive of associational freedoms."[30] The Chief Justice then turned to a determination of whether or not the Boy Scouts are entitled to protection because they engage in "expressive association."[31] His inquiry led to an examination of the Boy Scouts' mission statement. The gist of this document is essentially that the Boy Scouts seek to instill values in young people that will lead them to make ethical choices in their life experiences.[32]

---

and that "much of the activity central to the formation and maintenance of the association involves participation by strangers to that relationship." Id. at 621.

[25] Id. at 622.

[26] Id. at 648.

[27] Id. at 623.

[28] Id.

[29] Here citing New York State Club Assn., v. City of New York, 487 U.S. 1, 13 (1988).

[30] Citing Roberts, 486 U.S. at 623.

[31] Boy Scouts at 648.

[32] "It is the mission of the Boy Scouts of American to serve other by helping to install values in young people and, in other ways, to prepare them to make ethical choices over their lifetime in achieving their full potential.

Relying on the Scout's mission statement, the Chief Justice wrote that it seems indisputable that the Boy Scouts were seeking to transmit a system of values by engaging in expressive activity.[33]

Having decided that the Boy Scouts' stated mission causes them to engage in expressive activity, the next inquiry was whether the forced inclusion of Mr. Dale as an assistant scout master would significantly affect their ability to advocate public or private viewpoints.[34] This inquiry required the Court to briefly examine the Boy Scouts' views on homosexuality. A careful reading of the mission statement clearly reveals that the Boy Scouts do not expressly or explicitly mention sexual orientation in their Scout Oath or Scout Law.[35] But they claim that homosexual conduct is inconsistent with the important life values found in the Scout Oath and Scout Law. And the values that the Scouts claim to instill in their members are based on the same Oath and Law.[36] So from where do these values arise? In the view of this organization, the values they seek to instill are represented by the terms "morally straight" and "clean" that are, in their eyes, incompatible with homosexuality.[37]

Certainly, reasonable people can reach different conclusions on the meaning of the terms "morally straight" and "clean." Many people might believe that homosexual conduct falls within these parameters. Others firmly maintain that sexual orientation is no one else's business. Still others, apparently including the Boy Scouts, believe that homosexuality is incompatible with living a morally straight and clean life.

The high court observed that the New Jersey Supreme Court concluded that "exclusion of members solely on the basis of sexual orientation was

"The Scout Oath: "On my honor I will do my best to do my duty to God and my Country and to obey the Scout law; to help other people at all times; to keep my self physically strong; mentally awake, and morally strait.

"The Scout Law: "A Scout is trustworthy, obedient, loyal, cheerful, helpful, thrifty, friendly, brave, courteous, clean, kind and reverent."

[33] Boy Scouts at 650, citing Roberts at 636 (O'Connor concurring) ("Even the training of outdoor survival skills or participation in community service might become expressive when the activity is intended to develop good morals, reverence, patriotism, and desire for self-improvement").

[34] Boy Scouts at 650.

[35] Id.

[36] Id.

[37] Id.

inconsistent with the Boy Scouts' commitment to a diverse and 'representative membership' … and contradicts Boy Scouts' overarching objective to reach 'all eligible youth.'"[38] The New Jersey court said that the Scouts violated the States' discrimination law, in part, because the exclusion of homosexual members "appears antithetical to the organizations' goals and philosophy."[39]

Chief Justice Rehnquist would have none of this. His ringing response was to reject the entire notion that a Court could reject a private organization's philosophy. He said "it is not the role of the Courts to reject a group's express values because they disagree with those values and find them internally inconsistent."[40] He wrote, "as is true of all expressions of First Amendment freedoms, the Courts may not interfere on the ground that they view a particular expression as unwise or irrational."[41] He continued, "religious beliefs need not be acceptable, logical, consistent, or comprehensive to others in order to merit First Amendment protection."[42] The Boy Scouts claimed in their appellate briefs that they taught their members that homosexual conduct is not morally straight.[43] The court accepted that assertion as true.[44] Because the majority accepted that assertion as true, there was no need to inquire further. Why? Because it is not the business of the Court to determine if a particular view is unwise or irrational, and because the record clearly establishes the Scouts' view on homosexuality,[45] there was no need for the Court to inquire further. The Court concluded that the Boy Scouts' professed beliefs

---

[38] 160 N.J. at 618, 734 A.2d at 1226.

[39] Id.

[40] Id. at 651, citing Democratic Party of United States v. Wisconsin, 450 U.S. 107, 124 (1981) ("[A]s is true of all expressions of First Amendment freedoms, the Courts may not interfere on the grounds they view a particular expression as unwise or irrational").

[41] Boy Scouts at 651.

[42] Id., citing Thomas v. Review Board of Indiana Employment Security Division, 450 U.S. 707, 714 ("[R]eligious beliefs need not be acceptable, logical, consistent, or comprehensible to others in order to merit First Amendment protection").

[43] Boy Scouts at 651.

[44] Id.

[45] Id. at 651–652.

about homosexual conduct were sincere.[46] Finally, the majority cited the fact that the Boy Scouts had publicly and consistently expressed the same views with respect to homosexual conduct by its pleadings in prior litigation.[47]

The next question faced by the Court was whether Dale's presence as an assistant scout master would place a significantly high burden on the Boy Scouts' desire to not "promote homosexual conduct as a legitimate form of behavior."[48] The Chief Justice noted "As we give deference to an association's assertions regarding the nature of its expression, we must also give deference to the association's view of what would impair its expression."[49] Given Dale's widely publicized interview with the newspaper about his sexual orientation, the fact that he was co-president of the gay and lesbian organization at college, and remains a gay rights activist today, it is obvious that his presence would force the Scouts to send a message, against their will, that they accept and even highly regard homosexual conduct as a legitimate form of behavior.[50]

The High Court turned to the holding in *Hurley* as a basis of its belief that Dale's presence would force the Boy Scouts to send a message that they condone homosexual conduct.[51] Recall that *Hurley* involved the question of whether Massachusetts' Public Accommodation law would require the organizers of a private St. Patrick's Day parade to include among the marchers an Irish-American gay, lesbian, and bi-sexual group called GLIB.[52] GLIB contended that the parade organizers violated their First Amendment rights by denying them the opportunity to march. In that case, the High Court observed that the parade organizers did not

---

[46] Id. at 652 quoting the Scouts' 1993 position statement, "The Boy Scouts of American has always reflected the expectations that scouting families have had for the organization. We do not believe that homosexuals provide role models consistent with these expectations. Accordingly, we do not allow for the registration of avowed homosexuals as members or as leaders of the B.S.A."

[47] *See* Curren v. Mount Diablo Council of Boy Scouts of American, 48 Cal. App. 4th 670, 952 P.2nd 218 (1998).

[48] Boy Scouts at 653.

[49] Id. citing La Follette, note 4041, *Supra* at 123–124 for the proposition that when considering burdens on associational rights, a court may not substitute its judgment for that of a political party.

[50] Id. at 653.

[51] Id.

[52] Id.

wish to exclude the GLIB members because of their sexual orientation, but because they wanted to march behind a GLIB banner.[53] The Court stated:

> A contingent marching behind the organization's banner would at least bear witness to the fact that some Irish are gay, lesbian or bi-sexual, and the presence of the organized marchers would suggest their view that people of their sexual orientation have as much claim to unqualified social acceptance as heterosexuals. The parade organizers may not believe these facts about Irish sexuality to be so, or they may object to unqualified social acceptance of gays and lesbians or have some other reason of wishing to keep GLIB's message out of the parade. But whatever the reason, it boils down to the choice of a speaker not to propound a particular point-of-view, and that choice is presumed to lie beyond the government's power to control.[54]

Here, the High Court found that the Boy Scouts legitimately believe that homosexual conduct is inconsistent with the values it seeks to instill in its members. That is so, just as the presence of GLIB in Boston's St. Patrick's Day parade would have interfered with the parade organizer's First Amendment rights not to be forced to propound a particular point-of-view. Dale's presence as an assistant scout master in a Boy Scout troop would just as surely interfere with the Boy Scouts' choice not to suggest a view on homosexuality contrary to its own beliefs.[55]

Next, the High Court turned to the New Jersey Court's determination that the Boy Scouts' ability to disseminate its message would not be significantly affected by the forced inclusion of Dale as an assistant scout master. The New Jersey Court found:

> Boy Scout members do not associate for the purpose of disseminating the belief that homosexuality is immoral; Boy Scouts discourages its leaders from disseminating *any* views on sexual issues; and Boy Scouts included

---

[53] Id.

[54] Hurley, 515 U.S., at 574–575.

[55] Boy Scouts at 654.

sponsors and members who subscribe to different views in respect of homosexuality.[56]

Chief Justice Rehnquist entirely disagreed with the New Jersey Courts' conclusion for three reasons. First, he fiercely stated that associations did not have to associate "for the purpose of disseminating a certain message"[57] in order to be entitled to the protection of the First Amendment. It is enough that an association may engage in expressive activity that could be impaired by Dale's presence in order to be entitled to protection. He cited *Hurley* for the proposition that the gay group could be excluded from marching in a parade even when the purpose of the parade was not to espouse any views whatsoever about sexual orientation.[58]

Secondly, he said that even if the Boy Scouts discouraged leaders from disseminating views on sexual issues, "the First Amendment protects the Boy Scouts' method of expression."[59] Even if Scout leaders try to dodge questions of sexuality and teach only by example, their approach does not impeach the sincerity of their beliefs concerning homosexuality.[60]

Third, he found that the First Amendment does not require every member of a group to agree on every issue in order for the group's policy to be "expressive association."[61] Mr. Dale argues that the Boy Scouts do not revoke the membership of heterosexual scout leaders who openly disagree with the Boy Scouts' policy on sexual orientation. The court decided that even if true, this statement is irrelevant.[62] The fact that the Boy Scouts take an official position with respect to homosexual conduct is itself sufficient for First Amendment purposes. Said the Chief Justice, "the presence of a gay activist like Mr. Dale in a Scoutmaster's uniform would send a distinctly different message from the presence of a hetero-

[56] 160 N.J. at 612, 734 A.2d at 1223.

[57] Boy Scouts at 655.

[58] Id.

[59] Id.

[60] Id.

[61] Id.

[62] In the view of the Court, the record sheds some doubt on Dale's claim. "For example, the National Director of the Boy Scouts certified that 'any persons who advocate to Scouting youth that homosexual conduct is consistent' with Scouting values will not be registered as adult leaders." See Id. at 655 n.1.

sexual Scout master who is on the record as disagreeing with the Scouts' policy."[63] The Scouts clearly have a First Amendment right to choose one message and not the other. The fact that this organization tolerates dissent within its ranks does not mean that its views are stripped of their First Amendment protection.[64]

The next question faced by the Court was whether the imposition of New Jersey's Public Accommodations law requiring the Boy Scouts to accept Dale violates the Scouts' freedom of expression.[65] The Court was much concerned about the broad parameters of New Jersey's Public Accommodation law.[66] The Statute covers over 50 different types of places in its definition of a place of public accommodation.[67] The Court pointed out that in this case the New Jersey Supreme Court applied its public accommodation law to a private entity without even attempting to tie the term "place" to a physical location.[68] The law covers traditional places like taverns, hotels, shops, and libraries. But it also sweeps within its grasp imprecise locations such as summer camps and playing fields.[69]

The High Court declared in cases such as *Roberts* and *Duarte*[70] that the states have a compelling interest in eliminating discrimination against women in public accommodations. But the Court declared that in each of those cases enforcement of the public accommodation statute would not materially interfere with the ideas the organizations sought to express.[71] In *Roberts,* the Court said that the Jaycees had failed to demonstrate any serious burdens on the male members' freedom of expressive association. In *Duarte,*[72] the Court wrote:

---

[63] Id. at 656.

[64] Id.

[65] Id.

[66] See, Supra, note for the listing.

[67] Boy Scouts at 656.

[68] Id. at 657.

[69] Id.

[70] Board of Directors of Rotary International v. Rotary Club Duarte, 481 U.S. 537 (1987).

[71] Id. at 757.

[72] In Board of Directors of Rotary International v. Rotary Club Duarte, 481 U.S. 537 (1987), the high court considered a situation in which the charter of a local chapter of Rotary International was revoked by the national organization because it admitted female members. Here, the court concluded "the relationship among the members is not the kind of intimate or private relation that

> Impediments to the exercise of one's right to choose one's associates can violate the right of association protected by the First Amendment. In this case, however, the evidence fails to demonstrate that admitting men and women to Rotary Clubs will affect in any significant way the existing members' ability to carry out their various purposes.[73]

By contrast, New Jersey's Public Accommodations law directly impacts associational rights that enjoy First Amendment protection by compelling the Scouts to accept Mr. Dale.[74] This is so because his presence places an intolerable burden on the Scouts' freedom of expressive association. Why? Because his presence implies acceptance of homosexual conduct. The High Court stated that New Jersey's Public Accommodations law does not justify such a severe intrusion on the Boy Scouts' freedom of expressive association.[75] The dissent berates the majority because the latter fails to recognize that gayness is regarded by many citizens as compatible with a clean and morally straight lifestyle.[76] But the Chief Justice's retort was that the First Amendment protects expression, popular or unpopular, citing decisions in unpopular cases involving flag burning and the Ku Klux Klan.[77] He also mentioned that the Court must not be influenced by its personal views with respect to the Boy Scouts' treatment of gays, right or wrong.[78] The Court held by a close 5–4 vote that the First Amendment prohibits the State from imposing a requirement that Mr. Dale be made an assistant scoutmaster.[79]

---

warrants constitutional protection." Id. at 541. It emphasized the Rotary Club's inclusive membership policy, pointing to its own declaration that "the purpose of Rotary is to produce an inclusive, not exclusive membership." Id. at 546. Importantly, Rotary's membership policy was designed to be inclusive in order to enable the club to be a true cross section of the business and professional life of the community.

[73] Boy Scouts at 658.

[74] Id. at 659.

[75] Id.

[76] See Id. at 699–700.

[77] Id. at 660, citing Texas v. Johnson, 491 U.S. 397 (1989) (holding that there is a right to burn one's American flag), and Brandenburg v. Ohio, 395 U.S. 444 (1969) (holding that Ku Klux Klan leaders had a First Amendment right to advocate unlawfulness).

[78] Id. at 661.

[79] Id.

II. Dissent

Mr. Justice Stevens authored a ringing dissent to the majority's determination that Mr. Dale's presence would intrude on the Scouts' freedom of association. First, in perhaps a gentle jab at the majority, normally strong supporters of federalism, he said that New Jersey ought to be commended for its attempts to eradicate the cancer of discrimination from society.[80] The High Court, he wrote, simply failed to accord that State the respect it is due in our federal system.[81] Next, the dissent claims "it is plain as the light of day" that the terms "morally straight" and "clean" have nothing to do with homosexuality.[82] Further, it is just as clear that scoutmasters do not give information or advice about sexual matters, leaving that to the parents.[83] And finally the Boy Scouts' pronouncements simply declare that homosexuality is not "appropriate."[84] Consequently, this idea or principle of excluding gays does not appear to be a part of the Scouts' publicly taught values and creeds.[85] The dissent maintained that there was no connection between these essentially private policy statements and the Scouts' expressive interests[86] that justify the majority's decision. They seemed to think that the Scouts' failure to forcefully and publicly advocate their concern with gayness was somehow evidence of an acceptance of homosexuality or the lack of an expressive objection to the

[80] Id. at 663 citing Justice Brandeis' comment in New State Ice Co. v. Liebmann, 285 U.S. 262, 311 (1932) (dissenting), "To stay experimentation in things social and economic is a grave responsibility … It is one of the happy incidents of the federal system that a single courageous State may, if its citizens choose, serve as a laboratory; and try novel social and economic experiments without risk to the rest of the country." The Chief Justice's response to the Brandeis quote was that in *New Ice Age* he was speaking of experimentation in matters economic during the depression years. Id at 660. He wrote that Brandeis was a champion of free speech in matters of expression. He thought that the founders "believed that freedom to think as you will and to speak as you think are means indispensable to the spread and discovery of political truth," citing Whitney v. California, 274 U.S. 357, 375 (1927) (concurring). Id. at 661.

[81] Id. at 664.

[82] Id. at 668.

[83] Id. at 668–669.

[84] Id. at 773.

[85] Id. "Rather, … the policy appears to be no more than a private statement of a few BSA executives…." Id.

[86] Id. at 776.

practice of that lifestyle. Maybe the lesson for the Scouts is that they should have been more outspoken or bigoted toward gays?[87]

Next, the minority opinion maintained that in order to win an expressive association claim, the Boy Scouts must show *more* (emphasis added by present authors) than merely some expressive activity.[88] They must also establish a serious burden on the group's collective effort.[89] But Dale's presence was no serious burden on the Scouts, in their view. This was so because it was never demonstrated by the Scouts that he would in any way advocate his beliefs to the youngsters in his charge.[90]

Justice Stevens recognized that the Scouts had a First Amendment right to not talk about homosexuality to its youthful members. But, he said, that interest could be accomplished by directions to adult leaders to not discuss matters relating to sex and religion.[91] The Scouts' concern that Dale would use his position as a bully pulpit to convey his ideas on homosexuality has no basis in fact, he averred.[92] Plus, there is no indication that Mr. Dale would not follow all Scout policies.

Next, Mr. Justice Stevens took great issue with the majority's holding that Dale's presence would send a message that the Scouts endorsed a gay lifestyle.[93] He forcefully argued that the majority's reliance on *Hurley* was misplaced. Recall in *Hurley* that a gay group wished to march in a private organization's St. Patrick's Day parade with a large banner to express pride in their gayness.[94] The court said in that case that the parade organizers, a private group, could not be compelled to proclaim a belief with which

[87] At least that was the opinion of one writer. Writing of the New Jersey Supreme Court decision he said, "By the perverse logic of this decision, the Boy Scouts erred not in the direction of bigotry but rather in not being bigoted enough." Terence Pell, "Not Bigoted Enough," Washington Post, Aug. 23, 1999, at A17.

[88] Boy Scouts at 683, citing Jaycees, 468 U.S. at 626–627.

[89] Jaycees at 627.

[90] Boy Scouts at 682, 689.

[91] Id. at 688.

[92] Id. at 689. "BSA has not contended, nor does the record support, that Dale ever advocated a view on homosexuality to his troop before his membership was revoked." Id.

[93] Id. at 696. He forcefully argued that the majority's reliance simply on the fact that Dale was gay somehow sent a message endorsing homosexuality was wrong. Such a presumed message is the same as a "constitutionally prescribed symbol of inferiority." Id.

[94] 515 U.S. 557, 561 (1995).

it disagreed.[95] Justice Stevens said that Dale's presence at a scout meeting was nothing like marching in a parade with a banner.[96] Contrary to *Hurley*, Dale does not carry a banner nor openly advocate his views merely by attending troop meetings.[97] Mere joining or attendance at a meeting is not enough to rise to the level of expression.[98] Usually, an expressive association claim involves at least the "avowal and advocacy of a consistent position on some issue over time."[99] The fact that a gay man participates in an organization no more conveys a message than the participation by an openly gay person in baseball, tennis, or golf somehow sends a message in support of this lifestyle.[100]

Finally, the dissenters reminded us "unfavorable opinions about homosexuals have ancient roots."[101] And that as a result of free interaction between people, these ancient and outmoded unfavorable opinions have consistently been moderating.[102] The minority opinion cited examples of domestic partner legislation, greater understanding in religious faiths, and removal of homosexuality from a list of mental disorders to support this idea of moderation.[103] Indeed, it is apparent that the publicly avowed view toward gays is heavily tilted toward acceptance. In contrast, the authors of this present article take the position that sexual conduct between consenting adults is none of the State's concern. None at all! The majority's response to this was, of course, that the Scouts' position on homosexuality did not have to be rational or reasonable to fall under First Amendment protection.[104]

But what relevance does any of the foregoing have to do with voluntary association? Let us stipulate that Mr. Dale is a very honest, upright, religious, witty, and moral person whom we would trust to care for and

[95] Id. at 573–574.

[96] Boy Scouts at 694.

[97] Id. at 695.

[98] Id.

[99] Id. at 696.

[100] Id. at 697.

[101] Id. at 699.

[102] Id.

[103] Id. at 699–700.

[104] *See* Id. at 660.

educate our children. And we further posit that his sexual orientation has absolutely no effect on his abilities to be a wonderful scoutmaster. These provisos notwithstanding, it is still illicit for the government to compel one person to associate with another just because the latter is of good moral character. Perhaps we prefer associating with our friends who smoke cigarettes, drink beer, play poker, eat fatty steaks, tell dirty jokes, and watch pornographic movies. Could the government legitimately compel us to shun our disreputable friends and instead go camping with the sainted Mother Theresa, or even Mr. Dale, just because they are of good moral character? We think not; the whole idea is preposterous in a free society. In the end, whether gay leaders are compatible with family values is not the fundamental issue. Rather, it is whether an organization has the right to set its own membership rules. These specifications for joining may not fit with some of today's politically correct social norms. They might be hurtful to an individual's feelings. But at the end of the day the alternative to the right of exclusion is total state control of private association. We need not succumb to the tyranny of the supposed good intentions of the State of New Jersey. We think that James Madison would appreciate the Boy Scouts' moral courage in standing up for his First Amendment.[105] We now turn to the philosophy of free association.

III. Philosophy

According to the New Jersey Supreme Court, the Boy Scouts are guilty of an egregious offense against morality, propriety, and, most important, the law, in their decision to exclude gays as scoutmasters. This philosophical position taken on by the court in this decision is that discrimination, on the basis of an entire litany of criteria, is wrong and should be proscribed by law. But the finding of this court is philosophically flawed. Indeed, it is so dead from the neck up that even the adherents of this perspective are unable to carry through on their own principles, and apply them widely.

---

[105] As would Justice Brandeis, See note 8080, *Supra*, He thought the founders "believed that freedom to think as you will and speak as you think are means indispensable to the spread and discovery of political truth," Whitney v. California, 274 U.S. 357, 375 (1927) (concurring).

For example, while employers may not exclude, or discriminate against employees on the basis of race, gender, national origin, sexual preference, and so on, the latter are not at all proscribed by law from doing just that with regard to the former. That is, if the present authors decline to take a job with Brigham Young, Loyola, or Yeshiva Universities on the grounds that their religious mission offends us, we are still in full compliance with the law. But let any one of them apply a similar criterion in their hiring of professors, and all hell breaks loose, legally speaking. Needless to say, it would be a matter of outlawry for them to refuse to employ scholars for these reasons.

Take another case. Suppose the present authors decide to go out to dinner together, but eschew all Chinese, black, Jewish, and Italian restaurants, not on the ground that their culinary offerings do not appeal to us, but rather because we loathe the nationalities thereby represented. Are we thereby guilty of law breaking? We are not. But were any of these establishments to make similar choices with regard to employees or customers (e.g., by posting a sign on their premises stating "no Chinese, blacks, Jews or Italians will be allowed entry, either as patrons or workers"), it would be a paradigm case of law violation.

This fact, that the burden of nondiscrimination is uneven, has further interesting ramifications. For example, sellers are typically forbidden to discriminate, but not buyers; but even this is by no means the end of the story. A diner can patronize an Italian restaurant, avoiding one offering Chinese food, even if this is motivated by racial or ethnic hatred. But a Greek eating establish may not ban Turkish diners, nor vice versa, even when this decision is precipitated by similar emotions. On the other hand, were any of these restaurants to decide not to hire (e.g., *purchase* the services of) Jews or blacks, they would quickly be found to be in violation of antidiscrimination law.

If the same establishments were to avoid purchasing meats or vegetables from gays or females or Spaniards, their (legal) guilt would turn on the issue of whether they shop for these things in a supermarket (in which case they could discriminate to their heart's content) or let these things out to competitive bidding contracts (in which case they could not discriminate on race, sex, gender, or ethnicity; however, it would be legal for them to discriminate on the basis of price, e.g., accept the lowest bid.).

One of the criteria of good law is surely intellectual coherence, something under which such legislation does not pass muster.

Moreover, if it is really true that discrimination is a cancer,[106] which must, presumably, be wiped out entirely, then why do we countenance it in personal relations? For example, dating. Why does not the law force all those who wish to engage in this practice, whether gay or straight, *not* to discriminate on the basis of race? If blacks are 14% of the overall population, then every seventh date of a white person must be with a member of this community. Marriage and friendship patterns, too, must come under the eagle eye of the discrimination police. Present intermarriage rates are evidence of the fact that blatant discrimination takes place in this arena.

And, as it happens, *both* heterosexuals and homosexuals are "guilty" of sexual discrimination. Male homosexuals, for example, abjure women as bed partners, as do female heterosexuals. Female homosexuals forswear men, the same practice of male heterosexuals. All of this evil behavior must be proscribed, forthwith. It is only bisexuals who are acting lawfully. The logical implication of the court in the gay boy scouts' case is compulsory bisexuality for everyone. Until and unless they are willing to embrace this consistent application of their own philosophy, they are forced, by the laws of logic, to change their verdict.

Further, "All-boys schools are attacked for discrimination, but all-girls schools are consistent with the needs of diversity. All-white clubs are verboten, but all-black clubs are a healthy reflection of racial pride. All-Christian schools are pockets of bigotry, but all-atheist schools are essential to pluralism."[107] The law mandates that girls be accepted for boy's sports team, but the reverse does not apply. If it did, that is, were girl's sports teams forced to allow male participation, and if ability were still the determining factor for inclusion, this would pretty much spell the death knell for all female participation in athletics, with the possible exception of such activities as golf, and "ballet sports" such as gymnastics,

[106] N.J-4. S.A. 10:5.

[107] Lew Rockwell, The Right To Exclude, Sep. 6, 1999; WorldNetDaily.Com.

diving, and synchronized swimming.[108] Certainly, it would be the rare female who could hold her own vis a vis males in football, baseball, basketball, and so on.

Or consider the fact that the Black Muslim group of Malcolm X was not forced to admit whites; that religious groups such as Mormons, Jews, Catholics, and so on may legally exclude nonmembers from (certain aspects of) their services. Then there is the fact that there is a strict enforcement of male-only and female-only rest rooms: neither may "poach" upon the preserves of the other; each, that is, may exclude the other.

Conceivably, all of these decisions may be "justified." Perhaps employers are stronger or more powerful or have better bargaining power than employees.[109] Even if so, this is unrelated to racial or gender discrimination. If this is legally offensive, per se, then mere wealth should be irrelevant. After all, the rapist cannot defend his action on the ground that his victim is richer than himself. In any case, it is the *customer*, not the owner of the restaurant, "who is always right." If there is any imbalance of power in that scenario, it presumably cuts in precisely the opposite direction. For example, since the patron of an eating establishment holds a thumbs up or thumbs down vote, it should be, if anyone, the former not the latter who would have the right to freely pick and choose.

This court finding is also philosophically flawed in that it ignores the fact that private property rights are in effect a license to exclude. The entire point of such rights is to draw a line between "mine" and "thine." If a man cannot exclude others from his premises, there is a strong sense in which they are not *his* premises at all.

States Rockwell: "But liberty also means the right to exclude because only property owners have the right to decide questions of access. There is simply no right to crash a private dinner party, for example. The owners

[108] See on this Block, Walter, Whitehead, Roy and Hardin, Lu, "Gender Equity in Athletics: Should We Adopt a Non-Discriminatory Model?," *The University of Toledo Law Review*, Vol. 30, No. 2, Winter 1999, pp. 223–249; Whitehead, Roy, Walter E. Block and Patrick Tinsley. 2008. "Christian Landlords and the Free Exercise Clause: Sinners Need Not Apply," Oklahoma City University Law Review; Vol. 33, No. 1, Spring, pp. 115–150.

[109] This will come as a surprise to the employer of Michael Jordan, or of marginal farmers during harvest when they are desperate for workers.

of the house have the right to invite or not invite guests on any grounds they wish. Similarly, there is no right to invade a private organization, on the part of candidates unwelcome to the membership."[110] If private male-only golf courses cannot be forced to admit women, it would appear to be a legal stretch to compel the boy scouts to welcome gays in their senior ranks.

The New Jersey Supreme Court attempted to argue its way out of this conundrum by defining the Boy Scouts as a "public accommodation." But this is a philosophical howler of the first magnitude. For this organization is not at all "open to the entire public." Rather, it is receptive *only* to those members of the public who meet its membership criteria, and this most certainly does not include gay scoutmasters. Were the "public accommodation" doctrine pushed to its logical conclusion, moreover, it would spell the death knell of private property. For *any* property, with no exceptions, it is open to *some* members of the public; even private homes and clubs. To infer that if an owner is willing to engage his property with *some* people that he therefore must be forced to do so with *all* people is thus logically invalid.

If the real reason for this attack on the liberties of Americans is not and cannot be concern with discrimination (as shown by the fact that the court will not consistently apply this tyrannical principle), nor yet is it "public accommodation" (because this mischievous doctrine undermines all property rights), what then is the true explanation for this loss of our liberties?[111] In a word, it is concern with victims, but only with *some* victims, those embraced by the forces of political correctness. Asks Rockwell in this regard:

> What if the Boy Scouts had decided to exclude, say, racists as Scout masters. Would the courts have intervened on behalf of, for example, a Klan member's right to join? Not on your life. This is not an equal application of the law, but one that favors interest groups approved by government.

[110] Lew Rockwell, "The Right To Exclude," Sep. 6, 1999; www.WorldNetDaily.Com. See also his "Exclusion," *Rothbard-Rockwell Report*, Vol. 10, No. 10, p. 1, October 1999.

[111] It is surely a paradox that at a time when the U.S. armed forces are conducting an expedition ostensibly to promote the liberties of the Iraqis, liberties at home are in great danger.

In this regard, it is more than passing curious that gays, who have long been associated with the view that they should be allowed a sphere of privacy in the bedroom or in the bathhouse for "acts between consenting adults," are now intent upon violating the private spaces of those who do not welcome them.

The legal precedent for the present diminution of property rights is the 1948 Supreme Court decision abrogating restrictive covenants that mentioned race. *Shelley v. Kraemer*[112] mandated they not be enforced. But if property rights and contracts are undermined by judicial decisions, the rot infects our entire society. If civilization is built upon these twin pillars, to the extent they are diluted, our entire society is put at risk.

In sharp contrast to *Shelley v. Kraemer* is the following ringing endorsement of contractual and private property rights mandating that the state not "limit or abridge, directly or indirectly, the right of any person, who is willing or desires to sell, lease, or rent any part or all of his real property, to decline to sell, lease or rent such property to such person or persons as he, in his absolute discretion, chooses."[113] But in 1967, the U.S. Supreme Court struck that amendment down[114]—on the same grounds that the New Jersey court ruled against the Boy Scouts.

In the view of Rockwell, "Since then the right of free association[115] has experienced many blows, from the 1964 Civil Rights Act, which defined all business enterprises as a public accommodation to be controlled by government, straight to this New Jersey decision. If a group is politically powerful enough, it can have the tyrants in black robes override anyone's property rights."

---

[112] 334 U.S. 1 (1948).

[113] These words appear in a 1964 amendment to the California constitution. See on this Cushman, Cases In Constitutional Law, p. 554, Prentice Hall (5th Ed. 1994).

[114] Lew Rockwell, The Right To Exclude, Sep. 6, 1999; WorldNetDaily.Com.

[115] For a philosophical view on the right to discriminate, see Narveson, Jan, "Have we a right to non-discrimination?," *Business Ethics in Canada*, Deborah Poff and Wilfrid Waluchow, eds., Scarborough, ON: Prentice-Hall Canada, 1987, pp. 183–198; Block, Walter, "Discrimination: An Interdisciplinary Analysis," *The Journal of Business Ethics*, Vol. 11, 1992, pp. 241–254; Block, Walter, "Compromising the Uncompromisable: Discrimination," *American Journal of Economics and Sociology*, Vol. 57, No. 2, April, 1998, pp. 223–237.

Libertarians[116] oppose not only this attack by a gay man on that venerable institution, the Boy Scouts. They also dispute the entire philosophy upon which such a lawsuit rests upon. Nor is it only a matter of a "slippery slope." The iceberg is already upon us, not just its tip. If an organization such as the boy scouts can be successfully assaulted in the courts by a gay person, then reductios ad absurdum are all but impossible.

IV. Economics

Why is it that we have run so far off the rails in terms of antidiscrimination law? How is it that we have arrived at a point where compulsory bisexuality is the only practice consistent with legislation in this area? Can it really be required by law that parents be forced to send their impressionable adolescent boys to an organization featuring gay scoutmasters, forsooth?

There are many plausible explanations for this sorry state of affairs: a failure of the will, rampant immorality, sheer bloody minded busybodyness, an altogether perverse interpretation of the otherwise reasonable desire to help the underdog, philosophical confusion, and "bloody cheek" in the British expression. But we must not, in casting around for blame on this matter, neglect the dismal science. Economic illiteracy, too, goes a long way toward explaining why so many segments of our society should either have embraced the antidiscrimination idea with alacrity, or at least accorded it passive acceptance.

[116] For the libertarian philosophy which underscores the underlying intellectual basis of this section, indeed of the entire paper, see Rothbard, Murray N., *For a New Liberty*, Macmillan, New York, 1973; Rothbard, Murray N., *The Ethics of Liberty*, Humanities Press, Atlantic Highlands, N.J., 1982; Hoppe, Hans-Hermann, *A Theory of Socialism and Capitalism: Economics, Politics and Ethics*, Boston: Kluwer, 1989; Hoppe, Hans-Hermann, *The Economics and Ethics of Private Property: Studies in Political Economy and Philosophy*, Boston: Kluwer, 1993; Nozick, Robert, *Anarchy, State and Utopia*, New York: Basic Books, 1974; Block, Walter, *Defending the Undefendable*, New York: Fox and Wilkes, 1991; Block, Walter, "Libertarianism vs. Libertinism," *The Journal of Libertarian Studies: An Interdisciplinary Review*, Vol. 11, No. 1, 1994, pp. 117–128; Murray, Charles, *What It Means to be a Libertarian*, New York: Broadway Books, 1997; Narveson, Jan, *The Libertarian Idea*, Philadelphia: Temple University Press, 1988; De Jasay, Anthony, *The State*, Oxford: Basil Blackwell, 1985.

The major fallacy underlying the so-called civil rights movement is the idea that discrimination, particularly on the part of the rich and powerful,[117] is economically deleterious to the downtrodden; indeed, that this is an important source of poverty, if not the major explanation for this state of affairs.[118] Visions of employers turning away blacks from the factory door, or enforcing sweatshop conditions on economically powerless women, dance in the minds of those determined that discrimination shall not legally take place on the basis of race or sex, or ethnicity or sexual preference or any of a continually increasing number of considerations.

The only difficulty with this perspective is that it happens not to be true. Take, as a case in point, the wage "gap" between male and female workers. According to the most popular hypothesis, the fact that females earn only some 70 for every dollar garnered by a male is per se proof of

[117] There are three main sources of economic discrimination: on the part of employers, fellow employees, and customers. In keeping with popular sentiment on this matter, we shall confine our remarks to the former case, where discrimination, as we shall show, is powerless to harm the economically weak.

[118] On the economics of discrimination, see Becker, Gary, 1957, *The Economics of Discrimination*, Chicago: The University of Chicago Press; Block, Walter, 1982, "Economic Intervention, Discrimination, and Unforeseen Consequences," *Discrimination, Affirmative Action and Equal Opportunity*, edited by Walter Block and Michael Walker. Vancouver: The Fraser Institute; Block, Walter and Walter Williams, 1981, "Male-Female Earnings Differentials: A Critical Reappraisal," *Journal of Labor Research*, 2(2): 383–388; Block Walter and Michael Walker, 1985, *On Employment Equity: A Critique of the Abella Royal Commission Report on Equality in Employment*, Vancouver: The Fraser Institute; Demsetz, Harold, 1965, "Minorities in the Market Place," *North Carolina Law Review*, 43(2): 271–297; Epstein, Richard, *Forbidden Grounds*, New York: Cambridge University Press, 1992; Hoffman, Carl and John Reed, 1982, "When is Imbalance not Discrimination?" *Discrimination, Affirmative Action and Equal Opportunity*, edited by Walter Block and Michael Walker. Vancouver: The Fraser Institute; Hutt, William H., 1964, *The Economics of the Colour Bar*, London: Andre Deutsch; Paul, Ellen Frankel, 1989, *Equity and Gender: the Comparable Worth Debate*, New Brunswick, N.J.: Transaction; Sowell, Thomas, 1981, *Ethnic America*, New York: Basic Books; Sowell, Thomas, 1982, "*Weber* and *Bakke* and the presuppositions of 'Affirmative Action,'" *Discrimination, Affirmative Action and Equal Opportunity*, edited by Walter Block and Michael Walker. Vancouver: The Fraser Institute; Sowell, Thomas, 1983, *The Economics and Politics of Race: An International Perspective*, New York, Morrow; Sowell, Thomas, 1984, *Civil Rights: Rhetoric or Reality*, New York: William Morrow; Sowell, Thomas, 1975, *Race and Economics*, New York: Longman; Williams, Walter, E., 1982b, *The State Against Blacks*, New York, McGraw-Hill; Williams, Walter E., 1982a, "On Discrimination, Prejudice, Racial Income Differentials, and Affirmative Action," *Discrimination, Affirmative Action and Equal Opportunity*, edited by Walter Block and Michael Walker. Vancouver: The Fraser Institute.

male chauvinist employer exploitation.[119] The implicit claim is that, now that acknowledged male advantages over females in upper body strength are less and less economically relevant (true enough), there are no differences in productivity levels on average between the two genders. This is also, as it happens, a not unreasonable surmise. (If it were conceded that females were less productive in the market place than males, this would furnish an alternative explanation for the wage gap.) This situation gives rise to the following two-by-two matrix:

	Male	Female
Wages	$10	$7
Productivity	$10	$10

Here, males and females have equal productivity, at $10 per hour, respectively, but, based on a wage gap of 30%, the former earn $10 per hour while the latter suffer under wages of only $7 per hour.

But there are grave difficulties with such a scenario. Were it true, it could not long endure. For it implies that any employer who hires a woman will earn $3 per hour more in profit than were he to hire a man. Surely, under the conditions specified above, the firm dominated by female employees will be able to underbid and price out of the market all competitors with a different make up in their work forces. Surely, under these conditions, any but the most warped employer would prefer to hire a woman (thus raising her salary) to a man, and would continue doing so until the wages of each came to conform to the other. (Given our numerical example, wages in equilibrium would reach $10 for both genders; at this point, there would be no additional profits earned by the entrepreneur for hiring women that would not be available to him were he to hire men.)

What, then, is the true explanation for the undeniable fact that women's earnings are appreciably below that of their male counterparts? If the discrimination hypothesis must be confined to the dust-bin of economic history, what, then, can take its place? It is, in large part, the marital

[119] These numbers are for illustrative purposes only.

asymmetry hypothesis: men earn more money in the market place than women because marriage has asymmetrical effects on pay: it enhances that of the husband, and reduces that of the wife. Since most people are married for at least some years of their adult lives, this biases the statistical differentials upon which the feminists[120] have pegged their misbegotten "wage gap" complaints.

Why the asymmetry? This is because husbands and wives do not equally divide housekeeping and child-rearing responsibilities. Very much to the contrary, the wife assumes the lion's share of these tasks, and the husband, even including repairs and garbage removal, a very small proportion. In virtually all marriages, the shopping, cooking, cleaning, sewing, bed making, vacuuming, and dishwashing are almost entirely monopolized by the distaff side. And this goes in spades for diapering, PTA meetings, caring for sick children, and so on. And this is to say nothing of getting up in the middle of the night and being on call every few hours during the day in order to breast feed, a biological impossibility for men.

What is the implication of such a state of affairs? It is what economists call the doctrine of alternative costs. If you want to be a concert pianist, and practice your instrument 8 hours a day, you probably won't be very good at golf, or at chess, or at computers, or at hundreds of other things; you certainly will not be as productive in these other tasks but for your tie to the piano. If you load yourself up with house and child-care, compared to your otherwise equally productive in the marketplace husband, he will gain a march on you in the latter direction. If a woman expects, moreover, to seriously or totally reduce her labor force attachment from the time her first child is born until her third child is in high school, she is likely to invest her human capital in less well paid but presumably more secure arenas such as secretary, nurse, school teacher, rather than in the more remunerative chemistry, computers, or engineering, lest the natural atrophy of her skills during her time of zero or lesser labor force

[120] For a critique of feminism see: Levin, Michael, September 1984, "Comparable Worth: The Feminist Road to Socialism," *Commentary*; Levin, Michael, 1987, *Feminism and Freedom*, New York: Transaction Books; Sommers, Christina Hoff, *Who Stole Feminism?*, New York, Simon and Schuster, 1994.

participation hurt her financially. Given that her husband is the primary bread-winner for these years, she is far more likely to agree to be the "trailing spouse" in the job market, than the reverse, in order to maximize total family income.

What are the results of these considerations? It is that while *on average* women should earn just as much as men, given that the average woman is just as productive as the average man, matters are quite different when we take into account marital status. If wage ratio of all males to all females is 70%, it drops precipitously for those who have ever been *married*, and rises to virtual equality for those who have *never* benefited from the institution of marriage. Indeed, in many cases, the wage "gap" for the never marrieds vanishes almost entirely![121]

The same analysis applies to discrimination against any other group, such as blacks, gays, and members of the various ethnicities. Discrimination is not the economic bugaboo it is commonly supposed to be. Much discrimination was aimed at Jews and Orientals, and yet they had higher than average incomes; discrimination did not reduce their economic viability. Given that blacks and Hispanics are also the objects of discrimination, this cannot account for their relative poverty.

If a restaurant does not wish to serve an Oriental person, there will be competitors anxious to do just that. They will earn greater profits, other things equal, since they can "monopolize" customers from this sector of society. If a firm does not to choose to employ a gay person, he will find a job elsewhere. And his new employer, more likely than not, will be able to undersell and drive into bankruptcy the first one. No, there is nothing to fear from discriminators. They are a paper tiger. Fear of them is certainly not a justification for riding roughshod over the rights of the citizenry to do exactly as they wish, to choose their friends, business associations, and personal relationships, provided only that they keep their mitts off of other people and their property.

---

[121] Block, Walter, "Discrimination: An Interdisciplinary Analysis," *The Journal of Business Ethics*, Vol. 11, 1992, pp. 241–254; Block, Walter, "Compromising the Uncompromisable: Discrimination," *American Journal of Economics and Sociology*, Vol. 57, No. 2, April, 1998, pp. 223–237.

V. Statistical Evidence

What are the facts of the matter? In Table 1 listed are the ratios of female to male median incomes[122] (in 1997 dollars) for the years 1987–1997. As can be seen, the ratio for all males and females ranges from a low of 46.7% in 1987 to 55.1% in 1997; from 77.9% to 81.0% for the single, never married during these years; and from a low of 36.9% in 1987 to a high of 47.1% in 1997 for those who were married, widowed, separated, or divorced. The point at issue is not the slight rise in all these figures over this 11-year period, but rather the fact that the reason female wages lag behind male wages for the total population is that the ever marrieds pull down the average for them. That is, the never married female to male wage ratio for this period of 51.3% was so low because the ever-married ratio of 41.7% pulled it down. Had no one been touched by the institution of marriage, and nothing else changed, the presumption is that the female–male wage ratio would have been 81.8% for this roughly decade-long period.

These facts are certainly compatible with the marital asymmetry hypothesis that married, separated, divorced, or widowed females would earn far less than their male counterparts, and that this effect would be much weaker for those who were never married. These facts are not at all consistent with the discrimination model, for here, the market, or capitalism, or what not, for some reason[123] gives *all* females the "short end of the stick." If anything, the male chauvinist pig might, on this hypothesis, be presumed to have greater animus against unmarried females than married ones, since his motto is that all women should be "barefoot, pregnant, and in the kitchen," and this ideal is more nearly approached by the latter than the former. Accordingly, we would expect, if sexism were a strong explanatory variable, the very opposite: namely, that the never married females would have lower wages relative to their male counterparts

[122] Source for Table 1: U.S. Census Bureau, "Historical Income Tables – People," table P-11, Marital Status – People 18 Years Old and Over by Median Income and Gender; http://www.census.gov/hhes/income/histinc/p11.html.

[123] Presumably this is due to sheer nastiness and perversity.

than would obtain in the case of the ever marrieds. But any such contention is flat out contradicted by the empirical evidence.

Table 2 tells much the same marital asymmetry story as does Table 1, only in a different and complementary manner.[124] The reason that the female to male median income ratio is so high for those aged 15–24 is because relative few people in this age cohort are married. This ratio tends to decline as we move up the age ranges because more and more people have ever been married (this includes the separated, divorced, married, and widowed) as they become older. The facts, again, are perfectly congruent with the marital asymmetry hypothesis of the wage gap, but not at all with the discrimination hypothesis. Again, posit malevolent male chauvinist pigs who are in a position to impose their will on society, wage wise; they hate females with a purple passion, and wish above all else to do them ill in this regard. Why oh why would they be so *variable* in their detestation? Why not penalize all women *equally*, for the "crime" of being female? Why pass over young women, or never married women? The facts of the matter simply make no sense when perused through these particular eye-glasses.

Economic theory is universal: it applies to all epochs, and to all geographical areas and political jurisdictions. Let us, then, range more widely, and peruse the evidence supplied by a different country, Canada, going back over several decades. We shall consider female–male wage ratios based on income averages, or means, not medians, as has been shown so far. According to one report,[125] the female/male earnings ratio in Canada in 1971 for never marrieds was 99.2%; for ever marrieds, it was 33.2%, and for both, together, it was 37.4%. According to another report,[126] the never married female to male average annual earnings for full-time workers in Canada with a university degree was 109.8% in 1971; that is,

[124] The source for Table 2 is the U.S. Census Bureau, *The Official Statistics*, Statistical Abstract of the United States, 1998, p. 475, table No. 752, "Money Incomes of Persons – Selected Characteristics, by Income Level: 1995.

[125] Block, Walter, 1982, "Economic Intervention, Discrimination, and Unforeseen Consequences," *Discrimination, Affirmative Action and Equal Opportunity*, edited by Walter Block and Michael Walker. Vancouver: The Fraser Institute, table 3, p. 112.

[126] Block Walter and Michael Walker, 1985, *On Employment Equity: A Critique of the Abella Royal Commission Report on Equality in Employment*, Vancouver: The Fraser Institute, tables V, VI and VII, pp. 48, 50 and 51.

females actually earned almost 10% more than their male counterparts. In very sharp contrast, the equivalent figure for ever marrieds with these qualifications was 56.8% and for the entire sample 61.2%. And in 1982, Canadian women with these educational attainments who were never married earned 91.3% of their male counterparts, while their ever-married sisters registered only 64.4% in this regard. The ratio for the entire sample was 67.2%.

VI. Conclusion

In the free society, James Dale would no more be free to impose his presence upon the unwilling Boy Scouts than an avowed and militant heterosexual would be able to join the Rutgers University Lesbian/Gay Alliance; or that the Black Muslim organization would be forced to accept a white person as a member; or that a religious affiliated university would be compelled to allow an atheistic professor to join its theology faculty. Freedom of Association is a necessary condition of a civilized order; laws prohibiting discrimination violated this freedom, and must be repealed. All of them.

5

Sexual Harassment in the Workplace

Introduction

Employers often express such an unwarranted fear of sexual harassment claims that they ignore the problem and hope that it will just go away and never happen in their workplace. This fear results from a lack of understanding of the nature of sexual harassment claims, confusion about the *true meaning* of untidy terms like "severe," "hostile," and "pervasive," and ignorance of appropriate management steps to both prevent harassment in the workplace and provide for a legitimate defense to sexual harassment claims. This article examines the kinds of sexual harassment claims that arise under Title VII of the 1964 Civil Rights Act,[1] as amended by the Civil Rights Act of 1991, the two key federal statutes used to combat sexual harassment in the workplace, expresses concern about the First Amendment free speech conflicts that arise in the context of harassment claims, and discusses practical steps employers may take to reduce the likelihood of both sexual harassment in the workplace and their possible liability, and concludes with a philosophical and economic perspective on the issue.

[1] Ellis 42 U.S.C. Section 2000e to 2000e-17 (1982).

W. E. Block, R. Whitehead, *Philosophy of Law*, Palgrave Studies in Classical Liberalism,
https://doi.org/10.1007/978-3-030-28360-5_5

The Law

Under section 102(a) of the 1991 Civil Rights Act,[2] both punitive and compensatory damages and a jury trial are available to plaintiffs who win a sexual harassment suit. Title VII, administered by the Equal Employment Opportunity Commission (EEOC), prior to the 1991 Act, only provided for recovery of back pay and restoration of job benefits. The amount that may be recovered under the 1991 Act depends on the size of the firm and ranges from $50,000 to $300,000.[3] In addition, state court tort remedies are available for torts resulting from the harassing conduct such as battery, mental anguish, invasion of privacy, outrageous behavior, and wrongful discharge. The recovery under state law remedies is governed by the laws of the various states.

In applying current standards for sexual harassment cases, the courts are becoming more forceful in requiring employers to know about and effectively deal with harassment in the workplace. Employers are accountable for behavior they, "in the exercise of reasonable care," should have known was occurring.[4] Additionally, courts and the EEOC have imposed greater responsibility on management to develop plans to deal quickly and effectively with legitimate sexual harassment claims.[5]

What Does It Look Like

Sexual harassment in the office means unwelcome sexual advances, requests for sexual favors, and other verbal or physical conduct of a sexual nature when:

(a) Submission to such conduct is either explicitly or implicitly made a condition of an individual's employment;

---

[2] Pub. Law No. 102-66, Section 102(a)(1) (1992).

[3] Id.

[4] Ellison v. Brady, 924 F.2d 872 (9th Cir. 1991) and Jensen v. Eveleth Taconite Co., 824 F.Supp. 847 (D. Minn. 1993).

[5] Price Waterhouse v. Hopkins, 490 U.S. 228 (1989) and Ellison v. Brady, footnote 4, Supra.

(b) Submission to or rejection of such conduct by an individual is used as a basis for an employment decision effecting such individuals;
(c) Such conduct has a purpose or effect of substantially interfering with an individual's right to work in an environment free of intimidation, hostility, or threats stemming from acts or language of a sexual nature[6]; and/or
(d) the conduct interferes with an employee's ability to focus on the job responsibilities.[7]

Some behavior that has been found by the Equal Employment Opportunity Commission and the courts to constitute sexual harassment is:

(a) Sexual harassment may include sexual suggestive or obscene comments, threats, insults, slurs, jokes about gender-based traits of a person, or sexual propositions[8];
(b) Harassment may also include physical conduct such as intentional touching, pinching, brushing against another's body, suggesting or coercing sexual intercourse, or physical assault[9];
(c) Nonverbal behavior such as leering or staring at another's body, displaying sexually suggestive photographs, cartoons, or magazines[10];
(d) Sexual harassment may also include continuing to express sexual or social interest in an individual after being informed that the interest is unwelcome[11];
(e) Sexual harassment also occurs when an individual believes that she is required to consent to the foregoing behavior as a term or condition of her employment[12]; and

---

[6] The definition is an adaption of the EEOC Guidelines prohibiting sexual harassment under Title VII.

[7] Ellison v. Brady, 924 F.2d 872 (9th Cir. 1991).

[8] Lipsett v. University of Puerto Rico, 864 F. 2d 881 (1st Cir. 1988).

[9] Jones v. Wesco Investments, 846 F.2d 1154 (8th Cir. 1988).

[10] Robinson v. Jacksonville Shipyards, 760 F.Supp. 1486 (M.D. Fla. 1991).

[11] Ellison v. Brady, 924 F.2d 872 (9th Cir. 1991).

[12] Simmonds v. Lyons, 746 F.2d 265 (5th Cir. 1984).

(f) The Equal Employment Opportunity Commission also says that an employer is responsible for acts of nonemployees such as customers or service technicians when the employer knows, or should have known, of the unwelcome conduct and fails to take immediate or appropriate action.[13]

Determination of whether conduct amounts to sexual harassment is generally made on a case-by-case basis after looking at all the circumstances. It is apparent, however, that most definitions of sexual harassment turn on an abuse of power in a relationship of unequal power, for example, teacher and student, or supervisor and employee.

Two Kinds of Sexual Harassment Claims

The Courts and the Equal Employment Opportunity Commission recognize sexual harassment claims on two primary theories. The theories are called quid pro quo sexual harassment and hostile environment sexual harassment. Quid pro quo sexual harassment occurs when a superior conditions the granting of an economic or job benefit upon submission to sexual conduct or punishes the subordinate employee for refusing to comply with the sexual request.[14] Hostile environment harassment exists when sexual- or gender-related conduct "has a purpose or effect of unreasonable interfering with an individual's performance or creating an intimidating, hostile, or offensive environment."[15]

Quid pro quo sexual harassment also has a subcategory called reverse quid pro quo harassment. If an employee is coerced into submitting to unwelcome sexual advances in return for a job benefit, other employees who were qualified but denied the benefit can establish that sex was a condition for denying the benefit.[16] It is important to realize that both quid pro quo and hostile environment sexual harassment may occur in

[13] 29 C.F.R. Section 1604 11(b) (1992).

[14] Hall vs. Gus Construction Company, 842 F.2d 1010 (8th Cir. 1988).

[15] Meritor Savings Bank v. Vinson, 477 U.S. 57 91986.

[16] 29 C.F.R. Section 1604 (9) (1992).

the same instance and the two causes of action are not always clearly distinct and separate.

In quid pro quo harassment claims, a five-part test has been used by the Courts to decide whether the plaintiff has established a prima facie case. In quid pro quo cases, the plaintiff is required to show[17]:

(a) The plaintiff is a member of a protected group;
(b) The sexual advances were unwelcome;
(c) The harassment was sexually or gender motivated;
(d) The individual's reaction to the advances affected a tangible aspect of employment such as compensation, advancement, terms, conditions, or privileges; and,
(e) Respondeat superior identity has been established.

Once a prima facie case has been established, the burden of going forward shifts to the employer to articulate a nondiscriminatory reason for the employment decision. The employer may show that there is a basis for the same decision even if the harassment had not occurred. To prevail under a quid pro quo theory, some Courts require that the plaintiff show some economic injury, like a promotion or pay disparity, arising from the employers' denial of the employment benefit.[18] Here, the employer is strictly liable for the conduct of supervisory employees who are acting within the scope of their authority. Knowledge of the supervisor's activities is imputed to the employer under a theory that the supervisor is acting as the employer's agent.[19]

The hostile environment theory has frightened employers because many believe they are liable for harassment cases that have occurred without their actual knowledge. Further, hostile environment cases may, in cases where the harassment has some relation to the work environment, involve off job conduct by co-workers or supervisors.[20] Under the hostile environment theory, the plaintiff is required to show:

---

[17] Jones v. Flagship International, 793 F. 2d 714 (5th Cir. 1986).

[18] Carrero v. N.Y. Housing Authority, 890 F.2d 569, 579 (2d Cir. 1989).

[19] Kotcher v. Rosa and Sullivan Appliance, 957 F.2d 59 (2d Cir. 1992).

[20] Kaufman v. Applied Signal, 970 F.2d 178 (96th Cir. 1992).

(a) She belonged to protected group;
(b) She was subjected to unwelcome sexual harassment;
(c) The harassment was based upon sex or gender;
(d) The harassment affected a "term, condition, or privilege, of employment;"
(e) The employer knew or should have known of the harassment in question and failed to take the proper remedial or preventive action.[21]

Another important concern in hostile environment cases is that the sexual harassment claim need not be based on conduct that is solely sexual in nature, since intimidation and hostility toward gender can result from conduct other than explicit sexual advances. For example, name calling, urinating in a gas tank, and refusing to service a company truck driven by new female employees were considered relevant in establishing a hostile work environment based on gender even though the conduct was not explicitly sexual in nature.[22] In addition, in a hostile environment case, unlike a quid pro quo case, it is not necessary that the plaintiffs suffer any economic loss of employment benefits.[23] Finally, sexual or gender stereotyping can contribute to a hostile environment.[24] For example, a belief by a partner in an accounting firm that women are just too nice to deal with male clients in some kinds of business situations has been found to be gender stereotyping.

One of the major issues that may arise in a hostile environment case is whether the fact that the alleged victim voluntarily participated in the relevant sexual conduct is a defense to a sexual harassment claim. The question is answered in the leading case of *Meritor Savings Bank v. Vinson*,[25] in which the Supreme Court, speaking through Justice Rehnquist, decided that the test is not whether the victim voluntarily participated, in the sense that she was not forced to participate, but whether the sexual advances were unwelcome. In *Meritor Savings Bank,*

[21] Jones v. Wesco Investments, 846 F.2d 1154 (8th Cir. 1988).

[22] See Hall v. Gus Construction Company, 842 F.2d 1010 (8th Cir. 1988), and Andrews v. City of Philadelphia, 895 F.2d 1469, 1485 (3d Cir. 1990).

[23] Meritor Savings Bank v. Vinson, 477 U.S. 57, (1986).

[24] Ellison v. Brady, 924 F.2d 872 (9th Cir. 1991).

[25] Meritor Savings Bank v. Vinson, 477 U.S. 57 (1986).

the victim was fondled in front of other employees, apparently voluntarily visited motels and participated in sexual intercourse 40 or 50 times with her supervisor. The supervisor also followed her into the restroom during working hours and exposed himself to her. She said she anticipated because she was afraid of the supervisor and in order to attain job benefits that included unusually rapid promotions. When she eventually left because of the sexual harassment and filed a federal court action, the bank's defense was that it had no knowledge of the conduct of the supervisor because she didn't file a grievance and that the plaintiff had voluntarily participated in the sexual activity. However, the bank had an employee grievance procedure that did not specifically discuss sexual harassment nor inform an employee how to bypass a guilty superior. The Supreme Court decided that the test is not whether the victim voluntarily participates but whether the sexual attention is welcome.[26] Other cases have also said that advances that were initially welcome between individuals can become unwelcome if the victim changes her mind and makes it clear to the man that the advances are no longer welcome.[27]

The Eighth Circuit Court of Appeals has defined unwelcome sexual harassment to mean that "the employee did not solicit or invite it and the employee regards the conduct as undesirable or offensive."[28] A woman's consistent failure to respond to suggestive comments or jokes may be sufficient to express to a man that the conduct is unwelcome.[29] On the other hand, the conduct of the alleged victim is often relevant in determining whether the advances are welcome. The Supreme Court has held that evidence of the plaintiff's sexual provocative speech or dress may be relevant in determining whether the plaintiff found sexual advances unwelcome.[30] In another case, the Eighth Circuit found that nude photographs taken of the plaintiff, and appearing in a motorcycle publication, were not material to the issue of whether she found the office conduct of other employees hostile. Her private life away from work did not mean she

---

[26] Id. at 67.

[27] Ellison v. Brady, 924 F.2d 842 (9th Cir. 1991).

[28] Moylan v. Maries County, 792 F.2d 746, 749 (8th Cir. 1986). For a discussion of the term "unwelcome" see Swentek v. U.S. Air, Inc., 830 F.2d 552, 556–557 (4th Cir. 1987).

[29] Lipsett v. University of Puerto Rico, 864 F.2d 881 (1st Cir. 1988).

[30] Meritor, Supra, Reference 23 at 67.

acquiesced to sexual comments and advances on the job.[31] Finally, if the plaintiff voluntarily initiates or participates in a mutual exchange of sexual comments and jokes with co-workers, this may constitute evidence that the plaintiff welcomed that kind of conduct.[32]

In a hostile environment case, the harassing conduct must be sufficiently pervasive to alter the conditions of employment and create an abusive environment. Some authorities believe that conduct that keeps the employee from focusing her attention on her job meets this criterion. The plaintiff must also show a practice or pattern of harassment. Usually a single or isolated incident will not be sufficient to establish a hostile environment. Initially, the courts decided whether hostile environment existed based on a reasonable person standard. Recently, at least one court has said in cases involving female plaintiffs that the test is a "reasonable woman" standard. In that case, the court stated: "In order to shield employers from having to accommodate the idiosyncratic concerns of the hypersensitive employee, we hold that a female states a prima facie case of hostile environment when she alleges conduct which a reasonable woman would consider sufficiently severe and pervasive to alter the conditions of employment and create an abusive work environment."[33]

This reasonable person or reasonable woman standard was not uniformly applied, however, in the various federal circuits. The Supreme Court dealt with this problem in *Harris v. Forklift Systems, Inc.*[34] The defendant employer in *Harris* claimed that the plaintiff, a strong self-reliant woman, should not prevail because she was unable to show psychological damage resulting from the harassment. The company president called Harris "a dumb ass woman," asked her to visit a motel with him to talk about her raise, asked her to get coins out of his pocket, tossed objects on the floor for her to pick up, said she closed a sale by promising sex to the customer, and made sexual innuendos about her clothing. The Supreme Court rejected the employer's psychological harm defense and defined the appropriate standard as (1) whether a reasonable woman would find the harasser's conduct sufficiently severe or pervasive to alter

[31] Burns v. McGregor, 989 F. 2d 959 (8th Cir. 1993).

[32] Staton v. Maries County, 792 F.2d 746, 749 (8th Cir. 1986).

[33] Ellison v. Brady, 924 F.2d 872 (9th Cir.1991).

[34] Harris v. Forklift Systems, Inc. 114 S. Ct. 367 (1993).

conditions of employment and (2) whether subjectively the victim perceived the environment as abusive. The majority said that Title VII comes into play long before the harassing conduct causes a nervous breakdown. If the environment is hostile and abusive to an employee, there is no additional need for it also to be psychologically injurious. The two female members of the Court, Justices O'Connor and Ginsberg, maintained that conduct which prevented a woman from "focusing" on her job is sufficient to establish a sexually hostile environment. The test supported by Justices O'Connor and Ginsberg is seen by some as a sensible one because no reasonable firm wants its employees distracted from their duties. Finally, Justice Ginsberg set the benchmark for an understandable definition of hostile environment by saying that women should not have to put up with conditions not acceptable to men. To many this is a simple, yet powerful and comprehensible expression of a workable definition of hostile environment. But, even so, what are we to make of the requirements that the conduct be "severe" or "pervasive" enough to create a hostile or abusive environment for the plaintiff or a reasonable person? These terms are troubling to a First Amendment student because the neither the EEOC nor the courts bother to define them. The *Harris* description of the harassing conduct as preventing the victim from focusing on her job is about as good as it gets. But, "severe," "hostile," and "pervasive" are perplexing terms. Reasonable people, even of the same philosophical perspectives, will differ on what they mean. It's a bit like nailing Jell-O to the wall. We do know that these words have been construed to refer to crude political statements about a member of the congress,[35] a painting,[36] pinups,[37] a postcard,[38] and a telephone call.[39] Given the "Jell-Oness" of

[35] Several Navy officers, concerned about Congresswoman Pat Schroeder's role in the investigation of the "Tail Hook" Sexual Harassment incident, displayed a banner, at any on-base party, that said, "Hickory Dickory Dock, Pat Schroeder can suck my cock." See Volkh," *Freedom* of Speech and Workplace Harassment," 39 UCLA L. Rev. 1791, 1802 (1992).

[36] Complaint regarding a painting, hanging in the City Hall of Murfreesboro, Tennessee, that showed a woman with one breast exposed, Jennifer Goode, *It's Art vs. Sexual Harassment*, Tennessean, Mar. 1, 1996 at A1.

[37] See, Robinson v. Jacksonville Shipyards, 760 F.Supp. 1486 (M.D. Fla. 1991), a case that imposed liability for centerfolds.

[38] Bartlett v. United States, 835 F.Supp. 1246 (E.D. Wash. 1993).

[39] Intlekoter v. Turnage, 973 F. 2d 773.775 (9th Cir. 1992), relying in part on a telephone call at home from a co-worker to support a hostile environment claim.

the rule, it is difficult to judge how others will apply it. There is a real danger that some fact finders, or more likely regulators, will conclude that various religious or political statements, vulgar jokes,[40] or indecent art can be severe and pervasive enough to create a hostile environment. More so when the regulators find the expression personally disagreeable or politically incorrect. So, there is a real potential that sexual harassment law can be used to suppress protected speech. It is the nature of the employment context. The employer's natural response, given that he does not even know exactly what the terms mean, is to avoid possible liability, and will likely cause him to "shut the employees up." After all that is the safe approach! An employer concerned about sexual harassment liability can't profit from the employee's speech, he can only lose from it. This is precisely the chilling effect on protected speech that vague laws and regulations that use untidy words like "pervasive," "severe," and "stigmatize" have. Vagueness leads people to steer far wider from the forbidden zone of actual harassment than if the boundaries are clearly marked.[41] The employer's only safe recourse is a zero-tolerance policy. In any case, harassment law poses First Amendment problems regardless of how it is handled because speech that "stigmatizes" or "victimizes" someone does not always strip aside the speaker's First Amendment protections. Despite these troubling problems, the courts plow on in their quest to cleanse the workplace of "severe" and "pervasive" conduct and speech, whatever the terms mean. The next sexual harassment venture of the Supreme Court was to try to lay down some boundaries for alleged "supervisor" harassment.

Laying Down the Law for Supervisor Harassment

In two precedent-setting cases, the Supreme Court attempted to clarify the liability tests for employers when a supervisor is alleged to have sexually harassed an employee. They provide a roadmap for employer liability and possible defenses in two relatively common instances. First, when an

[40] Morgan v. Hertz Corp., 542 F.Supp. 123, 128 (W.D. Tenn. 1991), Condemning remarks like, "Did you get any last night," Aff'd 725 F. 2d 1070 (6th Cir. 1984).

[41] See, Volokh, footnote 34, Supra.

employee is victimized by a supervisor with immediate (or higher authority) over the employee. And, secondly, in situations when a supervisor creates a hostile work environment by making explicit threats to alter a subordinate's terms or conditions of employment, based on sex, but when rebuffed, does not act to fulfill the threat.

Faragher. After resigning as a lifeguard for the city of Boca Raton, Florida, Beth Faragher sued the city and her two immediate supervisors, alleging that the male supervisors had created a "sexually hostile atmosphere" by repeatedly subjecting her and other female employees to "uninvited and offensive touching," by making lewd remarks, and by speaking of women in offensive terms. She claimed this conduct constituted discrimination in the "terms, conditions, and privileges of employment" in violation of Title VII of the Civil Rights Act. Faragher never complained to higher city officials about the treatment. Another supervisor once told another female employee, "the city just doesn't care." There was no showing that higher-echelon officials of the city (employer) had actual knowledge of the two supervisor's conduct. It, however, had failed to disseminate its sexual harassment policy to beach employees, made no effort to keep track of the conduct of the two beach supervisors, and the city's policy failed to provide for a procedure to bypass harassing supervisors in filing a complaint. The lower courts split on the issue of the city's liability.

The Supreme Court decided that an employer is subject to vicarious liability to a victimized employee for an actionable hostile sexually environment claim created by a supervisor with immediate (or higher authority) over the employee, *Faragher v. City of Boca Raton*.[42] The term vicarious generally means performed, exercised, received, or suffered in place of another.[43] When the supervisor's harassment culminates in a tangible employment action, such as discharge, demotion, firing, failure to promote, reassignment with different responsibilities, undesirable working conditions, or a decision resulting in a significant reduction in benefits, the liability is absolute. This is so because tangible employment decisions are the means by which the supervisor brings the official power of the

[42] No. 97-282, (June 26, 1998).

[43] *The College Dictionary*, Random House, 1973.

enterprise (employer) to bear on the employee. A tangible employment decision, such as a retaliatory discharge for rebuffing sexual advances, requires an official act of the enterprise, a company act. For these reasons, a tangible employment action taken by the supervisor becomes, for Title VII purposes, an act of the employer.

The next question is whether there is the employer liability when the commission of supervisor sexual harassment does not result in a tangible employment action? Here, the answer is less obvious. However, the Court did provide important guidance for management on steps that may be taken to avoid liability. The Court did so by establishing two affirmative defenses that may be raised when no retaliation or loss of tangible job benefits has occurred.

The Employer Defenses

In *Faragher,* the court said that when no tangible job action is taken against the employee, the employer may raise two affirmative defenses to liability or the award of damages. The defenses consist of two necessary elements:

(a) That the employer exercised reasonable care to prevent and correct promptly any sexually harassing behavior, and
(b) That the complaining employee unreasonably failed to take advantage of any preventive or corrective opportunities provided by the employer to avoid harm.

Justice Souter wrote that the need for a stated sexually harassment policy and grievance procedure suitable to the employment circumstances may be addressed in litigating the first element of the defense, and that a demonstration that the complaining employee unreasonably failed to use the established complaint procedure will normally suffice to satisfy the second element. Applying the two affirmative defenses to the facts of *Faragher*, the court found as a matter of law that the city could not have exercised reasonable care because it failed to provide its sexually harassment policy to beach employees, made no attempt to keep track of the two beach supervisor's conduct, and its policy failed to provide a procedure to bypass harassing supervisors.

Burlington v. Ellerth. Kimberly Ellerth quit her job after 15 months as a salesperson with Burlington Industries, alleging she had been subjected to sexually harassment by a mid-level supervisor, Ted Slowik. Slowik had authority to hire and promote employees, subject to higher approval: he was not a policy maker. The plaintiff was subjected to repeated boorish and offensive sexual remarks and gestures and was threatened with a loss of job benefits. On one occasion when she failed to respond to remarks Slowik made about her breasts, he told her, "you know Kim, I could make your life very hard or very easy at Burlington." Ellerth rebuffed all of Slowik's advances, yet suffered no retaliation and was, in fact, promoted once. Moreover, she never informed anyone in authority of Slowik's conduct despite knowing about Burlington's sexually harassment policy.

Justice Kennedy again held that an employer is subject to vicarious liability to a victimized employee for an actionable hostile environment created by a supervisor with immediate, or successively higher, authority over an employee, *Burlington Industries v. Ellerth*.[44] The liability is absolute when the employee has suffered the loss of a tangible job benefit, like a promotion, for rebuffing the sexual harassment. Again the Court maintained that when no tangible job action has been taken against the employee, the employer may raise the two affirmative defenses of reasonable care to prevent and promptly correct sexually harassing behavior and the unreasonable failure of the employee to take advantage of preventative or corrective opportunities provided by the employer's sexual harassment policy. The Court remanded the case to the trial court for a determination of whether she has a claim for vicarious liability and whether the affirmative defenses apply.

Public Policy Goals of the Court

The decisions in *Faragher and Burlington* clearly illustrate several public policy goals of the Supreme Court. First, the Court is clearly sending a signal to employers that the actions of a supervisor, which affect a tangi-

[44] No. 97-569, June 26, 1998.

ble job benefit of the harassed employee, will trigger absolute employer liability because they are company acts. Secondly, the primary purpose of Title VII is "not to provide redress but to avoid harm." In *Albemarle Paper Co. v. Moody*,[45] the Court is advancing this primary purpose by demanding employers to publish, educate employees and supervisors about, and enforce sexual harassment grievance procedures. Finally, the Court is encouraging employees to mitigate any damage to their employment by requiring them to take advantage of those employer promolgated sexual harassment grievance procedures in order to avoid a hostile environment. It seeks to promote these goals by providing a reward in the form of an affirmative defense to employers who comply and to deny recourse to employees who refuse to follow properly drafted employer sexual harassment grievance procedures. Thus, the next important question is what kind of employer action is necessary to comply and avoid liability for supervisor harassment?

Managing Supervisor Sexual Harassment Liability

There are several steps the astute employer may take to limit liability for supervisor sexual harassment claims. First all supervisors should be informed, in writing, that their sexually harassment of a subordinate that affects a tangible job benefit, as previously defined, will result in absolute employer liability. This is so because the denial of a tangible job benefit, for the purposes of Title VII, becomes a company act. There are, in addition, several preventive steps that must be taken in regard to all employees. They are:

1. The employer should publish a strong well-articulated policy concerning sexual harassment;
2. All employees should be informed of and provided a copy of the policy;
3. The CEO should clearly and forcefully advise all employees that sexual harassment will not be tolerated.

---

[45] Albemarle Paper Co. v. Moody, 422 U.S. 405.

4. The complaint procedure should allow employees to report sexual harassment to someone other than the harassing supervisor.
5. Supervisors should be informed, in writing, that the employer is absolutely liable for their sexual harassment involving the loss of an employee's tangible job benefits, and
6. The employer should swiftly take appropriate remedial action by fairly investigating, taking effective action, protecting the victim from retaliation, and restoring any lost tangible job benefits in a timely manner.

Many astute employers have already taken some or all of these preventive steps. A careful reading of some previous sexual harassment decisions reveals that the courts, as a matter of policy, are requiring employers to educate their employees, adopt effective and fair complaint procedures, guard against retaliation, and effectively deal with sexual harassment complaints. For example, the courts will consider a policy that specifically addresses and effectively deals with sexual harassment when reviewing liability issues, *Meritor Savings Bank v. Vinson*,[46] *Barrett v. Omaha National Bank*,[47] and Whitehead, "*Sexual Harassment In The Office*."[48] Those employers whose sexual harassment policies and procedures do not comport with these decisions are well-advised to adopt the appropriate policies forthwith.

Other Employer Defenses

As previously stated, employers are very concerned about strict liability under the so-called hostile environment theory, correctly contending that the conduct complained of may have occurred without their knowledge. Given *Faragher* and *Ellerth*, what kind of action can the employer take that will constitute a legitimate defense against both quid pro quo and hostile environment sexual harassment claims? The law in this area is still developing, but most commentators agree there are several key steps that

[46] 447 U.S. 57 (1986).

[47] 726 F.2d at 427.

[48] Whitehead, Roy Jr., *The CPA Journal*, pp. 45–49, Feb. 1996.

employers can take to protect against liability. In fact, the Equal Employment Opportunity Commission, by regulation, mandates that the existence of a sexual harassment policy and complaint procedure is relevant and will directly affect the employer's liability.[49] Thus, the failure to provide a reasonable policy and complaint procedure for employees is convincing evidence that the employer has ignored the problem and will likely lead to employer liability for sexual harassment claims.

A careful reading of *Meritor Savings Bank* also shows that the Supreme Court will consider a policy effective that specifically addresses sexual harassment rather than merely discrimination when reviewing liability issues. We also know from *Meritor* that a procedure requiring the employee to complain to or through the person who is the harasser is an inadequate defense because it violates EEOC guidelines.

Perhaps the most instructive case for employers is *Barrett v. Omaha National Bank*.[50] Here, the Eighth Circuit found that an employer was not liable for sexual harassment of a co-employee's conduct because the employer conducted an immediate full investigation to learn what happened, informed the accused employee within four days of the complaint that his conduct would not be tolerated, placed him on 90-day probation, told him that he would be fired for any further misconduct, and carefully advised the alleged victim of the action the employer was taking and of her rights all during the investigation.

One can convincingly argue that the failure of an employer to provide a grievance procedure for sexual harassment is evidence of employer contribution to a hostile sexual environment and would result in liability. One of the distressing traps that employers have fallen into in the past is, despite their good motives, appearing to be insensitive to the victim of harassment. In one case, the Internal Revenue Service allowed the harasser to continue to send harassing letters to victim after he had been told by his superiors to stop. Then, when they failed to stop the harassing conduct, they actually transferred the victim, rather than the harasser, to another city.[51]

---

[49] 29 C.F.R. Section 1604 (F) (1992).

[50] 726 F.2d at 427, see also Nash v. Electrospace System, 9 F. 3d 401 (5th Cir. 1993).

[51] Ellison v. Brady, 924 F.2d 842 (9th Cir. 1991).

The bottom line is that an employer has an affirmative duty to take immediate action in sexual harassment matters and that an honest effort to comply with that affirmative duty is often going to be a satisfactory employer defense.

What responsibility, if any, does a victim of sexual harassment have, and how can the victim protect herself?[52] Many victims tolerate harassing behavior for a considerable period of time because they believe that if they don't say anything that the problem will just disappear. This is probably the worst approach to follow because the harassment may be motivated as much by the exercise of power over the victim as by sexual interest. Generally the victim should speak up and make quite clear to the harasser that the unwelcome conduct will not be tolerated. The victim should also keep careful records of what is happening, including times, dates, and locations. The victim should also create a record by writing a letter to the perpetrator or to a trusted friend carefully outlining what has occurred.[53]

To summarize to this point, employers clearly have a responsibility to develop effective sexual harassment policies to deal with sexual harassment in the workplace. Those employers who have not already developed a separate and effective sexual harassment policies are placing their financial assets at risk. The successful sexual harassment policy will be supported by the chief executive officer, offer a clear and convenient separate method of complaining about sexual harassment, provide for an immediate and fair investigation, and demonstrate to employees that sexual harassment will not be tolerated and that disciplinary action will be taken swiftly. Employers who establish and follow an appropriate sexual harassment policy will benefit from a lessened risk of employer liability. The employer who heeds Justice Ginsberg's admonition that women should not have to put up with behavior that is not acceptable to men will have little concern about sexual harassment in the office. But, is this the best way? We now turn to a property rights philosophical approach to escape government coercion.

---

[52] For simplicity, we have been speaking as if all victims are female and all harassers male. Actually both roles can be filled by either gender. See, Oncale v. Sundance Offshore Services, No. 96-5989 (S.Ct. 1998), and Kinman v. Omaha Public School District, 94 F.3d 463 (8th Cir. 1996).

[53] Hughes, Jean O. and Sandler, Bernie R., "In Case of Sexual Harassment, A guide for Women Students." The Project on the Status and Education of Women. Association of American Colleges (April 1986).

Philosophy

We have set the stage for our consideration of sexual harassment law by describing it, giving its rationale, citing cases, and offering advice to employees and employers as to how they can most likely avoid becoming enmeshed in lawsuits concerning this offense. We have in this way, to the best of our ability, analyzed it from a positive perspective. But to do so is only to set the stage for examining these legislative and judicial enactments from the normative point of view. We now leave off our description of these laws and how they work and take up a discussion of whether or not these laws are just and, even, logically coherent. In a word, the answer we offer is No.

It is now time to cast a baleful philosophical eye on the entire enterprise of sexual harassment legislation, prohibition of quid pro quo agreements, and legal opposition to hostile environments. We do so from the classical liberal perspective, one based on private property, contract, freedom of association, and free speech rights.[54] In this view, all human interaction should be voluntary. The law should prohibit only those acts that violate the rights of people to the sanctity of their persons and justly owned property. To relate this to the issue at hand, the law against rape is certainly a legitimate one. For when this act occurs, a man imposes physical force against a woman,[55] in opposition to her own will; this is an invasive act, one which attacks a woman's most important private prop-

---

[54] See generally Murray N. Rothbard *For a New Liberty*, Macmillan, New York, 1973; Murray N. Rothbard *The Ethics of Liberty*, New York: New York University Press, 1998; Hans-Hermann Hoppe, *A Theory of Socialism and Capitalism: Economics, Politics and Ethics*, Boston: Kluwer, 1989; Hans-Hermann Hoppe, *The Economics and Ethics of Private Property: Studies in Political Economy and Philosophy*, Boston: Kluwer, 1993; Robert Nozick, *Anarchy, State and Utopia*, New York: Basic Books, 1974; Walter Block, *Defending the Undefendable*, New York: Fox and Wilkes, 1991; Walter Block "Libertarianism vs. Libertinism," *The Journal of Libertarian Studies: An Interdisciplinary Review*, Vol. 11, No. 1, 1994, pp. 117–128; Charles Murray, *What It Means to be a Libertarian*, New York: Broadway Books, 1997; Jan Narveson, *The Libertarian Idea*, Philadelphia: Temple University Press, 1988; J. Patrick O'Brien and Dennis O. Olson, "The Great Alaskan Money Give Away Program," *Economic Inquiry*, 18 (July 1990): 604–15; Jerry W. Dauterive, William Barnett and Everett White, "A Taxonomy of Government Intervention," *The Journal of the Southwestern Society of Economists*, 1985.

[55] We will continue to speak as if only males can commit such acts, and only women can be victimized by them. Obviously, while these two categories may be the most statistically significant, they certainly do not exhaust the four different possibilities.

erty right, that in her own person.[56] This holds, too, for assault and battery, which encompasses even the slightest of unwanted touching.[57]

Let us now consider how a "hostile environment" stacks up in this regard. We argue that it is not a per se violation of human rights. One can readily imagine a scenario in which women are subjected to the most hostile of sexually tinged environments, where they are paid to accept such treatment, and do so willingly; for example, a strip bar. There, men taunt women; they ask them to disrobe; they make lewd and suggestive remarks about their figures, their clothes, their makeup; they tell off color jokes, and so on. It is hard to imagine an environment more sexually "hostile" than that. If we are to take seriously laws prohibiting a "hostile environment," all such establishments should be shut down, forthwith. From the fact that they are not, that is, that firms which provide such services are allowed to operate with legal impunity, we may deduce that the prohibition of a sexually "hostile environment" is honored more in the breach than in the fact.

Further, we may also conclude that there is something philosophically suspect about legislatively proscribing "hostile environments." It is as if rape or murder were declared illegitimate, except when it occurs legally. We have, here, in other words, a legal system with no less than an inner contradiction.[58] We as a society have not banned strip clubs, nor should we, since they are instances of "capitalist acts between consenting adults."[59] But strip clubs are a paradigm case of "sexual harassment."

[56] For the implications of this viewpoint on abortion law, see Walter Block, "Abortion, Woman and Fetus: Rights in Conflict?," *Reason*, April 1978, pp. 18–25; Walter Block, "Compromising the Uncompromisable: A Private Property Rights Theory of Abortion," manuscript; Walter Block, "Libertarianism, Positive Obligations and Property Abandonment: Children's Rights," manuscript.

[57] Citation to be supplied by Roy Whitehead.

[58] Suppose there were a private amusement facility called "murder park." Here, each customer would be issued a revolver with six bullets, and told to "have at" anyone else in the arena (surrounded by tall thick walls so that the mayhem would be confined to the premises) who was there for the purpose. There would be a "cease fire" for 10 minutes every hour so that the dead bodies could be hauled away, and the remaining combatants issued new ammunition. Such an establishment would not at all violate laws against murder, for this crime is the killing of people *against their will*. Here, on the contrary, all customers by purchasing a ticket demonstrate that they are engaging in the otherwise murderous interaction on a voluntary basis.

[59] This is the felicitous phrase of Robert Nozick, *Anarchy, State and Utopia*, New York: Basic Books, 1974, p. 163.

Therefore, logical consistency requires that since strip clubs are legal, then so should sexual harassment, for the latter is precisely and exactly what takes place in the former.

And no less is true of quid pro quo, the bête noire of the feminists. The essence of this sort of agreement is voluntary mutually beneficial trade, tit for tat, barter, or exchange: you give us this, and we will give you that. As such, quid pro quo is the very basis of the free enterprise system and, indeed, of the entire western cultural vision of society. There are, after all, only two possible ways for human beings to interact with one another: through seizing each other's person and property, or receiving them (or the use of them) only with the agreement of the other party, typically in return for something of one's own. Norman Rockwell drew a very famous *The Saturday Evening Post* magazine cover, depicting a milk deliveryman and pie deliveryman, each one sitting on his own truck and partaking of both food items. Nothing can better illustrate quid pro quo than the sort of peaceful trade that occurred immediately prior to this artistic rendering. We are certainly not ready to rule out all purchases and sales on the ground that they are living illustrations of quid quo pro in action. Given this, there are no logical grounds on the basis of which that we can insist that they not be allowed in this one aspect of the law.

Consider the fact that prostitution is legal in (some parts of) Nevada.[60] The implication is that, at least in these areas, it is licit to offer consideration for sexual services. But if so, then it is well within the law to make what would otherwise be considered lewd and lascivious offers to women; namely, money for sex.

Suppose that we, the authors of the present chapter, set ourselves up as the Blockhead corporation, located in Reno, Nevada, and wish to hire a female who would function half time as a secretary and half time as a prostitute. We advertise for the usual secretarial skills (typing, filing, correspondence, etc.), and also for those suitable to the other half of the job as well. After she is hired, we avail ourselves of both types of her accomplishments. We have now probably violated, and with a vengeance, every injunction in the panoply of the genus sexual harassment, species quid

[60] This applies to every county in the state of Nevada apart from Clark County; Nev. Rev. Stat. 201.300 (1998).

pro quo, and hostile environment. Nevertheless, we should not be considered law violators.[61] Prostitution is legal.[62] And this applies too, to

[61] Of course, if this is to be a licit commercial arrangement, there can be no fraud. That is, the employer must be crystal clear as to the contents of the contract. With a meeting of the minds over the specifics, any demands for sex as part of the job description would be fraudulent.

[62] There is a parallel between this phenomenon and blackmail, which also combines two acts, each of which is legal in isolation (asking for money; threatening to tell about an embarrassing secret—e.g., engage in gossip) but prohibited by law as blackmail when combined. For support of the status quo on this law, see Peter Alldridge, "'Attempted Murder of the Soul': Blackmail, Privacy and Secrets," *Oxford Journal of Legal Studies* Vol. 13, No. 3, pp. 368–387; Scott Altman, "A Patchwork Theory of Blackmail," *University of Pennsylvania Law Review*, Vol. 141, No. 5, May, 1993, pp. 1639–1661; Gary Becker, "The Case Against Blackmail," Jan. 1985, unpublished; James Boyle, "A Theory of Law and Information: Copyright, Spleens, Blackmail and Insider Trading," *California Law Review*, Vol. 80, No. 6, December 1992, pp. 1413–1540; Jennifer Gerarda Brown, "Blackmail as Private Justice," *University of Pennsylvania Law Review*, Vol. 141, No. 5, May, 1993, pp. 1935–1973; Debra J. Campbell, "Why Blackmail Should be Criminalized: A Reply to Walter Block and David Gordon," *Loyola of Los Angeles Law Review*, Vol. 21, No. 3, November 1988, pp. 883–892; Ronald Coase, "The 1987 McCorkle Lecture: Blackmail," *Virginia Law Review*, Vol. 74, No. 4, 1988, pp. 655–676; George Daly and J. Fred Giertz, "Externalities, Extortion, and Efficiency: Reply," 68 (65) *American Economic Review*, 736, 1978 (1975); Sidney W. DeLong, "Blackmailers, Bribe Takers, and the Second Paradox," *University of Pennsylvania Law Review*, Vol. 141, No. 5, May, 1993, pp. 1663–1693; Daniel Ellsberg, "The Theory and Practice of Blackmail," in *Bargaining: Formal Theories of Negotiation*, 343, Oran R. Young, ed., 1975; Richard Epstein, "Blackmail, Inc.," (1983) 50 *University of Chicago Law Review*, 553; Hugh Evans, "Why Blackmail Should be Banned," *Philosophy*, Vol. 65, 1990, pp. 89–94; Joel Feinberg, "The Paradox of Blackmail," 1 *Ratio Juris* 83 (1988); Joel Feinberg, *The Moral Limits of the Criminal Law: Harmless Wrongdoing*, 1988; Joel Feinberg, *Harmless Wrongdoing*, New York: Oxford University Press, 1990; George P. Fletcher, "Blackmail: The Paradigmatic Case," *University of Pennsylvania Law Review*, Vol. 141, No. 5, May, 1993, pp. 1617–1638; Charles Fried, *Contract As Promise*, 102 (1981); Douglas H. Ginsburg and Paul Shechtman," *University of Pennsylvania Law Review*, Vol. 141, No. 5, May, 1993, pp. 1849–1875; Wendy, J Gordon, "Truth and Consequences: The Force of Blackmail's Central Case," *University of Pennsylvania Law Review*, Vol. 141, No. 5, May, 1993, pp. 1741–1785; Michael Gorr, "Nozick's Argument Against Blackmail," 58 *Personalist* 187, 190, 1977; Michael Gorr, "Liberalism and the Paradox of Blackmail," *Philosophy and Public Affairs*, Vol. 21, 1992, pp. 43–66; Vinit Haksar, "Coercive Proposals," *Political Theory*, February 1976, pp. 65–79; Russell Hardin, "Blackmailing for Mutual Good," *University of Pennsylvania Law Review*, Vol. 141, No. 5, May, 1993, pp. 1787–1815; Michael Hepworth, *Blackmail: Publicity and Secrecy in Everyday Life*, London: Routledge and Kegan Paul, 1975, pp. 29–40; Joseph Isenbergh, "Blackmail from A to C," *University of Pennsylvania Law Review*, Vol. 141, No. 5, May, 1993, pp. 1905–1933; R.S. Jandoo and W. Arthur Harland, "Legally Aided Blackmail," *New Law Journal*, 27 April 1984, pp. 402–404; Leo Katz, "Blackmail and Other Forms of Arm-Twisting," *University of Pennsylvania Law Review*, Vol. 141, No. 5, May, 1993, pp. 1567–1615; William Landes and Richard A. Posner, "The Private Enforcement of Law," (1975) 4 *Journal of Legal Studies*, 1, 43; James Lindgren, "Unraveling the Paradox of Blackmail," 84 *Columbia Law Review*, 670 (1984a); James Lindgren, "More Blackmail Ink: a Critique of 'Blackmail, Inc.,' Epstein's Theory of Blackmail" (1984b) 16 *Connecticut Law Review* 909; James Lindgren, "In Defense of Keeping Blackmail A Crime: Responding to Block and Gordon," *Loyola of Los Angeles Law Review*, Vol. 20, No. 1, November 1986, pp. 35–44; James Lindgren, "Blackmail: On Waste, Morals and Ronald

secretarial services. Yet, it should not be the case that when we combine two perfectly legal contractual employment interactions, the sum total of them should be considered illegal. It is difficult for the logical mind to come to any such conclusion.[63]

Coase," 36 *UCLA Law Review*, 597, 1989; James Lindgren, "Kept in the Dark: Owen's view of Blackmail" (1989) 21 *Connecticut Law Review* 749; James Lindgren, "Secret Rights: A Comment on Campbell's Theory of Blackmail," *Connecticut Law Review*, Vol. 21, 1989, pp. 407–410; James Lindgren, "Blackmail: An Afterward," *University of Pennsylvania Law Review*, Vol. 141, No. 5, May, 1993b, pp. 1975–1989; James Lindgren, "The Theory, History and Practice of the Bribery-Extortion Distinction," *University of Pennsylvania Law Review*, Vol. 141, No. 5, May, 1993a, pp. 1695–1739; Daniel Lyons, "Welcome Threats and Coercive Offers," *Philosophy*, October 1975, pp. 425–436; Jeffrie G. Murphy, "Blackmail: A Preliminary Inquiry," 63 *Monist* 156 (1980); Robert Nozick, *Anarchy, State and Utopia*, New York: Basic Books, 1974; David Owens, "Should Blackmail be Banned?," *Philosophy*, Vol. 63, No. 246, 1979, pp. 501–514; Posner, Richard A., *Economic Analysis of Law*, fourth ed., Boston: Little Brown, 1992; Richard A. Posner, "Blackmail, Privacy and Freedom of Contract," *University of Pennsylvania Law Review*, Vol. 141, No. 5, May, 1993, pp. 1817–1847; Steven Shavell, "An Economic Analysis of Threats and Their Legality: Blackmail, Extortion and Robbery," *University of Pennsylvania Law Review*, Vol. 141, No. 5, May, 1993, pp. 1877–1903; L.G. Tooher, "Developments in the Law of Blackmail in England and Australia," 27 *International and Comparative Law Quarterly*, 337 (1978); Jeremy Waldron, "Blackmail as Complicity," 4 (Nov. 1992) unpublished.

[63] For a critique of the status quo ante on blackmail, see Eric Mack, "In Defense of Blackmail," 41 *Philosophical Studies* 274 (1982); Murray N. Rothbard, *Man, Economy and State*, Auburn AL: Mises Institute, 1993, p. 443, ft. 49; Walter Block, "The Blackmailer as Hero," *The Libertarian Forum*, December 1972, pp. 1–4; Walter Block, *Defending the Undefendable*, New York: Fox and Wilkes, 1976 (1991), pp. 44–49; Walter Block, and Gordon, David, "Extortion and the Exercise of Free Speech Rights: A Reply to Professors Posner, Epstein, Nozick and Lindgren," *Loyola of Los Angeles Law Review*, Vol. 19, No. 1, November 1985, pp. 37–54; Walter Block, "Trading Money for Silence," *University of Hawaii Law Review*, Vol. 8, No. 1, Spring 1986, pp. 57–73; Walter Block, "The Case for De-Criminalizing Blackmail: A Reply to Lindgren and Campbell," *Western State University Law Review*, Vol. 24, No. 2, Spring, 1997, pp. 225–246; Walter Block, "A Libertarian Theory of Blackmail: Reply to Leo Katz's 'Blackmail and Other Forms of Arm-Twisting,'" *Irish Jurist*, Vol. XXXIII, 1998, pp. 280–310; Walter Block, and McGee, Robert W., "Blackmail from A to Z," *Mercer Law Review*, Vol. 50, No. 2, Winter 1999, pp. 569–601; Walter Block and Robert McGee, "Blackmail as a Victimless Crime," *Bracton Law Journal*, Vol. 31, 1999, pp. 24–28; Walter Block, "Blackmail and Economic Analysis," *Thomas Jefferson Law Review*, Vol. 21, No. 2, October 1999, pp. 165–192; Walter Block, "Blackmailing for Mutual Good: A Reply to Russell Hardin," *Vermont Law Review*, Vol. 24, No. 1, Fall 1999, pp. 121–141; Walter Block, "The Crime of Blackmail: A Libertarian Critique," *Criminal Justice Ethics*, Vol. 18, No. 2, Summer/Fall 1999, pp. 3–10; Walter Block, "Replies to Levin and Kipnis on Blackmail," *Criminal Justice Ethics*, Vol. 18, No. 2, Summer/Fall 1999, pp. 23–28; Walter Block and Christopher E. Kent, "Blackmail," *Magill's Legal Guide*, Pasadena, CA: Salem Press, 1999, p. 109; Walter Block, Stephen Kinsella, and Hans-Hermann Hoppe, "Second Paradox of Blackmail," *Business Ethics Quarterly*, Vol. 10, No. 3, July 2000, pp. 593–622; Walter Block, "The Legalization of Blackmail: A Reply to Professor Gordon," *Seton Hall Law Review*, Vol. 30, No. 4, 2000, pp. 1182–1223; Walter Block, "Threats, Blackmail, Extortion and Robbery and Other Bad Things," *University of Tulsa Law Journal*, Vol. 35, No. 2, Winter 2000, pp. 333–351; Walter Block, "Blackmail *is* Private Justice,"

Nor is it any proper objection to our thesis to claim that prostitution is legal in only a small part of the country. There are two possible rejoinders to this. First, if quid pro quo contracts with females, and the imposition of an environment "hostile" to them can be demonstrated as behavior which violates no law (even if only in most of Nevada), then we have shown that there is nothing per se problematic about sexual harassment. If so, it should not be proscribed anywhere else, either. Second, a case on libertarian grounds can easily be made out in behalf of legalizing prostitution in all other jurisdictions. After all, if a woman really "owns her own body," an oft made contention of the feminist and prochoice forces,[64] then she can decide for herself to use it to provide sexual services to men for a fee. To deny this is to "turn back the clock" to an era in the United States when the signature of an adult woman on a contract would be considered null and void.

Suppose, however, that a foreman of the Blockhead Corporation, unbeknownst to us, makes a quid pro quo offer to a female employee: go to bed with him, and get a raise, or refuse, and be fired. Now, it has already been established that we, the owners of the corporation, have a right to do this, provided no physical threat or fraud occurs. And, if it is licit for us to engage in such activities, it is also legitimate for us to pass on to our foreman the right, also, to operate in this manner. We might do so, for example, in lieu of paying a higher salary.

But suppose our policy is *not* to allow quid pro quo (sex for money) contracts in our corporation on the part of our employees, but our foreman does this in any case, on his own initiative. Let us consider the libertarian analysis that applies in this case. Our answer is that while this man did not violate the rights of the woman, she, after all, is an adult, a free agent, able to make up her own mind about offers of this sort. If there was any transgression here, and there was not, it was he who transgressed against *us*, the owners of the firm, and not against the woman.

University of British Columbia Law Review, Vol. 34, No. 1, 2000, pp. 11–37; Walter Block, "Reply to Wexler: Libertarianism, Blackmail and Decency," *University of British Columbia Law Review*, Vol. 34, No. 1, 2000, pp. 49–53; Walter Block, "Toward a Libertarian Theory of Blackmail," *Journal of Libertarian Studies*, Vol. 15, No. 2, Winter 2001, pp. 55–88.

[64] But only as regards abortion. For a libertarian perspective on this issue, see footnote 56, Supra.

Rothbard's analysis of the analogous case of payola is worthy of quotation at length[65]:

> In a typical payola scandal, a record company bribes a disc jockey to play Record A. Presumably, the disc jockey would either not have played the record at all, or would have played Record A fewer times; therefore, Record A is being played at the expense of Records B, C and D which would have been played more frequently … Surely, in a moral sense, the public is being betrayed in its trust in the disc jockey's sincerity … But the public has no property right in the radio program, and so they have no legal complaint in the matter … The other record companies, the producers of Records B, C, and D, were also injured since their products were not played as frequently, but they, too, have no property rights in the program…
>
> Was anyone's property rights aggressed against by the disc jockey's taking of a bribe? Yes, … the disc jockey violated his contractual obligation to his employer … to play those records which in his view will most suit the public. Hence, the disc jockey violated the property of the station owner or sponsor…. (I)t is the disc jockey who accepts payola who has done something criminal and deserves to be prosecuted, but not the record company who paid the bribe.
>
> Furthermore, if the record company had bribed the employer directly … then there would have been no violation of anyone's property right and therefore properly no question of illegality. Of course the public could easily feel cheated if the truth came out, and would then be likely to change their listening custom to another station or sponsor.

As for the payola-accepting jockey, so for the foreman of Blockhead who uses this firm for his own advantage, against his employers' interest. The woman in the case no more has her rights violated than do the producers of Records B, C, and D, nor the listening public. Further, were the radio station to allow the jockey to accept payola from Record company A, in lieu of a higher wage, it would be entirely within its rights, since it and only it owns the right to play what it wishes. Similarly, if Blockhead pays the foreman with lower wages, but allows him the right to engage in

[65] Rothbard, *Ethics of Liberty*, 1998, pp. 129–130, footnote 54, Supra.

quid pro quo contracts with the female employee, then again no one's rights are violated.

There is an obvious point to be made here; it is that the owners of the firm own the right to engage in quid pro quo contracts with female employees. If they cede it to a foreman, for mutually agreeable consideration, well and good. But if he seizes this on his own, he is stealing from the *firm*. This, then, is the kernel of truth behind legal prohibitions of quid pro quo dealings on the part of employees: without the express permission of the employer, it amounts to theft from them. Thus, quid pro quo may be legitimately precluded from the workplace in certain circumstances, not due to any intrinsic impropriety, but because it is a prerogative of the firm, and its owners object to its use on the part of their male subordinates, without permission.

There is a bottom line in all of this; "hostility" is in the eye of the beholder. There is no such thing as an objectively defined "hostile environment." The "reasonable woman" standard is an exercise in logical futility, for female tastes in this (as in so much more) vary widely. One woman's "hostile environment" is another's ideal employment situation. The female comfortable working in Hooters might be very unhappy employed by a nunnery; one who can prosper in the milieu of a house of prostitution might feel out of place in a kindergarten. Similarly, those who yearn to work in a library, bank, elementary school, or law office might not find a safe and happy harbor as a waitress in a topless restaurant.[66]

Critique of the Law

Let us now consider in detail some of the specifics of this law discussed above in a purely descriptive manner. We shall intersperse commentary into the citation of the law. As we state above[67]: Sexual harassment in the

[66] Or maybe not. The point is, no one can say anything for sure on this matter apart from noting that tastes will differ.

[67] See text accompanying footnote 1, Supra.

office means unwelcome sexual advances, requests for sexual favors, and other verbal or physical conduct of a sexual nature when:

(a) "Submission to such conduct is either explicitly or implicitly made a condition of an individual's employment."[68]

This may be disregarded. If it is agreed to by consenting adults, there is no warrant for setting such a contract aside, any more than there is for any other such agreement.

(b) "Submission to or rejection of such conduct by an individual is used as a basis for an employment decision effecting such individuals."[69]

There is no other rational way in which the bordello employer can decide whom to employ.

(c) "Such conduct has a purpose or effect of substantially interfering with an individual's right to work in an environment free of intimidation, hostility, or threats stemming from acts or language of a sexual nature."[70]

A woman may indeed have such a right.[71] But if she does, she also has a right to renounce it, for a fee, if she so wishes. To deny the latter is to deny the former. That is, if the EEOC maintains that a female does not have the right to relinquish what would otherwise be her right not to be continually approached in a sexual manner, then she cannot she have that right in the first place, contrary to the views of this regulatory body.

(d) "The conduct interferes with an employee's ability to focus on the job responsibilities."[72]

---

[68] 29 CFR #1604.11(a)(1)(2001).

[69] Id. At #1604.11(a)(2).

[70] Id. At #1604.11(a)(3).

[71] If so, then so does a man; men and women have equal rights in the libertarian society.

[72] Ellison v. Brady, 924 F.2d 872, 877 (9th Cir. 1991).

Consider again the Blockhead firm located in Reno, Nevada (or anywhere else where prostitution is legal). None of our sexual advances can be considered "unwelcome" since the woman we hire will contractually agree to accept these overtures. It is an *explicit* part of the contract; by signing it, she obligates herself to perform these duties. We may indeed legitimately "threaten" her if she withholds sexual services because in such a case she is guilty of contract violation. Our "threat" would be similar to that of any (ordinary) employer whose secretary refuses to type and file, or whose bordello prostitute refuses to entertain men in bed: she will be fired and her salary goes unpaid. It is impossible, moreover, for our conduct to interfere with the employee's ability to focus on job responsibilities because these are *precisely* her job responsibilities.

We continue to cite from our previous description of the law: "Some behaviors found by the EEOC and the courts to constitute sexual harassment is:

(a) Sexually suggestive or obscene comments, threats, insults, slurs, jokes about gender-based traits of a person, or sexual propositions."[73]

But it is obvious, the politicians responsible for these laws notwithstanding, that this is precisely what occurs in a peep show emporium, or with regard to a Victoria's Secret catalogue. If the law does not prohibit these activities, and it does not, then it is intellectually incoherent for it to proscribe so-called sexual harassment.

(b) "Physical conduct such as intentional touching, pinching, brushing against another's body, suggesting or coercing sexual intercourse, or physical assault."[74]

Coercing sexual intercourse is rape. Intentional unwanted touching and pinching and brushing constitute battery. No responsible legal commentator opposes the prohibition of such per se criminal behavior. But "suggesting sexual intercourse" is surely an entirely different matter. If the

---

[73] Lipsett v. University of Puerto Rico, 864 F.2d 881, 906 (1st Cir. 1988).

[74] Jones v. Wesco Investments, 846 F.2d 1154, 1155 (8th Cir. 1988).

EEOC and the courts ever succeeded in eliminating such suggestions, this would sound the death knell for the human race. That the dating and mating game should be played out only in, perhaps, at least so far, bars, while legally prohibited from churches, universities, and the workplace, is certainly not mandated by the idea that coercion should be banned from human interaction.

The point is, "suggesting sexual intercourse" has widely been interpreted as promoting a "hostile environment," or constituting "sexual harassment," when it occurs on a college campus, especially if the suggester is a male professor, and the suggestee is a female student. Similar findings have been made for the business firm, particularly if the initiator of this suggestion is a male boss, and it is made to a female subordinate. And yet, as we have seen, "suggesting sexual intercourse" is the paradigm action at the Blockhead company. We have already established the legal validity of this firm's practices (at least in most parts of Nevada). Legal consistency requires that at the very least, "suggesting sexual intercourse" be allowed in these domains. But more. "Suggesting sexual intercourse," at least at some point in the heterosexual relationship, is the primary vehicle for the perpetuation of the human race. If this is deemed per se illegal "harassment," it can only serve the interests of those who oppose heterosexuality.

(c) "Non-verbal behavior such as leering or staring at another's body, displaying sexually suggestive photographs, cartoons, or magazines."[75]

Movies, television, and Broadway shows are nowadays replete with partial, frontal, and total nudity; it is unreasonable to expect that viewers would resist "leering or staring at another's body." Were such a law to be carried out in a logically consistent manner, not only could there be no such industries, women would be confined to wearing chadors, as is the practice of the Taliban in Afghanistan and in many of the Islamic countries. This is hardly the direction in which we really want to go.

[75] Robinson v. Jacksonville Shipyards, 760 F.Supp. 1486, 1494 (M.D. Fla. 1991).

(d) "Continued expression of sexual or social interest in an individual after being informed that the interest is unwelcome."[76]

There are many thousands and thousands of cases on record of successful marriages of several decades and more duration where the husband's initial overtures to the wife were at first rebuffed. But the male, as was his wont,[77] persevered. He was pressing and persistent. This might not please the feminists in the courts and in the EEOC, but this is part and parcel of male human nature.[78]

According to what might be called the heterosexual norm, or ethic, the man is the pursuer, the woman the pursued. She sets up roadblocks, he overcomes them. The female, not the male, is the coy one. But this model does not resonate well in these modern politically correct times. Here, the sexes are supposed to be equal. The woman has as much right to initiate contact as the man.[79]

---

[76] Ellison v. Brady, 924 F.2d 872, 874–875 (9th Cir. 1991).

[77] See on this J. H. Barkow, L. Cosmides and J.Tooby, eds., *The adapted mind: Evolutionary Psychology and the generation of culture*, New York: Oxford University Press, 1992; D. M. Buss, *The Evolution of Desire*, New York: Basic Books, 1994; Richard Dawkins, *The Selfish Gene*, New York: Oxford University Press, 1976/1989; R. H. Frank, *Passion within Reason: The Strategic Role of the Emotions*, NY: Norton, 1988; Mark Ridley, *The Red Queen: Sex and the evolution of human nature*, NY: MacMillan, 1993; D. Symons, *The Evolution of Human Sexuality*, New York: Oxford University Press, 1979; R. Trivers, *Social Evolution*, Reading, MA: Benjamin/Cummings, 1985; E. O. Wilson, *Sociobiology*, Cambridge, MA: Harvard University Press, 1975; R. Wright, "Feminists, meet Mr. Darwin," *New Republic*, November 28, 1994. Sociobiologically speaking, females are supposed to be flirtatious; males, pressing and persistent.

[78] There is a wealth of anecdotal evidence attesting to male assertiveness and female reticence. Some of it is in the form of humor. According to one joke: If a general says "yes," he means "yes." If he says "no," he means "no." If he says "maybe," he is not a general. If a diplomat says "yes," he means "maybe." If he says "maybe," he means "no." If he says "no," he is not a diplomat. If a girl (virgin) says "no," it means "maybe." If she says "maybe," it means "yes." If she says "yes," she is not a girl (virgin). And according to another bit of "folk wisdom": When a woman says "No," it means "Maybe." When she says "Maybe," it means "Yes." In sharp contrast, the feminists have launched a campaign around the motto "No means no." We wonder what planet are they from, in terms of an understanding of human nature. Anyone who believes that every time a woman declines a man's advances, she is serious about it only evidences his ignorance of the human condition.

[79] For a recent critique of the modern mores, and a defense of the more traditional ones, see Danielle Crittenden, *What Our Mothers Didn't Tell Us*, NY: Simon and Schuster, 1998; Richard Dooling, *Blue Streak: Swearing, Free Speech and Sexual Harassment*, New York: Random House, 1996; Fein, Ellen, and Sherrie Schneider, *The Rules: Time Tested Secrets for Capturing the Heart of Mr. Right*, New York: Warner Books, 1996.

Of course, it is possible to go too far in this direction. There is, after all, such a thing as harassment, in contrast to rape. Even if the male expression of interest is limited to sending flowers, notes by mail, and leaving telephone messages (as opposed to physical invasion), it is possible for enough to be more than enough. But, for such cases, we already have remedies on the books (obtaining a protective order and antistalking statutes) and hardly need the minions of politically correct EEOC feminists to improve matters.

To anticipate the burden of the next section, on how a free market can alleviate legitimate harassment problems, reflect on the following: mail sent by an unrequited suitor is now delivered by the public postal monopoly; were this industry fully privatized,[80] there is little doubt that firms would deal with "junk mail" far more efficaciously than at present. Telephone messages come courtesy of one of the most highly government regulated of industries. A bit more economic freedom, here, too, might well eventuate in the more efficient elimination of junk phone calls. Flowers are commonly delivered on public streets. Under full free enterprise for this industry,[81] there is little doubt that unwanted flower deliveries, too, would be better squelched.

---

[80] The case for privatizing the post office is offered by Douglas K. Adie, *The Mail Monopoly: Analyzing Canadian Postal Service*, Vancouver: The Fraser Institute, 1990; Douglas K. Adie, *Monopoly Mail: Privatizing the United States Postal Service*, New Brunswick, N.J.: Transaction, 1988; Douglas K. Adie, "Why Marginal Reform of the U.S. Postal Service Won't Succeed," in *Free the Mail: Ending the Postal Monopoly*, Peter J. Ferrara, ed., Washington, D.C.: The Cato Institute, 1990; Thomas G. Moore, "The Federal Postal Monopoly: History, Rationale, and Future," *Free The Mail: Ending the Postal Monopoly* ed. Peter J. Ferrara (Washington, D.C.: CATO Institute, 1990); George Priest, "The History of the Postal Monopoly in the United States," *Journal of Law and Economics*, 18, no. 33, 1975; Stuart M. Butler, "Privatizing Bulk Mail," *Management*, 6, No. 1, 1986; Stephen Moore, "Privatizing the U.S. Postal Service," in Stephen Moore and Stuart Butler, eds., *Privatization*, Washington: Heritage Foundation, 1987.

[81] See on this Walter Block, "Public Goods and Externalities: The Case of Roads," *The Journal of Libertarian Studies*, Vol. VII, No. 1, Spring 1983, pp. 1–34; Block, Walter E. and Matthew A. Block. 1996. "Roads, Bridges, Sunlight and Private Property Rights," Journal Des Economistes Et Des Etudes Humaines, Vol. VII, No. 2/3, June-September, pp. 351–362; Block, Walter E. 1998. "Roads, Bridges, Sunlight and Private Property: Reply to Gordon Tullock," Journal des Economistes et des Etudes Humaines, Vol. 8, No. 2/3, June-September, pp. 315–326; Walter Block, "Road Socialism," *International Journal of Value-Based Management*, 1996, Vol. 9, pp. 195–207; Walter Block, "Theories of Highway Safety," *Transportation Research Record*, #912, 1983b, pp. 7–10; Walter Block, "Congestion and Road Pricing," *The Journal of Libertarian Studies*, Vol. IV, No. 3, Fall 1980, pp. 299–330; Walter Block, "Free Market Transportation: Denationalizing the Roads," *Journal of Libertarian Studies*, Vol. III, No. 2, Summer 1979, pp. 209–238; Michelle Cadin and

(e) "Belief that an individual required to consent to the foregoing behavior as a term or condition of her employment."[82]

Sexually suggestive comments are precisely what the secretary—prostitute of Blockhead—signed up to tolerate. Nor were her duties limited just to tolerating off color comments either. There is no way that sexual intercourse can be "coerced" here anymore than in a house of prostitution. Nor need one resort to the Blockhead case to deal with "leering or staring at another's body." Such behavior occurs in every Hooters, every Playboy Club, in every topless establishment, in every restaurant where women wear micro mini skirts and other revealing costume. They are hired for the express purpose of being "leered" at, with their own consent. Were they not the sort of people to call forth this type of male behavior, they would be fired, or not hired in the first place.

The Economics of Harassment

Let us recapitulate. So far, we have been arguing that "sexual harassment" law is illogical, insofar as it involves voluntary, mutually agreeable behavior between consenting adults. That is, unless there is a fraudulent promise that normal heterosexual overtures will not take place in a given premises, any woman who is on the receiving end of such behavior is free to take a different job; that she stays in her present position, where such overtures occur, is an indication that she values the package of work plus

---

Walter Block, (1997), "Privatize the Public Highway System," *The Freeman*, February, Vol. 47, No. 2., pp. 96–97; Gerald Gunderson, "Privatization and the 19th-Century Turnpike," *Cato Journal*, Vol. 9, No. 1, Spring/Summer 1989, pp. 191–200; Dan Klein, J. Majewski and C. Baer, "Economy, Community and the Law: The Turnpike Movement in New York, 1797–1845, *The Journal of Economic History*, March 1993, pp. 106–122; Dan Klein and G.J. Fielding, "Private Toll Roads: Learning from the Nineteenth Century," *Transportation Quarterly*, July 1992, pp. 321–341; Dan Klein and G.J. Fielding, "How to Franchise Highways," *Journal of Transport Economics and Policy*, May 1993, pp. 113–130; Gabriel Roth, *The Private Provision of Public Services in Developing Countries*, Oxford: Oxford University Press, 1987; Gabriel Roth, *Paying for Roads: The Economics of Traffic Congestion*, Middlesex, England: Penguin, 1967; Murray N. Rothbard *For a New Liberty*, Macmillan, New York, 1973; William C. Woolridge, *Uncle Sam the Monopoly Man*, New Rochelle, N.Y.: Arlington House, 1970.

[82] Simmonds v. Lyons, 746 F.2d 265, 269 (5th Cir. 1984).

being "victimized" more highly than her next best alternative. Laws attempting to prohibit such occurrences thus constitute an ill-conceived response to what is a nonproblem: ordinary heterosexual male–female, water-cooler-type interaction. This does not at all mean that, in this view, modesty and decorum and nonaggressive male behavior are out of reach for the women who do not yearn to be artists' models, actresses, prostitutes, or topless waitresses. The solution, in this perspective, may not emanate from the courts and the EEOC, but it nonetheless plays an important role in our society.

Very much to the contrary of the usual supposition on these matters, the answer is provided by the free enterprise system. In order to see this, we must discuss some concepts in labor economics.

Heterosexual males vary in their presentations of themselves to heterosexual females, all the way from courtly behavior suitable to the knights of the Round Table to that of the boor and lout.[83] Consider the position of a manager of a firm with a large number of females on staff, who is called upon to deal with one of the latter.

As is well known in economics, wages tend to equal the marginal revenue productivity of the worker.[84] But this includes not only the amount that the employee himself can add to the bottom line, but his effect on the contribution of others.[85] Let loose a few churls in the establishment, even those who full well know their job, and the productivity of most if not all of the females will plummet. Thus, as an employer, you would either not hire the barbarian, or you would only be willing to pay him a very low wage (perhaps, even, a large negative one) which is but another way of saying you would not hire him at all. A firm which also employed a large number of females, particularly ones sensitive to crude male

[83] For the purpose of this analysis, we assume that anything worse, for example, from slight to heavy physical abuse to actual rape, does not exist; such acts are dealt with by the forces of law and order, not by ordinary businesses on the shop floor.

[84] See, for example, Morgan O. Reynolds, *Economics of Labor*, South-Western College Publishing, 1995.

[85] A significant part of the reason a Michael Jordan or a Kobe Bryant was so productive in basketball was not due entirely to their own points, rebounds, or steals total, but because they also made their teammates into better players. This phenomenon is hardly confined to that particular sport, or, indeed, to the realm of athletics in general.

behavior, and insisted upon hiring such men, would be consigned to the dust bin of economics: for example, bankruptcy.

The market, then, is women's best protector against untoward male behavior. The scalpel of the free enterprise system will better rid women of unwanted attention than the bludgeon of government law. For if the government errs (as we have been arguing), there is no automatic feedback mechanism which forces it to mend its ways. If it loses money, it can always make up for this shortfall by increasing taxes, or reducing other expenditures. In the private sector, in contrast, a loss of profit is absolutely crucial. The market is a better supplier, not of women's rights,[86] but of comfort in social settings than is the law (which can legitimately be used only to quell assault, battery, and rape).

Yet another example of business coming to the rescue of female sensibilities concerns restaurants, and other such establishments that are open to the public, and earns profit only from satisfied customers. Bouncers in a bar put a damper on verbiage that borders on abuse. The last thing an owner wants is for women to be made uncomfortable in his emporium. The search for profits leads the proprietor, as if by an "invisible hand,"[87] to do that which is in the interests of his female customers.

However, consider "wolf whistles" that typically occur on sidewalks. Feminists, and even others, take sharp exception to these outbursts. To them, this type of behavior shows male contempt for females; the interpretation is that the former see the latter only as a form of "meat" or sexual object.[88] But there is a reason why this objectionable behavior still occurs; nowhere is it written in stone that the market is supposed to come to the rescue of all maidenly sensibilities.

---

[86] This is because we have argued that women have a right not to "niceness" but only to security of their persons.

[87] Adam Smith, *An Inquiry into the Nature and Causes of the Wealth of Nations*, New York: Modern Library, 1776/1965; for a critique from the free enterprise perspective, see Murray N. Rothbard *The Logic of Action: Method, Money and the Austrian School*, Vol. I, Cheltenham, UK: Edward Elgar, 1997.

[88] We assume away, for argument's sake, the claim that although crude, and unwelcome, wolf whistles are not per se rights violating, and do sometimes serve their purpose of allowing men to introduce themselves to women. That is, we temporarily adopt the leftist perspective that to see a woman as a sexual object is to commit in effect an assault upon her.

These "wolf whistles" are preeminently launched by construction workers and their ilk. The economic analysis we have offered does not apply to such situations because of externalities: the victimized women and the victimizing men are not employed by the same firm. If they were, the arguments mentioned above would provide sufficient incentive for the employer to bring them to a quick halt. Most economists would characterize this as a "market failure."[89] But it is no such thing.[90] It is due not to a market failure, but to a failure to allow markets to operate in the first place. For example, if the streets were privately owned,[91] the proprietor of the sidewalk would have exactly the same financial incentive we have attributed to the owner of the bar and restaurant. Those women who were annoyed by wolf whistles would not frequent his street establishment; since his profits depend upon the number of satisfied customers, he would have every inducement to deal with street whistlers as with offensive lounge lizards.

Consider the kinds of establishments for which boorish men typically work, if not in organizations that employ numerous women. After all, there are an awful lot of men who act in this manner, and they have to work somewhere. Traditionally, the market solution is segregation: boorish men tend to be diverted to places where they will do the least harm to the fairer sex: in the forests, deep sea fishing, merchant seamen, steel mills, putting out fires, and so on. The problem is that with affirmative action[92] that breaks down such answers to the problem, such firms are

---

[89] See Gene Callahan, *Economics for Real People*, Auburn, AL: The Mises Institute, 2001 or any other introduction to microeconomics or public finance on this matter. That is, in the view of most practitioners of the dismal science, the economics of discrimination as depicted above accurately describes intra firm activity, but not that which occurs inter firm.

[90] For a critique of the externalities as market failure literature, see Hans-Hermann Hoppe, "Fallacies of the Public Goods Theory and the Production of Security," in *The Economics and Ethics of Private Property: Studies in Political Economy and Philosophy*, Boston: Kluwer, 1993; Jeffrey Hummel, 1990, 'National Goods vs. Public Goods: Defense, Disarmament and Free Riders,' *The Review of Austrian Economics*, Vol. IV, pp. 88–122; Walter Block, 1983, 'Public Goods and Externalities: The Case of Roads,' *The Journal of Libertarian Studies: An Interdisciplinary Review*, Vol. VII, No. 1, Spring, pp. 1–34.

[91] See footnote 82, Supra.

[92] For critiques, see Walter E. Williams, and Walter Block, "Male-Female Earnings Differentials: A Critical Reappraisal," *The Journal of Labor Research*, Vol. II, No. 2, Fall 1981, pp. 385–388; Walter Block E., and Michael A. Walker, eds., *Discrimination, Affirmative Action and Equal Opportunity*, Vancouver: The Fraser Institute, 1982.

forced to hire females. It is as if there were two groups of people who hated each other on sight (e.g., boorish men, and women who view their treatment of women as very harmful). The market, naturally enough, would tend to segregate them, so that they would not be continually at war with one another. Along comes government, not able to refrain from interfering, and pursues policies that put these two groups into close and unwelcome proximity with one another. The result, of course, is chaos.[93]

The same economic analysis that applies to cigarette smoking can be utilized in the present context. Perhaps this furnishes a better analogy. Here, there is one group of people (the smokers) that creates a nuisance (second-hand smoke), and another group that feels victimized. The government, in its infinite wisdom, bludgeons all establishments into adopting the same rules: previously, to set up smoking sections; but now, more and more, to ban indoor smoking entirely.[94] In sharp contrast, the market, driven by profit considerations (e.g., customer satisfaction), wields a scalpel. Some shops, such as those which supply health foods, ban smoking entirely. Others, such as pool halls, billiard rooms, bowling lanes, bars, and grills, place no rules whatsoever against this practice. And then,

---

[93] There is a slight disanalogy here, in that in the case described in the text, there is mutual hatred and abuse emanating from both groups, while in sexual harassment, one category of people are the harassers, and the other, the harassees. For Ronald, H. Coase, "The Problem of Social Cost," *Journal of Law and Economics*, October 1960, Vol. 3, pp. 1–44; however, this would be a valid analogy, in that in order to stop the harassers from victimizing the harassees, one would have to bring discomfort to the former. That is, for Coase, there can be no such thing as harassment: all such interactions are reciprocal. For critics of Coase see: Walter Block, "Coase and Demsetz on Private Property Rights," *The Journal of Libertarian Studies*, Vol. I, No. 2, Spring 1977, pp. 111–115; Walter Block, 1995 "Ethics, Efficiency, Coasean Property Rights and Psychic Income: A Reply to Harold Demsetz," *Review of Austrian Economics*, Vol. 8, No. 2, pp. 61–126; Walter Block, "O.J.'s Defense: A Reductio Ad Absurdum of the Economics of Ronald Coase and Richard Posner," *European Journal of Law and Economics*, 1996, Vol. 3, pp. 265–286; Walter Block, "Private Property Rights, Erroneous Interpretations, Morality and Economics: Reply to Demsetz," *Quarterly Journal of Austrian Economics*, 1999; Roy E. Cordato, "Subjective Value, Time Passage, and the Economics of Harmful Effects," *Hamline Law Review*, Vol. 12, No. 2, Spring 1989, pp. 229–244; Elisabeth Krecke, "Law and the Market Order: An Austrian Critique of the Economic Analysis of Law," in Robert W. McGee, ed., *Commentaries on Law and Economics: 1997*, pp. 86–108; Gary North, *The Coase Theorem*, Tyler, Texas: Institute for Christian Economics, 1992; Murray N. Rothbard "Law, Property Rights, and Air Pollution," *Economics and the Environment: A Reconciliation*, Walter Block, ed., Vancouver: The Fraser Institute, 233–79, 1990.

[94] Since January 1, 1998, California has banned smoking in virtually all indoor public places including bars, Reuter, Ted, "California Living: Snuff out that cigarette, please," *Christian Science Monitor*, January 12, 1988.

in the vast middle ground, there are a plethora of rules, stipulating smoking times, days, sections, and so on, all in an attempt to tailor their response to consumer demands.[95]

So far, we have analyzed male–female interaction from the former vantage point. Let us now consider the latter perspective. Suppose, now, that most females, as contended by those responsible for the repression of sexual "harassment," are very reticent and shy. For them, the ordinary behavior of robust heterosexual males is odious. Apart from refusing to "pollute" the work premises by hiring males, as we have just discussed, let us now discuss how the market will protect women from male overtures.

Again, the system works through competition. Not only are firms in competition with each other in the product or final goods markets which is well known, they also compete with one another when it comes to hiring workers. The preeminent form of rivalry is, of course, the wage paid. But employers also contend with each other over employees through the provision of working conditions.

Consider, as an analogy to our case in point, the question of air conditioning. The employer faces the choice of whether or not he should install this amenity on his premises for the enjoyment of his workers. If he does, he will undergo a cost. On the other hand, he will more likely satisfy, attract, and retain employees. The profit-maximizing firm will engage in this expense if he can thereby recoup these costs in the form of lower wages paid. Most employees would accept a reduced wage in an air-conditioned factory in preference to the otherwise identical job lacking such favorable working conditions. Those firms which do not install air conditioning have to pay higher wages.

Workers tend to sort themselves out based on their tastes for air conditioning. Those who spurn it tend to gravitate to old-fashioned types of surroundings, where they are paid more, and have to forego the benefits of cooler air. Those who like it, but only slightly, can be found in premises of either type. And those who cannot get along without it tend to aggregate in air-conditioned facilities, even at the cost of a wage cut.

---

[95] See Walter Block, "Tobacco Advertising," *International Journal of Value Based Management*, Vol. 10, No. 3, pp. 221–235, 1997.

Women, too, differ in their "taste"[96] or distaste for assertive/aggressive male behavior; for example, for what is considered by some to be a "hostile environment." There are some, call them Ls, who have a marked aversion to all such goings on. They tend to gravitate to work environments which preclude males altogether (e.g., a nunnery, a kindergarten). Others, at the opposite end of the continuum, call them Ps, relish these sorts of "hostile" environments. In the middle, the category of probably most females, call them Hs, are those who take an intermediate stance on this issue.

Assume that apart from this issue, the marketable skills of all three groups are equal. Then, with equal productivity, we would expect money wages not to differ between them. Now, let us introduce the issue of hostility of environment. Under the economic system of laissez faire capitalism, firms are free to institute a policy proscribing a hostile environment, or not. That is, completely as a private matter, they can offer contracts to males,[97] positing that if they are found guilty of sexual harassment, they will have to pay a penalty, for example, forego a bond they have to post upon being hired.[98] This will undoubtedly imply a cost, as in the air conditioning case, for there will be the additional disbursements in order to monitor the system, hiring hearing officers to determine guilt or innocence, to say nothing of the extra monetary and psychic costs imposed on males.

Let us now consider employer incentives to introduce such a system, given that he is "free to choose."[99] He would do so, if he could thereby reduce his costs in the form of lower wages he could thereby pay to appreciative females.

There are those, of course, who would object to the fact that women have to pay a compensating differential in the form of lower wages. After

---

[96] See Gary Becker, *Human Capital*, New York: The National Bureau of Economic Research, 1964; Gary Becker, *The Economics of Discrimination*, Chicago: The University of Chicago Press, 1957.

[97] We are still implicitly assuming that only males can make the work environment uncomfortable, and only females can be thereby be victimized. To assume all four possibilities would only complicate the analysis without changing it.

[98] Or be docked in salary, or be summarily fired, etc.

[99] This is the felicitous title of Milton & Rose Friedman, *Free to Choose*, Avon Books, New York, 1981.

all, they are the victims, not the aggressors. If this is market fairness, we want less of it, not more, they might say.

This objection misses the point, however. Here, we are discussing not the first case where there was a large majority of women, and males were made by the market to either toe the line or not be hired at all. Rather, we are now considering the case of a male-dominated industry or firm (think oil refinery, lumberjack, steel mill, coal mine, etc.) where the sensibilities of women work, mainly, to reduce the productivity of men. Under these circumstances, of course women will have to lose out, financially, in the market, compared to the situation where they had no such negative effects on the productivity of men. It is the same with all statistical "outliers." Men who are over 7 feet tall and weigh more than 300 pounds, or who are less than 5 feet tall and weigh in at under 100 pounds, cannot buy off the rack clothes. They must purchase tailor-made products, and these cost more. Similarly, it is costly to "tailor" the reactions of hordes of men to female sensibilities.

Responsibility

(f) "Employer responsibility for acts of nonemployees such as customers or service technicians, when the employer knows, or should have known, of the unwelcome conduct and fails to take immediate or appropriate action."[100]

Perhaps the most evil and insidious aspect of this whole episode is the requirement that one person be held accountable for the actions of another. Let us here accept, if only for the sake of argument, that there is indeed a crime of sexual harassment. Placing responsibility for such acts on those who have *not* committed them is highly improper. Whether it is employees of the firm, customers, and suppliers and their employees, it matters not one whit: under this law the employer will be found guilty even though he had no part whatsoever in the wrong doing.

[100] CFR #1604.11(d)(2001).

That alone ought to be enough to establish its illegitimacy, for the entire corpus of law is built on the bedrock that the guilty party, not anyone else, shall pay for his crime. Suppose a transportation firm hires a driver to convey passengers in its bus from one city to another in a safe and law-abiding manner. Instead, this employee drives recklessly, and hits another vehicle. In justice, only this negligent chauffer should be forced to compensate the victims. In actual point of fact, however, it is likely that the firm itself will be made liable.[101] This stems from an unjustified search for "deep pockets." Just because the malfeasant driver does not have enough money to fully compensate the victims does not render it appropriate to attack the bank account of a totally innocent person, the owner of the firm.[102]

The view underlying sexual harassment law, in contrast, is predicated upon vicarious liability or respondeat superior. Here, one person, the employer, can be held liable for the crimes or torts of another, even though the party of the first part did not ask the party of the second to commit the act. No greater injustice can be imagined.

Rothbard[103] goes so far as to characterize this as the "notorious theory of vicarious liability." States Thomas Baty: "In hard fact, the reason for the employer's liability is the damages are taken from a deep pocket."[104] And in the view of Prosser,[105] "Most courts have made little or no effort to explain the result, and have taken refuge in rather empty phrases, such as … the endlessly repeated formula of 'respondeat superior,' which in itself means nothing more than 'look to the man higher up.'"

---

[101] Assume there is no insurance policy in effect.

[102] A counter argument is that the employer was causally related to the accident, and therefore at least in part responsible for it, in that had he not hired this particular driver, it would not have occurred. This is subject to the reductio ad absurdum response that there are many other people also causally responsible for the accident, and it would be highly unjust to make them pay for it. For example, the accident would not have occurred had not the driver been able to buy clothes, and food; had the car or road not been built in the first place. Thus, we can also implicate in this accident those who mined the iron necessary to construct the bus.

[103] Murray N. Rothbard, "Law, Property Rights, and Air Pollution," *Economics and the Environment: A Reconciliation*, Walter Block, ed., Vancouver: The Fraser Institute, 1990.

[104] Id. at p. 247, and William L. Prosser, *Handbook of the Law of Torts*, 1971, 4th ed., p. 459.

[105] Ibid., cited Murray N. Rothbard, "Law, Property Rights, and Air Pollution," *Economics and the Environment: A Reconciliation*, Walter Block, ed., Vancouver: The Fraser Institute, 1990, p. 247.

In our own rendition of this aspect of the law,[106] we state, "…the employer is strictly liable for the conduct of supervisory employees who are acting within the scope of their authority." This of course was reportorial not advocated by us. And, indeed, there is a certain coherence to this way of putting the matter. For if the "employees … are acting within the scope of their authority" in their malfeasance, then, and to that extent, the employer *should be* responsible for their acts, in that he in effect *ordered* them to commit the tort. But that is not at all what the EEOC is mandating. Here, there is the far lesser requirement only that the employer "knows, or should have known, of the unwelcome conduct and fails to take immediate or appropriate action."

But this should not even be relevant. If A knows that B is about to rob a grocer, it is clear who should go to jail when this nefarious activity actually occurs. Obviously B is the guilty party, and A, a total innocent.

If the law is going to hold employers responsible for acts of employees, all in the search for deep pockets, there is no rational end to this process. Suppose an employee commits an actual rape of a co-worker. It is clear that, in a just society, only the rapist should go to jail. To incarcerate the employer would be an injustice. Obviously, only the rapist is guilty of the crime, and should do the time, and this holds true whether the rape occurs on the business premises or somewhere else.

But there are other anomalies in this situation. It is unreasonable to hold employers responsible for employees, since the latter are in effect agents of the former; but if we do, then logical consistency requires that we should hold all principles responsible for the acts of their agents. For example, following this line of "reasoning," we would hold the tenant or landlord responsible for the acts of the real estate broker; the investor for the acts of the stockbroker; business partners, or spouses, for that matter, for the acts of each other. Alternatively, if the reason we are holding the employer responsible for the acts of the employee is that the former is higher up in the sociological hierarchy than the latter, we might consider generalizing this relationship, too. If we did, we would then jail landlords for the acts of their tenants. But it is merely Marxist drivel to think that

[106] See p. 11, Supra, text accompanying footnote 18.

employers have more power than employees (tell that to Michael Jordan and Jerry Reinsdorf) or landlords than tenants (tell that to the landlord of Bill Gates or Donald Trump). This being the case, then, we might with equal illogic hold employees responsible for the acts of employers, or tenants responsible for those of their landlords.

Vicarious liability and respondeat superior are a search for deep pockets, not justice.

Qui Bono?

If sexual harassment laws are the unmitigated disaster we have made them out to be, we must now attempt to explain why we have them on the books.

One way to answer this question is to ask: Who benefits from this legislation? The underlying theory is that those who gain from these enactments were likely instrumental in their passage in the first place, and in their subsequent support.[107]

The point is, it is difficult to avoid the conclusion that sexual harassment law in general, and the idiosyncratic definition and interpretation of "hostile environments," are aimed at interfering, as much as possible, with normal male–female interaction. As we have seen, it is entirely unremarkable for heterosexual males to take the initiative in setting up relationships with heterosexual females. If they are to do so, they must necessarily at least sometimes make overtures which are "unwelcome." There is no way that they can they possibly know, for sure, before the fact, whether their suits shall be welcome or not, even apart from the traditional coyness of heterosexual females. To penalize heterosexual males for such behavior is surely an attempt to reduce it.

When looked at in this way, there are some obvious candidates to play the role of beneficiary of these laws: all those who gain from making it more difficult for heterosexual men and women to interact with one

[107] This is the methodology employed by Elvis Cole and all other great detectives; see Robert Crais, *Sunset Express*, New York: Hyperion, 1996. Apart from means and opportunity, the motive for the crime is often the best way to discern the identity of the criminal.

another in traditional courtship patterns. This would include lesbians, since if men were kept apart from women, some of the latter might become attached to female homosexuals, who they previously spurned; also female man haters, on ideological grounds. Homosexual men would gain in a similar manner, if heterosexual men are cut off from heterosexual women. The point is, there are always people on the margin of homo and hetero-sexuality; make things more difficult in one of these directions, and at least some of these will become inclined to the other direction.

As well, there are the feminists who oppose [male] freedom almost for the sake of opposing freedom.[108] The idea that men, mostly assertive, often boorish, should be able to approach women with impunity for the ultimate purpose of heterosexual intercourse must be anathema to them. To this rogue's gallery, we must add the over-populationists[109] and other radical wing environmentalists for whom the ideal of fewer people figures heavily in their solution to the earth's supposed problems. If men and women cannot get together as easily as before, they are likely to breed fewer children, something fervently to be wished for, at least in this quarter.

We do not at this time contend that these groups have been active in promoting the anti-"sexual harassment" agenda. This may indeed be the case. We only maintain that this is a likely avenue for future research into the question of who supports such legislation.

[108] See Michael Levin, *Feminism and Freedom*, New York: Transaction Books, 1987; Michael Levin, "Comparable Worth: The Feminist Road to Socialism," *Commentary*, September 1984.

[109] See Paul R. Ehrlich, *The Population Bomb*, New York: Sierra Club – Ballantine, 1968; Paul R. Ehrlich, and Anne H. Ehrlich, *The Population Explosion*, New York: Simon and Schuster, 1990; David Foreman, "Only Man's Presence Can Save Nature," *Harpers*, April 1990; Al Gore, *Earth in the Balance: Ecology and the Human Spirit*, Boston: Houghton-Mifflin, 1992. For rejoinders, see Daniel Coffey and Walter Block, "Postponing Armageddon: Why Population Growth Isn't Out of Control," *Humanomics*. Vol 15, No 4, 1999, pp. 66–79; Walter Block, "Population Growth: Is it a problem?" *Resolving Global Problems into the 21st century: How Can Science Help Proceedings of the Fourth National Conference of Canadian Pugwash*, Peter S. Ross, Sheila Riordon and Susan MacArtney, eds., Ottawa: CSP Publications, 1989, pp. 30–61; Julian Simon, (1990). "The Unreported Revolution in Population in Population Economics," *The Public Interest*. Fall: 89–100; Julian Simon, *The Ultimate Resource*, Princeton: Princeton University Press, 1981; David Friedman, *Laissez Faire in Population: the Least Bad Solution*, New York: Population Council, 1972; Peter T. Bauer, "Population Scares," *Commentary*, November 1987, 39–42.

Conclusion

We conclude, given the foregoing, that sexual harassment law is unjust, and ought to be repealed. We maintain that quid pro quo is part and parcel of economic freedom, and that this has value both instrumentally in creating a prosperous economy,[110] and intrinsically, for its own sake. In our view, the elimination of a "hostile environment" is something that the market can do, where there is an economic need for this, far more effectively and justly than can government.

[110] James Gwartney, Robert Lawson and Walter Block, *Economic Freedom of the World, 1975–1995*, Washington, D.C.: The Fraser Institute, 1996.

Part II

Education

6

Forcing Some to Pay for the Free Speech of Others

Introduction

Colleges love to compete by freely disclosing to students, and potential students, the costs of tuition and room and board.

They are often, however, less inclined to advertise mandatory student fees used to subsidize various academic, infrastructure, and student activities. Fees are typically collected for chemistry labs, the library, computer labs, new campus building, student health, athletics, and to fund student organizations. The fees are usually approved and justified by the governing board as relevant to the student's overall educational experience because they are used to promote campus diversity and extracurricular activity. The fees, even to groups that support on and off-campus political activity, are said to be germane to the University's educational mission. Some governing boards contend that to deny mandatory fees to student organizations that promote on campus and off-campus political activity violates that organization's freedom of speech. But, what of the freedom of speech of students who object to their mandatory fees being used to subsidize ideological or political views that they find offensive or disagreeable? Must they pay for speech that they find objectionable? Is their

W. E. Block, R. Whitehead, *Philosophy of Law*, Palgrave Studies in Classical Liberalism,
https://doi.org/10.1007/978-3-030-28360-5_6

objection and attempt to withhold their support somehow an infringement on the student organization's freedom of speech? And, is forcing objecting students to pay for others student's objectionable speech somehow germane to the university's educational mission? Finally, does the First Amendment require one student to pay for another's speech? This article reviews another in a long line of cases where university administrators demonstrate an embarrassing ignorance of the proscriptions of the First Amendment of the Constitution in dealing with student speech issues.[1] The case of *Southworth et al. v. Grebe et al.*[2] and several of its precedents are utilized as a framework to discuss these issues and demonstrate the court's methodology in reconciling the competing interests. We conclude with a more radical philosophical perspective on free speech and private property rights.

The Background

Full time students at the University of Wisconsin–Madison must pay a mandatory student activity fee of $165.75 per semester.[3] It's mandatory because students who refuse to pay cannot receive their grades or graduate. Wisconsin law gives both the Board of Regents and the student's control over funds generated by the mandatory student fee.[4] The Regents classify a portion of the student fees as nonallocable, which they control, and a portion as allocable. The nonallocable fees, that are not in issue here, cover expenses like debt service, fixed operating costs, student health services, and the recreational sport budget. On the other hand, the Associated Students of Madison (ASM), the representatives of the student body, has complete authority over distribution of most of the allocable funds that are at issue.[5]

[1] See, Doe v. University of Michigan, 721 F.Supp. 852 (E.D. Mich. 1989) and UWM Post, Inc. v. Board of Regents, 774 F.Supp. 1163 (E.D. Wisc. 1991).

[2] 151 F.3d 717 (7th Cir. 1998), Rehearing denied 157 F.3d 1124 (7th Cir. 1998).

[3] Id. At 719.

[4] Section 36.09 of the Wisconsin Code.

[5] 151 F.3d 717 at 719.

These ASM-controlled fees fund the General Student's Service Fund (GSSF) and the Associated Students of Madison's budget. Both the GSSF and the ASM distribute the mandatory student fees to other private organizations. The GSSF portion is distributed to private organizations by a committee of the ASM called the Student Services Finance Committee (SSFC). Registered student organizations, university departments, and even community-based service organizations qualify for funding from the GSSF. To obtain money, the requesting organization must apply to the SSFC that reviews the application. The SSFC then determines whether to grant or deny the request for money and also determines the amount of funding the private organization will receive. During the 1995–1996 school year, the SSFC distributed about $974,000 in student fees to private organizations.[6]

In addition to obtaining money from the GSSF and the ASM budget, a registered student organization may seek funding through a student referendum. With a student referendum, the students vote at large on whether or not to approve an assessment for a student group.[7] The Wisconsin Student Public Interest Research Group (WSPIRG) obtained $49,500 in student fees during the 1995–1996 academic year. Once the ASM and SSFC have made their funding decisions, the decisions are sent to the chancellor and the board of regents for their review and approval.[8]

The Complaint

Several students sued the university objecting to the funding of organizations which engage in political and ideological activities with fees collected from students who object to those activities. The objecting students presented evidence of 18 organizations that received student fees and engaged in political and ideological activities.[9] The organizations were the Wisconsin Student Public Interest Research Group; The Lesbian,

---

[6] Id.

[7] Id. At 720.

[8] Id.

[9] Id. at 718.

Gay and Bi-Sexual Campus Center; The Campus Women's Center; The University of Wisconsin Green; The Madison Aids Support Network; The International Socialist Organization; The Ten Percent Society; The Progressive Student Network; Amnesty International; United States Student Association; Community Action on Latin America; La Colectiva Cultural De Aztlin; The Militant Student Union of the University of Wisconsin; The Student Labor Action Coalition; Student Solidarity; Students of National Organization for Women; and Madison Treaty Rights Support Group.[10]

The uses to which the student fees were put included the Wisconsin Student Interest Public Research Group contributing directly to its off-campus parent organization for use in lobbying Congress and developing candidate and voter guides. They also published a voter's guide, which ranked congressional candidates based on their views on various kinds of federal legislation. The University of Wisconsin Greens lobbied the Wisconsin State Legislature and encouraged legislators to introduce three bills which would limit mining in the state. They also distributed literature for the Green Party and distributed campaign literature for Ralph Nader during his bid for President on the Green Party ticket. The International Socialists Organization advocated the overthrow of the government. They also sponsored along with other groups, a partisan rally at the state capitol at a congressman's office. The Campus Women's Center used its bi-monthly newsletter to advocate its political and ideological views. For example, in a newsletter, they published a lengthy article opposing the Informed Consent Bill that proposed certain state regulations on abortion. The article urged people to contact the Campus Women's Center to learn how they could work against the legislation.

The Ten Percent Society used its funding to establish an internet home page to advocate legislation authorizing same-sex marriages, and, in no uncertain terms, condemning attempts by the Wisconsin Legislature to ban them. Amnesty International worked publicly for the abolition of the death penalty.[11]

---

[10] Id. at 720.

[11] Id. at 721.

The Board of Regents properly did not contend that these and other organizations did not engage in political or ideological speech. The Regents, instead, argued that the First Amendment protects the rights of the organizations to engage in such speech.[12] Of course it does! As we shall see, however, the issue is whether objecting students can be compelled to pay for, for example, the speech of the Ten Percent Society. The objecting students contended that they were not asking to restrict the speech of any of the student organizations, they were merely asking that they should not be forced to financially subsidize speech with which they disagreed. They argued that the First Amendment does not guarantee that the government will subsidize speech contending, "There is no right to have speech subsidized by the Government."[13]

The Issue

The question for the appellate court was whether the Regents can force the objecting students to fund private organizations that engage in political and ideological activities, speech, and advocacy.[14]

The First Amendment provides: "Congress shall make no law respecting an establishment of religion, or prohibiting the free exercise thereof; or abridging the freedom of speech, or the press; or the right of the people to peaceably assemble, and petition the government for any regress of grievances."[15] The Supreme Court has long recognized two necessary corollaries to the First Amendment due to free speech: the right not to speak,[16] and the right not to be compelled to subsidize others' speech.[17]

---

[12] Id.

[13] See, Federal Election Commission v. Massachusetts Citizens for Life, 479 U.S. 238 (1986), "There is no right to have speech subsidized by the government."

[14] *Southworth* at 722.

[15] United States Constitution, Amend. I.

[16] West Virginia State Board of Education v. Barnette, 319 U.S. 624, 642 (1943). Were this to be followed in a logically consistent manner, it would vitiate against laws compelling cigarette manufacturers to carry health warnings on their products.

[17] *Abood v. Detroit Board of Education*, 431 U.S. 209 (1977) and *Keller v. State Bar of California*, 496 U.S. 1 (1990).

The Supreme Court has never determined whether or not these First Amendment corollaries protect objecting students from being forced by state universities to subsidize private, political, and ideological organizations. In *Rosenberger v. Rector and Visitors of the University of Virginia*,[18] however, the supreme court did provide guidance on the appropriate analysis for such a challenge. In that case, the university used student fees to pay for printing costs for nonreligious newspapers, but denied the plaintiff's request to fund their newspaper's religious viewpoint. The Supreme Court felt that the student activity fees created a fora of money and that once established the fora had to be made available on a viewpoint neutral basis. Because the University of Virginia discriminated on the basis of religious viewpoint of the newspaper, it had violated the First Amendment.[19]

Rosenberger did not directly consider the question of forcing objecting students to fund private organizations, however, the court briefly discussed the issue. Justice O'Connor, indicated, "Finally, although this question is not presented here, I note the possibility that the student fee is susceptible to a Free Speech Clause challenge by an objecting student that she should not be compelled to pay for speech with which she disagrees,"[20] citing *Keller v. State Bar of California* and *Abood v. Detroit Board of Education*.[21]

In *Abood*, employees of Detroit Board of Education challenged the constitutionality of an agency–shop agreement that required teachers who did not join the union to pay a service fee to the union. The teachers argued that the mandatory fee violated their First Amendment rights of free speech and free association.[22] The Court held that the Board of

[18] 515 U.S. 819 (1995).

[19] Id. at 825–27.

[20] Id. at 842.

[21] 431 U.S. 209 (1977) and 496 U.S. 1 (1980).

[22] For the argument that unions, per se, are a violation of the law of free association, see Baird, Charles; Block, Walter "Labor Relations, Unions and Collective Bargaining: A Political Economic Analysis," *Journal of Social Political and Economic Studies*, Vol. 16, No. 4, Winter 1991, pp. 477–507; DiLorenzo, Thomas, "Labor Markets and Liberty," *Proceedings of the Banff Conference*, Vol. III in the Rating Economic Freedom Series, Stephen Easton and Michael Walker, eds., Vancouver: The Fraser Institute, 1992. Kauffman, Bill, 1992, "The Child Labor Amendment Debate of the 1920s; or, Catholics and Mugwumps and Farmers," *The Journal of Libertarian Studies*, Vol. 10, No. 2, Fall,

Education could compel nonunion teachers to pay the service fee explaining that "such interferences as exists as constitutionally justified by the legislative assessment of the important contribution of the union shop to the system of labor relations established by Congress."[23] Thus, so "long as the union acts to promote the cause which justified bringing the group together, the individual cannot withdraw his financial support merely because he disagrees with the group's strategy." In the decision, the court recognized the "common cause" of both the union and non-union teachers.

The *Abood* court continued, "we do not hold that a union cannot constitutionally spend funds for the expression of political views, on behalf of political candidates, or toward the advancement of other ideological causes not germane to its duties as a collective bargaining representative. Rather, the Constitution requires only that such expenditures be financed from charges, dues, or assessments paid by employees who do not object to advancing those ideas and who are not coerced into doing so against their will…."[24]

Thirteen years later, in *Keller v. State Bar of California*,[25] the Supreme Court revisited the issue of compelled funding. In *Keller*, a group of lawyers challenged the use of mandatory state bar dues to fund lobbying on social issues. In *Keller*, the Supreme Court said that *Abood* meant that unions could not expend the dissenting individual's dues on ideological activities not germane to the purpose for which the compelled association

pp. 139–170; McGee, Robert W., "If Dwarf Tossing Is Outlawed, Only Outlaws Will Toss Dwarfs: Is Dwarf Tossing a Victimless Crime?," *American Journal of Jurisprudence*, Vol 38, 1993, 335–358. n. 61, DTU; n. 89; Petro, Sylvester, *The Labor Policy of the Free Society*, New York, Ronald Press, 1957; Poulson, Barry W., 1982, "Substantive Due Process and Labor Law," *The Journal of Libertarian Studies*, Vol. VI, No. 3–4, Summer/Fall, pp. 267–276; Reynolds, Morgan, 1982, "An Economic Analysis of the Norris-LaGuardia Act, the Wagner Act and the Labor Representation Industry," *The Journal of Libertarian Studies*, Vol. VI, No. 3–4, Summer/Fall, pp. 227–266; Reynolds, Morgan O., *Power and Privilege: Labor Unions in America*, New York: Manhattan Institute for Policy Research, 1984; Reynolds, Morgan O., 1987, *Making America Poorer: The Cost of Labor Law*, Washington, D.C.: Cato Institute.

[23] 431 U.S. 209 at 222.

[24] Id. at 235–36. This is all well and good. But it ignores the issue that some members of unions are coerced into joining these organizations themselves, "against their will." On this see op. cit., footnote 22.

[25] 496 U.S. 1 (1990).

was justified: collective bargaining. The court said in *Keller* that the compelled association and integrated bar was justified by the state's interest in regulating the legal profession and improving the quality of legal services. The State Bar may, therefore, constitutionally fund activities germane to the common purposes of regulating the bar and improving legal services out of the mandatory dues of all members. It may not, however, in such manner fund activities of an ideological nature, like lobbying the state legislature on social issues like gun control or nuclear weapons initiatives, which falls outside of the scope of those common activities. These issues clearly fall at the extreme end of the spectrum not germane to the bar's common cause.[26]

From *Keller*'s holding "the State Bar may therefore constitutionally fund activities germane to those goals…," and *Abood*'s qualification, the constitution requires that expenditures for ideological causes not germane be financed by voluntary funds, and the courts have named the analysis born of Abood as the "germaneness analysis."[27] Sadly, the holding in *Abood* did not provide much guidance or how it should be applied. *Keller*, however, did more by setting forth guidelines for deciding permissive expenditures. In *Keller*, the guiding standard is "whether the challenged expenditures are necessarily or reasonably incurred for the purpose of regulating the legal profession or improving the quality of the legal service available to the people of the state."[28]

Beyond *Abood* and *Keller*, the Supreme Court has addressed the issue of germaneness in several other cases. The most important is *Lehnert v. Ferris Faculty Association*,[29] where the Supreme Court considered the constitutionality of various union expenditures under the germaneness analysis originating in *Abood* and *Keller*. *Lehnert*, however, went further by explaining that the analysis required a three-step process. The three steps, or prongs, for determining whether union expenditures violate the objecting employees' First Amendment rights are:

---

[26] Id. at 13–14.

[27] *Southworth v. Grebe*, 151 F.3d 717, 723 (1998).

[28] 496 U.S. at 14.

[29] 500 U.S. 507 (1991).

1. The expenditure must be "germane to collective bargaining;"
2. Justified by the government's vital policy interest in labor and avoiding "free riders;"
3. Not significantly add to the burdening of free speech that is inherent in the allowance of an agency or union shop.[30]

The court announced that *Lehnert*'s three-prong analysis is the test that it would follow in deciding the *Southworth* case. The Supreme Court recently reaffirmed this test in *Airline Pilots Association v. Miller*,[31] where it again followed the *Lehnert* test to determine if pilots were entitled to a refund of part of their agency fees.

Germaneness

Under the *Lehnert* test of germaneness, the question is whether the challenged activity is germane to the Regent's asserted interest. The regents asserted an interest in education by contending that funding private organizations which engage in political and ideological activities is germane to education because the funding allows for more diverse campus expression and this, in turn, is educational. The court, however, indicated that "germaneness" cannot be read so broadly as to justify funding of private organizations which engage in political or ideological advocacy, activities, or speech.[32] In *Keller*, for example, the State Bar defended its funding of lobbying on nuclear weapons, abortion, and prayer in public schools arguing that it was authorized to fund those activities "in all manners pertaining to the science of jurisprudence or to the improvement to the administration of justice." The Supreme Court rejected such an over-

---

[30] Id. at 519.

[31] _____U.S._____, 118 S. Ct. 1761 (1998).

[32] *Even if* the Regent's views of germaneness were upheld, this would still not account for the left-wing ideological bias of the funding at the University of Wisconsin. In other words, given that politics and ideology *is* germane to the educational mission, why should this be almost totally confined to one end of the political–economic–philosophical spectrum. Why, that is, should there not be *equal* funding for groups such as the National Rifle Association, Phyllis Schlafley's Eagle Forum, The Mises Institute, the Libertarian Party, the Four H Clubs, the Boy Scouts, the Young Republicans, the American Conservative Union, the Objectivist Society, and so on.

encompassing reading of germaneness, holding instead that expenditures "to endorse or advocate a gun control or nuclear weapons freeze initiative," clearly fall at the "extreme end of the spectrum" of expenditures not germane and, therefore, unconstitutional.[33]

In *Lehnert*, the Supreme Court again rejected a broad interpretation of "germaneness." *Lehnert* involved a challenge to the union's use of dues to fund lobbying related to financial support of the public employees in general. The court held that "where, as here, the challenged lobbying activities relate not to the ratification or implementation of the center's collective bargaining, but to financial support of the employee's profession or of public employee's generally, the connection to the union's function as bargaining representative is too attenuated to justify compelled support by objecting employees."[34] The court concluded that "the state constitutionally may not compel its employees to subsidize legislative lobbying or other political union activities outside the limited context of contract ratification or implementation."[35]

In *Keller* and *Lehnert*, the Supreme Court rejected arguments that political and ideological speech is germane to the union contract interest involved. In fact, in *Lehnert*, the Supreme Court stated that germaneness cannot be read so broadly in the context of a private sector union as to "include political and ideological activities."[36]

To justify compelling objecting students to fund private organizations, the regents point to the expansive government interest they have in education, as compared to the limited union representation interest involved in *Abood* and *Keller* collective bargaining and oversight of the Bar. They argue that educational interests are so broad that more activities are germane, including political and ideological activities. The regents correctly recognize that breadth of "educational" activity because everything in a sense is educational. When presented with a similarly expansive interest in *Keller*, the advancement of law, the Supreme Court, however, rejected such a broad meaning of germaneness. The court indicated in *Keller* that

---

[33] 496 U.S. at 15–16.

[34] 500 U.S. at 520.

[35] 500 U.S. at 522.

[36] 500 U.S. at 516.

germaneness cannot be so broadly construed as to include forced funding of private, political, and ideological groups. The court pointed out that many of the campus groups mirror organizations which exist outside the university setting whose primary goal is promotion of ideological beliefs. The court considered any educational benefit that comes from this outside activity as secondary, and therefore not sufficiently germane to overcome the objecting student's constitutional rights. The court forcibly stated that the mere incantation of the rubric "Educational Profession" cannot justify a tactic, repugnant to the constitution, of requiring objecting students to fund private, political, and ideological organizations.[37]

Vital Policy Interests of the Government

The second prong under *Lehnert* considers whether the compelled fee is justified by a vital policy interest of the government.[38] In the context of unions, those policy interests include both labor peace and avoiding free riders, and with the bar "the state's interest in regulating the legal profession and improving the quality of legal services."[39] The court indicated that no doubt there's a vital interest in education, and that the government has an interest in allowing students to share in the governance of the university system. For the vital policy interests, however, to survive scrutiny under *Lehnert*, they must justify compelled funding of the private or quasi-private activity involved like the advancement of partisan political and ideological causes.

In *Lehnert*, a plurality of the Supreme Court analyzed the policy interest involved, labor peace, and providing representation for free riders, and concluded that "labor peace is not especially served by … charging objecting employees for lobbying, electoral or other political activities that do not relate to their collective bargaining agreement."[40] *Lehnert* further stated that the cause of labor peace would not be advanced "Because

[37] *Southworth v. Grebe*, 151 f. 3d 717, 725 (1998).

[38] 500 U.S. at 520.

[39] *Keller*, 496 U.S. at 13–14.

[40] 500 U.S. 521.

worker and union cannot be said to speak with one voice, it would not further cause harmonious industrial relations to compel objecting employees to finance union political activities as well as their own."[41]

The quotation above illustrates the importance of a common cause for justifying compelled funding. In the context of union cases, if the union and nonunion members share a common cause, like negotiating the terms and conditions of employment, a common vital policy interest may justify compelled funding.[42] But where that was missing, as in *Lehnert*, or when union funds are used solely for partisan campaign contributions, the expenditure cannot be justified. In the case of compelled student funding, while there may be a common educational cause in shared governance, there's no common cause between private organizations that rightly engage in highly emotional political and ideological speech, like advocating same-sex marriages, informed consent laws, or overthrow of the government, and the objecting students. The Southworth Court could discover no vital policy interests supporting compelled funding of these private organizations. The court, citing *Lehnert*, said, "And we might even conclude that far from serving the school's interest in education, forcing objecting students to fund objectionable organizations undermines that interest."[43] The next concern dealt with "free-rider" problem. The court indicated that universities are unlike unions that have the duty to represent fairly all employees, including those who do not belong to the union. The court said that the union's common cause of collective bargaining often "entails expenditure of much time and money"[44] on nonmembers (free riders). Conversely, in the university context, the private organizations to which the students object to funding do not act in a representative capacity for the students (because there is no

[41] Id.

[42] It is not necessarily true that union and nonunion members share the common cause of negotiating pay scales, working conditions, and so on. To buy into this is to believe that unions are necessary and/or sufficient to better the lives of workers. But remuneration and safety protection and so on are high and rising in such industries as computers, banking, and insurance, which have never been unionized, and low and/or falling in such smoke stack and rust belt industries as steel, autos, and rubber, which have been. Moreover, as wages and working conditions in the United States have been improving, the rate of unionization has been falling.

[43] 151 f.3d at 728.

[44] Id.

common cause) and have no obligation to fairly represent the students, as union does for nonunion members. Because the Regents policy allows nonstudents to join student organizations and attend campus activities, in fact, said the court, "Free riders might accurately describe those organizations that receive a share of the mandatory fees."[45] Also, many of the ideological and political activities and speech to which the students objected occurred off campus, further limiting any possible benefit to objecting students. The court found that the union free rider[46] concern was inapplicable in a student funding situation.

Burdening Free Speech

The free speech prong recognizes that any time the government forces individuals to fund private organizations, a burden on free speech and association may incidentally result, but that burden may be justified by an important governmental interest.[47] In *Lehnert*, the court explained that "although first amendment protection is in no way limited to controversial topics or emotionally charged issues, the extent of ones disagreement with the subject of compulsory speech is relevant to the degree of impingement upon free expression that compulsion will affect."[48]

[45] Id. at 729.

[46] For a critique of the free rider concept, particularly as the justification for public policy, see Hoppe, Hans-Hermann, "Fallacies of the Public Goods Theory and the Production of Security," in *The Economics and Ethics of Private Property: Studies in Political Economy and Philosophy*, Boston: Kluwer, 1993; Hoppe, Hans-Hermann, *The Private Production of Defense*, Auburn, AL: The Mises Institute, 1998; Hoppe, Hans-Hermann, 1989, *A Theory of Socialism and Capitalism*, Boston, Kluwer; Hummel, Jeffrey, 1990, "National Goods vs. Public Goods: Defense, Disarmament and Free Riders," *The Review of Austrian Economics*, Vol. IV, pp. 88–122; Block, Walter, 1983a, "Public Goods and Externalities: The Case of Roads," *The Journal of Libertarian Studies: An Interdisciplinary Review*, Vol. VII, No. 1, Spring, pp. 1–34; Block, Walter, 1989, "The Justification of Taxation in the Public Finance Literature: A Critique of Atkinson and Stiglitz, Due, Musgrave and Shoup," *Journal of Public Finance and Public Choice*, No. 3, Fall, pp. 141–158; Block, Walter, 1993a, "Canadian Public Finance Texts Cannot Justify Government Taxation: A Critique of Auld & Miller; Musgrave, Musgrave & Bird; McCready; and Wolf," *Canadian Public Administration*, Vol. 36, No. 1, Fall, pp. 225–262.

[47] Id.

[48] 500 U.S. at 521–22.

The Court explained: "The burden upon freedom of expression is particularly great where, as here, the compelled speech is in a public context. By utilizing the petitioner's funds for political lobbying and to garnish support of the public in its' endeavors, the union would use each dissenter as an instrument for fostering public adherence to an ideological point of view he finds unacceptable."[49] The First Amendment protects the individual's right of participation in these spheres from precisely this type of invasion. When the subject of compelled speech is the discussion of governmental affairs, which is a core of our First Amendment freedoms, "the burden upon the dissenters' rights extends far beyond the acceptance of the agency shop and is constitutionally impermissible."[50]

In *Southworth*, the speech to which the students object includes such emotionally charged issues as abortion, homosexuality, and the U.S. democratic system of government. The source of plaintiff's disagreement is their deeply held religious and personal beliefs. Consequently, *Lehnert*'s common cause requirement makes clear that the regent's funding policy cannot stand. The court said that the burden on the objecting student's speech is "particularly great" because of their deeply held beliefs. The funded organization's use of the funds to "garnish support of the public in its' endeavors," and as "an instrument for fostering public adherence and ideological view," which the students find objectionable offends the First Amendment.[51]

The Regents attempted to justify forcing the objecting students to fund these organizations because "hateful speech has a place in our society too."[52] Sure it is! The court said that it's true that hateful speech is protected, but the constitution does not mandate that the objecting citizens pay for it. According to James Madison, "to compel a man to furnish contributions and money for the propagation of opinions which he dis-

[49] Id.

[50] *Southworth v. Grebe*, 151F 3d at 729.

[51] Id. at 729.

[52] Id., see, Regan v. Taxation with Representation of Washington, 461 U.S. 540 (1983) that holds that the Constitution does not confer an entitlement to funds that might be necessary to realize all the advantages of Free Speech. It is ironic that a school with a "hate speech" code advances a "hateful speech" argument.

believes is sinful and tyrannical."[53] The students, like the objecting union members in *Abood*, have a first amendment interest in not being compelled to contribute to an organization whose First Amendment-protected expressive activities conflict with one's "freedom of belief."[54]

One of the Supreme Court's recent cases, *Glickman v. Wileman Brothers & Elliott*,[55] confirms the *Southworth* approach. The case involved Department of Agriculture regulations that imposed assessments on growers for the costs of administrative expenses for marketing orders. Among the expenses were the costs of generic advertising of California peaches and plums. The growers contended that the compelled funding abridged their First Amendment rights. The Supreme Court, citing *Abood and Keller*, found that unlike those cases, the administrative fees did "Not compel the producers to endorse or finance any political or ideological views."[56] In approving the assessment, the Court said, "The germaneness test is clearly satisfied because the generic advertising is unquestionably germane to the purposes of the marketing orders" and "In any event, the assessments are not used to fund ideological activities."[57] The marketing orders, one assumes, benefitted all the growers, including the Wileman brothers.[58]

---

[53] Abood, 431 U.S. at 234–235 n. 31 quoting Irving Brant, James Madison: The Nationalist 354 (1948).

[54] *Southworth*, 151F. 3d at 730.

[55] ____U.S.____, 117 S. Ct 2130 (1997).

[56] Id. at 2138.

[57] Id. at 2140.

[58] There are problems with this finding, however. If these expenditures really benefitted the Wileman brothers, why did they object? Obversely, their objection constitutes evidence that they did *not* benefit. Suppose A takes a shower and bills B, his neighbor, for the soap costs on the ground that B "benefits." Should B be compelled by a court to pay A? Not in a court of law which recognizes private property and contract rights. Under such jurisdictions, B is forced to pay only for goods and services he *agreed to purchase*, not for those which in the view of third parties, even Supreme Court judges, he "benefits." Were we to extend the doctrine that free riders must be forced to pay for their alleged benefits to its logical conclusion, we would open up a Pandora's Box. Anyone, pretty much, could charge anyone else for services rendered. If we brush our teeth and drink our mild and take our vitamins, this presumably benefits many people. Should we attempt to charge them for these services, we would be laughed out of any rational court. Thank goodness this pernicious doctrine has not been carried out consistently through our legal system.

One petition for rehearing,[59] the dissenting judges claimed that *Southworth* was wrongly decided because diversity of views are important on campus and that the dues only go to the student government, not directly to the organizations. Judge Rovnen wrote that the only "direct" speech being funded is the that of the student government. And, he said, under *Rosenberger*, the radically different views of the listed organizations cannot be attributed to the student government. Indeed, the student government constitutionally must determine funding in a content-neutral manner. He says, "because the speech cannot be attributed to the student government, it necessarily cannot be attributed to the students paying the fee to the student government."[60]

Of course diversity of views on a college campus is important. But, so is the First Amendment. The objecting students do not contest the First Amendment importance of contrasting views. They simply contend, and rightly so, that they don't have to pay for them. Does the First Amendment require Democrats to contribute to Republicans so they can get out their message? Obviously not. Secondly, to say that the student fees only fund the student government is disingenuous. The money certainly flows through the student government and would not be available to, say the International Socialist Organization, absent the mandatory fees. It has already been established in *Abood* there is no requirement that the dues be "earmarked" to the organizations, or whether the organizations purport to speak for all students.[61] Therefore, whether or not the student fees directly fund the political or ideological activities to which the students object is irrelevant; the First Amendment is offended by the Regents use of the objecting student' fees to subsidize organizations that engage in political and ideological activities.[62] To hold otherwise would, in effect, allow money laundering, that is, prohibited in, for example, campaign finance laws.

---

[59] Southworth v. Grebe, 157 F. 3d 1124 (1998).

[60] Id. at 1125.

[61] *Abood*, 431 U.S. at 237.

[62] *Southworth*, 151 F. 3d at 732.

Finally, on appeal to the U.S. Supreme Court,[63] the Regents argue that *Southworth* deprives students at the University of a diversity of viewpoints and violates the First Amendment because *Rosenberger* required the University of Virginia to fund a student newspaper with a religious viewpoint. Again, the Regent's attempt to shoehorn this case into *Rosenberger* is misplaced because, in that case, the Supreme Court made it clear it was only considering the issue of the constitutionality of "content based" regulations in ruling that the newspaper had to be funded. The court made it abundantly clear that compelled funding of views with which students disagreed was not an issue.[64]

Philosophical Considerations

It is now time to consider these issues from a more philosophical point of view, one best grounded, in our estimation, on the rights of private property and contract; for example, libertarianism. This is the view that all human interaction should take place on a voluntary basis, with no force or fraud committed against individuals who are themselves nonaggressing.[65]

Suppose that the authors of the present article set up a new entirely private institution, Block Whitehead University.[66] We charge a certain amount for tuition, and then, also, impose a student fee. As in the case of the University of Wisconsin–Madison, part of this is nonallocable, and

---

[63] Patrick Healy, U. of Wisconsin Will Ask Supreme Court to Uphold Broad Use of Mandatory Student Fees, The Chronicle of Higher Education, P. 7, col. 3, Nov. 9, 1998.

[64] 515 U.S. at 851. Justice O'Connor, concurring, "Finally, although the question is not presented here, I note the possibility that the student fee is susceptible to a Free Speech Clause challenge by an objecting student that she should not be compelled to pay for speech with which she disagrees."

[65] On this see Rothbard, Murray N., *For a New Liberty*, Macmillan, New York, 1973a; Rothbard, Murray N., *The Ethics of Liberty*, Humanities Press, Atlantic Highlands, N.J., 1982; Hoppe, Hans-Hermann, *A Theory of Socialism and Capitalism: Economics, Politics and Ethics*, Boston: Kluwer, 1989; Hoppe, Hans-Hermann, *The Economics and Ethics of Private Property: Studies in Political Economy and Philosophy*, Boston: Kluwer, 1993.

[66] Known, affectionately, as "Blockhead U."

noncontentious. But the other part is indeed allocable, and goes, via our handpicked pet student government, to a whole host of feminist, socialist, multicultural, homosexual, minority racist, deconstructionist, "peace," and Marxist groups. We attract some thousands of paying customers to our little establishment under these conditions. Whereupon a few of them protest that their payments are going toward the promotion of ideas they find detestable.

Would it be proper for a court to find in their favor and overturn our leftish brainwashing scheme? Not a bit of it. For ours is a private university. No one ever need enroll unless he agrees to be bound by our rules and procedures, *all* of them. And a high profile program of ours allocates a hefty portion of the student fee to these outside activities, all in the name of diversity. If a student does not wish to have his money spent for such purposes, he has an easy remedy: let him sign up elsewhere. We can do anything we wish[67] to and with our students, provided only that they agree to enroll under the conditions we set down. For example, we could demand that they push a peanut with their noses down the quad before every class. This may lead us directly to bankruptcy, but that is entirely another matter. Certainly, we may expose them to a series of biased and one-sided outside speakers, and use their money to finance our own pet projects, as is done in Wisconsin.

How, then, can we reconcile this position with our claim that the case of the Wisconsin student plaintiffs should be upheld? It is simple. Ours is a private venture, and that institution of higher learning is anything but. A public university is an exercise in coercion. A large part of its revenues come not from willing customers, but from compulsory levies. In the libertarian view, such enterprises should not exist at all; they should be privatized.

(As it happens, the authors of the present chapter are both employees of a public university. Is it hypocritical for us to advocate that our and all other such institution(s) be privatized, while continuing to work for one of them while it still remains public? If so, then we admit to hypocrisy; not only for education, but also for numerous other institutions with

[67] Subject, of course, to the usual proscriptions against murder, fraud, etc.

which we come into contact virtually every day: for example, streets, highways, sidewalks, post office.[68]

That is one way to look at the matter. But there is another entirely different way to interpret it: here, we are not at all hypocrites. Consider a libertarian living under a totalitarian regime, such as Cuba, North Vietnam, or the former U.S.S.R. If he wants to eat, he must work. But

[68] On the case for road privatization, see Block, Walter, "Public Goods and Externalities: The Case of Roads," *The Journal of Libertarian Studies*, Vol. VII, No. 1, Spring 1983a, pp. 1–34; Block, Walter E. and Matthew A. Block. 1996. "Roads, Bridges, Sunlight and Private Property Rights," Journal Des Economistes Et Des Etudes Humaines, Vol. VII, No. 2/3, June-September, pp. 351–362; Block, Walter E. 1998. "Roads, Bridges, Sunlight and Private Property: Reply to Gordon Tullock," Journal des Economistes et des Etudes Humaines, Vol. 8, No. 2/3, June-September, pp. 315–326; Block, Walter, "Road Socialism," *International Journal of Value-Based Management*, 1996, Vol. 9, pp. 195–207; Block, Walter, "Theories of Highway Safety," *Transportation Research Record*, #912, 1983b, pp. 7–10; Block, Walter, "Congestion and Road Pricing," *The Journal of Libertarian Studies*, Vol. IV, No. 3, Fall 1980, pp. 299–330; Block, Walter, "Free Market Transportation: Denationalizing the Roads," *Journal of Libertarian Studies*, Vol. III, No. 2, Summer 1979, pp. 209–238; Cadin, Michelle, and Block, Walter, (1997), "Privatize the Public Highway System," *The Freeman*, February, Vol. 47, No. 2., pp. 96–97; Gunderson, Gerald, "Privatization and the 19th-Century Turnpike," *Cato Journal*, Vol. 9, No. 1, Spring/Summer 1989, pp. 191–200; Klein, Dan, "The Voluntary Provision of Public Goods? The Turnpike Companies of Early America," *Economic Inquiry*, October 1990, pp. 788–812; Klein, Dan, Majewski, J., and Baer, C., "Economy, Community and the Law: The Turnpike Movement in New York, 1797–1845," *The Journal of Economic History*, March 1993a, pp. 106–122; Klein, Dan, Majewski, J., and Baer, C., "From Trunk to Branch: Toll Roads in New York, 1800–1860," *Essays in Economic and Business History*, 1993b, pp. 191–209; Klein, Dan and Fielding, G.J., "Private Toll Roads: Learning from the Nineteenth Century," *Transportation Quarterly*, July 1992, pp. 321–341; Klein, Dan and Fielding, G.J., "How to Franchise Highways," *Journal of Transport Economics and Policy*, May 1993a, pp. 113–130; Klein, Dan and Fielding, G.J., "High Occupancy/Toll Lanes: Phasing in Congestion Pricing a Lane at a Time," *Policy Study*, No. 170, Reason Foundation, November 1993b; Roth, Gabriel, *The Private Provision of Public Services in Developing Countries*, Oxford: Oxford University Press, 1987; Roth, Gabriel, *Paying for Roads: The Economics of Traffic Congestion*, Middlesex, England: Penguin, 1967; Roth, Gabriel, *A Self-financing Road System*, London, England, The Institute of Economic Affairs, 1966; Rothbard, Murray N., *For a New Liberty*, Macmillan, New York, 1973; Woolridge, William C., *Uncle Sam the Monopoly Man*, New Rochelle, N.Y.: Arlington House, 1970. On the case for the privatization of mail delivery, see Adie, Douglas K., *The Mail Monopoly: Analysing Canadian Postal Service*, Vancouver: The Fraser Institute, 1990; Adie, Douglas K., *Monopoly Mail: Privatizing the United States Postal Service*, New Brunswick, N.J.: Transaction, 1988; Adie, Douglas K., "Why Marginal Reform of the U.S. Postal Service Won't Succeed," in *Free the Mail: Ending the Postal Monopoly*, Peter J. Ferrara, ed., Washington, D.C.: The Cato Institute, 1990; Moore, Thomas Gale, "The Federal Postal Monopoly: History, Rationale and Future," in *Free the Mail: Ending the Postal Monopoly*, Peter J. Ferrara, ed., Washington, D.C.: The Cato Institute, 1990; Priest, George, "The History of the Postal Monopoly in the United States," *Journal of Law and Economics*, 18, no. 33, 1975; Butler, Stuart M., "Privatizing Bulk Mail," *Management*, 6, No. 1, 1986; Moore, Stephen, "Privatizing the U.S. Postal Service," in Stephen Moore and Stuart Butler, eds., *Privatization*, Washington: Heritage Foundation, 1987.

the only jobs legally available are those offered by the government, which he opposes on philosophical grounds. Yet he becomes an employee of the state, while still maintaining his libertarian principles. In so doing, he is not hypocritical, but rather in the position of a victim of a holdup man who gives up his money rather than being shot, but still cleaves to the view that the entire enterprise of theft is illegitimate.)

Were total educational privatization to occur, the solution to the problem of forcing tax paying students to yield part of their college fees for the promotion of ideas they find abhorrent would be simple: since there would be no public universities, the entire problem would evaporate. That is, given that while fully private but not public colleges may engage in such brainwashing activities, and that there are none of the latter, why then there will arise no issue of illegitimately forcing some students to pay to promote the views of others. The only time something of this sort can arise would be in a private school, and this, as we have already seen, would be entirely legitimate; for even though a given student finds a specific allocation of his money to be untoward, he has *agreed* to the entire process, by enrolling in that private institution of higher learning in the first place.

What of the argument that by being a citizen of the United States a student has implicitly agreed to pay taxes, and, based on our democratic institutions, to pay taxes for, among many other things, institutions of higher learning, and that they have determined through legitimate procedures that part of student fees financially support ideas which some find unwelcome, and that therefore these defrayals are every bit as much voluntary as those which occur in a purely private setting? In other words, that these payments are akin to club dues, only that the "club" is now the United States. There are grave problems with this contention. First and most superficially, the constitution nowhere provides for public education. (Roy, is this true? If so, can you support it with a citation? If not, I'll delete it). This being the case, public education is a usurpation, similar to nationalizing, say, the steel works or auto plants. This may well be appropriate for the commies, but certainly not in the "land of the free." Second, and more basically, no one signed the constitution (Roy: was it the declaration of independence that Hancock and his buddies signed?); therefore, it cannot be used as evidence of agreement, albeit indirectly, for the program of paying for the free speech of some at the expense of others.[69] As for student fees as voluntary club dues, this is how Schumpeter reacted to such a contention: "the theory which construes taxes on the analogy of club dues or of the purchase of the services of, say, a doctor only proves how far removed this part of the social science is from scientific habits of mind."[70]

But state universities obviously do exist. How, then, to analyze their actions from the libertarian perspective? That is, what is proper public policy *given* that there are government universities which compel some students to pay for the "free speech" of others?

In one scenario, that propagated by Milton Friedman in many areas of public policy, the goal is to make the particular government enterprise as efficient as possible, not to end it. For example, he favors school vouchers, rather than the complete, total, and immediate privatization of public education; the negative income tax instead of the elimination of welfare; flexible exchange rates and a 3% rule for monetary expansion in preference to market money (a gold standard); and the voluntary military during the Vietnam war as an alternative to ending hostilities.[71]

---

[69] See on this Benson, Bruce L., 1989, "Enforcement of Private Property Rights in Primitive Societies: Law Without Government," *The Journal of Libertarian Studies*, Vol. IX, No. 1, Winter, pp. 1–26; Spooner, Lysander, *No Treason*, Larkspur, Colorado, (1870) 1966; Tannehill, Morris and Linda, *The Market for Liberty*, New York: Laissez Faire Books, 1984; Rothbard, Murray N., *For a New Liberty*, Macmillan, New York, 1973a; Rothbard, Murray N., *The Ethics of Liberty*, Humanities Press, Atlantic Highlands, N.J., 1982; Hoppe, Hans-Hermann, *A Theory of Socialism and Capitalism: Economics, Politics and Ethics*, Boston: Kluwer, 1989; Hoppe, Hans-Hermann, *The Economics and Ethics of Private Property: Studies in Political Economy and Philosophy*, Boston: Kluwer, 1993; Barnett, Randy E., *The Structure of Liberty: Justice and the Rule of Law*, Oxford: Clarendon Press, 1998.

[70] Schumpeter, Joseph A., *Capitalism, Socialism and Democracy*, New York: Harper, 1942, p. 198.

[71] Friedman, Milton, "The Role of Government in Education," *Capitalism and Freedom*, Chicago: University of Chicago Press, 1962, pp. 85–107; Friedman, Milton, Tyranny of the status quo / by Milton & Rose Friedman, San Diego: Harcourt Brace Jovanovich, 1984; Friedman, Milton, There's no such thing as a free lunch, LaSalle, Ill.: Open Court, 1974; Friedman, Milton, Politics and tyranny: lessons in the pursuit of freedom, Friedman et al.; edited with an introduction by David J. Theroux. San Francisco, Calif.: Pacific Institute for Public Policy Research, c1984; Friedman, Milton, The optimum quantity of money, and other essays. Chicago, Aldine Pub. Co. [1969]; Friedman, Milton, Money mischief: episodes in monetary history New York: Harcourt Brace Jovanovich, c1992; Friedman, Milton, Money and economic development, New York, Praeger [1973]; Friedman, Milton, Monetarist economics, Oxford, UK; Cambridge, Mass., USA: Blackwell, 1991; Friedman, Milton, Free to choose: a personal statement / Milton and Rose

Friedman argues in behalf of such initiatives, first, that they will not only lead to full economic freedom, but that they are the best means toward this end. But it is not clear at all how making a government enterprise more efficient (e.g., more market "based," as opposed to genuinely an aspect of the market) will lead to its demise. One would have thought that an efficient state corporation is far more stable than an inefficient one.

How would we apply these Friedmanite solutions to the issue at hand? There might be a "voucher" setup on campus whereby each student is able to earmark his student fees for the outside speaker or program of his choice, the only restriction being that the part of these payments allotted for extracurricular academic programs be spent in *some* manner for this purpose. But the same argument applies in this case. If public education is the ultimate evil, then removing this burr under its saddle (e.g., the plaintiff students) will hardly render it more likely to fail. Yes, this plan would render it more difficult for the administration and the highly politicized students to impose their views of a proper extracurricular education on the majority, but that is neither here nor there. If we assume the legitimacy of their ideological views, why shouldn't they be imposed on the entire student body? And if we do not, why should they be able to dispose of not only the student fees for these programs, but of all the tax revenues which now flow into their control?

Let us approach this problem from an alternative direction by asking questions of a somewhat different sort. Should public elementary schools require that pupils wear school uniforms? Should public universities have tenure for their professors? Should diversity and multiculturalism be mainstays of education? Should affirmative action be employed in decisions over student admission, faculty hiring, and course coverage?

For the Friedmans of the world, these questions are straightforward, and admit of answers based on their likelihood of promoting the efficiency of these institutions. They are of course highly complex, and there are great problems of empirical measurement, but at least the research program is clear: engage in these initiatives if they promote societal well-being, and eschew them if they do not. As a heuristic device, for them,

---

Friedman. New York: Harcourt Brace Jovanovich, c1980; Friedman, Milton, Dollars and deficits; living with America's economic problems, Englewood Cliffs, N.J., Prentice-Hall [1968].

these questions might almost translate into a query about which policies would maximize revenue were this industry a private one; alternatively, they might be asking which policies would maximize GDP or some other measure of wealth.

For the libertarian however, in sharp contrast, matters are quite different. The answer to the question of what policies should be pursued by a public educational establishment is akin to asking him for day-to-day advice on how best to run a North Korean steel mill, or a Cuban sugarcane plantation, or a U.S.S.R automobile factory. The only answer, the ONLY answer, is to privatize these enterprises, and to allow market participants to make these decisions.[72]

This answer seems evasive. It would almost appear to be no answer at all: Clinton-like, it might be charged, the answer merely avoids the question. In order to refute such a criticism, we must consider "taxicab theory."[73] Suppose you are in the south quadrant of the city, get into a taxi and tell the driver to take you to the western sector. He responds: "I can drive from here only to the north or east, but not to the west." What do you do? Do you ask him to take you to the north as this is closer to your western destination than is your only other option, to the east? Not at all. Instead, you hop out of that cab as quickly as you can, thank your lucky stars you got away from a maniac, and throw in your lot with another driver who will take you where you want to go.

Similarly, when asked how the government can best run steel mills it shouldn't own in the first place, or how public schools can best promote education it should have nothing to do with, the only rational answer is to insist, parrot like if need be, that it is not a proper role for government to be engaging in these activities; that the question is an invalid which shouldn't even arise.

However, an objection could be launched against our own opposition to the administration of public universities commandeering student fees and using them to promote ideas and activities detested by the plaintiffs: why don't we stick to our knitting, and instead of criticizing these

[72] How many free market economists do it take to change a light bulb? None. They leave it to market forces.

[73] The authors wish to express a debt of gratitude to Michael Edelstein and Nando Peluci for this insight.

practices, content ourselves with calling for privatization? We were happy to remain "above the fray" with regard to the management of unjustified steel mills and universities. Why don't we follow our own advice in the present situation?

The reason is that we are here discussing *additional* funds, over and above those spent on tuition. In the Wisconsin case, the administrators are appropriating an extra $165.75 per semester, *apart* from the other monies paid by the students for tuition. It is as if the gunman has just stolen $20,000 from his victim, and now realizes that the latter has another $165.75 in his back pocket. Should the criminal return to the scene of the crime and relieve the poor unfortunate of those funds as well? We answer in the negative, and in so doing, certainly do not commit ourselves to the legitimacy of the first and larger seizure.

Conclusion

We started off this essay by calling into question the propriety of forcing some students to subsidize the carrying out of the free speech rights of others. We ended by calling for the privatization of public universities. How did we get from one point to the other? Why is the second goal an implication of the first?

The point is, there is nothing *per se* wrong with "forcing" some students to pay to support the views which others favor. It all depends upon whether there was mutual agreement, on all sides, that this sort of thing be carried out. We demonstrated that when this was done in the context of the purely private college, it was unobjectionable. Surely, as part of advanced education, it is totally reasonable for faculties to introduce students to ideas they might at first (and even always) consider abhorrent (which, as it happens, find favor with other students). This is part and parcel of the educational enterprise. No good teacher can shrink from this challenge. What is wrong, then, with doing this is not the thing itself, but the fact that the entire educational experience (at least in the public sector) is not one of complete voluntarism. We cannot ignore the more basic underlying issue and think that we have fully considered the relatively more superficial question of student fees being hijacked.

7

Direct Payment of Scholarships to Church-Related Colleges

I. Introduction

This article discusses a scholarship program designed for the purpose of enticing Arkansas's best and brightest students to attend Arkansas public and private institutions of higher education. While perhaps well-intentioned, the program suffers from fatal constitutional infirmities. In section "II. The Program," we discuss the program. Section "III. The Constitution" relates it to the Establishment Clause of the First Amendment and the Equal Protection Clause of the Fourteenth Amendment of the Constitution. We then examine in section "IV. The Cases" several cases as they relate to Titles VI of the Civil Rights Act. Section "V. Title VI and Disparate Impact" offers a proposal to achieve the ends of the program that is not offensive to the Constitution and the disparate impact requirements of Title VI. Section "VI. The Cure" offers a constitutional cure for this malady. In section "VII. Libertarian Philosophy," we introduce the libertarian philosophy and then discuss in section "VIII. Educational Philosophy" the educational policy implied by this philosophy. We conclude in section "IX. Conclusion."

W. E. Block, R. Whitehead, *Philosophy of Law*, Palgrave Studies in Classical Liberalism,
https://doi.org/10.1007/978-3-030-28360-5_7

II. The Program

The State of Arkansas provides a full academic scholarship to a state-approved public or private Arkansas Institution of Higher Education to graduates of Arkansas secondary schools who demonstrate "extraordinary academic ability."[1] The sole measure of the graduate's "extraordinary ability" is demonstrated by scoring 32 or above on the American College Test (ACT), 1410 or above on Scholastic Aptitude Test (SAT), or selection as a finalist in the National Merit Scholarship competition.[2] The purpose of the Governor's Scholarship Program, according to the enabling legislation, is "that outstanding students are an essential ingredient for the economic and social benefit of the State of Arkansas. Benefits accrue to the state when a majority of National Merit Scholars and superior students attend Arkansas institutions of higher learning and remain in the state."[3] The scholarship award dollar amount equals the tuition, room and board, and mandatory fees charged for a regular full-time course load student by the approved institution of higher education in which the student is enrolled.[4] There are eight public and seven private, church-related, approved institutions participating in the program.[5]

The dollar value of the scholarship award varies considerably between public and private institutions. It is estimated, for example, that a scholarship recipient enrolled in Hendrix, a private church-related institution, costs the state about $15,000 per year. In contrast, a distinguished scholar enrolled at Southern Arkansas University, a public institution, will cost the state about $4730 per year.[6] It is critical to understand that the scholarship funds are dispersed from the state *directly* to the approved public and private, church-related institutions.[7] No funds are sent to the parents

[1] Ark. Stat. Ann.§ 6-82-305.

[2] Ark. Stat. Ann. § 6-82-305(d).

[3] Ark. Stat. Ann. § 6-82-301.

[4] Ark. Stat. Ann. § 6-82-312(b).

[5] Arkansas Department of Higher Education, Students Enrollments, May 1999.

[6] Id.

[7] Arkansas Department of Higher Education, Program Rules and Procedures, Rule 5, hereinafter DHE.

or recipients.[8] The responsibility for selecting the scholarship recipients rests with the Director of the Arkansas Department of Higher Education.[9] In order to keep their scholarships, the Distinguished Scholars must pass at least 24 credit hours while maintaining a 3.25 cumulative grade average on a 4.0 scale per academic year.[10]

As a condition of participation in the program, each institution of higher education, public or church-related, has to agree to provide the state the same level of administrative services in administering the program. Among these services are appointing an institution representative to act as administrator of the program for that campus, to receive all disbursements, complete all forms and rosters, verify all data, and ensure compliance with all Department of Higher Education (DHE) program rules and regulations.[11] In addition, the institution, public or private, must maintain disbursement records, prepare an annual Institutional Financial Information Sheet for all programs administered by DHE, prepare a list of program drops outs, certify full-time enrollment, provide DHE with an institutional verification of compliance at least twice yearly, and finally, from time to time, submit to a DHE review of the institution's records to demonstrate its due diligence as a *steward of state funds*.[12]

The program has been popular with good students. The state awarded a total of 341 Distinguished Governor's Scholarships for the 1997–1998 and 1998–1999 academic years.[13] Of those, 187 (54.8%) chose to attend a public institution, and 154 (45.2%) chose to attend a private, church-related institution.[14] The approximate expenditure of state funds for the scholarship program has resulted in disbursements of $2,182,000 to the private, church-related, institutions and $1,334,000 to their public counterparts.[15] As a result, 62% of the total state-distinguished scholarship

[8] Id.

[9] Ark. Stat. Ann. § 6-82-304 (3).

[10] Ark. Stat. Ann. § 6-82-311(c).

[11] DHE Rules and Procedures, Rule 5, Supra footnote 7.

[12] Id.

[13] Arkansas Department of Higher Education, Student Enrollments, Supra footnote 5.

[14] Id.

[15] Id.

funds were forwarded directly to the former and 38% to the latter.[16] Of the scholarship recipients, 2 (0.6%) were African-American, 6 (1.8%) Asian, 3 (0.9%) Native American, 320 (93.8%) Caucasian, 1 (0.3%) Hispanic, and 9 (2.6%) other or unknown. Finally, 199 (58.4%) of the scholars were male, and 142 (41.6%) female.[17]

III. The Constitution

The First Amendment to the U.S. Constitution says that "Congress shall make no law respecting the establishment of a religion, or prohibiting the free exercise thereof."[18] It is settled that "the Fourteenth Amendment has rendered the legislatures of the states as incompetent as the Congress to enact such laws."[19] Consequently, the Arkansas General Assembly is constitutionally prohibited from enacting laws respecting an establishment of a religion. But what sort of state action offends the Establishment Clause? Does the distinguished scholarship program that provides for direct payment of state funds to private, church-related institutions of higher education offend the prohibitions of the First Amendment? The answer lies in the intent of the founders and the relevant cases.

First, let us visit James Madison. Thomas Jefferson's famous letter about a separation of church and state to the Danbury Baptist Association is often cited as the primary authority about the intent of the Establishment Clause. However, two Madison veto messages and a letter to the Baptist Churches of Neal's Creek and Black Creek, North Carolina, arguably are more revealing of the intent of the writers of the Constitution and the First Amendment. Jefferson's letter reflected his concern over the establishment of a state religion. Madison's veto messages and letter deal with situations like the Arkansas scholarship program and reveal his notion that religious societies should remain pure, for example, apart from government influence. In 1811, Congress passed a bill giving certain powers

[16] Id.

[17] Id.

[18] Amendment I, Constitution of the United States.

[19] Cantwell v. Connecticut, 314 U.S. 296, 303 (1940).

to an Episcopal Church in Virginia.[20] Among them was the authority to provide for the support of the poor, and the education of poor children.[21] On February 11, 1811, President Madison returned the bill to Congress with a veto message. Madison argued that the government had no authority over the affairs of the church because of the Establishment Clause. He said the bill violated the Constitution because it "would be a precedent for giving religious societies, as such, a legal agency in carrying into effect a legal and public duty."[22] Again, in February, 1811, Madison vetoed another bill that, in part, reserved a parcel of government land in the Mississippi Territory for the Baptist Church at Salem Meeting House. He maintained that the bill violates the principle of the Establishment Clause prohibiting the use of government money to support religious societies.[23] Shortly thereafter, Madison received a letter from two Baptist churches in North Carolina approving his veto of the Bill to provide support to the Mississippi Baptist church.[24] In his response, Madison wrote "having regarded the practical distinction between Religion and Civil Government as essential to the purity of both and as guaranteed by the Constitution of the United States, I could not have otherwise discharged my duty… ."[25] It is clear that Madison believed that government possesses no authority to impose a duty or responsibility on a religious body.[26] Nor, as

---

[20] The Debates and Proceedings of the Congress of the United States with an Appendix containing Important State papers and The Public Documents, and all the Laws of a Public Nature; with a Copious Index. Eleventh Congress—Third Session. Comprising the Period from December 3, 1810 to March 3, 1811, Inclusive. Compiled from Authentic Materials. Washington: Printed and published by Gales and Seaton, (1853), pp. 982–985.

[21] Id.

[22] Id.

[23] Id.

[24] Id.

[25] To be supplied.

[26] "June 3, 1811. To the Baptist Churches in Neal's Creek and on Black Creek, North Carolina. I have received, fellow-citizens, your address, approving my objection to tile (sic) Bill containing a grant of public land to the, Baptist Church at Salem Meeting House: Mississippi Territory. Having always regarded tile(sic) practical distinction between Religion and Civil Government as essential to the purity of both and as guaranteed by the Constitution of the United States. I could not have otherwise discharged my duty on the occasion which presented itself. Among the various religions societies in our Country, none has been more vigilant or constant in maintaining that distinction than the Society of which you make a part, and it is an honorable proof of your sincerity and integrity, that you are as ready to do so in a case favoring the interest of your brethren as in other cases. It is but dust, at the same time, to the Baptist Church at Salem Meeting House, to remark that their

evidenced in the Baptist Church at Salem Meeting House matter, to use government funds to directly support a religious society. Madison believed that the Constitution granted the government absolutely no power over religion. Religion was to be removed from government influence. And the best way to separate them is to forbid the government from imposing any responsibilities or duties on religious societies. To maintain this purity, government was given no Constitutional authority or cause to directly support religious societies. This attitude arose not from hostility to religion but from a desire to protect it from the heavy hand of government regulation. Why? Because we know that government regulation follows government funds. What better witness than Madison?

IV. The Cases

How has the Supreme Court dealt with this issue? In *Lemon v. Kurtzman*,[27] the Supreme Court announced a three-prong test that determines whether the Establishment Clause had been violated. According to *Lemon*, a statute does not violate the Establishment Clause when (1) it has a secular legislative purpose, (2) its primary effect neither advances nor inhibits religion, and (3) it does not excessively entangle government with religion. In *Lemon,* the high court considered a Pennsylvania state statute that authorized the state to "purchase certain secular educational services from nonpublic schools, directly reimbursing those schools solely for teacher's salaries, textbooks, and instructional materials."[28] Most of the schools were affiliated with the Roman Catholic Church.[29] These schools were subject to state audit and had to "identify the separate cost of the secular educational service" to receive reimbursement.[30]

application to the National legislature does not appear to have contemplated a grant to the land in question but on terms that might be equitable to the public as well as to themselves. Accept my friendly respects. James Madison." June 3, 1811. Source of Information: Letters And Other Writings of James Madison, Fourth President of The United States, In Four Volumes Published By the Order Of Congress, Vol. II, J.B. Lippincott & Co., Philadelphia, (1865), pp. 511–512.

[27] 403 U.S. 602, 612–613, (1971).

[28] Id. at 602–603.

[29] Id. at 602–603.

[30] Id. at 602–603.

Here, the high court decided that the state statute violated the Establishment Clause because "schools seeking reimbursement must maintain accounting procedures that require the State to establish the cost of the secular as distinguished from the religious instruction."[31] The court then warned of the dangers of providing state financial aid directly to a church-related school citing *Waltz v. Tax Commission* for the proposition that[32]:

> Obviously, a direct money subsidy would be a relationship pregnant with involvement and, as with most government grant programs, could encompass sustained and detailed administrative relationships for enforcement of statutory or administrative standards….

According to the court, the history of government grants reveal that they typically result in various measures of government control and surveillance.[33] Here, the state's power to audit, inspect, and evaluate a church-related school's expenditures crates an intimate and continuing relationship between church and state.[34] The Pennsylvania arrangement violated the First Amendment because the intent of the Establishment Clause is to protect religion from government interference or supervision.[35] Direct payments and state supervision would certainly violate Mr. Madison's expressed "purity" view of the proper relationship between church-related schools and the state.

In *Committee for Public Education & Religious Liberty v. Nyquist,*[36] the high court dealt with a program that provided direct money grants to certain nonpublic schools for repair and maintenance, reimbursed low-income parents for a portion of the cost of private school tuition, including sectarian school tuition, and granted other parents certain tax benefits.[37] The judges decided that the maintenance and repair provisions

---

[31] Id. at 620.

[32] 397 U.S. 664, 668 (1970).

[33] Lemon, 403 U.S. at 621.

[34] Id. at 622.

[35] Id. at 623.

[36] 413 U.S. 756 (1973).

[37] Id. at 757.

of the New York statute violated the Establishment Clause because its effect is to subsidize and advance the religious mission of sectarian schools.[38] The court also held that the tuition reimbursement plans, if given directly to sectarian schools, would similarly violate the Establishment Clause.[39] This was notwithstanding the fact that the grants were delivered to the parents rather than the schools, as the effect of the aid is unmistakably to provide financial support for nonpublic sectarian institutions.[40]

The *Nyquist* holding concerning payments to parents was substantially weakened with respect to vouchers by *Agostini v. Felton*.[41] Here, the high court stated, "we have departed from the rule … that all government aid that directly aids the educational function of religious schools is invalid."[42] The high court rejected the argument that government and religion are too closely linked merely because a school voucher program transfers money from the government to sectarian schools. It stated, "we reject the argument, primarily because funds cannot reach a sectarian school unless the parents or student decide independently of the government, to send their child to a sectarian school."[43] Consequently, *Agostini* supports the proposition that when parents or students choose to use funds provided to them by the state to attend a church-related school, the Establishment Clause is not offended. This is so because the state funds are paid to the student or parent rather than directly to the church-related school. The state, then, has no call to compel the church-related school to perform administrative tasks for it or submit to its audit. This benefit to the parent approach (it allows a tax deduction for parents for certain educational expenses whether they were incurred in private, church-related, or public schools) is also seen in *Mueller v. Allen*.[44] But, as near as we can tell, the

---

[38] Id. at 774–780.

[39] Id. at 780–789.

[40] Id. at 780.

[41] 521 U.S. 203 (1997).

[42] Id. at 223.

[43] Id. at 230.

[44] 463 U.S. 338 (1983). The court stressed that all the decisions in validating aid to parochial schools have involved direct transmission of assistance from the states to the schools themselves, 463 U.S. at 399.

decision left the *Nyquist* prohibition of aid "directly" paid to a church-related school unaffected.

In *School District of The City of Grand Rapids v. Ball*,[45] the Supreme Court dealt with a district that adopted a shared time and community education program with nonpublic schools. The program was conducted for nonpublic school children at state expense in classrooms located in and leased from the private schools. It offered state-funded classes during the regular school day that were intended to supplement, for the private school students, the "core curriculum" courses required by the state.[46] The shared time teachers were full-time employees of public schools.[47] Of the 41 private schools involved in the program, 40 were church-related schools.[48] The High Court decided that this initiative had the "primary or principal" effect of advancement of religion, and, therefore, violated the Establishment Clause.[49] According to the judges, "even the praiseworthy secular purpose of providing for the education of school children cannot validate government aid to parochial schools when the aid has the effect in promoting a single religion or religion generally or when the aid unduly untangles the government in matters religious."[50] They held that "the symbolic union of church and state inherent in the provision of secular state-provided public instruction in the religious school buildings threatens to convey a message of state support for religion to students in the general public."[51] Further, "the programs in effect subsidize the religious functions of parochial schools by taking over a substantial portion of their responsibility...."[52]

Perhaps the most instructive case for our purposes is *Whitters v. Washington Department Of Services For The Blind*.[53] In *Whitters*, the court

---

[45] 473 U.S. 373 (1984).

[46] Id. at 375.

[47] Id. at 376.

[48] Id. at 379.

[49] Id. at 397.

[50] Id.

[51] Id.

[52] Id., The court also said that the Establishment Clause "rests on the belief a union of government and religion tends to destroy government and degrade religion," 473 U.S. at 398.

[53] 374 U.S. 481 (1986).

ruled on an objection to the state of Washington's vocational rehabilitation program for the visually handicapped that financed petitioner's training at a Christian college. The record shows that assistance to *Whitters* was provided under a Washington state program that paid money directly to the student, who then transmitted it to the educational institution of his choice.[54] The Washington statute authorized the state to "provide for special education and/or training in the professions, business or trades so as to assist visually handicapped persons to overcome vocational handicaps and to obtain the maximum degree of self-support and self-care."[55] Whitters, who suffered from a progressive eye disease, was eligible for vocational rehabilitation assistance under the terms of the statute. He attended Inland Empire School of the Bible, a private Christian College in Spokane, Washington.[56] He was studying the Bible, ethics, speech, and Church administration in order to equip himself for a career as a pastor, missionary, or youth director.[57]

The Washington court ruled that the "principal or primary effect" of the state financial assistance to Whitters was to train him become a pastor, missionary, or church youth director.[58] In the view of the court, the state aid clearly had the primary effect of advancing religion and violated the Establishment Clause.[59] On appeal, the High Court reversed this decision. It said, "it is well settled that the Establishment Clause is not violated every time money previously in the possession of the state is conveyed to a religious institution.[60] For example, a state may issue a pay check to one of its employees, who may then donate all or part of that pay check to a religious institution, all without constitutional barrier; and the state may do so even knowing that the employee so intends to dispose of his salary."[61] The court continued, "it is equally well settled, on the other hand, the state may not grant aid to a religious school, whether cash

[54] Id. at 483.

[55] Id.

[56] Id.

[57] Id.

[58] Id. at 485.

[59] Id. at 484.

[60] Id. at 486.

[61] Id.

or in kind, where the effect of the aid is that of a 'direct subsidy' to the religious school from the state."[62] The issue "is whether, on the facts, the extension of aid to petitioner and the use of that aid by petitioner to support religious education is a permissible transfer similar to the hypothetical salary donation, described above or is an impermissible *direct* (emphasis added) subsidy."[63]

In the opinion of the Supreme Court, the facts central to the inquiry in the *Whitters* case are whether (1) " any aid provided under Washington's program that flows to religious institution does so only as a result as a genuine independent private choice of the aid recipient;" (2) it is not one of the "ingenious plans for channeling state aid to sectarian schools that periodically reach the court;" (3) "it creates no financial incentive for students to undertake sectarian education;" (4) "it does not tend to provide greater or broader recipients for recipients who apply their aid to religious education;" and (5) "in this case, the fact that aid goes to individuals means that the decision to support religious education is made by the individual, not the State."[64]

And, importantly, nothing in the record indicated that, if Whittier's petition succeeds, any significant portion of the aid spent on the Washington program as a whole will end up flowing to religious education. The court stated, "respondent is correct in pointing out that aid to a religious institution, unrestricted in its potential usage, if properly attributable to the state, is clearly prohibited under the Establishment Clause."[65] But the respondent's argument does not apply in this case because there was no *direct aid* to the religious school.[66] The court decided that, on the facts present, the Washington program did not constitute sufficiently direct support of religion so as to violate the Establishment Clause.[67] Justice Powell, concurring, said that the Washington scheme

---

[62] Id.

[63] Id.

[64] Id. at 488.

[65] Id. at 489.

[66] Id.

[67] Id.

was constitutionally permitted because the student or parent directly received the state payments, citing *Mueller v. Allen*.[68]

Before turning to the Arkansas Scholarship program, it will be helpful to review the common threads woven through these cases that bind them together. First, requiring church-related schools to maintain administrative and accounting procedures for review by the state offends the Establishment Clause, *Lemon v. Kurtzman*[69] and *Agostini v. Felton*.[70] Second, payment of financial aid directly to a church-related school offends the Establishment Clause, *Lemon v. Kurtzman*,[71] *Waltz v. Tax Commission*,[72] *Committee For Public Education And Religious Liberty v. Nyquist*,[73] *Grand Rapids School District v. Ball, Mueller v. Allen*,[74] and *Whitters v. Washington Department Of Services For The Blind*.[75] Third, when there is a disparity in the amount of state funds spent on public and church-related students, the establishment clause is offended, *Whitters v. Washington*.[76] Four, the establishment Clause is offended if the scholarship program creates a financial incentive for the student to attend a church-related school, *Whitters. v. Washington*.[77] And finally, and perhaps most troubling, is this program an ingenious scheme designed to channel state aid directly to church-related schools condemned by the decisions in *Committee For Public Education And Religious Liberty v. Nyquist*[78] and *Whitters v. Washington*?[79]

A reasonable interpretation will conclude the Arkansas Distinguished Scholarship Program offends the Establishment Clause for a wide variety

---

[68] Id. at 491, citing Muellen v. Allen. 463 U.S. 388, 399, (1983) for the proposition that payments directly to parents are constitutional because any benefit to religion results from "numerous private choices of individual parents of school-age children."

[69] 403 U.S. 602 (1971).

[70] 521 U.S. 203 (1997).

[71] 403 U.S. 602.

[72] 397 U.S. 664 (1970).

[73] 413 U.S. 756 (1973).

[74] 473 U.S. 373 (1984).

[75] 474 U.S. 481 (1986).

[76] Id.

[77] Id.

[78] See, 413 U.S. 756 (1973).

[79] See, 474 U.S. 481 (1986).

of reasons. First, the program requires church-related institutions to agree to perform administrative tasks and ensure compliance with state regulations. The institution must submit to a review of its records and demonstrate its due diligence as a *steward of state funds*.[80] One would reasonably believe that the administrators of church schools would strongly object to the grubby hands of State officials thumbing through their private school files. Does this mean they agree to having the Legislative Audit look at their books? In any case, the regulations clearly offend the Establishment Clause holdings under *Lemon*[81] and *Agostini*[82] that the state may not compel religious societies to perform state administrative tasks.

Second, the state funds are paid directly to church-related institutions. This direct aid offends the Establishment Clause under *Lemon*,[83] *Waltz*,[84] *Nyquist*,[85] and *Whitters*.[86] If there is one thing certain under these cases, it is that state money paid directly to a church-related school is unconstitutional. This is so because the scholarship funds are a direct subsidy condemned in all the cases cited.

Third, there is a considerable disparity between the amount of state funds per distinguished scholarship provided church-related institutions and public institutions under the program. Recall that Hendrix will typically receive $15,000 and Southern Arkansas $4730 per scholarship student.[87] There is also a disparity in the total funds sent to private and public schools. Church-related schools received $2,182,000 and public institutions $1,334,000 in the years 1998–1999.[88] This disparity in treatment of public and church-related institutions offends the Establishment Clause under *Whitters*.[89]

---

[80] DHE Rule 6.H, Supra footnote 7.

[81] 403 U.S. 602 (1971).

[82] 521 U.S. 203 (1997).

[83] 403 U.S. 602.

[84] 397 U.S. 664.

[85] 413 U.S. 756.

[86] 474 U.S. 481.

[87] Arkansas Department of Higher Education, Supra footnote 5.

[88] Id.

[89] 474 U.S. 481.

Four, the program clearly creates a financial incentive for the distinguished scholarship student to attend a church-related school. This is so because the program is open-ended. The state pays whatever the church-related institution considers a reasonable level of tuition and fees.[90] The state-sponsored creation of a considerable financial incentive to attend a church-related school is offensive to the Establishment Clause under *Whitters.*[91]

Finally and most controversially, the distinguished scholarship program, if newspaper reports are accurate, may be a scheme to channel state aid directly to church-related schools that offends the Establishment Clause under *Whitters.*[92] According to Doug Smith,[93] the impetus for the distinguished scholars program did not emanate from the Department of Higher Education. Rather, it was proposed by state senators. The DHE had little choice because 50 senators sponsored the enabling legislation. One of its sponsors is quoted as stating that the bill was brought to him by the President of the Independent Colleges and Universities Association and by the Association's lobbyist.[94] But the impetus for the program is of questionable relevance because the legislation is so blatantly unconstitutional. A legal challenge will almost certainly raise the issue of a scheme to support religious schools. It will be interesting to see why the association would want the state rummaging around in their private, church-related educational programs to determine stewardship of state funds. The North Carolina Baptists who wrote to Mr. Madison would surely be offended.[95]

Mr. Madison would also surely be taken aback. His two veto messages and letter to the Baptist Churches of Neal's Creek and Black Creek, North Carolina, in 1811, sent a powerful message that government has no (none at all) business regulating a religious society, giving a religious

[90] Ark. Stat. Ann. 6-82-312(b).

[91] 474 U.S. 481.

[92] Id.

[93] Doug Smith, "Pushing And Shoving For The State's Top Scholars," *Arkansas Times*, Aug. 27, 1999, at 13, Col. 3–4.

[94] Doug Smith, "Pushing and Shoving For The State's Top Scholars, *Arkansas Times*, Aug. 27, 1999, at 13, Col. 4.

[95] See, The Debates and Proceeding of the Congress of the United States, Supra footnotes 20–24.

society legal agency to carry into effect a public duty, nor giving direct aid to a religious society.[96] The distinguished Scholars Scholarship Program has the unique and dubious distinction of offending *all* of Madison's notions of separation of religion from influence and regulation by the government. This was not so because of hostility toward religion but to protect religion from the government. He believed that the Constitution granted government no power over religion. And it surely follows, as in the Arkansas example, that when a religious society accepts government funds in this manner, the heavy hand of government regulation is sure to follow.[97] It makes no constitutional difference that church-related schools volunteer for regulation. It still offends the Constitution!

As we shall soon see, this state of affairs is made regrettable because there exists a relatively simple, and constitutional pleasing, way to retain Arkansas's best and brightest students. But, before broaching that subject, one other serious problem with the distinguished Scholarship program requires examination.

V. Title VI and Disparate Impact

Only 2 (0.6%) of the 341 Distinguished Scholarship recipients are black, while about 17.3% of the state's undergraduate students have this background.[98] Title VI of the Civil Rights Act prohibits discrimination "on the ground of race ... under any program or activity receiving Federal financial assistance."[99] The sole basis for selection of the scholarship recipients is a score of 32 on the ACT, 1410 on the SAT, or being a finalist in the National Merit Scholarship competition.[100] It is undisputed that the state of Arkansas receives federal funds for numerous educational programs.[101]

---

[96] Id.

[97] Id.

[98] Arkansas Department of Higher Education, "Student Enrollments," page 27, May 1999.

[99] 42 U.S.C. 2000d.

[100] Ark. Stat. Ann. 6-82-302.

[101] See Supra footnote 2.

Does the program have a disparate impact on black students? In *Griggs v. Duke Power Company*,[102] the Supreme Court introduced the theory of disparate impact discrimination by holding that a plaintiff need not necessarily prove intentional discrimination in order to prove that an employer has violated Title VII of the Civil Rights Act. Since then, "facially neutral employment practices that have a significant adverse effect on protected classes have been held to violate the Act without proof … of discriminatory intent."[103] The theory is based on the idea that even unintentional discrimination can be "equivalent to intentional discrimination," because of the same results.[104] Finally, courts have applied the employment disparate impact theory to cases involving Title VI.[105]

To demonstrate a prima *facie case* of disparate impact discrimination, a student must first show that the selection practice followed has caused a disproportionate effect that excludes him from an educational opportunity.[106] If such a showing has been made, the burden shifts to the defendant who must demonstrate that the selection practice is justified by "educational necessity."[107] Finally, even if the defendant meets the burden, the complaining student may prevail by offering an effective alternative practice that results in less disproportionality while still serving the goals of the educational program.[108] The racially disproportionate effect is typically demonstrated by the use of statistical evidence comparing the racial composition of the candidates selected with the qualified candidates in the pool.[109]

Clearly, black students have been disproportionately impacted by the Distinguished Scholars standards. Only 2 of the 321 students selected, or 0.6%, were African-American.[110] The next inquiry is whether the sole

[102] 401 U.S. 424 (1971).

[103] See, Watson v. Fort Worth Bank and Trust, 487 U.S. 977, 986–87 (1988).

[104] Id. at 987.

[105] See Elston v. Talladega County Board of Education, 997 F. 2d 1394, 1407 (11th Cir. 1993).

[106] Wards Cove Packing Company v. Atonio, 490 U.S. 642, 656–57 (1989).

[107] Board of Education of the City School District of New York v. Harris, 444 U.S. 130, 151 (1979).

[108] See, Watson, 487 U.S. at 998.

[109] See, Wards Cove, 490 U.S. at 650–55.

[110] Arkansas Department of Higher Education.

standards adopted by the State, ACT, and SAT scores, and becoming a National Merit finalist, are justified by "educational necessity." The first inquiry is whether Arkansas has some independent basis for choosing the cutoff scores. For example, the state might establish a cutoff score by using a professional estimate of the requisite ability levels to succeed in the scholarship program.[111] We find no evidence of such a professional study. The enabling legislation was presented to the General Assembly in whole cloth without state agency input.[112] In order to survive a disparate impact challenge, the state must establish something more than a mere articulation of the basis (keep good students in Arkansas) for the cutoff score.[113] Importantly, recently the U.S. Department of Education proposed regulations that provide[114]:

> The use of any educational test which has a significant disparate impact on members of any particular race … is discriminatory, and a violation of Title VI and/or Title IX respectively, unless there is no practical alternative form of assessment which meets the educational institutions' needs, and would have a less disparate impact.

Recently, a district court ruled that the NCAA initial eligibility rules (Proposition 16) that solely utilized a minimum test score on the ACT or SAT for eligibility to play constituted a disparate impact on African-American student athletes.[115] The NCAA rule is remarkably similar to the Arkansas scholarship program in its operation and impact. The NCAA's justification for its policy was to increase the graduation rate for black student athletes and to close the gap between white and black athlete graduation rates.[116] But, alas for the NCAA, the court found that African-American athletes were already graduating at a greater rate than black students generally.[117] The practical effect of Proposition 16 was to restrict

[111] See, Watson 487 U.S. at 994–95.

[112] See, Smith, Supra footnote 92, concerning the drafting of the legislation.

[113] See Ark. Stat. Ann. 6-82-301, Supra footnote 3, for the stated purpose of the legislation.

[114] Walter Williams, "Killing The Messenger," Arkansas Democrat Gazette, Sept.1, 1999, B10, Col. 4.

[115] Cureton v. National Collegiate Athletic Association, No. 97-131 (E. Dist. Pa. Mar. 8, 1999).

[116] Id.

[117] Id.

the access of black athletes to the limited number of college athletic scholarships available.[118] The court questioned how this would decrease the graduation gap. According to the judge, proffering such a "back-end"(later graduation) balancing between graduation rates and entrance requirements violates the prohibition against using a "bottom line" (the blacks we accepted did well) defense against disparate impact in cases involving pass/fail selection procedures found in *Connecticut v. Teal.*[119] The court concluded by questioning why the NCAA didn't just adopt a rule that considered graduation rates equal to that of the student body.[120]

To state it another way, are there other practical remedies that could be adopted that will also achieve Arkansas' goal of retaining the State's best and brightest students? There is a recent Equal Protection case that is helpful in identifying other relevant factors that might be considered. In *Hopwood v. Texas,*[121] the court decided it was a violation of the Equal Protection Clause of the Fourteenth Amendment to take into account solely a person's race when making admission decisions.[122] The court said, however, that race may be considered along with a number of other factors such as playing the flute, understanding Chaos Theory, economic status, life experience, family educational background, whether parents are alumni, how fast a person can run with a football, marital status, disability status, ACT and SAT scores, and veteran's status.[123] Why not consider some of those other relevant factors as qualification standards for the distinguished Scholars Program?

VI. The Cure

It is easy for pointy-headed professors like us to criticize administrative policy. Of greater interest, perhaps, is how can the state accomplish its stated goal of retaining more of its best and brightest high school

[118] Id.

[119] 457 U.S. 440, 446 (1982).

[120] Cureton, No. 97-131.

[121] No. 94-50569 (5th Cir., Mar. 18, 1996).

[122] Id.

[123] Id.

graduates? There are three possible repairs to the program. First, the "direct aid" issue can be avoided by making direct payments to the graduating senior or his parents. Here, state funds would be expended based on the free choice of the student or parent. It is the obligation of the recipient to administratively assure the state that the funds are being properly used and that the recipient is meeting the required hours and grade point standards. If the G.I. Bill can pass constitutional muster, then so can this plan.

Second, each recipient could be given the same dollar amount of educational subsidy. Assume every award is $12,000. The recipient would be free to use these dollars to attend the institution of his choice. What if 80% of the students decide to attend church-related schools? That would be fine because it is their choice. What of the recipient who attends a public institution that costs $8000 per year? That would also be acceptable. Again, that is their choice. In this case, the state could demand that the money over and above tuition is spent for educational purposes like a computer, books, and so on.

Third, the Department of Higher Education can easily draft regulations to comply with Title VI by listing relevant factors other than ACT and SAT scores to be taken into account when awarding the scholarships. These three simple corrections will bring the program into legal and constitutional compliance.

VII. Libertarian Philosophy

In this section, we shall try to step back from the hurly burly of the specific educational proposals we have been considering, in order to develop a philosophical vision of education; having done so, we shall then use it as a basis upon which to criticize these initiatives. Our vision is based on the philosophy of libertarianism,[124] a doctrine which takes as its

[124] On libertarianism, see Barnett, Randy, "Pursuing Justice in a Free Society Part One: Power vs. Liberty," *Criminal Justice Ethics*, 4: 50–72, 1985; Benson, Bruce L., 1989, "Enforcement of Private Property Rights in Primitive Societies: Law Without Government," *The Journal of Libertarian Studies*, Vol. IX, No. 1, Winter, pp. 1–26; Benson, Bruce L., "The Spontaneous Evolution of Commercial Law," *Southern Economic Journal*, 55: 644–661, 1989; Benson, Bruce L., *The Enterprise*

fundamental axioms personal and private property rights and the principle of nonaggression.

Libertarianism is essentially a philosophy of law. It asks but one question, and gives but one answer. The question is: Under what conditions is the use of force legally justified? The answer is: Only in response to, or in retaliation or defense against, a prior invasion against justly held property, or the human person. The sole function of just law, from this perspective, is to mandate that people keep "their mitts to themselves"; that they be prevented from attacking the persons or private property rights of others. Individuals may lawfully interact with each other in any mutually agreeable manner possible. The one thing proscribed by law is coercive act.

How can we distinguish between a lawful defense, and an illicit attack? We start out with the primordial legal claim that people are proper owners of themselves.[125] If so, then at one fell swoop we eliminate from the

of Law: Justice Without the State, San Francisco: Pacific Research Institute for Public Policy, 1990; Block, Walter, *Defending the Undefendable*, New York: Fox and Wilkes, 1976; Block, Walter, "Libertarianism vs. Libertinism," *The Journal of Libertarian Studies: An Interdisciplinary Review*, Vol. 11, No. 1, 1994, pp. 117–128; Boaz, David, *Libertarianism: A Primer*, New York: Free Press, 1997; Friedman, David, *The Machinery of Freedom: Guide to a Radical Capitalism*, La Salle, IL: Open Court, 2nd ed., 1989; Gwartney, James D., and Stroup, Richard L., *What everyone should know about economics and prosperity*, Vancouver: The Fraser Institute, 1993; Herbert, Auberon, *The Right and Wrong of Compulsion by the State*, Indianapolis: Liberty Fund, 1978; Hospers, John, Libertarianism, Nash, Los Angeles, 1971; Hoppe, Hans-Hermann, *A Theory of Socialism and Capitalism: Economics, Politics and Ethics*, Boston: Dordrecht, 1989; Hoppe, Hans-Hermann, *The Economics and Ethics of Private Property: Studies in Political Economy and Philosophy*, Boston: Kluwer, 1993; Machan, Tibor, *Individuals and their Rights*, LaSalle, IL: Open Court, 1989; Machan, Tibor,, "Law, Justice and Natural Rights," *Western Ontario Law Review*, Vol. 14, 1975, pp. 119–126; Murray, Charles, *What it means to be a Libertarian*, New York, Broadway, 1997; Narveson, Jan, *The Libertarian Idea*, Philadelphia: Temple University Press, 1988; Nozick, Robert, *Anarchy, State and Utopia*, New York: Basic Books, 1974; Rothbard, Murray N., *For a New Liberty*, Macmillan, New York, 1978; Rothbard, Murray N., *The Ethics of Liberty*, Humanities Press, Atlantic Highlands, N.J., 1982; Spencer, Herbert, *The Man Versus the State*, Indianapolis, Liberty Classics, 1981; Spooner, Lysander, *No Treason*, Larkspur, Colorado, (1870) 1966; Tannehill, Morris and Linda, *The Market for Liberty*, New York, 1984; Woolridge, William C., *Uncle Sam the Monopoly Man*, New Rochelle, N.Y.: Arlington House, 1970; Morriss, Andrew P., "Miners, Vigilantes and Cattlemen: Overcoming Free Rider Problems in the Private Provision of Law," *University of Wyoming Land and Water Law Review*, Vol. XXXIII, No. 2, 1998, pp. 581–696; Anderson, Terry and Hill, P.J., "An American Experiment in Anarcho-Capitalism: the *not* so Wild, Wild West," *Journal of Libertarian Studies*, Vol. 3, No. 1, 1979, pp. 9–29.

[125] This is impossible to deny, since the denial could only take place by the use of lungs, lips, tongue, and other body parts. But if self-ownership is unjustified, no one would have any right to object. For an elaboration of this "argument from argument," see Hoppe, Hans-Hermann, *The Economics*

list of legal activities murder, rape, assault, battery, slavery, kidnaping, or any such attack on the person. If two men are fighting, then we declare criminal the man who began the altercation.

But people need more than their own bodies to survive, and law is nothing if not a means toward this end. How, then, can property other than the person be brought into the nexus of justified ownership, so that we can determine legal right and wrong in this arena? In the libertarian view, justice in property titles is accomplished, at the outset, by mixing one's labor with the land,[126] or other aspects of the natural environment such as animals. One owns oneself, and by capturing a fish or cow, or homesteading a forest, or farming some land, one then comes to own these things as well. In addition, legitimate private property rights can arise through trade, gift giving, voluntary associations, and so on. Thus, if A captures a fish from a stream, and B domesticates a cow, and they barter these items, A comes to own the cow, and B the fish, even though neither homesteaded these items. But in both cases, their claim title can be traced to original homesteading, plus the legitimate intermediation of voluntary trade. These considerations are sufficient to indicate that theft, trespassing, fraud, or any other such uninvited border crossing would be illegal in the libertarian society.

What is the libertarian view of government? If there is any justification for this institution, it is to uphold the law. Since the law consists solely of protecting personal and private property rights, the function of the state is limited to these goals. Accordingly, three institutions are justified: armies to ward off foreign aggression, police to serve the same role vis a vis domestic evildoers, and courts to determine who is the instigator of unjustified force, threat or fraud, and who the victim. And that describes *in its entirety* the proper scope of government under libertarianism.

How does education enter this picture? It does not. The government simply has no role to play in this field at all. In this philosophy, there would be as great a separation between education and state as is provided

and Ethics of Private Property: Studies in Political Economy and Philosophy, Boston: Kluwer, 1993, pp. 204–207.

[126] See on this Locke, John, *An Essay Concerning the True Origin, Extent and End of Civil Government*, V. 27–28, in *Two Treatises of Government*, P. Laslett, ed., Cambridge: Cambridge University Press, 1960, pp. 17–18.

for in the U.S. Constitution between church and state.[127] There are those, of course, who maintain that education is special, and that public sector schooling, whether at elementary or university level, is justified. Such a claim cannot be reconciled with a careful reading of the U.S. constitution. Education is not specifically mentioned in this document. It is commonly placed under its general welfare provisions. But this is "penumbra" mining, not strict constructionism. More important, a role for the state in schooling cannot be harmonized with libertarianism, since education per se is irrelevant to rights violations.

One argument in behalf of a governmental role in education is based on external economies, or neighborhood effects. States Friedman in this regard: "A stable and democratic society is impossible without a minimum degree of literacy and knowledge on the part of most citizens and without widespread acceptance of some common set of values. Education can contribute to both. In consequence, the gain from the education of a child contributes to your welfare by promoting a stable and democratic society. It is not feasible to identify the particular individuals (or families) benefitted and so to charge for the services rendered."[128]

There are difficulties with this position. First, it is entirely possible that there will be "a minimum degree of literacy and knowledge on the part of most citizens" in the total absence of public or compulsory education. These laws were not promulgated in the United States until the late nineteenth century.[129] Would Friedman care to maintain that the United States was not "a stable and democratic society" before that time, attained this distinction only after that time, and that this was due to public and/ or compulsory education? If not, we must reject this Friedmanite brand

[127] Apart, that is, in the limited government libertarian view, from protecting against murder, rape, theft, fraud, contract enforcement, and all the rest, which holds true in *all* endeavors. That is, the state has no more of a function in education than in the bubble gum or paper clip industry.

[128] Friedman, Milton, *Capitalism and Freedom*, Chicago: University of Chicago Press, 1962, p. 86.

[129] Rothbard, Murray N., *Education: Free and Compulsory*, Auburn, AL: The Mises Institute, 1999, pp. 40–41, states: "…in 1852, Massachusetts established the first comprehensive statewide, modern system of compulsory schooling in the United States…. In 1850, all the states had public schools, but only Massachusetts and Connecticut were imposing compulsion. The movement for compulsory schooling conquered all of America in the late 19th century. Massachusetts began the parade, and the other states all followed, mainly in the 1870s and 1880s." See also on this Joel Spring, *The American School*, and Sheldon Richman, *Separating School and State: How to Liberate America's Families* (Fairfax, Va.,: The Future of Freedom Foundation, 1994).

of educational socialism as incompatible with the libertarian version of the free society.

As well, Friedman's concern with a "widespread acceptance of some common set of values" ought to be seen as ominous not only for libertarians, but for anyone concerned with civil liberties; particularly despicable is the forcible inculcation of an ideology upon children. In point of fact, the main impetus for public schooling in the United States was a desire on the part of Protestant authorities to "civilize" unruly Catholic children[130] who came to this country with what was then considered an "alien" culture. Placing education in the public sector was an attempt to beat this out of them.

Suppose we concede to Friedman that "the education of a child contributes to your welfare"; that without coerced tax levies for this purpose, you would not voluntarily contribute, financially, to the education of other people's children. Does it then follow that the state is justified in forcing you to pay for schooling of the children of strangers? It does not. Rothbard offers the following remedy for this fallacy:

> A and B decide to pay for the building of a dam for their uses; C benefits though he did not pay. A and B educate themselves at their expense and C benefits by being able to deal with educated people, and so on. This is the problem of the Free Rider. Yet it is difficult to understand what the hullabaloo is all about. Am I to be specially taxed because I enjoy the sight of my neighbor's garden without paying for it? A's and B's purchase of a good reveals that *they* are willing to pay for it; if it indirectly benefits C as well, no one is the loser. If C feels that he would be deprived of the benefit in only A and B paid, then he is free to contribute too.... In fact, we are *all* free riders on the investment, and the technological development, of our ancestors. Must we wear sackcloth and ashes, or submit ourselves to State dictation, because of this happy fact?[131]

[130] Liggio, Leonard P., and Peden, Joseph R., 1978, "Social scientists, schooling and the acculturation of immigrants in 19th century America," *The Journal of Libertarian Studies*, Vol. 2, No. 1, Winter, pp. 69–84.

[131] Rothbard, Murray N., *The Logic of Action: Method, Money and the Austrian School*, Vol. I, Cheltenham, UK: Edward Elgar, 1997, p. 251.

Another argument in behalf of a governmental role in education stems from the constitutional concern with promoting the general welfare. Given that promotion of the general welfare is indeed a praiseworthy goal, does this imply that the best way to attain this is for the government to provide or finance this service? This holds true only in Cuba and North Korea, at the time of this writing. There, under coercive socialism, it is widely held that if something is to be done for the general welfare, state action is required. But surely our society benefits from computers, automobiles, toys, celery, massages, babysitting, rubber bands, and literally thousands of other such things absent any contribution by statist authorities. Why should it be any different for educational services? Indeed, it is no stretch to maintain the very opposite point of view: that if it is important that the public have access to a good or service, the *last* thing needed is the bumbling and inefficiency of the bureaucrat.

It is hardly an accident that the U.S. Post Office, the paradigm case of a government operation, is practically a synonym for outdated management and bankruptcy.[132] The motor vehicle bureau is known far and wide, too, as an emblem of state incompetency. Nor is it any accident that the market is able to run circles around governmental "business" operations. As Henry Hazlitt[133] explains, the free enterprise system benefits from a weeding out process: ineffective entrepreneurs are forced to change their ways, or risk bankruptcy. The same does not obtain in the civil service. There, as long as a certain modicum of honesty is attained, it is all but impossible to eliminate waste. Did the Edsel arise in a governmental auto works, it would be with us still.

[132] Adie, Douglas K., *The Mail Monopoly: Analysing Canadian Postal Service*, Vancouver: The Fraser Institute, 1990; Adie, Douglas K., *Monopoly Mail: Privatizing the United States Postal Service*, New Brunswick, N.J.: Transaction, 1988; Adie, Douglas K., "Why Marginal Reform of the U.S. Postal Service Won't Succeed," in *Free the Mail: Ending the Postal Monopoly*, Peter J. Ferrara, ed., Washington, D.C.: The Cato Institute, 1990; Moore, Thomas Gale, "The Federal Postal Monopoly: History, Rationale and Future," in *Free the Mail: Ending the Postal Monopoly*, Peter J. Ferrara, ed., Washington, D.C.: The Cato Institute, 1990; Priest, George, "The History of the Postal Monopoly in the United States," *Journal of Law and Economics*, 18, no. 33, 1975; Butler, Stuart M., "Privatizing Bulk Mail," *Management*, 6, No. 1, 1986; Moore, Stephen, "Privatizing the U.S. Postal Service," in Stephen Moore and Stuart Butler, eds., *Privatization*, Washington: Heritage Foundation, 1987.

[133] Hazlitt, Henry, *Economics in One Lesson*, Arlington House Publishers, New York, 1979.

VIII. Educational Philosophy

Given, then, that there is no warrant for governmental meddling in the educational system, how does this impact the scholarship program analyzed in the previous sections of this chapter? Simple: if there is to be no involvement by the state in the schooling industry, then by definition it would be precluded from awarding to scholarships to brilliant students. And this holds for *any* motivation, including an attempt to encourage these young people to stay within its jurisdiction during their college years, in the hope that they would remain there for the rest of their lives. (Roy, couldn't we attack this policy, in a previous section, on the ground that it violates the constitutional provision outlawing restrictions on trade across state lines? What is the provision of the constitution which prohibits a state from setting up tariff barriers against imports from other states? It occurs to me that this might be used to ban states from subsidizing local industries. Subsidies, after all, are only the opposite side of the coin of taxes. If the one is unconstitutional, then this ought to apply to the other. And if it does not, then, were I a judge, I'd find this in some "penumbra" or other.)

The problem with this answer is that it appears too facile by half. Were we to apply this consistently we would remove ourselves from much of what passes for public policy analysis and debate. For example: should there be a 55 mile per hour speed limit? Should drunken drivers be arrested? Should we have seat belt laws, or compel motorcycle helmets? The libertarian answer is, privatize all roads, streets, and highways, and allow their owners to decide these questions.[134] Or, should there be tenure

[134] For the case in behalf of road and highway privatization, see Block, Walter, "Public Goods and Externalities: The Case of Roads," *The Journal of Libertarian Studies*, Vol. VII, No. 1, Spring 1983a, pp. 1–34; Block, Walter E. and Matthew A. Block. 1996. "Roads, Bridges, Sunlight and Private Property Rights," Journal Des Economistes Et Des Etudes Humaines, Vol. VII, No. 2/3, June-September, pp. 351–362; Block, Walter E. 1998. "Roads, Bridges, Sunlight and Private Property: Reply to Gordon Tullock," Journal des Economistes et des Etudes Humaines, Vol. 8, No. 2/3, June-September, pp. 315–326; Block, Walter, "Road Socialism," *International Journal of Value-Based Management*, 1996, Vol. 9, pp. 195–207; Block, Walter, "Theories of Highway Safety," *Transportation Research Record*, #912, 1983b, pp. 7–10; Block, Walter, "Congestion and Road Pricing," *The Journal of Libertarian Studies*, Vol. IV, No. 3, Fall 1980, pp. 299–330; Block, Walter, "Free Market Transportation: Denationalizing the Roads," *Journal of Libertarian Studies*, Vol. III, No. 2, Summer 1979, pp. 209–238; Cadin, Michelle, and Block, Walter, (1997), "Privatize

at universities?[135] Should school children wear uniforms, or be subjected to any dress code at all? What kind of scholarships should be awarded to students? Should there be minimum ACT or SAT scores for scholar athletes? Should there be affirmative action in admissions, graduation rates? What about free speech at universities?[136] Or metal detectors at high schools? Again, the answer is obvious: privatize all schools, and allow the firms involved to decide these questions themselves, in much the same manner that restaurants now determine their menu offerings, decorations, table settings, color of walls, and so on without any input from the government bureaucracy or outside busybodies.

Or, should the road be widened in the public park, easing traffic but reducing green space? Should the park include a children's zoo? A restaurant? Would the addition of a golf course, or baseball field, at the cost of forests, be an improvement? Should a lake or stream be dredged? Again, the libertarian answer is consonant with Occam's Razor: in a world of private parks, these would be entrepreneurial decisions. They would no more be any outsider's business than the choice of colors offered by an

---

the Public Highway System," *The Freeman*, February, Vol. 47, No. 2., pp. 96–97; Cobin, John, M. (1999), Market Provisions of Highways: Lessons from Costanera Norte. *Planning and Markets*, Volume 2, Number 1; Gunderson, Gerald, "Privatization and the 19th-Century Turnpike," *Cato Journal*, Vol. 9, No. 1, Spring/Summer 1989, pp. 191–200; Jackman, W.T., *The Development of Transportation in Modern England*, Cambridge: Cambridge University Press, 1916; Klein, Dan, "The Voluntary Provision of Public Goods? The Turnpike Companies of Early America," *Economic Inquiry*, October 1990, pp. 788–812; Klein, Dan, Majewski, J., and Baer, C., "Economy, Community and the Law: The Turnpike Movement in New York, 1797–1845," *The Journal of Economic History*, March 1993a, pp. 106–122; Klein, Dan, Majewski, J., and Baer, C., "From Trunk to Branch: Toll Roads in New York, 1800–1860," *Essays in Economic and Business History*, 1993b, pp. 191–209; Klein, Dan and Fielding, G.J., "Private Toll Roads: Learning from the Nineteenth Century," *Transportation Quarterly*, July 1992, pp. 321–341.; Klein, Dan and Fielding, G.J., "How to Franchise Highways," *Journal of Transport Economics and Policy*, May 1993a, pp. 113–130; Klein, Dan and Fielding, G.J., "High Occupancy/Toll Lanes: Phasing in Congestion Pricing a Lane at a Time," *Policy Study*, No. 170, Reason Foundation, November 1993b; Roth, Gabriel, *The Private Provision of Public Services in Developing Countries*, Oxford: Oxford University Press, 1987; Roth, Gabriel, *Paying for Roads: The Economics of Traffic Congestion*, Middlesex, England: Penguin, 1967; Roth, Gabriel, *A Self-financing Road System*, London, England, The Institute of Economic Affairs, 1966; Rothbard, Murray N., *For a New Liberty*, Macmillan, New York, 1973; Woolridge, William C., *Uncle Sam the Monopoly Man*, New Rochelle, N.Y.: Arlington House, 1970.

135 See Block, Walter and McGee, Robert W., "Academic Tenure: A Law and Economics Analysis," *Harvard Journal of Law and Public Policy*, Vol. 14, No. 2, Spring 1991, pp. 545–563.

136 See Alan Kors and Harvey Silverglate, *The Shadow University: The Betrayal of Liberty on America's Campuses*, New York: The Free Press, 1998.

automobile company, or the decision of the Disney Company to give Mickey Mouse a greater role in an upcoming movie and Donald Duck a lesser one.

On the other hand, this is a temptation that should be resisted by the libertarian, lest he become enmeshed in issues irrelevant to this philosophy. For the libertarian really *has* no views on the best operation of government initiatives which should not exist in the first place. And this is buttressed by libertarian "taxi cab" theory[137]: suppose you were in the southern part of the city, and wanted to go the west end. You hop into a cab and say: "Please take me to the western part of the city." The cabbie replies: "Sorry, I only go to the north or to the east; I don't go to the west." What do you do? Do you pick the north, on the ground that it is at least closer to the west than is the east? (That would be equivalent to attempting to wrestle with the myriad of questions about public sector functioning mentioned above). No. You get *out* of that taxi, and into another one willing to head in the direction you wish. That is to say, there are good and sufficient reasons to resist the temptation to become embroiled in mainstream public policy debates.

Nevertheless, we are going to ignore this sound advice, and plunge into the thickets of public policy analysis of educational scholarships. Given then that public universities ought not to exist, and that if they did, they should not be giving scholarships,[138] what kind of scholarship would be *most* consistent with libertarianism?, we ask.

When government becomes involved in an activity for which it has no warrant, such as education, it is in effect *stealing* money from the taxpayers. This is because the citizenry is *compelled* to pay taxes, the purpose for which these levies are being demanded is illegitimate, and we have an accurate word to describe such occurrences: theft. This being the case, the key to the libertarian analysis of scholarships is to return the ill-gotten gains to their rightful owners, the long suffering taxpayer. Better that the money should not have been taken from the taxpayer to finance public education in the first place. But given that this mulcting has taken place,

[137] We owe this point to Michael R. Edelstein and Nando Pelusi.

[138] Or doing *anything* else, given that they should not exist in the first place.

the least bad solution from the libertarian point of view is to undo this injustice[139] to the extent feasible.

How can this be done? Simple. By awarding scholarships not on the basis of IQ, or ACT or SAT score, but rather on the basis of the size of the tax bill paid by the family, say, in the past five years. This means that when it comes to awarding the Governor's Scholarship if there is a choice between a rich kid with mediocre smarts, and a poor one of high intelligence, the nod should go to the former. It is *his* parents who were victimized by state theft. The whole point of the exercise, at least from the libertarian point of view, is to attain justice, not to encourage people to go to school and then later reside in any particular locale. And justice can be attained by returning stolen property to the *victim*, not to anyone else.

A word on admissions criteria, while we are playing the role of skunk at the garden party. This, too, would have to radically revised, under a libertarian administration, on the assumption that there were no way to rid society of pernicious public universities. Admission, too, would be on the basis of the tax bill. The children of the rich, be they as stupid as fence posts, would go to the flagship university of the state. Intelligent students of poor backgrounds would be consigned to the bottom of the status and quality heap, community colleges.

It cannot be denied that such a libertarian scholarship and admissions program would play havoc with higher education. But we come not to praise and "improve"; rather, to tear down. And there is perhaps no better way to ruin public universities than to prohibit them from segregating themselves on the basis of intelligence. Advocates of affirmative action act in accordance to this goal, albeit for very different reasons. Libertarians who do not shrink from the logical implications of their basic premises cannot but embrace this "modest proposal" as it pertains to scholarships and admissions policy.

[139] Undoing injustice is the core of libertarian punishment theory. On this see Kinsella, N. Stephan, "Inalienability and Punishment: A Reply to George Smith," *The Journal of Libertarian Studies*, Vol. 14, No. 1, Winter 1998–1999, pp. 79–94; Kinsella, Stephan, "Punishment and Proportionality: the Estoppel Approach," *The Journal of Libertarian Studies*, 1996, Vol. 12, No. 1, Spring, pp. 51–74; Benson, Bruce, "Restitution in Theory and Practice," *The Journal of Libertarian Studies*, 1996, Vol. 12, No. 1, Spring, pp. 75–98.

Consider the basis upon which we as a society allocate other goods and services supplied by the public sector; there is not a one of them which is parceled out on the basis of intelligence. Included in this list would be admission to museums, libraries, playgrounds, beaches, recreation centers, wilderness areas, sports arenas, plays such as "Shakespeare in the Park," golf courses, the post office, hospitals, roads, streets, highways, the list goes on and on. Most of these are either for "free,"[140] or require a modest fee, and then utilize "first come first served" if there is excess demand. Where is the case for intellectual elitism only for public institutions of learning?

One possible exception to this rule is the military draft, a sort of "negative" service supplied by the state: there is a minimum level of intelligence required for acceptance. But the cutoff point commonly used is pegged at such a low point of the IQ bell curve[141] that for all intents and purposes, discrimination on the basis of intelligence does not affect the majority of the population, as it does in the field of education.

It may be objected that present admissions policy is inclusive. People on pretty much any point of the bell curve for intelligence will be accepted by a public institution of higher learning at *some* level; that, in any case, the limitations are no more stringent than those imposed by military personnel procurement.[142] And this cannot be denied. However, there is all the world of difference in the *quality* of the educational service offered at the top tier (e.g., the University of California at Berkeley), the mid tier (e.g., California State University at Hayward), and the bottom tier (any community college). Similarly, students attending the top tiers of the public educational establishment are typically statistically overrepresented with regard to scholarship awards.

But this is clearly unjust. Those funneled into the community colleges pay their taxes like anyone else. And there are some highly intelligent children of the very poor who attend the elite public universities, where far more than a proportional amount of money is lavished upon them.

---

[140] A misnomer, since they are financed through taxes.

[141] Herrnstein, Richard J., and Murray, Charles, *The Bell Curve: Intelligence and Class Structure in American Life*, New York: The Free Press, 1994.

[142] That is, under a policy of "open admission," anyone acceptable for military service will find a spot open for him at some college or other.

Of course, it cannot be denied that the present system is consonant with a rough approximation of justice (defined here as returning stolen tax money to students in proportion to the level of theft from their parents). After all, there is a strong and positive correlation between wealth and intelligence.[143] But this is not nearly good enough, since our information as to tax theft is at least as good as that concerning intelligence. That is, tax return information is more highly correlated with the level of depredation imposed by the government than are intelligence tests.

IX. Conclusion

The libertarian philosophy limits government to at most protecting people and their property from aggression. Education is a completely separate matter. When the state involves itself in illegitimate roles, it is in effect stealing the money necessary to finance them. The return of stolen property is a basic element of justice. Ideally, the state ought to be prevented from a continuation of its criminal behavior. Stipulate that this is for some reason impossible, and the analysis turns to the best way of erasing the effects of the theft. This, clearly, would be to award students benefits (both admission to poor, medium, or luxury institutions and scholarships) in proportion to the taxes improperly mulcted from them and their parents. Hence, the libertarian opposition to basing these awards on SATs, ACTs, or any other indications unrelated or under related to tax theft.

As it happens, both authors of the present chapter are employed by the University of Central Arkansas, a public institution of higher learning. Are we acting inconsistently? On the one hand, we are herein on record in maintaining that state education is incompatible with libertarianism, a philosophy we espouse; on the other hand, we have chosen to involve ourselves with this institution. Nor can we even avail ourselves of the excuse that we had no choice. We had; we could have worked at a private

[143] Herrnstein, Richard J., and Murray, Charles, *The Bell Curve: Intelligence and Class Structure in American Life*, New York: The Free Press, 1994; Levin, Michael, *Why Race Matters*, Westport, CT: Praeger, 1977.

university, or in an industry which is less under the control of government, for example, as a lawyer or economic consultant, respectively. Did we cleave to our principles fully, it might be charged, we even had the choice of starving to death. Such might be the only option of a libertarian living in North Korea, Cuba, or the old USSR, where virtually every enterprise was under state control, and therefore off limits for the likes of us.

But to put matters this way is to radically misunderstand the libertarian message. The illegitimacy, here, is *not* being employed by a public educational institution, but rather *favoring* it, and working to support, justify, defend, and expand this pernicious system. We are no more precluded from associating with a state university than we are traveling on governmental highways, or mailing a letter,[144] given that we also favor the privatization of these institutions. The point is, the guilty parties are those responsible for aiding and abetting this system, and *only* them; not innocents enmeshed in it.

One defense open to all libertarians involved in any way with illegitimate government enterprises is that we are only in this way attempting to have returned to us money stolen from us in order to finance them in the first place. And this, as far as it goes, it is a reasonable refutation of the charge of hypocrisy. The trouble is, it does not go far enough. For suppose a libertarian to come to us from the "forehead of Zeus," or from Mars; that is, by definition, a person from whom by stipulation could never have been previously victimized by unjust taxation. He would *still* be justified in working for a state college (or walking on a government road, or mailing a letter). Remember, it is in effect *stolen* funds which have gone to support these enterprises. The people who control them are the *thieves*. They have no right to stop our innocent newborn libertarian from availing himself of these services, for *they* are the guilty parties, not he.[145]

[144] For the case in favor of privatizing the post office see, Supra footnote 129. For this argument in the case of roads, streets and highways, see Supra footnote 131.

[145] For more on this, see Whitehead, Roy, and Block, Walter, "Mandatory Student Fees: Forcing Some to Pay for the Free Speech of Others," 20 *Whittier Law Review* 776 (1999).

Part III

Environment

8

The Unintended Consequences of Environmental Justice

I. Background

Two recent significant actions, a court of appeals decision and interim permitting guidance issued by the Environmental Protection Agency (EPA),[1] have created dangerous waves in the turbulent waters of environmental permitting for plant sites. Unless reversed, they forecast a regulatory nightmare for American industry that will result in a dramatic increase in the legal and economic risks associated with siting of industrial facilities. One important question is whether individuals or environmental groups have an implied private right of action in federal court to challenge the permitting and permit renewal process without exhausting available remedies before state or federal permitting agencies. As we shall soon see, the answer is probably yes. The fact that, when Title VI of the Civil Rights Act is considered, all three branches of government are involved gives considerable impetuous toward future unfettered filings of private causes of action in environmental justice cases. Prior to these unexpected regulatory actions, it was generally accepted that the federal or state permitting agencies served as gatekeepers to which private

[1] Public L. 88-352, 76 Stat. 241 (1964).

W. E. Block, R. Whitehead, *Philosophy of Law*, Palgrave Studies in Classical Liberalism,
https://doi.org/10.1007/978-3-030-28360-5_8

individuals or groups must administratively submit their opposition. These agencies could then exercise discretion about how to deal with the challenge. Astute management accountants, auditors, engineers, controllers, lawyers, and company executives involved in the selection of plant sites must be prepared to adopt management approaches suggested in this article to deal with the new permitting developments.

Another question, even more basic, is what is environmental justice and how does it impact plant citing vis a vis rich and poor neighborhoods, white and black ones. This essay will address both these narrow and broad issues, the former first.

II. Increasing the Risks of Plant Siting

President Clinton set the stage for this increased risk when he forcefully stated that one of the national priorities should be to establish environmental justice for minority and low-income communities by issuing Executive Order 12,898 (February 11, 1994). The Order broadly provides that all communities and persons across this nation should live in a safe and healthful environment. Then on December 30, 1997, the 3d Circuit Court of Appeals entered the arena when it discovered that a private cause of action exists to challenge the plant permitting process. And in February 1998, the Environmental Protection Agency (EPA) seized the initiative when it, citing the President s Executive Order, issued interim guidance that clearly recognizes a private cause of action in both the site permitting and renewal process.

Both the court decision and EPA interim guidance are rooted in a strained interpretation of a well-known Civil Rights statute.[2] Title VI that says that no person in the United States shall, on the grounds of race,

[2] According to some commentators, this law has a "noble purpose" behind it: an end to discrimination. For an alternative view, one which maintains that people have a right to interact with whomever they please on a mutually voluntary basis, that is, they have a right to discriminate (e.g., the right of free association), see; Levin, 1987. 1997. Block, Walter E. 1992. "Discrimination: An Interdisciplinary Analysis," The Journal of Business Ethics, Vol. 11, pp. 241–254; Rothbard, Murray N. 1998 [1982]. The Ethics of Liberty, New York: New York University Press; Epstein, Richard A. 1992. Forbidden Grounds: The Case Against Employment Discrimination Laws, Cambridge: Harvard University Press; Levin, Michael. 1987. Feminism and Freedom, New York:

color, or national origin, be excluded from participation in, be denied the benefits of, or be subjected to discrimination under any program or activity receiving any financial assistance. Whether those words can be strained to infer a private right of action in an environmental siting case is subject to considerable conjecture.

III. The Case

In *Chester Residents Concerned For Quality Living v. Seif*, Secretary of the Pennsylvania Department of Environmental Protection, No. 97-1125 (3d Cir. December 30, 1997), the appellate court dealt with the issue of whether a private cause of action exists under Title VI to challenge the permitting process. The city of Chester is located in Delaware County, Pennsylvania, and has a population of approximately 42,000, of which 65% is black and 32% is white. Delaware County, excluding Chester, has a population of about 502,000, 6.2% black and 91% white. The environmental group, Chester Residents Concerned for Quality Living, contended that state and environmental authorities had granted five waste facility permits for sites for the City of Chester since 1987, while only granting only two in the rest of Delaware County. It further charged that Chester facilities have a total permit capacity of 2.1 million tons of waste per year, while the non-Chester counterpart is only 1400 tons.

The court was faced with the question of whether a private right of action exists under the Discriminatory Effect Regulations promulgated by a federal administrative agency (EPA) under Title VI of the Civil Rights Act of 1964. The trial court found that no right of action exists which would allow a private individual to enforce the EPA civil rights regulations. The lower court believed that the permitting agency acted as a gatekeeper for these complaints. Title VI and the EPA s civil rights regulations implementing Title VI condition a state Department of Environmental Policy's receipt of federal funding on its assurance that it complies with Title VI and the regulations (40 CFR §7.80(a) (1997)).

Transaction Books; Levin, Michael. 1997. Why Race Matters: Race Differences and What They Mean, New York: Praeger.

These regulations prohibit recipients of federal funding, like state permitting boards, from using criteria or methods which have the effect of subjecting individuals to discrimination because of race, color, national origin, or sex.

The Third Circuit Court of Appeals decided that, in the absence of a statutory authorization, there is a three-prong test to determine when it is appropriate to trigger a private right of action to enforce government regulations. The test requires the court to determine:

Whether the issue is properly within the scope of the enabling statute;
Whether the statute under which the rule is promulgated properly permits the implication of a private right of action; and
Whether implying a private right of action will further the purpose of the enabling statute.

The appellate court held there was no question that the EPA's discriminatory effect regulation satisfies the first prong. The court said it is clear that actions having an unjustifiable disparate impact on minorities can be redressed through agency regulations designed to implement the purpose of Title VI. Announcing that the second and third prongs determined whether a private right of action existed, the court maintained it had to consider the relevant factors of:

Whether there is any indication of legislative intent, explicit and implicit, either to create such a remedy or to deny one; and
Whether it is consistent with the underlying purpose of the legislative scheme to find such a remedy for the plaintiff.

The court reviewed the law and regulations and agreed that there is some weight to the argument that the EPA, or a state permitting agency, are only a gatekeeper to enforcement, with private parties submitting their objections to the agency to act at its discretion. The court failed to enlighten the litigants by citing any explicit examples of a legislative intent to confer a private cause of action. The court, however, decided that private lawsuits are consistent with the underlying legislative scheme of Title VI, and as a result, the purposes of Title VI would best be served by allowing a private right of action. In sum, the activist court inferred an implicit indication in the legislative history of an intent to create a private right of action. It also found a private right of action as desirable since this will further the purposes of the statute. This is because it will "deputize private attorney's general who will enforce Title VI and its implementing regulation."[3]

Certainly, the foregoing decision should serve to warn those who are involved in risk management and plant siting to carefully consider the discrimination issues raised in the Chester case. The case, however, leaves unresolved several important questions. Is there a cause of action, for example, in the renewal of a site license? Shortly after decision in the Chester case, the Environmental Protection Agency released interim guidance that seems to deal with that question.

IV. EPA Interim Guidance

Citing the Presidents Executive Order 12,898, Federal Actions To Address Environmental Justice In Minority and Low Income Populations, the Environmental Protection Agency issued Interim Guidance for Investigating Title VI Administrative Complaints Challenging Permits, on February 5, 1998. The EPA cites the Chester case and flatly states that individuals may file a private right of action in court to enforce the nondiscrimination requirements in Title VI or the EPA's implementing regulations without exhausting administrative remedies. This means that the EPA and state permitting agencies are no longer considered by the agency as gatekeepers and allow private individuals direct access to the federal courts. This approach will obviously lead to increased environmental permitting litigation. The statement of agency policy will also likely have considerable influence on courts in other circuits which are, or soon will be, considering the same question.

Another section of the interim guidance should be frightening to all the individuals involved in plant siting. In the section Investigations of Alleged Discriminatory Permit Renewals, the interim guidance provides:

---

[3] Chester V. Seif. No. 97-1125 (3d Cir. Dec. 30, 1997).

> Generally, permit renewals should be treated and analyzed as if they were facility permits, since permit renewal is, by definition, an occasion to review the overall operations of a permitted facility and make any necessary changes. Generally permit renewals are not issued without public notice and an opportunity for the public to challenge the propriety of granting a renewal under the relevant environmental laws and regulations.[4]

The potential legal and management impact of that interim guidance is enormous because it is clearly relevant to renewals. Under the interim guidance, claims could be brought directly in federal court long after permits have been issued. This will give retroactive reach to environmental justice claims to jeopardize existing permits. It clearly will cause considerable reluctance to invest capital in and preclude otherwise beneficial development in the very minority and low-income communities that Title VI was intended to benefit.

V. Dealing with the Regulations

Taken together, the action of the 3d Circuit Court of Appeals in recognizing a private cause of action and the EPA interim guidance for investigating Title VI administrative complaints challenging permits foretell an explosion of regulatory and judicial activity in site permitting and renewals. Management accountants, auditors, controllers, engineers, facility owners, and executives must be alert to plan new construction and expansion carefully. Management of plant site selection and petitions for permit renewal should, at a minimum, involve the following:

An evaluation of the population of the city and county surrounding the proposed plant location;
A survey and evaluation of other plant sites and facility permits in the city and county;
An evaluation of how those facilities and permits impact on the protected classes of race, color, national origin, or low-income populations; and

[4] U.S. Environmental Protection Agency, Interim Guidance for Investigating Title V Administrative Complaints Challenging Permits, February 5, 1998.

A carefully balancing of the advantages of the plant site against the potential liability under the holding of the Chester case and the Environmental Protection Agency Interim Guidance.

There is only one quick and sure way to reverse this trend toward enlisting private attorney's general and bring economic sanity to the siting process. It is for Congress to adopt legislation clearly indicating that a private cause of action is not appropriate. Sadly, given the present congressional leadership's demonstrated timidity to act when faced with the administration's considerable ability to demonetize those who disagree in the area of minority and environmental rights, such action is not likely.

VI. The Philosophy of "Environmental Justice"

There is, however, another way to deal with this issue. It is neither quick nor sure, but it may be deeper and longer lasting. It is to call into question the very philosophical base upon which all such programs are predicted, the notion of "environmental justice."

We place quotation marks around this phrase to indicate that it is ideologically charged. As defined by its advocates, it depicts a world where poor and black neighborhoods are as environmentally pleasant as rich and white ones.

Before indicating why and in what sense such a state of the world would actually be *unjust*, a few distinctions must first be drawn.

One is between a lack of environmental amenities which constitute rights violations and those which do not. For example, living in a medium-sized city, the main industries of which are computers, universities, hospitals, and other such "clean" endeavors will undoubtedly be more ecologically desirable than in a large city which produces steel, automobiles, and leather tanning—even if strict environmental regulations are imposed on both. This is because of de minimus considerations: be the firms ever so careful, there will inevitably be some small amount of deleterious seepage in the latter case which does not apply to the former. As long as this falls safely under the threshold of what constitutes invasive behavior (Rothbard, 1990), there is no rights violation.

The second distinction is between a person "coming to the nuisance" and the nuisance coming to the victim. For example, suppose A has been living a quiet bucolic existence out in the country, where his land, except for a few crickets, is utterly silent. All of a sudden an airport opens up next door and inundates A at all hours with noise pollution. This would be a clear violation of his rights, since he had in effect homesteaded acoustical amenities. When these were torn from Mr. A, it was as if a possession of his was stolen.[5] In contrast, if B builds a house on an empty plot near an airport, then it was this facility which had homesteaded the rights to make noise, not him to a quiet environment. Were Mr. B to then turn around and sue the airport, it would the latter who would be in the right.

The third distinction is between being victimized by pollution by permission and against one's will. Mr. C wants to open up a pig raising and mushroom farming emporium. Both of these activities give off foul odors. If Mr. C blithely opens up shop, without a bye-your-leave from any of his neighbors, he is clearly violating their rights. They had homesteaded the relevant olfactory amenities which are now illicitly being

[5] For Coase, Ronald H. 1960. "The Problem of Social Cost," Journal of Law and Economics, 3: 1–44; Posner, Richard A. 1986. Economic Analysis of Law, third ed., Boston: Little Brown; Posner, Richard A. 1987. "The Law and Economics Movement," American Economic Review, 77(2): 2–13; and, Demsetz, Harold. 1979. "Ethics and Efficiency in Property Rights Systems," in Time, Uncertainty and Disequilibrium: Explorations of Austrian Themes, Mario Rizzo, ed., Lexington Mass.: D.C. Heath and Co; this would be an impossibility. In their view whether I should have the right to silence the airport the right to make noise depends upon who values it more. For a critique of this position see, Block, Walter E. 1977. "Coase and Demsetz on Private Property Rights," The Journal of Libertarian Studies: An Interdisciplinary Review, Vol. I, No. 2, Spring, pp. 111–115; Block, Walter E. 1995. "Ethics, Efficiency, Coasean Property Rights and Psychic Income: A Reply to Demsetz," Review of Austrian Economics, Vol. 8, No. 2, pp. 61–125; http://www.mises.org/journals/rae/pdf/r82_4.pdf; Block, Walter 1996. "O.J.'s Defense: A Reductio Ad Absurdum of the Economics of Ronald Coase and Richard Posner," European Journal of Law and Economics, Vol. 3, pp. 265–286; Cordato, Roy E. 1989. "Subjective Value, Time Passage, and the Economics of Harmful Effects," Hamline Law Review, Vol. 12, No. 2, Spring, pp. 229–244; Cordato, Roy E. 1992a. "Knowledge Problems and the Problem of Social Cost" Journal of the History of Economic Thought, vol.14, Fall, pp. 209–224; Cordato, Roy E. 1992b. Welfare Economics and Externalities in an Open-Ended Universe: A Modern Austrian Perspective, Boston: Kluwer; Krecke, Elisabeth. 1996. "Law and the Market Order: An Austrian Critique of the Economic Analysis of Law," Journal des Economistes et des Etudes Humaines 7(1), March, pp. 19–37; North, Gary. 1992. The Coase Theorem, Tyler, TX: The Institute for Christian Economics; North, Gary. 2002. "Undermining Property Rights: Coase and Becker," The Journal of Libertarian Studies: An Interdisciplinary Review, Vol. 16, No. 4, Fall, pp. 75–100; http://www.mises.org/journals/jls/16_4/16_4_5.pdf.

seized. However, suppose C *purchases* the right to waft foul odors over the property of the only persons negatively impacted. That is, these neighbors *voluntarily* agree to accept on his lands what would otherwise be deemed an improper odoriferous trespass. Would C *then* be guilty of untoward behavior? Of course not. But what of the *tenant* of D, Mr. E, who vociferously objects? Is not C guilty of ruining the environment if not for D, then for E? Again, we must answer in the negative. For the tenant has no direct rights to ecological values; his ownership cannot stretch any further than those of his landlord, D. But D has for a fee given up his right to a smell-free environment. As such he cannot also rent it to E. So E has no such rights. Of course, presumably, the rent E will have to pay D under the new regime will tend to be lowered, or not raised as fast as would otherwise occur. But this is entirely another matter.

With these preliminary distinctions in mind, we are now ready to consider permits for plant siting[6] in poor or black areas. (The two words shall be used interchangeably, given that blacks are average poorer than whites.)

One conclusion follows right off the bat. No permits should be granted for any factory, whether in rich or poor areas, where the pollution created thereby surpasses the level deemed compatible with the private property rights of other people. To allow this would be rights violating, a bringing of the nuisance to the victim, not the other way around, and must therefore be rejected. What, then, of industrial equipment which does not exceed such thresholds, but does render the surrounding areas less desirable? This, by definition, should be legal. However in a free market, they will tend to be confined to poorer (e.g., blacker) areas. This holds, except, of course, in cases where the surrounding property owners are willing to accept such facilities, in return for financial compensation.

---

[6] We are assuming, but only for the sake of argument, that there is a case for plant siting; for example, a system whereby firms must first obtain the permission of the state to erect buildings. For the view that this is in effect prior restraint, that factories should be able to locate wherever their owners wish, subject only to a lawsuit if they violate the rights of others (e.g., pollute) see, Rothbard, Murray N. 1982. "Law, Property Rights, and Air Pollution," Cato Journal, Vol. 2, No. 1, Spring; reprinted in Economics and the Environment: A Reconciliation, Walter E. Block, ed., Vancouver: The Fraser Institute, 1990; http://www.mises.org/rothbard/lawproperty.pdf; http://mises.org/story/2120; Block, Walter, ed., Zoning: Its Costs and Relevance for the 1980s, Vancouver: The Fraser Institute, 1980; Block, Walter, "Zoning: A Tragic Public Policy," The Freeman, August 1981, pp. 470–477.

Many commentators look in horror at such a phenomenon.[7] After all, they will ask, why should people, just because they are poor, have to put up with less than fully desirable surroundings?[8] Our critics are asserting in effect that the poor have as much right to a home overlooking the city as the rich, and we are maintaining that this claim is without merit. The point is, once we abstract from rights violations, we are left only with that which is more or less pleasant. Our contention is that unless additional funds can be used to purchase those things which make life more enjoyable (e.g., better views, safer neighborhood, more acreage of plot, more square feet of housing space, limousines, etc.), there is little reason to work harder or smarter to earn extra money. And without such incentives, civilization tends to fall apart, and with it general economic well-being.

Then, of course, there is the sheer justice of the matter. Why *shouldn't* a Bill Gates or a Michael Jordan be able to afford better environments than those of us with less money? It is *their* wealth, and to deny them the right to spend it on any legitimate goods and services they may wish such as a better environment is in effect to steal from them. Why should the rest of us, who have made fewer contributions to the well-being of our fellow citizens, enjoy equally desirable neighborhoods as a Gates or a Jordan?

Let us now consider some specific cases. If it is unfair for blacks to have the short end of the stick environmentally speaking,[9] it must also be improper that they, on average, drive older automobiles, don't eat as "high off the hog," have fewer computers, take fewer luxurious cruises, and are less well represented in high-end private schools. If we as a society are required to right the wrongs of "environmental racism," we must also alter these other perhaps more subtle instances of "*economic* racism."

---

[7] Dr. Benjamin Chavis, Testimony before the U.S. House of Representatives Committee on the Judiciary, Subcommittee on Civil and Constitutional Rights, Oversight Hearing: Environmental Justice, March 3, 1993.

[8] Remember, we are now talking about environments which, although they may be less desirable, are not rights *violating*. This is the difference, for example, between a house in a valley, with no view, and one on top of a hill, looking down upon a spectacular panorama.

[9] Again, it is not that their *rights* are violated, only that their surroundings are not as desirable as richer, on the average, whites.

A moment's thought, however, will disabuse us of this notion. There is a good, sufficient, and *just* reason why whites should be better housed, fed, educated, transported, and so on than blacks. They are richer, on average. This has little or nothing to do with race,[10] and much to do with wealth. Michael Jordan, Mike Tyson, Spike Lee, Oprah Winfrey, Jimmy Brown, Richard Roundtree, Michael Johnson, Evander Hollyfield, Roy Jones, Dr. Dre, John Singleton, Ice Cube, Vernon Jordan, Naomi Campbell, Iman, Shaquille O'Neil, Carl Lewis, Robin Givens, Johnny Cochran, Eddy Murphy, Will Smith, Denzel Washington and Halle Berry can all have if they wish Rolls Royces, lobster every night, Choate and Harvard, private jets, and trips to Europe. The can also, if they choose, live in upscale neighborhoods with every environmental amenity known to man. In contrast, poor whites for the most part just like poor blacks must do without such benefits. They must also live in more environmentally challenged neighborhoods, because they lack the requisite funds to do better for themselves.[11]

Let us attack this issue from another perspective: consider the issue of who initiates "environmental racism." The presumption of the critics is and must be that "environmental racism" is initiated by whites, or by the power structure, or "society," or some such. After all, murder, rape, and

[10] For an economic analysis in support of this contention, see Becker, Gary. 1957. The Economics of Discrimination, Chicago: The University of Chicago Press; Sowell, Thomas. 1975. Race and Economics. New York: Longman; Sowell, Thomas. 1981. Markets and Minorities, New York, N.Y.: Basic Books; Sowell, Thomas. 1982. "Weber and Bakke and the presuppositions of 'Affirmative Action,'" Discrimination, Affirmative Action and Equal Opportunity, Walter E. Block and Michael Walker, eds., Vancouver: The Fraser Institute, pp. 37–63; Sowell, Thomas. 1983. The Economics and Politics of Race: An International Perspective. New York, Morrow; Sowell, Thomas. 1984. "Civil Rights: Rhetoric or Reality," New York: William Morrow; Sowell, Thomas. 2000. Basic Economics: A Citizen's Guide to the Economy. New York, N.Y.: Basic Books; Block, Walter E. 1992. "Discrimination: An Interdisciplinary Analysis," The Journal of Business Ethics, Vol. 11, pp. 241–254; Block, Walter and Williams, Walter, E. 1981. "Male-Female Earnings Differentials: A Critical Reappraisal," The Journal of Labor Research, Vol. II, No. 2, Fall, pp. 385–388; Epstein, Richard A. 1992. Forbidden Grounds: The Case Against Employment Discrimination Laws, Cambridge: Harvard University Press; Levin, Michael. 1987. Feminism and Freedom, New York: Transaction Books; Levin, Michael. 1997. Why Race Matters: Race Differences and What They Mean, New York: Praeger. Williams, Walter, E. 1982. The State Against Blacks, New York, McGraw-Hill; Rothbard, Murray N., For a New Liberty, Macmillan, New York, 1973.

[11] Of course, using international comparisons, poor people in the United States, white and black, live immeasurably better than their counterparts in many areas of the world. Virtually *everyone* in America now has air conditioning, color tv, refrigeration, a telephone, an automobile, and so on. The same, unfortunately, cannot be said for even the middle class in most countries on the globe.

theft are begun not by the victims, but by the perpetrators. Were this not the case, these acts would not be crimes at all but something very different. For example, murder would be converted into assisted suicide, rape into seduction, and theft into gift giving.[12] That is, if A asks B to kill him, and perhaps even pays him to do so, this may be a crime in some jurisdiction,[13] but it is certainly not first-degree murder; rather, it is assisted suicide. If a woman asks a man to have sex with her, however this is characterized, it cannot be considered rape. And if C *requests* that D "rob" him, it is not theft. C and D may be trying to steal from a third party, such as an insurance company, but that is another matter; D is no longer initiating a real holdup of C.

To put this into other words, if it is the blacks who are initiating "environmental racism," then this not only cannot be considered a crime, it cannot even be considered an injury to them.

How, then, and in what ways do the poor bring upon themselves "environmental racism"? It is simple. When offered a choice between a cheap dwelling with few environmental amenities, and an expensive one with many, they tend to choose the former. When moving into Manhattan, for example, a poor or black person will locate in Harlem, or in the lower east side, rather than on Fifth Avenue in the 60s. The latter offers a very

[12] Here is a parallel to the blackmail literature. An act can be considered blackmail no matter *who* initiates the threat (usually to release secret and embarrassing information) coupled with the demand (usually for money, or perhaps sexual services). This to say the least is an anomaly, at least compared to the way we treat murder, rape, and robbery. It is part of the case for the legalization of this activity. On this, see Block, Walter and David Gordon. 1985. "Extortion and the Exercise of Free Speech Rights: A Reply to Professors Posner, Epstein, Nozick and Lindgren," Loyola of Los Angeles Law Review, Vol. 19, No. 1, November, pp. 37–54; Block, Walter E. 1986. "Trading Money for Silence," University of Hawaii Law Review, Vol. 8, No. 1, Spring, pp. 57–73; reprinted as Block, Walter E. 1987. "Trading Money for Silence?" Economic Imperialism: The Economic Approach Applied Outside the Traditional Areas of Economics, Peter Bernholz and Gerard Radnitzky, eds., New York: Paragon House, pp. 157–218; Block, Walter E. 1997. "The Case for De-Criminalizing Blackmail: A Reply to Lindgren and Campbell," Western State University Law Review, Vol. 24, No. 2, spring, pp. 225–246; Mack, Eric. 1982. "In Defense of Blackmail," 41 Philosophical Studies 274; Rothbard, Murray N. 1982. The Ethics of Liberty, Humanities Press, Atlantic Highlands, N.J. pp. 124–126, 245–249; Rothbard, Murray N., Man, Economy and State, Auburn AL: Mises Institute, 1993.

[13] Not libertarian ones. On this, see Rothbard, 1982, ibid; Hoppe, Hans-Hermann. 1989. A Theory of Socialism and Capitalism. Economics, Politics, and Ethics, Boston: Kluwer Academic Publishers; Hoppe, Hans-Hermann, ed. 2003. "National Defense and the Theory of Externalities, Public Goods and Clubs." The Myth of National Defense: Essays on the Theory and History of Security Production, Hoppe, Hans-Hermann, ed., Auburn: Mises Institute.

nice environment, with access to Central Park, but at a very high price. The best that can be said for the former areas, environmentally speaking, is that rents are relatively cheap there. Not only does this phenomenon apply to neighborhoods, it applies to towns as well. Very few poor people can be found in Scarsdale, N.Y., or Indian Wells, California, towns with many environmental amenities, where a small house sells for a half million dollars or more. Rather, they locate in poor towns, such as College Station, Arkansas, or Lake Charles, Louisiana, where housing is far cheaper and environmental benefits far fewer.

So, if the poor, of their own volition, move to less attractive areas so as to take advantage of the cheaper real estate prices available there, how can "environmental racism" be considered an attack on them? It cannot. As it happens, matters are very much to the contrary. For suppose that the self-styled green antiracists have their way, and succeed in rendering all neighborhoods, areas, towns, and so on *equal*, environmentally speaking. This would mean that real estate prices, too, would tend toward a rough similarity. But this would prevent blacks from stretching their dollars further, by occupying environmentally deprived areas. The green self-proclaimed antiracists, then, are no friends of the black or poor communities.

Advocates of "environmental racism," were they to be logically consistent, would have to favor spreading rich and poor people, blacks and whites, homogeneously throughout the environment. Bill Gates and Michael Jordan will have to live cheek by jowl with the homeless, and denizens of the Bowery, no matter what are their desires in this regard. This is justice?

One way to promote "environmental racism" is, as we have seen, for the poverty stricken to seek out cheap real estate with few environmental amenities. But the direction of causation can also take place in the opposite direction. That is, sometimes a factory, plant, or mill initiates matters, by locating in a poor area.

On superficial examination, this would appear to be more like the murder, rape, or theft cases discussed above. Here, the presumed "bad guy" is at least initiating the harm. But this too should be legally unobjectionable, despite surface appearances.

First of all, the incursion of the commercial endeavor must be with the permission of the *owners* of the property in question. Only they can sell to a newcomer, and they would only do so if in their own minds, they benefitted more from the sale price than they lost from the alienation of their holdings. The tenants occupying the areas surrounding the new enterprise will of course lose out, given our assumption that these new structures are not environmentally attractive. But if so, their rent levels will fall, and we are in effect back at our first case, where poor racial minorities *voluntarily* trade environmental amenities for cold hard cash.

Secondly, various self-styled spokesmen for blacks and poor people (e.g., Wilson, 1985) have long and bitterly complained about the fact that factories are *deserting* inner city areas. They characterize *this* as a form of racism. It would thus appear that the verdict is already in, all that needs to be done is to specify the particular charge: capitalism is guilty of racism no matter what it does. If factories *leave* black areas, they are racist in that they are not providing enough jobs; if they stay there, or enter for the first time, then they are *environmental* racists.[14]

What we may take from this discussion is the fact that plant location is a double-edged sword for the poor. Yes, it reduces environmental amenities, but, other things equal, it increases job availability. It is only under a free enterprise system that poor blacks (and everyone else for that matter) are allowed to make such tradeoffs for themselves. Plant location regulation, whether based on the fallacious notion of "environmental racism" or racism due to factory desertion, denies this. If the cause of the environmental disparity is economic rather than racism, the tactic of prohibiting industrial development in minority and poor areas will harm the very communities that proponents of the "environmental racism" theory propose to aid.

[14]Wilson (Wilson, William Julius. 1987. The Truly Disadvantaged: The Inner City, the Underclass, and Public Policy. University Of Chicago Press) is entirely mistaken in thinking that firms would leave the inner city out of a racist desire to exacerbate black unemployment. They relocate out of these areas, on the contrary, because union-inspired minimum wage laws render such operations unprofitable (Becker, Gary. 1995. "It's simple: Hike the minimum wage, and you put people out of work." Business Week. March 6, p. 22; http://www.bloomberg.com/bw/stories/1995-03-05/its-simple-hike-the-minimum-wage-and-you-put-people-out-of-work). Often, they relocate to the south or to third world countries which are relatively free of such obstructions to enterprise. A high incidence of crime in these areas provides another disincentive.

9

Environmental Justice Risks in the Petroleum Industry

I. The Hazard

In practically all of its various forms, petroleum is potentially hazardous to the environment. As a result, virtually every activity engaged in by the petroleum industry can have profound environmental implications. For many years, environmental considerations have played a role in decisions regarding the siting of petroleum production, refining, or storage facilities. Recent case law and regulatory developments in "environmental justice," however, assure that environmental considerations that affect minority communities will play an increasingly critical economic role in both the permitting process and, perhaps most importantly, the permit renewal process. This article discusses the recent developments, suggests preventive management techniques to deal with the new challenges, and proposes a better process of environmental justice in order to benefit minority populations living near the sites. The article will accomplish this by addressing the legal and regulatory environmental barriers to the petroleum site permitting and renewal process, reviewing the Environmental Protection Agency's "environmental justice" compliance guidance, and suggesting pre-permit management techniques to educate

W. E. Block, R. Whitehead, *Philosophy of Law*, Palgrave Studies in Classical Liberalism,
https://doi.org/10.1007/978-3-030-28360-5_9

citizens of the affected community so as to minimize the hidden contingent costs of "environmental justice" complaints.

II. Background

To incorporate environmental considerations into capital budgeting, a company must constantly monitor changes in environmental law. Astute petroleum executives, attorneys, controllers, auditors, investors, and management accountants must be able to identify potential hidden environmental costs resulting from compliance with environmental regulations. The Institute of Management Accountants has recognized this need by issuing two helpful statements, No. 4W, Implementing Corporate Environmental Strategies, and No. 4Z, Tools and Techniques of Environmental Accounting for Business Decisions.

Few contemporary issues are more emotionally charged than environmentalism and its underlying values. Legitimate policy controversies are generally portrayed as battles between victimized citizens and corporate polluters. In this context, it is difficult not to side with the environmentalists.[1]

This context, however, often represents a misleading and false dichotomy, which may actually operate to direct beneficial social and economic resources away from the poor, minority communities that the regulations were intended to benefit.[2] It is reasonable to assume that the type of community most likely to accept a new factory would be a town where more jobs are needed and increased tax revenue from the facility would benefit the area. There is scant evidence that the Environmental Protection Agency ("EPA") takes into account the wishes or needs of the affected minority community in the decision making process.[3] Decision makers must be aware that their good faith motives and community support for a facility may not be determinative with government regulators and the courts.

[1] See Frank B. Cross, The Subtle Vices Behind Environmental Values, 8 DUKE ENVTL. L. & POL'Y F. 151, 151 (1997).

[2] See id. at 151.

[3] For example, in the Louisiana Shintech matter (see infra Part IX) 73% of the black residents and 100% of the black public officials favored the plant. See Robyn Blumner, Standing in the Way of Jobs, WASH. TIMES, Oct. 3, 1998, at C7.

III. Studies

Throughout the 1970s and 1980s, a variety of empirical studies purported to find evidence of environmental injustice. One of the first studies examined population data for Houston, Texas area communities where landfills and incinerators were located.[4] The study concluded that minority neighborhoods supported a disproportionate number of waste facilities.[5] A second study, conducted by the U.S. General Accounting Office in 1983, analyzed population demographics in communities adjacent to waste facilities in the Southeast.[6] This study also reported that a disproportionate number of such facilities were located in minority and/or poor communities.[7] Another frequently cited study was published by the Commission for Racial Justice of the United Church of Christ in 1987.[8] It too reported evidence of environmental racism.[9]

Although many of these studies have been frequently cited in order to bolster the position taken by advocates of the environmental justice cause, some experts have questioned the results of the studies on the basis of methodological flaws. One such problem has to do with the studies' definition for "minority communities" which classifies any community as a minority community if it has a higher proportion of nonwhite residents than that reflected in national statistics.[10] As a result, the studies categorize some communities as "minority" even if they have a large majority of nonminority residents. A related problem is that the studies focus on the minority proportion of the population in high pollution areas, rather

[4] Robert D. Bullard, Solid Waste Sites and the Black Houston Community, 53 SOC. INQUIRY 273 (1983).

[5] See id. at 285.

[6] U.S. GENERAL ACCOUNTING OFFICE, GAO REPT. No. RCED-83-168, SITING OF HAZARDOUS WASTE LANDFILLS AND THEIR CORRELATION WITH RACIAL AND ECONOMIC STATUS OF SURROUNDING COMMUNITIES REPORT (1983).

[7] See generally id.

[8] THE UNITED CHURCH OF CHRIST COMM'N FOR RACIAL JUSTICE, TOXIC WASTES AND RACE IN THE UNITED STATES: A NATIONAL REPORT ON THE RACIAL AND SOCIOECONOMIC CHARACTERISTICS OF COMMUNITIES WITH HAZARDOUS WASTE SITES (1987).

[9] See generally id.

[10] See Laura Pulido, A Critical Review of the Methodology of Environmental Racism Research, 28 ANTIPODE 142 (1996).

than population densities. As a result, the studies ignore the actual number of minority or low-income residents exposed to hazardous waste.[11]

Still another potential flaw-of these studies is the potential for significant aggregation error resulting from defining geographic areas too broadly.[12]

These studies have also failed to consider the timing of hazardous material sitings relative to shifts in the population.[13] In other words, due to the dynamic nature of the housing market, population shifts toward a higher proportion of minority and/or poor residents may have occurred after the siting of hazardous material facilities in some locations.[14] In fact, one article suggests that economic factors, not environmental racism, are the real cause of the observed population differences surrounding hazardous materials facilities.[15] Another problem with much of the environmental justice research is that the studies focus exclusively on the number of facilities located in minority/poor neighborhoods, failing to consider the amount and type of pollution actually involved.[16]

IV. A Definition

The Environmental Protection Agency defines environmental justice as fair treatment for people of all races, cultures, and incomes, regarding the development of environmental laws, regulations, and policies.[17] Since the early 1990s, there has been a steady increase in the incidence of claims that minority and low-income populations bear a disproportionate amount of negative health and environmental effects from pollution,

---

[11] See id.

[12] See id.

[13] See Vicki Been, Locally Undesirable Land Uses in Minority Neighborhoods: Disproportionate Siting or Market Dynamics?, 103 YALE L.J. 1383, 1385 (1994).

[14] See id. at 1388.

[15] Thomas Lambert & Christopher Boerner, Environmental Inequity: Economic Causes, Economic Solutions, 14 YALE J. REG. 195 (1997).

[16] Andrew Holmes & Larry B. Cowart, Environmental Racism: The New Liability for Industrial Site Selection, REAL ESTATE ISSUES, Apr. 1996, at 1.

[17] See generally 40 C.F.R. § 7.30 (1999) (prohibiting discrimination under any EPA program or activity).

often as a result of environmental racism—the intentional siting of hazardous waste facilities in predominately minority and low-income areas.[18] Now the President, the EPA, and the courts have acted to expand greatly the definition of "environmental justice" to include not only the evils of intentional discrimination, but also unintended "disparate impact" discrimination.[19]

Disparate impact discrimination flows from practices that are not intended to discriminate, but for some reason have an unintended, but discriminatory, disparate effect on a protected class.[20] For example, an employer may have a policy that it only hires the relatives of current employees. Well-intentioned reasons may exist for this policy, such as increasing employees' loyalty to and knowledge of the company.

However, if all the current employees are white, the policy will have a discriminatory disparate impact on qualified blacks, who will never be employed at this company. The Clinton Administration and the EPA seem to believe that there is a vast conspiracy between state environmental regulators and regulated industries to impose a disparate impact by locating industrial facilities in low-income and minority neighborhoods.[21]

V. Setting the Stage

Whether or not claims of environmental racism are adequately supported by sound scientific research, President Clinton moved environmental justice to the forefront of the national agenda when he issued Executive Order 12898 on February 11, 1994.[22] This Order broadly provides that "disproportionately high and adverse human health or environmental effects … on minority populations and low-income populations,"[23] shall

[18] "S See Blumner, supra footnote 3, at C7.

[19] See id.

[20] See id.

[21] See id.

[22] Exec. Order No. 12, 898, 3 C.F.R. 859 (1995), reprinted as amended in 42 U.S.C. § 4321 (1994 & Supp. IV 1998).

[23] Id. at 859.

be identified and addressed. The Order further requires each cabinet of the government to make environmental justice a part of its mission.[24]

In the past, it was generally accepted that federal or state permitting agencies served as gatekeepers to which private individuals or groups must submit their opposition to siting permits. These agencies could then exercise discretion in dealing with such challenges. However, several recent significant developments, in the form of a court of appeals decision,[25] an EPA policy statement,[26] and a controversial EPA decision in the Louisiana Shintech case,[27] have the potential to open the flood-gates for additional private actions in environmental permitting for plant sites. The obvious result would be a dramatic increase in the legal and contingent economic costs associated with siting of industrial facilities.

VI. New Developments

The first critical question is whether private individuals or environmental activists have an implied private cause of action in federal court to challenge the permitting and permit renewal process without first exhausting available remedies with state or federal permitting agencies.

The Third Circuit Court of Appeals provided an affirmative answer to this question when it discovered that a private cause of action does exist to challenge the plant permitting process.[28] In February 1998, the Environmental Protection Agency seized the initiative when, citing the President's Executive Order, it issued a policy statement in the form of an interim guidance that clearly recognizes a private cause of action in

[24] See id.

[25] Chester Residents Concerned for Quality Living v. Seif, 132 F.3d 925 (3d Cir. 1997).

[26] OFFICE OF ENVIRONMENTAL JUSTICE, UNITED STATES ENVIRONMENTAL PROTECTION AGENCY, INTERIM GUIDANCE FOR INVESTIGATING TITLE VI ADMINISTRATIVE COMPLAINTS CHALLENGING PERMITS (1998); http://www.epa.gov/oeca/oej/titlevi/html [hereinafter INTERIM GUIDANCE].

[27] In re Shintech, 746 So. 2d 601 (La. Ct. App. 1999).

[28] See Chester Residents Concerned for Quality Living v. Seif, 132 F.3d 925, 932–37 (3d Cir. 1997).

both initial site permitting, and more surprisingly, the permit renewal processes.[29]

Both the court decision and the EPA interim guidance are rooted in an interpretation of The Civil Rights Act of 1964 (the "Act").[30] Title VI of the Act says that "no person in the United States shall, on the grounds of race, color, or national origin, be excluded from participation in, be denied the benefits of, or be subjected to discrimination under any program or activity receiving Federal financial assistance."[31] Whether the Act infers a private right of action in an environmental siting case has been the subject of considerable conjecture.[32]

VII. The Chester Case and Private Permit Challenges

When decided, Chester Residents Concerned for Quality Living v. Seif[33] was widely regarded as having the same effect on environmental law as the Brown v. Board of Education [34] desegregation case did on education law. Although the appeal of the Chester decision was recently vacated by the U.S. Supreme Court as moot because the contested facility decided to surrender the challenged permit in question,[35] the initial decision provides a valuable roadmap to follow for courts evaluating private causes of action. It is beneficial to understand the case because, the theory espoused

[29] See INTERIM GUIDANCE, supra footnote 26, at 3.

[30] 42 U.S.C. §§ 2000d to 2000d-7 (1994).

[31] U.S.C. § 2000d.

[32] See generally Chowdhury v. Reading Hosp. and Med. Ctr., 677 F.2d 317 (3d Cir. 1982) (alleging racial discrimination in denial of staff privileges at federally-assisted hospital); Guardians Ass'n v. Civil Serv. Comm'n of New York, 463 U.S. 582 (1983) (asserting discriminatory impact of police appointments made based on written examination scores); Alexander v. Choate, 469 U.S. 287 (1985) (claiming that limitation on number of allowed hospital days funded under Medicaid has a disproportionate and discriminatory effect on the handicapped).

[33] 132 F.3d 925 (3d Cir. 1997).

[34] Brown v. Board of Educ., 347 U.S. 483 (1954).

[35] See Seif v. Chester, 524 U.S. 974 (1998) (citing United States v. Munsingwear, 340 U.S. 36 (1950) for the proposition that the withdrawal of the permit application rendered the case moot).

by the court is recognized by other federal circuits, is cited in EPA permitting regulations, and similar cases will surely arise again.

In *Chester*, the appellate court dealt with the issue of whether a private cause of action exists under Title VI to challenge the permitting process.[36] "The City of Chester is located in Delaware County, Pennsylvania, and has a population of approximately 42,000, of which 65% is black and 32% is white. Delaware County, excluding Chester, has a population of about 502,000 of which 6.2% is black and 91% is white."[37] The environmental group, Chester Residents Concerned for Quality Living, contended that state and environmental authorities had

> granted five waste facility permits for sites in the City of Chester since 1987, while only granting two permits for sites in the rest of Delaware County. It further alleges that the Chester facilities have a total permit capacity of 2.1 million tons of waste per year, while the non-Chester facilities have a total permit capacity of only 1,400 tons of waste per year.[38]

The court was faced with the question of whether a private right of action exists under the Discriminatory Effect Regulations promulgated by a federal administrative agency (EPA) under Title VI of the Civil Rights Act of 1964.[39] The original trial court found that no private right of action exists that would allow a private individual to enforce the EPA civil rights regulations,[40] thus affirming that the state permitting agency acts as a gatekeeper for such complaints. Title VI and the EPA's civil rights implementing regulations condition the receipt of federal funding by a state's permitting agency on its assurance that it complies with Title VI and the regulations.[41] "[T]hese regulations prohibit recipients of federal funding from using 'criteria or methods … which have the effect of

[36] See Chester, 132 F.3d at 927.

[37] See id. at 927, n. 1.

[38] id.

[39] See id.

[40] See Chester Residents Concerned for Quality Living v. Seif, 944 F.Supp. 413, 417 (E.D. Pa. 1996).

[41] See 40 C.F.R. § 7.80(a) (1999).

subjecting individuals to discrimination because of their race, color, national origin, or sex....'"[42]

On appeal, the Third Circuit decided that in the absence of a specific statutory authorization, there is a three-pronged test—to determine when it is appropriate to imply a private right of action to enforce government regulations.[43] The test requires the court to determine "(1) 'whether the issue is properly within the scope of the enabling statute'; (2) 'whether the statute under which the rule was promulgated properly permits the implication of a private right of action'; and (3) 'whether implying a private right of action will further the purpose of the enabling statute.'"[44]

The appellate court said that "[t]here [was] no question that the EPA's discriminatory effect regulation satisfies the first prong."[45] The court also said it is clear that "'actions having an unjustifiable disparate impact on minorities [can] be redressed through agency regulations designed to implement the purpose of Title VI.'"[46] Announcing that the second and third prongs determined whether a private right of action existed,[47] the court found that it had to consider the relevant factors of "(1) whether there is 'any indication of legislative intent, explicit and implicit, either to create such a remedy or to deny one'; and (2) whether it is 'consistent with the underlying purposes of the legislative scheme to imply such a remedy for the plaintiff.'"[48]

The court reviewed the law and regulations and agreed that there was some weight to the argument that the EPA, or a state permitting agency, acts only "as a gatekeeper to enforcement, with private parties submitting their allegations to the agency and its discretion."[49] The court failed to

---

[42] Chester Residents Concerned for Quality Living v. Seif, 132 F.3d 925, 928 (3d Cir. 1997) (quoting 40 C.F.R. § 7.35(b) (1997)).

[43] See id. at 933.

[44] "Id. (quoting Polaroid Corp. v. Disney, 862 F.2d 987, 994 (3d Cir. 1988)).

[45] id.

[46] Id. (quoting Alexander v. Choate, 469 U.S. 287, 293 (1985)).

[47] See id.

[48] Chester Residents Concerned for Quality Living v. Seif, 132 F.3d 925, 933 (3d Cir. 1997) (quoting Cort v. Ash, 422 U.S. 66, 78 (1975)).

[49] Id. at 935.

enlighten the litigants by citing any explicit examples of a legislative intent to confer a private cause of action.[50] It decided that private lawsuits are consistent with the underlying legislative scheme of Title VI.[51] The court also said that a private right of action is desirable "because it will deputize private attorneys general who will enforce section 602 and its implementing regulations,"[52] and will further the purposes of Title VI.[53]

The foregoing decision should serve as a signal to those involved in risk management and siting decisions to consider carefully the discrimination issues involving disparate impact raised in the Chester case. The case, however, leaves unresolved several important questions. Is there a cause of action, for example, in the renewal of a site license? The interim guidance released by the EPA shortly after the Chester decision deals with that question.

VIII. EPA Interim Guidance Follows Chester

On February 5, 1998, in connection with the President's Executive Order 12898, Federal Actions To Address Environmental Justice In Minority Populations and Low Income Populations, the EPA issued its Interim Guidance for Investigating Title VI Administrative Complaints Challenging Permits ("the Guidance"). The EPA cites the Chester case with approval and flatly states that "individuals may file a private right of action in court to enforce the nondiscrimination requirements in Title VI or EPA's implementing regulations without exhausting administrative remedies."[54] With the interim guidance, this means that the EPA and state permitting agencies are no longer considered by the agency as gate-keepers; private individuals now gain direct access to the federal courts.

[50] See id. at 936.

[51] See id.

[52] id.

[53] See id.

[54] See INTERIM GUIDANCE, supra footnote 26, at 4.

The Agency announced a five-step framework for determining whether a disparate impact exists, that is subject to this private cause of action.[55] The steps are:

1. To identify the population affected by the permit that triggered the complaint. The affected population is that which suffers the adverse impacts of the permitted activity;
2. To determine the racial and/or ethnic composition of the affected population;
3. To identify which other permitted facilities, if any, are to be included in the analysis and the racial and/or ethnic composition of the population already affected by those permits. This is referred to as the universe of facilities;
4. To conduct a disparate impact analysis to determine whether persons protected under Title VI are being impacted by the facility at a disparate rate. The EPA expects the rates of impact for the protected population and comparison populations to be relatively comparable; and
5. To use arithmetic or statistical analysis to determine whether the disparity is significant under Title VI. After calculations, the EPA may make a prima facie disparate impact finding, subject to the recipient's opportunity to rebut.[56]

The recipient will have an opportunity to "justify" the decision to issue a permit, based on legitimate, substantial interests of the recipient, notwithstanding the resulting disparate impact.[57] Demonstrating that the permit complies with applicable environmental regulations will not ordinarily be considered a legitimate justification.[58] Rather, an articulable value to the recipient must be found.[59]

The types of factors that will be considered in determining the sufficiency of the justification can include the seriousness of the disparate

[55] See id. at 9–11.

[56] See id.

[57] See id. at 12.

[58] See id.

[59] See INTERIM GUIDANCE, supra footnote 26, at 12.

impact, whether the permit is a renewal (with demonstrated benefits) or for a new facility (with more speculative benefits), and whether any of the articulated benefits associated with the permit can be expected to assist the affected minority community that is a subject of the complaint.[60] An offered justification will not be considered acceptable if there is a less discriminatory alternative that lessens the adverse disparate impact.[61] This approach obviously will lead to increased environmental permitting litigation. The statement of agency policy will likely have considerable influence on courts who are, or soon will be, considering the same question as in Chester.

Another section of the Guidance should be of even greater concern to all managers involved in decisions to seek permit renewals. In the section, "Investigations of Allegedly Discriminatory Permit Renewals," the Guidance provides:

> Generally, permit renewals should be treated and analyzed as if they were facility permits, since permit renewal is, by definition, an occasion to review the overall operations of a permitted facility and make any necessary changes. Generally, permit renewals are not issued without public notice and an opportunity for the public to challenge the propriety of granting a renewal under the relevant environmental laws and regulations.[62]

The potential legal and management impact of the Guidance is enormous because it is clearly relevant to permit renewals. Consequently, under the Guidance, disparate impact claims may be brought directly in federal court long after permits have been issued. "Jeopardizing existing permits by giving retroactive reach to environmental justice claims is likely to cause considerable reluctance in related capital investment decisions. Although unfortunate, a likely result is the abandonment of otherwise beneficial economic development in the same minority and low-income communities that Title VI was intended to benefit."[63] In fact,

---

[60] See id.

[61] See id.

[62] Id. at 8.

[63] See Henry Payne, 'Environmental Justice,' Kills Jobs for the Poor, WALL ST. J., Sept. 16, 1997, at A22.

Detroit Mayor Dennis Archer is pushing to scale back federal involvement in environmental justice cases because he wants to attract industry to minority neighborhoods.[64] Press reports indicate that some manufacturers are avoiding black areas because of the interim guidance.[65]

IX. The EPA Guidance in Action: The Shintech and Select Steel Decisions

The "minority community economic development be damned" approach is illustrated by the EPA's Shintech decision in February 1998.[66] This case illustrated that a permit already granted by Louisiana's Department of Environmental Quality could be delayed.[67] The stated reason was that polluting industries locate in minority areas because their residents are powerless to stop them. The action was taken despite local National Association for the Advancement of Colored People (NAACP) polls that showed that 73% of the black residents of Convent favored the plant location.[68] According to a lawyer representing town residents, the EPA and opposing nonresident activists also ignored the favorable opinions of all the locally elected black officials.[69] The community residents were excited because the average wage paid by Shintech was $12.00 to $15.00 per hour compared to the prevailing community wages of $6.00 per hour.[70] Shortly after the EPA's decision, Shintech abandoned the project and moved to another location.[71]

The Shintech decision has generated considerable criticism from governors, mayors, and chambers of commerce because it is viewed as failing

[64] See Lynette Clemetson, A Green Bottom Line, NEWSWEEK, Nov. 2, 1998, at 53.

[65] See Blumner, supra footnote 3, at C7.

[66] See United States Environmental Protection Agency, In re: Shintech Inc., Order Responding to Petititoners' Requests That the Administrator Object to Issuance of State Operating Permits, Permit Nos. 2466-VO, 2467-VO, 2468-VO; http://www.epa.gov/rgytgrnj/programs/artd/air/title5/t5memos/shin1997.pdf [hereinafter Shintech].

[67] See id. at 21.

[68] See Payne, supra footnote 63, at A22.

[69] See id.

[70] See id.

[71] See Vicki Ferstel, Environmental Justice Under Scrutiny, BATON ROUGE ADV., Feb. 7, 2000, at lB.

to follow the interim guidance by taking into account the demonstrated economic benefits of the facility for the community.[72] Sadly

> when government actions are driven by public perception and pressure groups, those actions generally are responding to middle class concerns and ignoring the problems of the poor.[73]

A result favorable to industry was handed down in an October 30, 1998, decision concerning Select Steel Corporation.[74] In Select Steel, the EPA's Office of Civil Rights carefully followed the five-step framework previously discussed.[75] The private complaint charged that the Michigan Department of Environment Quality's permit for a steel recycling mill would lead to a discriminatory, disparate impact on minority residents in Genesee County.[76] The EPA followed the interim guidance's framework by determining the affected population,[77] determining the demographics of the affected population,[78] determining the universe of the facilities and the total affected population, and conducting a disparate impact analysis.[79] The EPA found that there was no affected population that suffered "adverse" impacts within the meaning of Title VI.[80] The EPA dismissed the private complaint.[81] The decision was obviously influenced by the Michigan Department of Environmental Quality's careful investigation of the permit application that generally followed the EPA's guidance. The decision signals that a permit applicant that initially applies the interim

---

[72] See John H. Cushman Jr., Pollution Policy is Unfair Burden, States Tell E.P.A., N.Y. TIMES, May 10, 1998, at Al.

[73] Cross, supra footnote 1, at 157.

[74] See OFFICE OF CIVIL RIGHTS, UNITED STATES ENVIRONMENTAL PROTECTION AGENCY, INVESTIGATIVE REPORT FOR TITLE VI ADMINISTRATIVE COMPLAINT FILE No. 5R-98-R5 (SELECT STEEL COMPLAINT); http://www.epa.gov/reg5oopa/pdf/sel-steel.pdf [hereinafter SELECT STEEL COMPLAINT].

[75] See supra text accompanying footnote 56.

[76] See SELECT STEEL COMPLAINT, supra footnote 74, at 1.

[77] See id. at 12.

[78] See id.

[79] See id.

[80] See id. at 25–27.

[81] See id. at 40.

guidance's five-step approach in preparing the application will likely receive a reasoned response from the EPA.

X. Managing Environmental Justice Issues

Taken together, the president's executive order, the philosophy of the Chester case recognizing a private cause of action, the EPA's interim guidance for investigating Title VI private administrative complaints challenging permits, and the EPA's application of the Guidance foretell an explosion of regulatory and judicial activity in site permitting and renewals. All parties involved, including managers, controllers, investors, creditors, and auditors would be wise to consider the impact of these developments. These developing concerns must be carefully managed. First, the five-step framework established by the interim guidance and the EPA decisions in Shintech and Select Steel provide helpful guidance. Recall that the EPA decision in Select Steel complimented the Michigan state agency for essentially following the interim guidance. So the following, at a minimum, should be accomplished prior to requesting a permit:

- An evaluation of the population of the city and county surrounding the property in question to determine the racial and ethnic composition that will be affected by the permit.
- A survey and evaluation of other plant sites and facility permits in the city and county.
- An evaluation of the impact of those facilities and permits on the protected classes of race, color, national origin, or low-income populations; and,
- A disparate impact analysis to determine whether protected persons affected by the new facility will suffer a disparate impact and whether the impact is significant.

Even if disparate impact is found, bear in mind that the permit may still be "justified" based on a legitimate, substantial interest of the recipient.[82] Factors that may be considered are the seriousness of the disparate

[82] See INTERIM GUIDANCE, supra footnote 26, at 12.

impact, whether the permit is a renewal (with demonstrated benefits), or, perhaps most importantly, whether the articulated benefits can be expected to assist the minority community.[83] Surely, as Mayor Dennis Archer advocates, jobs and tax revenues can be considered a substantial benefit.[84]

One other very practical concern that is not often addressed is how to educate the affected community about the facility and its impact on them.[85] Many applicants for permits allow activists with no connection to the community to capture the issue and dominate the discussion.[86] "Environmental activists tend to be white, middle-aged, middle-class professionals—not young, blue collar workers or blacks."[87] They often do not reflect the concerns of the poor minority residents. How then do you beat the activists to the hearts and minds of citizens of the affected community? One often overlooked way is to utilize Section 101 of the National Environmental Policy Act of 1969 ("NEPA").[88] The section focuses on "productive harmony" as the goal of federal actions, including "social, economic, and other requirements of present and future generations of Americans."[89] The section advocates the importance of citizen participation and perspective through an interactive, integrated process to improve final decisions, and discovering the "widest range of beneficial uses of the environment."[90] A way to preempt and manage intrusion has been developed by the environmental consulting firm of James Kent and Associates of Aspen, Colorado.[91] By going into the community and informally identifying the leaders and disruptive issues prior to the permitting

[83] See id.

[84] See Clemetson, supra footnote 64, at 53.

[85] See Clemetson, supra footnote 64, at 53.

[86] See id.

[87] Id.

[88] 42 U.S.C. §§ 4321–4370d (1994 & Supp. IV 1998).

[89] 42 U.S.C. § 4321.

[90] Id.

[91] See Interview with James Kent and Associates of Aspen, Colorado (transcript on file with authors) [hereinafter Interview].

process, the firm helps its clients avoid the kind of activist interference that evolved in the Shintech case.[92]

Pre-permit application contact with community members provides opportunities to integrate the project successfully with local leaders and networks.[93] The community contacts allow the permit applicant to institute "issue tracking" mechanisms so citizens can understand how their interests are being addressed, thereby building public support for the project and focusing decision making on the informed interests of the community.[94] Recognizing the values of the local community allows for the social and physical environment to be linked together into a plan that will accommodate their interests and achieve the "productive harmony" contemplated by section 101 of the Act.[95] Such action will signal to the regulators that the permit applicant is accommodating the "community interests" and, as in the Select Steel case, is likely to receive a favorable response from the regulators.[96]

Some might express concern about the costs associated with initially following the five-step framework of the interim guidance[97] or the section 101 citizen participation advocated by the Kent firm.[98] The alternative, however, of a contested permit surely is much more costly in terms of money, personnel, and resources. The funds expended on pre-permit management are money well-spent. In addition, business decision makers will find that community support makes for a smoother transition in other, nonenvironmental facets of siting a facility in a new town. It is in a business' best interest to get the community involved, and the diminu-

[92] See id.

[93] See id.

[94] See id.

[95] See id.

[96] A prominent theme in a review of the National Environmental Policy Acts effectiveness is "issue stacking." The term refers to issues identified at the professional or community level that are catalogued, saved, and analyzed in the Environmental Impact Statement process, thereby providing many opportunities for early resolution and building community support. See Lynton Caldwell, Beyond NEPA: Future Significance of the National Environmental Policy Act, 22 HARVARD ENVTL. L. REv. 203, 203–09 (1998).

[97] See supra text accompanying footnote 56.

[98] See Interview, supra footnote 91.

tion of a threat of a suit is just one of many reasons for better community involvement.

XI. Philosophical Difficulties

Another way to manage the problem might be to encourage petroleum companies to reward or compensate communities for hosting a facility such as an oil refinery. A compensation system ensures that all who benefit from the facility pay the full cost that the facility imposes on society.[99] However, there are philosophical difficulties with "encouraging" companies to pay communities for foisting oil refining facilities on them. First of all, such "encouragement" often translates into the legal obligation for firms to make pay-offs at some point in time for such purposes. After all, if it is sound public policy to "encourage" the petroleum industry to compensate host communities, it will reasonably be asked why this should not be formalized in law. Moreover, suppose an oil refiner refuses to do that which it is "encouraged" to do. This would promote uneven results, and the calls to require that firms live up to their compensatory duty will be overwhelming.

Secondly, and more basically, the direction of compensation is by no means clear. There is indeed a case for forcing (or "encouraging") an oil company to make a payment to the locality. After all, operating in that vicinity will help the firm or it would not have chosen to locate there. On the other hand, the town gains as well, or it would not welcome the company with open arms. More to the point, the people in the area benefit from this commercial immigrant. With regard to paying this "compensation," there are three options open to the new petroleum firm: it can offer wages below, equal to, or in excess of, those already prevailing. If the oil company proffers less salary than presently being earned by the local workers, they will spurn this opportunity. Even a roughly comparable salary (with due consideration given to the nonmonetary aspects of the job) will likely be insufficient to woo them away from their present

[99] See STEPHEN HUEBNER, ARE STORM CLOUDS BREWING ON THE ENVIRONMENTAL JUSTICE HORIZON? 21–22 (1998).

employment; why leave your job for something that is not preferable in any way? Only if the wage and working conditions package is better than those that are already prevailing will the new corporation be able to attract a labor force. Typically, the improvement must be substantial to overcome the status quo.[100] Thus, if there is any compensating to be done, there is at least as good a case that the local community should be compensating the petroleum firm; the direction of compensation should actually be reversed.

But all talk of compensation, in either direction stems from economic illiteracy. All commercial interaction, whether in the goods or labor market, is mutually beneficial in the ex-ante sense. Both parties to a trade expect to gain from it in some form, and this is their motivation for entering into a transaction. Suppose, for example, that a housewife purchases a fish for $4. She would not have done so if she places a value on this item of less than this amount. Assume that she values it at $5. Then she earns a profit of $1 on the deal. But the identical reasoning applies on the other side of the equation. The retailer would never have sold the fish at this price unless he valued it at less than this amount. Let us suppose that he assigned a value to it of $3. Then he earns a profit of $1 on the exchange. So, who should compensate whom for this sale? The entire question is ludicrous. Both gain from it.[101] It is the same with the location of the oil industry in the town; there is no warrant for compensation in either direction, for the market is a mutually beneficial institution.

Suppose, however, that there is a winner and a loser. While this cannot occur ex-ante, it certainly could take place ex-post. For example, suppose the seller, but not the housewife, later comes to regret his decision. That is, the price of fish rises to $50 right after the sale at $5 takes place, and the fish monger comes running after the housewife, demanding compensation (or a rescission of the sale). What are we to make of such a claim?

---

[100] As we have seen, the pay offered by Shintech was about $15.00 per hour compared to the prevailing $6.00 community wage.

[101] In the ex-ante sense, that is. In the ex-post sense, the housewife may later learn that her family had fish for lunch, and doesn't want to eat it for dinner as well. Had she known that, she would not have made the purchase for any positive price. Thus, she loses her entire expenditure. Similarly, a fish shortage might suddenly ensue, driving the market price of fish up to $50. The seller, then, would greatly regret his precipitate sale. The ex-ante gains from trade are always positive, necessarily so. Ex-post, they are only usually positive, depending on the skills of the market participants.

It is abject nonsense, since the commercial interaction was "for keepsies" in the terminology of the playground, and not unilaterally revocable.[102] The bottom line here is that it is a misunderstanding of the market to think that compensation should be "encouraged" or legally mandated just because gains from trade are made. Gains from trade are always made in the free market, and by both sides. If compensation had to be made under such conditions, the death knell of free enterprise would begin to toll.

XII. Vote with Feet

We have seen above that, according to an NAACP poll in Louisiana, 73% of the black residents favored a new oil industry plant in their town.[103] Some people may object and argue that there are falsehoods in polls. Similarly, the views of black politicians welcoming Shintech may also be disparaged by left-wing environmentalists [104] within the EPA noting that elected officials are chosen on the basis of many criteria. Therefore, their views on any one issue such as siting a plant may not be representative of those of their constituents.[105]. But there is one indication of black accep-

[102] Similarly, it would be just as wrong to "encourage" or force, the fishmonger to return the housewife's money to her if she later came to regret her purchase, say, because her family was tired of fish. Now it might be that the seller will do this in any case, in order to keep a loyal customer, for example, for the goodwill involved. But it should be no part of public policy to "encourage" him to do so, and certainly not to require any such act on his part.

[103] See Payne, supra footnote 63, at A22.

[104] "Left wing environmentalist" is by no means a tautology, nor, by the same token, is "free market environmentalist" an oxymoron. For instances of the latter, see generally, Terry L Anderson & Peter J. Hill, Property Rights as a Common Pool Resource, in BUREAUCRACY VS. ENVIRONMENT: THE ENVIRONMENTAL COSTS OF BUREAUCRATIC GOVERNANCE (John Baden and Richard L. Stroup eds., 1981); TERRY L ANDERSON & DONALD R. LEAL, FREE MARKET ENVIRONMENTALISM (1991).

[105] It is interesting to compare the dollar vote of the marketplace with the ballot box vote of the political system in this regard. In the latter, "consumers" are allowed to express themselves only once every two or four years; in the former, every day. In the political system, the choice is limited to a "package deal." One must vote for Clinton or Bush overall, for example, and cannot pick Clinton on monetary, trade, and farm policy, and Bush on labor, taxes, and "ethics." In very sharp contrast, in the economic market it is possible to focus one's vote. This may be done so narrowly as to distinguish between colors and brands of cars and ties, for example. For the case that voters are not at all akin to consumers, examine the claim of the Public Choice School. See JAMES

tance of the "environmental racism," of plant location in their areas which cannot so easily be dismissed: "voting with one's feet."

Consider again the fact that black response to hazardous material sittings has been to move toward these locations after they have been set up.[106] This shows, perhaps in a way that no other evidence can, the true evaluation on the part of poor blacks of these plant locations; it is one of enthusiastic approbation.

It was no coincidence that there was only one-way Jewish traffic with regard to Nazi Germany in the late 1930s; no Jews wanted to enter, all wanted to leave. Similarly, immigration in the 1950s was to the United States and from Cuba, not the other way around. Likewise, the movement across the Berlin Wall was from East to West, not from West to East.[107] Another indication of where life was better concerned blacks in the U.S. south during the Jim Crow decades. Very few moved from Detroit, Chicago, New York, and Philadelphia to Alabama, Mississippi, and Arkansas; the overwhelming majority moved in the opposite direction. The point is, when people are free to migrate, can telephone or write encouraging messages to their friends and family still "back home," and the migration continues, this is some of the strongest evidence we have as social scientists that geographical relocation is an improvement.[108]

M. BUCHANAN & GORDON TULLOCK, THE CALCULUS OF CONSENT: LOGICAL FOUNDATIONS OF CONSTITUTIONAL DEMOCRACY (1971); WALTER BLOCK & THOMAS DiLORENZO, A CRITIQUE OF THE PUBLIC CHOICE THEORY OF THE STATE, Addleton Academic Publishers (2017).

[106] See Lambert & Boerner, supra footnote 15 passim.

[107] On the importance of voluntary migration patterns as an indication of the underlying social welfare involved, see generally THOMAS SOWELL, MIGRATIONS AND CULTURES: A WORLD VIEW (1996).

[108] Very few people will question the fact the Jews were better off away from the Nazis, Cubans escaping Castro, Germans out from under the yoke of the Communists, and blacks free of Jim Crow restrictions. But the same analysis can be applied to several other much more controversial cases. For example, black migration patterns were toward the Republic of South Africa in pre-Mandela days. This suggests that as bad as the white apartheid regime was for these peoples, it was an improvement over the neighboring black-run countries. Similarly, the migration from the countryside to the cities during the Industrial Revolution indicates that these changes constituted an improvement in the lives of the poor, not a retrogression. On this latter case, see generally CAPITALISM AND THE HISTORIANS (F. A. Hayek ed., 1954), which includes essays by T. S. Ashton, L. M. Hacker, W. H. Hutt, and B. de Jouvenel.

The fact that poor and black people are attracted to the higher paying jobs in the petroleum industry is very strong evidence that they regard the package of slightly dirtier air and higher wages as preferable to the slightly cleaner air and lower wages back where they came from. Nothing could more dramatically indicate that in the eyes of ostensible "victims" of environmental racism, this was a good thing. In effect, the blacks are saying, "if this is environmental racism, we want more of it."

XIII. Paternalism

However, these arguments are not good enough for the EPA and others who complain about "environmental racism." For not only are they left-wing environmentalists, they are paternalists as well—a poisonous combination.

What is paternalism? It is the view that the elites[109] know better what benefits the people (particularly the poor and blacks) than do they themselves. Since the elites know better, they also adopt the right to impose their vision on these people "for their own good." Nowhere is this mind set more clearly articulated than in the debate now raging over social security.[110] The underlying premise of this program is that the people have too high a rate of time preference (or are too stupid) to be able to save for their old age. Therefore, the government is justified in forcing them to do "in their own interest" what they (perversely) do not now believe to be in their own interest.[111]

For example, "…there is some justification for the government to mandate, as the Chilean government does in its private system, sufficient saving during working years so that most people will have a privately provided old age income that exceeds the designated income floor."[112] The minor objection to Barro is that it is somewhat misleading to call the

[109] See THOMAS SOWELL, THE VISION OF THE ANOINTED (1995) (calling elites "the anointed").

[110] See Robert J. Barro, Don't Tinker with Social Security. Reinvent It, 4 HOOVER DIGEST 11 (1998).

[111] See id.

[112] Id.

Chilean system "private" in that it stems from the barrel of the government's gun.[113] A more serious one is that it implies that unless savings "exceeds' the designated income floor," the government will step in with "a welfare program" (e.g., rob the parsimonious Peter to pay the spendthrift Paul). But why should the government engage in massive theft from the more thrifty? Another difficulty has to do with the rate of time preference. Why do the paternalists of the world assume that one time preference is better than another, and that the government can unerringly hit upon the "correct" one. Certainly, no reasons are given in support of this curious contention.

Perhaps the most serious objection of all to paternalism, at least from the point of view of its adherents, is that this doctrine is logically incompatible with our democratic institutions. And this applies to all paternalism, whether concerned with child labor, minimum wages, maximum hours, savings, or, in the present case, "environmental racism." If there are people so stupid, so childlike, so unsophisticated, so unworldly, so simple-minded, so credulous, so unwary, that their savings or geographical locational decisions cannot be relied upon, then why and how can they be entrusted with the vote? Why should we not, according to this very mischievous argument, take away the suffrage from all blacks, all poor people, and all those whose savings rate is not to the liking of our rulers? Needless to say, down this path lies totalitarianism and fascism. All men of goodwill, of necessity, would have to pull back from this logical abyss with horror. But then the same may be said of the "environmental racism" which is an integral part of this perspective.

XIV. Conclusion

But we have not yet plumbed the depths of this philosophy. So far we have only scratched the surface, showing how "environmental racism" law is a legal and administrative nightmare, will harm its supposed ben-

[113] Try not saving as much as this government thinks is good for you and see what happens. To be sure, it is reasonable to distinguish between a program imposed by the government and one run by it, but the former is not private and the latter public. Both are within the purview of the government.

eficiaries, constitutes a "taking"[114] against the petroleum industry, attacks private property rights, and is paternalistic. It is now time to take off the gloves and challenge the underpinnings of the EPA's version of "environmental justice" by taking a people friendly, economically responsible and environmentally concerned approach to the siting of facilities.

[114] See generally RICHARD A. EPSTEIN, TAKINGS: PRIVATE PROPERTY AND THE POWER OF EMINENT DOMAIN (1985).

10

Environmental Takings: The Case for Full Water Privatization

1. Introduction

In the summer of 2001, the eyes of the nation were focused with considerable discontent on the California electrical power crisis. But, alas, a worse crisis is lurking in the arid West.[1] The demand for water exceeds the supply. What about the most beneficial use of water in California and the West? Even some Californians are said to use water for purposes other than adult beverages. All sorts of troubling issues arise in the allocation of precious water. Recently, in the Klamath Basin of Oregon, the Bureau of Reclamation breached a 1909 contract to provide water to farmers to protect the sucker fish, a bottom-feeding scavenger. The government's action may result in as many as 1400 farmers filing for bankruptcy.[2] It has

[1] *See generally*, Mort Rosenbum, *As All Eyes Turn to the Power Crunch, a Worse Crises Looms: Water*, www.tbo.com/ap/breaking/MGA4ZWIKNMC.html (Last visited Jan. 21, 2002). Rosenbum contends that the planet has no more water than it did a millennia ago. But with today's rocketing growth, conflicting needs of farms, cities, industry, recreation, and government wetlands protection, there exists the potential for bitter water wars. But where have these wars happened? Nowhere, according to Bjorn Lomborg, *The Skeptical Environmentalist*, 149 (2001). He says the water problem is logistical rather than a shortage.

[2] *See*, Michael Kelly, *Evicted by Environmentalists*, Washington Post, July 11, 2001, at A19, Col. 1. Mr. Kelly points out that all the battles over the Endangered Species Act are episodes in a continu-

W. E. Block, R. Whitehead, *Philosophy of Law*, Palgrave Studies in Classical Liberalism,
https://doi.org/10.1007/978-3-030-28360-5_10

already driven some of them to acts of civil disobedience by cutting open the dam gates to release water into their parched fields.[3] How should be water be allocated? Should it go to farmers to raise crops or should the Federal government intercede under the Endangered Species Act and impose water use restrictions to protect endangered fish species.[4] If water is taken from the user, who should suffer?[5] Should this be all of society, or solely the impacted farmers? Some concerned commentators contend that there is a significant public policy danger in requiring compensation for environmental takings because the government engages in many actions that reduce property values. They contend that to require the government to pay negatively affected owners is a recipe for inaction on important environmental issues.[6] This section of the article responds by examining the thorny legal and ethical questions that arise when agricultural water users have the contractually-conferred right to access water taken from them because the Federal government imposes water use restrictions under the Endangered Species Act. The case of *Tulare Lake Basin Storage District v. United States*[7] entangled the court in the thorny issues raised above and presents a unique medium to use to decide whether the taking of contractually-conferred water rights constitutes a

---

ing war of values fundamental to the nation. This war is best understood as taking place between increasingly poor and powerless rural voters and those voters in increasingly rich and powerful urban-suburban areas. Because few people are still in direct contact, and competition with nature, and directly affected by environmental decisions, the balance of power has shifted away from the rural residents who are today's stewards of the land, to the urban voters.

[3] *See*, Kimberley L. Strassel, *Thoreau the Bums Out: Oregon's Farmers Embrace Civil Disobedience*, Wall Street Journal, July 12, 2001, at A21, Col. 4.

[4] It has come to the point in the west where "endangered species protection is the most significant factor in water shortages," says Janet Raloff, *Endangered Species Are Keeping Some Landowners Thirsty*, Science News, Vol. 160, No. 22, Dec. 1, 2001, p. 344.

[5] The leftists want capitalists and the rich to suffer for the sake of the poor and the greens want property owners to suffer, "for the sake of lower animals and inanimate nature," states George Reisman, *Capitalism: a treatise on economics*, 102, Jameson Books, 1996.

[6] For this proposition, *See generally*, the editorial, *Taking Lake Tahoe*, Washington Post, Jan. 20, 2002, at p. B6, where the editors articulate the constitutionally suspect position that the determination to compensate landowners should be a policy judgment, not a constitutional command. But when does a policy judgment made by a government agency trump the Constitution? The *Post*'s proposition is nonsense on stilts and the answer is easy; never.

[7] 49 Fed.Cl. 313 (2001).

"taking" of protected property under the Fifth Amendment of the United States Constitution.[8]

2. Facts

This controversy commenced with efforts by the Fish and Wildlife Service to protect the Delta smelt and the winter-run Chinook salmon, two species of fish said to be in jeopardy of extinction.[9] The effort to protect the fish, specifically by restricting water out-flows in California's primary water distribution system, bring into conflict the Endangered Species Act and California's century-old regime of private water rights. The science that the Fish and Wildlife service is relying on by increasing water flows to protect the fish is questionable.[10] But that issue is beyond the scope of this article.[11]

The California water system involves a transport of water from water-rich areas in Northern California to the more arid parts of the state.[12] Various water projects and aqueduct systems have been built to facilitate that goal. Two of them, the Central Valley Project (CVP) and the State

[8] U.S. CONST. amend. V. states, "…nor shall private property be taken for public use, without just compensation." See, generally, Epstein, Richard A., *Takings: Private Property and the Power of Eminent Domain*, Harvard University Press, Cambridge, Massachusetts and London, England, 1985.

[9] Tulare Lake Basin Storage District v. United States, 49 Fed. Cl. 313 (2001).

[10] The National Academy of Sciences has concluded that federal biologists had "no substantial scientific foundation" for their efforts to protect endangered fish by withholding water in the Klamath Basin. *See* Michael Grunwald, *Scientific Report Roils a Salmon War*, Washington Post, Feb. 4, 2002, A1, Col. 1. The Academy concluded that the data "has not shown a clear connection between the water level in upper Klamath Lake and conditions adverse to the welfare of the suckers." It noted that "the best year ever recorded for sucker survival was a low-water year." Chuck Cushman of the American Land Rights Association is quoted as saying of the Fish and Wildlife biologists, "You can't trust the science, because you can't trust the scientists. They've got a biased point of view, and there is no way to fight back."

[11] But faith in the ethics of government agencies has been destroyed in the West by instances of "bio-fraud" on the part of government employees in cases involving the alleged planting of lynx and grizzly fur in an attempt to establish evidence of a habit under the Endangered Species Act. *See*, Valerie Richardson, *'Biofraud' Angers West, Taints Federal Stewards*, The Washington Times, Jan. 21, 2002. She relates that many Westerners view the Endangered Species Act as a device to move people off the land they developed and love.

[12] 49 Fed. Cl. at 314.

Water Project (SWP) are the focus of this case. In order to operate the two projects, water is diverted from the Feather and Sacramento Rivers, captured by the pumping systems located at the southern edge of the Sacramento-San Joaquin Delta, and then distributed through a series of canals to end-users in Southern California.[13]

Both Bureau of Reclamation (BOR) and Department of Water Resources (DWR) are granted water permits by the State Water Resources Control Board (the Board), a state agency given the ultimate authority of controlling, appropriating, using, and distributing state waters.[14] BOR and DWR in turn contract with county water districts, conferring on them the right to withdraw or use certain quantities of water.[15] The plaintiff farmers in this case contract directly with the state water project.[16]

The water projects are required to be financially self-sustaining, with the cost of construction and maintenance to be paid entirely by those who ultimately receive the water. The water contractors are thus obligated to pay to maintain the operation of the system regardless of the amount of water actually received for their benefit.[17] Because the amount of water available to users in a particular year is largely a function of natural causes, however, permits explicitly provide that the state will not be liable for shortages due to drought or other causes beyond its control.[18]

Against this backdrop of water transportation entitlements, Congress passed the Endangered Species Act of 1973 (ESA).[19] That Act was designed to "halt and reverse the trend toward species extinction, whatever the cost," *Tennessee Valley Authority v. Hill.*[20] In *Tennessee Valley,* the

[13] Id.

[14] Id. at 315.

[15] Id. at 315.

[16] Id.

[17] Id.

[18] Id.

[19] 16 U.S.C., sections 1531–1544 (1994).

[20] 437 U.S. 153, 184 (1978). Here the court considered the famous snail darter case and decided to allow enforcement of the Act whatever the cost. Whatever the cost seems a bit extreme. Should there not be some balancing of the opposing interests? Some consideration, for example, of the interests of creatures with opposable thumbs who happen to be the stewards of private property. Some consideration of the millions of taxpayer dollars spent on a nearly completed dam? This is exactly what Justice Powell advocated in his dissent. He wrote, "This decision casts a long shadow over even the most important projects, serving vital needs of society and national defense, when-

court was confronted with the situation that millions of federal dollars had already been appropriated and spent on a dam on the Tennessee River. The majority decided that the Congress had spoken in the plainest words, making it clear that endangered species were to be accorded the highest priority.[21] The majority decided that Congress intended to give the act precedence over the primary missions of government agencies.[22] Accordingly, the ESA requires them to consult with the Secretary of the Interior about actions that might harm endangered species.[23] In fulfillment of the duties assigned to it under the ESA, the National Marine Fishery Service (NMFS) initiated discussion with the Federal Bureau of Reclamation and the California State Department of Water Resources to determine the impact of the Central Valley Project and the State Water Project on the winter-run Chinook salmon.[24] As a result, the NMFS issued a biological opinion on February 14, 1992, concluding that the proposed operation of SWP and CVP was likely to jeopardize the continued existence of the salmon population. Included in the Agency's finding was a reasonable and prudent alternative (RPA) designed to protect the fish by restricting the time and matter of pumping the water out of the Delta.[25] As a result, water that otherwise would have been available for distribution to the farmers was made unavailable.

Sadly, the whole process was repeated the following year, with the addition of a biological opinion from the U.S. Fish and Wildlife Service that the Delta smelt was at risk. Again, reasonable and prudent alterna-

---

ever it is determined that continued operation would threaten extinction of an endangered species or its habitat" 437 U.S. 195–196. He continued, "I view it as the duty of this court to adopt a permissible construction that accords with some modicum of common sense and the public weal" 437 U.S. 196.

[21] 437 U.S. at 183.

[22] Id at 181.

[23] This consultation is to "insure that any action authorized, funded, or carried out by such agency ... is not likely to jeopardize the continued existence of any endangered species or threatened species..." 16 U.S.C. section 1536(a)(2) (1994).

[24] 49 Fed.Cl. at 315.

[25] Where activities of a federal agency are seen to jeopardize the continued existence of listed species or cause the destruction or adverse modification of critical habitats, the Act directs the secretary to suggest "reasonable and prudent alternatives" to avoid such harms; *see* 16 U.S.C. section 1536 (b) (3) (A) (1994).

tives were adopted that again restricted the time and manner in which water could be pumped into the Delta, thereby further limiting the water available to the distribution system.[26]

On March 19, 1992, the State Water Resources Control Board addressed the National Marine Fishery Service's first biological opinion. Recognizing that the Bureau of Reclamation and Department of Water Resources could not comply with the reasonable and prudent alternative and still meet the water quality standards imposed on them by their permits by the State Water Resources Control Board, the Board concluded that the Federal requirements under the Endangered Species Act overrode the contractual terms set forth in the permits.[27] In order to maintain the quality of the water, the State Water Resources Control Board adopted the National Marine Fishery Service's reasonable and prudent alternative that resulted in a considerable restriction on the amount of water that the plaintiffs could draw from the project.[28]

The reasonable and prudent alternative implemented deprived the Tulare Lake Basin Water District of at least 9770 acre-feet of water in 1992, at least 26,000 acre-feet of water in 1993, and at least 23,050 acre-feet[29] of water in 1994. The Kearn County water agency lost a minimum of 319,428 acre-feet over the same period.[30]

3. The Issue

The Fifth Amendment to the United States Constitution concludes with a phrase: "Nor shall private property be taken for public use, without just compensation." The purpose of that clause, according to the leading case of *Armstrong v. United States* is, "to bar government from forcing some

[26] 49 Fed.Cl. at 315.

[27] Id.

[28] Id. at 315.

[29] An acre-foot of water is the amount necessary to raise the level of water of a pond with the area of an acre by one foot. It is equal to 43,560 cubic feet or 325,851 gallons or 1233 cubic meters.

[30] Id.

people alone to bear public burdens which, in all fairness and justice, should be borne by the public as a whole."[31]

The issue is not whether the Federal Government has statutory authority to protect the winter-run Chinook salmon and Delta smelt under the Endangered Species Act. It may. Rather, the critical issue is whether it may impose the cost of their protection solely on the plaintiff farmers.[32]

---

[31] 364 U.S. 40, 49 (1960). Here, a contractor had a state lien on an uncompleted vessel and the material furnished for its construction. The builder of the vessel had a contract that allowed the United States to require the builder to transfer title to the government on default. The United States contended that after default it was immune from paying the contractor's liens. Justice Black wrote, "[T]he total destruction by the Government of all value of these liens, which constitute compensable property, has every element of a Fifth Amendment 'taking' and is not a mere 'consequential' taking" 364 U.S. at 48.

[32] A similar issue arises with regard to rent control. Given, arguendo, that it is a governmental responsibility to guarantee the poor, cheap rental accommodation, it by no means logically follows that the entire expense of this program be the responsibility of landlords alone, as opposed to the general taxpayer. After all, we have similar policies concerning feeding the poor, and manage to acquit this "responsibility" without saddling grocers and restaurateurs, alone, with the entire expense. For the general case against rent control, see: Arnott, Richard J., and Mintz, Jack M., *Rent Control: The International Experience*, Kingston Ontario: John Deutsch Institute, 1987; Baird, Charles, *Rent Control: The Perennial Folly*, Washington D.C.: The Cato Institute, 1980; Block, Walter, and Edgar Olsen, eds., *Rent Control: Myths and Realities*, Vancouver, The Fraser Institute, 1981; Block, Walter, "A critique of the legal and philosophical case for rent control," *Journal of Business Ethics*; Block, Walter, "Rent Control: A Tale of Two Canadian Cities," *Mid Atlantic Journal of Business*, Vol. 25, No. 7, 1989, pp. 85–88; Block, Walter, "An Analysis and Evaluation of *Rental Housing in the City of New York: Supply and Conditions 1975–1978* by Peter Marcuse," *International Journal for Housing Science*, Vol. 4, Number 4, Fall 1980, pp. 343–359; Block, Walter, "The Negative Impact of Government Policies on the Built Environment," *International Journal of Housing Science*, Vol. 5, No. 2, Spring 1981, pp. 131–140; Block, Walter, "Rent Control: A Case Study of British Columbia," *Mid Atlantic Journal of Business*, Vol. 30, No. 3, December 1994, pp. 299–304; Block, Walter, "Housing is Not a basic human right," *Canadian Housing*, Vol. 6, No. 1. Spring 1989, pp. 30–31; Block, Walter, "Rent Controls – Who Benefits and Who Is Hurt," *Housing in Canada: A Continuing Challenge*, Paul Cosgrove and Raymond V. Hession, eds., Don Mills, Ontario: The Canadian Real Estate Association, 1982, pp. 197–209; Block, Walter," On Rent Control," David Henderson, ed., *The Fortune Encyclopedia of Economics*, New York: Warner Books, 1993, pp. 421–425; Block, Walter, Horton, Joseph, and Shorter, Ethan "Rent Control: An Economic Abomination," *International Journal of Value Based Management*, Vol. 11, No. 3, 1998, pp. 253–263; Downs, Anthony, *Residential Rent Controls: An Evaluation*, Washington: The Urban Land Institute, 1988; Grant, R.W., *Rent Control and the War Against the Poor*, Manhattan Beach: Quandary House, 1989; Johnson, M. Bruce, ed., *Resolving the Housing Crisis: Government Policy, Decontrol, and the Public Interest*, San Francisco: The Pacific Institute, 1982; Salins, Peter D., *The Ecology of Housing Destruction: Economic Effects of Public Intervention in the Housing Market*, New York: New York University Press, 1980; Tucker, William, *The Excluded Americans: Homelessness and Housing Policies*, Washington D.C., Regnery Gateway, 1990.

4. Discussion

The government and supporting Amici Curiae, a noteworthy collection of white, middle-class urban environmental groups,[33] including the Sierra Club, Defenders of Wildlife, Environmental Law Foundation, and various and sundry paternalistic law professors,[34] contended that a taking did not occur under the Fifth Amendment for three reasons. First, they maintained that the implementation of the RPAs merely frustrated the contract's purpose and did not therefore effectuate a taking.[35] Second, they argued that the needed criteria for a regulatory taking, specifically the existence of a reasonable, investment-backed expectation and a significant decrease in economic value, have not been met.[36] Finally, they contended that the government cannot be liable for a taking when it does no more than impose a limit on plaintiff's title that the background principles of California state law would otherwise require.[37]

A. Frustration

The government argued that it may not be held liable to the farmers for lawful actions that, although they may injure or destroy contract rights

[33] For a comment on the makeup of some activist environmental groups *see generally*, Frank Cross, *The Subtle Vices Behind Environmental Values*, 8 Duke Envl L. & Policy Forum 151 (1997). Also, *see generally*, Block, Walter, ed., *Economics and the Environment: A Reconciliation*, Vancouver: The Fraser Institute, 1990; Block, Walter, "Environmentalism and Freedom: The Case for Private Property Rights," *Journal of Business Ethics*, Vol. 17, No. 6, December 1998, pp. 1887–1899; Block, Walter and Roy Whitehead, "The Unintended Consequences of Environmental Justice," *Forensic Science International*, Vol. 100, Nos. 1 and 2, March 1999, pp. 57–67; DiLorenzo, Thomas, "Does Capitalism Cause Pollution?," St. Louis, Washington University: Center for the Study of American Business, Contemporary Issues Series 38, 1990; Hill, Peter J., and Meiners, Roger E., eds., *Who Owns the Environment?*, New York: Rowman and Littlefield, 1998; McGee, Robert, and Block, Walter, "Pollution Trading Permits as a Form of Market Socialism, and the Search for a Real Market Solution to Environmental Pollution," *Fordham University Law and Environmental Journal*, Vol. VI, No. 1, Fall 1994, pp. 51–77; Rothbard, Murray N., "Law, Property Rights, and Air Pollution," *Economics and the Environment: A Reconciliation*, Walter Block, ed., Vancouver: The Fraser Institute, 1990; Stroup, Richard L., and John C. Goodman, et al., (1991) *Progressive Environmentalism: A Pro-Human, Pro-Science, Pro-Free Enterprise Agenda for Change*, Dallas, TX: National Center for Policy Analysis, Task Force Report.

[34] 49 Fed.Cl. at 314.

[35] Id. at 317.

[36] Id.

[37] Id.

do not *take* them as the phrase is understood in the constitutional sense.[38] No *taking* occurs, the government says, when "expectations under a contract are merely frustrated by lawful government action not directed against the taking claimant," *767 Third Avenue Association v. United States*.[39] The government contends that the RPA represents a legitimate exercise of federal authority that does no more than frustrate rather than appropriate, the plaintiff's contractual rights in the water.[40]

Unfortunately, for the government's contention, but happily for the long compelling tradition of liberty and property rights found in the Constitution, the plaintiffs in this case can claim an identifiable interest in the stipulated volume of water. The government's frustration argument only applies when the claimant has a contractual right to buy at a certain price, but cannot claim actual ownership of the property because title has not passed to the party seeking compensation, *Omnia v. United States*.[41] The Omnia Company in May 1917, during World War I, by assignment, became the owner of a contract that gave it the right to buy steel from Allegheny Steel Company.[42] In October 1917, before any deliveries under the contract, the government requisitioned the company's entire production of steel.[43] In holding that the contract had merely been frustrated, rather than *taken*, the high court addressed the situation where a litigant claims a right to buy property but cannot claim actual ownership of the property because title to the property has not passed to the party seeking compensation.[44] The *Tulare* court said that unlike *Omnia*, "where the

---

[38] Id.

[39] 48 F.3d 1575, 1581 (Fed. Cir. 1995). There, the lessor claimed reimbursement from the U.S. government for leases breached by a foreign government (Socialist Federal Republic of Yugoslavia) after the foreign government's offices were ordered closed and its assets frozen. The court said, "[L]essor had no compensable investment backed expectation to be free from government interference, within the meaning of the just compensation clause, regarding its rights under lease with entities of foreign government, since lessor leased office space to foreign government entities with notice that the United States was statutorily and constitutionally authorized to take action against foreign government by closing its offices and blocking its assets, and the United States had done so in the past."

[40] 49 Fed.Cl. at 317.

[41] 261 U.S. 502 (1923).

[42] Id. At 507.

[43] Id.

[44] Id. At 510. The high court said, "[T]hat provision has always been understood as referring only to a direct appropriation, and not to consequential injuries resulting from the exercise of lawful power." Obviously, the power was used to prosecute the war.

steel company could only claim a contract expectancy but not an ownership right in the steel, our plaintiffs can claim an identifiable interest in a stipulated volume of water."[45] Here, the farmers possessed an actual property interest in receiving a volume of water rather than merely a future expectancy.[46] Under California law, the title of water always remains with the state, the rights to the water's use is transferred first by permit to the Department of Water Resources, and then by contract to end-users, such as the plaintiffs.[47] Those contracts confer on plaintiffs the right to the exclusive use of a prescribed quantity of water, consistent with terms of the permits.[48] The right to use of the water remains in place until formally changed by administrative process. Thus, it is clear that the plaintiff's contract right in the water's use is superior to all competing interests. The expectation in receiving the water is therefore deemed a property interest sufficiently matured to characterize it as an actual interest in the subject water rather than a mere expectation of its use.[49]

B. Nature of Taking

Courts have traditionally divided their analysis of Fifth Amendment takings into two categories: physical takings and regulatory takings. A physical taking occurs when the government's action amounts to a physical occupation or invasion of the property, including the function equivalent of a "practical ouster of the owner's possession," *Loretto v. Teleprompter Manhattan CATV Corporation.*[50] A regulatory taking arises, on the other hand, when the government's regulation restricts the use to which the owner may put his property. In deciding whether a regulatory taking has occurred courts generally employ the balancing set out in *Penn Central*

[45] 49 Fed.Cl. at 317.

[46] Id. at 318.

[47] Id.

[48] Id.

[49] Id.

[50] 458 U.S. 419 (1982). Here, the high court decided that a New York law requiring landlords to allow cable television wires and facilities on their property was a "taking" of property compensable under the Fifth Amendment. Justice Marshal wrote, "[W]e affirm the traditional rule that a permanent physical invasion of property is a taking" 458 U.S. at 441.

Transportation Company v. New York,[51] by balancing the character of the government's regulation and the reasonableness of the property owner's investment-backed expectations.[52] On the other hand, regulations that are found to be too restrictive, those that deprive the property of its entire economical beneficial productive use, commonly identified as categorical takings are treated like physical takings and require no such balancing, *Lucas v. South Carolina Coastal Council*.[53] There the state sought to limit the use of petitioner's beachfront lots in the interest of restricting coastal zone development.[54] The trial court found that the lots had been rendered valueless by the regulations.[55] The high court said, "[W]e think, in short, that there are good reasons for our frequently expressed belief that when the owner of real property has been called upon to sacrifice *all* economically beneficial uses in the name of the common good, that is to leave his property economically idle, he has suffered a taking.[56]"

Precedent indicates that the distinction between a physical invasion and a governmental activity that merely impairs the use of that property turns on whether intrusion is "so immediate and direct as to subtract from the owner's full enjoyment of the property and to limit his exploita-

[51] 438 U.S. 104, 124–125 (1978).

[52] Here, the city of New York's Landmarks Law prevented the owner from using air space above Grand Central Terminal for an office building of over 50 stories because the city considered they would adversely affect the architectural features of the landmark building. The high court decided that the Landmarks Law did not effect a taking of private property because "[w]here (1) the law does not interfere with the owner's present use of the building, (2) the law does not necessarily prohibit occupancy of any of the airspace above the landmark building, and (3) the law does not deny all use of the air rights above the landmark," a taking does not follow. 438 U.S. at 115. The court continued that a taking also had not occurred because, "[T]he restrictions imposed are substantially related to the promotion of the general welfare and not only permit reasonable beneficial use of the landmark site but also afford appellants opportunities to enhance not only the terminal site proper but also other properties." 438 U.S. at 139.

[53] 505 U.S. 1003, 1015 (1992).

[54] Id. at 1020. There is always a risk that regulations, by requiring private property to be left substantially in its natural state, as in *Lucas*, carry a risk that private property is being pressed into some form of public service "under the guise of mitigating public harm" 505 U.S. 1018. Here, the court foresaw the situation discussed in footnote 89 *Infra*, where the Fish and Wildlife Service used the "guise" of Incidental Take Statements to prohibit the grazing of cattle where there was no evidence of the presence of endangered species on the land.

[55] Id. at 1019.

[56] Id.

tion of it," *United States v. Causby*.[57] In *Causby*, the court ruled that frequent flights of airplanes immediately above a landowner's property constitute a taking, comparing such actions to a more traditional physical taking. The court said, "If, by reason of the frequency and altitude of the flights, respondents could not use this land for any purpose, their loss would be complete. It would be as complete as if the United States had entered on the surface of the land and taken exclusive possession of it."[58]

While water rights present an unusual taking situation, the cited *Causby* example is an instructive one. In the context of water rights, a government regulation that places a restriction on use completely eviscerates the property right itself, since the user's sole entitlement is to the use of the water, *Eddy v. Simpson*.[59] In that California case, the court said, "the right of property in water is usufructuary, and consists not so much of the fluid itself as to the advantage of its use.[60]" Unlike other property where use restrictions may limit some, but not all of the incidences of ownership, the denial of a right to use water accomplishes an extinction of all value of it. Thus, in this case, by limiting the farmer's use of water to that which they were contractually entitled, the government substituted itself as the beneficiary of the water contract and totally displaced the contract holder.[61] The complete occupation of the farmer's water rights clearly mirrors the physical invasion present in *Causby*. The federal government has rendered the farmer's right to the water valueless and has affected a physical taking under the Fifth Amendment.[62] The Supreme Court long ago held that water rights can be subject to a physical taking. In a 1931 decision, the high court ruled that when the government diverted water from the petitioner's mill for production of power elsewhere a compensable taking occurred, *International Paper Co. v. United States*.[63]

[57] 328 U.S. 256, 265 (1946).

[58] Id. at 261.

[59] 3 Cal. 249, 252–253 (1853).

[60] Id. at 253.

[61] 49 Fed.Cl. at 319.

[62] Id.

[63] 282 U.S. 399, 407 (1931). There, in determining whether the government's acquisition of a corporation's entire right to use water power constituted a taking, the court noted that the "peti-

C. Ownership at Time of Taking

The next inquiry in a takings case is whether in fact the farmers owned the property at the time of the taking.[64] The government contends that background principles of state law and California's public trust doctrine render the farmer's loss noncompensable.[65] Under the terms of the applicable contract, the state was protected from liability for any damages resulting from the shortage of water available for distribution by the DWR. The court quickly pointed out that this case involved the federal government as the defendant and it enjoyed no such contractual immunity from liability.[66]

The government then contended that the farmers have no vested property interest in the water if its intended use violates a public trust.[67] That contention may be valid if the use is a nuisance that, for example, pollutes the state's groundwater, *Rith Energy v. United States*.[68] But the farmer's use of their water rights in this case is not a nuisance.[69] The government also argued that, given the determination under the Endangered Species Act, the farmer's use of the water is unreasonable and violates the public trust.[70] The court refused to accept this contention. First, the allocation of water covered by the contract had already been made by the Water Resources Control Board and that determination clearly defined the

---

tioner's right was to the use of water; and when all the water that it used was withdrawn from the petitioner's mill and turned elsewhere by government requisition for the production of power it is hard to see what more the government could do to take that use." *See*, also Ivanhoe Irrigation District v. McCracken, 357 U.S. 275, 285 (1958), where the court said of an interference with water rights, "depriving the owner of its profitable use was the imposition of such servitude as would constitute an appropriation of property for which compensation should be made."

[64] 49 Fed.Cl. at 320.

[65] Id.

[66] Id.

[67] Id. at 321.

[68] 44 Fed.Cl. 108 (1999), *aff'd* 247 F.3d 1355 (Fed.Cir 2001). There, the court rejected the takings claim of a surface miner when it was determined that the mining operation did violence to the state's citizens by polluting the state's groundwater.

[69] 49 Fed.Cl. at 323. Growing food and fiber appears to fit into those activities that should be supported as contributing to the public good.

[70] Id.

scope of the farmer's property rights.[71] The court also pointed out that this is not a case under state nuisance law. The farmer's use of the water for producing food and fiber is a legitimate one not harmful to the public trust.[72]

5. Conclusion

This case highlights the conflict between the "Holy Grail" of some urban environmentalists,[73] the Endangered Species Act, and the noble liberty and property interests enjoyed by all Americans, even rube farmers, protected by the Fifth Amendment. The use of the term "Holy Grail" is not a misnomer. Witness the fact that river water was denied firefighters in a recent fire in the Northern Cascades because of concerns that its use would violate the Endangered Species Act.[74] Four of the firefighters, including two females, died horrible deaths in the raging flames.[75] No reasonable person wishes to see fish and animals become extinct. But, when we decide to protect endangered species at the expense of private property interests, who should bear the burden?[76] Should the cost be borne solely by the impacted farmers? Or should all of society shoulder the burden? We believe this case strikes a reasonable balance and has set the stage for a new era of environmental responsibility.[77] Because as the

[71] Id.

[72] Id.

[73] *See generally*, Frank Cross, *The Subtle Vices Behind Environmental Values*, 8 Duke Envl L. & Policy forum 151 (1997), for the idea that many staunch environmentalists are middle-class urban dwellers. See Kelly, footnote 3, *Supra*, for support of the proposition that environmental regulations are increasingly reflective of the values of urban dwellers who have little connection with the land or nature. Why should they care about the cost of protecting fish and fuzzy creatures? They have nothing to lose and don't have to pay. And it makes them feel good.

[74] *See*, Chris Solomon, *Why Thirty Mile Fire Raged Without Water*, Seattle Times, August 1, 2001, at A 7, Col. 3.

[75] *See*, Walter Block, *Four Firemen Perish*, www.lewrockwell.com/orgin.block2.html (Last visited Apr. 8, 2002).

[76] And when we realize that *human life* hangs in the balance, it is not clear that there is any justification for this policy at all.

[77] *See*, "What the claims court has potentially done is to set the stage for a new era of environmental responsibility. The key problem in America's environmental debate is that most people have no

Supreme Court foresaw in *Armstrong*,[78] if we truly believe it is in the public interest to take private property to protect endangered species,[79] we should all willingly share in and bear the resulting economic costs.[80] Finally, these pitched battles between farmers and federal[81] agencies often arise because of the paternalistic approach of the government. Rather than consulting with the impacted community, as a fair reading of Section 101 of the National Environmental Policy Act mandates,[82] government agencies often rely solely on so-called scientific opinion to justify top-down management.[83] The top-down management is certain to create conflict with and is insultingly paternalistic toward the impacted community,[84] because private property owners have a compelling self-

---

concept of how much it costs to protect natural resources, and feel there is nothing to lose from more regulations," editorial, *The Earth Rebalanced*, The Wall Street Journal, Jul. 10, 2001, at A18.

[78] 346 U.S. 40, 49 (1960). One purpose of the Fifth Amendment is "to bar the government from forcing some people alone to bear public burdens which, in all fairness and justice, should be borne by the public as a whole."

[79] For the case that private property rights are a far more reliable means toward this end, as well as being more in accord with our traditions of relying upon this institution, see footnote 33, supra.

[80] That is exactly the issue awaiting resolution before the Supreme Court in *Tahoe-Sierra Preservation Council v. Tahoe Regional Planning Agency*, No. 99-15614 (9th Cir. June 2000), where the landowners were prevented from developing their lots for several years to protect against runoff into the lake. The 9th Circuit reversed the trial court's holding that the temporary deprivation of a beneficial use of the property was compensable. But why should it make any difference if the taking has not been finalized because of the idle meanderings of an administrative agency of the city, state, or federal government? This delay provides an incentive for the administrative agency to postpone, sometimes for decades as in the *Tahoe* case, a final decision. Meanwhile, the owner has been deprived of the use of his property. And the courts can use this delay to "play the owner like a yo-yo and never give him his day in court," Timothy Sandefur, *The Obstacle of the Takings Clause*, Ideas on Liberty, Vol. 52, No. 1, Jan. 2002, p. 45–46.

[81] *See generally*, Lanton Caldwell, *Beyond NEPA: Future Significance of the National Environmental Policy Act*, 22 Harvard Envl. L. Review 203, 203–209 (1998), about how to provide early opportunities for resolution of disputes and building community support by using the productive harmony provisions of section 101 of the Act.

[82] *See*, Kevin Preister and Jim Kent, *Using Social Ecology to Meet the Productive Harmony Intent of the National Environmental Policy Act*, 7 Hastings West-Northwest Journal of Environmental Law and Policy 235, 239–241 (2001), for a detailed discussion of the use of section 101 of The National Environmental Policy Act to achieve productive harmony with the impacted community.

[83] Roy Whitehead and Walter Block, *Environmental Justice Risks in the Petroleum Industry*, 24 William and Mary Environmental Law and Policy Review 67, 81 (2000).

[84] *See generally*, Richard Merritt and Roy Whitehead, *Including the Excluded Population in Marine Corps Environmental Decisions*, The Marine Corps Gazette, Oct. 2000, pp. 42–44. In the Louisiana Shintech case, for example, over 70% of the black elected community representatives favored the plastics plant location. White, middle-class, urban environmentalists, paternalistic members of

interest in protecting the environment.[85] What sane private property owner wants to destroy the beneficial use of his property?[86] It is encouraging for advocates of private property rights to see that the courts are catching on to the trampling of private property rights by leftist environmentalists and their captive[87] ideology driven government agencies[88] in the guise[89] of protecting endangered species.

---

congress, and the EPA objected to the location and drove the plant elsewhere without regard to community economic needs and wishes.

[85] For the contention that private property rights and a system of private causes of action are preferable to government regulation in preventing violence against the environment, *See*, Walter Block, *Environmentalism and Economic Freedom: The Case For Private Property Rights*, Journal of Business Ethics, Vol. 17, No. 6, Dec. 1998, pp. 1887–1899.

[86] "The concept of private property rights, although much reviled by self styled defenders of the environment, is the key to its protection. "When people are allowed full title to property, they treat it as if they own it; that is, they tend to protect it. When property rights are unprotected, allowing others to violate them with impunity, they tend to do so. Spoiling the environment is the result," *See*, Walter Block, Economics and the Environment: a Reconciliation, 284, Vancouver: The Fraser Institute, 1990.

[87] Just as private "entrepreneurs in the marketplace recognize and fill demands for goods and services, politicians and bureaucrats discover opportunities to meet the demands of their constituencies," Terry Anderson, *The Market Process and Environmental Amenities, Economics and the Environment: A Reconciliation* 141, *The Fraser Institute*, 1990. Bureaucrats, like the officials involved in the Tulare case who provide services to environmental interest groups, do not have to pay the opportunity costs of expended resources. "They can increase their own utility by increasing budgetary discretion, power, and wealth" at the expense of hayseed, private property owning farmers. See, Anderson, p. 141.

[88] The aforementioned bio-fraud article, *Supra*, footnote 11, alleged the planting of lynx fur. "The lynx fur scandal underscores everything that's wrong with the Fish and Wildlife Service and the Forest Service. It shows how the agencies succumbed to the Clinton-era ideology ahead of science. It demonstrates the undue influence environmental groups have over the departments," says Kimberley Strassell, *The Missing Lynx*, The Wall Street Journal, Jan. 24, 2002, at A18, Col. 4. She quotes Jim Beers, a 30-year veteran of the Fish and Wildlife Service: "In recent years the agency eliminated all the real requirements, pushed out people that didn't fit the anti-hunting, anti-fishing, anti-land- management profile. They've got to get back to science." She relates that anti-development environmental groups that have captured a government agency, "quickly realized how easy it is to exploit the law. Getting a plant or animal listed meant putting large areas of rural America off limits." Finally, the article reveals that the former director of the Fish and Wildlife Service and the Forest Service "have gone to work for the left-wing, activist National Wildlife Federation."

[89] The use of the term "guise" is not a misnomer. The *Lucas* court, footnote 54, *Supra*, expressed a concern that private property might be pressed into some form of public service "under the guise of mitigating public harm." Recently, the 9th Circuit Court of Appeals dealt with a situation where the Fish and Wildlife Service used Incidental Take Statements to prohibit the grazing of cattle where there was absolutely no evidence that endangered species existed on the land. The court found that the Service acted in an arbitrary and capricious manner by imposing terms and conditions on the land without evidence of the existence of an endangered species. *See generally, Arizona Cattle Growers Association v. U.S. Fish and Wildlife Service, Bureau of Land Management*, 273 F.3d

II. Water Privatization

1. Introduction

Private property rights have benefited every arena of human experience they have touched.[90] The economy of the U.S.S.R. fell apart mainly because of the absence of this system.[91] The US economy is one of the foremost in the world largely due to its relatively greater reliance on this institution.[92]

And yet, there are vast areas of human existence where private property rights play no role at all: oceans, seas, rivers, and other bodies of water. But why should we expect that there would be any better results from such "water socialism" than we have experienced from socialism on land? Indeed, the evidence is all around us attesting to this fact: whales are an endangered species; fish stocks are precipitously declining; oil spills are a recurring problem; droughts are becoming more and more serious, and not only in the underdeveloped countries of the world; rivers are polluted, some so seriously that they actually catch fire; lakes are becoming overcrowded with boaters, swimmers, fishermen, and so on, and there is no market mechanism to allocate this scarce resource amongst the competing users; deep sea mining (manganese modules) is in a state of suspended animation due to unclear titles; the legal status of offshore oil

1229 (9th Cir. 2001). This sort of "guise" practice hardly contributes to the public trust in government agencies.

[90] Bethell, Tom, *The Noblest Triumph: Property and Prosperity Through the Ages*, New York: St. Martin's Press, 1998; Pipes, Richard, *Property and Freedom: The story of how through the centuries private ownership has promoted liberty and the rule of law*, New York: Knopf, 2000.

[91] F.A. Hayek, "Socialist Calculation I, II, & III," *Individualism and Economic Order*, Chicago: University of Chicago Press, 1948; Hoppe, Hans-Hermann, *A Theory of Socialism and Capitalism*, Boston, Kluwer, 1989; Mises, Ludwig, *Socialism*, Indianapolis: Liberty Fund, 1981 (1969); Block, Walter, "Socialist Psychology: Values and Motivations," *Cultural Dynamics*, Vol. V, No. 3, 1992, pp. 260–286; Boettke, Peter J., *Why Perestroika Failed: The Politics and Economics of Socialist Transformation*, London: Routledge, 1993; Boettke, Peter J., ed., *The Collapse of Development Planning*, New York: New York University Press, 1994; Boettke, Peter J., and Anderson, Gary, "Perestroika and Public Choice: the economics of autocratic succession in a rent seeking society," *Public Choice*, 75, no. 2, February 1993, 101–118; Boettke, Peter J., and Anderson Gary, "Soviet Venality: The USSR as a Mercantilist State, *Public Choice*, 1997.

[92] Gwartney, James, Robert Lawson and Walter Block, *Economic Freedom of the World, 1975–1995*, Vancouver, B.C. Canada: the Fraser Institute, 1996.

drilling rigs is unclear. Most revealing, water covers some 79% of the earth's surface,[93] but accounts for only a small percentage of world GDP.[94] While no one expects an exact proportionality between surface coverage and contribution to economic welfare, such a strong disparity suggests that the economic system pursued in these two realms may not be totally unrelated to these results.

Our claim is that we have no warrant to believe that socialism, the absence of private property rights, is any more workable on land than on water; that it is time; it is long past time, to explore ways in which this institution can be applied to aqueous resources.

2. Case for Privatization

Privatization is the process of transferring governmental ownership, management, and control from governmental to private hands. The case for privatization, in general, is straightforward. It consists of utilitarian and de-ontological reasons extolling the benefits of this course of action.

What is the utilitarian case? Individual firms, owned by private persons, are better able to promote consumer sovereignty[95] than are statist agglomerations. This comes about mainly through the weeding out process[96]: those entrepreneurs who cannot satisfy customers are forced into bankruptcy through such competition.

Similarly, the de-ontological case for privatization is simple and straightforward. Individuals, but not governments, can come to own

[93] States *The New Encyclopaedia Britannica*, 15th ed., [1998 rev.], Chicago: Encyclopedia Britannica, c1998, volume 4, page 320, Article Title: "Earth": "The planet's total surface area is roughly 509,600,000 square km (197,000,000 square miles), of which about 29 percent, or 148,000,000 square km (57,000,000 square miles), is land. The balance of the surface is covered by the oceans and smaller seas."

[94] Dowling, Mike, "Interactive Table of World Nations Sorted by Gross Domestic Product," available from http://www.mrdowling.com/800gdp.html; Internet; updated Tuesday, September 5, 2000.

[95] See Hutt, William H., "The Concept of Consumers' Sovereignty," *Economic Journal*, March, 1940, pp. 66–77 on this. For the related concept, individual sovereignty, which is even more in accord with libertarian free enterprise principles, see Rothbard, Murray N., *Man, Economy and State*, Auburn AL: Ludwig von Mises Institute, [1962] 1993, pp. 560–566.

[96] Hazlitt, Henry, *Economics in One Lesson*, Arlington House Publishers, New York, 1979.

land and other resources through homesteading,[97] the only method which can justify ownership on the basis of the libertarian legal code.[98] Any attempt on the part of the state to engage in this activity is fatally compromised by its essentially coercive nature. Government ownership of resources is only legitimate in the statist philosophy of coercive socialism or fascism. (We here abstract from the limited government libertarian perspective which makes an exception for what it characterizes as legitimate state functions: armies to repel foreign invaders, police to

[97] Block, Walter, "Earning Happiness Through Homesteading Unowned Land: a comment on 'Buying Misery with Federal Land' by Richard Stroup," *Journal of Social Political and Economic Studies*, Vol. 15, No. 2, Summer 1990, pp. 237–253; Hoppe, Hans-Hermann, *The Economics and Ethics of Private Property: Studies in Political Economy and Philosophy*, Boston: Kluwer, 1993; Locke, John, *An Essay Concerning the True Origin, Extent and End of Civil Government*, V. 27–28, in *Two Treatises of Government*, P. Laslett, ed., Cambridge: Cambridge University Press, 1960, pp. 17–18; Locke, John, Second Treatise of Civil Government, Chicago: Henry Regnery, 1955; Rothbard, Murray N., Power and Market: Government and the Economy, Menlo Park Cal.: Institute for Humane Studies, 1970; Rothbard, Murray N., For a New Liberty, Macmillan, New York, 1978; Rothbard, Murray N., The Ethics of Liberty, New York: New York University Press, 1998 (1982).

[98] Anderson, Terry and Hill, P.J., "An American Experiment in Anarcho-Capitalism: the *not* so Wild, Wild West," *Journal of Libertarian Studies* Vol. 3, No. 1, 1979, pp. 9–29; Barnett, Randy E., *The Structure of Liberty: Justice and the Rule of Law*, Oxford: Clarendon Press, 1998; Benson, Bruce L., 1989, Enforcement of Private Property Rights in Primitive Societies: Law Without Government," *The Journal of Libertarian Studies*, Vol. IX, No. 1, Winter, pp. 1–26; Cuzán, Alfred G., "Do We Ever Really Get Out of Anarchy?," *Journal of Libertarian Studies*, Vol. 3, No. 2 (Summer, 1979); De Jasay, Anthony, *Against Politics: On Government, Anarchy, and Order*, London, Routledge, 1997; Friedman, David, *The Machinery of Freedom: Guide to a Radical Capitalism*, La Salle, IL: Open Court, 2nd ed., 1989; Hoppe, Hans-Hermann, *Democracy, the God that Failed: The Economics and Politics of Monarchy, Democracy and Natural Order*, New Brunswick, N.J. Transaction Publishers, 2001; Hummel, Jeffrey Rogers, National Goods Versus Public Goods: Defense, Disarmament, and Free Riders, 4 *Rev. Austrian Econ.* 88 (1990); Kinsella, Stephan, "Estoppel: A New Justification for Individual Rights," *Reason Papers* No. 17 (Fall 1992), p. 61; Morriss, Andrew P., "Miners, Vigilantes and Cattlemen: Overcoming Free Rider Problems in the Private Provision of Law," *Land and Water Law Review*, Vol. XXXIII, No, 2, 1998, pp. 581–696; Oppenheimer, Franz, *The State*, New York: Free Life Editions, (1914), 1975; Rothbard, Murray N., *The Ethics of Liberty*, Humanities Press, Atlantic Highlands, N.J., 1982; Skoble, Aeon J. "The Anarchism Controversy," in *Liberty for the 21st Century: Essays in Contemporary Libertarian Thought*, eds. Tibor Machan and Douglas Rasmussen, Lanham MD: Rowman and Littlefield, 1995, pp. 77–96; Sechrest, Larry J., "Rand, Anarchy, and Taxes," *The Journal of Ayn Rand Studies*, Vol. I, No. 1, Fall 1999, pp. 87–105; Spooner, Lysander, *No Treason*, Larkspur, Colorado, (1870) 1966; Stringham, Edward, "Justice Without Government," *Journal of Libertarian Studies*, Vol. 14, No. 1, Winter 1998–1999, pp. 53–77; Tinsley, Patrick, "With Liberty and Justice for All: A Case for Private Police," *Journal of Libertarian Studies*, Vol. 14, No. 1, Winter 1998–1999, pp. 95–100; Tannehill, Morris and Linda, *The Market for Liberty*, New York: Laissez Faire Books, 1984; Woolridge, William C., *Uncle Sam the Monopoly Man*, New Rochelle, N.Y.: Arlington House, 1970.

reduce invasive acts on the part of local miscreants, and courts to determine who is who in this regard.)[99]

If the case for privatization is a simple one, so too does this apply to many specific instances of this doctrine. For example, the privatization of public housing,[100] state enterprises in western countries,[101] in the U.S.S.R. and other former communist countries,[102] and the Post

---

[99] For an articulation of the minarchist free market philosophy, see Machan, Tibor, 1978, "Against non-libertarian natural rights," *The Journal of Libertarian Studies*, Vol. 2, No. 3, Fall, pp. 233–238; Murray, Charles, *What It Means to be a Libertarian*, New York: Broadway Books, 1997; Read, Leonard, E. *Anything That's Peaceful*, Irvington-on-Hudson, N.Y.: Foundation for Economic Education, 1964.

[100] Jacobs, Jane (1989), *The Death and Life of Great American Cities*, New York: Vintage.

[101] Hanke, Steve H., ed., 1987, *Privatization and Development*, San Francisco: Institute for Contemporary Studies; Walker, Michael A., ed., *Privatization: Tactics and Techniques*, The Fraser Institute, Vancouver, B.C., 1988; Ohashi. T.M., T.P. Roth, Z.A. Spindler, M.L. McMillan, & K.H. Norrie, *Privatization Theory & Practice*, The Fraser Institute, Vancouver, B.C., 1980; Pirie, Madson, 1986, *Privatization in Theory and Practice*, London: Adam Smith Institute; Benson, Bruce L., *To Serve and Protect: Privatization and Community in Criminal Justice*, New York, N.Y.: University Press, 1998; Anderson, Terry L., and Peter J. Hill, "Privatizing the Commons: An Improvement," 50 S. Econ. J. 438 (1983); Butler, Eamonn, ed., 1988, *The Mechanics of Privatization*, London: Adam Smith Institute.

[102] Boettke, Peter J. "The Austrian Critique and the Demise of Socialism: The Soviet Case," in *Austrian Economics: Perspectives on the Past and Prospects for the Future*. Vol. 17, Richard M. Ebeling, ed., Hillsdale, MI: Hillsdale College Press, 1991, pp. 181–232; Conway, David. *A Farewell to Marx: An Outline and Appraisal of His Theories*, Middlesex, England: Penguin Books, 1987; Cubeddu, Raimondo. *The Philosophy of the Austrian School*. New York: Routledge, 1993, pp. 109–158; Dorn, James, "Markets True and False in Yugoslavia," *Journal of Libertarian Studies*, Fall 1978, 2(3), pp. 243–268; Ebeling, Richard M. "Economic Calculation Under Socialism: Ludwig von Mises and His Predecessors," in Jeffrey Herbener, ed., *The Meaning of Ludwig von Mises*, Norwell, MA: Klewer Academic Press, 1993, pp. 56–101; Foss, Nicolai Juul, "Information and the Market Economy: A Note on a Common Marxist Fallacy," *Review of Austrian Economics*, 1995, 8(2), pp. 127–136; Gordon, David. *Resurrecting Marx: The Analytical Marxists on Freedom, Exploitation, and Justice*, New Brunswick, NJ: Transaction, 1990; Hayek, Friedrich A. "Socialism and War: Essays, Documents, Reviews," *The Collected works of F. A. Hayek*, vol.10, B. Caldwell, ed., 1997; Heilbroner, Robert. "Analysis and Vision in the History of Monetary Economic Thought," *Journal of Economic Literature*, September 1990, 28, pp. 1097–1114; Hoppe, Hans-Hermann, "De-Socialization in a United Germany," *Review of Austrian Economics*, 1991, 5(2), pp. 77–106; Horwitz, Steven. "Money, Money Prices, and the Socialist Calculation Debates," *Advances in Austrian Economics*, Vol. 3, 1996, pp. 59–77; Keizer, Willem. 1997. "Schumpeter's Walrasian Stand in the Socialist Calculation Debate." In Austrian Economics in Debate, edited by Willem Keizer, Bert Riben and Rudy Van Zijp. London: Routledge; Klein, Peter G. "Economic Calculation and the Limits of Organization" *Review of Austrian Economics*, 1996 9(2), pp. 3–28; Lavoie, Don. *Rivalry and Central Planning: The Socialist Calculation Debate Reconsidered*, New York: Cambridge University Press, 1985; Lewin, Peter. "The Firm, Money and Economic Calculation," *American Journal of Economics and Sociology*, October 1998; Maltsev, Yuri N. *Requiem for Marx*. Auburn, AL: Ludwig von Mises Institute, 1993; Mises, Ludwig von. *Socialism*, Indianapolis: LibertyPress/

Office.[103] Privatization for roads, highways streets and sidewalks are perhaps more conceptually complex, but even here, there is a plethora of literature attesting to the benefits and justification of this initiative.[104]

LibertyClassics, 1981; O'Driscoll, Gerald P., Jr. *Economics as a Coordination Problem*, Kansas City: Sheed Andrews and McMeel, 1977, pp. 1–15; Reisman, George. *Capitalism: A Treatise on Economics*, Ottawa, Illinois: Jameson Books, 1996, pp. 135–139, 267–282; Reynolds, Morgan O. "The Impossibility of Socialist Economy," *The Quarterly Journal of Austrian Economics*, Summer 1998, 1.2, pp. 29–43; Rothbard, Murray N. "How and How Not to Desocialize," *Review of Austrian Economics*, 1992, 6(1) pp. 65–78; Salerno, Joseph T. "Ludwig von Mises as a Social Rationalist," *Review of Austrian Economics*, 1990, 4, pp. 26–54; Steele, David Ramsey, *From Marx to Mises: Post-Capitalist Society and the Challenge of Economic Calculation*, La Salle, IL: Open Court, 1992; Vaughn, Karen I. "Economic Calculation Under Socialism: the Austrian Contribution," *Economic Inquiry*, June 1980, 18 (20), pp. 535–554.

[103] Adie, Douglas K., "Why Marginal Reform of the U.S. Postal Service Won't Succeed," in *Free the Mail: Ending the Postal Monopoly*, Peter J. Ferrara, ed., Washington, D.C.: The Cato Institute, 1990; Moore, Thomas Gale, "The Federal Postal Monopoly: History, Rationale and Future," in *Free the Mail: Ending the Postal Monopoly*, Peter J. Ferrara, ed., Washington, D.C.: The Cato Institute, 1990; Priest, George, "The History of the Postal Monopoly in the United States," *Journal of Law and Economics*, 18, no. 33, 1975; Butler, Stuart M., "Privatizing Bulk Mail," *Management*, 6, No. 1, 1986; Moore, Stephen, "Privatizing the U.S. Postal Service," in Stephen Moore and Stuart Butler, eds., *Privatization*, Washington: Heritage Foundation, 1987.

[104] Beito, David T. and Linda Royster Beito, "Rival Road Builders: Private Toll Roads in Nevada, 1852–1880," *Nevada Historical Society Quarterly* 41 (Summer 1998), 71–91; Block, Walter, "Free Market Transportation: Denationalizing the Roads," *Journal of Libertarian Studies: An Interdisciplinary Review*, Vol. III, No. 2, Summer 1979, pp. 209–238; Block, Walter, "Congestion and Road Pricing," *The Journal of Libertarian Studies: An Interdisciplinary Review*, Vol. IV, No. 3, Fall 1980, pp. 299–330; Block, Walter, "Public Goods and Externalities: The Case of Roads," *The Journal of Libertarian Studies: An Interdisciplinary Review*, Vol. VII, No. 1, Spring 1983, pp. 1–34; Block, Walter, "Theories of Highway Safety," *Transportation Research Record*, #912, 1983, pp. 7–10; Block, Walter "Road Socialism," *International Journal of Value-Based Management*, 1996, Vol. 9, pp. 195–207; Block, Walter and Block, Matthew, "Roads, Bridges, Sunlight and Private Property Rights," *Journal Des Economistes Et Des Etudes Humaines*, Vol. VII, No. 2/3, June-September 1996, pp. 351–362; Block, Walter, "Roads, Bridges, Sunlight and Private Property: Reply to Gordon Tullock," *Journal des Economistes et des Etudes Humaines*, Vol. 8, No. 2/3, June-September 1998, pp. 315–326; Foldvary, Fred, *Public Goods and Private Communities: The Market Provision of Social Services* (Edward Elgar, 1994); Cadin, Michelle, and Block, Walter, (1997), "Privatize the Public Highway System," *The Freeman*, February, Vol. 47, No. 2., pp. 96–97; Cobin, John, M. (1999), Market Provisions of Highways: Lessons from Costanera Norte. Planning and Markets, Volume 2, Number 1; Klein, Dan, Majewski, J., and Baer, C., "From Trunk to Branch: Toll Roads in New York, 1800–1860," *Essays in Economic and Business History*, 1993, pp. 191–209; Klein, Dan and Fielding, G.J., "Private Toll Roads: Learning from the Nineteenth Century," *Transportation Quarterly*, July 1992, pp. 321–341; Lemennicier, Bertrand, "La Privatisation des rues," *Journal Des Economistes Et Des Etudes Humaines*, Vol. VII, No. 2/3, June-September 1996, pp. 363–376; Semmens, John, "The Privatization of Highway Facilities," *Transportation Research Forum*, (November, 1983); Semmens, John, "Why We Need Highway Privatization," Laissez Faire Institute (March 1991); Semmens, John, "Privatizing Vehicle Registrations, Driver's Licenses and Auto Insurance," *Transportation Quarterly* (Fall 1995).

Perhaps the most difficult case to make in behalf of privatization is that for water. This is why this section of the chapter will be devoted to the argument on behalf of applying the institution of private property to water resources. Under this rubric shall be included anything[105] which admit of moisture: aquifers, brooks, canals, channels, drinking water, drainage, ditches, ducts, estuaries, flumes, ground water, irrigation ditches, icebergs, lakes, lagoons, oases, oceans, ponds, puddles, reservoirs, rivers, runoff, seas, springs, streams, swamps, underground water, water basins, water courses, waterfalls, water mains, water sheds, water tables, water traps on public golf courses, waterways, wetlands, and so on.[106] In addition, privatization of air and water, where appropriate, is a necessary if not sufficient condition for reducing the harm done to mankind by clouds, flooding, fog, hurricanes, storms, tidal waves, tornados, torrential rain, tsunamis, typhoons, whirlpools, winds, and so on.

Why is it necessary that extra care and thoroughness be taken in the attempt to build the case for privatizing water? There are several reasons.

3. Opposition to Water Privatization

A. Rare

It has rarely if ever been done. Apart from a few small private lakes and ponds used for fishing, boating and swimming, there are no cases[107] of

[105] However, it must be underscored that only scarce resources are candidates for property ownership. On this see, Callahan, Gene, "Rethinking Patent Law," Mises Institute, July 18, 2000, http://www.mises.org/fullstory.asp?control=468&FS=Rethinking+Patent+Law; Cole, Julio H., "Patents and Copyrights: Do the Benefits Exceed the Costs?," http://www.economia.ufm.edu.gt/Catedraticos/jhcole/Cole%20_MPS_.pdf; Kinsella, N. Stephan, "Against Intellectual Property," *Journal of Libertarian Studies*, forthcoming; Kinsella, N. Stephan, "Is IP property or not?," *National Post*, February 22, 2001; Kinsella, N. Stephan, "In Defense of Napster and Against the Second Homesteading Rule," LewRockwell.com, September 4, 2000, http://www.lewrockwell.com/orig/kinsella2.html; McElroy, Wendy, http://www.zetetics.com/mac/intpro1.htm; http://www.zetetics.com/mac/intpro2.htm; Mercer, Ilana, "How Things Would Work in a Copyright-free Universe," *National Post*, Jan. 26. 2001; Moore D. Adam, "A Lockean Theory of Intellectual Property," Fall, 1977, 21 *Hamline Law Review* 65.

[106] The head police character in the movie the "Fugitive" demanded of his minions that they search every "house, barn, shed, palace, outhouse, doghouse, etc.…" Our goal is to be as exhaustive as he was.

[107] We here abstract from such things as backyard swimming pools, jacuzis, bath tubs, showers, water faucets, cesspools, water fountains, septic tanks, and so on, which already fall under private control.

private ownership, even in countries ostensibly devoted to free enterprise, but which in actuality practice various versions of "water socialism."

B. Unexplored

It has not even been explored in the literature. There is, of course, a wealth of information available concerning water resources, but very little indeed in favor of full privatization.

C. Out of Fashion

It is not in keeping with the intellectual climate of opinion. People balk at privatization for roads and other facilities mentioned above on the rare occasions it is acknowledged at all, in what might be characterized as the mainstream literature. It is probably no exaggeration to predict that when and if the typical public policy wonk hears of the thesis which motivates the present enterprise, to wit, to privatize bodies of water as fully as land masses, he will dismiss it out of hand as a particularly noxious form of lunacy.

D. Interconnectedness

According to that old song, "the hip bone is connected to the thigh bone, is connected to…" In like manner, most bodies of water are joined with most others. That is, although we call the various oceans of the world by different names (e.g., Atlantic, Pacific, Indian), they all touch upon and flow into each other at their common boundaries. Even a seemingly isolated lake is not totally separated from other bodies of water insofar as it has streams feeding into and out of it. These water avenues, lead to still others and eventually to the sea, where they are linked to all others.

But the colors of the rainbow also shade into one another.[108] Yet we have no trouble distinguishing one from the other, except of course at

[108] Similarly for the boundaries between radio and TV stations on the electromagnetic spectrum. For the case in favor of privatization in this regard, see Coase, Ronald H., "The Federal Communications Commission," 2 *Journal of Law and Economics*, 1, 1959.

their very boundaries. And with precision scientific instruments, we can at least mark off an agreed upon fence post. Land, too, is all inter connected, apart from where it ends at water's edge. And, for a time, our society had difficulty marking off one man's holdings from that of another. But with the advent of fencing materials, particularly barbed wire, this became easier and easier.[109]

No, the interconnectedness of even all bodies of water constitutes no overwhelming objection to privatization. The reason we have no "fences" to place in the water is not because this is an impossible idea: it is rather due to the fact that absent aqueous property rights, there has been no financial incentive to engage in research to this end. But imagine the opposite. Suppose, that is, that property rights in bodies of water were recognized by law. It takes no great leap of imagination to suppose that scientists and engineers would soon be able to offer new technology which could distinguish between "mine and thine."

Nor need these water fences be used only to demarcate the property holdings of one firm from that of another. They can also be used to corral fish, whales, and other ocean livestock. For all too long, these creatures have been free to roam the range of the oceans. It is time, it is past time, for we humans to do for them what we have done for land-based animals[110]: to tame and domesticate them,[111] and to bring them within the purview of economic rationality.[112]

Not only is water connected in the horizontal realm, so to speak, the same pertains in the vertical. That is, the three quarters of the earth's surface on which water rests is the horizontal axis, while the vertical dimen-

[109] Anderson and Leal, op. cit., report on the function of cowboys as "human fences."

[110] For the argument that elephants, rhinos, and other endangered species would benefit from being barnyardized, for example, fenced in with electrically charged wires, see Anderson and Leal, op. cit., Simmons, Randy, and Kreuter, Urs, "Herd Mentality: Banning Ivory Sales is No Way to Save the Elephant," *Policy Review*, Fall 1989, pp. 46–49; Block, Walter, "Environmental Problems, Private Property Rights Solutions," *Economics and the Environment: A Reconciliation*, Vancouver: The Fraser Institute, 1990, pp. 281–332; Block, Walter, "Environmentalism and Freedom: The Case for Private Property Rights," *Journal of Business Ethics*, Vol. 17, No. 6, December 1998, pp. 1887–1899.

[111] For the argument that this is symbiotic, for example, beneficial to both mankind and animal and fish species, see Heffner, Henry E., "The Symbiotic Nature of Animal Research," *Perspectives in Biology and Medicine*, Vol. 43. No. 1, Autumn 1999.

[112] It is time, too, to jettison such socialist and profoundly anti-private property rights songs as "Home, home on the range," and "Where the deer and the antelope play."

sion refers to the fact that a molecule is at one time water in the ocean, at another it evaporates and travels into the clouds, whereupon it rains down onto the surface of the earth, either on land or in the sea, but eventually comes to rest in the latter, after traveling through the river system. It is thus insufficient to ascertain only who is the owner of water in the sea; this must also be determined, if we are to specify a complete system, for water while it is on its way up to the sky though evaporation, while it is in a (temporary) state of "rest" in the clouds, and when it is on its way down again in the form of rain.

But these are mere technical issues. Where there is a will (and a legal system which supports it), there is a way. The reason this has not yet occurred is not entirely due to costs; a large part of the blame must rest, also, with the fact that we have not pushed the private property rights envelope far enough, yet, in terms of water.

E. Arrogance[113]

The idea that man should own the oceans and the seas will appear as arrogance to some people. The "tower of Babel" story in the Bible[114] would appear to be apropos. When man's pride and ambition got him above himself, God struck back by making it difficult to him to communicate with his fellows.

But why should land be any different from water? If it is not morally sinful to aspire to ownership of the former, why should this apply to the latter? One might, with as much reason, claim that walking is justified, but that driving a car, sailing a boat, or, perish the thought, flying an airplane are perversions, or somehow impious.

F. Legal Nightmare

Suppose a river, such as the Mississippi, changes its course, and starts moving over previously dry land. Or that any river overflows, flooding surrounding farms and neighboring houses. If the river in question were

[113] We owe this objection to Marybeth Block.

[114] See also Aristophanes' theory of love.

privately owned, a charge could be made that this would create a legal nightmare.

This is only legally problematic, however, because there are no precedents, and there are no precedents, in turn, because rivers are presently unowned. Their mismanagement hence now constitutes an "act of God." Instead of blaming the Deity, we would do well to attempt to address these dangers and inconveniences. Just as there should be no "fish freedom" the same should apply to rivers. Flooding and course changes[115] should be seen for the mismanagement they are. The reason there has been no private investment in taming these unruly bodies of water is that there are no economic incentives to do so. It would not pay for any single farmer located on the banks of a river to attempt to take on so gargantuan a task. Neoclassical economists would characterize this as a "market failure," since such a farmer would not be able to recoup an amount even near to his total investment. But these so-called external economies stem not from anything intrinsic to the situation; rather, they are the result of lack of ownership and responsibility.

Of course, there will be complications when this arena of the law is recognized. Absent any contract to the contrary, for example, a river owner should not be liable for all damages caused, say, by flooding due to heavy rain,[116] but only for those in excess of the amount that otherwise would have ensued. For example, if it can be shown that ordinarily, under river socialism, a storm of a certain severity would cause $100 in damages, and that in the actual event it caused only $75, then plaintiff should not be able to collect anything at all from the river owner. On the other hand, if under our assumptions $125 worth of harm was inflicted upon

[115] This applies only to *unwelcome* flooding and course changes. But railroads and highways (see footnote 13 *supra*) sometimes change their location. If there is an economic need for this in the case of a river, and it is accomplished at minimal cost, then this constitutes an exception to the claim made in the text.

[116] We assume, for the moment, that the level of technology, or of the law, is such that the clouds themselves are not owned, and that thus no one is liable for their excessive and unwarranted rain on the river. For some people, to blame rain or storm on the state is only a joke. This is not the case at present. Had the government not taken as much of the GDP as it has, to fritter it away on warfare and welfare state considerations (and for numbered bank accounts in Switzerland), there would have been just that much more available to address private needs. Some of this, undoubtedly, would have been spent in an effort to domesticate weather conditions.

owners whose property abuts the river, then the defendant would be responsible for at most $25.

G. "Equity"

Another argument against private ownership is that the rich would hog it all up, and leave the short end of the stick for the poor. There is no doubt that this fear motivates, at least in part, the U.N. Law of the Sea Treaty, according to which "the oceans are the common heritage of all of mankind,"[117] and that therefore no individual nation, let alone private person, should be allowed to own any of it. The fear on the part of the U.N. bureaucrats who hail from the underdeveloped nations is that they do not have the requisite technology to mine manganese nodules at the bottom of the ocean, for example, and that it is "unfair" for those with this ability to be able to make us of it on their own accounts. Another way of putting this matter is that the landlocked nations would be at a disadvantage vis-a-vis those which border on the sea, and that the former are poorer than the latter, and thus it would be "inequitable" to allow a competitive race to take advantage of such watery resources.

The implication seems to be better that no one should be able to own aqueous possessions than that the rich be afforded this opportunity. One difficulty with this position is that it equates "equity" or "fairness" with "egalitarianism." But nothing could be further from the truth. If it were so, then advocates of this position would be willing to give up their own "excessive" intelligence, or IQ points, were this possible, to their less intellectually well-endowed brethren. That no one has even taken this position shows that even its advocates shrink in horror from the logical implications of their own system.

Insofar as is the economic well-being of the poor of the earth is concerned, it is clear that the wealth of the less fortunate would be enhanced, not worsened, by allowing economic opportunity to the rich. This is because economic development is a positive, not a zero sum game. Under capitalism, the wherewithal enjoyed by both parties to a transaction, at

[117] https://www.un.org/Depts/los/convention_agreements/texts/unclos/closindx.htm.

least in the ex-ante sense, is increased. The rich do not increase their income at the expense of the poor; rather, their income rises by *enriching* the less well to do. It is no accident that the poor in the more capitalist west enjoy a standard of living that is the envy of those at the bottom of the income distribution, and even in the middle of it, in countries infected by coercive socialism.[118]

H. Monopoly

There is the fear that under private ownership of seas, there could be monopolistic encroachment. For example, A owns an island which is completely surrounded by ocean,[119] and B owns the surrounding patch of water. Thus, A would be trapped on his island prison. Some property rights for A!

But a moment's reflection should convince us that this is an unlikely if not an impossible situation.[120] First of all, the primary and first user of the waterway surrounding island A is likely to be A himself. According to homesteading theory, A would thus be the rightful owner of the surrounding aqueous area, not B. Second, if B first homesteaded the water, and only then, later, did A come upon the island to take up ownership over it, the latter would never have done so unless his access and egress rights were clearly specified in such a manner so as to not preclude the economic viability of ownership of the island in the first place. Third, there are airplanes and helicopters available, at least in the modern era.[121]

---

[118] See on this, Gwartney, James, Robert Lawson and Walter Block, *Economic Freedom of the World, 1975–1995* Vancouver, B.C. Canada: the Fraser Institute, 1996.

[119] This is by definition.

[120] A similar objection with regard to private roads and streets has been dealt with in Block, Walter, "Free Market Transportation: Denationalizing the Roads," *Journal of Libertarian Studies: An Interdisciplinary Review*, Vol. III, No. 2, Summer 1979, pp. 209–238, see footnote 13, *supra*.

[121] This of course invites discussion of ownership of the relevant air travel rights, a topic we address below.

4. Full and Complete Privatization

Notwithstanding all the objections in the foregoing, there are good and sufficient reasons to contemplate the privatization of bodies of water. With this introduction, we are now in a position to consider some of them.

The thesis of the present chapter is that all bodies of water should be fully and completely privatized. Consider the ocean in this regard. This would mean not merely that fishing should be limited to those who purchase rights to do so, but that the whole kit and caboodle would be treated in much the same way as are land holdings.[122] That is, the surface of the ocean would be owned, just as railroads presently are, at least in the United States, and just as roads and highways would be, at least as contemplated by authors who advocate such a situation.[123] This is not to say that it is contemplated that all of the oceans, every single cubic foot of them, should immediately be privatized. Many of them are as presently worthless as is some of the more out of the way acreage in Alaska, Antarctica, and Siberia.[124] All we are deliberating upon is the *legal status* of these places. At present, it is impossible to own them, because both the

---

[122] There are several publications whose titles indicate they are compatible with this very radical enterprise, but they are misnomers. For example, Anderson, Terry L., and Leal, Donald R., *Free Market Environmentalism*, San Francisco: Pacific Research Institute, 1991 call their chapter 9 "Homesteading the Oceans," a policy taken seriously in the present paper, but these authors discuss only schemes to quasi-privatize fish; similarly the title employed by Runoflsson, Birgir, "Fencing the Oceans," *Regulation*, Summer 1997. pp. 57–62 is misleading in that it also advocates only individual transferable quotas (ITQs) in fish, as its subtitle ("A Rights-Based Approach to Privatizing Fisheries") makes clear. A similar analysis applies to Eckert, Ross D., *The Enclosure of Ocean Resources: Economics and the Law of the Sea*, Stanford, CA: Hoover Institution Press, 1979. For a critique of tradeable emissions rights (TERs), the air analogue of ITQs in the water, see McGee, Robert W. and Walter Block, "Pollution Trading Permits as a Form of Market Socialism, and the Search for a Real Market Solution to Environmental Pollution," *Fordham University Law and Environmental Journal*, Vol. VI, No. 1, Fall 1994, pp. 51–77. Jeffreys, Kent, "Who Should Own the Ocean," *Competitive Enterprise Institute Update*, No. 8, August 1991, pp. 1–2, perhaps comes the closest of the material cited in this footnote to my own vision of full water privatization, but even it focuses mainly on the problem of over fishing, and contemplates "permitting … outright ownership of limited ocean areas. For example, offshore rigs…" But why not outright ownership of *all* as opposed to "limited" ocean areas? Private ownership of offshore rigs, moreover, is already a staple of present sea law.

[123] See footnote 13, *supra*.

[124] Actually, these are particularly inept examples, in that land in none of these three places is fully open for private holdings.

law does not allow it, and, in many cases,[125] ownership is not yet economically viable. What is being advocated is a change in the *law*, such that those parts of the watery domain for which private property is now economically workable would be allowed at once to be owned, and that more and more of them could come to be owned when their economic status changed so as to make this a paying proposition.

One clear benefit would be that world GDP would rise. At present, the oceans and seas, as we have seen, account for a large part of the earth's surface, but only a small percentage[126] of the world GDP. It need not be the case that each and every acre of the earth's surface should account for the same proportionate contribution to GDP as does every other. Deserts are less productive than fertile land. But at least a large part of the vast disparity between productivity on land and in and on water must be due to the beneficial effects of private property rights on land which do not apply to water.[127]

On land, man went through the hunting and gathering stage, during which his standard of living was appropriate to the Stone Age. When he graduated from this precarious existence to one of farming, his standard of living exploded in an upward direction, as did sustainable population size. After that came manufacturing, and then the information age, with similar upward spurts in how well man could live, and how many of this species could be supported.

As far as the seas are concerned, however, we are still back in a cave man type of development, where hunting and gathering are in the main the only avenues open to us. It was not until the institution of private property took hold on the land that farming, herding, and later developments could be supported. It is a well-known fact, at least within the free market environmental community,[128] that the cow prospered, due to private property rights which could avert the tragedy of the commons, while

[125] Apart from those areas of the seas which are located near population centers. There is no doubt that did the law but allow it, for example, private individuals would be willing, and more than willing, to own the Hudson River.

[126] See text accompanying footnote 93.

[127] See on this the large "tragedy of the commons" literature. Indeed, one could expand this so as to include the literature on the failure of socialism, "water socialism" in this case.

[128] See footnotes 110 and 122, *supra*.

the bison almost perished as a species due to lack of the same. Nowadays, happily, this problem has been remedied with regard to the buffalo.[129] But the whale, the porpoise, edible fish, and other sea species are dealt with, at present, in precisely the same manner that almost accounted for the disappearance of the bison.

ITQs, of course, are a vast improvement over nonownership, with attendant and uneconomic over fishing. But they constitute only a quasi-private property rights system, not the pure form of this institution. In order to see this, consider imposing ITQs on buffalo, or elephants. This would mean that these animals would still be free to roam as they wished, but it would be legal for only certain people to be able to hunt them. The point is we would still be in the hunting stage of human existence with regard to such species. But if economic history has taught us anything, it is that herding is far more efficient than hunting (e.g., corralling fish in the open ocean is far more effective than fishing, or hunting, for them).

This scenario assumes, of course, that the necessary complementary technological breakthroughs occur, such as either genetic branding, or perhaps better yet, electrified fences, which can keep the denizens of the deep penned in where deep-sea fish farmers want them. Yes, this seems unlikely at present, given that under present law there would be no economic benefit to such inventions. But this is due, in turn, not to any primordial fact of nature or law. Rather, it is because the law has not yet been changed so as to recognize even the possible future scenario where ocean privatization would be economic. The public policy recommendation stemming from this analysis is merely that the law should now be changed so as to recognize fish ownership in a given cubic area of ocean when and if such an act becomes technically viable. Then, whether or not it actually occurs is only an empirical question. It will, if and only if the complementary technology is forthcoming to make it feasible. But under this ideal state of affairs, there would be no legal impediment, as there now is, in this direction. That is, suppose that the needed innovations never occur, or are always too expensive, compared to the gains to be made by herding fish instead of hunting them. Then, of course, there can

[129] And other previously endangered species also, such as the elephant, the rhinoceros, and the alligator.

be no private property rights used in this manner in the ocean, as a matter of fact. But as a matter of *law*, things would still be different under the present proposal. There would always be the contrary to fact conditional in operation that *if* technology were such, *then* it would be legal to fence in parts of the ocean for these purposes. Under this state of affairs, there would be no legal impediments to the development of the requisite technology.[130]

[130] It is on this point that the Chicago School analysis of property rights goes wrong. In that perspective, private property rights only arise when technology, an exogenous force, makes them economically practicable. There can *be* no private property rights in the ocean unless and until electric sea fences are invented. Science is the dog; the law is the tail that is wagged. In contrast, in the libertarian vision that underlies the present paper, technology is endogenous. It is the tail that is wagged by the legal dog. Private property rights to *anything* will *always* be recognized in law, as a matter of course, stemming from homesteading: when and if ocean owners stake claims, based on mixing their labor with this element, for which new presently non-existing technology is available, then it will be recognized. The difference in this case is a subtle one: in the libertarian legal code, the law gives incentives for such innovations, by guaranteeing recognition of such property titles when they are achieved; in the Chicagoite tradition, the law does not. For the Chicago view of property rights, see Posner, Richard A., "Killing or Wounding to Protect a Property Interest," 14 *Journal of Law & Economics* 201 (1971); Posner, Richard A., *Economic Analysis of Law* (5th ed., Aspen Law & Business, 1998); Coase, Ronald, H., "The Problem of Social Cost," *Journal of Law and Economics*, October 1960, Vol. 3, pp. 1–44; Demsetz, Harold, "Some Aspects of Property Rights," *Journal of Law and Economics*, Vol. IX, October 1966; Demsetz, Harold, "Toward a Theory of Property Rights," *American Economic Review*, 57: 347–359, 1967. For the libertarian critique, see Block, Walter, "O.J.'s Defense: A Reductio Ad Absurdum of the Economics of Ronald Coase and Richard Posner," *European Journal of Law and Economics*, 1996, Vol. 3, pp. 265–286; Cordato, Roy, E., "Knowledge Problems and the Problem of Social Cost," *Journal of the History of Economic Thought* 14 Fall 1992a; Cordato, Roy E., "Subjective Value, Time Passage, and the Economics of Harmful Effects," *Hamline Law Review*, Vol. 12, No. 2, Spring 1989, pp. 229–244; Cordato, Roy E., *Welfare Economics and Externalities in an Open-Ended Universe: A Modern Austrian Perspective*, Boston: Kluwer, 1992b; Krecke, Elisabeth, "Law and the Market Order: An Austrian Critique of the Economic Analysis of Law," *Journal des Economistes et des Etudes Humaines* 7(1), March 1996, pp. 19–37; *Commentaries on Law & Economics*, 1997 Yearbook, ed., Robert W. McGee, pp. 86–109; North, Gary, *Tools of Dominion: The Case Laws of Exodus*, Tyler, TX: Institute for Christian Economics, 1990; North, Gary, *The Coase Theorem*, Tyler, TX: The Institute for Christian Economics, 1992. For the debate between Block and Demsetz on these matters see Block, Walter, "Coase and Demsetz on Private Property Rights," *The Journal of Libertarian Studies: An Interdisciplinary Review*, Vol. I, No. 2, Spring 1977, pp. 111–115; Demsetz, Harold, "Ethics and Efficiency in Property Rights Systems," in *Time, Uncertainty and Disequilibrium: Explorations of Austrian Themes*, Mario Rizzo, ed., Lexington Mass.: D.C. Heath and Co., 1979; Block, Walter, "Ethics, Efficiency, Coasean Property Rights and Psychic Income: A Reply to Demsetz," *Review of Austrian Economics*, Vol. 8, No. 2, 1995, pp. 61–125; Demsetz, Harold, "Block's Erroneous Interpretations," The Review of Austrian Economics, Vol. 10, No. 2, 1997, pp. 101–109; Block, Walter, "Private Property Rights, Erroneous Interpretations, Morality and Economics: Reply to Demsetz," *Quarterly Journal of Austrian Economics*, Vol. 3, No. 1, Spring 2000, pp. 63–78.

Another benefit would be making the earth a more habitable place in which to live. Consider in this regard clouds, flooding, fog, hurricanes, storms, tidal waves, tornados, torrential rain, tsunamis, typhoons, whirlpools, winds, and so on. At present, these are considered acts of God. If the oceans and the air, from which and in which these disasters emanate, were allowed by law to be owned by firms or individuals, at least in principle, this might well set up the first steps in mankind's long journey to quelling these "natural" disasters. How else could this ever be done, other than by employing the institution of private property rights, which is responsible for so much else we include under the category of "good works?"

5. Foundations

A. Libertarian

Let us now consider a theory of ownership in bodies of water that can be characterized as "libertarian," or "Lockean" or as one based on homesteading. An almost entirely accurate rendition of this philosophy is offered by Trelease, Frank J.[131]:

> The Code is designed for an easterner seeking a new water law for his state. He should clearly understand this choice. To help him, I offer an analogy to another resource with which he is quite familiar, and which like water must be wisely used, protected, sometimes preserved from use, and which must be shifted from old uses to new and more desirable uses as times and needs change. *Think land.* Land is just as valuable and indispensable a resource as water. Our lives and our wealth depend upon it. The government, the ultimate source of title, wishes to see that the resource is put to its highest and best use. It could do this administratively. A 'land bureaucrat' could allow its temporary use for particular regulated purposes at will or for a term of years, but when a new or better use is seen, reallocate it by moving off the present tenant and installing a new one. Instead, the gov-

[131] "The Model Water Code, The Wise Administrator and the Goddam (sic!) Bureaucrat," 14 *Nat. Resources J.* 207 (1974) [this can also be found in Trelease, Frank J., *Water Law, Cases and Materials*, third ed., American Casebook Series, St. Paul, MN: West Publishing Co., 1979, p. 9].

ernment allocates the land in discrete and identifiable parcels, as private property. The land laws make these property rights very firm and secure. Land is then available for use by individuals to produce wealth. Since each person will try to make the best use of it that he can, the total of individual wealth will approach the production of maximum national wealth. Yet new and more productive uses by a different person may come to be seen desirable. Since the land is a valuable asset, if it were to be transferred to another person without compensation, the first holder would be impoverished and the latter enriched. Therefore, the laws provide that the property rights are not only secure but are voluntarily transferable. The land can be bought by the new user for the new purpose by paying the owner a price. In most cases the government is willing to let the change occur because it knows the new use is better than the old, since otherwise the buyer could not afford to pay the seller the capitalized values of the seller's use plus a profit…

How is the situation different if we say 'water' instead of 'land' in the above paragraph?

Although Trelease does not answer his own question, based on the context it seems a rhetorical one. The clear answer is that there is no difference whatsoever between land and water as far as privatization is concerned. This is the essence of the libertarian theory of water privatization: aqueous resources should be treated exactly the way land would be dealt with, in a fully free enterprise society.[132]

B. Riparian, Appropriation

In contrast to this libertarian view, there are two main legal precedents at work in the US as concerns water rights. These are the main competitors with the libertarian theory. They are, respectively, riparian ownership, in which the rights to the use of a body of water is given to the abutting landowners, and appropriation, wherein use of the water establishes not ownership, but the right to continued use.

---

[132]Trelease himself, ibid., makes several concessions as regards land ownership for "zoning, land use planning laws," and condemnation for "a public purpose." This would be incompatible with the libertarian legal code, whether on land or in water.

States Posner in this regard:

In the eastern states, where water is plentiful, water rights are communalized to a significant extent, the basic rule being that riparian owners (i.e., the owners of the shore of a body of water) are each entitled to make reasonable use of the water—a use that does not interfere unduly with the uses of the other riparians. In the western states, where water is scarce, exclusive rights can be obtained by appropriation (use).[133]

And in the view of Trelease:

Riparian rights are governed by the common law. The modern form of riparian law gives each owner of land bordering on the stream a right to make a reasonable use of the water and impose liability on the upper riparian owner who unreasonably interferes with that use. The right exists whether or not the water is actually used, and a use may be initiated at any time. The use must usually be made on the riparian land and within the watershed of the stream. A non-riparian who uses water is liable to any riparian he injures and conversely a riparian who initiates a use which interferes with a prior non-riparian use is subject to no liability. Some states do not give effect to attempts of riparian proprietors to grant their water rights to non-riparians.

Appropriative rights are governed primarily by statute. An appropriation may be described as a state administrative grant that allows the use of a specific quantity of water for a specific beneficial purpose if water is available in the source free from the claims of others with earlier appropriations. The right is initiated by an application for a permit. The place of use is not restricted to riparian land or even to the watershed. The right may be sold and its use or place of use changed, and it may cease to exist if it is not used.

Riparian law, developed in the green countrysides of England and Eastern America, seems to be based on the unspoken premise that if rights to the use of water are restricted to those persons who have access to it through the ownership of the banks and if those persons will restrict their demands on the water to reasonable uses, there will be enough for all. Appropriation law, developed in the arid West, is usually thought of as a

---

[133] Posner, Richard A., *Economic Analysis of Law*, third ed., Boston: Little Brown, 1986, pp. 34–35.

Table 10.1 Summary of the appropriation, riparian and libertarian perspectives

	Appropriation	Riparian	Libertarian
1. How established	Use	Abutting land ownership	Use*
2. Can sell?	Yes	No	Yes
3. What get?	Specific quantity	Reasonable use	Whatever
4. Permanent?	Yes		Yes
5. Absentee owner?		Yes	Yes
6. Where must use	Anywhere	On riparian land only	Anywhere
7. Application	Streams, rivers	Streams, rivers	All bodies of water

> system for water-short areas. Where there is not enough for everyone, the rule of priority insures that those who obtain rights will not have their water taken by others who start later. The theory is that as demands arise water rights to supply them will be given out until the water is exhausted, after which those with new demands must purchase rights.[134]

In contrast with these "mainstream" theories of water ownership, the libertarian theory of property in water is more radical than either of them; in that, it applies to *all* bodies of water, not just streams or rivers, as do the other two. It is very similar to appropriation; after all, "appropriation" is practically a synonym for "homesteading." But there are subtle differences between the two. How do the three systems compare with one another: the riparian, the appropriation, and the libertarian. Table 10.1 affords a summary look.

As can be seen, the appropriation and the libertarian system are very similar. Let us explore their differences, if only to defend against the claim that they are identical. One clear difference is in terms of 7. Application. Appropriation applies only to streams and rivers (as does the riparian theory of rights), while the libertarian applies to all bodies of water, including those two but also oceans, seas, and so on. Another difference concerns 3. What get? In actual practice, the appropriation owners each

[134]Trelease, Frank J., *Water Law, Cases and Materials*, third ed., American Casebook Series, St. Paul, MN: West Publishing Co., 1979, pp. 10–11.

get a small share of the total water available. While this might upon some occasions be the libertarian conclusion as well, it is also possible under the latter system, but not the former, for one person or firm to take over ownership of an entire body of water. If Henry Hudson not only discovered the Hudson River, but had also mixed his labor with it in its entirety before anyone else came upon the scene, then under the libertarian provision, he could be the owner of this entire river.

11

The Value of Private Water Rights

Introduction

As the world's resources become increasingly scarce with the passage of time and increase in population, different theories emerge as to which avenues of remedy would be most effective. Privatization of the world's natural resources has been occurring for a millennia. However, as social, political, and economic systems have emerged and faded throughout history, there has been a greater push for privatization. Currently, as the world's population passes the six billion mark and environmental degradation continues to occur, some advocate privatization as a solution to many of the world's problems.

The world's oceans, apart from the territorial seas and exclusive economic zones of nations, are classified as the high seas. Neither individuals nor nations have property rights in the high seas. Partly as a result of this communal ownership, the tragedy of the commons has come into play and fisheries have been depleted whilst other marine animal and plant life suffer as well. If an entrepreneurial system were instituted in the world's

W. E. Block, R. Whitehead, *Philosophy of Law*, Palgrave Studies in Classical Liberalism,
https://doi.org/10.1007/978-3-030-28360-5_11

oceans, it is arguable that pollution would decrease and plant and animal species would be conserved. To understand how such a system would successfully function, it is necessary to first examine the history and practice of private water rights and usage in the United States. Parallels can then be drawn and possibilities can be explored for the application of U.S.-based water doctrine to the oceans.

Part I of this chapter begins with a discussion of the historical background of the development of water rights in the arid regions of the Western United States. The historical picture is framed to highlight the importance of the public policy and tax implications that arise when an entrepreneur purchases arid real property with a reasonable expectation that rights to scarce water will attach to the property in the future. In *Gladden v. Comm'r Internal Revenue*,[1] the Internal Revenue Service ("IRS") and the U.S. Tax Court contended that the original purchaser could not count the premium paid for the future water rights when determining the tax basis for the sale of those rights.[2] The Court of Appeals reversed and put forth a different view including in the cost basis some of the value of after-acquired water rights.[3] The Ninth Circuit decision is reasonable and meets public policy goals because it encourages private ownership of water rights.

In Part II of this chapter, a general case for private property rights in bodies of water is made. It begins by mentioning the environmental problems that result from the present system of socialized water ownership. Four philosophical stances on environmental issues in general are outlined focusing on water privatization. We then discuss and assess how privatization of bodies of water can be of use in solving these problems, utilizing some conjectural examples.

---

[1] *See generally* 262 F. 3d 851 (9th Cir. 2001).

[2] Id. at 852.

[3] *See* id.

I. Legal Perspective on Water Rights

A. Historical Approaches to the Appropriation of Water Rights

The general right to use Western water occurs within the rules set out by the so-called prior appropriation doctrine (the doctrine).[4] The doctrine grew out of the California Gold Rush era of 1848–1860.[5] Gold mining required a great deal of water. As one commentator has explained:

> The discovery of gold in the Sierra foothills of California in January 1848 and the great mining industry that followed had a profound influence, not only upon the political and economic growth of California, but upon the development of water law in this state and throughout the entire West. The association of gold and water came about because much of the gold was extracted from the ground by means of hydraulic or pacer mining processes in which the use of water was essential. Rights to use the water therefore became fundamentally important.[6]

Hydraulic mining made considerable economic sense to the gold miners because it reduced manual labor.[7] Rather than engaging in laborious, expensive, and often dangerous digging, they could rapidly wash away the overlying clay and soil to get to the gold.[8] The cost of digging and panning a cubic yard of dirt was $20, but only 20 cents using the hydraulic method.[9] It is a small wonder that the minors sought a water use doctrine to support their search for gold. The prior appropriation doctrine

---

[4] *See* Marc Reisner & Sarah Bates, Overtapped Oasis: Reform Or Revolution For Western Water 62 (1990).

[5] Id.

[6] Id. *citing* W. Hutchins, The California Law Of Water Rights 41 (1956). SOURCE NOT IN PACKET.

[7] Donald Pisani, To Reclaim A Divided West: Water, Law, And Public Policy 1848–1902, 17 (1992).

[8] Id.

[9] Id. at 18.

naturally fit the bill.[10] It provided certainty that water would be available for the appropriator's needs.[11] The prior appropriation doctrine is based on the idea that the first person to put water to a beneficial use has a superior right to the water.[12] This is so even if the use is not contiguous to a stream.[13] Consequently, the doctrine of prior appropriation is based on first in use and first in time appropriation, rather than ownership of the adjacent upland.[14] It is generally accepted that nine Western states follow a strict prior appropriation doctrine. They are Alaska, Arizona, Colorado, Idaho, Montana, Nevada, New Mexico, Utah, and Wyoming.[15] As previously indicated, water rights are vested when water is diverted for a beneficial use.[16] The parameters of beneficial use are sometimes problematic for definitional purposes. One commentator on Western water rights recently wrote that as a practical matter the term, "beneficial use" really means any use at all.[17] Most states, however, have a statutory definition that includes examples of economic and socially beneficial purposes.[18] The right to receive water under the doctrine does not depend on balancing the most economically or socially desirable use.[19] Finally, senior appropriators are entitled to take their entire entitlement as long as there is available water in the stream.[20] This first in time, first in right, philosophy can be extremely harsh on junior appropriators who may receive no water in dry years.[21] In some cases, the application of strict prior

---

[10] It worked for the early miners who first diverted the water and to early irrigators who needed a reliable water source for their crops. *See* Reisner & Bates, *supra* footnote 4, at 64.

[11] Id. But this certainty did not require the reallocation of water for competing community needs that might arise later on like city water supplies. Id. at 65. "[T]he prior appropriation doctrine is so firmly entrenched in Western laws and customs that its abolition is almost unthinkable." Id.

[12] Id. at 62, 63.

[13] Id. at 62–63.

[14] Reisner & Bates, *supra* footnote 4, at 63.

[15] Id. at 63.

[16] Id.

[17] Robert Glennon, Water Follies: Groundwater Pumping And The Fate Of America's Fresh Water 16 (2002).

[18] Reisner & Bates, *supra* footnote 4 at 63, *citing* Colo. Rev. Stat. § 37-92-102(3) (2002) (balancing use of water by mankind with reasonable preservation of nature).

[19] Id.

[20] Id.

[21] Id.

appropriation may result in de-watering of streams,[22] or the lowering of the water table and land surface.[23]

Early Western courts and legislatures wanted to stimulate the growing mining industry that was largely developing on federal lands.[24] Almost all the court cases involving water rights between 1850 and 1870 addressed the use of water for mining.[25] Additionally, water-driven mining practices such as hydraulic mining were expanded over the years as water was diverted great distances from the available streams.[26] During this period, the courts struggled to decide whether the public policy would be best served by prior appropriation or some other doctrine. Eventually, the right of prior appropriation was recognized in two cases involving the diversion of water by the initial claimant at the expense of downstream miners.[27] As the case law developed, the doctrine of prior appropriation had been generally accepted in the West around 1860.[28] That meant that the first claimant had an exclusive right to use the water, regardless of the amount appropriated.[29] All other users had to wait for the initial claimant, who had an exclusive right to take water first.[30] The initial claimant could use the water anywhere, any distance from the stream, even if the use caused the stream to run dry.[31] By 1865, this water use doctrine had reached the U.S. Supreme Court, which decided to recognize the local laws, customs, and decisions in the West that supported prior appropriation.[32] Having briefly framed the historical picture of water rights in the West, it is necessary to address the question of valuation of those rights.

---

[22] Glennon, *supra* footnote 16, at 17 (noting is some cases there are more rights than actual water).

[23] Id. at 32–33 (showing that the land surface has dropped several feet in southern Arizona due to land subsidence caused by taking the underlying water).

[24] Pisani, *supra* footnote 7, at 11.

[25] Id. at 223.

[26] Id.

[27] *See* Eddy v. Simpson, 3 Cal. 249, 252, 253 (Cal. 1853), and Irwin v. Phillips, 5 Cal. 140, 145 (Cal. 1855).

[28] *See* Pisani, *supra* footnote 7, at 31.

[29] Id.

[30] Id.

[31] Id.

[32] *See* Sparrow v. Strong, 70 U.S. 97, 104 (1865).

Questions about the supply of and future access to precious water for agricultural and industrial purposes are a pressing national concern.[33] IRS regulations and the policies of other government agencies including the Environmental Protection Agency ("EPA") and the U.S. Fish and Wildlife Service influence answers to these questions. The policies of these agencies affect the willingness of private property entrepreneurs to invest capital in an expectation of obtaining and maintaining those water rights.[34] The government agencies including the IRS can best serve the nation's water interests by encouraging private investment in water rights and in all other property rights. To that end, we examine the case of *Gladden v. Commissioner*,[35] in which the Ninth Circuit Court of Appeals reversed a decision by the Tax Court and resolved an issue of first impression. The contentious issue in the case was whether water rights that are "not legally vested" at the time of purchase can be attributed to a private partnership's cost basis in land.[36]

B. Underlying Facts of the Gladdens' Decision

The Gladdens were half-partners in the Saddle Mountain Ranch Partnership (the Partnership), which farmed land in the Harquahala Valley, Arizona.[37] In 1976, the Partnership purchased 880 acres of land at a cost of $675,000.[38] When purchased, the land had no appurtenant water rights, but fell geographically within the boundaries of the

[33] *See* Roy Whitehead, Jr. & Walter Block, *Environmental Takings of Private Water Rights: The Case for Water Privatization*, 32 Envtl. L. Rep. 11162, 11162 (2002) (citing Bjorn Lomborg, The Skeptical Environmentalist: Measuring the Real State Of The World 149 (2001)) (indicating that there is no shortage of water and that a perceived water shortage is caused by logistical problems).

[34] *See* id. at 1170 (discussing the utility of private ownership of water and other property); *see also* Walter Block, *Environmentalism and Economic Freedom: The Case for Private Property Rights*, available at http://cba.loyno.edu/faculty/Block/Blockarticles/environmentalism.htm (last updated June 12, 2001) (arguing that although environmental protectionism and economic freedom have an "inverse" relationship, the two concepts may still be reconciled).

[35] *See generally Gladden*, 262 F.3d 851.

[36] Id. at 853.

[37] Id. at 852.

[38] Id.

Harquahala Valley Irrigation District ("HID").[39] HID was a municipal corporation that was formed in 1964 for the basic purpose of acquiring water rights and distributing water for irrigation.[40] The Colorado River Basin Project Act ("the Act") was approved in 1968 by Congress and established the Central Arizona Project, which focused on importing water to the Harquahala Valley from the Colorado River.[41] The Act restricted the availability of water by providing that water "shall not be made available directly or indirectly for the irrigation of lands not having a recent irrigation history…."[42] The Partnership's land was not affected by the Act as it had a "recent irrigation history" at the time of purchase.[43] At its inception, the Act prevented landowners within the irrigation district from separating their water rights from the land; they could only sell their water rights "as part of a sale of the land to which [the rights] were appurtenant."[44] This practice continued until 1993, when the Federal Government contracted with the HID to allow water rights to be sold independently from the land, if sold to the government.[45] The Partnership took part in this agreement and sold its water rights for $1,088,132, keeping a share of the sale price in the amount of $543,566.[46] The Gladdens listed this amount as a capital gain on their 1993 tax return; "[t]hey offset this gain by the portion of the original purchase price for the land that they claimed was paid for the expectation of water rights."[47] This calculation resulted in a reportable taxable capital gain of $130,762 for the Gladdens.[48]

---

[39] Id.

[40] *Gladden*, 262 F.3d at 852.

[41] Id.

[42] 43 U.S.C. § 1524(a) (1986).

[43] Id.

[44] Id.

[45] Id.

[46] Id.

[47] Id.

[48] *Gladden*, 262 F.3d at 852.

C. The Procedural History of the Tax Court Decision

The Tax Commissioner did not agree with the capital gain as calculated by the Gladdens. The Commissioner calculated that "the Gladdens' share of the sale of the water rights was properly characterized as a $543,566 receipt of ordinary income, with no offset for any price paid for an expectancy in the water rights."[49] The Gladdens petitioned the Tax Court for review on the grounds that the water rights constituted a capital asset.[50] They claimed that there had been a "sale or exchange" according to the Tax Code and that it was thus proper to distribute some portion of their tax basis in the land to the sale of the water rights.[51] They contended that "because it was impossible to determine what portion of the basis should be allocated to the water rights, capital gain from the sale of the water rights should not be recognized until all of the cost basis in the land had been recovered."[52]

The Tax Court granted summary judgment in favor of the Gladdens on the first two issues, holding that the sale of the water rights was considered a sale of a capital asset, in accordance with the Tax Code.[53] The Court found for the Commissioner on a third issue because the partnership had purchased the land prior to acquiring water rights and therefore could not use a portion of their land-based tax to the sale of those rights.[54] The question is thus presented of whether an entrepreneur[55] would reasonably consider the potential for future water rights when making a choice to invest in real property.

---

[49] Id. (issuing a notice of deficiency to the Gladdens for $110,809).

[50] Id.

[51] Id.

[52] Id.

[53] *Gladden*, 262 F.3d at 852–3.

[54] Id. at 853.

[55] *See* Gene Callahan, Economics For Real People 77–78 (Mises Inst. 2002) (using the term "entrepreneur" to represent those individuals who "search for potential profit opportunities that are not being taken advantage of").

D. Grounds for the Court of Appeals Reversal in Favor of the Gladdens

The Court of Appeals found that the defining issue in *Gladden* to be whether any of the cost basis in the land purchased by the partnership in 1976 could be proportioned to water rights that were expected, but not legally vested, at the time of purchase.[56] The Court began its analysis by looking to the *Code of Federal Regulations*:

> When a part of a larger property is sold, the cost or other basis of the entire property shall be equitably apportioned among the several parts, and the gain realized or loss sustained on the part of the entire property sold is the difference between the selling price and the cost or other basis allocated to such part.[57]

This regulation provides that when property is acquired in a "lump-sum purchase but then divided and sold off in parts, the cost basis of the property should generally be allocated over the several parts."[58] The *Gladden* court illustrated this line of reasoning by comparing the example of a land developer who subdivides a large tract of land into smaller parcels.[59] When the developer later sells off the parcels, "he must allocate his cost basis in the overall property among the smaller parcels" to determine his capital gain or loss on the sale of those properties.[60] In *Gladden*, the rule would have applied if the water rights were vested when the Partnership first purchased the land. A precedent illustrating this principle is supplied by the *Inaja Land Co. v. Commissioner*[61] decision, in which the court held that "where property is acquired for a lump-sum and subsequently disposed of a portion at a time, there must be an allocation of

---

[56] *Gladden*, 262 F.3d at 853.

[57] Id. (quoting 26 C.F.R. § 1.61-6(a) (2002)).

[58] *Gladden*, 262 F.3d at 853.

[59] Id.

[60] Id. (*citing* Homes by Ayres v. Comm'r, 795 F.2d 832, 835 (9th Cir. 1986)).

[61] 9 T.C. 727 (1947).

the cost or other basis over the several units and gain or loss computed on the disposition of each part…."[62]

C.F.R. § 1-61-6(a) could have been applied to the Gladdens' situation if the Partnership had purchased the land with no expectation that it would ever gain Colorado River water rights.[63] It is unsuitable in any such case to permit a partnership to apportion any of the cost of their original land purchase to the sale of the after-acquired rights. For example, in *Plow Realty Co. of Texas v. Commissioner*,[64] the land had originally been valued solely for its cattle grazing qualities.[65] In that case, the Tax Court held that a subsequent sale of mineral rights to have a zero amount cost basis.[66]

Gladden falls between the recognized case law precedents. The Gladdens' "water rights were not vested at the time the partnership purchased its land, but the purchase was made with a realistic expectation that water rights would eventually attach to the land."[67] A reasonable person would believe that the expectation of access to water in such an arid climate as Arizona would add to the purchase price. The Tax Court, however, ruled that because the "the water rights were not vested when the land was purchased, they were [actually] acquired in a 'separate transaction' from the land purchase for purposes of determining their tax basis."[68] Consequently, according to the Tax Court, because the water rights were acquired at no cost, the Gladdens had a zero cost basis in them.[69] By deciding as it did, the Tax Court created a clear precedent that "a taxpayer could never apportion any of his cost basis in land to the sale of an appurtenant water right that was not fully vested in the land at the

---

[62] Id. at 735.

[63] *Gladden*, 262 F.3d at 854 (explaining that the original price of the property would not have made it eligible for any expectancy of water rights to the Colorado River).

[64] 4 T.C. 600 (1945).

[65] Id. at 609.

[66] Id. (indicating that at the time the contracts were entered into, oil had not been discovered on the grazing land and that there was no expectation of future mineral rights included in the purchase price).

[67] *Gladden*, 262 F.3d at 854.

[68] Id.

[69] Id.

time of the purchase, even though in practical economic terms that expectation had a real value at the time of purchase."[70]

The Ninth Circuit held that the Tax Court's rule was unsound for three reasons. First, "[w]here land is purchased at a premium based on the expectation of a future water right, separating the land and the water rights for the purposes of allocating basis would cause the land to have an artificially high basis and water rights to have an artificially non-existent basis."[71] The following example demonstrates this principle.

Consider a case where two parcels of land are the same, except Blackacre has a future expectation of water rights and Greenacre is expected to remain arid. Consequently, Blackacre has a sale price of $2000 per acre while Greenacre's is only $1000 per acre. Suppose each parcel is purchased by different taxpayers and both eventually receive water rights. Assume that both taxpayers sell their water rights for $1000 in one year and their land for $1000 the following year. According to the Tax Court's holding, the owner of Greenacre would report a $1000 capital gain in the first year and no gain or loss in the second year, properly reflecting economic reality. In contrast, Blackacre would have to report a $1000 capital gain the first year and a $1000 loss the second year, when in fact neither outcome occurred.[72] These figures exemplify the nonsensical results.

The Ninth Circuit's second reason was that the Tax Court's ruling could potentially conflict with existing precedent. In *Piper v. Commissioner*,[73] a taxpayer traded securities in one company for common stock and common stock subscription warrants in another company.[74] When the taxpayer sold the common stock, he was allowed to attribute some of his original basis to the warrants. The Tax Court stated that "[i]t can not be said that the warrants had no value simply because they could not be exercised to immediate financial advantage at the time they were issued … the

[70] Id.

[71] Id.

[72] Id. at 854 (illustrating why the Tax Court's ruling contravenes some notions of common sense).

[73] 5 T.C. 1104 (1945).

[74] Id. at 1108.

fact that they were highly speculative and entirely prospective is no basis … for denying to them any value."[75]

Thirdly, the Ninth Circuit relied on a Revenue Ruling in reaching its decision.[76] This Ruling addressed a situation where a farmer bought ten cows that were artificially impregnated with transplanted embryos.[77] The fair market value of the cows before their impregnation was $80, but the farmer paid $250 for each cow.[78] He subsequently sold the adult cows after they gave birth at a price of $80 apiece and kept their calves.[79] The IRS ruled that the farmer could not recognize any gain or loss on the sale of the cows based on the purchase price; instead, only $80 was properly proportioned to the cost basis of the cows themselves.[80] According to the Ruling, the remaining $170 that the farmer paid was due to the value of the embryos, and that amount was therefore properly treated as the farmer's basis in those embryos.[81] The outcome in this case paralleled the result in *Gladden* because both the farmer and the Gladdens had cost bases related to future expectations.[82]

In *Gladden*, the Ninth Circuit also dealt with the Commissioner's contention that a United States Court of Claims case was controlling. In *Niagara Mohawk Power Co. v. United States*,[83] the Court of Claims held that a company that acquired water rights through merger with another company could not use the fair market value of those rights at the time of acquisition as its cost basis.[84] In *Niagara Mohawk*, the Court stated that the correct determination for valuation of water rights was the cost of acquisition, measured by the worth of the securities exchanged to gain

---

[75] Id. at 1110 (analyzing why the respondent erred in attributing the entire cost to the value of stock).

[76] *See Gladden*, 262 F.3d at 855 (citing Rev. Rul. 86-24, 1986-1 C.B. 80).

[77] Id. (delving into an explanation of the facts of this Revenue Ruling).

[78] Id.

[79] Id.

[80] Id.

[81] Id.

[82] Id. *Cf.* Sherwood v. Walker, 33 N.W. 919, 923 (Mich. 1887) (holding that cows used specifically for breeding are more valuable than barren cows).

[83] 207 Ct. Cl. 576 (1975).

[84] Id. at 588.

the rights.[85] The United States Court of Appeals, however, quickly seized on *Niagara Mohawk* as supportive rather than inconsistent with its own holding.[86] The Commissioner argued that the Gladdens had acquired the water rights at no cost and therefore the proper basis was zero.[87] However, the Commissioner's argument contained significant shortcomings. If the Gladdens paid a premium for their land, it is arguable that they did so based on an expectation that they would receive water rights. They expected to receive valuable water just as the farmer in Revenue Ruling 86-24 expected to receive valuable calves from the cows.[88] The Gladdens had a reasonable expectation that the water would be valuable and would constitute a significant factor in the land's assessment.[89] As entrepreneurs, they were seeking a previously untapped valuable commodity. An additional case that influenced the Gladden holding is *Day v. Commissioner.*[90] There, the Tax Court recognized that groundwater rights appurtenant to land had an effect on the value of the land and treated the revenue from sale of those rights as a capital gain.[91]

E. Properly Calculating the Cost Basis for the Sale of Land With and Without Future Expectation of Water Rights

Having decided that the Gladdens could distribute some portion of the cost of land to the sale of its accompanying water rights, the Court turned to the issue of the percentage amount that could be applied.[92] The Gladdens sought to apply the entire cost of the land, indicating that it

---

[85] Id. at 592.

[86] *Gladden*, 262 F.3d at 855 (stating that the water rights in *Niagara Mohawk Power Corp.* was the value *actually* paid).

[87] Id.

[88] Id.

[89] Id. (commenting that expectation of water rights was just as reasonable as the expectation that a cow purchased by a farmer would produce calves).

[90] 54 T.C. 1417 (1970).

[91] Id. at 1423. The court recognized that the expenditure of capital investment was for the purpose of acquiring "underlying water which very substantially affected the value of the land." Id. at 1427.

[92] *Gladden*, 262 F.3d at 855.

would be impossible or impractical to apportion a precise basis to water rights alone.[93] Further, the Gladdens contended they were entitled to recover the entire cost basis in the land prior to the reporting of any capital gain.[94] This argument had been previously addressed in *Inaja Land Co. v. Commissioner*,[95] where the court held that taxpayers "should not be charged with gain on pure conjecture unsupported by any foundation of ascertainable fact."[96] However, the Court of Appeals was not clear as to the possibility or practicality of legitimately discovering the premium price the Gladdens had paid for the expectation of future water rights.[97] The Court posited that one possibility was to estimate the premium paid for the water rights by comparing the purchase price of the Gladdens' land to the purchase price of similar land without a "recent history of irrigation[.]"[98] Thus, such similar land would not contain any expectation of future water rights.[99] The difference in cost of acquisition would be the premium paid for the expectation of future water rights.[100] This is certainly a reasonable calculation technique.

F. Ultimate Outcome of the Gladdens' Decision and Its Implications

The Court's decision in *Gladden* was both legally and economically reasonable. It is an unquestionable assumption that purchasers of private land would readily pay a premium for the expectation of future water rights, which would clearly enhance the utility of the property for agricultural, residential, or industrial purposes. The cost of the land without water rights must be factored into any purchasing decision in order to

---

[93] Id. at 856.

[94] Id.

[95] 9 T.C. 727 (1947).

[96] Id. at 736. *See also* Burnet v. Logan, 283 U.S. 404, 413 (1931) (stating the proposition that "income tax law is concerned only with realized losses, as with realized gains") (quoting Lucas v. American Code Co., 280 U.S. 445, 449 (1930)).

[97] *See Gladden*, 262 F.3d at 856.

[98] Id.

[99] Id.

[100] Id.

determine the appropriate cost basis.[101] The basis allocated to the future water rights should be calculated as the additional premium paid for the water rights just as the basis allocated to the bovine embryos was the premium paid for the expectation of the cows producing calves.[102] Breeding cows are clearly more valuable than barren ones, just as water-enhanced land is clearly more valuable to the private investor than arid land.[103] Given a choice, an entrepreneur would certainly choose the option and commodity that would produce the greatest economic benefit.[104] The Court's holding in *Gladden* will encourage private investment in property that is currently arid, but has an expectation of future water rights. In the current economic climate, many resources have become private commodities. In some cases, an increase in private investment has had beneficial results. The same principle is applicable to water regulation.[105] The *Gladden* court suggestion that comparable sales be used to determine the premium paid in the purchase price for the future water rights was astute.[106] The economic difference between the purchase prices of comparable land with and land without any future expectation of water will at least roughly reveal the market premium paid for the rights.

(1) the expectation of future water rights is helpful in providing a greater explanation of its connection to part I of the introduction, begin-

---

[101] *See* Id. (according to the calculation of the *Gladden* court).

[102] *See generally* Rev. Rul. 86–24, 1986-1 C.B. 80 (showing it is proper to allocate part of the cost of the embryo).

[103] *See generally*, Sherwood v. Walker, 33 N.W. 919, 923 (Mich. 1887) (holding that cows used specifically for breeding are more valuable than barren cows). Under the *Gladden* context, the opposite outcome would result in the case of land near a rising river or flooding lake.

[104] *See* Callahan, *supra* footnote 51.

[105] *See generally*, Walter Block et al., *Human Organ Transportation: Economic and Legal Issues*, 3 Quinnipiac Health L.J. 87, 99 (1999/2000) (arguing that a free market system of organ donations requires financial incentives); *see also* Roy Whitehead, Jr. & Walter Block, *Environmental Justice: Risks in the Petroleum Industry*, 24 Wm. & Mary Envtl. L. & Pol'y Rev. 67, 82 (2000) (suggesting a system in which a community hosting an oil refinery should be rewarded or compensated); Roy Whitehead, Jr. & Walter Block, *Should the Government be Allowed to Engage in Racial, Sexual or Other Acts of Discrimination*, 22 N. Ill. U. L. Rev. 53, 66–68 (2001) (analyzing the utility of the disbursement of government funds directly to parents and students who in turn may choose to utilize the educational aid attend church-related schools); Roy Whitehead, Jr. & Walter Block, *Mandatory Student Fees: Forcing Some to Pay for the Free Speech of Others*, 20 Whittier L. Rev. 759778–781 (1999) (arguing that privatization of public universities would lead to greater "economic freedom" for students).

[106] *See Gladden*, 262 F.3d at 856.

ning of Part II, and conclusion; (2) development of the analysis in Part II.A to include greater explanation of, support for, and critique of the competing perspectives outlined there (for instance, that there are still spills and pollution does not indicate that government regulation cannot ameliorate environmental problems; similarly, conclusively referring to ITQs and the like as market socialism, and that this will lead to economic demise, does not do these positions any justice). In order for this section to be useful, the competing views must be meaningfully described and then precisely discredited; (3) supporting your thesis that "Privatization of waters is environmentally and economically sound" (for instance, a discussion of some of the vast literature on the tragedy of the commons on the pros and cons of privatization, why privatization will provide incentives to protect endangered species (isn't there a significant externality problem except for a few high-tourist areas?); why privatization will provide environmental protection incentives (again, isn't there a significant externality problem for most areas?); isn't this resource already in "the economic sphere of interaction"? how would in increase GDP?); (4) engaging in a "reality"-check on Part II.B, particularly its second half (for example, water diversion and electrically fencing or marking fish (we recognize that this is hypothetical, but it is only a useful hypo to the extent it may be achievable in the foreseeable future)); and (5) discussion and analysis of initial allocation issues.

II. Economic and Philosophical Perspective on Water Rights

The foregoing material makes the case for water privatization as best we can make it, confining ourselves to legal analysis alone. That is, the paper to this point has demonstrated, to the best of our ability, utilizing legal findings, court cases, property law, and so on, the viability of rights in bodies of water. But while this is necessary, in our opinion, otherwise we would not have included this material in our chapter, it is not sufficient; had we thought so, we would have ended at this point in our brief. Also needed, in our view, is an economic and philosophical grounding of water rights, to which we now proceed. Why?

For one thing, it is to obviate the charge against us of legal positivism: the claim, false in our opinion, that the only possible law is man-made law; that courts and legislatures are the be all and end all of law. In contrast, we buy into the notion that there is such a thing as natural law,[107] and that when this and man-made law conflict, it is to the detriment of the latter. Surely, the Nuremberg trials[108] established this, quite properly rejecting the defendant's claims that they were "only following orders," or that what they were doing was not only legal under Nazi jurisprudence and law, but also actually required.

A. Extant Problems Under the Current System of Water Rights Regulation

In recent decades through the present day, as awareness of environmental issues has increased and become prevalent in many circles of society, much discussion has and continues to take place regarding air and water pollution, oil spills, endangered aquatic species, disappearing forests, global warming, ozone layer depletion, and dying marine plant and animal life.[109] Many of these concerns are directly or indirectly tied to water issues. Regardless of individual motivation, most people would like to see the calamities tied to environmental degradation curtailed, if not entirely solved. However, disagreement arises regarding methods of achieving these goals. Four main perspectives exist in common parlance. The moderate left-wing stance advocates address these problems by placing them under government control;[110] this is generally accepted as the public

---

[107] See Benson, Bruce L. 1993. "The Impetus for Recognizing Private Property and Adopting Ethical Behavior in a Market Economy: Natural Law, Government Law, or Evolving Self-Interest," Spring, 6 Rev. Austrian Econ. 43–80, http://www.mises.org/journals/rae/pdf/rae6_2_2.pdf; van Dun, Frank. 2001. "Natural Law, Liberalism, and Christianity." *Journal of Libertarian Studies*, Volume 15, Number 3; summer, pp. 1–36; http://www.mises.org/journals/jls/15_3/15_3_1.pdf; accessed on 12/14/03.

[108] http://www.yale.edu/lawweb/avalon/imt/imt.htm; http://www.law.umkc.edu/faculty/projects/ftrials/nuremberg/nuremberg.htm; accessed on 12/14/03.

[109] *See* for example, Stroup, *infra* footnote 119; Tipon, *infra* footnote 116.

[110] *See generally* Al Gore, Earth in the Balance: Ecology and the Human Spirit, 300–301 (Houghton-Mifflin 1992) (discussing a Global Marshall Plan with global agreements for all nations to bring environmental technologies to the Third World).

policy status quo. Some extreme left-wing solution proponents suggest extensive limitations on technology and reversion to the pre-industrial times, hoping that plants and animals will be able to regenerate and recover in many areas where they have been overly lost, due to human ambition and industrial development.[111] The generally accepted moderate right-wing position is to institute "quasi market" institutions such as transferable emission permits from everything from pollution to fishing permits,[112] institute marketable permit systems, and promote emissions trading.[113] The extreme right-wing position is referred to as "free market environmentalism," which envisions virtually all ecological problems as a breakdown in, or failure to support private property rights and the advocates a much more privatized market system to alleviate this condition.[114]

Entrusting the water pollution and endangered species problems to the government is ineffective because the planet continues to suffer from spills, pollution, endangered marine species, and dying plant life under

---

[111] *See* Barry Commoner, Making Peace with the Planet 101–102 (Pantheon Books 1990); Jeremy Rifkin, Entropy: A New World View (Bantam 1980); Murray Bookchin, *Death of a Small Planet: It's Growth That's Killing Us*, The Progressive 19–23 (1989); David M. Graber, *Bill McKibben's Mother Nature as a Hothouse Flower: The End of Nature*, L.A. Times, Oct. 22, 1989, available at 1989 WL 2232834 (book review) (describing this view in greater detail).

[112] *See, for example*, Christopher J. Carr & Harry N. Scheiber, *Dealing With a Resource Crisis: Regulatory Regimes for Managing the World's Marine Fisheries*, 21 Stan. Envtl. L.J. 45, 48 (2002) (discussing individual transferable quotas (ITQ) which, "[i]n the case of fisheries, ITQs and other property rights are assigned within the framework of scientifically managed regimes with quotas, seasonal regulations, gear restrictions ... [p]rivatization is thus a dimension of fishery management reforms that is being adopted around the world to meet the resource crisis").

[113] *See* Robert W. Hahn & Gordon L. Hester, *Where Did All the Markets Go?: An Analysis of EPA's Emissions Trading Program*, 6 Yale J. on Reg. 109, 113 (1989) (describing an emissions trading program which "allows the exchange of emission rights both externally (between firms) and internally (within a single firm)"); Robert W. Hahn & Robert N. Stavins, *Incentive-Based Environmental Regulation: A New ERA from an Old Idea?*, 18 Ecology L.Q. 1, 9 (1991) (suggesting a system where the "allowable overall level of pollution is established and then allotted in the form of permits among firms").

[114] *See* Whitehead, *supra* footnote 101, at 82; Walter Block, *Drowning in Manitoba, Water Privatization in Walkerton, Ontario* (Aug. 3, 2001), available at http://www.lewrockwell.com/block/block4.html (last visited Aug. 26, 2003); Walter Block, *Water Privatization* (2002), available at http://www.mises.org/journals/scholar/waterprivate.pdf (last visited Aug. 26, 2003). National Center for Policy Analysis, Progressive Environmentalism: A Pro-Human, Pro-Science, Pro-Free enterprise Agenda for Change (1991), available at http://www.ncpa.org/studies/s162/s162.html (last visited Aug. 26, 2003).

current levels of government involvement.[115] Cessation of technology and reversion to primitive living would certainly end additional pollution, leaving animal and plant life to be controlled predominantly through natural selection. However, human nature is naturally progressive, not retrogressive, as are all living organisms. Hence, the implementation of such a strategy contravenes common sense notions to which generally rational individuals would agree. Alternative methods of control of natural resources use, such as tradable fishing permits and individual transferable quotas ("ITQs"), would limit the amount of a certain species that could be caught and would allow for ease of fishery management and sustainable practices.[116] This type of system presents an improvement over complete nonownership, which heavily contributes to the tragedy of the commons. In the case of fish, there exists massive and perhaps irreparable overfishing of certain stocks.[117] Tradable pollution

---

[115] (2) development of the analysis in Part II.A to include greater explanation of, support for, and critique of the competing perspectives outlined there (for instance, that there are still spills and pollution does not indicate that government regulation cannot ameliorate environmental problems; we readily concede that just because there are at present still spills and pollution does not indicate that government regulation cannot possibly ameliorate environmental problems. To suppose that the state could do so would not appear to be a contradiction in terms, at least at first glance. But at least, weak claim, this state of affairs constitutes strong evidence in that regard. That is, the fact that the government has for several decades attempted such remedies, and the problem remains unsolved, indicates, by induction, that it is not likely to succeed in future, or, indeed, ever. It is our view that the only way to properly address spills and pollution, and so on, is through a strong defense of private property rights. And here is where our strong claim comes in: government is necessarily unable to defend private property rights, since its very inception, and continued operation, is logically incompatible with such a situation. For the state is necessarily a coercive institution, not a contractual one. Were it entirely based on voluntary contract, it would be a government no more; instead, it would take on the role of a private company. For a defense of this latter claim, the defense of which is beyond the scope of the present paper, see Hoppe, Hans-Hermann. 1993. *The Economics and Ethics of Private Property. Studies in Political Economy and Philosophy*, Boston: Kluwer Academic Publishers; Hoppe, Hans-Hermann. 2001. *Democracy – The God That Failed: The Economics and Politics of Monarchy, Democracy, and Natural Order*, Rutgers University, N.J.: Transaction Publishers; Hoppe, Hans-Hermann, ed. 2003. The Myth of National Defense: Essays on the Theory and History of Security Production. Auburn, AL: The Ludwig von Mises Institute; Rothbard, Murray N., *The Ethics of Liberty*, Humanities Press, Atlantic Highlands, N.J., 1982; Oppenheimer, Franz. 1914. *The State*, New York: Vanguard Press; Benson, Bruce L., 1989, Enforcement of Private Property Rights in Primitive Societies: Law Without Government," *The Journal of Libertarian Studies*, Vol. IX, No. 1, Winter, pp. 1–26.

[116] *See* Tipton, *infra* footnote 116, at 397–400 (discussing the advantages of an ITQ system).

[117] Id. at 386 (referring to the Magnuson Act, which was passed due to Congressional fears that "overfishing would cause irreversible environmental and economic damage before effective international fisheries agreements could be negotiated and implemented.") Id.

permits may present a more feasible alternative in the current economic and political climate than the command and control modalities advocated by the moderate left (e.g., minimum mileage per gallon standards, and industrial restrictions under the Clean Air Act).[118] However, this system resembles nothing so much as market socialism,[119] the system practiced in Eastern Europe until the political changes of recent decades. Avoiding the pitfalls that led to the economic demise of the Soviet system in the last century, arguably we can promote a system that will address environmental problems in a manner amenable to industry and advocacy groups.

Similarly, referring to ITQs and the like as market socialism, and that this will lead to economic demise, does not do these positions any justice. In order for this section to be useful, the competing views must be meaningfully described and then precisely discredited.

Are we too harsh in characterizing ITQs as "market socialism?" First, what, precisely, are individual transferable quotas? This is a system whereby no fisherman owns the ocean, each of them is assigned a certain maximum quota, or weight of fish they can catch in a given time period.

> An individual transferable quota (ITQ) is an allocated privilege of landing a specified portion of the total annual fish catch in the form of quota shares. This differs from the traditional open-access approach to commercial fisheries. ITQs divide the total annual catch quota into smaller individual portions. ITQs are generally transferable, which means fishing vessel owners can sell their ITQ certificates or buy others' certificates or, in some cases, lease their quota shares depending on how much (or whether) they want to participate in the fishery. ITQs are not considered property, but a privilege

---

[118] *See Incentive-based Environmental Regulation, supra* footnote 107, at 8 (advocating the possible benefits of marketable permit systems for the cost-minimization of the allocation of pollution control burdens). The principles advocated here could readily be applied to fisheries and tradable quota permits.

[119] *See* Peter Boettke, The Political Economy of Socialism: The Formative Years 1918–1928 (Kluwer 1990); Robert W. McGee & Walter Block, *Pollution Trading Permits as a Form of Market Socialism and the Search for a Real Market Solution to Environmental Pollution*, 6 Fordham Envtl. L.J. 51 (1994) (discussing the "reliance on command rather than market incentives which is really just a form of market socialism…"). *See generally* Morgan O. Reynolds, *The Impossibility of Socialist Economy, or, A Cat Cannot Swim the Atlantic Ocean*, 1 Q. J. Austrian Econ. 29 1998) (socialism does not work in practice).

to catch a share of the total allowable catch of fish or shellfish in a given year.[120]

Second, what is "market socialism?" Market socialism[121] is a system that attempts to use markets, within a context of governmental[122] or non-ownership, of a resource. It is an economic system that places prices and markets in a subservient position to the overall goal of central control of recourses. Here is a more formal definition:

> Market socialism: A type of economy based on—(1) government, rather than individual, ownership of many resources, especially those like heavy manufacturing, energy reserves, widely used raw materials (lumber, steel),

[120] http://www.ncseonline.org/nle/crsreports/marine/mar-1.cfm?&CFID=11584823&CFTOKEN=88289486; accessed on 12/14/03.

[121] For more on this see, Bardhan, Pranab K. "On Tackling the Soft Budget Constraint in Market Socialism," in John Roemer and Pranab Bardhan, eds., *Market Socialism: The Current Debate* (New York: Oxford University Press, 1993); Bergson, Abram. "Market Socialism Revisited," *Journal of Political Economy* 75(5): 655–673, October 1967; Lange, Oskar. "On the Economic Theory of Socialism," *Review of Economic Studies* 4(1): 53–71, October 1936, and 4(2): 123–142, February 1937. Issued in book form with contributions by Benjamin Lippincott, ed., and Fred M. Taylor: University of Minnesota Press, 1938. Reprinted by McGraw-Hill, 1964; Murrell, Peter. "Incentives and Income under Market Socialism," *Journal of Comparative Economics* 8(3): 261–276, September 1984; Putterman, Louis. "The Public as Principal: Agency under Common Ownership Market Socialism," in John Roemer and Pranab Bardhan, eds., *Market Socialism: The Current Debate* (New York: Oxford University Press, 1993); Roemer, John E., and Pranab Bardhan. "Market Socialism: A Case for Rejuvenation," *Journal of Economic Perspectives* 6(3): 101–116, Summer 1992; Roemer, John E., and Joaquim Silvestre. "Investment Policy and Market Socialism," in John Roemer and Pranab Bardhan, eds., *Market Socialism: The Current Debate* (New York: Oxford University Press, 1993); Stauber, Leland G. "The Implications of Market Socialism in the United States," *Polity* 8(1): 38–62, Fall 1975; Stauber, Leland G. *A New Program for Democratic Socialism*. Carbondale, Ill.: Four Willows Press, 1987; Stauber, Leland G. "A Concrete Proposal for a Market Socialism for Large Enterprises: Reactions from West and East and Further Discussion," *Coexistence* 30(3): 213–235, September 1993; Yunker, James A. "Capital Management under Market Socialism," *Review of Social Economy* 32(2): 196–210, October 1974; Yunker, James A. "A Survey of Market Socialist Forms," *Annals of Public and Cooperative Economy* 46(2): 131–162, April-June 1975; Yunker, James A. "A Market Socialist Critique of Capitalism's Dynamic Performance," *Journal of Economic Issues* 20(1): 63–86, March 1986; Yunker, James A. "Would Democracy Survive under Market Socialism?" *Polity* 18(4): 678–695, Summer 1986; Yunker, James A. "A New Perspective on Market Socialism," *Comparative Economic Studies* 30(2): 69–116, Summer 1988; Yunker, James A. 1995. "Post-Lange Market Socialism: An Evaluation of Profit-Oriented Proposals." *Journal of Economic Issues*, September; http://www.wiu.edu/users/miecon/wiu/yunker/postlang.htm; accessed on 12/14/03.

[122] Educational or school vouchers are also examples of market socialism, in that they constitute an attempt to use markets, within a system of public or government-owned schools.

> and transportation systems, that are deemed critical to the operation of the economy; (2) answering three questions of allocation with a combination of central planning by government and decentralized decision-making by individual factories and the owners of non-critical resources; (3) the limited use of markets to exchange farm products and retail consumer goods; (4) economic and monetary incentives, such as bonus, paid to the workers of government-owned facilities to encourage efficiency and increased productivity.[123]

So, are ITQs an example of market socialism? It would seem difficult to deny that they are. For ITQs function in the absence of private property in the underlying resource, the ocean, and, yet, markets, or, better yet, quasi-markets operate in this context, in that people can buy and sell the rights to catch a certain amount of fish.

Let us put this matter in other words, by use of a diagram, for further clarification. A given system can have, or fail to have, private property rights, and, also, can have, or fail to have, markets, where things can be bought and sold. This gives rise to a two by two matrix:

	Private Property Rights	No Private Property Rights
Markets	I	II
No Markets	III	IV

I. An economic system that features both private property rights and markets is one of laissez faire capitalism. At the other end of the spectrum is pure socialism, IV, which allows for neither. III is a contradiction in terms, and is included only for purposes of symmetry; if markets are not allowed, then, and to that extent, are private property rights abrogated.

Under rubric II, we find market socialism, where markets are allowed, but people are not permitted ownership in that which is traded. ITQs, educational vouchers, tradeable emissions rights and the economic system promulgated by Oskar Lange, and practiced, to some degree, by Tito's Yugoslavia, all fit comfortably in this category. ITQs are correctly characterized in this way since they may be bought and sold, but the property rights underlying them, territory in the ocean, are presently

[123] http://64.127.80.59/cgi-bin/gls.pl; accessed on 12/13/03.

forbidden to private individuals. When and if educational vouchers to public schools were bought and sold, they too would apply, since, by definition, there would be markets in these tickets, but the public schools cannot be privately owned, by their very nature. It is much the same with tradeable emissions rights.[124] Here, too, there are markets; people can buy and sell "rights" to pollute; but, since pollution is a trespass, it is incompatible with full private property rights. Likewise, Lange advocated,[125] and Tito's Yugoslavia to some degree followed,[126] a plan where government owned virtually all of the means of production, but quasi-markets were nevertheless encouraged.

B. The Possible Benefits of Water Privatization

How can an individual be forced to keep waters clean and protect the associated dependent plant and animal? This can be answered by an age-old, simple question: What is in it for me? Ideally, the advantages of cleaner waters teeming with fish and filled with coral reefs and abundant plant life would provide more than sufficient motivation for some to invest in the endeavor. Unfortunately, as Adam Smith noted well over a century ago, benevolence is not enough.[127] However, if these advantages could be packaged with other self-interested goals, motivation would vastly increase.

Under our modern economic system, landowners derive profit from the land they own just as cattle ranchers derive profit from their livestock. Why shouldn't these basic principles of a private economy apply to the

[124] Robert W. McGee & Walter Block, *Pollution Trading Permits as a Form of Market Socialism and the Search for a Real Market Solution to Environmental Pollution*, 6 Fordham Envtl. L.J. 51 (1994) (discussing the "reliance on command rather than market incentives which is really just a form of market socialism…").

[125] http://cscs.umich.edu/~crshalizi/notebooks/socialism.html; http://www.wiu.edu/users/miecon/wiu/yunker/postlang.htm, accessed on 12/15/03.

[126] http://reference.allrefer.com/country-guide-study/yugoslavia/yugoslavia92.html; http://www.bartleby.com/65/ti/Tito-Jos.html, accessed on 12/15/03.

[127] *See* Russell B. Korobkin and Thomas S. Ulen, *Law and Behavioral Science: Removing the Rationality Assumption from Law and Economics*, 88 Cal. L. Rev. 1051, 1064 (2000) (citing Adam Smith, An Inquiry into the Nature and Causes of the Wealth of Nations 15 (James E. Thorold Rogers ed., Clarendon Press 1869)).

ocean and the owners of fish stock? Harkening back to one of the classic arguments in tragedy of the commons discussions, individuals given ownership over areas of ocean would thus have a strong and direct incentive to keep them clean.[128] Under a privatized system, anyone who then polluted or otherwise mistreated a privately owned area of ocean would have violated private property rights. The private owner would have an incentive to investigate, even if there was a cost involved. Private ownership of waters would also compel the use of cleaner and safer boats because the private owners of the waterways through which the vessels traveled would presumably charge more for those which were dirty and unsafe based on the likelihood of higher levels of pollution being discharged. Hence, the addition of toxic pollutants, harmful to marine plant and animal life, like oil, would be significantly reduced. To address oil spills as an example, other than bad publicity and the cost of the oil lost, fuel companies have no incentive to take precautions against spills because they have free use and access to the waterways. Again, this is a classic example of the environmental degradation that occurs because of the tragedy of the commons.

Another advantage to privatization would be that just as people breed and raise cattle on private land, they could breed and raise fish in privately owned segments of the oceans. With the financial motivation, different species could be managed and fostered leading to possible recoveries and delisting of endangered aquatic species.[129] A privatized system could all but eradicate poaching and overfishing as fish would be managed in a sustainable manner.[130] A real-life example is that of practices toward cows

[128] *See* Tipton, *infra* footnote 116, at 410 (stating that "[b]y implementing a system which provides quasi-property rights to vessel owners, the ITQ system establishes an economic incentive for fishermen to protect the common resource").

[129] The Endangered Species Act, 16 U.S.C. §§ 1531–1544 (1973), contains detailed provisions, which are supplemented by the Federal Register, for the processes of listing and delisting endangered and threatened plant and animal species. The listing process is described in § 1533 of that Act.

[130] *See* Carrie A. Tipton, *Protecting Tomorrow's Harvest: Developing a National System of Individual Transferable Quotas to Conserve Ocean Resources*, 14 Va. Envtl. L.J. 381, 381–82 (1995) (stating that "the real catastrophe of the seas is the lack of conservation techniques for renewable fish resources"). There are no empiric examples of farmers "over-cowing," that is, we do not treat cows as we do fish because of the private property rights that apply to the former, but not the latter. As far as cows are concerned, we have a farming relationship with them. But with regard to fish (and recently buf-

versus buffalo. Arguably, cows are not endangered because they are owned and managed as private property. Livestock farmers thus have a vested interest in caring for these animals and controlling their breeding practices. In contrast, buffalo, until recently, were not privately owned. Buffalo have faced the longstanding threat of extinction partly because there was no profit incentive to protect them.[131] The current buffalo farms, while frequently used to provide buffalo meat for human consumption, do contribute to the continuation of the species.[132] Private ownership in ocean grounds and species could enhance the numbers in existing fish species and could produce recreation sites in the oceans such as fishing or snorkeling parks.

For the privatization of water to be effectively instituted in a market system, property rights must be clearly defined, defended against outside incursion, and made divestible.[133] If property rights are clearly defined, prospective owners are able to determine to which resources they have access.[134] In a context faced by a party like the Gladdens, knowledge of resources would aid in the determination of property value pricing assessment on behalf of both buyers and sellers. Individuals' vested interests in property rights will also determine the enforcement of an appropriate valuation system. For example, if a prospective owner were to have rights to the coral reef on their property, but was unable to prevent unauthorized scuba diving there, the cost would probably exceed the benefits. Thus, the owner would be less likely to care for the reef. However, if the

falo), we hunt, but do not farm them. Humankind made a massive shift in subsistence practices when farming became more prevalent than hunting; some might refer to this as the beginning of modern civilization. When a similar breakthrough is applied to aquatic species as well as those currently confined to farmyards, this will be another shift worthy of note.

[131] Id. at 382 (indicating "those who sacrifice to conserve do not reap the benefits of such conservation"). Under the current fishery system, "each market participant has an incentive to collect as much of the fishery resource as possible, because the escapable nature of the resource combined with the lack of tangible, divisible property rights for fishery participants ensure that any fish not collected by one fisherman will be collected by another." Id.

[132] *See generally* Janie McDaniel et al., *Where Did the Buffalo?* (1998), at www.horseshoe-mt-bison.com/where.htm (last visited Aug. 26, 2003) ("90% of bison raised today are owned by private individuals" according to NBA, National Bison Association).

[133] *See* Richard L. Stroup, *Environmentalism, Free-Market* (2002), available at http://www.econlib.org/library/Enc/EnvironmentalismFreeMarket.html (last visited Aug. 26, 2003) (arguing that a well-functioning environmental market requires a "'3-D' property rights").

[134] Id.

property rights included the authorization to exclude nonpaying scuba divers, private owners would be more likely to protect and perform maintenance activities on site. Diving would also be subject to greater regulation.

Property rights should be divestible or transferable for the maximum benefit of the owner and the resource.[135] If not, the alternative is that owners would not be able to consider their complete opportunity costs. If an owner was unable to obtain the full value of the property by manipulating the natural resources for the highest economically valued use, a policy of nontransferability would imply inefficiency. In the oceanic setting, if an owner was prohibited from altering the property use from recreational diving to a more lucrative use such as marine research or mining, then the prospective economic benefits from the more profitable uses would not be available for consideration in determining the overall property value.[136]

Privatization of waters is environmentally and economically sound.[137] As discussed above, hypothetically it would largely decrease the amount of pollution and the risk to endangered species. Privatization of water would allow the global community to incorporate a resource that covers 75% of the earth's surface into the economic sphere of interaction.[138] As a result, it would vastly enhance the world's gross domestic product (GDP).[139] On the other hand, since this has never been attempted, the

---

[135] Id.

[136] Id. (stating that "[a]s long as the third D, divestibility, is present, property rights provide long-term incentives for maximizing the value of property").

[137] *See generally*, Terry L. Anderson, Water Crisis: Ending the Policy Drought 73–91 (1983) (concerning the privatization of in-stream flows). Terry L. Anderson & Pamela S. Snyder, Water Markets: Priming the Invisible Pump 114 (1997) (stating that "environmental entrepreneurs … play an important role in creating private rights and capturing the benefits of the environmental amenities…"). Id. at 114 (all addressing arguments about feasibility).

[138] It cannot be denied that the oceans are in some limited sense now part of the economic sphere of interaction. At present, this is akin to the economic system that prevailed on the land during our pre-history, when humans were all but limited to hunting and gathering. What is being proposed in the text is that we replicate this move from hunting and gathering to farming which took place on land, and, now, apply to bodies of water. The point is man will not have arrived at a modern system of economics on the oceans unless and until he moves from hunting and gathering to farming. But this requires as a necessary condition the legalization of private property in the seas.

[139] The Random House Dictionary of the English Language 843 (Stuart Berg Flexner & Leonore Crary Havck eds., 2d ed. 1987). (defining gross domestic product, "gross national product exclud-

logistics of sectioning the oceans, rivers, lakes, and other waters into private properties seems impossible. However, as history demonstrates, sectioning off large portions of land into private properties was once an obstacle to private land ownership. Yet even without the advanced technology that is readily available today, such as geographic information systems and data that would help to plot property lines, private ownership and the free market economy has flourished.

Before taking this analysis any further, let us pause to consider a few possible objections to the thesis we are now advancing.

One possible criticism is that the "tragedy of the commons" vitiates against our thesis. There is indeed a vast literature on this subject;[140] however, the main thrust of it is precisely to *support* our viewpoint, not to undermine it. The tragedy of the commons comes about as a result of property being held in *common*. When this occurs, whether in the form of everyone owning a right to fish in the ocean, or to hunt buffalo on the land, each economic actor has an incentive to overact. He loses at least a small value by desisting, and gains nothing thereby. In very sharp contrast, if he owns the resource outright, his incentives are very different. Now, if he forebears, he still owns the resource in question, and can utilize it in future. Thus, sustainable development is compatible with privatization, but not with its absence; for example, common ownership.[141]

Another possible criticism stems from the so-called problem of externalities: the claim that the existence of "problems" of this sort somehow vitiates privatization. Nothing could be further from the truth. Nor is our claim limited to saying that it does not apply here. No, make the stronger claim that the entire concept is fallacious. There are two kinds of externalities, pecuniary and nonpecuniary (real), and each may take on a positive or a negative aspect. This gives rise to a two by two matrix:

ing payments on foreign investments.") Gross national product is "the total monetary value of all final goods and services produced in a country during one year." Id.

[140] Hardin, Garrett. 1968. "Tragedy of the Commons," *Science*; Anderson, Terry L., and Peter J. Hill, "Privatizing the Commons: An Improvement," 50 S. Econ. J. 438 (1983); Ostrom, Elinor. 1990. *Governing the Commons*, Cambridge Press; Rose, Carol. 1986. "The Comedy of the Commons," *University of Chicago Law Review*, pp. 711–781.

[141] See text discussion, above, near footnote 124.

Externalities	Pecuniary	NonPecuniary (real)
Positive	I	II
Negative	III	IV

I is the realm of pecuniary external economies or positive pecuniary externalities, II that of nonpecuniary or real external economies or positive externalities, III stands for pecuniary external diseconomies or negative pecuniary externalities, and IV for nonpecuniary or real external diseconomies or negative externalities. The columns may be disposed of forthwith, as sources of "problems," or "market failure." For a pecuniary externality means that A undertakes an act limited to buying or selling or some other form of finance that benefits B, and yet the law does not allow A to bill B for such. For example, A buys a loaf of bread, thus raising, very slightly, the prices of this product plus all those that precede it as factors of production (flour, salt, sugar, tractors, etc.), as well as complements (e.g., butter). But this harms those who must now purchase this foodstuff at the slightly higher price, all other consumers (negative pecuniary externality), and helps those who sell it, for example, the owners of bakeries, and so on (positive pecuniary externality). To call this a market failure goes too far, way too far, since *all* commercial transactions partake of this phenomenon.

Similarly, we must give short shrift to both positive and negative nonpecuniary externalities. Consider the latter, first. A bathes regularly, or mows his lawn, thus increasing the value of his neighbors' homes. Or, becomes educated, or pays for national defense, thus conferring unrequitable benefits upon all and sundry. But he cannot charge his neighbor for such services, so market critics claim there will be less than optimal investments made in such directions. A moment's thought, however, will disabuse us of any such notion. For it commits the fallacy of supposing that tastes are objective. But we know full well that "one man's meat is another man's poison": the pacifist will hardly benefit from expenditures on armaments; the misanthrope will not count himself lucky to be placed next to "nice" neighbors. Some think that public education confers benefits on nonparticipants; others may regard these expenditures as the promotion of feminism, Marxism, or greenism, and oppose all three. How, then, can they be rationally thought to benefit from being forced to promote philosophies they regard as abhorrent?

The most usual example of nonpecuniary external diseconomies resorted to by anti-market economists is smoke pollution. But this is not an externality at all; or, rather, it is, but only because government refuses to interpret such activities as trespass of smoke particles.[142] Did but the law change in this respect, pollution would no longer be an externality; rather, it would be an internality. For if it were but illegal, the victim *would* be able to charge the perpetrator with damages for past pollution, and to obtain an injunction to prevent future such occurrences. Thus, in one fell swoop, the so-called externality would be "internalized."[143]

Having dealt with objections to ocean privatization on the grounds of "externalities," we return to our main thrust and focus on its practicalities. It is possible to hypothesize that the use of today's technology would allow for the division of the ocean without necessitating a maze of fences. An owner's property could extend from the ocean floor to the surface of the water. The depth of the water and its natural contents would naturally affect the price at which it could be purchased. With advancing technology, it may be feasible to utilize electronic fences,[144] allowing water

[142] Horwitz, Morton J. 1977. *The Transformation of American Law: 1780–1860*, Cambridge: Harvard University Press; Rothbard, Murray N., "Law, Property Rights, and Air Pollution," *Cato Journal*, Vol. 2, No. 1, Spring, 1982, reprinted in *Economics and the Environment: A Reconciliation*, Walter Block, ed., Vancouver: The Fraser Institute, 1990. http://www.mises.org/rothbard/lawproperty.pdf, accessed on 12/12/03; Block, Walter. 1990. "Environmental Problems, Private Property Rights Solutions," *Economics and the Environment: A Reconciliation*, Walter Block, ed., Vancouver: The Fraser Institute, pp. 281–332.

[143] For a critique of the "externalities" doctrine from a free market perspective, see Cordato, Roy E., *Welfare Economics and Externalities in an Open-Ended Universe: A Modern Austrian Perspective*, Boston: Kluwer, 1992; Block, Walter, 1990. "Resource Misallocation, Externalities and Environmentalism in the U.S. and Canada," *Proceedings of the 24th Pacific Northwest Regional Economic Conference*, 91–94; Block, Walter. 1983. "Public Goods and Externalities: The Case of Roads," *The Journal of Libertarian Studies: An Interdisciplinary Review*, Vol. VII, No. 1, Spring, pp. 1–34; http://www.mises.org/journals/jls/7_1/7_1_1.pdf, accessed on 12/12/03; Hummel, Jeffrey, "National Goods vs. Public Goods: Defense, Disarmament and Free Riders," *The Review of Austrian Economics*, Vol. IV, 1990, pp. 88–122.

[144] (4) engaging in a "reality"-check on Part II.B, particularly its second half (e.g., water diversion and electrically fencing or marking fish (we recognize that this is hypothetical, but it is only a useful hypo to the extent it may be achievable in the foreseeable future)). What of the possible objection that electric fencing in the sea, or fish marking, are only useful hypotheticals to the extent they may be achievable in the foreseeable future? First, it is not clear that such techniques would *not* be achievable in the foreseeable future, if property rights in oceans were legalized. To be sure, such

divisions between different property owners; a mechanism, which has served us well on land.[145]

Furthering the example of how water privatization could function, all registered boats could be required to contain a computer chip for identification purposes. A monitoring device could then be mounted to the ocean floor in each individual property section that could recognize these chips and transmit a profile of the vessel, its path through the property, and the duration it remained, to a monitoring system. A bill could then be automatically generated and sent to the owner of the vessel based on use of the water owner's property. The monitoring chip could be positioned in the center of the property and designed to encompass detection points covering the property boundaries. If a water owner wished to charge different prices for traverse through different depths, detector chips could be installed on the property that would only detect a boat's path at a certain distance. Another advantage to this technology would be to facilitate detection of trespassers. As a consumer check on the system, ship owners could install a satellite mapping system that would chart the boat's entire path and duration of travel. While purely hypothetical, this example raises some interesting points regarding the advantages of water privatization.

Another possible conjecture is that free enterprise in the oceans could reduce underwater injuries. For example, while not extremely common in the high seas as they exist today, injuries resulting from shark attacks could be reduced. The existence of a profit motive would drive the

---

technology is not even on the drawing boards, at present. But with the proper legal context, and the incentive to earn vast amount of profit by fencing in the seas, it is difficult to maintain that such technologies would not be relatively quickly forthcoming. Second, even if such techniques would not be achievable in the foreseeable future, we still take the position that they are very worthwhile to discuss, at least for theoretical legal purposes. We are at present with regard to the ocean in a similar position to the one we were in regarding Western lands before the advent of barbed wire. Would it have made sense to entertain the notion of a hypothetical "barbed wire," say, 200 years before this product were invented, just as a matter of legal theory? Of course, it would have.

145 *See generally* Terry L. Anderson & Donald R. Leal, Free Market Environmentalism 30 (1991) (stating that part of the reason that "tomorrow" is so far away is because the legal regime is not yet in place that would reward such innovation). Without private property in aqueous resources, it is to no one's financial self-interest to invent water "fences." Id. In the past, before the advent of barbed wire, distinguishing "mine from thine" on the land seemed improbable. Id. Fences, in those days, consisted of cowboys, and branding irons. Id.

development of both technological and monitoring advances that would serve to protect humans from that perceived threat. Owners who use their property as a recreational commodity could provide monitoring gear (even if it is only a wristband) that would work with the device already mounted to the ocean floor. The detector device on the ocean floor would identify each wristband as a customer of that particular property owner. In conjunction with that system, owners could also maintain a sensor device that would detect unidentified motion in the particular quadrant. The sensor would then alert hypothetical electronic fences of the future to be employed or to issue a power surge that would ward off attacks. Again, this scenario is purely conjectural and requires some suspension of our reality, but it is not outside the realm of possibility. As technology advances and the trends toward privatization in many environmental arenas continue, speculation abounds as to what exactly the future may hold.

Viewing fish as a commodity, breeders could install electric fences to herd their charges just as barbed wire does for cows in upland pastures. For migratory species, the owner could electronically mark the herd so its movements and final destination, whether it be a spawning ground or a fisherman's net could be tracked. Based on the prevalence of sonar and other technological advances utilized by the fishing industry today, further advancements for the abovementioned purposes are far from unimaginable. The human mind is capable of accomplishing great feats, particularly when a specific incentive encourages such activity.

Conclusion

Private property promotes prosperity.[146] Harkening back to the first section of this article, this is the reason why private parties like the Gladdens invest in water rights. Generally speaking, the wealthier a country is, the greater the degree of environmental protections and amenities it can

[146] *See generally* Walter Block, 2 Q.J. Austrian Econ. 65 (Fall 1999) (reviewing Tom Bethell, The Noblest Triumph: Property and Prosperity Through the Ages (1998)) http://www.mises.org/journals/qjae/pdf/qjae2_3_3.pdf (last visited Aug. 26, 2003).

afford. (Whether this is done in the real world is debatable in some settings). This insight applies to water as much as it does to anything other natural resource that can be traded or sold. Water accounts for approximately 75% of the earth's surface. If these massive areas were to be privatized, arguably the standard of living would be dramatically affected worldwide. The environmental benefits of privatization would improve the sanitation and availability of clean water throughout the world. In addition, it is entirely possible that species of marine animals, which are currently listed as endangered, would be spared from the threat of immediate extinction. Organized farm breeding of fish and other aquatic life would create an abundant food source that could contribute to the subsistence of many different world populations. However, before this process can begin, an overhaul of the existing legislation must be undertaken and accomplished. The legal protection of aquatic private property must be ensured.

Part IV

Health

12

Human Organ Transplantation: Economic and Legal Issues

Imagine that a member of your family faced sure death unless a body part could be found and quickly transplanted. Your doctor and the hospital have the know-how to perform the procedure but lack the human raw materials with which to do the job. To what lengths would you be able to go to obtain the body part? And, since the supply is usually smaller than the demand, who should decide who gets the human organ and on what basis? Should a free market be allowed? Or, should a government bureaucracy make the decision? Is this a matter requiring a national standard that justifies preemption by the federal government? Or, is it a matter of state's rights that fits neatly under the Supreme Court's recent Federalism[1] cases? What about "equity" and ability to pay? Should body parts be provided regardless of wealth? This article examines those questions and concludes that the free market is the most just and beneficial system possible.

[1] In *Alden v. Maine*, 67 U.S.L.W. 4601, the Supreme Court ruled that the states were protected from federal wage and hours legislation by its sovereign immunity. In two cases, *Florida v. College Savings Bank*, 67 U.S. L.W. 4830 and *College Savings Bank v. Florida*, 67 U.S.L.W. 4590, the Supreme Court determined that Congress exceeded its constitutional mandate when it authorized private suits against a sovereign state for patent infringement and Lanham Act violations. Why can't a state control the transplantation of body parts under these theories?

W. E. Block, R. Whitehead, *Philosophy of Law*, Palgrave Studies in Classical Liberalism,
https://doi.org/10.1007/978-3-030-28360-5_12

A bitter struggle to control the nation's most precious medical resource, body parts, rages between state governments, the federal government, medical agencies, doctors, and the often forgotten donors and donees. State legislatures, dissatisfied with the federal government's attempt to seize complete control of this market, have begun passing laws that would bar donated body parts from being shipped beyond their borders to sick people elsewhere in the country.[2] These laws have been enacted in an attempt to thwart the paternalistic effort by the Clinton Administration to control transplantation. What is paternalism? It is the view that the elites, who gain power through controlling regulatory compliance, know better what benefits the people than they do themselves. And, since they know better, they have the right to impose their ideology on the entire community. The plan would force, without regard to local need, organ recovery networks and transport centers around the nation to share their precious organs nationwide under a government mandated regulatory compliance scheme.

One example of a state's reaction is illustrated by Governor Tommy G. Thompson of Wisconsin who said, "They changed the rule, so I introduced legislation." He continued, "in this state, we go out and aggressively encourage people to be donors, with me doing the public service announcements. If I'm going to do that, I want those organs to stay in the state and take care of patients that need it in Wisconsin."[3] Four other states, Louisiana, Oklahoma, South Carolina, and Florida have adopted laws similar to Wisconsin's. Legislation has also been introduced in Arizona and Texas.[4] These laws are regarded by some as provincial. "Oklahoma has been castigated," said the Director of the Oklahoma Sharing Network. "We have been called narrow-minded, self-centered, not caring for others. Actually, our law is pretty moderate. It says we can't by-pass local patients unless we get a pay-back for the organ." The Clinton Administration has fired back at the states by including a preemption clause in the final regulations that will, if judicially sanctioned, thwart their efforts.[5]

---

[2] See, Sheryl C. Stolbery, "Fight Over Organs Shifts From States to Washington," The New York Times, March 11, 1999, at C1, Col. 2.

[3] Id.

[4] Id.

[5] 42 C.F.R. Section 121.12 (1998). The Secretary is clearly concerned that the final rule might run afoul of the Supreme Court's recent "Federalism" cases discussed Infra, at footnotes 50 and 51. She

More than 61,000 Americans now await body parts.[6] But only about 20,000 transplants are performed each year because the demand for human organs far outweighs the supply.[7] Under the current system for sharing parts, the nation is divided in 63 areas composing of 11 regions, and there are huge disparities in waiting times from area to area and region to region.[8]

For instance, for patients with blood type O, who represent 47% of the nation's liver transplant candidates, the median waiting period in New York City is 511 days, while in nearby Northern New Jersey it is only 56 days.[9]

Early in 1999, Donna Shalala, the Secretary of Health and Human Services, announced her intention to even out queues by giving body parts to the most sick patients first, regardless of location. She claimed the current system put geography ahead of medical need. But the plan, issued in the form of a federal regulation, caused such a bitter fight among doctors, hospitals, and patients that Congress delayed its effective date until October 1, 1999. So what was the system?

The System that Was

In 1999, the organ donation system was 15 years old; it began with the 1984 law called the Organ Procurement and Transportation Act (NOTA),[10] which gives the Department of Health and Human Services the authority to regulate the national organ distribution system. The law prohibited the buying and selling of organs and declared them a national

---

attempts to foreclose such an inquiry by claiming that any state input in the program would result in less sharing of body parts and violate Medicare and Medicaid reimbursement rules. She says that the value of a federal program outweighs the state's policy interests, see generally 63 Fed. Register 16321 (Apr. 2, 1999).

[6] Supra, footnote 1. Providing rough support for this figure, Lori Noyes, "Organ Donor and Transplant Facts," *Organ Transplant Ring*, November, 1998, p. 3, estimates 62,000.

[7] 63 Fed. Register 16296 (Apr. 2, 1998).

[8] Supra, footnote 1.

[9] Id.

[10] Pub. L. 101–666, Title II, Sec. 202, Codified at 42 U.S.C. 274 (6) (2) (D).

resource. The law, in effect, prohibits a free market for body parts.[11] The system works this way: a private, nonprofit organization, United Network for Organ Sharing, contracts with the Health and Human Services agencies to distribute donated body parts, through the Organ Procurement and Transportation Network (OPTN).[12] The network has divided the country into 11 regions; within them, there are 63 local organ procurement organizations, whose job it is to obtain and distribute this material.[13]

Under the old rules, organs are offered first within the local area, then region wide, then nationally.[14] The system, however, is incredibly confusing. Dallas and Fort Worth, for instance, share an airport and are only 30 miles apart, yet they belong to different organ procurement organizations and do not share with one another. If there are extra livers or kidneys in Fort Worth, they are first offered to patients in Houston, four hours away.[15]

With its rule, the Clinton Administration ordered the organ sharing network to come up with a better distribution system. It threatened that if network officials did not change the system on their own, the Department of Health and Human Services would do it for them. Thus, because of the Clinton Administration's initiative, many officials and doctors with local organ procurement organizations have begun to press their state legislatures to pass laws that would keep organs within state boundaries.[16]

The Final Rule

The Department of Health and Human Services has released what it calls the Final Rule.[17] Its stated purpose is to encourage organ donation, develop an organ allocation system that functions as much as technologically feasible on a nationwide basis, providing the basis for effective fed-

[11] Id.

[12] 63 Fed. Register 16300.

[13] Id.

[14] 63 Fed. Register 16298.

[15] Supra, footnote 1.

[16] Supra, footnote 1.

[17] 42 C.F.R. 121 (1998).

eral oversight of the OPTN and better information to patients, families, and health care providers.[18] Under the Final Rule, the OPTN is required to develop equitable allocation policies that provide transplant material to those with the greatest urgency in accordance with sound medical judgment.[19] The intent is to increase the likelihood of patients obtaining a match; it gives all patients equal chances to obtain organs compared to others in similar situations, wherever they may live in the United States.[20] It is intended that mere location will not be a primary factor determining a place on the queue. Instead, organs will be allocated according to objective standards of medical status and need.[21]

Under the Final Rule, human organs donated for transplantation are a public trust.[22] Consequently, the government argues that it must control the process to ensure that donated material is equitably allocated among all patients without regard of their economic status.[23] The preamble of the Final Rule states that, at the national level, the current policies treat patients inequitably because they create enormous geographic disparities in waiting time.[24]

The principle that donated body parts are national resources implies that (1) in principle, and to the extent technically and practically achievable, any citizen or resident of the United States in need of a transplant should be considered as a potential recipient of each retrieved organ on a basis equal to that of a someone who lives nearer to the source of the organ or tissue. Body parts ought to be distributed on the basis of objective priority criteria, not on the basis of location or wealth, and (2) the current practices in this area do not give patients, their families, and physicians the timely information they need to help in selecting a transplant hospital,[25] and this must be rectified.

---

[18] 63 Fed. Register 16295 (1998).

[19] Id.

[20] 63 Fed. Register 16297 (1998).

[21] Id.

[22] 63 Fed. Register 16298 (1998).

[23] Id.

[24] Id.

[25] Id.

Share across Geographical Lines?

During the rule-making process, many patients and advocates argued that human tissues should follow the patient.[26] That is, regardless of where a patient lives or lists, he should have the same chance or receiving an organ as if living or listing elsewhere.[27] They contended that local preference prevents this proper result. They ask, why should patients who list in areas that, for some reason, obtain more organs in relation to the local demand, benefit over patients from other areas who have equal or greater medical need?[28]

Some argued that the feasibility of national organ sharing is limited by the cold ischemic time (the time that an organ remains viable).[29] Some commentators argue that the travel time to and from large cities, where most transplant heart specialists are located, readily permits a national allocation scheme.[30] Opponents of the national scheme maintained that local donations will suffer if the donors know that their organs may be shipped out on a nationwide basis. It was also suggested that local doctors would be less aggressive in obtaining body parts if they knew that they would have to be shared nationally.[31]

Which is to be preferred, helping the sickest first or those most likely to survive the greatest number of years?[32] Many witnesses at the public hearing agreed on two broad points: first, from the perspective of individual patient who is at risk of eminent death, the "sickest first" policy is the only choice; and second, there are patients that are so likely to die that

[26] 63 Fed. Register 16304 (1998).

[27] Id.

[28] Id.

[29] Id.

[30] Id.

[31] Id.

[32] In battle conditions, army doctors use triage: painkillers, only, for soldiers not likely to survive, little attention for the ones likely to recover on their own, and heavy investment of medical resources for the middle group, where the rate of return on such effort is expected to be the highest. In effect if not by intention, present institutional arrangements put the entire society on a war footing. In sharp contrast, markets allocate scarce goods and services in accord with wealth (e.g., based directly or indirectly on past earnings; that is, contributions to the betterment of economic welfare.) Cadillacs, that is, go to those who can afford them, not those who "need" them most; Geos end up in the hands of the relatively poor, not drivers who can better utilize them.

it would be futile to help them and thus waste tissue that could have saved someone else.[33]

The available evidence shows that for most patients, higher medical urgency does not reduce the likelihood of post-transplant survival. Thus, less ill patients should not receive a higher priority.[34] Although current OPTN policies vary by organ, the predominant thrust of OPTN is nevertheless to give priority on the basis of the greatest medical need.[35]

What is the government's responsibility to provide access to transplantation services to all Americans, regardless to economic status? During the rule-making process, access was described in terms of the person's ability to pay, which almost always required health insurance.[36] A few state-supported hospitals testified that they accept all patients regardless of income.[37] But the great weight of testimony was that most transplant hospitals require that the patient demonstrate the ability to pay.[38] As a result, many commentators argued that the promise to honor the altruistic gift of an organ to whoever needs it most is being violated.[39] Secretary Shalala concluded that the department and OPTN should give more emphasis to social-economic equity in transplantation decisions. National treasures, she maintains, should not carry a price tag.[40]

Government's Expectations

Secretary Shalala opined that the rule would have three major effects.[41] They are:

---

[33] Id.

[34] Id.

[35] Id.

[36] 63 Fed. Register 16305 (1998).

[37] Id.

[38] Id.

[39] Id.

[40] Id. But what is the logical effect of this thinking on the market? Can a poor person go to Auto Zone, select a part for his car and refuse to pay based on an equity or economic status? Certainly not! This is nonsense!

[41] 63 Fed. Register 16324 (1998).

1. First, it establishes terms of public oversight and accountability for the entire organ transplantation system, and the OPTN in particular. She believes that this reform creates major public benefits in the categories of "good government," preserving public trust and confidence in organ allocation, and assuring the rule of law. The benefit of the proposed rule is substantial and may well lie primarily in the future problems avoided (e.g., reduction in organ donation if the public were to lose confidence in the fairness of the OPTN in allocating ordinances) rather than the specific current problem to be resolved.[42]
2. This rule requires creation of a system of patient-oriented information on transplant program performance. The Secretary maintains that the new rule will provide better times and numbers, and percentage of transplant center organ turn-downs of organs for nonmedical reasons, to patients and physicians. Finally, information is needed that is easy to use for patients, physicians, and families who wish to compare center performance on any of these dimensions.[43]
3. Third, this rule will improve equity by creating performance goals against which the OPTN can reform current allocation policies. Equity is a goal. As it is achieved, benefits accrue to members of society at large, to donor families, to transplant candidates, and to transplant recipients. The Secretary regards a system that allocates organs to those most in need based on sound medical judgment, but with little regard to geography, as reasonable and as a profound benefit to society quite apart from those that are life-saving.[44]

Allocation of Body Parts

The rule provides that organ allocation policies and procedures must be in accordance with sound medical judgment,[45] and will be designated and implemented as follows: (1) to allocate organs among transplant candidates in order of decreasing medical urgency, with waiting time used to break ties

[42] Id.

[43] Id.

[44] Id.

[45] 42 C.F.R. Section 121.8 (a) (3) (i) 1998.

within medical status groups.[46] Neither place of residence nor of listing shall be a major determinant of availability.[47] For each status category, Intra-Transplant Program Variance in the performance indicator "waiting and status" shall be as small as can be reasonably achieved.[48] Priority shall be given to reducing the waiting time variance in the most medically urgent status categories before reducing it in less urgent status categories.[49]

Recall that the states are attempting the pass legislation to "save" body parts for their citizens. The governor of Wisconsin argues that the federal program "pre-preempts state's rights."[50] The Final Rule deals with the Governor Thompsons of the world by invoking the Supremacy Clause of the U.S. Constitution; it mandates preemption of any local law in the area of body parts. The regulation states: "no state or local governing entity shall establish or continue in effect any law, rule, regulation, or other requirement that restricts in any way the ability of any transplant hospital, OPTN or other party to comply with organ allocation policies of the OPTN or other policies of the OPTN that have been approved by the Secretary under this part."[51] Will this preemption clause survive the recent Supreme Court Federalism cases that support State's rights?[52] Is there a national purpose at play here?[53]

---

[46] Id.

[47] Id.

[48] Id.

[49] Id.

[50] Supra, footnote 1.

[51] 42 C.F.R. Section 121.12.

[52] Several recent cases decided by the Supreme Court may signal a resurgent federalism. The court has recently ruled, for example, that the Federal Government may not compel a state sheriff to perform federal gun background checks, Printz v. United States, 521 U.S. 898 (1997). In three cases decided on June 23, 1999, Alden v. Maine, 67 U.S.L.W. 4601, Florida v. College Savings Bank, 67 U.S.L.W. 4580, (involving a holding that Congress lacked the Article I power to override state sovereignty in a suit against the state under the Fair Labor Standards Act) and College Savings Bank v. Florida, 67 U.S.L.W. 4590, (concerning the a patent suit by the bank against the state under U.S. patent law), the high court ruled that Congress exceeded its authority under Article I when it authorized suits against the states. The cases demonstrate that the high court meant what it said in Seminole Indian Tribe v. Florida, 517 U.S. 44 (1996). In Seminole, the court said that Congress may not abrogate state powers under its Article I authority. Could it follow that Congress, and the president, may not abrogate the states' authority to control the distribution of body parts within their jurisdiction?

[53] This Federalism issue may arise because of a feeling by the court that the lack of a compelling threat to the entire county like the Great Depression, World War II, and the Cold War, no longer

An Economic Introduction

Organ transplantation has been part of medical technology for over 40 years, beginning in the 1950s with the first consistent successes in kidney transplantation. Recent advances in technology which are advancing the frontiers of transplantation dramatically, however, are now poised to combine with another powerful force—that of free markets—to impel society to confront the mechanism by which providers and users of human organs are brought together. The purpose of this section of the chapter is to address the economic questions affecting trade in body parts.

Inside the human body, there are 25 different organs and tissues that can be transplanted under current technology, including bone, bone cartilage, bone marrow, corneas, heart, kidneys, intestines, lungs, and livers. Organ transplantation is not some sort of experimental new science. Success rates for such surgeries are as high as 95+%; and for many diseases, a transplant is the standard method of treatment.[54] The amount of resources available in a human body is amazing, but yet, ten people die every day in the United States while waiting for an organ transplant that never comes. The queue grows each day, but the number of organ donors does not.

Two basic organizational principles are in competition for facilitating the transfer of body parts from provider to user: (1) the present system—that of donation—and (2) a legal, free market reflecting the forces of supply and demand, with the characteristics of any free market. This chapter will first consider the present system and then move to the capitalist alternative.

The Donation System

Currently, to become an organ donor, one must sign a "donor card." This allows for the specification of which tissues are to be transplanted. The age of an organ supplied can range anywhere from those of a newborn to

exist. We no longer need federal supervision of all things, great and small, to exist very well. See, generally an article by the Dean of Stanford Law School, Kathleen M. Sullivan, "Federal Power, Undimmed," The New York Times, June 27, 1999, at A 21, Col. 3.

[54] Scott Russell, *The Body as Property*, (New York: Viking Press, 1981), p. 112.

senior citizens. Unfortunately, signing a donor card does not automatically qualify a person—even an adult; the family of the deceased must also know of and agree to the procedure. To become an actual donor, a person must be in good health and death must be sudden—possibly through accident or stroke. The person must also be declared brain dead; in this condition, the functioning of the brain has ceased—permanently and irreversibly. In this state, the heart and lungs of the "deceased" person continue to function with support of mechanical ventilators. When doctors extract an organ, they surgically remove it through routine medical procedures and normal funeral arrangements can then be made (including open casket).

There are hundreds of institutions which are privately funded (additional ones are supported through tax revenues) that specialize in the donation and transplantation of organs. These institutions include: American Heart Association, American Society of Transplant Physicians, American Association of Critical-Care Nurses, and The North American Transplant Coordinators Organization. They locate and transplant body parts for citizens in need and also keep a networking list of current persons in need.

The major problem associated with the process is lack of supply. According to surveys, more than 85% of the public believes in and supports organ donation, but only about one-third of available organs are ever donated.[55] Different measures can be taken to encourage more citizens to donate. At present, when a new driver gets his license, there is a place on the back in which he can sign up to be an organ donor. This is a very simple process and very time efficient; nevertheless, very few people sign up, relative to the great demand.

Apart from psychic gains, donors have no possible way of benefitting from this system. They simply sign papers and eventually die, but do not improve their financial situation. They never even know if their organs have been taken. The practice is restricted, though, because eligibility requires one to be related to the recipient, whether by blood, marriage, friendship, or as members of the same community.

[55] Noyes, *Organ Transplant Ring*, p. 2.

Market Organization

Under present arrangements, a doctor informs the family of the death of their loved one and asks if they will allow him to harvest the organs in almost the same breath. When a family has just learned their loved one has passed away, the last thing they want to think about is people cutting them open and removing various body parts. This situation may supply dramatic plots for hospital shows such as *ER* and *Chicago Hope*—this might well be the only virtue of extant law—but in terms of saving the lives of desperate patients, it is an abysmal failure.

Consider the following situation: the daughter of a very wealthy man is found to have a malfunctioning kidney. There is a long waiting list of people in need of kidneys, and this child is placed at the end of the queue. The girl's father places an advertisement in the newspaper as well as on the internet offering $100,000 to whoever can deliver a compatible kidney to them the fastest. Is it wrong for the father to offer money for an organ? Many people would object, because this would put his daughter ahead of those who have been waiting for a transplant for a long time.

When we wreck our automobiles, we do not drive them off a cliff or bury them because they are no longer of use to us; we parcel them out (salvage them), we restore life to other automobiles by providing parts which will allow them to last longer. Yet, thousands of people die each year of natural causes with perfectly good "salvageable" organs; and thousands of other people die each year because one of their "parts" are broken and are in desperate need of another one to replace it. A person does not need his organs after death. These internal components merely take up space and wilt away with the rest of the body. The healthy, extractable organs could be used again and would greatly enhance the life span of persons in need of a transplant. Some could be preserved for later use, and others could be quickly transferred to persons in need.

A market for human organs is an eminently reasonable concept. At this point in time, it is not legal to exchange body parts for money. If someone needs an organ, his name is placed on a waiting list until one becomes available. If someone wishes to donate a body part, he is able to agree to do so; upon his demise, the transfer is made. At present, a relatively low proportion of the organs potentially available for this purpose are in fact donated. Why? The reason is that our law prohibits economic incentives. There is simply no financial gain in donating organs. Only a free market organization of this transaction can satisfy this motive. Absolutely crucial to the functioning of any market, this one specifically included, is the existence of such incentives. In the present situation, many people will not donate their organs because they do not like the idea of pieces of them being removed from their bodies after their death. For these potential donors, financial incentives are absolutely imperative. It is all well and good to rely on benevolence, *in part*. This presumably accounts for the small supply of human tissues presently available. But why not supplement this with the more ordinary financial incentives? After all, we do not rely solely on benevolence to put food on the table, or clothes on our back. If we did, we would be as poorly fed and ill clad as those at the end of the queue who suffer needless months on a dialysis machine, or actually die as a result of the hatred for commerce implicit in the legal status quo.

There is a great demand right now for organ donations, and the supply of organs is very low. If legalization of a market in human body parts occurred, the initial price of organs would of course rise; but as more and more organs are donated, and we moved toward an equilibrium price, we would never again be faced with the specter of people dying for the lack of that which is potentially readily available.

If a market for human organs were allowed, many people would benefit. It would become a market as for everything else, such as cars or carrots. Suppliers would be reimbursed for their organs and would therefore be more likely to leave them to the medically needy upon their demise. We rely upon monetary incentives in many other walks of life to good effect. The laws of economics apply here as well. The father would place the advertisement in the newspaper and on the internet, and then choose the respondent asking the lowest price, assuming equal quality, availability, convenience, and so on. But isn't this practice unfair to the other people in need of organs and already waiting for them? If so, it is also unjust to potential suppliers, because they cannot benefit from this transaction, either. One would also have to argue that people who could not afford a car or a carrot were being cheated, and that the dealers who did not sell to a particular customer were being robbed as well. Obviously, this is irrational. A man must earn his right to purchase any consumer good, and this applies to human body parts as to all else.

Can it be cogently urged that transplant material is a matter of life and death, and that therefore we ought to suspend the market in this one case? Not at all. For one thing, body parts are not at all the only thing necessary for survival; there are also doctors, milk, penicillin, MRIs, ambulances, steel, just to name a few things. For another, if the world wide collapse of socialism has taught us anything, it is that the last best chance for maintaining life, for example, a strong economy is *not* to eschew the "magic of the marketplace." If we want to ensure a continuing adequate supply of cars and carrots, the *last* thing we ought to do is to apply to these goods the mechanisms now used for the transfer of human body parts.

Objections to Market Organization

Some argue that the selling of organs would put transplants out of reach for many and allow the rich to outbid all others. It, of course, cannot be denied that in any market system, those with the most assets will jump to the head of the donee queue. But the poor will *also* benefit. Consider, again, cars and carrots. Under the market system, the wealthy have first call on these items, too. But the impoverished in this country need never fear the famines endemic to countries—such as in Africa—which embrace socialism. And those at the bottom of the U.S. income distribution have more and better access to automobiles than even the middle class of most nations. Death does not discriminate very much, at present, for transplants. Both rich and poor patients die from a lack of organs and needlessly and tragically go to the grave. Under markets, this simply will not occur. Vastly enhanced supplies will be forthcoming given economic incentives. No patient at *any* income level will be consigned to death for lack of human tissue.

Wealth is the product of man's capacity to produce goods and services desired by others. Those who argue that money is earned by the strong at the expense of the weak are simply mistaken.[56] It is false to claim that money was made by the man who invented the computer at the expense of those who did not. It is not the wealthy man's "fault" that he is wealthy, or that other men did not use their intelligence to produce great value. Likewise, one cannot claim that the organ was bought by the wealthy man at the expense of those who are not wealthy. He did not buy the organ at the expense of anyone; he bought it for his own benefit, and to that of the seller.

One argument against a free market in body parts is that citizens would go around murdering one another to obtain organs to sell or to give to a loved one in medical need.[57] Society *already* experiences these problems, however, in such areas as domestic violence and aggravated robbery. There is no reason to suppose that this would be exacerbated in a new, legal human commodity market. The same mechanisms of law enforcement and criminal jurisprudence are available to deal with such events in any event, should they occur.

If anything, there is good and sufficient reason to believe that such "body snatching" dangers would be *lessened* under a regime of economic freedom. Consider diagram 1 in this regard. Here, supply and demand conditions are such that at the present zero price allowed to be paid by donee to donor, there is a shortage of some 60,000, as 80,000 people wish to have this operation, but it is given to only roughly 20,000. What would be the equilibrium price in such a setting, that which would equate supply and demand, and clear the market? Any estimate must be a very

[56] This is the core error in Marx. For a remedy to this fallacy, see Mises, Ludwig von, "Economic Calculation in the Socialist Commonwealth," in Hayek, F.A., ed., *Collectivist Economic Planning*, Clifton, N.J.: Kelley, 1975 (1933); Mises, Ludwig von, *Socialism*, Indianapolis: Liberty Fund, 1981 (1969); Bohm-Bawerk, Eugen, *Capital and Interest*, South Holland, IL: Libertarian Press, George D. Hunke and Hans F. Sennholz, trans., 1959 (1884); see particularly Part I, Chapter XII, "Exploitation Theory of Socialism-Communism"; Rothbard, Murray N., *Classical Economics: An Austrian Perspective on the History of Economic Thought*, Hants, England: Edward Elgar, 1995; Hoppe, Hans-Hermann, 1990, "Marxist and Austrian Class Analysis," *The Journal of Libertarian Studies*, Vol. 9, No. 2, Fall, pp. 79–94; Foss, Nicolai Juul, 1995 "Information and the Market Economy: A Note on a Common Marxist Fallacy," *Review of Austrian Economics*, Vol. 8, No. 2, pp. 127–136; Rothbard, Murray N., "Karl Marx: Communist as Religious Eschatologist," *Review of Austrian Economics*, Vol. 4, 1990, pp. 123–179.

[57] The economically illiterate writers of the T.V. show "Law and Order" (mis)lead their audience into believing that this sort of behavior results from free enterprise.

rough approximation, since in the absence of a legal market, we have no empirical experience, and economic theory alone is insufficient to determine an exact price. Let us suppose[58] then, just for the sake of argument, that the price for the average human tissue suitable for transplant is $10,000. This then would furnish the incentive for the body (part) snatcher under free enterprise. However, the present situation is far worse. For it is not at all the case that there are now 50,000 organs that can be bought and sold, the precise amount, in our hypothetical example, which would generate the price of $10,000. Rather, there are only 20,000 such body parts available. Extending a vertical line from this point on the quantity axis yields a price of $100,000, *not* the $10,000 which would occur with laissez faire. And what is the economic significance of this price? This is the *present* black market or illegal price which serves as the incentive for the criminal. The point is, the greater the potential profit, the more likely is the theft of human organs. Thus, our present price regulations actually *exacerbate* the threat of organ theft. Were we to decriminalize this market, such horrors would *decrease*; we could in one fell swoop *reduce* the profit incentive for body snatchers.

But at least, it will be said, no "profits" are being made from organ transplantation under the present system. Most commentators preach that a market for human organs would be immoral, wrong, and unfair. Happily, they are unwilling to extend this basic economic error to more ordinary goods and services. Were they to do so, and were their arguments implemented, we would to that extent approach the institutional arrangements responsible for ending the Soviet economic system.

There is one anomalous group in this sad scenario: healthcare professionals; they are virtually the only ones completely satisfied with the status quo prohibitions and price controls.[59] But there is a reason for this

[58] Three scientists were marooned on an island with plenty of canned goods, but no can opener. The first, a chemist proposed to heat the cans to a certain temperature, whereupon they would burst, without destroying their contents. The second, a physical engineer, agreed with the goal, but proposed a different means: dropping the cans onto a rock from a precise height, to this same end. At this point they both turned to the third man, an economist, who opined, assume we have a can opener….

[59] It is a staple of basic economic analysis that price controls boomerang, and hurt the very people they were ostensibly designed to aid. Most economists hold strong beliefs about the deleterious effects of minimum wages, rent controls, and tariffs, for example. On this, see Frey, Walker. But

stance. They are the only ones "profiting" from the current system, aside from very few desperate patients who miraculously pass through the waiting list and actually receive an organ. These healthcare professionals are making a fortune from organ and tissue transplantation. "The organs and tissues from a brain-dead but otherwise healthy patient can generate over $2,000,000 in business for the medical industry. The total amount of money spent in the United States on organ and tissue transplants and follow-up care is around $8,000,000,000 per year and climbing rapidly" (Organ Keeper, background).[60]

Reasons for a Free Market

Legalization of trade in body parts would provide a positive reassurance to each individual that when they were deceased, their organs would be used to prolong the life of another human being. This feeling in and of itself might provide some additional incentive to create a drastic increase in the number of organs supplied. There would also be a great comfort in

these insights have not yet percolated into the consciousness of the general public. For an appreciation of markets in bodily organs, see Barnett, Andy H., Frank Adams and David L. Kaserman, "Markets for Organs: The Question of Supply," *Contemporary Economic Policy*, forthcoming; Barnett, Andy H., Roger Blair and David L. Kaserman, "The Economics and Ethics of a Market for Organs," *Society*, September/October, 1996, pp. 8–17; Barnett, Andy H., T. Randolph Beard and David L. Kaserman, "Scope, Learning, and Cross-Subsidy: Organ Transplants in a Multi-Division Hospital – An Extension," *Southern Economic Journal*, January 1996, pp. 760–67; Barnett, Andy H., David L. Kaserman, "The 'Rush to Transplant' and Organ Shortages," *Economic Inquiry*, July 1995, pp. 506–515. Reprinted in Price Theory and its Applications, edited by F.M. Scherer and Bernard Saffran, Edward Elgar Publishing, 1999; Barnett, Andy H., T. Randolph Beard and David Kaserman, "The Medical Community's Opposition to Organ Markets: Ethics or Economics," *The Review of Industrial Organization*, December 1993, pp. 669–678; Barnett, Andy H., T. Randolph Beard and David Kaserman, "Inefficient Pricing Can Kill: The Case of Regulation in the Dialysis Industry," *Southern Economic Journal*, October 1993, pp. 393–404. Reprinted in Foundations of Industrial Organization, edited by Robert Ekelund, Edward Elgar Publishing, 1998; Barnett, Andy H., David Kaserman, "The Shortage of Organs for Transplantation: Exploring the Alternatives," *Issues in Law & Medicine*, Fall 1993, pp. 117–137; Barnett, Andy H., David Kaserman and Roger Blair," Improving Organ Donation: Compensation versus Markets," *Inquiry*, Fall 1992, pp. 372–378; Barnett, Andy H., David Kaserman, "An Economic Analysis of Transplant Organs: A Comment and Extension," *Atlantic Economic Journal*, June 1991, pp. 57–63.

[60] Organ Keeper is an organization who believes that there should be a market for human organs, and to protest the lack of one, they have become "organ keepers" and share information as well as their own beliefs through the internet. See on this http://organkeeper.com/backgrnd.html.

knowing that each individual's family would have a means to provide for funeral expenses, and possibly bring in enough money from the sale to aid it in other estate costs, if the family donated an organ to someone in need. Instead of spending, say, $6000 on a funeral, relatives could sell an organ to someone in need and defray their expenses, in the same way that other types of inherited wealth is used by heirs. Some might consider it immoral to make a "profit" from a loved one's death,[61] but selling an organ would help prolong another person's life and could also help relieve the financial burden of the donor family.

A free market would also shield physicians from having to issue Solomon-like judgments with which many are uncomfortable and under which many physicians reluctantly labor.[62] Most organ donations are made by relatives of donees in need.[63] In these cases, the incentive stems from the fact that there are close family ties involved. Sometimes, not very often, the donation comes from a friend. In such cases, the doctor plays an important role in the decision to donate. He must base his decisions on the conflicting obligations to the donor and the patient. These moral obligations have been widely discussed,[64] but no clear norms have been set to guide doctors in this decision-making process. Legalization would aid the doctor, because the donor would already know the incentives available and the decision to donate would already have been made.

Legalization of trade in body parts would produce more jobs in the fact that there would be a demand for workers to locate and transplant organs from donors and to recipients. Free trade, in itself could provide an added cash flow in our market system. Overall, this legalization would save lives and positively boost our economy.

[61] These people would presumably be very happy in North Korea or Cuba, where such sentiments are in the ascendency.

[62] If they are *not* uncomfortable in this role, this is even *more* reason to preclude them from it.

[63] Sean Elliott of the National Basketball Champion San Antonio Spurs is a recent case in point.

[64] Caplan, Arthur, "Ethical and Policy Issues in the Procurement of Cadaveric Organs for Transplantation," *New England Journal of Medicine*, 311, 1984, pp. 981–983; Childress, James F., "Ethical Criteria for Procuring and Distributing Organs for Transplantation," *Journal of Health, Politics, Policy and Law*, 14:1, 1989, pp. 87–113.

Conclusion

Putting a dead body in a coffin, six feet under the surface of the earth is not profitable to anyone except the undertaker, but it is, unfortunately, a part of our tradition. A funeral today (on average) costs a deceased person's relatives about $6000.[65] It is part of "tradition" to lay our loved ones at rest, but it is not a moral tradition. It is not considered "immoral" to allow a seven-year old child to die of liver failure after waiting three years on a transplant list, while at the same time people were dying with perfectly good livers and taking them to the grave with them. Evidently, it is not considered "immoral" to lay someone to rest who had a perfectly good liver, which could save a child whose liver is about to cause his death.

Let us conclude with our numerical example: the advertisement the father placed in the newspaper and on the internet is responded to by several men, asking various prices for the kidney, ranging from $250,000 to $150,000. The father tries to negotiate with the sellers, and succeeds in getting the price dropped to $120,000. The arrangement is made, and the little girl receives her kidney. The donor receives his $120,000. Everyone involved in this transaction benefits. Those who did not receive the kidney are not losing anything from this deal, and those who did not sell a kidney did not lose anything. As with all such "capitalist acts between (other) consenting adults,"[66] they simply did not benefit from it.

Our laws should allow free trade of healthy human organs. Our current laws regarding organ transplantation do not sufficiently provide for society's needs. People are dying because we cannot efficiently use the resources readily available. We, in the United States, operate basically in a free market. This means that prices, quantities, qualities, supply, and demand are set by the producers and consumers. Legalizing the free trade of organs would allow our nation to efficiently control one of our most precious, natural resources—life itself, in many cases. It is the responsibility of politicians, bureaucrats, and judges to get out of the way of citizens who, through private arrangements, can organize markets to save precious lives. If they do not, they are complicit in the resulting deaths.

[65] Johns, Albert, "Planning May Help Families Minimize the High Cost of Funerals," *Las Vegas Review Journal*, May 24, 1998, Lifestyle Section, pp. 1–2.

[66] Nozick, Robert, *Anarchy, State and Utopia*, New York: Basic Books, 1974.

13

America's Failing Drug Control Laws

I. Introduction: Welcome to the War

Imagine you are boarding a plane with $6000.00 in cash to purchase goods for your legitimate landscaping business. Or perhaps you loaned your car to a friend who was arrested for smoking pot in the vehicle. Maybe you are a grandmother living in public housing with a grandchild who, without your knowledge, unwisely sold drugs several blocks from your apartment. You might be suffering from cancer and desire to use marijuana to alleviate your pain. You might be a 16-year-old kid who dreams of singing in the school choir. In any of these seemingly innocent

---

Congress is daily demanding accountability for failed corporate executives in the private sector. Where is the demand for accountability for the managers of failed government agencies like, we contend, the Drug Enforcement Administration? The media gleefully identifies Chief Executives of failing private corporations. Everyone has heard of Kenneth Lay of Enron. Who among us has heard of the government officials responsible for failed agencies such as the Immigration and Naturalization Service, The Department of Transportation's Security Program, The Bureau of Indian Affairs, and the State Department and its incompetent visa officials? We contend that the public interest demands that the administrators of government agencies also be held accountable. We trust that this article will advance that public interest.

W. E. Block, R. Whitehead, *Philosophy of Law*, Palgrave Studies in Classical Liberalism,
https://doi.org/10.1007/978-3-030-28360-5_13

circumstances, will you expect your precious property interests protected by the Constitution to be subject to forfeiture to the government? Not in this country! Not in America where we are all protected by the presumption of innocence, the Fifth and Fourteenth Amendment Due Process Clauses, and the Eighth Amendment Excessive Fines provisions. Well, as we shall see, you are very wrong!

Forfeiting Property: The Thing Is Guilty

The linchpin of government drug forfeiture is the legal fiction that civil asset forfeiture is an in rem action by the sovereign against the thing.[1] To illustrate this ancient approach consider *Calero-Toledo v. Pearson Yacht Leasing Company*.[2] In March 1971, a yacht company leased a pleasure craft to two residents of Puerto Rico.[3] In May 1972, a single marijuana cigarette was discovered on board.[4] In July 1972, Puerto Rican authorities seized the craft pursuant to the Puerto Rican Controlled Substances Act.[5] On appeal, the Supreme Court was faced with the issue of whether the lessor's yacht could be constitutionally forfeited without notice and hearing when the lessor was neither involved in or knew of the illegal act.[6] In affirming the forfeiture, Justice Brennan wrote that, "First, seizure under the Puerto Rican statutes serves significant governmental purposes: seizure permits Puerto Rico to asset *in rem* jurisdiction over the property in order to conduct forfeiture proceedings, thereby fostering the public interest in preventing continued illicit use of the property and in enforc-

[1] *See*, *The Palmyra*, 25 U.S. (12 Wheat.) 1, 14–15 (1827). There the court said, "The thing is here primarily considered as the offender, or rather the offense is attached primarily to the thing … [T]he proceedings in rem stands independent of, and wholly unaffected by any criminal proceedings in personam." "No personal conviction … is necessary to enforce a forfeiture." Id. at 15.

[2] 416 U.S. 663 (1973).

[3] Id. at 665.

[4] Id.

[5] Title 24, section 2512 (a) (4) and (b) provide: "(a) The following shall be subject to forfeiture to the Commonwealth: (4) All conveyances, including aircraft, vehicles, mounts, or vessels, which are used, or intended for use, to transport, or in any manner to facilitate the transportation, sale, receipt, possession, or concealment of property described in clauses (1) and (2) of this subsection."

[6] 416 U.S. at 664.

ing criminal sanctions. Second, pre-seizure notice and hearing might frustrate the interests served by the statutes, since the property seized -as here, a yacht- will often be of a sort that could be removed to another jurisdiction, destroyed, or concealed, if advance warning of confiscation is given. And finally … seizure is not initiated by self-interested private parties; rather Commonwealth officials determine whether seizure is appropriate under the Puerto Rican statutes."[7] Note the court's handy reliance on characterizing the action as *in rem* to avoid the constitutional issues that arise when the action is *in personam*. Finally, the court seems to place great reliance on the fact that the forfeiture was initiated by disinterested government officials. But are those officials really disinterested when the forfeited property inures to their benefit?[8] Also consider that the rule is based on a custom established to deal with problems of the eighteenth century.[9] The wonder is that it has survived to imperil our times. On this haunting thought, Oliver Wendell Holmes said:

> The customs, beliefs, or needs of a primitive time establish a rule or a formula. In the course of centuries the custom, belief, or necessity disappears, but the rule remains. The reason which gave rise to the rule has been forgotten, and ingenious minds set themselves to inquire how it is to be accounted far. Some ground or policy is thought of, which seems to explain or reconcile it with the present state of things; and then the rule adapts itself to the new reasons which have been found for it, and enters a new career.[10]

A troubling illustration of the highest court in America's application of the Holmes comment to the primitive law of forfeiture is found in a case involving an innocent wife wronged by a straying husband. In *Bennis v.*

---

[7] Id. at 679.

[8] Prior to our American revolution, the much despised Writs of Assistance allowed officers of the Crown to collect a commission on forfeited goods. *See*, Eric Blumenson & Eva Nilsen, *Policing For Profit: The Drug War's Hidden Economic Agenda*, 65 U. Chi. L. Rev. 35 at 75 nn. 143–44 (1998). Founding father John Adams described James Otis' 1761 courtroom argument against the Writs of Assistance as "Then and there the child of independence was born." *See*, DAVID McCULLOUGH, *JOHN ADAMS*, SIMON & SCHUSTER (2001) p. 62.

[9] See footnote 3, Supra.

[10] *See*, Oliver Wendell Holmes, The Common Law 5 (1881).

Michigan,[11] the high court came face to face with a situation involving forfeiture of a fancy, new car, owned by an innocent spouse.[12] The facts reveal that the straying husband drove the marital car to a seedy part of town where he solicited a willing prostitute to engage in intimacy in the front seat.[13] Sadly, this voluntary but illegal act of commerce was observed by a police officer, who arrested the husband.[14] In due course, the county prosecutor seized the car and filed a complaint alleging that the vehicle was a public nuisance.[15] Mrs. Bennis provided undisputed testimony that the car was jointly owned and that she had neither knowledge of, nor consented to the illegal use of the automobile.[16] At this point, one would think that the twice wronged Mrs. Bennis would get her car back. Not if she lives in Michigan.

In *State ex rel. Wayne Co. Prosecutor v. Bennis*,[17] the Michigan Supreme Court affirmed the trial judge's determination that the vehicle was a nuisance and upheld his order of forfeiture. The already wronged wife argued that her interest should not be twice harmed because forfeiture of her interest in the car violates due process since the state has no legitimate interest in punishing an innocent person.[18] In response, the Michigan high court cited the age-old legal fiction that "[t]he subject property was itself the offending party, not the wife, and, consequently, the property was to be punished."[19] The court rejected the innocent wife's contention that the Fourteenth Amendment[20] prevented forfeiture of her interest in the car. Interestingly, the court also considered that she had no cause to complain because she either explicitly or implicitly entrusted her husband with

[11] 516 U.S. 442 (1996).

[12] Id. at 443.

[13] Id.

[14] Id.

[15] Mich. Comp. Laws, section 600.3801; Mich. Stat. Ann., section 27A3801 provides: "Any building, vehicle, boat, aircraft, or place used for the purpose of … prostitution … is declared a nuisance … and nuisances shall be enjoined and abated…."

[16] 516 U.S. at 468.

[17] 447 Mich. 719, 527 N.W.2d 483 (1994).

[18] 447 Mich. at 722, 527 N.W.2d at 486.

[19] Citing our old friend, *The Palmyra*, 25 U.S. (Wheat) 1, 14 (1827) at 527 N.W.2d at 494n.32.

[20] "…nor shall any state deprive any person of life, liberty, or property, without due process of law."

use of the car.[21] We can be sure that she did not explicitly entrust the car to the straying husband for the use to which it was put. The now twice wronged wife chose to seek a more rational form of justice in the U.S. Supreme Court. And she did so with some hope of success because the high court had suggested in dictum, that some culpability or negligence allowing the property to be misused must be present for forfeiture purposes.[22]

Mrs. Bennis was again disappointed. Writing for the majority, Chief Justice Rehnquist accepted Michigan's theory that the innocent wife had no protection from forfeiture.[23] The majority relied on a variety of nineteenth and early twentieth century cases that allowed forfeiture of ships used for piracy,[24] equipment used for bootlegging,[25] and vessels used to run illegal liquor.[26] All of the cited cases used the primitive legal fiction that the *in rem* forfeiture was of the "guilty" property and that the innocence of the owner was irrelevant. The majority wrote that "[i]t is not unknown or indeed uncommon for the law to visit upon the owner of property the unpleasant consequences of the unauthorized action of one to whom he has entrusted it," citing *Van Oster v. Kansas*.[27] The court concluded that this "long and unbroken line of cases holds that the owner's interest in property may be forfeited by reason of the use to which the property is put even though the owner did not know that it was to be put to such use."[28] The majority then found a way to reconcile the ancient relic rule of the *Palmyra* with today's modern world by writing that this

[21] 447 Mich. at 741, 527 N.W. 2d at 494.

[22] *See, Austin v. United States*, 509 U.S. 602, 619 (1993), where the court said that holding an owner accountable for another's activities rests "on the notion that the owner has been negligent in allowing his property to be misused and that he is properly punished for that negligence." And in *Pearson Yacht*, 416 U.S. 63, 689–90 (1974), the court suggested that the owner might be protected if he took "reasonable steps" to prevent wrongful use of the property.

[23] 516 U.S. at 453.

[24] *See* once again, *The Palmyra*, 25 U.S. 1, 12 (Wheat) (1827).

[25] *Dobbin's Distillery v. United States*, 96 U.S. 395, 401 (1878).

[26] *Harmony v. United States*, 43 U.S. 210 (1844).

[27] 272 U.S. 465 (1926). Here, the case concerned an innocent buyer whose seller retained possession of the car long enough to use it to transport illegal liquor before turning it over to the buyer. The innocent buyer lost the car to forfeiture.

[28] 516 U.S. at 446.

line of cases is "too firmly fixed in the punitive and remedial jurisprudence of the country to be now displaced."[29]

Concurring in the result, Justice Thomas expressed considerable concern with what he regarded as the "unfair" and "intensely undesirable" result.[30] He admitted that "one unaware of the history of forfeiture laws and 200 years of this Court's precedent regarding such laws might well assume that such a scheme is lawless—a violation of due process."[31] He decided, however, that "the federal Constitution does not prohibit everything that is intensely undesirable."[32] And he cautioned or perhaps foresaw:

> Improperly used, forfeiture could become more like a roulette wheel employed to raise revenue from innocent but hapless owners whose property is unforeseeably misused, or a tool wielded to punish those who associate with criminals, than a component of a system of justice. When the property sought to be forfeited has been entrusted by its owner to one who uses it for a crime, the Constitution apparently assigns to the States and to the political branches of the Federal Government the primary responsibility for avoiding the result.[33]

Despite the Justice Thomas' belated concern, the much-wronged Mrs. Bennis still lost her car. But the decision at least compelled a heated dissent.[34] The dissenters were concerned with the absurd results that might arise from the decision. Justice Stevens wrote that "[W]ithout some form of exception for innocent owners, the potential breath of forfeiture actions … would have catastrophic effects on the nation's economy."[35] For example, "airplanes could be forfeited if a passenger had a marijuana cigarette in his luggage."[36]

---

[29] Id. at 448.

[30] Id. at 454.

[31] Id.

[32] Id. at 455.

[33] Id. at 457.

[34] Justices Stevens, Breyer, Kennedy, and Souter.

[35] 516 U.S. at 559n.1.

[36] 516 U.S. at 560.

Satisfying the Demand for Forfeited Property

We all wish to believe that our supposedly over-worked, often under-funded, and truly under-appreciated public defenders against crime are solely motivated by a constitutionally mandated desire to see to our general welfare. One of the truly unfortunate byproducts of the so-called War on Drugs is a nagging concern that the stronger motivation might be raising money for their own purposes. This concern dates from the day that the drug laws were amended to provide law enforcement personnel an economic stake in forfeiture law.[37] This "economic stake" arose from legislation that allowed federal law enforcement officials to keep the proceeds from drug forfeitures rather than placing the proceeds in the general treasury.[38] Then, to enhance the "economic stake," state and local police were allowed to keep a large share of the forfeiture proceeds.[39] The proceeds from drug forfeitures may be used for several purposes including paying informants and the salaries of local police.[40] There is always a demand for more money in law enforcement.[41] Now the forfeiture laws have created a ready supply: just go out and find some property to forfeit.

Some civil libertarians might question whether raising money is compatible with administering justice. So far, the question has not much concerned the courts in drug cases.[42] The Supreme Court has expressed the opinion that "[T]he Government has a pecuniary interest in forfeiture

---

[37] For a compelling, and sometimes troubling discussion of law enforcement's "economic stake" in forfeiture law *See generally*, Eric Blumenson & Eva Nilsen, *Policing for Profit: The Drug War's Hidden Economic Agenda*, 65 Chicago Law Review 35 (1998). *See also*, Anti-Drug Abuse Act of 1986, codified at 21 U.S.C., section 853(p) (1994), that allows the forfeiture of substitute property if the assets subject to seizure is no longer available. Now almost any property is fair game even if it cannot be connected to the crime.

[38] Comprehensive Crime Control Act of 1984, codified at 28 USC, section 524 (1994).

[39] The federal government may share forfeited property with any state or local law enforcement agency that participated in any act leading to forfeiture of property authorized by 19 USC, section 1616a(c).

[40] 28 U.S.C. section 524(c)(1)(F) and Directive 90–5, *The Attorney General's Guidelines on Seized and Forfeited Property* (July 1990).

[41] As there is in virtually all other fields of endeavor known to man.

[42] Some have argued that the courts have adopted a premise that drugs are so bad for society that "almost any law or law enforcement measure is validated," Steven Wisotsky, *Not Thinking Like a Lawyer: The Case of Drugs in the Courts*, 5 Norte Dame J Legal Ethics & Pub Pol 651, 658 (1991).

that goes beyond separating a criminal from his ill-gotten gains … the sums of money … are substantial, and the Government's interest in using the profits of crime to fund these activities should not be discounted."[43] But, alas, the rewards of forfeiture might in some, perhaps even isolated instances, be too tempting for the police who consider themselves underpaid. A commander of a task force in Oakland, California, is said to have told his officers that "A lot of dirty money drug money would be passing through their hands, and it would really not matter if they kept some of it for themselves, because the suspects are in no position to complain."[44] And he is of course correct. So-called reverse stings have become a major tactic to raise funds for law enforcement. These stings involve police officers posing as drug dealers and selling to unwitting buyers. The benefit to the police is that they can then seize and forfeit the hapless buyers' cash.[45] Often, the police prefer to arrest buyers with lots of cash rather than the dealers with the drugs.[46] This approach clearly does little to get the drugs off the street. One police officer is quoted as saying that forfeiture laws give law enforcement a powerful financial incentive to "allow the drug market to continue."[47] The motive of financial gain is again found in the policy of the Washington, D.C. police, who set up roadblocks to seize cash from people coming into the city to buy drugs.[48]

There are many horrifying examples of drug raids, at least motivated in part by a financial interest to seize property, going bad and resulting in the death or maiming of innocent citizens. There is even a web site devoted to the subject.[49] Perhaps the most frightening example to

---

[43] *Caplin & Drysdale, Chartered v. United States*, 419 U.S. 617, 629 (1989), and in a footnote in our often cited *Calero-Toledo*, 416 U.S. at 687 n26, "Seizure and forfeiture statutes also help compensate the Government for its enforcement efforts."

[44] *United States v. Reese*, 3 F.3d 870, 874 (9th Cir. 1993).

[45] *See* J. Mitchell Miller & Lance Selva, *Drug Enforcement's Double-Edged Sword: An Assessment of Asset Forfeiture Programs*, 11 Justice Q 313, 319 (1992).

[46] Id. at 325.

[47] Id. at 333.

[48] This policy was followed because police have a "financial incentive to impose roadblocks on the southbound lanes of I-95, which carry cash to make drug buys, rather than the northbound lanes, which carry the drugs, after all, seized cash will end up forfeited to the police department, while seized drugs can only be destroyed," Richard Miniter, *Ill Gotten Gains*, 25 Reason 32, 34 (Aug/Sept 1993), quoting Patrick Murphy, former Police Commissioner of New York City.

[49] http://home.earthlink.net/~ynot/victims.html (last opened March 29, 2002).

ordinary citizens concerns Donald Scott, a then 61-year-old resident of the exclusive community of Malibu, California. Scott's ranch of over 200 acres in a wealthy community attracted the attention of law enforcement when an informant reported marijuana plants on the property. The information was not properly corroborated.[50] Nor was there any indication that Scott was a dangerous person.[51] On October 2, 1992, at least 30 officers executed a search warrant by kicking in the door and running through the Scott home. Mrs. Scott's screams led to Scott picking up a pistol to defend her. The masked intruders, in front of his wife, shot Mr. Scott dead. Oh yes, a minor point, a search of the house and the surrounding 200 acres revealed zero, not one, marijuana plant.[52] The District Attorney's investigative report found that much of the information used to obtain the warrant was false.[53] Was this an honest mistake that could be marked down as an aggressive law enforcement plan to stamp out dangerous drugs? Shockingly, no! The District Attorney concluded that a purpose of the operation was to obtain the proceeds from the forfeiture of Scott's $5 million dollar ranch.[54] This financial motive was also evidenced by the fact that at the briefing before the raid officers were provided a property appraisal of the ranch with comparable sales of adjoining property.[55]

How can these Writ of Assistance[56] compatible problems be solved? Clearly, the best way is to remove the basis of the law enforcement demand for forfeited property. This might best be accomplished by entirely suspending forfeiture. We recognize that it is politically unlikely that Congress and law enforcement, having tasted the sweet nectar of drug forfeitures, can ever be completely weaned. As a second best policy, we then suggest that the forfeited assets go instead to the general treasury.

---

[50] *Report on the Death of Donald Scott*, 37–41 (Office of District Attorney, Ventura County, California, Mar. 30, 1993). The Border Patrol had conducted two ground reconnaissance trips into the property and found no marijuana plants.

[51] Id. at 11.

[52] Id. at 37–41.

[53] The supporting affidavit falsely stated that ground surveillance had confirmed the presence of marijuana plants. Id. at 42.

[54] Id. at 16, 50–52.

[55] Id. at 16.

[56] *See* Supra, footnote 10, about Writs of Assistance.

One final note on this. The parallels between the War on Drugs and the failed prohibition of alcohol are striking. The more aggressive law enforcement becomes with programs like forfeiture, the more profit the dealer makes because he can mark-up the price of his goods to cover the risk. This makes drug dealing even more profitable every time the government introduces a new weapon in the War on Drugs.[57]

Is the Reform Act Really a Reform?

A casual observer might say to the present authors, stop whining! Congress has already taken steps to reform the abuses of which you complain. Can't we just move on? It is true that Congress has passed and the president has signed the Civil Asset Reform Act of 2000.[58] The Act (1) purports to shift the burden of proof from the respondent to the government. The government now must show by a preponderance of the evidence that the property is subject to forfeiture[59]; (2) requires a "substantial connection" between the property and the offense[60]; (3) provides for appointment of counsel for indigents in certain narrow circumstances[61]; (4) offers an "innocent owner" defense in some instances[62]; (5) contains a "hardship" provision allowing return of the seized property to the claimant pending a hearing[63]; (6) allows for compensation when the property is damaged or destroyed by the government[64]; (7) eliminates the requirement for the claimant to post bond to maintain his claim[65]; and (8) mandates notice of the seizure to the owner within 60 days.[66] This sounds like a good Act

---

[57] *See* Steven Wisotsky, *Crackdown: The Emerging 'Drug Exception' to the Bill of Rights,* 38 Hastings L.J. 889, 895 (1987).

[58] Pub. L. No., 106-185, section 2, 2000 U.S.C.C.A.N. (114 Stat 202, 225) codified at 18 U.S.C. section 983.

[59] 18 U.S.C. section 983(c)(1).

[60] 18 U.S.C. section 983(c)(3).

[61] 18 U.S.C. section 983(b)(1).

[62] 18 U.S.C. section 983(d).

[63] 18 U.S.C. section 983((f)(1).

[64] Amending the Federal Tort Claims Act at 28 U.S.C. section 2680 (c).

[65] 18 U.S.C. section 983 (a)(2)(E).

[66] 18 U.S.C. section 983 (a).

for the forfeiture claimant seeking to regain or protect his property does it not?

But there are serious drawbacks to this so-called reform. At first glance, shifting the burden of proof from the claimant to the government seems to be a wholesome change. But the new burden of proof, preponderance of the evidence, has little potential to thwart abuse. The Act still allows the seizing law enforcement agency to have a financial interest in the booty received from the forfeiture.[67] The new burden is unlikely to cause law enforcement to drop their interest in obtaining needed funding. As we have suggested, the real reform will occur when the forfeited funds are ended, or at least placed in the general treasury. A worrisome question is that the Act also requires that the Government show a "substantial connection between the property and the offense."[68] But, sadly, the statute does not define "substantial connection." What does "substantial connection" mean and how closely connected must the property be to the offense? Will it protect you if you allow someone to borrow your car who then drives it to a bar where he smokes marijuana? This test is unclear, at best. Finally, how many people will really benefit from the Act by challenging forfeitures? Few we think because most forfeiture actions are never contested.[69]

The Act limits government appointed counsel to "those individuals who already benefit from this accommodation in connection with a related criminal case."[70] The exception is larger than the grant. The Act provides *no* appointed counsel rights in civil cases unless a home is

---

[67] It is reported that an attempt by Congressman Henry Hyde to rectify the troubling problems of asset distribution, conflicts of interest, and accountability that we discuss here were thwarted largely by the vigorous opposition of the law enforcement community. See Eric Blumenson & Eva Nilsen, *Policing for Profit: The Drug War's Hidden Economic Agenda*, 65 The University of Chicago Law Review 35, 107–108 (1998).

[68] 18 U.S.C. section 983(c)(1).

[69] One study shows that 89% of all forfeitures were uncontested and that 80% of all forfeitures occur administratively, *See* Supra footnote 67, Blumensen & Nilsen, *Policing For Profit: The Drug War's Hidden Economic Agenda*, 35, 50 n61. And, of course, the Supreme Court recently told us that prisoners are not even entitled to actual notice of the forfeiture of drug-tainted property. Due process only requires notice reasonably calculated to apprise the prisoner of the forfeiture proceedings. *See, Dusenberry v. United States*, 534 U.S. 161 (2002). One can only speculate on how many prisoners ever receive notice.

[70] 18 U.S.C. section 983(b)(1).

involved.[71] The Act will encourage law enforcement officials focused on forfeiture to pursue civil rather than criminal sanctions to avoid dealing with pesky appointed counsel.

It is indeed praiseworthy that the Act provides an innocent owner defense in all federal civil forfeiture cases.[72] An innocent owner is one who "did not know of the conduct giving rise to the forfeiture," or, when he discovered the illegal conduct, did "all that reasonably could be expected under the circumstances to terminate such use of the property."[73] To be protected under the Act, the owner has to take good faith efforts to stop the illegal use of the property or notify law enforcement authorities.[74] The Act also is commendable because it contains language that protects a person, who at the time he acquired the property was "a bona fide purchaser or seller for value and did not know the property was subject to forfeiture."[75]

Finally, there arises the most troubling question about the effectiveness of the Act. The Act says a claim to protect the property from forfeiture will not be denied when (1) "the property is the claimant's primary residence;" (2) "the claimant has no reasonable alternative means of shelter;" and (3) "the property is not, and is *not traceable to* (emphasis added), the proceeds of any criminal offense."[76] The Act's protection of bona fide purchasers sounds good until the vague term "is not traceable to the proceeds of any criminal offense" is considered. The real effect of that provision is to negate all that was said before and impose strict liability on persons who either did not know, or had no reason to be aware of the proceeds of a criminal offense. It sounds exactly like the strict liability imposed on aged tenants for the unknown acts of their grandchildren in a recent Department of Housing and Urban Development (HUD) case.[77] What public policy interest is served by depriving

---

[71] 18 U.S.C. section 983(b)(1).

[72] 18 U.S.C. section 983(d).

[73] Id.

[74] Id.

[75] 18 U.S.C. 983(d)(3)(A).

[76] 18 U.S.C. section 983(d)(3)(B).

[77] *See Department of Housing and Urban Development v. Rucker*, 535 U.S.__, 152 L. Ed 2d 258 (2002).

innocent family members of an abode to shield them from the elements[78] when the criminal no longer has an interest in the residence? Sadly, as we have demonstrated, the reform Act is not as effective in dealing with past abuse of drug forfeiture as widely advertised. There are still substantial and unresolved questions concerning the true purpose and fairness of drug-related forfeitures. The profit motive for law enforcement is still all too present. Sadly, the Act has by no reasonable measure cured the wrongs of which we complain. And that is largely because government agencies still have a financial interest in drug forfeitures, justice be damned.

Eviction for the Unknown Sins of Grandchildren

In order to combat drug use in public and other low-income housing, Congress passed the Anti-Drug Abuse Act of 1988.[79] The amended Act says that each public housing agency shall utilize leases that provide that any criminal drug-related activity on or off the premises, engaged in by a tenant, *any* (emphasis added) member of the tenant's household, or any guest or other person under the tenant's control, shall be cause for eviction.[80] The Department of Housing and Urban Development read the statute to require lease terms that permitted eviction of a tenant anytime a member of a tenant's household or guest engaged in drug-related criminal activity, regardless of whether the tenant knew, or had reason to know of it.[81] In the case of *Department of Housing and Urban Development v. Rucker*,[82] the Supreme Court faced two issues. First, whether the statute required lease terms authorizing the eviction of innocent tenants for

---

[78] In this and subsequent discussion of HUD and public sector housing, we abstract from the problems, moral and economic, which emanate from this policy. On this see Tucker, William, *The Excluded Americans: Homelessness and Housing Policy*, Chicago: Regnery-Gateway, 1990; Jacobs, Jane (1989), *The Death and Life of Great American Cities*, New York: Vintage.

[79] Codified as 42 U.S.C., section 11901 (3) (1994).

[80] 42 U.S.C., section 1437d (l)(6) (1994, Supp. V).

[81] *See*, 56 Fed. Reg. 51560, 51567 (1991), the strict liability regulation says that there is authority to evict when the tenant did not know, could not foresee, or could not control the other occupants.

[82] 535 U.S.__, 152 L. Ed 2d 258 (2002).

drug-related acts of others, and if so, whether the statute was constitutional under the Due Process Clause of the Fourteenth Amendment.[83]

The facts giving rise to the case are these. The grandsons of tenants, 71-year-old William Lee and 63-year-old Barbara Hill were apprehended in the apartment parking lot smoking marijuana, and the mentally retarded daughter of 64-year-old Pearl Rucker, who lived with her, was discovered with cocaine and a crack pipe three blocks from the apartment, and three times within a three-month period, 76-year-old, semi-paralyzed, Herman Walker's caregiver and two others were found possessing cocaine in his apartment.[84] On these facts, the 9th Circuit sitting en banc decided that HUDs interpretation allowing the eviction of "innocent tenants" was inconsistent with Congressional intent.[85] The en banc court believed that the statute did not address the level of personal knowledge or fault required for eviction.[86] The appellate court was also concerned with questions about the Fourteenth Amendment because HUD's interpretation allows tenants to be deprived of a property interest without any relationship to individual wrongdoing.[87]

Chief Justice Rehnquist writing for the high court said the statute "unambiguously requires lease terms with the discretion to evict tenants for drug-related activity of household members and guests whether or not the tenant knew, or should have known, about the activity."[88] The word "any" as used in the controlling statute has an expansive meaning and includes the tenants in this case. He said, "[T]hus, any drug-related activity engaged in by the specified persons is grounds for termination, not just drug-related activity that the tenant knew, or should have known, about."[89] The decision is troubling because what can aged grandparents

---

[83] Id. at 535 U.S.___, 152 L. Ed 2d 264, 265.

[84] Id. at 535 U.S.__, 152 L. Ed at 266. *See generally*, Charles Lane, *Supreme Court Upholds Public Housing Drug Law*, Washington Post, March 27, 2002, A4., for the ages and physical capacity of the tenants.

[85] 237 F.3d 1113 (2001).

[86] Id. at 1120.

[87] Id.

[88] 535 U.S.__, 152 L. Ed 2d at 266.

[89] Id. at 535 U.S.__, 152 L. Ed 2d at 267. 237 F.3d 1124–25 (citing *Scales v. United States*, 367 U.S. 201, 224–25 (1961) and *Southwestern Telegraph & Telephone Co. v. Danaher*, 238 U.S. 482 (1915)).

do to control their grandchildren? One wonders if the court considered what their own grandparents knew of their long-past teenage follies? Do they have any idea what their own grandchildren are doing tonight? Strict liability for old people means that the government and the court do not care what they knew or did not know. How can you control behavior when you don't know of it? Where is Pearl Rucker supposed to take her mentally retarded daughter? The Hilton? More likely she will reside on the street. Just mark them down as another casualty of the paternalistic War on Drugs.

The Court next turned to the tenant's due process claim and pointed out that the cases cited by the court of appeals, *Scales* and *Southwestern Telegraph & Telephone*, both dealt with the acts of the government as a sovereign either criminally punishing or civilly regulating the behavior of the general population.[90] Here, said the court, the Fourteenth Amendment is not implicated because the government is not attempting to criminally punish or civilly regulate the tenants as members of the general populace. Said the court, "[I]t is instead acting as landlord of the property it owns, invoking a clause in a lease to which respondents have agreed and which Congress has expressly required."[91] The court apparently believed that because HUD cloaked itself in the guise of a private landlord, the Constitution did not apply. But whatever cloak it wears, the government is acting as a sovereign and is bound by the Constitution. Is not an eviction of elderly tenants such as these a civil regulation of the behavior of a member of the general population? Is regulating an elderly person to a life on the street not government action? This case is another indication that the courts are so concerned with the problems concerning illegal drugs that they turn a blind eye to the abuses flowing from the War on Drugs.[92]

[90] Id. at 152 L. Ed 2d 269. In *Scales v. United States*, 367 U.S. 201, 224–25 (1961), the government criminally charged Scales with knowing membership in an organization that advocated the overthrow of the government, 367 U.S. 203, 224 (1961). In *Southwestern Telegraph& Telephone Co. v. Danaher*, 238 U.S. 482 (1915, an Arkansas statute forbade discrimination amongst customers of a telephone service.

[91] *Rucker* at 152 L.Ed. 2d at 269.

[92] *See* Supra, footnote 43.

The Legislative Mandated Necessity to Die in Pain

The state of California recently passed an initiative called the Compassionate Use Act of 1996.[93] The Act was designed to allow seriously ill citizens to use marijuana for medical purposes and created an exception to the state law prohibiting the possession and growing of this substance.[94] The state prohibitions against marijuana no longer apply to an ill patient or the caregiver who obtains the approval of a medical doctor.[95] Given that there is a ready market for such services for patients, several groups opened dispensaries to dispense marijuana to meet the needs of the patients.[96] The United States quickly sued in federal district court to enjoin these activities as a violation of the federal Controlled Substances Act.[97] The federal Act contains no "medical necessity" exception. The sole exception is for government approved research projects.[98]

The Cooperative argued that the language of the Act is subject to additional implied exceptions, including the common law exception of medical necessity.[99] The 9th Circuit Court of Appeals decided that the medical necessity defense was a cognizable defense and remanded the case to the district court.[100] On *certiorari*, the Supreme Court did not bother to trouble itself with the medical necessity defense. Justice Thomas said "to resolve the question presented, we need only to recognize that the medical necessity exception is at odds with the terms of the Controlled Substances Act. The statute, to be sure, does not explicitly abrogate the defense. But its provisions leave no doubt that the defense is unavailable."[101] He continued, "[U]nder any conception of legal necessity, one principle

---

[93] Cal. Health & Safety Code Ann., section 11362.5 (West. Supp. 2001).

[94] Id.

[95] Id.

[96] See, *United States v. Cannabis Cultivators Club*, 5 F. Supp. 2d 1086, 1092 (ND Cal. 1998).

[97] Specifically prohibiting the distribution, manufacturing, and possessing with the intent to distribute a controlled substance. 21 USC 841(a).

[98] 21 U.S.C. 823(f).

[99] *United States v. Oakland Cannabis Buyers Cooperative*, 532 U.S. at 483 (2001).

[100] 190 F.3d at 1115–15. The Court of Appeals instructed the lower court to consider the criteria for a medical necessity exception to the Act. 190 F.3d at 1115.

[101] 532 U.S. at 491.

is clear: the defense cannot succeed when the legislature itself has made a determination of values."[102]

The court was convinced that by listing government approved research projects as the sole exception to the Act, Congress had determined that marijuana had no medical benefits worthy of exemption.[103] There was, however, creditable evidence presented at the court of appeals that some people have medical conditions for which the use of marijuana is necessary to treat or alleviate pain and other symptoms.[104] The high court's response was that given Congress had already determined by statute that there was no basis for a medical necessity exception, it was an error for the court of appeals to even consider such evidence.[105] But, by analogy, Congress has determined that, for example, age discrimination in employment and discrimination against the disabled is contrary to our values. But the Supreme Court has said that states cannot be sued for violation of some of these federal statutes based on their sovereign immunity.[106] Why is allowing for a medical necessity any different? And it is clear that Asa Hutchinson has no intention of ending this War. On February 13, 2002, according to press reports, he was loudly jeered by city of San Francisco leaders while making a speech at the Commonwealth Club. They shouted "liar" when he said "science has told us so far there is no medical benefit for smoking marijuana."[107] The audience was unhappy because hours before the speech federal agents raided the Harm Reduction Center that provided marijuana treatment to 200 patients a day referred by doctors for pain reduction treatment.[108] The timing raises interesting moral questions about the DEA's recent enforcement decisions. A recent editorial entitled "Disinformation" was sharply critical of the Drug Enforcement Administration (DEA) ads recently used during the Super Bowl and the NCAA Final Four that claim that drug users are supporting

[102] Id.

[103] Id. at 493.

[104] 190 F.3d at 1115.

[105] 532 U.S. at 495.

[106] *See*, *Seminole Tribe of Fla. v. Florida*, 514 U.S. 44, 55 (1996).

[107] Margie Mason, *City Berates DEA Chief For Pot Bust*, The Washington Times, Feb. 14, 2002, A10.

[108] Id.

terrorists. The editorial suggested instead that the government's War on Drugs is responsible for inflating the price of drugs, thereby "funneling huge profits to terrorist organizations."[109] The editorial suggested that the ad should say of Asa Hutchinson, " I arranged for someone's terminally ill mother to experience excruciating pain until she dies."[110]

"Special Needs" for a War on Choir Singing

Recently the Supreme Court dealt with the question of whether school districts may constitutionally conduct warrantless searches of all public school children participating in extracurricular activities.[111] The 10th Circuit had decided that the school's testing program violated the Fourth Amendment,[112] because a school "must demonstrate there is some identifiable drug abuse problem among a significant number of those subject to testing, such that testing that group of students will actually redress its drug problem."[113] In *Earls*, the high court majority reversed the 10th Circuit and decided that school districts may conduct such suspicionless searches based on a "special needs" exception to the requirement that the government must have probable cause.[114] What makes the decision most troubling for privacy advocates is that the so-called special needs exception had generally been reserved for suspicionless drug testing of people who are performing jobs that have the potential to do great harm to the public like airline pilots, railroad engineers, DEA agents, and others involved in regulated industries.[115]

---

[109] *See*, Editorial, *The Arkansas Times*, March 29, 2002, p. 22. col. 1.

[110] Id.

[111] *Board of Education of Pattawatomic County v. Earls*, 70 U.S.L.W. 4737 (U.S. Jun. 27, 2002) (No. 01-332).

[112] Establishing "[t]he right of the people to be secure in their persons, houses, papers, and effects, against unreasonable searches and seizures."

[113] 242 F.3d 1264, 1270 (2001).

[114] Id.

[115] On this approach to avoiding the Fourth Amendment *See Skinner v. Railway Labor Executive's Assn.*, 489 U.S. 602, 609 (1989) (the government seeks to prevent the development of unsafe conditions) and *Treasury Employees v. Von Raab*, 489 U.S. 656, 667–668 (1989).

We think the decision also reflects the court's attitude, previously discussed,[116] that drugs are bad and we have got to do something.[117] Justice Thomas' decision clearly denies any notion that children have an expectation of privacy in school. The kids in the choir obviously don't have to shower and change clothes in public like the ballplayers in *Vernonia School District v. Acton*.[118] But he says they "are routinely required to submit to physical examinations and vaccinations against disease,"[119] and "some of these clubs and activities require occasional off-campus travel and communal undress."[120] But those minimal exposures hardly rise to the level of the exposure found in the typical football dressing room. The good Justice then makes perhaps the most outlandish claim of all, that having to urinate in a cup with a faculty member listening, only constitutes a "negligible" intrusion.[121] Even Justice Beyer in his concurring opinion says that there is no agreement that urine sampling is a "negligible" infringement of privacy.[122] Forget the embarrassment for the targeted kid for a moment, what about the intrusion on the sensibilities of the teacher. Who in their right mind (except some fetish monger) wants to listen to 50 kids urinate in cups? To the majority, however, urine tests are no different than math tests. Finally, subjecting the shy and the modest, the choir member or computer club nerd, to the same privacy infringements as the well-built, aggressive football player,[123] is just silly and can be harmful.[124]

[116] On this contention that the courts have allowed their concern about drugs to color their approach to Constitutional issues, *See* Supra footnote 42.

[117] Even Justice Beyer (concurring) says "I cannot know whether the school's drug testing program will work." 70 U.S.L.W. at 4742. Another relevant indication of the court's we don't know what to do but we have got to do something, even if it's wrong, approach.

[118] 515 U.S. 646, 657, where the majority goes to great length to describe the expectation of nudity and lack of privacy in the football team's dressing room. They say an "element of 'communal undress' is inherent in athletic competition." Id. Apparently the purpose is to argue that nudity is common to and accepted by teenagers. But is it amongst the shy and modest, in the choir and computer club? The Court has been watching too many Britney Spears videos.

[119] 70 U.S.L.W. at 4739.

[120] Id.

[121] Id. at 4740. After having admitted that "[U]rination is an excretory function traditionally shielded by great privacy." Id. (citation omitted). Now, apparently everywhere but at public schools.

[122] Id at 4742.

[123] "School sports are not for the bashful." Vernonia, 515 U.S. at 657. But the choir, sewing, or computer club might be. The majority is mixing the well-known apples and oranges.

[124] Justice Ginsberg (dissenting) makes this point citing a brief by the American Academy of Pediatrics. 70 U.S.L.W. at 4744.

In *Chandler v. Miller*,[125] a case involving the drug testing of political candidates, Justice Ginsberg said of the "special needs" exception, "The proffered special need for drug testing must be substantial."[126] The majority in that case decided that Georgia had not demonstrated a substantial problem of drug use by its elected officials. It is puzzling where the majority finds a substantial state interest in *Earls*. Only three of 797 students of the rural Oklahoma school tested positive. The school board president said that some people called him to discuss the drug problem.[127] So what, where is objective evidence of the problem? Even the school superintendent repeatedly described the drug use situation as not "major."[128] The argument that there was a compelling state interest greater than in *Chandler* in winning a drug war is difficult to support when there is no smoke of battle present. The majority appears to have gutted the balancing test of *Chandler* in favor of making the government interest in forbidding drug use (as slight as it is here) the only relevant "special needs" factor.

But Justice Thomas was not much deterred by the lack of evidence of a real drug problem. Not in the least. He apparently believes that even if there is no current problem, there might be a future one to be deterred. He says, "Indeed, it would make little sense to require a school district to wait for a substantial portion of its students to begin using drugs before it was allowed to institute a drug testing program designed to deter drugs."[129] This is an additional clue that the balancing test of *Chandler* and *Vernonia School District v. Acton* has been scrapped in favor of considering only the hysterical government interest in stamping out drug use.

And for good measure, the majority cuts the head off the public safety requirement that formally governed many of the "special needs" exceptions. Students, says the majority, are a danger to themselves because of their tendency to use drugs.[130] And that self-danger is enough to support suspicionless drug testing. The decision is troubling because it suspends

[125] 520 U.S. 305 (1997).

[126] Id. at 321.

[127] 70 U.S.L.W. at 4740.

[128] 70 U.S.L.W. at 4743.

[129] Id.

[130] Id. "[t]he need to prevent and deter the substantial harm of childhood drug use provides the necessary immediacy for the school testing policy." Id. So a problem is not needed? It is enough that

the Constitutional Fourth Amendment requirements in favor of "we got to do something" attitude toward drug use. Again the remedy is worse than the bite. Finally, is this an appropriate way to educate kids? Should we not teach them to respect the Constitution and value liberty? To make a kid urinate in a cup just to sing in the choir is silly, offensive, and everyone, including the kid, knows it. As Justice Beyer said, one of the tasks of schools is to teach the habits and manners of civility.[131] This is hardly accomplished by treating schools as prisons and kids as prisoners. We now turn to a potential remedy for the current drug war situation.

II. A Case for the Legalization of Drugs

The so-called War on Drugs in the United States has been an abject failure. The government spends billions of dollars in an attempt to stop the smuggling of drugs across the border, to stop the sale of these substances within the country, and to warn teens of the dangerous side effects. According to the Budget of the United States Government, the 2001 proposal for drug control programs is approximately 19.2 billion dollars.[132] By many estimates, usage has gone down, for both legal and illegal substances. Still, the use of illegal substances continues, and new reports suggest that children are likely to try drugs for the first time with their parents. In fact, "one in five people in treatment for substance abuse say they took drugs with their parents."[133] The War on Drugs is a costly project, and the results of the current efforts have not been promising. Both citizens and the government need to ask whether or not society would be better off if drugs were legal. Under a system of legalization, usage could be monitored; drugs would become safer; crime would decrease; and the

some other school, somewhere, has a problem like that of the out of control student use found in *Veronoia*. See *Vernonia*, 515 U.S. at 648.

[131] 70 U.S.L.W. at 4742 (Justice Beyer concurring) citing C. Beard & M. Beard, New Basic History of the United States 228 (1968).

[132] Budget of the United States Government, Fiscal Year 2001. Accessed November 5, 2000. http://w3.access.gpo.gov/usbudget/fy2001/pdf/budget.pdf.

[133] Adam Marcus. *Health Scout, Drug Use a Family Affair*. Thursday, August 24, 2000. Accessed November 4, 2000. http://www.healthscout.com/cgibin/WebObjects/Af?id=101667&ap=107.

risk of overdose would be greatly reduced. Studies also suggest that in addition to providing these benefits to society, the health problems of the country would not increase significantly, and the productivity of the country would not suffer.

In order to present a comprehensive argument for the legalization of drugs, the issue needs to be approached from several points of view. The discussion will begin with an examination of whether or not the prohibition of these substances infringes on the liberty of the person. From there, the discussion will proceed with arguments from a sociological and psychological perspective. The effect of legal drugs on a first time user and an addict will be addressed. The issue of legalization will then be examined from an economic point of view. Economic analysis provides a valid, rational, and objective argument for the legalization of drugs.

In order to focus this topic more narrowly, cocaine and crack will be used as representative drugs. These substances are purely recreational and therefore avoid all of the arguments for marijuana that revolve around medicinal uses. Also, the two drugs are different versions of the same chemical. Economic analysis can predict their relative consumption based on the strength of each substance, the high that each creates, and the legal penalties for possession.

Crack is a form of cocaine that can be smoked. It is relatively easy to manufacture, without requiring expensive equipment. Powdered cocaine hydrochloride is mixed with baking soda to form a paste, which is then heated until it is dry. This process of heating the mixture removes the hydrochloride salt, leaving the crack in a rock-like form.[134] In contrast to cocaine, which is either snorted or injected, crack is smoked in a marijuana or tobacco cigarette or a small glass pipe. Cocaine and crack have the same effect on the brain since both cause increases in the levels of dopamine, but crack smoke is quickly absorbed in the lining of the lungs and enters the brain in larger doses than cocaine. This creates an intense high that lasts for approximately 15 minutes, followed by a "crash" in which the user experiences depression and an intense drive to smoke more crack. While early street reports indicated that crack was 90% pure

---

[134] Steven R. Belenko, *Crack and the Evolution of Anti-Drug Policy* (Connecticut: Greenwood Press, 1993), 3.

cocaine, research has determined that crack still contains high levels of adulterants, making crack only 5 to 40% pure cocaine.[135] Cocaine abuse causes several symptoms including severe weight loss, insomnia, and psychosis. "Overdose reactions, more common with intravenous abuse, are marked by tremors, delirium, and convulsions. Fatalities do occur after either acute respiratory failure or circulatory collapse."[136]

According to the Statistical Abstract of the United States, in 1997, 0.7% of the population, aged 12 and older, reported that they were current cocaine users. In the same year, 0.3% of the same age group reported that they currently used crack.[137]

The Sourcebook of Criminal Justice Statistics finds that within the city of New Orleans in 1997, 45.8% of arrested males and 31.7% of arrested females tested positive for cocaine use.[138] One might wonder why the numbers of cocaine users are much higher for arrestees than for the general population. One reason might be that the data from the Statistical Abstract of the United States came from a self-reported household survey. It is likely that many people were afraid of honestly disclosing their cocaine or crack use. When the prisoners were arrested, they were given drug tests which are much more accurate than self-reported data. Another possibility may be that people with a history of crime, who are less afraid of imprisonment, are more likely to engage in other illegal behaviors. A law-abiding citizen, who would be deterred by the threat of jail time, might be less likely to use illegal drugs. Alternatively, it is possible that people who use cocaine and crack are more violent, and therefore commit more crimes. When discussing the effect of a system of legalization, the statistics regarding these drugs and crime will need to be examined in further detail.

Let us begin by examining whether or not the prohibition of cocaine and crack infringes on the liberty of the person. Two arguments must be

[135] Steven R. Belenko, *Crack and the Evolution of Anti-Drug Policy* (Connecticut: Greenwood Press, 1993): 6.

[136] George Beschner and Alfred S. Friedman, *Teen Drug Use* (Massachusetts: Lexington Books, 1986): 55.

[137] U.S. Census Bureau, *Statistical Abstract of the United States* (Washington: G. P. O., 1999): 152.

[138] Michael J. Hindelang, *Sourcebook of Criminal Justice Statistics* (Washington, D. C.: U.S. Department of Justice, Bureau of Justice Statistics, 1999): 371.

addressed: (1) Does the government have to right to infringe on your liberty if you are engaging in a behavior that is harmful to yourself? and (2) Are you really at liberty to make a rational choice for yourself when you are already addicted to cocaine or crack? In his work, *On Liberty*, John Stuart Mill examines the effect of laws against the sale of poisons, which is equally applicable to the sale of drugs, and thus the terms will be used interchangeably. He specifically states that these laws infringe upon the liberty of the person wishing to purchase the drugs. One might object by saying that it is the government's duty to protect people from accidentally injuring or killing themselves. To this, Mill replies that "when there is not a certainty, but only a danger of mischief, no one but the person himself can judge of the sufficiency of the motive of which may prompt him to incur the risk."[139] Mill suggests that labeling drugs would be a convenient way of informing the person of possible dangers without infringing on the person's liberty. Also, Mill states that by requiring the seller to enter into a register the name of the buyer, the amount of the sale, the quality of the goods, and so on, that the sale of the drugs can be monitored. This would not hinder the legal sale of drugs, but would make improper use of these substances more difficult.[140]

If one agrees that in general the government should not infringe on your right to engage in recreational activities, should the government be allowed to step in if the activity is harmful to yourself? Walter Block compares the use of drugs to the issue of wearing a seat belt. Is the infringement on human freedom small enough and the social good large enough to warrant government intrusion? Block argues that you cannot quantify these variables and that they involve interpersonal utility comparisons. Moreover, Block notes that there are many things, besides drugs and driving without seat belts, that are harmful—including chocolate, hang gliding, boxing, and automobile racing. If the government is allowed to prevent you from harming yourself, these activities would have to be outlawed.[141]

---

[139] John Stuart Mill, *On Liberty* (New York: W. W. Norton & Company, 1975): 89.

[140] John Stuart Mill, *On Liberty* (New York: W. W. Norton & Company, 1975): 90.

[141] Walter Block, "Drug Prohibition and Individual Virtue," *Review of Political Economy* 8, 4 (1996): 435; see also Block, Walter (1993). *Drug Prohibition: A legal and economic Analysis. Journal of Business Ethics*; vol. 12; pp. 689–700; Carpenter, Ted Galen. (December, 1985). *The U.S. Campaign*

In the previous discussion, we assumed that the individual knows that the action in which he is engaging is harmful, even potentially deadly. People can choose whether or not they would enjoy the benefits of hang gliding more than the risks, and the government should not prevent them from engaging in this activity. The question arises as to whether or not cocaine or crack addicts know that what they are doing is harmful. At the point that the person becomes addicted, is he at liberty to choose no longer to engage in this harmful behavior? Is he, in a sense, forced to continue the behavior? From an economic point of view, if you are forced to trade, you cannot gain from the exchange. Block finds this problematic because even under the threat of "your money or your life," you still have the opportunity to gain. "If you value your life over your money, you are better off if you are allowed to choose life over money. Consider an addict offered one ounce of his favorite narcotic for $100. Are we to say that he would be better off, from his own perspective, if he could not make this choice? If the person in danger of being murdered is made better off by being given a choice, why does this not apply to the addict?"[142] In this sense, the addict is not genuinely forced, and therefore is seen to be at liberty to make the decision for himself.

Legalizing cocaine and crack would have significant sociological and psychological effects on society. Lawrence Kohlberg identified common stages of moral development for people. Not everyone reaches all of the stages; many people stop at stage four, the stage that Kohlberg defines as the law and order stage. Justice at this stage is defined "in terms of a system, a social *order* of roles and rules that are shared and accepted by the entire community and that constitute the community."[143] Good actions

---

Against International Narcotics Trafficking: A Cure Worse Than the Disease. The Cato Institute, Washington D.C.; Cussen, Meaghan and Walter Block, "Drug Legalization: A Public Policy Analysis," *American Journal of Economics and Sociology*, Vol. 59, No 3, July 2000, pp. 525–536; Holloway, Jason and Block, Walter. (April, 1998). *Should Drugs be Legalized? West Coast Libertarian*; vol. 18, #2; pp. 6–7; Szasz, Thomas Stephen, *Ceremonial chemistry: the ritual persecution of drugs, addicts, and pushers*. Holmes Beach, Fla.: Learning Publications, 1985; Szasz, Thomas Stephen, *Our right to drugs: the case for a free market*, New York: Praeger, 1992; Thorton, Mark. (1991). *Alcohol Prohibition was a Failure* (The Cato Institute, Washington D.C.).

142 Walter Block, "Drug Prohibition and Individual Virtue," *Review of Political Economy* 8, 4 (1996): 435.

143 Lawrence Kohlberg, *Essays on Moral Development, Volume I: The Philosophy of Moral Development* (San Francisco: Harper and Row, Publishers, 1981): 150.

are oriented toward authority figures, and people obey the law for the sake of obeying the law. These people follow laws without questioning them. Under this theory, one might argue that many people have not tried drugs simply because they are illegal. Even if cocaine and crack were completely safe, individuals who have reached the law and order stage would still not try these substances as long as they remained illegal. If cocaine and crack were legalized, people would be more inclined to try them. The overall usage in the country would, therefore, increase.

An interesting psychological aspect of legal drug use is the "gateway effect." Individuals, it is argued, begin using drugs that are legal, and these substances are a "gateway" to illegal drug use.[144] A person might begin using cigarettes, which are legal, accessible, and inexpensive. He may find that he likes the stimulant aspect of nicotine and begin abusing other tobacco products. Ultimately, he may begin using illegal stimulants, such as speed, to get the same high. If cocaine or crack were legalized, individuals may begin using these substances and progress to products, such as heroin, that might remain illegal. This evidence, accompanied with Kohlberg's theory on the law and order stage, would seem to suggest that cocaine and crack should remain illegal. Economic analysis, however, offers an alternative point of view.

In order to effectively present this argument from an economic perspective, some basic microeconomic concepts are required. In economics, demand refers to the quantity of a good that a buyer is willing and able to buy at various prices. Similarly, supply refers to the amount of the good that a seller is willing and able to sell at various prices. An inverse relationship exists between price and quantity demanded—as the price of the good increases, buyers are willing and able to buy less of the good. Buyers are less willing to purchase more units of the good at a higher price because as they purchase additional units of the good, the buyer begins to experience diminishing marginal utility from the good. The additional units only have enough value for the buyer at a lower price. Conversely, a positive relationship exists between price and the quantity of the good that suppliers are willing and able to supply. A particular sup-

[144] Rosalie Liccardo Pacula, "Economic Modeling of the Gateway Effect," *Health Economics* 6, 5 (1997): 521.

plier may only be willing to supply ten units of a good at a certain price, but if the price increases, his incentive to supply more of the good increases. Ultimately, the main point to understand is that at a low price, buyers are willing and able to buy more, while sellers are willing and able to sell less. On the other hand, at a high price, buyers are willing and able to buy less and sellers are willing and able to sell more. This model works for any good, including cocaine. This basic economic analysis will be useful in observing the effects of various laws (or lack of laws) on the price of cocaine or crack, and understanding what effect changes in price will have on consumption and production patterns.

Having established the economic laws of supply and demand, these laws can be applied to the market for cocaine and crack. Economic analysis can be used to compare the price, demand, and supply in the illegal markets as well as in an expected legal market. It is important to understand how sellers set the prices for their drugs. First, in the sale of any good, the seller has to consider the costs of production. These may include costs for equipment, inputs, or labor. For an illegal good such as cocaine or crack, however, these production costs are quite low. Production of crack does not require any special equipment and can be produced in a short period of time by one person. For cocaine, "of uncertain quality that now sells on the street for $10, the cost of production is five to ten cents."[145] The major costs in selling an illegal good such as cocaine include the threat of discovery, risk of seizure, and risk of punishment that may include fines and jail time. These are all costs to the seller that are taken into account in setting the price for illegal substances. Clearly, if cocaine and crack were legalized, these costs would disappear. New costs of advertising, for example, may arise in the new legal market, but the elimination of risk to sellers would mean that the price of these substances would greatly decrease.

In the illegal market for cocaine and crack, buyers also face costs that exceed the dollar value of the good. First, there are costs associated with finding someone willing to sell you an illegal substance. These costs include the risk of assault and arrest. If a user is imprisoned, he or she will

[145] William A. Niskanen, "Economists and Drug Policy," *Carnegie-Rochester Conference Series on Public Policy* 36 (1992): 233.

not earn an income for that period of time. The total monetary penalty for someone earning a higher income is therefore greater than for someone earning a lower income.[146] The foregone wages and other foregone uses of one's time can be seen as a cost to the person who is imprisoned. "Second, the costs of use include the risks of drugs of uncertain potency, adulterants, and of some use techniques."[147] Because cocaine and crack are illegal, it is more difficult to obtain information about the drug which is being purchased. They are not controlled by government standards, and suppliers are not required to disclose the strength of the drug or the quantities of adulterants. "Cutting agents can turn out to be any of various sugars, local anesthetics, or amphetamines; on occasion, rat poison has been used."[148] Buyers who purchase these substances risk being poisoned by the adulterants and are left with no legal recourse to sue the seller. Under a legal market, there would be government standards set for cocaine and crack. Brand names would likely appear, and sellers would be required to label their product with a list of the ingredients and the potency. A recommended dosage could be set for cocaine and crack, similar to the way dosages are determined for cold medicines. Warnings could also be placed on the containers to inform users of the side effects of the substance, both in the short and long term. All of these measures would reduce the costs to buyers of cocaine and crack. By eliminating the risks associated with finding the product, and decreasing the risk associated with the chemical composition of the substance, the cost of taking the drug would decrease for the buyer.

One might argue that as the price of drugs falls, the quantity demanded of these substances will be greater. Remember that as price falls, the amount of a good that buyers are willing and able to buy will increase. An economic rebuttal to this argument is that to an addict drugs are a necessity, not a luxury. Therefore, drugs have a low price elasticity of demand

[146] John R. Lott, "An Attempt at Measuring the Total Monetary Penalty from Drug Convictions: The Importance of an Individual's Reputation," *Journal of Legal Studies* 21, 1 (1992): 185.

[147] William A. Niskanen, "Economists and Drug Policy," *Carnegie-Rochester Conference Series on Public Policy* 36 (1992): 234.

[148] Roger LeRoy Miller, Daniel K. Benjamin, and Douglass C. North, *The Economics of Public Issues* Massachusetts: Addison-Wesley, 1999): 37.

(change in consumption relative to change in price) for the addict.[149] Whether the price is increased or decreased, the addict is not likely to change his consumption by much. The price of cocaine or crack in a legal market, *ceterus paribus*, would fall since these goods currently include a premium for the dealer to compensate him for the risk involved in supplying the product. By one estimate, legalization would lead to a 60% reduction in retail drug prices.[150] With this fall in price, the sellers would be willing to sell less and buyers would, theoretically, be willing to buy more. The cost for current addicts is based on the costs associated with finding a dealer in an illegal market, threat of arrest, and the danger of taking substances of unknown purity. Under a legal system, these costs to buyers would be reduced or eliminated. From the buyer's point of view, the cost of the drug will decrease, and they will be willing and able to purchase more of the good at each price. In fact, consumption of drugs may double under a system of legalization.[151] Estimates by other economists, however, indicate that the consumption of cocaine would increase only about 50%.[152] As stated earlier, the change in demand for addicts may not change much with a change in price, but new users are likely to enter the market. Occasional users may also increase their consumption to be more frequent users.

If the taint of illegality is removed, demand would likely increase. Supply, however, would likely increase at a much faster rate due to the significant reduction in costs to suppliers as a result of the elimination of the risk of being apprehended, convicted, and punished. In Fig. 13.1, D_1 and S_1 represent the market demand and supply before legalization, and the market-clearing price is P_1. After legalization, demand and supply would shift to D_2 and S_2, and the market-clearing price would decrease to P_2, which is significantly lower than P_1.

---

[149] Walter Block, "Drug Prohibition and Individual Virtue," *Review of Political Economy* 8, 4 (1996): 435.

[150] Henry Saffer and Frank J. Chaloupka, "The Demand for Illicit Drugs," *In Abstracts of Working Papers in Economics (AWPE)* (1996): 14.

[151] William A. Niskanen, "Economists and Drug Policy," *Carnegie-Rochester Conference Series on Public Policy* 36 (1992): 241.

[152] Henry Saffer and Frank J. Chaloupka, "The Demand for Illicit Drugs," *In Abstracts of Working Papers in Economics (AWPE)* (1996): 14.

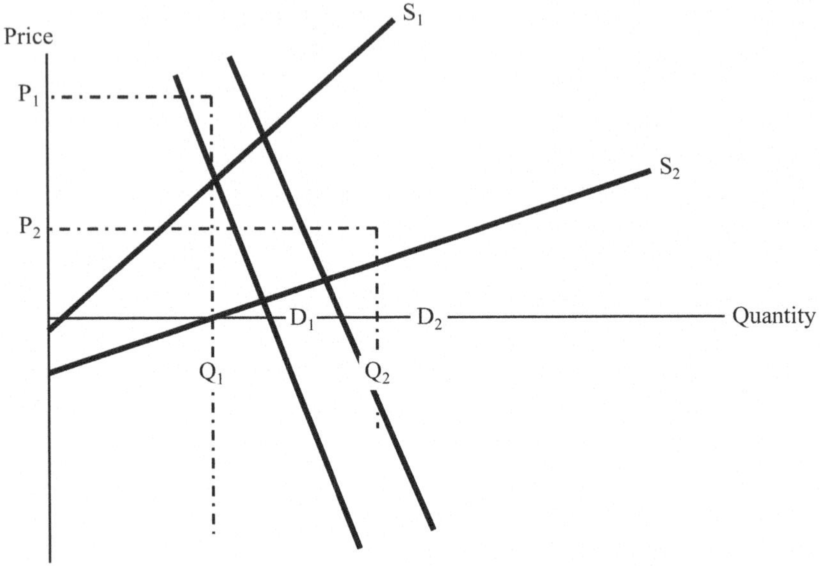

Fig. 13.1 Supply and demand for drugs under legalization and prohibition

The idea of increased consumption is enough for many people to argue that drugs should remain illegal. After all, Americans have invested a great deal of money and effort in the War on Drugs with the goal of reducing consumption. The positive benefits of a legal drug system, however, need to be considered. First, use of these substances could be carefully monitored. Currently, many countries are unable to monitor illegal drug deals even in their prisons. In 1994, the United Kingdom reported that 45% of its inmates were using drugs in prison.[153] Canadian prisons experienced similar problems; drugs are sold for 500% of their street value behind bars and many prisoners reported that their consumption actually increased while they were incarcerated.[154] One would imagine that prisoners' actions could be constantly monitored, and yet, illegal substance use is quite prevalent. Under a legal system,

[153] "A Shock to the System: Drugs in Prison," *The Economist* 340, 7974 (1996): 54.

[154] Kevin Marron, "High Times Doing Hard Times: Packed with Dealers and Substance Abusers, Canada's Prisons Have Become a Lucrative Market for the Drug Trade," *Maclean's* 109, 13 (1996): 50.

however, use of cocaine and crack could be monitored and recorded. As John Stuart Mill suggested, sellers could be required to document the specific details of their exchanges. This would not hinder the legal sale, but would make improper use of these substances more difficult.[155]

It is particularly important to note that monitoring the sales of legal cocaine and crack would also mean that the quality or purity would be controlled and subject to certain standards. Guidelines would prevent sellers from placing dangerous adulterants of unknown quantities into their products. Labeling the substances would also warn users of the possible dangers and side effects, and recommended dosages would likely mean fewer accidental overdoses. Users would purchase their drugs from authorized dealers because of the security of knowing that the cocaine and crack are high quality.

Even if it is true that consumption doubles, society will not likely notice a difference in health care costs or accidental deaths, but any difference is likely to be negative. "A careful review of the available studies indicates that many of the adverse health effects of current drug use, maybe most of these effects, are due to the side effects of prohibition of these drugs—overdose, adulterants, more risky use techniques, and a reluctance to seek early medical treatment."[156] This is not meant to suggest that there are not health risks associated with using cocaine and crack. In fact, the side effects of these substances, even when they are of known purity and consumed in small quantities, can be great. There is every reason to believe, however, that the major risks associated with consuming these substances, as stated earlier, would be reduced under a system of legalization. Even if the number of cocaine and crack users increased, "the potential net effects appear to be small, and may be negative."[157]

Another common concern with legalized drug use that people often cite is that productivity of individuals would decrease. Unfortunately, few studies have been done on this issue, and clearly, more research needs to

155 John Stuart Mill, *On Liberty* (New York: W. W. Norton & Company, 1975): 89.

156 William A. Niskanen, "Economists and Drug Policy," *Carnegie-Rochester Conference Series on Public Policy* 36 (1992): 240.

157 William A. Niskanen, "Economists and Drug Policy," *Carnegie-Rochester Conference Series on Public Policy* 36 (1992): 243.

be conducted. One small study concluded that "drug use (at least once in the prior year) appears to *increase* wages about 7 percent and that hard drug use may increase wages as much as 20 percent."[158] Although this single study does not provide sufficient evidence to conclude that drug use has a positive effect on wages, it does indicate that it may not cause the sort of economic problems that individuals fear.

A positive benefit to consider is that under a system of legalized crack and cocaine, crime will decrease. There are three types of crime associated with cocaine and crack use: systemic crime, psychopharmacologically driven crime, and economically compulsive crime. Systemic crime arises out of the process of drug distribution. It includes turf wars between dealers, "homicides committed within dealing hierarchies as a means of enforcing normative codes, robberies of drug dealers and the usually violent retaliation by the dealer or their bosses."[159] This is the most common type of crime associated with drug use, and has been referred to "as a means to achieve 'economic regulation and control' in an illicit market."[160] A study in New York in 1988 found that "of 118 crack-related homicides that were studied, 85 percent were systemic in nature."[161] If cocaine and crack were legal, sellers and buyers could take their grievances to court, and disputes could be resolved by a judge. By legalizing these substances, systemic crime would be reduced, or possibly eliminated.

The second type of crime associated with cocaine and crack use is psychopharmacologically driven crime. This type of crime occurs when the behavior of a person is significantly altered, by becoming violent or irrational due to effect of the stimulant. Current data suggest that this is the least common type of crime associated with cocaine and crack. The same

---

[158] William A. Niskanen, "Economists and Drug Policy," *Carnegie-Rochester Conference Series on Public Policy* 36 (1992): 237.

[159] United States Sentencing Commission. *Special Report to the Congress: Cocaine and Federal Sentencing Policy*. 95. February 1995. Accessed October 1, 2000. http://www.ussc.gov/crackexec.htm.

[160] United States Sentencing Commission. *Special Report to the Congress: Cocaine and Federal Sentencing Policy*. 95. February 1995. Accessed October 1, 2000. http://www.ussc.gov/crackexec.htm.

[161] United States Sentencing Commission. *Special Report to the Congress: Cocaine and Federal Sentencing Policy*. 96. February 1995. Accessed October 1, 2000. http://www.ussc.gov/crackexec.htm.

New York study found that "only three of the 118 exclusively crack-related homicides in the study were psychopharmacological in nature, and in two of these three cases the victim precipitated the crime."[162] By minimizing the harmful effects of cocaine and crack by using government standards and mandatory labels, the risk of violent behavior associated with these drugs might be reduced.

The final type of crime associated with cocaine and crack use is economically driven crime. When individuals commit crimes to obtain money to pay for their habit they are said to have committed economically driven crime. Although this occurs on a small scale, a study found that most street users "reported that some of their living expenses and over 90 percent of their drug use were financed by [retail drug sales], suggesting that street users rely on frequent, relatively small drug sales to support their crack cocaine habit."[163] Under a system of legalization, the price of drugs would decrease, due to the elimination of risk to sellers, and the need to commit crime to pay for cocaine and crack would be greatly reduced. If cocaine and crack were legalized, therefore, all three types of crime associated with this drug use would be reduced or eliminated.

The sellers in a legal cocaine or crack market will likely be different from the sellers who currently deal in the illegal market. In any market, the sellers will be those with a competitive advantage over their competitors. In an illegal market, those who already have prison records or who have nothing to lose by going to jail will have a competitive advantage over people who might sell, but who would be seriously hurt by the legal punishment.[164] In a legal market, the sellers with the competitive advantage might be the pharmaceutical companies, the tobacco companies, and the pharmacies. Pharmaceutical companies currently have the technology to produce and package drugs in a uniform and safe manner. They have economies of scale

---

[162] United States Sentencing Commission. *Special Report to the Congress: Cocaine and Federal Sentencing Policy*. 99. February 1995. Accessed October 1, 2000. http://www.ussc.gov/crackexec.htm.

[163] United States Sentencing Commission. *Special Report to the Congress: Cocaine and Federal Sentencing Policy*. 101. February 1995. Accessed October 1, 2000. http://www.ussc.gov/crackexec.htm.

[164] Roger LeRoy Miller, Daniel K. Benjamin, and Douglass C. North, *The Economics of Public Issues* Massachusetts: Addison-Wesley, 1999): 33.

since they already have the machinery and labor to manufacture products in large quantities. They are also accustomed to dealing with the laws established by the Food and Drug Administration. The company would be allowed to place their particular brand name on the cocaine or crack produced, and their reputation for quality would be carried over to this new drug. Tobacco companies may compete with the pharmaceutical companies to produce these substances. Tobacco companies may be likely producers of cocaine and crack since they already have the experience of producing an addictive substance. They may start to advertise, as they do with cigarettes, that their cocaine or crack contains no additives. Tobacco companies also have an advantage in producing cigarettes with low tar or low levels of nicotine as well as cigarettes which contain much higher levels. These companies may begin to manufacture cocaine and crack with different potencies and market one version as being safer.

Pharmacies are also currently in the business of dispensing drugs. Again, their reputation would be important when a buyer is choosing to purchase a drug. Many pharmacies advertise that they provide full product information about possible side effects and drug interactions. People purchasing products like cocaine and crack will want to know this information, and only a pharmacist will know if their other prescription medicines will react negatively with these substances.

As stated earlier, the price of cocaine and crack in a legal market ought to fall because the element of risk for the seller has been removed. The companies who produce these goods will also likely generate economies of scale which will lower the price of the drugs even further. There is nothing in this argument, however, that would prevent the government from imposing exorbitant taxes on the sale of drugs. The government already heavily taxes legal substances such as cigarettes. In this case, the price would increase for the buyer, but the seller would not generate any extra revenue since the seller would not benefit from the taxes. The seller would continue to sell at the current volume, but the buyer would theoretically buy less since the price is higher due to the tax. This is commonly called a sin tax and used by politicians to imply that something is bad and therefore should be taxed. Actually, from an economic point of view, this is simply capitalizing on the low price elasticity of demand for cocaine and crack. In reality, the tax would not likely deter consumption of addicts by any large amount, as they would continue to consume the drug at near current rates. Because the price would increase without decreasing consumption by much, revenue would be generated. By one estimate, "the excise tax on legal drugs would generate tax revenue, probably about $4 billion a year."[165] This money could be used to establish treatment facilities or to fund an advertising campaign, similar to the current ads against cigarettes that would warn people of the harmful effects of these substances.

After examining the issue of the legalization of drugs from several points of view, one can draw the conclusion that the current policy is ineffective and in need of reform. Given that the government spends billions of dollars on a program that is largely failing, individuals and society need to consider legalizing addictive substances like cocaine and crack. Under a system of legalization, usage could be monitored; drugs would become safer; crime would decrease; and the risk of overdose would be greatly reduced. Studies also suggest that in addition to providing these positive benefits to society, the health problems of the country would not increase significantly, and the productivity of the country would not suffer if drugs were legalized. In addition, revenue could be generated from taxing drugs, and this money could be used to inform people of the possible dangers of consuming these products. Social influence through television advertising and warning labels have been effective in reducing consumption of cigarettes and alcohol, particularly among pregnant women. There is no reason to believe that this same social influence would not apply to the consumption of drugs. No one denies that drugs are harmful. The case presented here, however, argues that while cocaine and crack may be harmful, they should not be illegal.

III. An Objection

Let us consider an objection to the foregoing made by Alan Keyes, candidate for president on the Republican ticket for the 2000 election. In his "Drug war threatens U.S."[166] Keyes sets forth his views on this public

---

[165] William A. Niskanen, "Economists and Drug Policy," *Carnegie-Rochester Conference Series on Public Policy* 36 (1992): 243.

[166] http://www.worldnetdaily.com/bluesky_keyes/20000603_xcake_drug_war_t.shtml.

policy. His perspective is particularly germane to our interests since of all the presidential candidates, Keyes is by far the most outspoken advocate of individual responsibility; and this, in turn, might be considered an argument in favor of legalization. After all, prohibition is at bottom a paternalist law, implying that the people cannot be trusted to look after themselves. However, even though Keyes acknowledges that legalization would appear to stem from his own philosophical premises,[167] he does not at all conclude that addictive substances should be made legal.

He starts off by conceding that the "war on drugs" has gotten out of hand, and has committed many abuses: "In its current form, then, the war on drugs is indeed a threat to our liberty." But this does not logically imply, he contends, that it ought to be repealed. Rather, borrowing a leaf from former President Clinton's view on affirmative action, with a little boost from Jesse Jackson, this war ought to be mended, not ended. Keyes states: "Does this mean that we should adopt the position that drug laws, and their reasonable and constitutional enforcement, are threats to our liberty? I don't think so. Rather, it means that we must insist that the drug enforcement effort cease violating the constitutional rights of citizens. There is no reason that the pursuit, apprehension, prosecution and punishment of drug traffickers need be any less solicitous of the constitutional rights of the suspected criminals than are the corresponding actions directed against suspected murderers and embezzlers."

But there are problems here. First of all, mere "insistence" will not do. There are good and sufficient reasons why the drug war has resulted in unwarranted seizures of property, rampant violation of privacy, and other violations of liberty. Keyes seems to think that these results of the war are incidental, not necessary. He is mistaken. The reason for the escalation is that the war has within it the seeds of its own destruction. Every time the Drug Enforcement Agency interdicts a shipment of contraband material, it drives up its price. But with the higher price, the criminal classes are given even greater impetus and incentives to pursue their activities. *Of*

[167] He states: "In fact, many people expect me to agree with the moral case against drug laws because I believe that respect by government for the moral capacity of free citizens is so central to the preservation of our way of life. I am indeed a moral libertarian—and I think America is founded on moral libertarian principles. But this does not mean that I believe our drug laws must be repealed on moral.

course, this will lead to an exacerbation of hostilities, from both sides. The drug runners will escalate their weaponry, and bribery, and the police charged with eradicating them will have no choice but to step up their efforts as well. It is no wonder that under these circumstances the niceties of our Constitutional protections will take a back seat. It is all well and good for Keyes to regret these excesses, and even to call for their removal, but a moment's reflection on the underlying causes of these abuses indicates that this is just so much idle chatter. It is akin to decrying man's inhumanity to man, or drunkenness, or jealousy, with a resolution that things be put right. These things, too, have strong causal antecedents, and all the protestations in the world will not put them right.

Secondly, his analogy between addictive substances on the one hand, and murderers and embezzlers cannot be maintained. When the police capture either of the latter types of criminals, there is simply no impetus automatically created which promotes these activities. Indeed, the very opposite is the case. That is, the power of the police is demonstrated and would-be malefactors are in effect given a warning to cease or desist, or face the penalties attached to capture.

Why the difference? In the case of addictive drugs, there is a vast market of people who demand these products. With less offered, due to a capture, basic supply and demand analysis implies a higher price, attendant higher profits, and hence more incentive to continue in, and even expand the scope of business. But who demands embezzlement? Apart from Murder Inc., for which there *is* a demand, the same considerations do not apply to such capital crimes. And, not only does killing for hire account for a very small proportion of all murders, but the masses of people—in contrast to addictive drugs—are strongly opposed to such acts. That is, far more people engage in the recreational use of drugs than commit murder or embezzlement. These are powerful disanalogies.

A more powerful argument for opposing drug legalization, in the view of Keyes, has to do with morality. To summarize: liberty is a most important goal for society, but it cannot be achieved or maintained without a core of morality underlying it. However, addictive drugs corrode morality, and hence liberty, at one remove. So, therefore, there is a logical contradiction in urging drug legalization on grounds of liberty, when to do so undermines the very liberty we are relying upon in the argument. But let us put this in Keyes's own words, lest we be accused of misunderstanding or improperly characterizing his perspective. He states:

> There can be no liberty unless the moral foundation of liberty is safeguarded…
>
> There was a time when we could avoid this negative effect of drug laws by doing without them—because the foundations of moral education made them unnecessary. There was a time when the great and decisive majority of young Americans were raised in morally upright families, God-fearing churches and sound schools, through which they were formed in moral precepts that led them to have contempt for the abuse of conscience and liberty that drugs represent. As long as these institutions were permitted to do their proper work, the rising generations simply did not have the problems of character that make young people vulnerable to the abuse of drugs. Because this was the condition of society for much of our history, the proliferation of drug laws in America did not occur until the latter half of the 20th century.
>
> When a society begins to generate new laws, it is almost always a sign that it has previously begun to generate new evils. The rise of American drug laws has been a response to the rise of the new problem of drug abuse. This problem, in turn, arose because of our diminished national willingness to attend to the moral elements of education and child rearing.
>
> This is why the undeniably negative implication of the drug laws cannot be escaped by simply repealing them. We have placed ourselves in this position by decades of moral laxity. The root of the drug problem was our excessive permissiveness in the moral formation of our children. But having allowed this to happen, we have limited the choices open to us now. A repeal of the drug laws will inevitably be interpreted as a further grant of permission for this kind of behavior. Whatever rhetoric of confidence in the moral capacity of our people cloaks such a repeal, it will in fact reinforce the moral destruction we are suffering. Accordingly, because we are not in the innocent condition that preceded the need for drug laws, but are rather in the morally compromised condition that continues to demand a collective response to the moral damage we have permitted, it is essential that we maintain the laws.

What we have here, then, in microcosm, is a debate between those who advocate the supremacy of liberty vis-a-vis virtue (e.g., libertarians) and those who see virtue as the mother, not the daughter, of liberty (e.g., conservatives).[168]

There are several grave drawbacks to the Keyes' conservative position.

1. Overgeneralization

If addictive substances are immoral, and will lead to a weakening of the social will to maintain liberty, there are many more instances of this abuse than drugs. Cigarettes, alcohol, fatty foods, chess, sports, hang gliding, gambling, sex can all be addictive, at least for some persons. Logical consistency dictates that Keyes must favor prohibiting *all* of these goods or activities. He cannot pick and choose; all must go by the boards. But if so, what of people's liberty to do as they please, as long as they do not violate the rights of others?[169]

2. Pessimism

Keyes is far too pessimistic. He believes we will lose our liberties if drugs are legal because so many people will come under their influence, and zombies cannot be counted upon to uphold our rule of law. One problem with this is that there are *already* many addicts of heroin, cocaine, and other such substances, and, while there are always risks to liberty, they do not seem to be emanating from this quarter. Rather, the greatest dangers to our freedom now that the risk of thermonuclear war has receded, stem from excessive regulation, high taxes, and political correctness. But drug legalization is part and parcel of too much government control. Keyes' position is part of the problem in this regard, not part of the solution.

3. Alcohol

Why the radical difference in the position of conservatives such as Keyes on drugs and alcohol. *Both* are addictive. *Both* tend to deflect the atten-

[168] For an extended discussion of this issue, see Carey, George W., ed., *Freedom and Virtue: The Conservative / Libertarian Debate*, Wilmington DE: Intercollegiate Studies Institute, 1998 [1984].

[169] See on this Mill, John Stuart, *On Liberty*, N.Y.: Prometheus, 1986 [1859].

tion of users from the niceties of protecting liberty. *Both* have all sorts of negative social, economic, and political repercussions. If our moral fiber is so greatly attenuated that society's investment in liberty cannot afford to legalize drugs, why not go back to the prohibitionism of alcohol for this reason? That these two products would be treated so differently is either evidence of failure to carry a chain of thinking to its logical conclusion, enslavement to the status quo, or hypocrisy.

States Keyes: "Drug abuse, and the public response to it, raises a similar challenge. Because freedom doesn't just require that we refrain from assaulting each other. It also requires that we acknowledge our duty to participate as rational agents in the great project of self-government. That means that one of the requirements of freedom is a *clear head* (emphasis added).

Clear head? But alcohol certainly addles the brain, as much or more than, say, marijuana. Have we learned nothing from our disastrous experience with prohibition?

4. History

As a matter of historical fact, our drug laws were enacted not in order to safeguard freedom, but as a racist anti-oriental measure. The prime target of this legislation were Chinese opium dens.

5. Imprimatur

States Keyes: "A repeal of the drug laws will inevitably be interpreted as a further grant of permission for this kind of behavior. Whatever rhetoric of confidence in the moral capacity of our people cloaks such a repeal, it will in fact reinforce the moral destruction we are suffering. Accordingly, because we are not in the innocent condition that preceded the need for drug laws, but are rather in the morally compromised condition that continues to demand a collective response to the moral damage we have permitted, it is essential that we maintain the laws."

The idea, here, is that man-made law puts some sort of societal imprimatur on behavior. If legal, it is approved; if illegal, disapproved. Since reasonable men can disapprove of addictive drugs, it is only responsible to ban them by law.

But if the law ought to prohibit everything of which moral men disapprove, again, there will be a very long list of proscribed activities and products. Further, if the law has such a powerful effect on moral behavior, and moral behavior is the bedrock of liberty, then not only should the law prohibit that which is bad, it ought, also, to compel what is good. For example, we ought to have compulsory prayers, religion, teeth brushing, milk drinking, and so on. But if we do this, we will have gone a long way from promoting liberty, presumably the point of the entire exercise.

6. Licentiousness

Keyes accuses the legalization argument with a "confusion of liberty with licentiousness." He continues: "Liberty is not an abstract right to do whatever we feel like without regard to the consequences. It especially does not mean this in those areas where the consequence of abuse is to destroy liberty. If we want to hold on to liberty, then we must limit those abuses that will destroy it. We can't have it both ways. This means that at some level, in the laws of a free society, limits must be set which respect the requirements of freedom."

On the contrary, there is no "confusion of liberty with licentiousness" in the libertarian position.[170] Rather, in this perspective, liberty exists not only to protect nondebatable activities (e.g., brushing teeth, eating apples, tying shoelaces) but also "licentious" ones, such as engaging in what might be considered immoral victimless crimes, such as the use of addictive drugs, alcohol, pornography, prostitution, gambling, and so on. If liberty can only protect us when we engage in the former set of acts, but not the latter, then what good is it? It is simply not liberty at all.

[170] See on this Block, Walter, "Libertarianism vs. Libertinism," *The Journal of Libertarian Studies: An Interdisciplinary Review*, Vol. 11, No. 1, 1994, pp. 117–128.

But it is a straw man argument to interpret this view as supporting the doing of "whatever we feel like without regard to the consequences." There is no such thing as liberty, for instance, to engage in murder, rape, theft, arson, for to do these things is to violate the equal liberty of others to be free of aggression and invasive violence.[171] In our view, decriminalization of voluntary drug use will enhance liberty for all. It is time to approach the drug war from a philosophical and economic perspective and to disarm the drug warriors and abate their violence to liberty.

[171] See Rothbard, Murray N., *For a New Liberty*, Macmillan, New York, 1973; Rothbard, Murray N., *The Ethics of Liberty*, New York: New York University Press, 1998 (1982).

Part V

Crime

14

Taking the Assets of the Criminal to Compensate Victims of Violence

I. Legal Analysis

Over 30 years ago, New York was terrorized by a serial killer, David Berkowitz, immortalized by the media as the "Son of Sam."[1] By the time Berkowitz was apprehended, publicity about the case had created an enormous monetary value in the rights to his criminal story. New York's appalled legislature sought to prevent Berkowitz and other criminals from exploiting for profit the tales of their sensational crimes while their victims remained uncompensated. The statute resulting from the legislature's praiseworthy efforts to strip the criminal of his crime-related profits and compensate the victim was called the "Son of Sam Law."[2] Its efforts are praiseworthy because criminals should not profit from their violence against victims. And surely victims deserve to be compensated for the damages caused to them by the criminal's violence. Today, over 40 states, including California, have some form of the "Son of Sam" law. The New York law provided that if any person "accused or convicted of a

[1] On July 9, 2002, Berkowitz was denied parole by New York authorities. He claims that a neighbor's dog ordered the killings. *See*, In The News, *Arkansas Democrat-Gazette*, July 10, 2002, at A1.

[2] Simon and Schuster v. Members of the N.Y. State Crime Victims Board, 502 U.S. 105 (1991).

W. E. Block, R. Whitehead, *Philosophy of Law*, Palgrave Studies in Classical Liberalism,
https://doi.org/10.1007/978-3-030-28360-5_14

crime in this state"[3] was "due money under contract with respect to a re-enactment"[4] of the crime "by the way of a movie, book, magazine article, tape recording, phonograph record, radio or television presentation, or live entertainment of any kind,"[5] or for expressions of a person's faults or feelings about the crime, the contract must be reported to the New York State Crime Victims Board, and the money due must be paid over to the New York board to be placed in an escrow account, primarily for the benefit of the victims who, within five years thereafter, won money judgments against the criminal.[6] Convicted persons, included those who had "voluntarily and intelligently admitted"[7] crimes for which they were not prosecuted.[8]

We contend that all people who abhor violence should favor stripping the criminal of his profits and compensating the hapless victim. To that end we explore the recent California case, we call "Son of Sinatra" to discover a constitutionally pleasing way to accomplish this result. We discuss the constitutional problems that arise when states set out to seize assets of the criminal that have a connection with his storytelling about the crime. Often, and sometimes as discussed here, the attempt fails because of the application of the Free Speech Clause[9] of the constitution as applied to the states by the Fourteenth Amendment.[10] The state of California is one of those jurisdictions that seek to relieve the criminal of his ill-gained profits and to attach the assets of the criminal to compensate the victim. California's Son of Sinatra case commenced in 1963 when Keenan and Amsler, in conspiracy with Irvin, kidnapped Sinatra, Jr., from his Nevada hotel room and drove him to Los Angeles.[11] Sinatra was held until his famous singer father, fondly referred to as Ole blue eyes,

[3] Id. at 108.

[4] Id.

[5] Id.

[6] Id. at 109.

[7] Id.

[8] Id. at 110.

[9] "Congress shall make no law … abridging the freedom of speech, or the press…."

[10] "Nor be deprived of life, liberty, or property without due process of law."

[11] Keenan v. Superior Court (Sinatra, Jr.) 27 Cal. 4th 413, 418 (2002).

paid a considerable ransom.[12] All three conspirators were later apprehended and convicted of felony offenses and incarcerated under California law.[13] To add insult to injury, the kidnapers made media statements after their arrests, now admitted to be false, that Sinatra, Jr. had assisted in his own kidnapping to extort money from his rich and famous father.[14]

This controversy results from a business arrangement by Keenan and his accomplices with a newspaper reporter to interview Keenan about the Sinatra kidnapping.[15] The purpose was to produce a story for sale to the print, broadcast, and film media.[16] Revenues obtained from telling the kidnapping story were to be split among the reporter, the kidnapers, and the publication.[17] Subsequently, an article entitled, "Snatching Sinatra," written by the reporter, Gilstrap, appeared in the January 1990 issue of *New Times Los Angeles* (not the *Los Angeles Times* newspaper).[18]

Thereafter, other magazines reported that Columbia Pictures had bought the motion picture rights to "Snatching Sinatra" for some 1.5 million dollars.[19] Subsequently, in February 1998, Sinatra, Jr., made a demand on Columbia Pictures to withhold from the kidnapers, and from the reporter and *New Times* as the kidnapers' representatives, any monies otherwise due them for the motion picture rights.[20] Columbia Pictures denied the request and refused to withhold the money without a court order.[21]

Having praised such attempts by the states to deny any profits from their crimes to such criminals, we nevertheless are compelled to explore the possible constitutional infirmities of the California equivalent of the New York "Son of Sam Law." The first prong of the California statute imposes an involuntary trust, in favor of injured and uncompensated

---

[12] Id.

[13] Id.

[14] Id.

[15] Id. at 419.

[16] Id.

[17] Id.

[18] Id.

[19] Id.

[20] Id.

[21] Id.

crime victims as "beneficiaries" of a convicted felons "proceeds" from expressive "materials" (books, films, magazine, and newspaper articles, video and sound recordings, radio and television appearances, and live presentations) that "include or are based on the 'story' of a felony for which the felon was convicted, except where the materials mention the felony only in passing as in a footnote or bibliography."[22]

The second prong of the California statute approaches the financial exploitation of crime from an alternative and distinctly different angle. This section involves the theory of involuntary trust and is applied to "profits," received by the felon, or his representative, from the sale or transfer of any "thing" or right, the value of which is "enhanced by the notoriety gained from the commission of a felony for which a convicted felon was convicted."[23] Recently, the statute's involuntary trust provisions were extended to "profiteers of the felony," that is "any persons who derive income by selling memorabilia, property, rights, or things for value enhanced by their felony-notoriety."[24]

The California "Son of Sam" statute raised the primary issue of whether the "Son of Sam Law" facially violates constitutional protections of free speech by appropriating, as compensation for crime victims, all monies due to a convicted felon from expressive materials that might include the story of the crime.[25] In order to decide the question, the California court turned to the controlling US Supreme Court decision in *Simon and Schuster v. Members of NY State Crime Victims Board*.[26] There, the New York statute took, for the benefit of crime victims, all monies due a criminal under contract with respect to a "re-enactment" of the crime, or from the expression of his or her personal thoughts or feelings about the crime in a film, broadcast, print, recording, or live performance format.[27]

The high court determined that the New York law was invalid on its face, reasoning that the statute was a direct regulation of speech based on content and must fall unless it satisfied a strict level of constitutional

[22] Ca. Stats. section 2225 (a)(4),(6),(7),(9), (b),(1).

[23] Section 2225 (a)(10).

[24] Section 2225(a)(3)(B).

[25] Keenan at 415.

[26] 502 U.S. 105 (1991).

[27] Keenan at 417.

scrutiny. The New York law failed the test because, although the state had a compelling interest in compensating crime victims from the fruits of the crime, the statute in question was not narrowly tailored to that purpose.[28] The high court decided that the New York statute was over inclusive because it swept in protected speech. The majority held that two aspects of the New York law regulated speech too broadly for the state's compelling purpose:

1. First, the law applied to expressive works in which one merely admitted crime for which he or she had not been convicted.[29]
2. Second, it confiscated all profits from expressive works in which one made even incidental or tangential mention of his or her past crimes for non-exploited purposes.[30]

The *Sinatra* court likewise reasoned that California's Son of Sam Law imposed a content-based financial penalty on protected speech. And like its New York counter point, fails to satisfy strict scrutiny because it too is over inclusive. The statute contains the fundamental defect identified in *Simon and Schuster*; it reaches beyond a criminal's profits from a crime or its exploitation to reach all income from a criminal's speech or expression on any theme or subject if the story of the crime is included.[31]

Sinatra Jr.'s complaint alleged that under Section 2225 all monies due to the kidnapers, or their representatives, Gilstrap and the *New Times* for preparation for sale of the story of Sinatra, Jr.'s kidnapping, the sale of the rights to the story, or the sale of the materials that included or were based on the story were "proceeds"[32] as defined by 2225(a) (9) and "profits"[33] as defined by the same statute. Thus, they were subject to an involuntary trust in favor of Sinatra, Jr., who was considered a statutory beneficiary.[34]

---

[28] Simon and Schuster at 121–123.

[29] Id. at 121.

[30] Id.

[31] Sinatra at 418.

[32] Id. at 419.

[33] Id.

[34] Id.

The complaint also asked that Columbia Pictures and the *New Times* hold present and future proceeds and profits in trust for Sinatra, Jr.[35]

In *Simon and Schuster*, six justices, in an opinion by Justice O'Connor, noted that a statute is presumptively inconsistent with the First Amendment if it imposes a financial burden on speakers because of the content of their speech.[36] The majority was clearly concerned that the government's ability to impose content-based burdens on speech raises the specter that it may effectively drive protected ideas or viewpoints from the market place.[37] The majority said the First Amendment "presumptively places this sort of discrimination beyond the power of the government."[38]

New York's Son of Sam Law was presumptively an invalid content-based burden on speech because "it singles out income derived from expressive activity for burden the state places on no other income,[39] … it's directed only at works with a specified content,"[40] and "plainly imposes a financial dis-incentive only on speech with a particular content."[41] Next, because the "Son of Sam" statute penalizes speech on the basis of content, the high court concluded that it could survive strict constitutional scrutiny only if, "the state must show that its regulation is necessary to conserve a compelling state interest and is narrowly drawn to achieve that end."[42]

The high court continued by indicating that the state had no compelling interest in shielding readers and victims from negative emotional responses to a criminal's public retelling of his deeds. This is so because

---

[35] Id.

[36] 502 U.S. at 115–116, citing Leathers v. Medlock, 499 U.S. 439, 447 (1991). In *Leathers*, the high court dealt with an Arkansas law that imposed a tax on the cable media that exempted the print media. The court said, "[T]hese cases demonstrate that differential taxation of First Amendment speakers is constitutionally suspect when it threatens to suppress the expression of particular ideas or viewpoints. Absent a compelling justification, the government may not exercise its taxing power to single out the press." 499 U.S. at 447.

[37] Simon and Schuster at 115–116.

[38] Id. at 115–116.

[39] Id. at 116.

[40] Id. at 116.

[41] Id. at 116.

[42] Id. at 118.

the protection of offensive and disagreeable ideas is at the core of the First Amendment.[43] Constitutionally, states do have a compelling interest in "insuring that victims of crime are compensated by those who harm them,"[44] and "preventing wrongdoers from dissipating their assets before the victims can recover."[45] Additionally, the state has a legitimate interest in "insuring that criminals do not profit from their crimes,"[46] and in transferring the fruits of the crime from the criminals to their victims.[47]

New York asserted a compelling interest in preventing criminals from retaining the profits of storytelling about their crimes before their victims were compensated.[48] However, as the high court said, the state did not show why it had a greater interest in compensating crime victims from profits of such storytelling than from reaching the criminal's other assets.[49] "Nor could the state justify … a distinction between his expressive activity and any other activity in connection with its interest in transferring the fruits of crime from the criminals to their victims."[50] The majority reached two conclusions. One, that the state had a compelling interest in compensating victims from fruits of the crime.[51] But alas, little interest in limiting such compensation solely to the proceeds of the wrongdoer's storytelling about the crime.[52]

Second, the high court then determined that the statute was in fact over inclusive. It cited two factors that illustrated the statute's over breath:

1. "The statute applies to works on any subject provided that they express the author's thoughts or recollections about his crime, however, tangentially or incidentally;"[53] and

---

[43] Id. at 118.

[44] Id. at 119.

[45] Id.

[46] Id.

[47] Id. at 119–120.

[48] Id. at 119–120.

[49] Id.

[50] Id. at 119–120.

[51] Id. at 120–121.

[52] Id.

[53] Id. at 121.

2. "The statute's broad definition of person convicted of a crime enables the board to escrow the income of any author who admits in his work to having committed a crime, whether or not the author was actually ever accused or convicted."[54]

To illustrate the over breath of the two provisions, the court discussed several works of literature that would potentially fall within the provisions of the New York law. The court reasoned that had the "Son of Sam" law been in effect at the time and place of publication, it would have escrowed payments for such works as *The Autobiography of Malcolm X*, that describes crimes committed by the civil rights leader before he became a public figure[55]; *Civil Disobedience*, in which Thoreau acknowledges his refusal to pay taxes and talks about his experiences in jail[56]; and *The Confessions of St. Augustine*, where the author writes of his past crimes and corruption of his soul, one crime which involved the taking of pears from a neighboring orchard.[57] The court considered that the prohibited works subject to escrow under the law might include the writings of authors such as Emma Goldman and Martin Luther King, Jr.[58] The list of individuals whose autobiographies would be subject to the statute as written would include Sir Walter Raleigh, who was convicted of treason after a show trial in 1603[59]; Jesse Jackson who was arrested in 1963 for trespass and resisting arrest after attempting to be served at a lunch counter in North Carolina[60]; and Bertrand Russell who was jailed for seven days at the age of 89 for participating in a sit-down protest against nuclear weapons.[61] The majority was clearly troubled by the possibility that the "Son of Sam" law threatens a wide range of protected literature. Some of that threatened literature might not enable a criminal to profit from his crime.[62]

---

[54] Id.

[55] Id.

[56] Id.

[57] Id.

[58] Id.

[59] Id.

[60] Id. at 120.

[61] Id. at 121.

[62] Id. at 121–122.

As the high court majority wrote, New York's Son of Sam law "has singled out speech on a particular subject to bear a financial burden that it places on no other speech and no other income."[63] The state's interest in compensating victims from fruits of crime is a compelling one, but the Son of Sam law is not narrowly tailored to achieve that objective because it places a heavy burden on storytelling that it places on no other speech or income.[64] As a result, the court opined that New York's law was "inconsistent with the First Amendment."[65]

Having steeped itself in the juices of *Simon v. Schuster*, the California Supreme Court then turned to the trying task of determining whether or not the California statutory provisions fit within the proscriptions therein set out. First, the court reasoned that the California statute, like that explored in *Simon and Schuster*, places a direct financial disincentive on speech or expression about a particular subject. The California statute clearly targets and confiscates a convicted felon's proceeds from expressive things like books, films, articles, recordings, broadcast interviews, or performances that include telling the story of the felon's crime.[66] While certain classes of speech like obscenity, fighting words, and some forms of defamation, may be subject to state viewpoint neutral regulation because of their direct and injurious nature, discussions of a crime have never been included in this limited category.[67]

The legislative history of the California statute confirmed that the purpose of the statute was to insure that the "fruits" of the crimes, including proceeds from exploiting the story of those crimes, would be used to compensate crime victims.[68] The legislature declared that, "victims of felonies have a special relationship to proceeds from the sale of stories about those felonies which are written by persons convicted of committing them."[69]

---

[63] Id. at 116.

[64] Id. at 123.

[65] Id. at 123.

[66] Sinatra at 428, citing Chaplinsky v. New Hampshire, 315 U.S. 568, 571–72 (1992) and R.A.V. v. St. Paul, 505 U.S. 377, 382–390 (1992) for the proposition that discussions of crime have never been subject to restrictions on speech like defamation and fighting words.

[67] Id. at 428.

[68] Id. at 429.

[69] Id. citing Cal. Civil Code, section 2224.

Given that the state has a compelling interest in compensating victims, the question that most troubled the majority was whether Section 2225 was properly narrowly tailored to insure that fruits of the crime are used to compensate the victims of crime.[70]

The court was convinced, however, that Section 2225 like the New York law in *Simon and Schuster*, was over inclusive and was invalid under the First Amendment.[71] The California court reasoned that the statute penalized the content of speech to an extent far beyond that necessary to transfer the fruits of crime from criminals to their uncompensated victims.[72] The court said that even if fruits of the crime may include royalties from exploiting the story of one's crimes, the relevant section does not confine itself to such income.[73] Instead, it confiscates *all* (emphasis added) of the convicted felon's proceeds from speech or expression on any theme or subject that includes the story of the felony, except by mere passing mention.[74] By this financial disincentive, the California law discourages the creation and dissemination of a wide range of ideas and expressive works which have little or no relationship to the exploitation by the criminal of his deeds.[75]

Citing *Simon and Schuster*, the California court expressed its concern that this law infringed upon the essential values of the First Amendment. The court said the constitutional problem with the New York law was that in order to serve a relatively narrow interest, compensating crime victims from fruits of the crime, the New York statute targeted, segregated, and confiscated *all* (emphasis added) income from, and thus unduly discouraged, a wide range of expressive works containing protected speech on themes and subjects of legitimate interest to the public.[76] This was so simply because the content of the material included reference to past crimes.[77]

---

[70] Sinatra at 430.

[71] Id. at 431.

[72] Id.

[73] Id.

[74] Id. at 431.

[75] Id. at 432.

[76] Id. at 433.

[77] Id.

The California majority concluded by again complaining that had section 2225 been in effect at the time and place of publication, the statute would have applied to numerous works of the authors, previously discussed,[78] whose discussions of important matters of public interest make substantial, and often vividly descriptive references to prior felonies in which they were involved.[79] The court said that a statute operating in this fashion disturbs and discourages protected speech to a degree substantially beyond that necessary to serve the state's compelling interest in compensating crime victims from fruits of the crime.[80] A convicted felon, for example, might tell stories about his crimes for several constitutionally pleasing reasons other than personal profit. It may very well be of public interest for the criminal to express views on punishment, assaults and batteries in prison, the cause of sex crimes, or an evaluation of the role of lawyers in the criminal justice system. All these approaches may have no causal connection with the exploitation of the crime involved. Accordingly, the court concluded that by precluding these types of storytelling, Section 2225(b) (1) is facially invalid under the First Amendment of the United States Constitution.[81]

Sadly, for public confidence, the court's decision has the potential to give an impression that the criminal may profit from his crimes while the poor victim goes uncompensated for the violence imposed on him. Justice Brown, in an attempt to mute this unappealing idea offered a concurring opinion agreeing with the result in *Sinatra*. But troubled by the very real possibility that the decision would be interpreted by the public as encouraging the idea that violent crime can pay, he wrote separately to express his view that a properly drafted statute can constitutionally separate criminals from their profits.[82] He suggests that profits derived from their crimes can be collected by the state for the benefit of victims while at the same time complying with the requirements of the First Amendment. Justice Brown reasoned that *Simon and Schuster* reflected

[78] *See* Supra footnotes 55–62.

[79] Id.

[80] Id.

[81] Id. at 436.

[82] Id. at 438.

the praiseworthy notion that crime could (1) neither impoverish the victim nor enrich the criminal.[83] He believed that the Supreme Court's opinion clearly recognized the compelling interest in "insuring that victims of crime are compensated by those who harm them."[84] Toward the other end, the high court acknowledged the compelling interest in insuring that criminals do not profit from their crimes. The effect of these two interests is to insure that criminals do not profit from their crimes and that the victims are restored to their status quo.

Justice Brown stressed that the Supreme Court deemed the New York law unconstitutional because it imposed a financial burden on speakers due to the content of their speech.[85] In *Simon and Schuster*, the high court said that "the state has a compelling interest in compensating victims from fruits of the crime, but little if any interest in limiting such compensation to proceeds of the wrongdoer's speech about the crime."[86] Justice Brown points out that the state's compelling interest in compensating victims from the proceeds of crime would be better served by making available to the victim all the criminal's assets, however, and wherever derived.[87]

Justice Brown astutely observes that *Simon and Schuster* does not "stand for the proposition that the government cannot recruit the proceeds of expressive activity relating to a crime. Rather, the government cannot single out those proceeds for special treatment while ignoring other assets."[88] Consequently, when the state goes after all of the criminal's assets, it may thus constitutionally order restriction from all sources including, but not limited to, the defendant's income from storytelling. The law was designed to prevent a criminal from enjoying *any* of his wealth while his victim remains uncompensated.[89]

The reason the New York law was defective was that it did not fully deprive criminals of all their profits, only those that resulted from story-

[83] Id.

[84] Id.

[85] Simon and Schuster at 115–116.

[86] Id. at 120–121.

[87] Sinatra at 440.

[88] Id., citing United States v. Seale, 20 F 3rd 1279, 1285, FN.7. (1994).

[89] Sinatra at 441.

telling. The law's message was not that crime doesn't pay but that *speaking* about it doesn't pay. Deterring transgression is a compelling state interest. Deterring speech is not.

Justice Brown contends that California's limitation on the law's scope solely to storytelling is the fatal flaw of the so-called Son of Sam provision.

The majority in *Simon and Schuster* observed that statutes may be content neutral, and thus avoid strict scrutiny where they are intended to serve purposes unrelated to the content of regulated speech, notwithstanding their incidental effect on speakers or messages.[90] Consequently, contends Justice Brown, a law that neutrally seizes *all* (emphasis added) profits from crime comports with *Simon and Schuster* and thus with the First Amendment.[91]

Consequently, a state may constitutionally seize assets by pursuing its compelling interest of compensating victims, in which case the government may seize assets from any source, including assets that are not fruits of the crime, up to the amount of the victim's damage. Additionally, a state may constitutionally seize assets by pursuing the compelling interest of depriving criminals of assets that are fruits of the crime. There is no reason why a state must select only one compelling interest to pursue. It may pursue all interests separately, seizing all assets up to the amount of damage under the compensation rationale and then all fruits flowing from the crime under the ill-gained profits rationale. Since each phrase would neutrally seize assets in furtherance of a compelling state interest, the law would avoid the constitutional bear traps encountered in *Simon and Schuster* and *Sinatra.*

Finally, we note that several state statutes allow the pursuit of assets wherever located and however obtained.[92] States that adopt Justice Brown's astute idea of allowing the pursuit of all assets will likely avoid the First Amendment trap encountered in *Sinatra.*

---

[90] Id. at 122.

[91] Sinatra at 443.

[92] Me. Rev. Stat. Ann. tit. 14, section 752-E, Wyo. Stat. Ann. section 1-40-302, W.Va. Code, section 14-2B-3.

II. Philosophical Analysis

We now turn to a philosophical discussion of compensating the victims of violence. This section of the chapter will attempt to first articulate and then apply the libertarian theory of political economy[93] to the issues of free speech rights and the status of the criminal vis a vis his victim, and compensation owed by the former to the latter.

Let us first make clear that the libertarian theory of punishment[94] is one of compensation for the victim; that is, the perpetrator is punished

---

[93] See on this the following: Barnett, Randy E., *The Structure of Liberty: Justice and the Rule of Law*, Oxford: Clarendon Press, 1998; Benson, Bruce L., 1989, Enforcement of Private Property Rights in Primitive Societies: Law Without Government," *The Journal of Libertarian Studies*, Vol. IX, No. 1, Winter, pp. 1–26; Block, Walter, *Defending the Undefendable*, New York: Fox and Wilkes, 1985; Block, Walter, "Libertarianism vs. Libertinism," *The Journal of Libertarian Studies: An Interdisciplinary Review*, Vol. 11, No. 1, 1994, pp. 117–128; Cuzán, Alfred G., "Do We Ever Really Get Out of Anarchy?," *Journal of Libertarian Studies*, Vol. 3, No. 2, pp. 151–158 (Summer, 1979); Dauterive, Jerry W., William Barnett and Everett White, "A Taxonomy of Government Intervention," *The Journal of the Southwestern Society of Economists*, 1985; De Jasay, Anthony, *The State*, Oxford: Basil Blackwell, 1985; De Jasay, Anthony, *Against Politics: On Government, Anarchy, and Order*, London, Routledge, 1997; Friedman, David, *The Machinery of Freedom: Guide to a Radical Capitalism*, La Salle, IL: Open Court, 2nd ed., 1989; Hoppe, Hans-Hermann, *A Theory of Socialism and Capitalism: Economics, Politics and Ethics*, Boston: Kluwer, 1989; Hoppe, Hans-Hermann, *The Economics and Ethics of Private Property: Studies in Political Economy and Philosophy*, Boston: Kluwer, 1993; Hummel, Jeffrey Rogers, National Goods Versus Public Goods: Defense, Disarmament, and Free Riders, 4 *Rev. Austrian Econ.* 88 (1990); Kinsella, Stephan, "New Rationalist Directions in Libertarian Rights Theory," 12:2 *Journal of Libertarian Studies* 313–26 (Fall 1996); Kinsella, Stephan, "Legislation and the Discovery of Law in a Free Society," 11 *Journal of Libertarian Studies* 132 (Summer 1995); Kinsella, Stephan, "The Undeniable Morality of Capitalism," 25 *St. Mary's Law Journal* 1419 (1994); Kinsella, Stephan, "Estoppel: A New Justification for Individual Rights," *Reason Papers* No. 17 (Fall 1992), p. 61; Rothbard, Murray N., *For a New Liberty*, Macmillan, New York, 1978; Rothbard, Murray N., *The Ethics of Liberty*, New York: New York University Press, 1998; Rothbard, Murray N., "Society Without a State," J. R. Pennock and J. W. Chapman (eds.), *Anarchism: Nomos XIX*. New York: New York University Press, 1978, pp. 191–207; Skoble, Aeon J. "The Anarchism Controversy," in *Liberty for the 21st Century: Essays in Contemporary Libertarian Thought*, eds. Tibor Machan and Douglas Rasmussen, Lanham MD: Rowman and Littlefield, 1995, pp. 77–96; Sechrest, Larry J., "Rand, Anarchy, and Taxes," *The Journal of Ayn Rand Studies*, Vol. I, No. 1, Fall 1999, pp. 87–105; Stringham, Edward, "Justice Without Government," *Journal of Libertarian Studies*, Vol. 14, No. 1, Winter 1998–1999, pp. 53–77; Tinsley, Patrick, "With Liberty and Justice for All: A Case for Private Police," *Journal of Libertarian Studies*, Vol. 14, No. 1, Winter 1998–1999, pp. 95–100.

[94] Barnett, Randy, "Pursuing Justice in a Free Society Part One: Power vs. Liberty," *Criminal Justice Ethics*, 4: 50–72, 1985; Barnett, Randy, and Hagel, John, eds., *Assessing the Criminal*, Cambridge MA: Ballinger, 1977; Block, Walter, Radical Libertarianism: Punishment Theory for the State, *Festschrift for Antony de Jasay*, forthcoming; Kinsella, Stephan, "A Libertarian Theory of Punishment and Rights," 30 *Loy. L.A. L. Rev.* 607–45 (1997); Kinsella, Stephan, "New Rationalist Directions

by forcing him to compensate the injured party to the extent of the rights violation perpetrated upon him. This is in sharp contrast to the competing models, for example, crime prevention, rehabilitation, and so on. The reason for this is that libertarianism is predicated on an attempt to attain *justice*, not the desiderata of the schools of thought that support these alternatives, such as utilitarianism.

If all we wanted to do was prevent crime, we need not catch, prosecute, and incarcerate the real criminal in any given case. We could, instead, pick a believable candidate for the "role"[95] of offender. As long as we did this surreptitiously enough, arguendo, we could reduce felonies in this entirely unjust manner. We could do so far more efficiently than at present. Under our usual procedures, we must spend significant amounts of time finding and trying the evildoer; under this alternative system, we need only go out on the street and wait until a likely candidate comes along, and then grab him. Alternatively, we could engage in the preventive detention of all high crime cohorts,[96] despite the fact that they had not been found guilty of violating any law. This, too, would "solve" the problem of wrongdoing, but without an iota of justice involved; indeed, under the very opposite of principles.

This will not do, for the libertarian. Here, crime, preeminently, is a disparagement of the particular victims' rights, by a specific perpetrator. It is not an attack upon society as a whole, except insofar as an attack on any one person places another in fear; but, in this particular case, it was only that one person who must be made whole again,[97] not others. And, while it is impossible to place the victim back on the plane of life he was

in Libertarian Rights Theory," 12:2 *Journal of Libertarian Studies* 313–26 (Fall 1996); http://www.mises.org/journals/jls/12_2/12_2_5.pdf; Kinsella, Stephan, "Legislation and the Discovery of Law in a Free Society," 11 *Journal of Libertarian Studies* 132 (Summer 1995); Kinsella, Stephan, "The Undeniable Morality of Capitalism," 25 *St. Mary's Law Journal* 1419 (1994) (review essay of Hans-Hermann Hoppe, *The Economics and Ethics of Private Property* (1993)); Kinsella, Stephan, "Estoppel: A New Justification for Individual Rights," *Reason Papers* No. 17 (Fall 1992), p. 61; Rothbard, Murray N., *For a New Liberty*, Macmillan, New York, 1978; Rothbard, Murray N., *The Ethics of Liberty*, New York: New York University Press, 1998.

[95] For example, a man in his 20s, not a grandmother of 80.

[96] Such as black male teenagers.

[97] Barnett, Randy E., *The Structure of Liberty: Justice and the Rule of Law*, Oxford: Clarendon Press, 1998.

following before the outrage, justice consists of at least attempting to do so as far as possible.

In contrast, the problem with punishment for any purpose other than victim compensation is that while it may indeed visit justice upon the perpetrator, it, does nothing for the victim in this regard. Worse, the latter is called upon to pay for this punishment (e.g., incarceration), as is so often the case in the modern era, then injustice is perpetrated upon the victim twice over. Insult is added to injury as first the victim is forced to do the bidding of the criminal, and then of the state, when he must pay taxes for the care, feeding, upkeep, and yes, punishment of the thug. It cannot be denied, of course, that the criminal richly deserves castigation. This indeed occurs under the principle of compensation to the victim, as it is the criminal himself, not the state, courtesy of money mulcted from taxpayers, who must perform the compensation function under the libertarian legal code.

Criminal rehabilitation is even worse from a perspective that focuses on victim compensation such as libertarianism. At least under punishment theory, the victim is protected from further incursions. This occurs in two senses: once, while the criminal is in jail undergoing his punishment, he is out of circulation at least for the duration, and can count upon no further depredations. Secondly, it is possible he will learn his lesson (if his treatment was severe enough) and that if publicized this will serve as an object lesson for all other would-be malefactors. However, under rehabilitation, if successful, only the general public safety is enhanced; this does nothing for the present victim, surely a miscarriage of justice. And if, more likely, it is unsuccessful, not even that benefit is derived. Moreover, even if the perpetrator is reformed, justice is still not done to him,[98] as he is actually *rewarded* for his misdeeds, by being morally improved. The fact that his incarceration includes color television, recreation rooms, air conditioning, wholesome food, and so on only constitutes an additional moral outrage.[99] If rehabilitation occurs as a

---

[98] Kinsella, Stephan, "Estoppel: A New Justification for Individual Rights," *Reason Papers* No. 17 (Fall 1992), p. 61; Kinsella, Stephan, "Punishment and Proportionality: The Estoppel Approach," 12:1 *Journal of Libertarian Studies* 51 (Spring 1996).

[99] One reason that rehabilitation does not work too well under modern institutions is that financial reward is not predicated upon a reduced recidivism rate. That is, those prisons that do a good job

result, or alongside, of restitution, well and good, but this cannot be the be-all and end-all of punishment.

According to libertarianism, man is a self-owner. There are no "human rights" as such, over and above the fact that an individual's most important and primary property rights consists of his ownership over his own person. To interfere with that right is to engage in an illicit taking, for example, to participate in a theft. So in effect, murder is the theft of a life, kidnapping is the (temporary) theft of a man's body, slavery is the permanent theft of the human person, rape is the theft of sexual services of a woman, and assault and battery is akin to the theft of bodily integrity.

Why put things in such an artificial, unaccustomed, and metaphorical manner? Why not adopt the more typical and usual language that drives a wedge between theft of a good (e.g., a car, a television set) and trespass upon or invasion of another person's body? The main reason for doing so is to facilitate communication regarding the libertarian theory of punishment. It is preeminently a compensation theory, and this process instinctively makes more sense to most people for inanimate objects than for violations of "human rights."

For example, while compensation for the theft of a car might be easily comprehended, matters are far less clear in this regard concerning murder, rape, and so on. Let us then establish clearly how libertarian compensation theory might work as far as inanimate matters are concerned, as a launching pad for later dealing with violation of animate human beings.

The formula for assessing proper compensation is "two teeth for a tooth,"[100] plus expenses of capturing the criminal, plus a risk or fright assessment. Why is it precisely "two teeth for a tooth," rather than 1.9 or

in this regard are not automatically rewarded with extra profits, nor are those that fail penalized monetarily. Compare this with virtually every other good or service in the economy: plumbing, peanut butter, parsley, pizza. The reason there are no problems with regard to these items is that entrepreneurs who succeed in providing us with a high quality level of these products at low cost, and thus satisfy the profit and loss test, are duly rewarded. Those who do not suffer automatic losses, and, if they do not mend the error of their ways, bankruptcy. It is due to this automatic feedback mechanism that satisfactory results emanate. But no such process is operational in the prison "industry." Inmates are given parole when presumably "rehabilitated," and if they commit other crimes, those responsible for unleashing these monsters on an unsuspecting public pay no price for their errors.

[100] Rothbard, Murray N., *The Ethics of Liberty*, New York: New York University Press, 1998, p. 94, ft. 6.

2.1 "teeth?" Simple. Consider the car theft. When the robber is apprehended, the first thing that must be done, in justice, is to remove the automobile from his ill-gotten horde of gains. That is the first "tooth." Secondly, what the carjacker did to the owner of the vehicle must in turn be done to him. Simple justice requires no less. Since he transferred ownership of an automobile from the proper owner of it to himself, precisely, this, then, must be done to *him*. For example, the car thief must be forced to disgorge a vehicle of similar value (or some other equivalent consideration) to the victim. That is the second "tooth." Thus, so far, we have arrived at exactly 2.0 "teeth," no more, no less.

But there is more to be done, far more. First of all, there were the costs imposed by the criminal on honest men, of searching for and capturing him. These expenditures, too, must be defrayed, and paid by the villain.[101] It is only if he has an instant attack of remorse, and immediately

[101] These costs would be paid by the perpetrator not to the victim, but rather to the forces of law and order which would be private in a fully libertarian society. See on this Anderson, Terry and Hill, P.J., "An American Experiment in Anarcho-Capitalism: the *not* so Wild, Wild West," *Journal of Libertarian Studies* Vol. 3, No. 1, 1979, pp. 9–29; Benson, Bruce L., 1989, Enforcement of Private Property Rights in Primitive Societies: Law Without Government," *The Journal of Libertarian Studies*, Vol. IX, No. 1, Winter, pp. 1–26; Benson, Bruce L., "The Spontaneous Evolution of Commercial Law," *Southern Economic Journal*, 55: 644–661, 1989; Benson, Bruce L., *The Enterprise of Law: Justice Without the State*, San Francisco: Pacific Research Institute for Public Policy, 1990; Benson, Bruce L., "The Impetus for Recognizing Private Property and Adopting Ethical Behavior in a Market Economy: Natural Law, Government Law, or Evolving Self-Interest," 6 Rev. Austrian Econ. 43 (1993); Benson, Bruce, *To Serve and Protect*, New York: New York University Press, 1998; Bernstein, Lisa, "Opting out of the Legal System: Extralegal Contractual Relationships in the Diamond Industry," *Journal of Legal Studies*, Vol. 21, 1992; Friedman, David, *The Machinery of Freedom: Guide to a Radical Capitalism*, La Salle, IL: Open Court, 2nd ed., 1989; Hadfield, Gillian K., "Privatizing Commercial Law," *Regulation*, Vol. 24, No. 1, Spring 2001, pp. 40–45; Hoppe, Hans-Hermann, *The Economics and Ethics of Private Property: Studies in Political Economy and Philosophy*, Boston: Kluwer, 1993; Hoppe, Hans-Hermann, "The Private Production of Defense," *Journal of Libertarian Studies*, Vol. 14, No. 1, Winter 1998–1999, pp. 27–52; Hummel, Jeffrey Rogers, National Goods Versus Public Goods: Defense, Disarmament, and Free Riders, 4 *Rev. Austrian Econ.* 88 (1990); Kinsella, Stephan, "Legislation and the Discovery of Law in a Free Society," 11 *Journal of Libertarian Studies* 132 (Summer 1995); Macey, Jonathan and Maureen O'Hara, "Regulating Exchanges and Alternative Trading Systems: A Law and Economics Perspective," *Journal of Legal Studies*, Vol. 18, 1999; Milgrom, Paul, Douglass North and Barry Weingast, "The Role of Institutions in the Revival of Trade: The Medieval Law Merchant, Private Judges and the Champagne Fairs," *Economics and Politics*, Vol. 2, 1990; Morriss, Andrew P., "Miners, Vigilantes and Cattlemen: Overcoming Free Rider Problems in the Private Provision of Law," *Land and Water Law Review*, Vol. XXXIII, No, 2, 1998, pp. 581–696; Rothbard, Murray N., *For a New Liberty*, Macmillan, New York, 1978; Rothbard, Murray N., *The Ethics of Liberty*, Humanities Press, Atlantic Highlands, N.J., 1982; Rothbard, Murray N., "Society Without a

turns himself and the stolen automobile in to the police that the fiend would undertake no obligation at all on this score.

Secondly, and perhaps more controversially, when the carjacker engaged in his evil deed, the motorist had no idea of what would happen to him. Likely, he feared for his very life. To allow such a malefactor to escape with merely the return of the stolen goods to the rightful owner, and by paying over a car or something else of similar value of his own, and compensating the police forces for their manpower and other costs, would be a travesty of justice. It would only *begin* to pay the compensatory debt he owes. No. The car stealer and possible kidnapper and/or murderer, must be placed in fear of his *own* life, precisely what he imposed on his victim. How can the criminal learn what it is like to have his life threatened? The only possible just solution to this imbalance is to make the criminal occupy as similar a position as possible. One way this could be attained is to force him to play a game of Russian roulette, where the proportion between the number of bullets and empty chambers would be commensurate with the severity of the threat imposed upon the victim.

Suppose, then, that the car was stolen from the owners' garage while they were out of town on vacation. When they returned, their only fear was that the criminal, having once gotten away with his foul deed, would return again to brutalize them again. Conceivably, under these circumstances, they might wish to move out of town, leaving no forwarding address, losing their jobs and friends, in an effort to put as much distance, emotional, physical, and geographical, between them and a repeat of this unsavory event. Then, with this only "slight" scaring, the fright penalty imposed might be one of pulling the trigger on a gun with 100 chambers, and only two or three of them loaded with a bullet. An intermediate scenario might be one where an armed thief stole the automobile from the street in front of the house, or, worse, from a locked garage, while the family was at home, but not involved directly. This might call for, respec-

State." J. R. Pennock and J. W. Chapman (eds.), *Anarchism: Nomos XIX*. New York: New York University Press, 1978, pp. 191–207; Stringham, Edward, "Justice Without Government," *Journal of Libertarian Studies*, Vol. 14, No. 1, Winter 1998–1999, pp. 53–77; Tinsley, Patrick, "With Liberty and Justice for All: A Case for Private Police," *Journal of Libertarian Studies*, Vol. 14, No. 1, Winter 1998–1999, pp. 95–100; Tannehill, Morris and Linda, *The Market for Liberty*, New York: Laissez Faire Books, 1984; Woolridge, William C., *Uncle Sam the Monopoly Man*, New Rochelle, N.Y.: Arlington House, 1970.

tively, 5 and 10 loaded chambers out of 100. And what of the case where the car door was forcibly opened while the motorist was behind the wheel, a gun was stuck in his face, he was thrust, bodily, out of his car and onto the street, in a dangerous neighborhood? An argument could be made for as many as half the chambers filled with bullets. The point is there is a continuum. The more heavily armed and thus threatening the mugger, the more frightening the situation (victim present, molested), the higher the proportion of bullets in the chambers of the Russian roulette gun there would be.

Where does the compensation come in? This must be answered, since the treatment outlined above sounds more like direct punishment than compensation. The compensation enters the picture when we reflect upon the option that that victim has the opportunity to let the criminal off the hook if he pays him off to do so. Suppose there is a *very* wealthy car thief, Bill Gates himself. He commits criminal acts, and then *laughs* at the libertarian comeuppance, given that it is limited to two teeth plus expenses. But when the fright consideration is brought to bear, he might be willing to give up virtually his entire fortune not to be forced to play Russian roulette, even with a relatively low proportion of bullets to chambers.

This one proviso alone, completely apart from any other consideration, ought to put paid to the notion that a strictly compensatory model, along libertarian lines as sketched out above, would not *also* contain provision for crime reduction, the presumed goal of the utilitarian. If the prospect of even a small probability that the death penalty[102] might be imposed for even relatively minor crimes does not put a severe dent in criminal behavior, then nothing will.[103]

We have now established at least an outline of libertarian punishment theory. Let us now use it to address the issue analyzed in the first section of this chapter: to wit, the propriety of allowing "Son of Sam" and others

---

[102] For an analysis of the retardant effects of the death penalty on crime, see Ehrlich, Isaac, The Deterrent Effect of Criminal Law Enforcement *Journal of Legal Studies*, Vol. L (2), June 1972, pp. 259–276; Ehrlich, Isaac, Participation in Illegitimate Activities – A Theoretical and Empirical Investigation, *Journal of Political Economy*, Vol. 81 (3), May/June 1973, pp. 521–565.

[103] The death penalty, of course, would have limited deterrent effect on those willing to commit suicide in the course of their murderous activities.

of that ilk to benefit from the sale of their life stories to the press. In order to do this, we must first apply libertarian punishment theory to their specific crimes, for example, murder. How would libertarianism address this issue? True to the insight that we must extrapolate from crimes against property to crimes against persons (since the former is typically more straightforward than the latter), we proceed in this vein.

What, then, is the murderer doing when he kills his victim, if we are to characterize this crime against the person in the same manner as violence against property? Simple. He is stealing a life. But we have already established the model for dealing with theft: two teeth for a tooth, plus expenses, plus a fright penalty. All we need do, now, is apply that insight to the present context.

We are immediately faced with a difficulty when we try to effectuate the first "tooth" in this process. Unfortunately, present medical technology does not allow for the transfer of a life out of the body of the live murderer and into that of the dead victim. We can of course execute the live murderer, but at our present levels of ability, we are not at all able to transfer his life into the victim's dead body. Relieving A, the murderer, of his (now) improperly kept-to-himself life may indeed punish him, but will do little good for B, the victim, in terms of compensation. Thus, we are in a position to impose punishment on A, but not grant compensation to B, our goal.

Fortunately, we have a "weapon" at our disposal: our imaginations. Use of concocted scenarios[104] may shed light on the justice of the matter, even if technology is not now, and may never be, at the level of accomplishment necessary to effectuate this solution. Imagine, then, that we do indeed *have* a machine which is able not only to relieve A of his illicitly cleaved to life, but *also* to transfer this life out of A and into B. This latter person, it will be appreciated, is the only one in this little scenario *deserving* of this life, in that this is the first part ("tooth") of a just compensator remedy for the crime of murder.

[104] The late Robert Nozick is the past master of utilizing imaginary machines, and scenarios, in an attempt to shed light on what would otherwise be intractable philosophical challenges. See on this, Nozick, Robert. 1974. *Anarchy, State, and Utopia*. New York: Basic Books.

Consider the diagram below. At the first level, we have a live murderer (IA—happy face) and a dead victim (IB—sad face). We flick a switch, and viola! emerges from our machine a live ("re-enlifed") victim (IIB—happy face) and a dead murderer (IIA—sad face). Is there anyone so rash, even a staunch opponent of capital punishment, who would oppose the forcing of A into the machine, the pulling of the switch, and the resultant state of affairs?[105] Presumably, the only basis upon which to deny this would be an opposition to justice, or, a hatred so severe of imaginary constructions that a person so minded would be willing to defend a very unjust state of affairs. For, surely, the ideal punishment for murderer is (at least) to force him to give back to his victim the life he stole from him.

Unfortunately, the second tooth of our process would be difficult to implement, given that A has but one life, not to "give to his country," but, more pertinently, to offer to his *victim*. If, however, people were like the proverbial cat, and had "nine lives," then this tooth, too, could apply. The murderer would immediately give up a second life as the "second tooth." He might well also forfeit a third life (to say nothing of the monetary expenses necessary to compensate his capturers), assuming that the fright portion of the penalty works out in such a manner.

Having taken this science fictionist trip, let us now return to reality, even though it is a dimension with less justice in it, due to the absence of this wonderful life transfer machine. Without it, but thanks to our imagination of it, we can now see our way more clearly toward a just solution of what to do with the murderer, and his "right" to sell his story to the press. His right to his very life is forfeit. That much is clear, thanks to the machine. But if this life cannot be transferred to the dead victim, can it be transferred at all? Yes, indeed, it can. It can be transmitted not to the victim himself, of course, but rather to his heir. A murders B. A's very life now belongs to C, the heir of B. C can do with A's life *whatever* he wishes. If he desires to do so, he may have B executed [106] privately. He may do so

[105] We assume, arguendo, that we know for sure that A did indeed murder B. Or, if not, then that the person responsible for pulling the switch, guilty of the miscarriage of justice implicit in taking the life of an innocent man, A, by forcing him to undergo the rigors of this machine, will, in turn, be placed in this very contraption and thereby forced to give his own life back to A.

[106] C may not torture A to death, or even torture him at all, unless A was guilty of doing that to B. This is because such acts are different than murder, and do not constitute a valid "tooth."

publicly, in a large theater, and charge ticket prices for admission. Or, C may *enslave* A, and force him to do his bidding for the rest of his life. Yet another option is for C to sell A's body parts to those in need of transplants, to help compensate for the loss of B's life.[107]

We have established that A's life is forfeit. He owes it to *someone*. Unfortunately, due to a lack of advanced medical technology,[108] he cannot give it to B, the man he murdered. But B left heirs, C, to whom go all his worldly possessions. But *one* of B's possessions, in justice, is A's life. Therefore, that life of A's now properly belongs to C.

We may now more directly approach the problem of murderers selling their life stories with which we are faced. Suppose, then, that there are journalists interested in telling the story of A (and his "interaction" with

[107] For an analysis of markets in used body parts, see Barnett, Andy H., Frank Adams and David L. Kaserman, "Markets for Organs: The Question of Supply," *Contemporary Economic Policy*, forthcoming; Barnett, Andy H., Roger Blair and David L. Kaserman, "The Economics and Ethics of a Market for Organs," *Society*, September/October, 1996, pp. 8–17; Barnett, Andy H., T. Randolph Beard and David L. Kaserman, "Scope, Learning, and Cross-Subsidy: Organ Transplants in a Multi-Division Hospital – An Extension," *Southern Economic Journal*, January 1996, pp. 760–67; Barnett, Andy H., David L. Kaserman, "The 'Rush to Transplant' and Organ Shortages," *Economic Inquiry*, July 1995, pp. 506–515; reprinted in Price Theory and its Applications, edited by F.M. Scherer and Bernard Saffran, Edward Elgar Publishing, 1999; Barnett, Andy H., T. Randolph Beard and David Kaserman, "The Medical Community's Opposition to Organ Markets: Ethics or Economics," *The Review of Industrial Organization*, December 1993, pp. 669–678; Barnett, Andy H., T. Randolph Beard and David Kaserman, "Inefficient Pricing Can Kill: The Case of Regulation in the Dialysis Industry," *Southern Economic Journal*, October 1993, pp. 393–404. Reprinted in Foundations of Industrial Organization, edited by Robert Ekelund, Edward Elgar Publishing, 1998; Barnett, Andy H., David Kaserman, "The Shortage of Organs for Transplantation: Exploring the Alternatives," *Issues in Law & Medicine*, Fall 1993, pp. 117–137; Barnett, Andy H., David Kaserman and Roger Blair, "Improving Organ Donation: Compensation versus Markets," *Inquiry*, Fall 1992, pp. 372–378; Barnett, Andy H., David Kaserman, "An Economic Analysis of Transplant Organs: A Comment and Extension," *Atlantic Economic Journal*, June 1991, pp. 57–63; Barnett, William II, Michael Saliba and Deborah Walker, "A Free Market in Kidneys: Efficient and Equitable," *The Independent Review: A Journal of Political Economy*, Volume V, Number 3, Winter 2001, pp. 373–385; Barnett, William, The Market for Used Human Body Parts, The Free Market, Vol. 6, No. 2, 1988; Block, Walter, Roy Whitehead, Clint Johnson, Mana Davidson, Alan White and Stacy Chandler, "Human Organ Transplantation: Economic and Legal Issues," *Quinnipiac College School of Law Health Journal*, Vol. 3, 1999–2000, pp. 87–110; Block, Walter, "The Case for a Free Market in Body Parts," *Essays in the Economics of Liberty: The Free Market Reader*, Llewellyn Rockwell, ed., California: The Ludwig von Mises Institute, 1988, pp. 266–272; Clay, Megan and Walter Block. 2002. "A Free Market for Human Organs," *The Journal of Social, Political and Economic Studies*, Vol. 27, No. 2, Summer, pp. 227–236.

[108] If the government would stop wasting so much of our valuable resources, we might well be on our way to solving this medical problem, instead of only being able to contemplate it as a matter of science fiction.

B) and are willing to offer A $1 million for this privilege. What should ensue in the just society? Should A be allowed to enter into such a contract? There is no question of A making this decision on his own, let alone keeping *any*, and certainly not *all* of this money for himself. No, indeed, no. Remember, A is now C's slave.[109] It is thus up to C, not A, whether or not A will give the interview to the journalist. If A sees any financial reward from his cooperation with the writer, it will stem from C's generosity, not A's rights, for A has none, not even the right not to be killed that all other people possess; remember, A's life is forfeit and actually and properly owned *not* by himself, but by C.

Suppose A refuses to do the interview against the wishes of C. That is, C wants A to tell his story to the journalist, but A is unwilling. There is a simple remedy open to C in such a situation: he can threaten to (legally) kill A unless A complies with C's wishes on the matter. Do not forget: thanks to the life transfer machine example, A's life no longer properly belongs to him, A. Instead, it now belongs to C. Thus C, not A, must make the decision as to whether or not the interview between A and the writer occurs, and who is to receive the monetary proceeds offered by the latter for the story.

Now, consider a lesser crime: car theft. A steals B's car, but does not have the wherewithal to pay him, B, back one car let alone two.[110] A, then, is resting "comfortably" in a jail which is very different from the ones now in operation. It is dedicated to forcing A to work at hard labor (e.g., a chain gang) in order to pay B what he owes him. There will be no air conditioning, no game rooms, no television; there will be nutritious but poorly tasting fodder as food. There will be hard labor for, say, 16 hours per day, six and a half days per week. A, in other words, is undergoing something very much akin to slavery, only on a temporary basis, until he pays off his entire debt to B.

[109] A is a justified slave in that this is part and parcel of his proper compensation—punishment to C, for a capital crime against B. This is in sharp contrast to the slavery which occurred in the United States, where *innocent* people, not murderers, were seized and enslaved against their will.

[110] We assume no costs of capture, and that the trial by Russian roulette concluded without loss of A's life. We also abstract from the possibility of B allowing A to skip this game, in return for even greater compensation owed to B.

Along comes our proverbial journalist into this idyllic scene, who wants to do a story on A, again for $1 million. How does the libertarian punishment—compensation theory—apply here? In this case, B may again force A to tell his story, whether he agrees to do so or not, on the ground that B is owed, say, $200,000, and this debt must be paid off as quickly as possible.[111] And, of course, the *first* $200,000 of this $1 million goes to B. It is only after he has fully paid off his debt to B, and is once again a free man, that A may make such decisions for himself, and keep money paid him over and above what he owes.

Consider an objection to our thesis: but this Draconian punishment proposal violates the free speech rights of A to tell his story to the press. The reply is that *only* free men can have free speech rights. Free speech is something that is (properly) denied to those who are (legitimate) slaves. There simply are no free speech rights on or with other people's property. Suppose D comes to E's house, at three in the morning when the latter is trying to sleep, and proceeds to read in a very loud voice the Declaration of Independence. E objects, and orders D to leave the premises. D refuses, on the ground that his free speech rights are being abridged by E. This is a ludicrous "debate." As anyone can see, free speech rights protect people against incursions of the exercise of free speech on their *own* property, not on the property of others. But not only *on* their own property, also *with* their own property. But the prisoner, in the libertarian model, is not properly a self-owner. He can either be enslaved permanently (for a capital crime) or temporarily (until he pays off his debt). But in *neither* case does the issue of his free speech rights even arise. This is because, as long as he is a prisoner, he is owned by *others* and it is they and they alone who control his free speech rights.

In conclusion, the issue of convicts speaking freely and pocketing money for doing so does not even arise. As non-self-owners, they are prohibited from engaging in any such activity. The *real* issue is whether or not they may be *forced* to speak against their will by their masters, and it is our conclusion that they may.

---

[111] Hence, the 16-hour a day, six and a half day week, with cheap food, clothes, and so on.

I. A = alive murderer B = dead
victim

------------------------ ------------------
--
! . . ! ! . .
!
! . ! ! .
!
! \..../ ! ! ......
!
! ! ! / \
!
!----------------------! !-----------------
-!

II. A = dead murderer B = alive
victim

------------------------- -----------------
--
! ! !
!
! . . ! ! . . !
! . ! ! .
!
! ! ! \....../ ! ! ......
! ! !
! / \ ! !
!
!------------------------! ! ----------------!

☺☺ ☹☹

15

Resolving the Abortion Controversy

I. Background

In this article, we advocate a liberty and private property rights approach to the issue of abortion. While some contend that the famous cases of *Roe v. Wade*[1] and *Planned Parenthood v. Casey*[2] settles for evermore the question of whether a woman had a legal right to an abortion, a great deal of controversy still lingers. This is so because abortion has become all too

Block wishes to thank David Kennedy, Anthony Sullivan, and the Trustees of the Earhart Foundation for the financial support necessary to write this article. The opinions expressed herein, of course, reflect the thinking of the authors alone.
This article is dedicated to the anti-abortionists most akin to the abolitionists in the early part of the nineteenth century who not only wrote and spoke out against slavery, but actually did something to stop it: namely, those who physically interfered with abortion clinics and with abortionists. But, as will be explained below, this applies only to those who help stop abortions when eviction is an option.
The authors of the present article wish to congratulate the editors of the *Appalachian Journal of Law* for their courage in publishing it. This article was accepted for publication previously by both the *Thomas M. Cooley Law Review* and the *Manitoba Law Journal*; in each case, the editors reneged and refused publication despite their initial acceptance. We now, also, thank Palgrave Macmillan for allowing us to include this chapter in the present book.

[1] 410 U.S. 113 (1973).

[2] 505 U.S. 833 (1992).

W. E. Block, R. Whitehead, *Philosophy of Law*, Palgrave Studies in Classical Liberalism,
https://doi.org/10.1007/978-3-030-28360-5_15

commonplace. About 35% of all American women will obtain an abortion during their childbearing years.[3] This easy availability fuels the ire of and represents the equivalent of a holocaust to anti-abortion advocates.[4] Some believe that 39 million lives have been snuffed out by abortion since *Roe* was decided.[5] President George W. Bush is critical of the easy availability of abortions.[6] Critics claim his administration is engaged in a war against women's reproductive rights by appointing anti-abortion advocates to the federal standing advisory committee of the FDA on reproductive health and trying to establish a link between breast cancer and abortion.[7] Many believe that the current Republican majorities, as slim as they are in the House and Senate, will lead to a push for the abolition of a woman's right to an abortion.

Some members of the Senate have made it clear that they intend to do what they can to overcome the holding of *Roe v. Wade*.[8] Anti-abortion activists believe that there are two key steps that must be achieved in order to overturn *Roe v. Wade*.[9] First, they must establish by law, government policy, and most important, in the minds of voters, that a fetus[10] is a human being.[11] If a fetus is human,[12] it warrants the equal protection of

---

[3] *See generally*, Roger Simon, *The Argument that Never Ends, U.S. News*, www.usnews.com/usnews/issue/030120/usnews/20roe.htm (Jan. 20, 2003).

[4] Id.

[5] Id.

[6] *See* id., where White House Chief of Staff Andrew Card is quoted as saying that ending abortion is "a high moral priority" for the president.

[7] Caryl Rivers & Rosalind C. Barnett, *The War Against Reproductive Rights*, Boston Globe A15, (Mar. 1, 2003).

[8] *See generally* Jim VandeHei, *GOP Looks To Move Its Social Agenda*, Wash. Post A1 (Nov. 25, 2002).

[9] Id.

[10] The question of whether the mother is carrying a fetus or an unborn child is an emotionally charged one in the abortion debate. Witness the uproar that followed when the *Boston Globe* described an unborn child killed in the mother's womb by a stray gunshot as a fetus. Several readers were "horrified" by the *Globe*'s alleged insensitivity for the life of what they regarded as a living baby. They thought the *Globe* was taking sides in the abortion debate. The paper's concern about the outburst of criticism required a response by its ombudsman. The paper's editors decided in the future to use terms "like the child the woman was bearing," rather than fetus. *See* Christine Chinlund, *Fetus or Baby*, Boston Globe A13 (Feb. 17, 2003).

[11] Supra footnote 4. *See also*, Meghan Cox Gurdon, *Mother of All Rights*, Wall St. J., Jan. 21, 2003, where the author writes, "Abortion doctors dispatch unwanted 'fetuses,' but at crowded fertility clinics those same organized clusters of cells are referred to as 'babies.' Well, which is it?"

[12] In Mississippi, "it" is a person. The Mississippi Supreme Court recently decided that a non-viable fetus was a person for the purposes of the state's wrongful death statute. *See Federal Credit Union v.*

the law afforded to the mother. Secondly, anti-abortion activists seek to get more conservative judges appointed.[13] On the other hand, those opposed to whittling away the so-called privacy right to abortion announced in *Roe v. Wade*, desperately seek to thwart the confirmation of conservative judges. Witness the brutal and unprecedented filibuster of an appeals court judge in the case of Miguel Estrada.

II. The Guiding Cases

Before turning to our discussion of the liberty and property interest involved in the abortion question, we commence with a discussion of the guiding cases of *Roe v. Wade*[14] and *Planned Parenthood v. Casey*.[15] Roe was a pregnant single woman who brought an action challenging the Texas criminal abortion laws that prevented procuring or attempting an abortion except on medical advice for the purpose of saving the mother's life.[16] The only exception to the Texas criminal proscription was the purpose of saving the life of the mother.[17] Roe claimed she was entitled to terminate her pregnancy by an abortion performed by a competent physician under safe medical conditions.[18] She could not obtain an abortion in Texas because her life was not threatened by the pregnancy.[19] This plaintiff alleged she could not afford to travel to a jurisdiction where abortions were legal.[20] She said that the Texas statutes infringed upon her right of personnel privacy under the First, Fourth, Fifth, Ninth, and Fourteenth Amendments of the Constitution.[21] In effect, she claimed that the Texas statute infringed the right of a pregnant woman to termi-

Tucker, 853 So.2d 104 (Miss. 2003).

[13] Supra footnote 4.

[14] *Roe*, 410 U.S. 113.

[15] *Planned Parenthood*, 505 U.S. 833.

[16] *Roe*, 410 U.S. at 120.

[17] Id. at 118.

[18] Id. at 120.

[19] Id.

[20] Id.

[21] Id.

nate her pregnancy.[22] This right is discovered, according to Roe, in the personal liberty rights found in the Fourteenth Amendment's Due Process Clause and/or in the personal, marital, familial, and sexual privacy protected by the Bill of Rights.[23]

Speaking for the majority, Justice Blackman indicated that there are three "recognized" important life and health risks associated with abortion.[24] They are: "a. the skill of the physician, b. the environment in which the abortion is performed, and above all c. [t]he duration of pregnancy, as determined by uterine size and confirmed by menstrual history."[25]

Given the foregoing, the Court decided that the state has at least three legitimate interests in regulating abortion. One is to see that the abortion is performed under conditions that insure safety for the patient.[26] This interest includes the physician and his staff, facilities used, and the availability of adequate care for any complication or emergency that might arise either during or after the procedure.[27] Justice Blackman pointed out that this interest is justified by the high mortality rate at nonregulated "abortion mills."[28] As a consequence, the government has an interest in protecting the health of the mother.

Finally, the state has an interest, or even a duty, to protect prenatal life.[29] Justice Blackman indicated that some wish that this interest commenced at conception.[30] If life begins at conception, obviously, the only legitimate justification for abortion would be to protect the life of the

---

[22] Id. at 129.

[23] Id. *See generally*, *Griswold v. Connecticut*, 381 U.S. 479, 481–486, where the Court decides that the Connecticut statute forbidding the use of contraceptives violates the right of marital privacy which is within the penumbra of specific guarantees of marital rights. The Court concludes that the idea of allowing the police to search the marital bedroom for evidence of the use of contraceptives is repulsive to the privacy that protects the marriage relationship. Id. at 486.

[24] Id. at 145.

[25] Id. (internal quotation marks excluded).

[26] Id. at 150.

[27] Id.

[28] Id.

[29] Id.

[30] Id.

mother.[31] But the Court did not adopt that approach. The majority decided that they could give recognition to a less rigid rule to determine when a potential life is involved.[32]

The Court said that while the Constitution does not mention any specific right to privacy, it has long recognized a right of personal privacy and that there is some guarantee of zones of privacy under the Constitution.[33] In any event, the right of privacy, wherever found, includes a woman's decision on whether or not to have an abortion.[34] All sorts of detrimental results might naturally flow from the state denying a woman's right to an abortion. Among them are psychological harm, lack of childcare, the trauma of the unwanted child, the stigma of being an unwed mother, the mental and physical health of the mother, the resources of the mother, and the mother's ability to care for the child.[35]

Roe argued that a reasonable consideration of these factors made the woman's right to an abortion absolute.[36] In other words, she could terminate her pregnancy at any time for whatever reason she chose. The Court disagreed.[37]

The Court held that at some point in the pregnancy, the state's interest in safeguarding health, maintaining medical standards, and protecting the life of the fetus, become compelling enough to sustain legitimate regulation of the factors that govern the abortion decision.[38] As a consequence, the mother's privacy interests are not absolute.

The Court continued, "We, therefore, conclude that the right of personal privacy includes the abortion decision, but that this right is not unqualified and must be considered against important state interests in regulation."[39] The majority believed that at some point, the government's

---

[31] Id. (otherwise, abortion would clearly be murder.)

[32] Id. at 150–152.

[33] Id. *See Griswold v. Connecticut*, 381 U.S. 479, (1965) (holding that a privacy right to use contraceptives fit within the penumbra of rights found in the Bill of Rights).

[34] *Roe*, 410 U.S. at 153.

[35] Id.

[36] Id.

[37] Id.

[38] Id. at 154.

[39] Id.

interest in protection of health, medical standards, and prenatal life, became compelling enough to justify regulations that limited the woman's right to an abortion.[40] It is long established that when fundamental rights are involved that any regulations impacting those rights are only justified when there is a compelling state interest.[41] But the government has a compelling interest in protecting health and prenatal life that justifies regulation, according to this finding.[42]

The Court next took up the question of whether or not a fetus is a "person" within the meaning of the Fourteenth Amendment of the Constitution.[43] This is a critical issue because if a fetus[44] is a person from the moment of conception,[45] then a right-to-life would be guaranteed by the Fourteenth Amendment.[46] Sadly, for judges, there is little authority in the Constitution for deciding on a definition of a "person."[47] In almost all instances, this word is used in the post-natal sense.[48] As a consequence, the Court was convinced that the word "person" does not refer to the

[40] Id. at 155.

[41] Id. (citing *Kramer v. Union Free Sch. Dist.*, 395 U.S. 621, 627 (1969)).

[42] Id. at 156.

[43] Id. at 157.

[44] Recently, the Michigan Court of Appeals took up the question of whether an expectant mother who stabbed to death her boyfriend could use a "defense of others defense" because she feared for her fetus. The fetus was in its sixteenth or seventeenth week and would not be considered viable under *Roe v. Wade*. One of the issues was whether an unborn child was a person entitled to the defense. The trial court ruled that there had to be a "living human being independent of the mother." The Michigan Court of Appeals decided that the defense could be used because the state's public policy was to protect a fetus from an intentional act. They found the basis for the public policy in the Michigan's Fetal Protection Act. *See People of the State of Michigan v. Kurr*, 253 Mich. App. 317 (Mich. App. 2002), appeal denied, 467 Mich. 943 (2003).

[45] One commentator sums up the question in stark terms. "If the fetus isn't human, then getting an abortion is no different than getting a tattoo or a nose job. It's a victimless procedure that is nobody's business and should be legal. If a fetus is human, then the logical conclusion is inescapable: abortion by definition is homicide and should be illegal except when, to save her own life, the mother aborts in self-defense." *See* Norah Vincent, *Wrong Focus on Abortion Issue*, Los Angeles Times (Jan. 9, 2002). (available at www.latimes.com/news/opinion/la-oe-vincent9jan09).

[46] *Roe* at 156–157. *See* Supra footnote 4, where the Simon article points out that to some in our society abortion represents an American holocaust resulting in the "mass murder of the unborn that has claimed more than 39 million lives since the Supreme Court made abortion legal on Jan. 22, 1973."

[47] Id. at 157.

[48] Id.

unborn.[49] That said, the Court's conclusion that a fetus is not a person does not foreclose the state's interest in regulating abortion. Why? Because at some point in the life cycle, the fetus surely becomes a person entitled to life.[50]

The pregnant woman is not alone in her privacy. She is joined by and possesses an embryo and later a fetus, and it is appropriate according to the legal philosophy we are examining, for the state, at some point, to develop an interest in the health of both the mother and that of the potential human life.[51]

Texas argued that life begins at conception.[52] The Court indicated that it need not resolve the difficult question of when life begins because even those trained in philosophy and theology are unable to agree on an answer.[53] And it refused to speculate on the correct answer.[54]

The Court pointed out that on the question of when life begins, the common law found great significance in quickening.[55] On the other hand, physicians and scientists have regarded quickening with less interest and have generally focused on conception, live birth, or some interim point in which the fetus becomes "viable."[56] The Court concluded that viability [57] usually occurs at about 28 weeks but, in some cases, may occur earlier.[58]

The majority announced that it would not agree that by adopting the Texas theory that life begins at conception that the state may override the privacy rights of the pregnant woman.[59] The Court, however, also announced that the government had a legitimate interest in protecting the health of the pregnant woman and the potentiality of the human life

---

[49] Id. at 158.

[50] Id. at 159.

[51] Id.

[52] Id.

[53] Id.

[54] Id.

[55] Id. at 160.

[56] Id.

[57] Id. (the ability to live outside the womb.)

[58] Id.

[59] Id. at 162.

she bears.[60] How best to do that was the tricky question. The Court recognized that the interest of a woman seeking an abortion and the interest of the potential life in her womb may conflict with one another. At some point during the woman's pregnancy, the interests of each party become "compelling."[61] The question to be resolved is "When is that point?"

First, the Court dealt with the health of the mother. It announced that with respect to the state's legitimate interest of helping her, the "compelling" point, in light of present medical knowledge,[62] is at approximately the end of the first trimester.[63] From this point on, the state may monitor the abortion procedure to the extent that the regulation relates to the preservation and protection of maternal health.[64]

It follows, on the other hand, that for the period of pregnancy prior to the "compelling" point, the doctor and the pregnant woman are free to determine whether or not the patient's pregnancy should be terminated.[65] If they so decide, the woman is entitled to an abortion, free from any interference from the state.[66]

Next, the Court dealt with the interests of what is called "potential life."[67] Consequently, the state's legitimate interest in potential life, the so-called compelling point, is at viability.[68] At this stage of the pregnancy, the state has a compelling interest in the potential human life contained in the woman's womb.[69] The Court decided that the Texas penal code was too restrictive because it made no distinction between abortions performed early in pregnancy, before the viability of life, and those per-

---

[60] Id.

[61] Id. at 162–163.

[62] Does this mean that medical advances might result in a different "point?" See below for a discussion of this question.

[63] Id. at 163 (The court said this is a reasonable point because mortality in abortion prior to this point is less than mortality in normal childbirth).

[64] Id. (The court listed examples of permissible regulation as "qualifications" of the doctor, "licensure" of the doctor, and designation of the facility as a clinic or a hospital.)

[65] Id.

[66] Id.

[67] Id.

[68] Id. (The ability to live outside the womb.)

[69] Id. (Once the state has a compelling interest in the viable life it may regulate abortion.)

formed later.[70] Secondly, it was too restrictive in that it limited abortion to a single reason, "saving" the mother's life.[71]

The Court indicated that its decision allowed the state to place more stringent restrictions on the availability of abortion as the length of the pregnancy increases, as long as they are tailored to consider the "compelling" interest of both the mother and potential life.

III. Reconsidering Roe: *Planned Parenthood v. Casey*

Roe v. Wade was decided in 1973. For 19 years, the Court's determination that the Constitution protects a woman's right to terminate her pregnancy in its early stages was sharply questioned. Finally, in 1992 in the case of *Planned Parenthood of Southeastern Pennsylvania v. Casey*,[72] the Supreme Court was given an opportunity to reexamine the principles that undergird *Roe*. Recall that *Roe* decided that a woman's decision to terminate her pregnancy is a "liberty" protected by the substantive rights found in the Due Process Clause of the Fourteenth Amendment. Obviously, the Fourteenth Amendment does not specifically describe the limits of the substantive rights contained therein. Consequently, the adjudication of substantive due process rights requires the Supreme Court to exercise its judgment in determining boundaries between the individual's liberty and the demands of society in protecting the unborn.

---

[70] Id. at 164.

[71] Id. at 164–165. Here, the court summarized and repeated its decision. The court indicated: "A state criminal abortion statute of the current Texas type, that excepts from criminality only a life-saving procedure on behalf of the mother, without regard to pregnancy stage and without recognition of the other interests involved, is violating of the Due Process Clause of the Fourteenth Amendment. (a) For the stage prior to approximately the end of the first trimester, the abortion decision and its effectuation must be left to the medical judgment of the pregnant woman's attending physician. (b) For the stage subsequent to approximately the end of the first trimester, the State, in promoting its interest in the health of the mother, may, if it chooses, regulate the abortion procedure in ways that are reasonably related to maternal health. (c) For the stage subsequent to viability, the State in promoting its interest in the potentiality of human life may, if it chooses, regulate and even proscribe, abortion except where it is necessary, in appropriate medical judgment, for the preservation of the life or health of the mother."

[72] 505 U.S. 833 (1992).

Those boundaries were again explored in *Planned Parenthood.* The issues raised in *Planned Parenthood* were framed by six provisions of the Pennsylvania Abortion Act of 1982. Briefly, they are that the Act requires that: (1) the woman seeking the abortion give her informed consent prior to the abortion procedure; (2) that she be provided certain information at least 24-hours before the abortion is performed[73]; (3) that in the case of a minor, she have the consent of one of her parents[74]; (4) that a married woman who seeks an abortion must indicate in writing that she has notified her husband of the intended abortion[75]; (5) compliance is exempted with the first three requirements in the event of a "medical emergency"[76]; and (6) there are reporting requirements placed upon facilities that provide abortion services.[77] The district court found that all provisions at issue were unconstitutional.[78] The Court of Appeals for the Third Circuit upheld all the regulations except for the husband notification requirement.[79]

The High Court commenced its analysis by stating that the Due Process Clause of the Fourteenth Amendment provides a constitutional protection of a woman's decision to terminate her pregnancy.[80] The Court indicated the controlling word in the Fourteenth Amendment that governs a woman's right to an abortion is "liberty."[81] The Court commenced its analysis by reaffirming what it called the three essential holdings of *Roe*:

1. The right of a woman to have an abortion before viability and without undue interference from the state.[82] (As previously indicated, before viability, the state's interest will not support the imposition of a sub-

[73] Id. at 844.

[74] Id.

[75] Id.

[76] Id.

[77] Id.

[78] *Planned Parenthood v. Casey, 744* F.Supp. 1323 (E.D. Pa. 1990), *aff'd in part and rev'd in part,* 947 F.2d 682 (3d. cir. 1991), *aff'd in part rev'd in part,* 505 U.S. 833 (1992).

[79] *Planned Parenthood v. Casey,* 947 F.2d 682 (1991), *aff'd in part and rev'd in part,* 505 U.S. 833 (1992).

[80] *Planned Parenthood,* supra footnote 73 at 846.

[81] Id.

[82] Id.

stantial obstacle to the woman's elective right to an elective procedure.)

2. The state's power to restrict abortions after fetal viability, when the law has exceptions for pregnancy problems that might endanger the woman's life or health.[83]
3. The state has a legitimate interest from the outset of pregnancy in protecting the health of the woman and the life of the fetus that may become a child.[84]

The Court clearly indicated that it continued to follow each of the foregoing three principles.[85] The majority concluded that any reservations the justices may have expressed about the central holding of *Roe* are clearly outweighed by the individual liberty interests involved when they are combined with the force of the doctrine of *stare decisis*.[86] The Court pointed out that although much criticized, *Roe* has not been proven "unworkable."[87]

The High Court said that even if the three principle holdings of *Roe* were in error that would only concern the strengths of the state's interest in fetal protection. That is, the central recognition afforded women's liberty interest by the Constitution would stand even if *Roe* was overruled.[88] According to the Court, the liberty interest, which supports the *Roe* decision includes:

> '[T]he interest in independence in making certain kinds of important decisions.' While the outer limits of this aspect of protected liberty have not been marked by the Court, it is clear that among the decisions that an individual may make without unjustified government interference are personal decisions relating to marriage, procreation, contraception, family relationships, and child rearing and education.[89]

---

[83] Id.

[84] Id.

[85] Id.

[86] Id. at 853.

[87] Id. at 855.

[88] Id. at 858.

[89] Id. at 858. (citing *Carey v. Population Serv.*, 431 U.S. at 684–685 (citations omitted)).

The High Court forcefully stated that there is a constitutional liberty interest on the part of a woman to have some freedom to terminate her pregnancy.[90] As a consequence, the Court believed it was unable to repudiate the constitutional basis on which Roe was decided.[91] But that right is not completely free from reasonable state regulation that protects the interest of both the woman and the unborn child.[92] And, as the Court said in *Roe*, at the point of viability the government has an interest of sufficient force to regulate the right of the woman to terminate her pregnancy.[93]

The Court then faced the central criticism that the line drawn by the *Roe* court to allow government intervention, the viability of the fetus, was somewhat puzzling.[94] The *Planned Parenthood* court's response was that the claims of women to retain the ultimate control over their destiny and their bodies, claims implicit in the very meaning of liberty, required it to decide when the unborn child was viable.[95] The Court said, "Liberty must not be extinguished for want of a line that is clear."[96] But the duty of the court required it to draw a line.

The Court forcefully concluded that the line should be drawn at viability. Thus, before that time a woman has a right to choose to have an abortion.[97] There are two reasons to abide by that principle. First, while there is always a risk that the judicial act of line drawing may seem arbitrary, *Roe* was a reasonable decision reached with great care.[98] The great doctrine of *stare decisis* requires that the Court adhere to the principles announced in *Roe*. Secondly, viability is the time when there is a possibility of maintaining and nourishing a life outside the womb. Consequently,

[90] Id. at 869.

[91] Id.

[92] Id.

[93] Id.

[94] Id.

[95] Id.

[96] Id.

[97] Id. at 870.

[98] Id.

the independent existence of a second life can reasonably be the object of state protection that now overrides the liberty interest of the woman.[99]

The Court was much concerned that overturning *Roe*'s limitation on state power would result in serious inequity to people who had relied on the decision for close to two decades. The judges pointed out that men and women have organized intimate relationships and made choices that define themselves and their places in society relying on the availability of an abortion in the event that contraception should fail.[100] The majority believed that the ability of women to participate equally in the economic and social life of the nation had been greatly advanced by their capacity to control their reproductive lives.[101] Overruling Roe would come at a great cost for people who have adopted their thinking and their lifestyles on the basis of the holding of that case.[102]

It is possible that maternal health care advances after the *Roe* decision may very well allow safe abortions at a later time than the current viability standard.[103] Also, post *Roe*, neonatal care may have advanced viability to a point somewhat earlier in time.[104] However, these possible changes only go to the time limits of the competing interests of the mother and the potential life.[105] They have no bearing on the correctness of the critical holding of *Roe* that viability—at whatever stage in the pregnancy this applies—marks the earliest point in which the state's interest in fetal development is sufficient to justify a legislative ban on abortion.[106]

Additionally, the Court was much concerned that overruling *Roe*'s central finding, in addition to being contrary to the doctrine of *stare decisis*, would also weaken the Court's authority to exercise judicial power and function as a supreme court of the land. After all, the Court's authority depends greatly on its reputation for fairness and consistency. Decisions like *Roe*, said the judges, are entitled to a strong and effective use of the

[99] Id. *See Roe*, 410 U.S. at 163.

[100] *Planned Parenthood*, 505 U.S. at 856.

[101] Id.

[102] Id. at 856.

[103] Id. at 860.

[104] Id.

[105] Id. at 861.

[106] Id. at 860.

doctrine of precedence to counter the resistance to implementation.[107] Overturning the central ideas found in *Roe* would result in a great loss of confidence and unnecessarily damage the Court's reputation.

The judges then announced a number of guiding principles that should control their assessment of the Pennsylvania statute. They are (1) to protect the central liberty rights recognized by *Roe* and at the same time to accommodate the state's compelling interest in protecting potential life, an undue burden standard should be employed.[108] An undue burden exists and is an invalid law, if its purpose or effect is to place substantial obstacles in the path of a woman seeking an abortion before her fetus attains viability.[109] (2) The Court rejected *Roe*'s rigid trimester framework.[110] It declared that the state might take reasonable measures to insure that the woman's choice about whether to have an abortion is informed.[111] Measures, however, designed to advance this informed choice interest should not be invalidated when their purpose is to persuade the woman to choose childbirth over abortion.[112] (3) Finally, the government may attempt to further the health and safety of a woman seeking an abortion but may not impose health regulations that present a substantial obstacle to the woman's ability to obtain an abortion.[113] (4) Adoption of any of these broad standards does not overrule *Roe*'s critical holding that a state may not prohibit any woman from making the ultimate decision to terminate her pregnancy prior to the potential life's viability.[114] Finally, it was decided that the government may regulate or proscribe, but only after viability has been reached.[115]

The majority then applied this reasoning to the Pennsylvania law. First, the High Court determined that the state's medical emergency definition, intended to assure compliance with the abortion regulations, would

---

[107] Id. at 865.

[108] Id. at 878.

[109] Id. at 870.

[110] Id. at 878.

[111] Id.

[112] Id.

[113] Id.

[114] Id. at 879.

[115] Id.

not in any way impose a threat to a woman's life or health.[116] Consequently, it does not violate the essential holdings of *Roe*. Second, the husband notification provision constitutes an undue burden of the woman's interest in an abortion and is therefore invalid.[117] The Court was clearly concerned that a number of women might be prevented from obtaining an abortion because of this provision. The judiciary was not convinced that the father's interest in the fetal welfare was equal to the mother's protected liberty interest.[118] Obviously, the state regulation with respect to the fetus will have a greater impact on the pregnant woman's body than it will on her husband.

The Court also found the state's informed consent provision that required consultation before the procedure was not an undue burden on the woman's right to terminate a pregnancy.[119] It said that requiring the woman be informed of the availability of information relating to the consequences to the fetus does not interfere with her constitutional right of privacy and does not override her right to an abortion.[120]

Despite the controversy surrounding the implementation of *Roe*, the Court was firmly convinced that it was in the continuing national interest to uphold the core values of that opinion. As previously indicated, those core values are embedded in the "liberty" interest found within the Fourteenth Amendment. The reference to a liberty interest is important, but generally ignored. It indicates that the majority did not rest their decision solely on the right of privacy, which requires a balancing of interests. Instead it rested on "liberty" that is specifically mentioned in our constitution. Liberty interests of the individual are presumed constitutional, and the burden is on the government. The government bears the

---

[116] Id. at 880.

[117] Id. at 895.

[118] Id. at 881.

[119] Id. at 883. On this issue the High Court on February 24, 2003, refused to hear the appeal of a 7th Circuit decision which held that a requirement that a woman get face-to-face counseling at least 18 hours prior to obtaining an abortion was constitutional and did not unreasonably interfere with her liberty interest in an abortion. A lower court had found that about 10% of women who received counseling changed their mind about getting an abortion. *See, A Woman's Choice-East Side Women's Clinic v. Newman*, 305 F.3d 684 (2002), *cert. denied, A Woman's Choice-East Side Women's Clinic v. Brizzi*, 537 U.S. 1192 (2003).

[120] Id.

burden of proving the necessity of restricting a liberty interest. This was recognized by the *Casey* opinion by the quote, "Neither the Bill of Rights nor the specific practices of states at the time of the adoption of the Fourteenth Amendment marks the outer limits of the substantive sphere of liberty which the Fourteenth Amendment protects. See U.S. Const., Amend. 9."[121]

Why is our reliance on a liberty interest wise? Because that appears to be the way of the Supreme Court. In *Lawrence v. Texas*,[122] Justice Kennedy's opinion concerning the conduct of two gay men in their own home is based on "liberty" not privacy. He begins:

> *Liberty* protects the person from unwarranted governmental intrusions into a dwelling or other private places. In our tradition the state is not omnipresent in the home. And there are other spheres of our lives and existence, outside the home, where the state should not be a dominant presence. Freedom extends beyond spatial bounds. *Liberty* presumes an autonomy of self that includes freedom of thought, belief, expression, and certain intimate conduct. The instant case involves *liberty* of the person both in its spatial and transcendent dimensions.[123]

Clearly, Justice Kennedy has shifted the burden of proof. If liberty is the issue, the government is compelled to justify any restriction of the individual's liberty as necessary. If privacy is the issue, the burden is on the individual to show that the right of privacy being exercised is somehow a fundamental right. This is not to say that the government may never restrict liberty. Surely, behavior that is violent to the rights of others may be prohibited without violating liberty rights. This is why it is so necessary to properly define the status of fetus or unborn child. Is it not reasonable to suppose that among those other spheres of liberty referred to by Justice Kennedy is the abortion decision and the liberty interests of the mother and the fetus? This we attempt.

Having explored the current legal status of the issue of abortion, we now turn to a compromise for the seemingly uncompromisable conflict

[121] Id. at 848.

[122] 539 U.S. 558 (2003).

[123] Id. at 562.

that daily rages between fierce, and often violent, anti-abortion critics of *Roe v. Wade*, like Operation Rescue and the pro-choice forces of groups such as Planned Parenthood.

IV. Introduction to the Compromise

There is a strong analogy between the anti-abortionists active in the modern era and the abolitionists[124] who tried to end slavery in the pre-Civil War[125] period. Each attempts (attempted) to safeguard the well-being and even the very lives of a particularly helpless group of people.

If anything, the present day pro-life forces are in a worse position than their nineteenth century counterparts. For one thing, the fetus is far more helpless than was the black slave. The latter could "run away" with the help of the Underground Railroad and other such institutions. No three-week old fetus has the maturity to initiate or even remotely cooperate in any such venture. True, the pro-lifers can try to convince a pregnant woman not to abort, but in order to save the baby's life they have to convince the potentially evil doer mother,[126] not, of course, the fetus. In contrast, the organizers of the Underground Railroad did not have to convince the masters of anything—not very likely, in any case—but only the slaves, a far less difficult task.

Another analogy in this regard is that between abortion and the Nazi holocaust. Both incidents are associated with massive slaughter of innocents. If the immorality of an act is correlated with the helplessness and innocence of the victims, then the moral outrage now directed at Nazis

---

[124] Afgen, *The Abolitionist*, http://afgen.com/slave1.html, (last accessed Feb. 16, 2005); InfoPlease, *abolitionists*, http://www.infoplease.com/ce6/history/A0802190.html, (last updated Feb. 16, 2005).

[125] Strictly speaking, a "Civil War" is conducted between two contending forces, each of whom wishes to rule the entire country. A more accurate description of the conflagration of 1861–1865 would thus be "War between the States." Pejoratives on the other side of this debate are "War of Northern Aggression" and "First War of Southern Secession." For intellectual support of the latter two, *see* Thomas DiLorenzo, *The Real Lincoln: A New Look at Abraham Lincoln, His Agenda, and an Unnecessary War* (Random H. & Hummel 2002); Jeffrey Rogers, *Emancipating Slaves, Enslaving Free Men: A History of the American Civil War* (Open Ct. 1996).

[126] Who, by analog, now takes on the position of the slave master, not the slave.

might better be vented in the direction of pro-choicers. For surely, the Jews who were slaughtered, no matter how innocent of any wrong doing themselves, were at least more responsible for their fate than the fetuses victimized by abortion.[127]

This practice attacks the weakest and most defenseless members of our society. It is one thing to do away with adults, as in the case of the Jewish Holocaust, the Bosnian "ethnic cleansing," or the mass murder in Rwanda. The suffering is pitiful, but at least for the most part, the victims were adults. In the event, they were unable to protect themselves against their enemies. But they had this option, at least theoretically.

The only group of sufferers whose plight even remotely approaches that of the fetus is the abused (small) child. This is surely one of the most pitiful sets of victims, but even they, in contrast, have had some years of life. The fetus stands alone, even compared to these other unfortunates.[128]

It is for this reason we maintain that abortion is an abomination. It is a massive killer. More people[129] die annually as a result of it (1,591,000) than perish from heart disease (720,058), cancer (505,322), stroke

[127] This is meant not to "blame the victims" of the holocaust, but to underscore the even greater blamelessness, or, better, helplessness, of the fetus.

[128] An anti-abortion exhibit displayed at Boise State University has drawn the ire of Rabbi Daniel B. Fink, of the Ahavath Beth Israel synagogue in Boise, Idaho. The presentation features three horrific pictures, one of Jewish victims of the Nazi holocaust, a second one of a black man being lynched, presumably by the KKK, and the third of an aborted fetus. The first is labeled as "Ungentile," the second as "Unwhite," and third as "Unborn." Rabbi Fink objects on the ground that this depiction is "racist, anti-Semitic," and "exploitative" (*see* Richard Morgan, *Sense and Censorship*, The Chronicles of Higher Education A6 (Apr. 12, 2002)). He opposes the equation of these three sorry episodes in human history. We, too, object; but likely for reasons opposite to his. In our view, what we do to very young human beings is far worse than what we do to either of these two other groups of people, and thus should not be equated with them. And this for two reasons: one, fetuses are more helpless than either Jews or blacks; two, far more of them have been murdered. Lynched blacks number "only" in the thousands. There were "only" six million Jews who perished in the holocaust. But, given that somewhat more than 1.5 million fetuses are killed every year in the United States alone, it takes only four short years to reach totals attained by the Nazis regarding the Jews.

[129] For the purpose of this article, fetuses are counted as people. Reasons are given for this stance below.

(144,088), or all accidents (91,983).[130] Adding insult to injury, death occurs in these cases because of the purposeful action of other people.[131]

There is another parallel between the position occupied by the pro-lifers in the modern period and the abolitionists in the 1840s. Then, the war that was to take place 25 years hence would "solve" the problem. But in the interim, between 1840 and 1865, the abolitionists did what they could to bring this event about; at the very least, they prepared the way for it on philosophical grounds.

In the present case, it is the contention of this article, new medical technology will "solve" the abortion problem. But this will obtain only if pro-lifers borrow a leaf from their abolitionist forebears. That is, they must work morally and philosophically to pave the way for this eventuality. The thesis of the present article is that, on a pragmatic level, the only way to resolve this vexing question, in a way that will satisfy both sides—at least partially—is to rely on new medical technology.[132] These breakthroughs will, hopefully, allow the pregnant woman who wishes to exercise her rights to free choice one additional option: to rid herself of the burden of bearing the fetus without endangering its life. This is not a pipedream because research in this area is proceeding apace. According to a report in *The New Republic*, scientists are perfecting a process called "ectogenesis" that allows a fetus to gestate in an artificial womb, separate from its biological mother.[133]

---

[130] Source *Statistical Abstract of the United States*, 1993; table #128, page 93 for heart disease, cancer, stroke, and accidents in 1990. Data for abortion from tables #112, 113, page 83 in 1988. The Canadian death figures for 1991 are as follows: abortion, 70,463, circulatory system illnesses, 75,089, cancer, 52,425, respiratory ailments, 16,272, accidents and adverse effects, 12,057 (*Canada Yearbook,* 1994, table #4.4 page 149), abortion, 70,463 (*Statistics Canada: Therapeutic Abortions*, 1991, 82–219). Thus, abortion is the leading cause of death in the United States and the second leading cause in Canada. For more statistical data on the number of abortions conducted in the United States, see http://www.abortiontv.com/AbortionStatistics.htm#United%20States; http://www.abortionfacts.com/statistics/statistics.asp (accessed on 3/6/03).

[131] Further, baby murder leads to a callous indifference to all life. A society which treats the least of us in so cavalier a fashion tends to find it easier to do away with older people against their will as well. All of life becomes cheaper.

[132] "…the time of viability is, to a large extent, determined by the advances in technology." James J. Mulligan, *Choose Life*, 59 (The Pope John 51 Center 1991).

[133] *See* Sacha Zimmerman, *The Future of the Abortion Debate*, The New Republic (Aug. 18, 2003). (The article suggests that this process might be available in five years.)

However, just because aborting the fetus is abominable, it does not follow that it should be prohibited by law. Under a just, for example, libertarian law code,[134] there are numerous despicable acts, which are not legally proscribed, since they do not constitute "invasions" or "border crossings." Abortion falls into this category. It is a failure to come to the aid of or an unwillingness to become a "good Samaritan." The woman who refuses to carry her fetus to term is in exactly the same position as a person who refuses to rescue a drowning swimmer. Abortion is not, in and of itself, an act invasive of other people or their property rights, even when fetuses are considered persons.

There is perhaps no more intractable dilemma facing us today than abortion. Not since pre-civil war days has our country been so divided over a moral issue. The position adumbrated in this article, hopefully, provides a clear way out, a compromise not otherwise obtainable.

Let us begin at the beginning. At what point does human life begin? There are really only two reasonable possibilities: at conception or at birth; all other points of development in between are merely points along a continuum which begins and ends with these two options. At any point before the fertilization, there is only a sperm and an egg. Neither, without the other, is capable of developing into anything else, let alone anything human.[135] But the fertilized egg most certainly will become a human being, if kept in the womb for nine months.[136] At any point after birth,

---

[134] Hans-Hermann Hoppe, *A Theory of Socialism and Capitalism: Economics, Politics and Ethics* (Dordrecht, 1989); Hans-Hermann Hoppe, *The Economics and Ethics of Private Property: Studies in Political Economy and Philosophy* (Kluwer 1993); Murray N. Rothbard, *The Ethics of Liberty* (Humanities Press 1982); Murray N. Rothbard, *For a New Liberty: The Libertarian Manifesto* (Collier Macmillan 1973); Bruce L. Benson, *The Impetus for Recognizing Private Property and Adopting Ethical Behavior in a Market Economy: Natural Law Government Law or Evolving Self Interest*, 6 Rev. Austrian Econ. 43; Walter Block, *Defending the Undefendable* (Fox and Wilkes 1991); Williamson N. Evers, *Toward a reformulation of the law of contracts*, 1 The J. of Libertarian Studies 3 (Winter 1977).; Williamson N. Evers, *Social contract: a critique*, 1 The J. of Libertarian Studies 185 (Summer 1977); Tibor R. Machan, *Social Contract as a Basis of Norms: A Critique*, 7 The J. of Libertarian Studies 141 (Spring 1983); George H. Smith, *William Wollaston on property rights*, 2 The J. of Libertarian Studies 217 (Fall 1978).

[135] When, and if, parthenogenesis ever develops for the human egg, or sperm, this statement will have to be reexamined.

[136] With the advanced technology that the next few decades are sure to bring, it will be possible for the fertilized egg to develop outside the womb as well: in the laboratory, in a host mother, and so on.

there is similarly no question: if a baby is not a human being, then no one is.

So which is it? Does life begin at the beginning point of this nine-month continuum or at the end of it? We take the former position. We maintain that the fetus is an alive human being from day one onward, with all the rights pertaining to any other member of the species.[137]

We take this position for two reasons. First, if not interfered with, without any further effort, the fetus is already on its way to human status. Surely an entity, which after a nine-month "sleep" will wake up as a human being, has already attained that status. Consider the alternative. Here, the fetus of 35 weeks and several days, although viable outside the womb in virtually all cases given present technology, has no rights at all. It can be killed with legal impunity. It will be a fully rights bearing baby in a mere matter of hours, and yet now it can be "disposed of." Compare two entities, assuming that this was technologically possible: one, the newborn babe, still attached to its umbilical cord, a few seconds old. The other, its sibling, is still in the womb but due out in a matter of minutes. No two entities could be more alike, biologically, spiritually, or in any other way. Yet, in the "pro-choice" philosophy, it would be murder to kill the one and a matter of complete judicial irrelevance to kill the other. Surely, this is a travesty not only of justice but also of common sense.[138]

The second reason is a logical—rhetorical—pedagogical one. Paradoxically, considering the foregoing, we shall be defending the "pro-choice" position. It behooves us, then, to place every obstacle in our own way lest we become involved in a process of demolishing straw men. That is, given it is our view that a woman has a right to rid herself of the fetus at any point in this process, for any reason deemed sufficient by herself alone, matters would be far too easy for us if human life began only at birth. For then the decision to terminate the pregnancy would be nondebatable. However, if we can show, as we intend to do, that it would be

[137] Steven Luper, *Invulnerability: On Securing Happiness*, 106 (Open Ct. 1996), states: "Of course, it does not follow that the death of a fetus is unfortunate. For that conclusion we would need to assume that fetuses are selves." This is perhaps one of the most extreme articulations of the pro-choice view.

[138] Contrast this with the case of partial birth abortions.

licit for her to end the pregnancy even given that the fetus has all human rights, the analysis would be the more logically robust.

Since we end up taking a "free choice" position, in order to make our case as difficult for ourselves as possible, we begin by conceding to the anti-abortionist side that human life begins in the very early stages of pregnancy[139] and not after birth.[140] Given this, how can we defend the mother's right to kill the fetus?

Simple. She owns her own body, and the unwanted fetus growing within it is in effect a trespasser or parasite. This may sound harsh, but when the property rights in question are thoroughly analyzed, it is the only possible conclusion that may be reached. To see this point, consider the following case:

Suppose one day you wake up to find yourself attached to another person, for example, Thompson's[141] by now famous violinist, through your kidneys. You have two healthy organs, and the other person has none that are functioning. During the night, while you slept, doctors performed an operation connecting that person to your kidneys through a sort of umbilical cord, and there you lie. This operation was conducted without the permission or even knowledge of either "patient."

What rights and obligations do you have with regard to this violinist? First, let us stipulate that the person in question is a complete innocent. Last night he was in a hospital bed; this morning he woke up in your bed attached to you. He is not a rapist. You were "raped," but this was not done by your bedmate; instead, it was the act of evil doctors who have since vanished from the scene. What you are confronted with is the result of the rape, namely, this person lying in bed with you attached to your kidneys[142] completely dependent upon you for his life.

---

[139] Actually, with the fertilized egg.

[140] Judith Jarvis Thompson, *A Defense of Abortion*, 1 Phil. and Pub. Affairs 47 (1971), (reprinted in *Moral problems* (James Rachels, ed., 2nd ed., Harper and Row, 1975)), seems ambivalent as to whether "a line can be drawn" between the human and the non-human being. Roger Wertheimer, *Understanding the Abortion Argument*, 1 Phil. and Pub. Affairs 69 (1971), makes this question a central focus of his analysis.

[141] Judith Jarvis Thompson, *Rights, Restitution and Risk* (Harvard University Press 1986); Judith Jarvis Thompson, *The Realm of Bights* (Harvard University Press, 1990).

[142] For the argument in favor of legalizing markets in used body parts, *see generally*, A. F. Adams, A. H. Barnett, & D. L. Kaserman, *Markets of Organs: "The Question of Supply*, 17 Contemporary

What can you do with this person? Suppose he goes back to sleep and is thus totally helpless. Can you just slit his throat? That would be murder and must therefore be opposed.[143] Killing him is aggressive; it constitutes initiatory violence. Even if you can get away with it on practical grounds, it should certainly not be allowed on the basis of legal principles.

What can you do? Do you have to let him stay attached for nine months or for any particular length of time? Instead of slitting his throat, can you sever the connection between the two of you—which would also cause his death? If you did that, you would still be guilty of the initiation of coercion, surely a crime, specifically, murder. What you must do is notify somebody—the association "Friends of Kidney Victims" or a hospital or the Salvation Army or the Church and have them sever the connection between you two, without thereby killing this dependent.

Econ. Policy 147 (Apr. 1999); W. L. Anderson & A. H. Barnett, *Waiting for Transplants*, 17 The Free Mkt. 1 (1999); A. H. Barnett, T. R. Beard & D. L. Kaserman, *The Medical Community's Opposition to Organ Markets: Ethics or Economics?*, 8 Rev. of Indus. Org. 669 (1993); A. H. Barnett, R. D. Blair & D. L. Kaserman, *Improving Organ Donations: Compensation Versus Markets*, 29 Inquiry 372 (Fall 1992); A. H. Barnett, & D. L. Kaserman, *The 'Rush to Transplant' and Organ Shortages*, 33 Econ. Inquiry 506 (July 1995); W. Barnett II, *The Market in Used Human Body Parts*, 6 The Free Mkt 5 (1988); William Barnett & Michael Saliba, *A Free Market for Kidneys: Options, Futures, Forward and Spot*, —Managerial Fin—, (forthcoming); W Barnett, II, M. Saliba & D. Walker, *A Free Market in Kidneys: Efficient and Equitable*, 5 The Indep. Rev. 373 (2001); D. Barney Jr. & L. Reynolds, *An Economic analysis of Transplant Organs*, 17 A. Econ. J. 12 (September 1989); R. D. Blair & D. L. Kaserman, *The Economics and Ethics of Alternative Cadaveric Organ Procurement Policies*, 8 Yale J. on Reg. 403 (1991); W. Block, *The Case for a Free Market in Body Parts*, 6 The Free Mkt. 3 (1988); Walter Block, Roy Whitehead, Clint Johnson, Mana Davidson, Alan White & Stacy Chandler, *Human Organ Transplantation: Economic and Legal Issues*, 3 Quinnipiac Health L.J. 87, (1999–2000); A. L. Caplan, *If I Were a Rich Man Could I Buy a Pancreas? And Other Essays on the Ethics of Health Care* (Indiana University Press 1992); C. T. Carlstrom & C. D. Rollow, *The Rationing of Transplantable Organs: A Troubled Lineup*, 17 Cato J. 163 (Fall 1997); W. DeJong, J. Drachman, S. L. Gortmaker, et al., *Options for Increasing Organ Donations: The Potential Role for Financial Incentives, Standardized Hospital Procedures, and Public Education to Promote Family Discussion*, 73 The Milbank Q. 463 (1995);H. Hansmann, *The Economics and Ethics of Markets for Human Organs*, J. Health, Pol., and Policy and L. 57 (Spring 1989); D. L. Kaserman & A. H. Barnett, *An Economic Analysis of Transplant Organs: A Comment and Extension*, 19 A. Econ. J. 57 (June 1991);Dennis Prince, *Organ for Sale—Not Wurlitzer*, http://www.auctionwatch.com/awdaily/dailynews/1-090399.html (1999); J. R. Richards, *Nephrarious Goings On: Kidney Sales and Moral Arguments*, 21 J. of Medicine and Philosophy 375 (August 1996); S. Rottenberg, *The Production and Exchange of Used Body Parts*, 2 Towards Liberty 322 (1971); R. Schwindt, & A. R. Vining *Proposal for a Future Delivery Market for Transplant Organs*, 11 J. Health Policy and L. 483 (Fall 1986); A. R. Vining, & R. Schwindt, *Have a Heart: Increasing the Supply of Transplant Organs for Infants and Children*, 7 J. Policy Analysis and Mgt. 706 (1988).

[143] Christine Overall, *Ethics and Human Reproduction: A Feminist Analysis* (Allen and Unwin 1987), reaches a similar conclusion.

If a parent abandons a newborn in the woods or shoves a five-year-old out into a blizzard, he is doing something akin to that of slitting the cord between you and the kidney victim who is attached to you. It is incumbent upon the individual to at least make a phone call to an orphanage, or put the child on the proverbial Church steps,[144] or be in touch with whatever organization functions in this capacity in any given society. It is only if no help is forthcoming from any such quarter that these actions can possibly not be interpreted as murder.

This case is not analogous to the one where an individual is invited on an airplane trip, and then halfway, while he is up in the air, the owner states that the invitation was only for 15 minutes and that the time is now up … so stop trespassing and leave forthwith, sans parachute. There is an implicit contract in force in that instance.[145] In contrast, there *can be* no such contract in the case of pregnancy, at the very least because there is simply no child to have a contract *with* at the point of intercourse when the child is created.[146] The fetus does not yet exist, and even when it does, it is impossible to have a contract (implicit or otherwise) with a one-week-old baby.[147]

Consider another mental experiment. It is 100 years in the future. With modern technology, it is possible to take a fetus at any stage of development out of the womb and place it in a test tube or a host mother or in some other way for the mother to abandon the fetus without killing or even harming it in the least. Suppose that under these circumstances, a woman had an abortion—that is, she refused to notify anyone or use the "Church steps,"[148]—when she could as easily have saved the life of

[144] We consider below whether, and if so to what extent, this requirement is inconsistent with the libertarian proscription against positive obligations.

[145] One must of course tread carefully through the minefield of implicit contracts, but it would appear that here we have a paradigm case of this type of "agreement." Surely no one would ever enter an airplane (or a car, train, etc.), if he were liable to be pushed out while at full speed.

[146] We abstract from the possibility of the mother having a contract with the father to raise the child.

[147] One could of course have an *obligation* to a small child, but cannot be bound by an implicit contract to such a person. This is because *explicit* contracts with babies (without parent or guardian consent) are impermissible, and an implicit contract is merely the embodiment of an explicit one.

[148] There is an episode of the television show M*A*S*H where Hawkeye and Fr. Mulcahy brought a baby born to a Korean woman but fathered by an American G.I. to a monastery-orphanage for safekeeping since no one else would care for it. We owe this example to Hannah Block.

this fetus by engaging in this modern technology. Under these conditions, the individual would be guilty of an initiatory aggressive act that would certainly be contrary to all known principles of law. Under these assumptions, one would have to evict the fetus, not abort it.

V. Evictionism

The word "abort" is used in different ways. It is absolutely crucial that a distinction be made between killing and eviction.[149] This future technology would allow the individual to do the one without the other. If and when it becomes possible, the individual would have an obligation, similar to the one owed to the person you woke up in bed with in the

---

[149] Not every analyst of abortion seems aware of this distinction. Those who have utilized it include: Robert A. Frietas Jr., *Fetal Adoption: A Technological Solution to the Problem of Abortion Ethics*, The Humanist 22 (May/June 1980); Raymond N. Herbenick, *Remarks on Abortion, Abandonment and Adoption Opportunities*, 5 Phil. and Pub. Affairs 98 (1975); John Morreall, *Of Marsupials and Men: A Thought Experiment on Abortion*, 37 Dialogos 16 (1981); Susan T. Nicholson, *The Roman Catholic Doctrine of Therapeutic Abortion*, Feminism and Phil. 392 (Nary Vetterling-Braqgin, Frederick A. Elliston, & Jane English eds., Littlefield, Adams, 1978); Christine Overall, *Ethics and Human Reproduction: A Feminist Analysis* (Allen and Unwin, 1987); Ellen Frankel Paul & Jeffrey Paul, *Self Ownership, Abortion and Infanticide*, 5 J. Med. Ethics 134 (1979); Murray N. Rothbard, *For a New Liberty: The Libertarian Manifesto* 108 (Collier Macmillan 1973); Judith Jarvis Thompson, *A Defense of Abortion*, 1 Phil. and Pub. Affairs 47 (reprinted in *Moral problems* (James Rachels, ed., 2nd ed. Harper and Row 1975)); Daniel I.Wikler, *Ought We to Save Aborted Fetuses?* 90 Ethics 64 (1973); Walter Block, *Abortion, Woman and Fetus: Rights in Conflict?*, Reason 18 (April 1978).

Steven L Ross., *Abortion and the Death of the Fetus*, 11 Phil. and Pub. Affairs 232 (1982), offers somewhat awkward subscript nomenclature for this distinction. His "abortion1" depicts the case "where the pregnancy but not the life of the fetus would be ended." This is what we have been calling "eviction." His "abortion2" refers to the case "where the fetus would be killed despite the fact that this was not at all necessary to our accomplishing (abortion1)." This, we would characterize as out and out murder. Ross' "abortion" refers to "current practice, where separation and death occur more or less simultaneously." This is the complex, two-stage affair of eviction plus killing to which we refer as plain "abortion."

Abortion has been defined as "the removal of a non-viable fetus from the uterus; or, the killing and removal but non killing of a viable fetus" Mulligan, *Choose Life* at 353. What about removal but non-killing of a viable fetus? That is eviction.

See generally, John Hart Ely, *The Wages of Crying Wolf: A Comment on Roe v. Wade, 82* Yale L.J. 920, 935 (1973); Richard A. Epstein, *Substantive Due Process by Any Other Name: The Abortion Cases*, The Supreme Court Review 1973 (Phillip B. Kurland, et al., eds. University of Chicago Press 1974); Joel Feinberg, *Matters of Life and Death: New Introductory Essays in Moral Philosophy* (Tom Regan ed., Random H. 1981); Lawrence Tribe, Abortion: The Clash of Absolutes (W.W. Norton 1990).

attached kidney case, not to kill but merely to evict.[150] If this were not done, it would be similar to abandoning the baby in the woods.

From these examples is derived the principle that when one evicts a trespasser, or deals with any other violator of rights, one is obliged to do so in a certain way; it must be done in the least invasive manner possible consistent with upholding property rights. If a trespasser is on your lawn and you have a bazooka, you are not entitled to blow him away—not as a first step in any case. That is far too extreme and incompatible with the doctrine of private property rights. The homeowner has the right to make sure that the outsider does not trespass further, but he must be evicted in the gentlest manner possible. Suppose a viable baby was removed from the womb, and the doctor killed it afterward.[151] It seems crystal clear that would be first-degree, premeditated murder and ought to be dealt with accordingly. It is an understatement of the highest order to say that this is hardly the gentlest manner possible.

Whether or not it can be argued that this level of technology exists now or for what term of the pregnancy is unimportant. One hundred years ago, there was no question of any such technology. At that time the question arose, "Does the individual have to carry this perhaps unwanted visitor that was not contracted for to a term of nine months?" Based on the private property rights philosophy, the individual then had the right to evict the trespasser in the most gentle manner possible. If there was no gentle manner feasible, an individual's property rights to her womb transcend the so-called right to life of anyone else. No one has a "right to life."[152]

---

[150] We assume, in order to strengthen the analogy, that "modern technology" would allow you to detach yourself from the kidney victim without killing him.

[151] Partial birth abortions consist of allowing the baby's head to protrude, but then to kill it by removing its brains with suction.

[152] That would imply positive rights. Others would have an obligation to help. For a libertarian critique of this Good Samaritan or brother's keepers' philosophy, *see* Hans-Hermann Hoppe, *A Theory of Socialism and Capitalism: Economics*, Pol. and Ethics (Dordrecht 1989); Hans-Hermann Hoppe, *The Economics and Ethics of Private Property: Studies in Political Economy and Philosophy* (Kluwer 1993); Murray N. Rothbard, *The Ethics of Liberty* (Humanities Press 1982); Murray N. Rothbard, *For a New Liberty: The Libertarian Manifesto* (Collier Macmillan 1973); Robert Nozick, *Anarchy, State, and Utopia* (Basic Books 1974).

Individuals only have a right not to be aggressed against. The fetus is not being aggressed against by eviction from a woman's womb, which is her property; that is, this "facility" is owned by the woman not the fetus. On the contrary, the fetus aggressor, albeit not purposefully, is the initiator of violence.

All fetuses have equal rights. They are all equally innocent. Consider those who are created as the result of rape. Clearly, here, there was no agreement or consent or invitation between the mother and the baby. But such a fetus is still a trespasser; it is in effect a parasite to the woman who does not want that fetus in her body. She has a right to evict it.

The private property rights position on this issue is thus a moderate one. Pro-abortion radical feminists and others, who think they have a right to kill fetuses, even if it is possible to evict them without harm, represent one extreme[153] in this debate. They hold the view that it is the pregnant woman's right to determine whether or not that fetus will live. Nor does this apply only in the case of rape. This position defends a woman's choice to abort when intercourse for the purpose of procreation occurs voluntarily, but later on, she decides not to carry the baby to term. Women have a right to kill their unborn children, even if medical technology exists which would save it, in this view.

On the other side of the spectrum are the anti-abortionists, who would violate the woman's right to her own body to the extent of insisting that a trespasser, a parasite, be allowed to remain there for nine months against her will.[154]

This position is also unjustified, from a libertarian point of view. The position herein advocated is to allow for eviction, not killing; it does not support trespassers "rights" over those of the legitimate owner of the maternal property in question.

Causation is not directly a legal concern. The law is a normative science; causation is at most an element in a positive science. It is a category mistake to conflate causation and rights violations. We are not now involved with positive causality, only with normative rights violations. All

---

[153] Steven L Ross., *Abortion and the Death of the Fetus*, 11 Phil. and Pub. Affairs 232 (1982).

[154] Doris Gordon, *Abortion and Rights: Applying Libertarian Principles Correctly*, 1 Stud. in Prolife Feminism 121 (spring 1995).

sorts of harm is *caused* by people, and these actions would not be proscribed because they are all well within our rights. Certainly, in the case of rape there is no such cause. The woman is a totally innocent victim. She did not cause that baby to come into being. The reason that fetus came into being was "caused" by the rapist. The key is not causation. Our perspective does not deal with cause but rather with rights violations. The key is not who caused the death, it is rather who violated the rights of the individual. Rights are not violated by evicting a parasite or trespasser.

The bottom line, here, is the question of legality: under what conditions is it justified to use force? In our own personal view, abortion is an evil; we oppose it. It would be nice if all women carried babies to term, and that as a result there were fewer, or better yet, no people killed in this manner. We are pro-people. We also oppose drugs, alcohol, cigarette smoking, and chocolate eating. We try hard not to do any of these things. However, we would not impose a penalty on ourselves or anyone else for engaging in these actions. It is the same with abortion. The real question is, "What penalties should be imposed for engaging in this practice?" Not whether or not it is virtuous or moral to indulge in them.

The anti-abortionist position, to be logically consistent, would have to hold this action as premeditated, first-degree murder. If the death penalty is justified in any case, it is justified in this one. It should apply to the woman who gets an abortion and to the doctor or whoever performs it. If that kind of penalty is not imposed, there is an inconsistency that is incompatible with just principles of law. The logic of the premises is not being followed.

The position put forth here, in contrast, is one of eviction not of killing. However, if the only way to evict is by killing the fetus, then the woman's right to her property—that is, her womb—must be held above the valuable life of the fetus. At least in cases of rape, it is clear that the fetus is a trespasser and a parasite. This, then, is true in every case because all fetuses have the same rights.

Let us put this in other words. Must A agree to stay attached to B, who has no functioning kidney, for the rest of his life? Hardly. Individual B is a parasite, no matter how personally innocent. Must A agree to maintain this bizarre experiment for nine months, if that is how long it will take to uncover a new donor for B? Not at all. Any such requirement would entail slavery of A, for whatever the duration.

Nor, at the other extreme, may A simply haul off and shoot B to death. The latter is not guilty of any wrongdoing. Our theory would require that A detach himself from B in the gentlest manner possible, so as to give him the best chance for survival. This would entail, presumably, a visit to the hospital that very day, where they could be surgically disconnected, and the status quo ante achieved.

If this discussion is correct, we deduce that the pregnant woman may remove the fetus from her body in a manner that does the least harm to it possible. That is, she may evict but not kill it. True, 100 years ago, the only way to rid herself of the unborn human within her would have been to put it to death; 100 years from now, it will presumably be possible to transfer it to a test tube or a host mother without disturbing it in the slightest.

At present, however, this policy prescription serves as a true compromise between the pro-choice and pro-life camps. The former gains half a victory: the woman may rid herself of the fetus, as is desired by the pro-choicers, but they will be disappointed in that she does not also have the right to kill it. Likewise, the latter also comes away with half a loaf; this side of the debate welcomes the fact that the baby will live, even if they cannot, under the compromise, force the biological mother to bear the child, as they would wish.

VI. Compromise

This compromise, or eviction position, is a true intermediary between the two more well-known abortion theories, pro-life and pro-choice. It and it alone can be justified; the others cannot.

The key to the solution is to focus on the private property rights in question. In this case, it is the mother's womb; given that the fetus is unwanted, it is in effect a trespasser or a parasite. The mother, then, has a right to evict it—in the gentlest manner possible—but not to kill it.

One hundred years ago, this would not have had much practical import; eviction necessarily meant killing. One hundred years from now, presumably, we will have the medical technology necessary to preserve the life of the fetus outside the natural mothers' womb during any stage in its development (whether in a test tube or in the womb of a host mother, etc.) Right now, medical technology can preserve the lives of some evicted fetuses but not all. This factor alone would render evictionism a true compromise.

But there are various other dimensions to it. These may best be brought out with the help of the following chart, which depicts three possible answers to a series of important questions, not merely two, as is usually supposed:

A. Pro-abortion (pro-choice)
B. Eviction (pro-property rights)
C. Anti-abortion (pro-life)

1. Is the mother compelled to bring the fetus to term; that is, to carry it for nine months?
   A. no B. no C. yes
2. Can the mother evict the fetus from her womb?
   A. yes B. yes C. no
3. Can the mother kill the fetus? (Would that new pill—RU 486—which kills and then flushes out the fetus, be legal?)
   A. yes B. no C. no
4. Given century old technology, can the mother unilaterally determine that the fetus shall die?
   A. yes B. yes C. no
5. Given present technology, can the mother unilaterally determine that the fetus shall die?
   A. yes B. sometimes C. no
6. Given future technology, can the mother unilaterally determine that the fetus shall die?
   A. yes B. no C. no

Pundits, editorialists, moralists, lawyers, judges, and advocacy groups have all been arguing over columns one and three. They ignore column two, which is a principled compromise that contains at least a potential solution to this seemingly intractable problem.

Evictionism also solves the challenge of anti-girl baby abortions. In China, India, and elsewhere, cultural phenomena influence women to abort baby girls in favor of their male counterparts. There are many difficulties in this arena, where modern leftist radical[155] feminism meets ancient culture and Malthusian[156] over populationist hysteria. Left feminists urge that women be free to choose whether to abort or not. Heavily populated countries such as China have instituted laws, which mandate the maximum number of children each mother may bear (typically, one). As a result, women in these third world societies have been making decisions all right but not in the direction presumably favored by Marxist feminists; to wit, they have been choosing to kill almost exclusively their baby girls.

There are numerous problems here apart from the sheer human tragedy of massive murder of the innocents involved in all abortions. For one thing, the radical feminists seem to have been hoisted by their own petard.[157] They have championed "choice" in these matters, and the decision of women has been, if anything, the exact opposite of what they would have asked of these women, had they been able to make that choice for them.[158]

---

[155] There is no reason to allow socialist women's organizations to co-opt the honorific "feminism." On the contrary, there are also feminists of almost diametric opposite viewpoints. See Wendy McElroy, *A Site for Individualist Feminism and Individualist Anarchism*, http://zetetics.com/mac/ (Last updated Feb. 16, 2005); Joan Kennedy Taylor, *Reclaiming the Mainstream: Individualist Feminism Rediscovered* (Prometheus 1992).

[156] Paul Ehrlich, *The Population Bomb* (Sierra Club- Ballantine 1968); Al Gore, *Earth in the Balance: Ecology and the Human Spirit* (Houghton-Mifflin 1992).

[157] There are some who would not look upon this result exactly as a "problem." See e.g., Michael Levin, *Comparable Worth: The Feminist Road to Socialism*, Commentary (Sept. 1984); Michael Levin, *Feminism and Freedom* (Transaction Books 1987).

[158] States Christine Overall, *Ethics and Human Reproduction: A Feminist Analysis*, 20 (Allen and Unwin, 1987), "…sex pre-selection based on intrinsic sex preference is always irrational and wrong … except to avoid offspring with sex linked diseases."

Further, Overall maintains that "The technology of sex pre-selection enables people, particularly men, to act upon their biases against women; it is not an exaggeration to regard the potential results as a form of genocide—that is, a wrongful form of sexual discrimination that reduces the relative number of females. Id. at 31. Robyn Rowland, *Motherhood, Patriarchal Power, Alienation and the Issue of "Choice" in Sex Pre-Selection*, in *Man-Made Women*, 75 (Gena Corea et al., eds., Indiana

Another predicament has to do with sociobiology.[159] Females, not males, are the limiting factor in population growth.[160] It is for this reason that the farmer keeps 25 cows and one bull, not the reverse. Any society, then, which limits its female population, is dooming itself ultimately to extinction. One reaction to this might be to adopt a "laissez-faire" attitude of "so be it": if a group of people wishes to abort females and thus eventually vanish, let them get on with it; they have the right to make such choices, and if they result in the demise of their society, there will be no one but themselves to blame. Possibly, long before group extinction, it will be realized that this behavior is not exactly pro-survival and will be ended voluntarily. If so, they will endure; if not, they will not. In either case, their fate is in their own hands.

Yet another concerns the kind of society that will be in existence roughly 20 years after such decisions are made. It will be one with hundreds of males for every female: surely a recipe for disaster, at least from a social and psychological perspective.[161] The result can only be massive homosexuality, or polyandry, or massive emigration, which will only start the problem off on another round elsewhere, if these mores are carried with them.

True, under evictionism, the "traditionalist" mothers would have chosen to evict, not abort, their female children. But this gratuitous killing of girl babies would be ended, since the ones who were evicted for this reason would grow up to be adults in any case, albeit in a test tube or host mother, not in the pregnant woman herself.

University Press 1987), refers to sex pre-selection, cloning, ectogenesis, surrogate motherhood as "...technology which could mean the death of the female."

[159] Edward O. Wilson, *Sociobiology* (Harvard University Press 1980).

[160] For the view that population growth is not a danger, for example, that there is no overpopulation threat, *see* Julian Simon, *The Ultimate Resource* (Princeton University Press 1981); Walter Block, *Population Growth: Is it a problem*? in *Resolving Global Problems into the 21st century: How Can Science Help Proceedings of the Fourth National Conference of Canadian Pugwash*, 30 (CSP Publications 1989); Daniel Coffey & Walter Block, *Postponing Armageddon: Why Population Growth Isn't Out of Control*, 15 *Humanomics* 66 (1999).

[161] Sowell tells of the Japanese males who emigrated to the United States in the nineteenth century, and were prohibited by immigration law from bringing women who might have become their wives with them. *See generally* Thomas Sowell, *Race and Economics* (Longman 1975); Thomas Sowell, *Ethnic America* (Basic Books 1981); Thomas Sowell, *The Economics and Politics of Pace: An International Perspective* (Morrow 1983).

If so, none of these difficulties would arise, not the socio-biological ones or the social and psychological. As well, the left wing woman's movement would be saved from an extremely embarrassing result, which, one might reason, would make them more receptive than otherwise to evictionism.

VII. Pragmatic Issues

Given, then, that abortion is an immoral,[162] but not legally punishable offense, what can be done, short of using the majesty of the law, to stop this monumental slaughter of human infants? Paradoxically, one must embrace the notion of evictionism, and then count upon developing technology to save these countless baby lives.

Even on a pragmatic basis, the frontal attack on abortion simply does not work. Anti-abortionists have long pleaded with the political process to stop this unconscionable slaughter—all to virtually no avail.[163] The popularity of the present law, as revealed by numerous public opinion polls, indicates, moreover, that this state of affairs is likely to continue for the foreseeable future.

The mistake has been to confront the problem totally and directly; for example, to insist upon an end to abortion. This has not worked, will not work, and at least on the moral grounds we are now defending, should

[162] An argument can be made that abortion as a last resort in the case of rape or incest, or to save the mother's life, is not immoral. But utilization of this procedure as a means of birth control hardly qualifies. However, the fetus who is a product of rape or incest is every bit as deserving of the right not to be aggressed against as any other fetus. Thus, abortion in even these cases would be unjustified according to libertarian law. Eviction, of course, would be justified for incest and rape. And the same applies to cases where the pregnant mother's life is in danger: she may evict, but not evict and then murder, for example, abort, unless medical technology is not advanced far enough to distinguish between the two. In any case, the present article is devoted not to an analysis of the moral status of abortion, but rather concerns something very different: what the law on this issue should be from the point of view of justice.

[163] One indication of the fact that the anti-abortionists are losing the battle—apart from the sheer numbers killed—is the increasingly harsh treatment to which they are subjected to by the law and police when they attempt to blockade and picket abortion centers. In some jurisdictions, for example, British Columbia, Canada, it is now illegal for peaceful pickets to come with several hundred feet of an abortion "clinic." This pro-abortion "bubble law" is in sharp contrast with labor legislation in the province; in that case, there are very few limitations on picketing.

not work. All is not lost, however, in the fight to save the poor children who have had their lives cruelly snuffed out through this process. There is an alternative that may prove successful. (Given the vast amount of good to be attained by saving the lives of fetuses, anything may well be better than current efforts).

How will embracing the evictionism analysis help with saving precious human lives? Simple. With advanced medical technology, based on breakthroughs which are even now almost an everyday occurrence, it is extremely likely that a greater and greater number of fetuses will be able to be safely transported from the (original) mother's womb to another safe and supportive place: to a surrogate mother, to the uterus of an animal, to a mechanical or laboratory contrivance ("test tube"), to some other alternative which cannot even be imagined today. Is there any doubt that this will come to pass if it has not yet already occurred—in 25, 50, or 100 years from now?

What will abortion law be like on that day? If there is little or no change from what prevails at present, the fetuses of the future will face the same fate as those today, despite the advances in medical technology that could otherwise have saved their lives.

With no distinction between eviction and abortion, and with the latter legal as it is at present, a woman who wishes to rid herself of an unwanted pre-birth child will be able to do so with impunity. Even though there are (will be) facilities standing by, which could preserve the life of her fetus, she now is and will continue to be under no legal compulsion to choose this option.

But suppose that there were a very different legal regime in operation. How would the fetus fare under laws that prohibited abortion but allowed eviction? On the assumption that this law was obeyed,[164] the unborn child would be in a far better position. For now, if its mother wanted to rid herself of him, he would be guaranteed an alternative place of incubation.[165] Previously, in contrast, the maternal decision to kill off her child would have prevailed.

[164] It would take us too far a-field to make any other assumption.

[165] This guarantee would have to be financially supported by the pro-life community, or through similar charitable, efforts. Based on the vociferous opposition to abortion, there seems little doubt that this could easily be done. According to expert estimates, the black market price for an adoption

From a pragmatic point of view, then, "pro eviction" may well be a better strategy than "pro-life." That is, if maximizing the number of babies saved is the goal,[166] it is far more likely to be attained if the pro-life forces throw their weight behind a law which allows eviction, than to remain in their present path and to continue to hold out for a law which prohibits abortion.

Why is this? There are several reasons.[167]

1. The present tactic simply is not working. Right now, despite the best efforts of all concerned, like it or not, the pro-choice movement has won out. Legal abortions may now be obtained with about as much difficulty as prescription drugs. Nor is the prognostication for any change in the foreseeable future. According to public opinion polls, an imperfect but not fully misleading indication of future legislative enactments, this cannot be denied.

It is a basic aphorism of life that when you are losing, it often pays to consider a different strategy. This applies to sports, to examination taking, to love making, to playing a musical instrument—in a word, to just about every human endeavor imaginable. It would be amazing if one arena—saving the lives of human infants—were an exception to this general rule. It is time; it is long past time that we pro-lifers at least consider the possibility that there may be a different means, which is better tailored to obtain the ultimate end—the safeguarding of innocent lives.

2. Evictionism is a compromise position. It lies part way between the status quo, where babies are slaughtered with as much compunction as we would swat a fly, and the present official goal of the pro-life move-

is some $25,000. There is little doubt that were this market legalized, a lion's share of these funds would be diverted toward saving the lives of fetuses. *See generally* Richard A. Posner, *Economic Analysis of Law, 139* (3rd ed., Little Brown 1986); Nancy C. Baker, *Baby Selling: the Scandal of Black market Adoptions* (Vanguard Press 1978).

[166] Is there any other pro-life desiderata worth mentioning in the same breath? Hardly.

[167] In this section, we particularly ignore, for argument's sake, the moral issues. We focus on only one question: which course of action will maximize the preservation of human (e.g., fetal) life. Let it not be argued that this is not a worthwhile endeavor. To be sure, morality is paramount. But such concerns should not be allowed to completely blind us to *other* monumental tasks, that is, in this case, saving life.

ment, which is to force all[168] pregnant women to carry their unborn child for nine months and then deliver them.

Under evictionism, each side gets half a loaf. The pro-lifers are assured[169] that fetuses are not done away with in a cavalier manner. Had they their 'druthers, they would also insist that the natural mother bring the baby to term after a gestation period of nine months. This, they cannot have, under the terms of the evictionism compromise.

Similarly, the pro-choicers obtain some but not all of what they want. They wish the mother not only the right to cut short the pregnancy term but also to have a life and death say over the fate of the child they bear. Under evictionism, they could only retain the former; the latter would be denied them. That is, the mother could end the pregnancy any time she wished,[170] but once she did so, the determination of life or death for her progeny would be out of her hands.

3. Moving from the present law of practically unlimited abortions, to the pro-lifers' ideal of (practically) none, is an all or none proposition. It is like betting the mortgage on one flip of the coin. It is an exceedingly high-risk strategy. If it prevails, well and good.[171] The pro-life community will have attained all it wants. If the change in law fails to occur, this movement will be pushed back to the status quo where it attains neither of its two goals (e.g., saving the fetus' life, the legitimate goal, and forcing the mother to bear the child, the illegitimate one from the libertarian point of view). Since the lives of potentially millions of babies are at stake, it may well prove better to adopt a more risk reducing stance: instead of holding out for the full loaf of bread, content oneself with half a loaf, given the greater likelihood of achieving the latter. This advice is certainly buttressed by past experience. Millions of dollars have been raised and spent. The courts have pretty much concluded, at least since

[168] In some cases, an exception would be made for the cases of rape, incest, or to save the mother's life.

[169] This is based upon the assumption, of course, of medical technological availability.

[170] As technology progresses, the time when eviction will be able to be completed safely will be extended more and more; eventually, there can be little doubt, transplants of the baby from the natural womb to a substitute will be a feasible even as late as the ninth month, and as early as a few days after conception.

[171] Well and good for the pro-lifers, that is. But not for the libertarian, for whom evictionism is not a compromise, but rather the only system fully consistent with liberty and human rights.

Roe v. Wade, that a woman has the right to abort. Thousands of protests at abortion centers have been held. A few abortionists have even been killed. But at least so far, it is safe to say, the conscience of the nation has not been changed. On the contrary, the protesters who hold the vigils are widely seen as "extremists," something that does not bode well for the prospect of saving these helpless young lives.

4. Eviction has not failed. As it happens, it has never been tried. The main reason for this is that it is almost totally unknown as an option.[172] Now it may well be that this option, too, shall fail. If so, it will not be the first time in the history of the world that justice did not prevail. But should this occur, little will have been lost. The pro-life movement will be in no worse position, life-saving wise, than now prevails. And at least we shall have had the satisfaction of striking out in a new *ex ante* promising direction. Perhaps, out of this failure, should it indeed occur, new ideas for subsequent attempts shall be born. But at this point in time, all this is a bit premature. No one knows if this strategy will succeed or not. It seems reasonable to at least give it a try, given that extant methods seem to be running up against the proverbial brick wall.

5. Eviction, even though characterized above as constituting "only half a loaf," is all that the pro-life position, properly construed, really requires or is entitled to. As the very name implies, saving lives—nothing more, nothing less—is really what the pro-life movement is all about. All else, even if compatible with this end, is simply extraneous. And if incompatible, it must be jettisoned as not only irrelevant but as a positive danger to the main goal.

There is simply no reason why pro-lifers should prefer the traditional means of giving birth. They must of course oppose abortion, but for them eviction should be a perfect substitute even for normal births. All that should matter is that the fetus be safely born. If this is done the natural way, well and good. But if this goal is achieved in *any other* way (e.g., surrogacy, etc.), it should be a matter of complete indifference to advocates of the pro-life position. Life is life is life; where it occurs is only a matter of housing.[173]

---

[172] *See* Walter Block, *Abortion, Woman and Fetus: Rights in Conflict?*, Reason 18 (April 1978).

[173] We assume, needless to say, that surrogacy "housing" is not inferior to the natural kind. Whether it is or not is an issue too far a-field to be considered here. It is also irrelevant, given our main pur-

Even were this not so, pro-lifers cannot afford to spread themselves out too thinly. There are many good deeds simply crying out to be accomplished. For this movement to spend any effort whatsoever on promoting traditional birth methods implies just that much less can be utilized on their unique mission. Actually, to do so would be a betrayal of that philosophy. Worse, if this is done in the name of pro-life and with financial resources donated to that specific cause, then it amounts to no less than fraud.

But this may be a bit of overkill. It is not clear that there is any responsible person in the pro-life community who advocates eschewing the main life-saving mission; even in part, so as to increase the likelihood of natural births. Again, it seems more reasonable to suppose that the reason both goals have been pursued in the past is due to a failure to see that there really *are* two separate and distinguishable elements in the demand that abortion be stopped: normal births and live babies.

What of the argument that the best policy may be to wait to support evictionism until the new technology kicks in? In that way the pro-life movement can, as it were, have its cake and eat it too.

This is a problematical strategy for several reasons. One, the new technology is already "kicking in." If ever this were a reasonable tactic, it is no longer so. Two, why not use the extra time to organize? The other side certainly will. Three, it will be a lot easier to convince people of evictionism if advocacy of such a position is, and is widely seen to be, a defense for its own sake rather than merely as a second best policy. Long-term advocacy is usually more effective than being a Johnny-come-lately.

What of the argument that anti-abortion will save lives now and forever more; eviction will only save lives in the future, as technology develops. Therefore, embrace anti-abortionism, not evictionism (again, eschewing morality and focusing only on life saving). This argument, too, is fallacious. First, we have witnessed the utter failure of the pro-life movement to achieve its goals. Second, under a legal system of eviction, the requisite technology will develop faster than otherwise. The anti-abortionists will only be faced with a technical problem, not a political

pose: to shed philosophical light on the implications of a private property rights analysis of abortion.

one, which they have so far been losing, with no prospect of a victory in sight.

Thus, the present stance of the pro-life forces is a highly risky one; by keeping their heads in the sand regarding evictionism, they are endangering the lives of millions of babies, the very opposite of their goal. Yes, if they win, they win right now. But if they lose, they lose forever more or at least as long as it takes to convince a majority of the pro-life anti-abortion case.

This, then, is the pragmatic case for taking on the banner of evictionism and eschewing the demand that the natural mother be forced to carry the fetus for nine months and then give birth to it. Had the pro-lifers seen the difference between these two very different claims say, 50 years ago, it is just possible that many infants consigned to death today would already be saved. That was not to be. However, if a sea change can occur today, fetuses of the future may be spared the fate suffered by all too many at present.

If evictionism were to be instituted at present, at one fell swoop, one-ninth or perhaps two-ninths of all babies would be immediately saved. Partial birth abortions would immediately become a thing of the past. Moreover, within a few years, a third ninth of babies could be saved, as medical technology is enhanced. And so on. This process would continue until *all* fetuses would be kept alive.

VIII. Implications

In this section, we explore the implications of the libertarian eviction theory for several related issues and questions.

1. Suppose Eviction Costs More than Abortion; Who Pays?

If it costs more to engage in this technology, there is no positive obligation for the mother to pay the extra amount. This should be done by the Church or a group called the Friends of Babies or some pro-life type of group specifically set up for, and devoted to, this very purpose. However, the individual does have the obligation to make use of such modern technology. Consider a pregnant woman who refuses to avail herself of medical breakthroughs.[174] She has the right to refrain on her own accounts but not to kill (e.g., make it impossible for someone else, with a test tube incubator) her child.

2. Evictionism more dangerous

Suppose eviction is more dangerous than abortion, should the mother be forced to undergo the former procedure? No, not a bit of it. The libertarian position is a true compromise, as it happens; some things go one way, others things not. On this issue, the private property analysis sides with the pro-choicers. Under libertarianism, there are no positive obligations. Thus, the mother is only to be forced to undergo an eviction procedure (on the assumption that she prefers aborting her child) when there is no increase in hazard to herself.

3. What Should Be the Legal Status of RU-486?

The abortion pill is known as RU-486 in France and a combination of mifepristone and misoprostol in the United States. But whatever its name, it has been declared by our Food and Drug Administration to be safe, effective, and relatively risk free. The controversy surrounding this drug, however, arises from none of these sources. Instead, it emanates from the fact that this drug works not by making it impossible for the egg and sperm to come together, but, rather, by in effect killing off the fertilized egg, otherwise known as the fetus.

Our position on this drug should by now be clear. In the past, when fetal outplacement was impossible, the RU-486 was the most gentle (well, no more invasive than any other form of eviction) form of ridding the woman of an unwanted fetus. Therefore, it was justified. In the future, when it will be technologically feasible to more gently remove the fetus from the womb without harming it or the mother, use of this drug would be considered murder. At the present day—is not it ever this way?—things are more complicated. Our own technological knowledge admits of no answer to this question. But at least we have a principle to guide us through this moral thicket: if and to the extent, outward transfer is possible, then and to that extent the drug should be prohibited for pregnant women.

[174] Shades of Jehovah's Witnesses.

Of course, an eviction pill, not an abortion pill, would be totally justified. That is, medicine, which results in the expelling of a healthy fetus (able to be hosted by a surrogate), would be entirely compatible with libertarian law.

4. Child Abuse

What about preventing the pregnant mother from the "child abuse" of drinking wine or smoking cigarettes?

This is hard to answer, given the present medical uncertainty about the harm committed thereby. Instead, take a more radical case,[175] for which no one can be found who would deny that the substance harms the fetus: crack. If giving crack to an infant would amount to child abuse, then the same conclusion must be reached for the fetus. But abuse for a child, under libertarianism, would imply at the very least [176] that the victim be forcibly removed if by doing so the situation of the fetus would improve.

5. Does the Pregnant Woman Have the Right to Commit Suicide?

In the ordinary case, the answer is clear. Since libertarianism prohibits only the initiation of violence against another person or his property, and since suicide is violence against the self, not another person, this form of killing is legally justified.[177] Dr. Kevorkian would not be incarcerated in a libertarian society.

When the pregnant woman commits suicide, however, she of course ends the life of a person other than herself. Does this count as the initiation of violence against another person? Not at all, since the fetus, as we have seen, is the aggressor, trespassing on *her* property, that is, herself.

---

[175] Or assume for the sake of argument that for a pregnant woman to indulge in alcohol or cigarette smoking constitutes child abuse.

[176] For libertarian punishment theory in general, *see* Murray N. Rothbard, *The Ethics of Liberty* (Humanities Press 1982); Murray N. Rothbard, *For a New Liberty: The Libertarian Manifesto* (Collier Macmillan 1973); *Assessing the Criminal* (Randy Barnett & John Hagel eds., Balinger 1977). Specifically, the punishment for child abusers should be even more severe than that accorded those who engage in such attacks upon adults, if only because of their greater helplessness and dependency.

[177] Not morally however. On this, *see* Walter Block, *Libertarianism vs. Libertinism*, 11 J. Libertarian Stud.: An Interdisciplinary Rev. 117 (1994). For an alternative anti-libertarian view on suicide, *see* Milton Friedman, *Say "No" to Intolerance*, 4 Liberty Mag. 17 (1991).

In the past, when there was no possibility of preserving a fetus outside the mother's womb, the libertarian would have placed no legal barriers in the way of her suicide. Nowadays, of course, the position is a bit unclear. However, in the future, when medical technology allows for eviction, the mother must be prevented by law from committing suicide *before* transferring her child to another host. She cannot be kept waiting, certainly not for nine months or so. On the other hand, for reasons discussed below under the heading of "positive obligations," she can be kept waiting for a "reasonable" amount of time, for example, a few hours, analogous to her duty to inform others of a child available for adoption.

Of course, there is a distinct limit to the effectiveness of legal sanctions for those who wish to commit suicide. As a practical matter, pregnant women in that position will presumably do exactly as they please. But our task is to clarify what the law should be, and in this case, it would prohibit suicide until an eviction team can be (reasonably quickly) brought to bear.

IX. Objections

With these remarks, we have now presented the case for evictionism, the compromise between the pro-life (no eviction allowed) and the pro-choice (killing is allowed, even when not required to evict) positions. It now remains for us to defend this perspective against criticisms. As with all moderate philosophies, the libertarian must vindicate itself vis-à-vis objections from not one, but both of the other two sides of this debate. It is to this task that we now turn.

1. Transplant Analogy Misses the Mark

Some might object to the kidney "transplant" analogy on the ground that the woman is responsible for the pregnancy and must bear the full consequences of the act responsible for this state of affairs, while Mr. A, Thompson's violinist who lacks a kidney, is a completely innocent party. But the woman, conceivably, could be ignorant of the causes of pregnancy; many were, in previous centuries. As well, the mother who was victimized by rape has in no way consented. And yet, her child has the same rights as all other children conceived in voluntary circumstances.

Even on the assumption that the woman voluntarily agreed to engage in sexual intercourse, knowing full well that it might result in pregnancy, it by no means follows that she should be forced to bear the child to term. Under the libertarian code of law, we may be punished only for initiating violence against a nonaggressor, or for contract breaking, which amounts to the same thing. Yet, it is the unwanted fetus, not the mother, who is "initiating violence" by trespassing on private property (the womb). As for contract breaking, if the mother were paid to have a child by the father or by a third party, then and only then would eviction or abortion constitute a rights violation, not of the fetus but of the person who paid her. At the point of intercourse, there was simply no child or fetus in existence with whom she could have contracted, assuming that a person of such tender age would be in a position to engage in an agreement in the first place.

Further, there is something perverse in interpreting the requirement that people take responsibility for what they do in this manner. If a pregnant woman cannot evict her fetus on such a ground, what of the person who ate too many French fries? Logic would imply the illegitimacy of him obtaining an angioplasty. For if you eat too many fatty foods you are on your way toward having a heart attack, availing yourself of a coronary bypass or other such operation would be to fail to "take responsibility" for your initial actions. This is an obvious bit of nonsense. Yet, precisely this argument applies to the eviction case.

2. Positive Obligations

Another argument against the libertarian view is that it amounts to a demand for positive obligations.

Before confronting this charge head on, let us place it in context. Our claim, here, is that if we are indeed guilty of making an exception to the general libertarian stricture against positive obligations, it is a very narrow and limited one. All that is required is that the pregnant woman notifies an evictionist that she wishes to rid herself of the fetus. In the case of the post-birth child, the "positive" requirement would be that the parent not simply hides the child in an attic or basement and refuse to feed it until it dies. Instead, the "obligation" is to engage in a public notification (to the newspaper or radio or church or orphanage or evictionist) to the effect that the parent in question no longer wishes to support his child. It is only if no one else in the entire world desires to take charge of the baby that it may legitimately die of neglect, under the libertarian code.

But even such a minimalist exception is still incompatible with the prohibition against compulsory Good Samaritanism. In order to see why such a charge does not apply, we must be clear on the relationship between parents and children under libertarianism.[178] A child falls part way between animals or land and other people. One may not own other adults; slavery represents an initiation of violence.[179] One may own animals and real estate outright, after homesteading[180]—mixing one's labor with them. After the homesteading period is over, ownership is no longer conditional; it applies even to absentee owners. With regard to children, the intermediate case, one may not own them outright; one may own the right to raise them, by homesteading, or mixing labor with them, or by hiring others to do so in one's stead; but here, all one owns is the right to continue this process. Once the support of children (whether in the womb or not) ceases, however, any rights of parenthood cease. One may abandon a child, but if so, gives up all rights pertaining thereto. There is no such thing as an absentee parent; once parental duties are relinquished, parental rights vanish.

---

[178] Bill Kauffman, *The Child Labor Amendment Debate of the 1920's; or, Catholics and Mugwumps and Farmers*, 10 J. of Libertarian Stud. 139 (Fall 1992); Williamson M. Evers, *Rawls and children*, 2 J. Libertarian Stud. 109 (Summer 1978); Williamson M. Evers, *The law of omissions and neglect of children*, 2 J. Libertarian Stud. 1 (Winter 1978); Walter Block, *The Employer of Child Labor*, in *Defending the Undefendable*, 247 (Fleet Press 1976); Murray N. Rothbard, *The Ethics of Liberty*, 97–112 (Humanities Press 1982).

[179] For an analysis of "voluntary slavery," *see* Walter Block, *Voluntary Slavery*, 1 The Libertarian Connection 9 (Apr. 1969); Walter Block, *Toward a Libertarian Theory of Inalienability: A Critique of Rothbard, Barnett, Gordon, Smith, Kinsella and Epstein*, 17 J. Libertarian Stud. (Spring 2003); Walter Block, *Alienability, Inalienability, Paternalism and the Law: Reply to Kronman*, 28 Am. J. Crim. L. 351 (Summer 2001); Walter Block, *Market Inalienability Once Again: Reply to Radin*, 22 Thomas Jefferson L. Rev., 37 (Fall 1999).

[180] John Locke, *An Essay Concerning the True Origin, Extent and End of Civil Government*, in *Two Treatises of Government*, 17 (P. Laslett ed., Cambridge University Press 1960); Hans-Hermann Hoppe, *The Economics and Ethics of Private Property: Studies in Political Economy and Philosophy* (Kluwer 1993); Murray N. Rothbard, *The Ethics of Liberty* (Humanities Press 1982); Murray N. Rothbard, *For a New Liberty: The Libertarian Manifesto*, (Collier Macmillan 1973).

So, what are we to say of a parent who no longer wishes to support his child's life, indeed, wishes for death for the child, and acts in this manner by hiding and failing to feed it, yet refuses to relinquish command of the child? This would appear to be as clear a case of murder as ever there was. Thus, it is not a positive obligation at all to be required to notify the public that you are about to relinquish your control over what was previously your baby. Once you stop caring for it, the child is no longer yours.

In effect, if not explicitly, when you took over the care of the baby,[181] you assented to an implicit obligation requiring you to continue to do so or to notify someone else of this fact. To fail to do so thus smacks of rights violation,[182] rather than being forced to assume a positive obligation.[183]

There are more pragmatic ways of reconciling the absence of "positive obligations" with saving a baby's life: medical technology once more rides to the rescue. When and if there is a way to evict the baby which is no more harmful, inconvenient, costly (or to pay the differential to the mum), risky, whatever; then, she should not be allowed to legally refuse the eviction, and we *still* do not have to concede that there are positive obligations placed on her.

Are there any positive obligations incumbent upon the kidney host person in the Thompson example? He cannot stab the kidney dependent violinist, but can he unhook the connection without so much as a by your leave? As a matter of practicality, as a nonphysician, if he just cut the

---

[181] Pre- or post-birth.

[182] This way of putting the matter would not apply to the rape victim or to Thompson's forced host to the violinist. *See* Judith Jarvis Thompson, *Rights, Restitution and Risk* (Harvard University Press 1986).

[183] Hiding a newborn baby and starving it to death is akin to giving up land, but refusing to allow another homesteader access. Is the abandoner of the land really required to notify others of this fact? No, ordinarily, but then, land does not exactly have the same rights as people, at least under the libertarian code of law. But yes, the abandoner of land most certainly has the obligation of publicly notifying people of his new non- ownership status if he has put up no trespassing signs, fences, and so on, on his (ex)holdings. This is because if he refuses to do so, he is actively preventing others from claiming non-owned land. In keeping the baby (land), but not allowing anyone else to homestead (own) it, you are in effect pre-empting the rights of others to do so. No one may properly prevent others from homesteading virgin territory. A person who sets up a fence around a square mile of land, does not himself homestead, work, or even claim the territory internal to that perimeter, and yet prevents others from so doing, is pre-empting virgin territory, contrary to homesteading theory. It is our claim that the parent who will not care for his child, and yet prevents other from doing so by hiding the baby from them, is guilty of a similar crime.

cord, *both* host and parasite[184] would likely die. As a result, he must get to a hospital or doctor to do the unhooking; and while the medical team does that, they can connect the parasite to another host or to a dialysis machine. But suppose the host is also a skilled physician in his own right. Then, by assumption, he can do the uncoupling all by his lonesome. Would he be guilty of murder if he did so (without giving even as much as a five-minute warning to the violinist)? Our answer is that he would be guilty of murder. He would be doing far more than acting in mere self-defense. He would not be removing the (innocent) predator in the gentlest manner possible.

3. Returning Stolen Property

Consider another criticism that could be leveled against the eviction theory. This one charges an incompatibility between the libertarian position on abortion and on the ethics of stolen property.[185] What is the latter claim?

Suppose that A is the rightful owner of a VCR. For the Lockean, he built it out of materials available to all in nature.[186] For the Nozickian, he traded for it using other property or labor services to which he was entitled.[187] For the Marxist, A was the legitimate owner of the VCR because this was his share of the communal labor effort.[188] No matter what the justification, we assume that A had legitimate proprietary rights over this machine. B, then, comes upon the scene and steals the VCR away from A, whereupon he sells it to C, offering a fake bill of sale. C is totally innocent, at least in terms of *mens rea*; C is not a fence, not the knowing purchaser of stolen goods. On the contrary, C, too, like A, is a victim.

We, the forces of good or of law and order, now come upon the scene. We are the observer from on high. We know that the scenario as depicted above is correct. Unfortunately, there are limits to our powers. Justice

---

[184] "Parasite" has such a "bad press" in our common lexicon that we hesitate to imply this word to describe the fetus or kidney-dependent person. Yet, the appellation fits, fully. We use it in the hope and expectation that the reader can uncouple the negative pejoratives usually associated with this phase, and concentrate solely on the property rights relationships.

[185] This was argued, forcefully, by Patrick English.

[186] John Locke, *An Essay Concerning the True Origin, Extent and End of Civil Government*, in *Two Treatises of Government*, 17 (P. Laslett ed., Cambridge University Press 1960).

[187] Robert Nozick, *Anarchy, State, and Utopia* (Basic Books 1974).

[188] Karl Marx, *Capital* (Modern Lib 1906).

would consist of our seizing of B, and forcing him to remit the funds he had mulcted from C, and returning the VCR to A, the rightful owner. As it happens, however, while our knowledge of these occurrences is impeccable, B has eluded us; he is not to be found. All that remain to us is the VCR, now in C's possession, and A, the rightful owner, who looks longingly at his property now held by C.

What is the just course of action? C objects to our transferring of this property from himself to A on the ground that he, C, purchased it in good faith from B. He even has the contract to prove it. Unfortunately, for him, this contract was drawn by B, the admitted thief. It seems clear under these circumstances that C is out of luck.[189] The VCR must be taken out of his hands and put into those of A, the original owner. Were B ever to be found, C would have recourse to him; since B by stipulation is unavailable, C must bear the loss.

Where is the analogy to abortion? Here, B is the rapist who, unfortunately, escapes justice. But which is which as far as A and C are concerned? Who must bear the cost of the "theft": the mother or the fetus?

The right-to-life critic of the eviction theory maintains that it is the fetus which properly takes on the role of A and the mother, C. That is, given that someone must suffer an uncompensated loss (because the guilty party, B, the one from whom any compensation would be derived, has disappeared), it should be the mother. She should be forced to bear the child until her pregnancy is terminated with a birth. Yes, she is guiltless; totally. The victim of a rape cannot be construed in any manner, shape, or form as having agreed to give birth to a child. She is as innocent as C, as in the previous case. And this is precisely the point; when B absconds, whether the rapist or the thief, *someone* must endure an uncompensated loss. This stems from the nature of reality. Innocent people must sometimes be forced to bear losses, and the case of rape is one such.

There is, however, a reply available to the evictionist: A is really the mother, and C is really the fetus. It is thus the latter, not the former, who must be forced to endure the uncompensated loss. Why is the mother really the A (rightful owner of the VCR) of our story? This is because it is

---

[189] We assume there is no theft insurance policy in effect; otherwise, it is the insurance company which is left holding the bag.

she, and she alone, who is the rightful owner of the property in question, the womb.

4. Endangerment

Here is another argument for preventing the pregnant woman from evicting her fetus. This, presumably, would apply under a state of technology that allows for viable evictions or under the lack thereof.[190]

The claim is that the pregnant woman is not quite the innocent victim some theories might see her as. On the contrary, she endangered the fetus by giving it life. That is, merely by conceiving of the fetus, she put it in danger.[191]

Ordinarily, for this libertarian view, there are no positive obligations. Good Samaritan laws compelling a person to save someone else's life are illegitimate. However, if you first endanger a person, say, by throwing him in the path of a car, *then* it becomes legally incumbent upon you to pull the victim away, out of the path of the onrushing car.[192]

Although clever—too clever by half—this argument fails.

Getting pregnant is not equivalent to endangering a person. Rather, it is enhancing the person, or creating him de novo, by giving him life. The danger, if danger there be, comes not from being pregnant but from being evicted (rather, being aborted).

What is the proper analogy to getting pregnant and then evicting? This is akin to first pushing someone out of the path of an onrushing car

---

[190] It is an element of moral reasoning that it be timeless in this sense. That is, applicable to all state of the world, epochs, levels of technological development. Murder is wrong in the past of cave man days, at the present, and in the future of space-man days. Were this not to apply, we could scarcely hold murder to be ethically proscribed. On this, *see* Walter Block, *Neglect of the Marketplace: The Questionable Economics of America's Bishops*, 2 Notre Dame J.L. Ethics & Pub. Policy 125 (1985); Walter Block, *The U.S. Bishops and Their Critics: An Economic and Ethical Perspective* (The Fraser Inst. 1986).

[191] It is now subject to the risk that the mother might rid herself of it and either kill it (before the advent of eviction) or discomfort it (by making it move to a presumably less preferable locale). In contrast, presumably, before conception, the fetus (does it even make sense to speak of a fetus before fertilization?) was in no such "danger."

[192] This argument was made to the senior author by Karen Selick. According to Orson Scott Card & Kathryn H. Kidd, *Lovelock*, 281 (Tor Books 1994), "I also have a responsibility to protect it from all harm, because I brought it to life…" The character Lovelock makes this statement with regard to the baby Faith in this novel, under conditions while not exactly the same as we are discussing, are eerily similar.

(where death would have been certain—as certain as not getting pregnant would not give life to this particular person) and then, pushing so hard that you push the saved person in an adjacent lake, whereupon he starts to drown. The "victim" then complains, "Hey, you pushed me into the lake, you are therefore required to get me out of here."[193] The proper response is that if we get you out of the lake it will be over and above the call of duty; we do not owe it to you. The proper interpretation of our act is not "endangering you," but rather "saving your life," at least for the few seconds between being pushed out of the way of the car and the time when you fell into the lake.

This defense of eviction succeeds easily when the extant level of technology allows for the saving of the baby's life in a test tube or host mother. Here, by stipulation, the evicting mother is not at all endangering the baby; rather, she is merely transferring it to another "home." But what about the case when medical technology is not sufficiently developed to achieve this end? Then, is not the eviction identical to the abortion? And can it be seriously denied that an abortion harms or endangers the fetus?

Our reply is that when the mother conceived the baby, gave it life, the correct way to look upon this act is as if she pushed a person away from the path of an onrushing car. In so doing, the erstwhile victim of the automobile is pushed into the lake, where he proceeds to drown. It would be nice if the rescuer thereupon went into the lake to perform a further life-saving effort; this would be virtuous; this would be highly moral. But in a libertarian society of no positive obligations, there can be no legal requirement toward this end. Similarly, after giving the fetus the boon of life, it would be highly desirable if the mother were to carry through with nine months of pregnancy and then further support until the child reached adulthood. This would be nice; this would be moral; this would be virtuous; this would be ideal. But it is simply not legally required, at least in a libertarian society.

5. "Plucking"

Consider the following:

> Close your eyes for a moment and imagine that, due to advances in medical technology or mutation caused by a nuclear war, the relevant cutaneous and

[193] For example, "Hey, you got pregnant with me, you created my life, you endangered me, you have to save me now."

membranous shields became transparent from conception to parturition, so that when a mother put aside her modesty and her clothing the developing fetus would be in full public view. Or suppose, instead, or in addition, that anyone could at any time pluck a fetus from its womb, air it, observe it, fondle it, and then stick it back in after a few minutes. What then would we think of aborting a fetus? And what does that say about what you now think?[194]

Obviously, men of good will would change what they now think about abortion and be more likely to embrace libertarian evictionism. If the fetus is viable at any time out there on its own, then how can killing it be just? Evicting it, when the mother no longer wishes to be burdened by it, yes, however morally repugnant; but out and out murder? Not at all.

This, unfortunately, is not at all the conclusion self-styled feminists wish to draw from Wertheimer's plucking scenario. On the contrary, they recoil in horror from so reasonable an inference. States Overall:

Wertheimer predicted that if the developing embryo/fetus could be viewed and manipulated, attitudes toward it would change. About this he was quite correct; but what he did not foresee was that those changes might be morally undesirable. As the capacity to manipulate the embryo/fetus grows, the increasing tendency to commodify it and to view it as a work of art or an ongoing experiment should be resisted. Instead of treating the embryo/fetus as a distinct, separate, independent entity, it should be seen in a more holistic fashion as connected with its mother, who is not a danger to it but the source of its ongoing sustenance.[195]

Seldom have more fallacies and refusal to face reality been packed into a smaller paragraph. First, Wertheimer's point was not at all that the baby would be seen as an art or an experiment; rather, it was to save its life by arguing against abortion. Second, commoditization[196] has nothing whatever to do with the case.[197] Whether the pre-birth adoption would be

[194] Roger Wertheimer, *Understanding the Abortion Argument*, 1 Phil. and Pub. Affairs 86 (1971); cited in Christine Overall, 1987. *Ethics and Human Reproduction: A Feminist Analysis*, 40 (Allen & Unwin).

[195] Overall, infra footnote 205 at 61.

[196] For another viciously anti-commercial creed, *see* Patricia Baird, *Proceed with Care: Final Report of the Royal Commission on New Reproductive Technologies*, 2 volumes, Ottawa, Canada: Minister of government Services, 1993.

[197] For another unwarranted attack on commoditization, *see* Margaret Jane Radin, *Market-Inalienability* 100 Harv. L. Rev. 1849 (June 1987). For a reply *see* Walter Block, *Market Inalienability*

done for money or not is entirely irrelevant.[198] Third, the essence of the argument was that under this scenario, for the first time, the young human being need *not* be seen as part and parcel of the mother; remember, with modern or perhaps futuristic technology, it will be able to do quite nicely outside of her womb. Therefore, the genetic or natural or even host mother is no longer a (necessary) "source of its ongoing sustenance." Last, and most important, the mother of the fetus most certainly is "a danger to it," specifically in the case where she wishes to abort her child.

6. Parental Rights

There is an argument against mere eviction, as opposed to abortion, which claims that the parents have the right not to bring life forth unless they wish to do so. This point is made most forcefully by Ross who states: "The fetus is the only thing that someone—a parent—may with equal comprehensibility and legitimacy want dead."[199] He defends this perspective on the grounds that parents have such an intimate relationship with their offspring:

> If upon entering a clinic women were told, 'We can take the fetus out of your womb without any harm to you or it, keep it alive elsewhere for nine months, and then see it placed in a good home, many would, understandably, be quite unsatisfied. What they want is not to be saved from the 'inconvenience of pregnancy' or 'the task of raising a certain (existing) child'; what they want is *not to be parents*, that is, they do not want there to *be* a child they fail or succeed in raising. Are these people monsters? Hardly. Certainly anyone who wants the violinist they unplug themselves from, or a full-grown child they abandon, dead *is* incomprehensibly malicious. But it is precisely because our relationship to the fetus is not like either of these that the desire it be dead makes sense.[200]

Once Again: Reply to Radin, 22 *Thomas Jefferson L. Rev.* 37 (Fall 1999).

[198] The presumption, however, is that if an act is legally justified, then it is licit whether done for money or not. True, there are some things that by their very nature cannot be done on a commercial basis. For example, it is a logical contradiction to pay for the true friendship or true love. For there to *be* true friendship or true love, it cannot be done for money. However, in every other case, if something is legitimate to do for free, it is legitimate to do for profit.

[199] Steven L. Ross, *Abortion and the Death of the Fetus*, 11 Phil. and Pub. Affairs 236 (1982).

[200] Id. at 238.

Elsewhere, Ross maintains, "one can simply want there to be no child at all," and describes this as "a deeply felt personal preference subscribed to by some, yet intelligible to all."[201]

Well, it may be intelligible to most of us, at least to all those who have ever wished someone else dead. But mere intelligibility is hardly sufficient to establish a just legal code. If it were, we would have to repeal the law against murder.[202]

Overall provides a good antidote to the excesses of Ross. She maintains, "This kind of feeling does not justify killing the embryo/fetus."[203] Why not? Because for Overall, "the mother does not own (the fetus) and therefore is not entitled to have it killed."[204] This is precisely in keeping with the libertarian view of the matter. There, the mother can only own the right to continue to parent the baby and can do so only by continuing this practice. Once she stops this support of her child, let alone wants to kill the fetus, all of her "homesteading" rights over it cease forthwith.

Overall, although she clearly sees the errors of Ross and Englehardt, unfortunately does not accept the entire libertarian package. For one thing, she balks in the case of the "embryo/fetus (which) is irretrievably deformed or damaged by the abortion process."[205] For another, she rejects "embryo adoption" because "at all points during pregnancy (it) is not yet technically possible and in any case raises its own moral problems: Should all aborted embryo/fetuses be candidates for adoption? What about those

---

[201] Id. For a view supportive of Ross', *see* Tristam H. Englehardt, Jr., *Viability and the Use of the Fetus*, in *Ethics and Public Policy*, 307 (Tom Beauchamp & Terry P. Pinkard eds., Prentice-Hall 1980).

[202] What should be the legal status of those who physically interfere with abortionists (this analysis is limited to cases where eviction is possible) that is, either by destroying abortion centers, or killing abortionists? States Rothbard, *The Ethics of Liberty* at 77, "…if every man has the right to defend his person and property against attack, then he must also have the right to hire or accept the aid of other people to do such defending: he may employ or accept defenders just as he may employ or accept the volunteer services of gardeners on his lawn." Extrapolating from this, the implication is that, while the fetus is in no position to "employ or accept defenders," defenders may indeed come to the aid of those who are about to be murdered. Thus, it would be entirely appropriate, according to our understanding of the libertarian legal code, to kill those in the act of murdering fetuses and/or to destroy the means they use to this end, for example, abortion clinics. But remember the caveat: this applies *only* to cases where eviction is not an option; otherwise, the mother's property rights in her own person take precedence.

[203] Overall, *Ethics and Human Reproduction: A Feminist Analysis* at 81.

[204] Id. at 82.

[205] Id.

with defects? What women should be able to become their adoptive mothers? How should the decision be made?"[206]

We cannot deny that these are reasonable questions. But they all have libertarian answers. Yes, all aborted embryo/fetuses should be candidates for adoption. This should include those with defects. Only if not a single solitary person on the whole earth wants to adopt such an infant should it be allowed to die. (This is surely unlikely in the extreme, unless the entire pro-life movement is totally hypocritical.) Any woman (or man) should be allowed to become the adoptive parent, provided of course that the laws against child abuse be strictly upheld.[207] The decision should be made by the institution called upon by the pregnant woman (upon pain of violating the law) to do so. Presumably, this would be a hospital, or a church, or some other organization set up to undertake such actions. Nor (contrary to Overall) would there be any law in the free society preventing the highest money bidder from becoming the adoptive parent.

X. Conclusion

We have attempted to explain the pro-life and pro-choice positions and to discuss their strong and weak points. We described a compromise, called evictionism, and showed how it is a true intermediary between the two more well-known positions on abortion. We have demonstrated how it can be justified, while they cannot.

The key to the solution is to focus on the private property rights in question. In this case, it is the mother's womb; given that the fetus is unwanted, it is in effect a trespasser, or a parasite. The mother, then, has a right to evict it—in the gentlest manner possible—but not to kill it, if technology permits her not to do so.

What remains, on a practical level, is to enact legislation based on this libertarian philosophy. That, in our opinion, constitutes the last best hope for saving millions of innocents from merciless slaughter, without in the slightest violating the rights of any pregnant woman.

---

[206] Id. at 84.

[207] In the libertarian society, such behavior would be subject to very severe negative sanction; presumably, less of it will therefore occur.

16

The IRS Joins the Boardroom

I. Introduction

The First Circuit Court of Appeals in *United States v. Textron*, No. 07-2631, issued a critically important tax decision giving the Internal Revenue Service (IRS) access to Textron's tax accrual planning work papers. The case is a major victory for the IRS and in effect gives this government agency a seat in the room when tax accrual work papers are prepared. In *Textron*, the Court held En Banc[1] that the taxpayer could not, in response to an IRS summons, withhold from production to the IRS its tax accrual work papers under the long-recognized work product doctrine.[2] The decision, which reversed the district court, was reached by

[1] That is, by the full court.

[2] See on this: Anderson, Jeff A.; Cadieux, Gina E.; Hays, George, E.; Hingerty, Michael B. 1982–1983. "Work Product Doctrine." Cornell Law Review, 68, pp. 762–881; http://heinonline.org/HOL/Page?handle=hein.journals/clqv68&div=50&g_sent=1&collection=journals#. Cohn, Sherman L. 1982–1983. "The Work-Product Doctrine: Protection, Not Privilege." Georgetown Law Journal 71, pp. 917–989. Allen, Ronald J., Mark F. Grady, Daniel D. Polsby and Michael S. Yashko. 1990. "A Positive Theory of the Attorney-Client Privilege and the Work Product Doctrine." *The Journal of Legal Studies*, Vol. 19, No. 2 (June), pp. 359–397; http://www.jstor.org/stable/724425?seq=1#page_scan_tab_contents. Giesel, Grace M. 2012. "Alternative Litigation

W. E. Block, R. Whitehead, *Philosophy of Law*, Palgrave Studies in Classical Liberalism,
https://doi.org/10.1007/978-3-030-28360-5_16

a narrow margin of a five judge panel, with three judges representing the majority over the two judges, who wrote the dissenting opinion.

This decision was troubling to a number of large corporations and corporate counsel because it chills the taxpayer's thorough analysis of the accounting and legal implications of financial decision making by placing those corporate thought processes directly into the hands of the IRS. Textron filed a Writ of Certiorari with the U.S. Supreme Court. Textron's writ was supported by an unusually large number of friends of the court briefs filed on its behalf by corporations and organizations such as the U.S. Chamber of Commerce, the Washington Legal Foundation, the International Civil Defense Lawyers, the U.S. Steel Corporation, the Product Liability Advisory Council, and Graybar Electric Company. Many commentators expected the high court to take the case to resolve the issues we will discuss in this article. To the surprise of many accountants and lawyers, the high court recently decided not to hear the case, *Textron v. United States*.[3] The failure of the high court to do so will clearly encourage the IRS to continue to aggressively seek access to the information provided by the taxpayer to its accountants, auditors, and lawyers. The case is clearly a game changer in civil tax litigation because it invites the government into the corporation's financial planning conferences.

In this chapter, we explore the critical question of what did the Textron case hold and what can the taxpayer do to protect his work papers. Clearly, the First Circuit majority was not impressed by Textron's argument that tax accrual work papers are protected from disclosure by the work product doctrine. This case has severely limited the taxpayer's protection from discovery under the work product doctrine by the finding that it does not apply when there is a statutory requirement that the papers be prepared under securities law and that the taxpayer's primary motive is an unqualified audit opinion. The Court was not receptive to an argument that accrual work papers can have a dual purpose that includes both the ordinary course of business and the possibility of future litigation. The Court was greatly influenced by the practical problems

---

Finance and the Work-Product Doctrine." *Wake Forest Law Review*, Vol. 47, No. 5, https://papers.ssrn.com/sol3/papers.cfm?abstract_id=2220983.

[3] Sup. Ct. no. 09-750 (5/24/2010).

faced by the IRS in discovering the underreporting of corporate taxes which the Court complained was endemic. The Court said it was fair and in the public interest for the IRS to have access to these papers to insure the proper collection of taxes. The Court was also influenced by the fact that the IRS was investigating nine leveraged lease transactions entered into by Textron that were the same or substantially similar to the Sale-In/Lease-Out ("SILO").[4]

II. Background

This article discusses the question of whether the work product doctrine shields from an Internal Revenue Service (IRS) summons the tax accrual work papers prepared by lawyers, accountants, and others in Textron's tax department. The work papers were prepared to support Textron's calculation of tax reserves for its audited corporate financial statements. Textron is a major aerospace and defense conglomerate, with well over 100 subsidiaries, whose consolidated tax return is audited by the IRS on a regular basis. Textron is required by federal securities law to have public financial statements certified by an independent auditor. To comply with the securities law financial reporting requirements, Textron must calculate the reserves to be entered on the company's books to account for contingent tax liabilities. Contingent liabilities necessarily include estimates of potential tax liability if the IRS decides to challenge debatable positions taken by the taxpayer. An independent auditor, in this case Ernst & Young, then examines the work papers to determine the reasonableness and adequacy of Textron's reserve account for contingent tax liabilities. Tax accrual work papers are obviously a valuable resource for the Internal Revenue Service because they pinpoint the soft spots in the corporation's tax return and provide an item by item analysis of the corporation's potential exposure to additional tax liability.

The present case began with the 2003 IRS audit of Textron's liability for the years 1998–2001. The IRS issued a summons to examine all of Textron's books, papers, records, or other data which may be relevant or

[4]Transactions listed in Notice 2005–2013 ("listed transactions").

material to the inquiry involving the SILO transactions. The summons also asked for related work papers created by Ernst & Young when reviewing the adequacy of Textron's reserves.

Textron challenged the summons as lacking a legitimate purpose and claimed that the attorney-client, tax practitioner privilege, and a qualified privilege for litigation materials based on the work product doctrine, protected the material from disclosure. Textron claimed that the real effect of the summons would be to allow the IRS access to materials that might result in litigation. Unconvinced, the IRS brought an enforcement action in Federal District Court in Rhode Island.

The District Court decided the papers were protected by the work product privilege. It concluded that the work papers were prepared "because of" the prospect of litigation. On appeal, a divided panel of the First Circuit upheld the District Court's decision. The First Circuit then granted the government's petition for a re-hearing En Blanc, vacated the panel decision, and obtained additional briefs from the parties and interested friends of the court. Let us now turn to the En Blanc decision.

III. Discussion

There were four decisive questions that arose during the First Circuit's En Blanc review of the Textron case. First, does the work product doctrine only apply to materials that are expressly prepared for litigation? What if the documents are prepared as a necessary part of the ordinary course of business? Second, may tax accrual work papers qualify for work product protection? Third, does the fear of making tax accrual materials available to the IRS discourage sound preparation of the work papers? And, fourth, is it somehow unfair for the government to have access to the taxpayer's tax accrual spreadsheets?

The work product privilege arose from the Supreme Court's decision in *Hickman v. Taylor*,[5] and focuses on the materials lawyers typically prepare for the purpose of actually litigating cases. The *Hickman* case concerned on-going litigation in which one side filed a discovery request

[5] 329 U.S. 495 (1947), at 510–11.

seeking from opposing counsel memorandum concerning witness interviews that had been conducted after receiving notice of possible litigation. The Court pointed out that *Hickman v. Taylor* addressed "the extent to which a party may inquire into oral and written statements of witnesses, or other information, secured by an adverse party's counsel in the course of preparation of possible litigation after a claim has arisen." *Hickman* described the work product doctrine as protecting documents that "are prepared in anticipation of litigation or for trial." Here, said the Second Circuit panel, the critical difference between *Hickman* and *Textron* is that the immediate motive of Textron in preparing the tax accrual work papers was to fix the amount of tax reserves on their books and to obtain an unqualified financial opinion from the auditor. Just because the taxpayer wants to be adequately reserved for possible tax liability does not necessarily mean that the taxpayer is preparing for litigation. Finally, of great importance to the reviewing court was that the district trial judge did not say the accrual work papers were prepared for use in possible litigation.

The Appellate Court found that it is not enough to trigger the work product doctrine protection that the subject matter of the document related to a subject that might conceivable be litigated. Rather, as the U.S. Supreme Court has explained, "the literal language of the work products doctrine means that it protects materials prepared for any litigation or trial as long as they are prepared by a party to the subsequent litigation," see *Federal Trade Commission v. Grolier, Inc.*[6] The Court decided that from the outset, the focus of work product doctrine has been on materials prepared for use in litigation, either underway or anticipated. It is only work done in anticipation of, or for a trial, that is protected under the doctrine. Nor, said the Court, is it enough to trigger the work product doctrine that the contested materials were prepared by lawyers or represent legal thinking. This is because many corporate papers are routinely prepared and reviewed by lawyers. According to *Hickman v. Taylor*, supra, reports if made in ordinary course of business are not privileged. Finally, the Court said that a set of tax reserve figures, calculated for purpose of accurately stating a company's financial condition has in ordinary

[6] 462 U.S. 19 (1983).

parlance only that purpose: to support a finance statement and the independent audit of it. The Court concluded that the Textron work papers were required by statutory and audit requirements and were not necessarily protected by the work product doctrine. But that was not the end of the inquiry.

The Court next discussed the purpose of tax accrual work papers and whether or not they should be given work product protection. These judges pointed out that the tax audit work papers must be prepared by exchange-listed companies to comply with securities law and accounting principles for certified financial statements. Citing the famous case of *United States v. Arthur Young*,[7] the Court reasoned that the purpose of the tax accrual work papers is clearly not necessarily bundled with any sort of preparation for litigation. The Court said that the *Young* case made this point in refusing to create an accountant's work privilege for tax audit papers. In describing the auditor's function, the *Young* court stated:

> The auditor is ethically and professionally obligated to ascertain for himself as far as possible whether the corporation's contingent tax liabilities have been accurately stated.... Responsible corporate management would not risk a qualified evaluation of a corporate taxpayer's financial posture to forge cover for questionable positions reflected in prior tax return. *Arthur Young*, 465 U.S. 818–19.

The Court concluded that under the *Young* test, the purpose of work papers were to make book accounting entries, prepare financial statements, and obtain an unqualified audit from Ernst & Young. Consequently, the primary motivation was to ascertain sound business practice rather than to make preparation for future litigation.

Third, the Court was not convinced that the revelation of the tax accrual work papers in this case would raise the concern the work product doctrine is intended to remedy. These jurists said that the evidence in this case squarely supports the IRS's position. The work doctrine privilege is aimed at protecting the litigation process, specifically work done by counsel to

[7] 465 U.S. 805, 812 (1983); held that auditors have both a public responsibility to insure that financial statements are properly certified, and a corresponding private responsible to their client, to insure that the financial statements are properly certified.

assist in litigating the case. It is not a privilege intended to help the lawyer prepare corporate documents or other materials created in the ordinary course of business. So, said the Court, the rationale for the rule stops at this point because allowing IRS access to the tax accrual work papers simply did not discourage sound preparation for the Ernst & Young audit. This is so in this case because there was a legal obligation to soundly prepare such papers to comply with the securities law and accounting principles in order to have the financial statements certified by the auditor, see *Arthur Young* (supra). The Court indicated that responsible corporate management was required to prepare the work papers in order to obtain an unqualified evaluation of its financial condition from the auditors.

Fourth, the Court discussed whether the Internal Revenue Service's concern about widespread corporate abuse of tax laws and tax shelter abuse was well-founded. The Court averred that Textron apparently thinks it is unfair for the government to have access to its spreadsheets. But said the court, tax collection is not a game. Underpaying taxes is a threat to the public interest based on fair tax collections. Consequently, if a blueprint to Textron's possible improper deductions can be found in that firm's files, it is properly available to the government unless otherwise privileged. Having already decided that the work product doctrine does not apply, the Court indicated that the purpose of discovery is to assist in the proponent, in this case the IRS, in discovering the truth. Because the appropriate collection of revenues is essential to the operation of government, it is imperative and fair that the tax accrual work papers be furnished to the IRS.

Finally, the Court was satisfied that the government's concern about widespread corporate abuse of tax laws is well-founded. The Court opined that the underreporting of corporate taxes was likely endemic and serious. Textron's return was massive in length consisting of over 4000 pages. The IRS asked for the work papers only after finding a specific type of SILO transaction that had been commonly abused by taxpayers. It is because the proper collection of revenues is essential to government that administrative discovery is fair in this case. Shockingly, the court notes in a discussion of the tax accrual work papers that in some instances, the spreadsheet entries estimated the probability of IRS success in collecting the taxes on the SILO transactions at 100%. It is black letter law that a taxpayer is generally not allowed to report a position for which it does not have some reasonable basis. How likely is it that a corporation like Textron would have a reasonable basis for taking a position when its own work papers indicate that it has a no chance of winning on the merits? It sounds like the majority is convinced it is fair for the IRS to get the work sheets.

IV. Fairness

The ruling for the government gives the IRS further support for its policy to seek tax accrual work papers when taxpayers have entered into listed transactions and may cause the IRS to reconsider its "policy of restraint" in seeking tax accrual work papers in other situations. Also, we expect that the several states will take note of this decision and commence to aggressively seek accrual information.

This decision is obviously of concern to corporate accountants and lawyers, because it effectively deprives them of a way to protect their clients from having the IRS privy to preparation of tax work papers. But here, we think, that the appellate court was convinced that the work product doctrine had become an obstacle to the fair collection of taxes. The facts are not friendly to Textron. They want to hide from the IRS's prying eyes SILO transactions that their own advisors believed were not supportable if challenged by the IRS. The Court did not think that was fair to the government and other taxpayers. Finally, it is important to understand that this case does not stand for the proposition that work papers prepared for actual litigation are not protected. The Court clearly said that work papers prepared in anticipation of litigation are still protected. The court flatly rejected Textron's position that the work papers had a dual purpose of ordinary business and anticipated litigation. The Court was unconvinced that the primary motive for presentation of the work papers was anticipation of litigation.

V. Dealing with the Decision

What is the taxpayer to do now? First, in some respects, the Textron decision can produce perverse results. This is because when a taxpayer knows that the IRS might have a seat at the table, some taxpayers will be tempted not to disclose information to auditors and lawyers that could result in an IRS intervention. This withholding could actually result in a weaker tax enforcement system. But we expect that most corporations and taxpayers like Textron will try to clearly label work papers as materials prepared in anticipation of litigation, try to carefully segregate aggressive tax issues from less sensitive matters to limit the scope of any litigation, and involve external lawyers and accountants in an attempt to protect accrual work papers. Lastly, Congress ought to consider legislation that would allow taxpayers to obtain waivers to release certain kinds of information to third party auditors and lawyers without waiving the work product doctrine in regard to the IRS. The use of such waivers might result in a stronger tax enforcement system.

Finally, in a related development, the IRS recently issued Announcement 2010–2017, which indicates that the IRS plans to require the filing of a new schedule for reporting uncertain tax positions pursuant to FIN 48 (or other accounting standards such as IFRS) for tax returns relating to calendar year 2010 and for fiscal years that begin in 2010. This disclosure would be required by a business taxpayer with total assets in excess of $10 million. The recent denial of the Writ of Certiorari certainly strengthens the IRS's position in obtaining accrual information.

VI. Further Considerations

A. The Fourth Amendment

The Fourth Amendment[8] to the U.S. Constitution states:

> The right of the people to be secure in their persons, houses, papers, and effects, against unreasonable searches and seizures, shall not be violated, and no Warrants shall issue, but upon probable cause, supported by Oath or affirmation, and particularly describing the place to be searched, and the persons or things to be seized.

---

[8] https://www.google.com/search?site=&source=hp&q=Fourth+Amendment&oq=Fourth+Amendment&gs_l=hp.3..0l10.2293.2293.0.5755.2.2.0.0.0.0.174.277.0j2.2.0....0...1c.1.64.hp..0.1.173.0.pxuDwKbilEc.

If the IRS claim in *Textron* is not a violation of the Fourth Amendment, it is difficult to see what would be. Under present law, this corporation, and of course all others, is required to pay taxes, but that is it. It is not entailed to proffer to government authorities anything more than that. When and if it pays what the law requires, that ends its legal responsibility. For the IRS to thrust itself, forcibly, into the deliberations of a private company, before not only was it not found guilty of criminal behavior, it was not even accused of the same, constitutes a failure to uphold the rule of law.[9]

B. *Nemo judex in causa sua*

We also take not of the fact that the *Textron* case was tried in a government court. Here, two out of three of the parties were an agency of the state: the IRS and the Court. According to that old aphorism: he who is a judge in his own case cannot be trusted to be unbiased.

The principles of natural justice mandate that no one should be a judge in his own case. In this particular instance, one branch of government, the Court, presumes to judge another branch of government, the IRS. Not only does this constitute an appearance of bias, it is the paradigm case of such a violation of natural justice. Another aphorism is that not only must the Emperor's wife be pure, she must be seen to be pure. In like manner, justice must not only be actually done, it must also be widely seen to be done. It is difficult to see how this can be attained under present circumstances.

No truer words were ever said on this matter than these:

> The maxim that *no man is to be judge in his own case* should be held sacred. And that is not to be confined to a cause in which he is a party, but applies to a cause in which he has an interest....
>
> This will be a lesson to all ... tribunals to take care, not only that in their decrees they are not influenced by their personal interests, but to avoid the appearance of labouring under such an influence.[10]

---

[9] See on this Hayek, Friedrich A. 1976. *Law, Legislation and Liberty*. Vol. 2: *The Mirage of Social Justice*. Chicago: University of Chicago Press.

[10] Source: http://www.duhaime.org/LegalDictionary/N/NemoJudexInParteSua.aspx.

In Canada, the Supreme Court had occasion to reflect on the maxim in Brosseau v Alberta Securities Commission, Justice l'Heureux-Dubé:

> The maxim *nemo judex in causa sua debet esse* underlies the doctrine of reasonable apprehension of bias.
>
> It translates into the principle that no one ought to be a judge in his own cause. In this case, it is contended that the Chairman, in acting as both investigator and adjudicator in the same case, created a reasonable apprehension of bias.
>
> As a general principle, this is not permitted in law because the taint of bias would destroy the integrity of proceedings conducted in such a manner.

What we are saying is that whenever there is a law case between a branch of government such as the IRS,[11] that Federal and State courts in the United States, *all* of them, ought to recuse themselves on the basis of bias, possible or actual.[12] Who, then, should judge such legal altercations? This is unclear. Perhaps a Canadian court. Or the U.N. Or, maybe, even, horrors, a *private court*, such as the American Arbitration Association, or the Jewish Bet Din, or the Catholic Ecclesiastical court. We only say that it should not be a court which is part of the U.S. government, or that of any of the 50 states, if the maxim "No one should be a judge in his own case" is to be upheld.

---

[11] Indeed, *any* branch of government.

[12] On recusal, see McKeown, M. Margaret. 2010–2011. "To Judge or Not to Judge: Transparency and Recusal in the Federal System." *Review of Litigation*, Vol. 30; http://heinonline.org/HOL/Contents?handle=hein.journals/rol30&id=1&size=2&index=&collection=journals. Goldberg, Deborah, James J. Sample and David Pozen. "The Best Defense: Why Elected Courts Should Lead Recusal Reform." *Washburn Law Journal*, Vol. 46, No. 3, pp. 503–534, 2007; https://papers.ssrn.com/sol3/papers.cfm?abstract_id=997320. Sample, James J. and David Pozen. "Making Judicial Recusal More Rigorous." *Judges' Journal*, Vol. 46, pp. 17–24, Winter 2007, https://papers.ssrn.com/sol3/papers.cfm?abstract_id=997311. Day, Terri. "Buying Justice: Caperton v. A.T. Massey: Campaign Dollars, Mandatory Recusal and Due Process, 28 *Mississippi College Law Review* 359 (2009); https://papers.ssrn.com/sol3/papers.cfm?abstract_id=2497450. Osborn, Rebekah L. "Current development 2005–2006: Beliefs on the Bench: Recusal for Religious Reasons and the Model Code of Judicial Conduct," Summer, 2006, 19 *Geo. J. Legal Ethics* 895. Bassett, Debra Lyn. "Recusal and the Supreme Court." *Hastings Law Journal*, Vol. 56, p. 657, 2005, https://papers.ssrn.com/sol3/papers.cfm?abstract_id=594870.

C. IRS-gate

The IRS attempt to trespass into the private affairs of Textron comes with particular ill grace given IRS-gate. The former head of this organization Lois Lerner was found with her hand in the cookie jar related to her targeting of the Tea Party and other right wing groups.[13] Thus, the IRS shot itself in the foot[14] when it engaged in such nefarious partisan activities. If there is any justice in the word, this organization deserves to be transferred to the dust-bin of history.

VII. Conclusion

We see no warrant for inviting the IRS into the boardrooms of the nation's corporations on fishing expeditions. If a firm breaks the (tax) law, if extant tax law is to be upheld,[15] the proper procedure is to sue them afterwards, not coercively intrude on them before. Given the dire recent history of the IRS,[16] not only should they not be allowed to meddle in the deliberations of the business community, there is a strong case for disbanding this organization entirely, and, if revenue neutrality is to be achieved,[17] substituting for this intrusive bureaucracy a sales or value-added tax.

[13] Lederman, Leandra. 2016. "IRS Reform: Politics as Usual?" https://papers.ssrn.com/sol3/papers.cfm?abstract_id=2745370. Norquist, Grover. End the IRS Before It Ends Us: How to Restore a Low Tax, High Growth.... https://www.amazon.com/gp/search?index=books&linkCode=qs&keywords=9781455585816. Hackney, Philip T. 2015. "Should the IRS Never 'Target' Taxpayers? An Examination of the IRS Tea Party Affair." *Valparaiso University Law Review*, Vol. 49, (p. 453) https://papers.ssrn.com/sol3/papers.cfm?abstract_id=2587424.

[14] If not higher up.

[15] It would take us too far afield to engage in a critique of this proposition.

[16] Lois Lerner and IRS-Gate attacking the Tea Party in an unwarranted, biased manner.

[17] Itself a dubious proposition.

Credits

We thank the publishers of these articles which appeared in the following law reviews and law journals for reprint permission. We thank Nathan Fryzek and Christian Torsell for obtaining these permissions. We thank our co-authors as well: Lu Hardin, Patrick Tinsley, Clint Johnson, Mana Davidson, Alan White, Stacy Chandler, Katherine Wingfield and Pam Spikes.

Part I: Discrimination

Chapter 1. Whitehead, Roy, Walter Block and Lu Hardin. 1999. "Gender Equity in Athletics: Should We Adopt a Non-Discriminatory Model?" *The University of Toledo Law Review*, Vol. 30, No. 2, Winter, pp. 223–249; http://141.164.133.3/faculty/Block/Blockarticles/genderequity.htm; http://tinyurl.com/ypvz5h

Chapter 2. Whitehead, Roy and Walter Block. 2001. "Should the Government be Allowed to Engage in Racial, Sexual or Other Acts of Discrimination?" *Northern Illinois University Law Review*, Vol. 22, No. 1, Fall, pp. 53–84; http://www.walterblock.com/publications/government_discrimination.pdf (32)

W. E. Block, R. Whitehead, *Philosophy of Law*, Palgrave Studies in Classical Liberalism,
https://doi.org/10.1007/978-3-030-28360-5

Chapter 3. Whitehead, Roy, Walter Block and Patrick Tinsley. 2008. "Christian Landlords and the Free Exercise Clause: Sinners Need Not Apply," *Oklahoma City University Law Review*, Vol. 33, No. 1, Spring, pp. 115–150; http://141.164.133.3/faculty/Block/Articles%20for%20web/Christian%20Landlords.doc

Chapter 4 Whitehead, Roy and Walter Block. 2004. "The Boy Scouts, Freedom of Association and the Right to Discriminate: A Legal, Philosophical and Economic Analysis," *Oklahoma City Law Review*, Vol. 29, No. 3, Fall, pp. 851–882; http://tinyurl.com/24qjht

Chapter 5. Whitehead, Roy and Walter Block. 2002. "Sexual Harassment in the Workplace: A Property Rights Perspective," *University of Utah Journal of Law and Family Studies*, Vol. 4, pp. 226–263; http://141.164.133.3/faculty/Block/Articles%20for%20web/Sexual%20Harassment%20in%20the%20Workplace.doc

Part II: Education

Chapter 6. Whitehead, Roy and Walter Block. 1999. "Mandatory Student Fees: Forcing Some to Pay for the Free Speech of Others," *Whittier Law Review*, Vol. 20, No. 4, pp. 759–781; http://141.164.133.3/faculty/Block/Blockarticles/mfearningdifferentials.htm; http://141.164.133.3/faculty/Block/Blockarticles/mandatoryfees.htm

Chapter 7. Whitehead, Roy and Walter Block. 2000. "Direct Payment of State Scholarship Funds to Church-Related Colleges Offends the Constitution and Title VI," *Brigham Young University Journal of Public Law*, Vol. 14, No. 2, pp. 191–207; http://tinyurl.com/2dwelf; http://141.164.133.3/faculty/Block/Blockarticles/directpymt.htm

Part III: Environment

Chapter 8. Block, Walter and Roy Whitehead. 1999. "The Unintended Consequences of Environmental Justice," *Forensic Science International*, Vol. 100, Nos. 1 and 2, March, pp. 57–67; http://141.164.133.3/faculty/Block/Articles%20for%20web/Consequences%20of%20Enviromental%20Justice.doc

Chapter 9. Whitehead, Roy and Walter Block. 2000. "Environmental Justice Risks in the Petroleum Industry," *William and Mary Environmental Law and Policy Review*, Vol. 24, No. 1, Winter, pp. 67–88; https://scholarship.law.wm.edu/cgi/viewcontent.cgi?article=1246&context=wmelpr

Chapter 10. Whitehead, Roy and Walter Block. 2002. "Environmental Takings of Private Water Rights: the Case for Full Water Privatization," *Environmental Law Reporter*, October, pp. 11162–11176; https://www.researchgate.net/publication/228125587_Environmental_Takings_of_Private_Water_Rights__The_Case_for_Water_Privatization?ev=prf_pub

Chapter 11. Whitehead, Roy, Catherine Gould and Walter Block. 2004. "The value of private water rights: from a legal and economic perspective," *Albany Law Environmental Outlook Journal*, Vol. 9, No. 2, pp. 315–343; http://tinyurl.com/36p9he; http://141.164.133.3/faculty/Block/Articles%20for%20web/The%20value%20of%20Private%20Water%20Rights.doc

Part IV: Health

Chapter 12. Block, Walter, Roy Whitehead, Clint Johnson, Mana Davidson, Alan White and Stacy Chandler. 1999–2000. "Human Organ Transplantation: Economic and Legal Issues," *Quinnipiac College School of Law Health Journal*, Vol. 3, pp. 87–110; http://141.164.133.3/faculty/Block/Articles%20for%20web/Human%20Oragn%20Transplantation.doc; http://www.walterblock.com/publications/human_organ_transplantation.pdf

Chapter 13. Block, Walter, Katherine Wingfield and Roy Whitehead. 2003. "Re-Evaluating America's Failing Drug Control Laws: A Legal, Philosophical, and Economic Proposal," *Oklahoma City Law Review*, Vol. 28, No. 1, Spring, pp. 119–159; http://141.164.133.3/faculty/Block/Articles%20for%20web/Drug%20control%20Laws.doc

Part V: Crime

Chapter 14. Whitehead, Roy and Walter Block. 2003. "Taking the assets of the criminal to compensate victims of violence: a legal and philosophical approach," *Wayne State University Law School Journal of Law in Society*, Vol. 5, No. 1, Fall, pp. 229–254; http://www.walterblock.com/publications/block_taking-assets.pdf

Chapter 15. Block, Walter and Roy Whitehead. 2005. "Compromising the Uncompromisable: A Private Property Rights Approach to Resolving the Abortion Controversy," *Appalachian Law Review*, 4 (2), pp. 1–45; http://www.walterblock.com/publications/block-Whitehead_abortion-2005.pdf

Chapter 16. Whitehead, Roy, Pam Spikes and Walter E. Block. 2016–2017. "IRS joins the boardroom," *Rutgers Law Record: The Digital Journal of Rutgers School of Law*, Vol. 44, pp. 145–159; http://lawrecord.com/files/44_Rutgers_L_Rec_145.pdf

References

Anderson, Terry L., and Hill, Peter J., "Property Rights as a Common Pool Resource," *Bureaucracy vs. Environment: The Environmental Costs of Bureaucratic Governance*, John Baden and Richard L. Stroup, eds., Ann Arbor: University of Michigan Press, 1981.

Anderson, Terry L., and Leal, Donald R., *Free Market Environmentalism*, San Francisco: Pacific Research Institute, 1991.

Baird, Patricia, *Proceed with Care: Final Report of the Royal Commission on New Reproductive Technologies*, 2 volumes, Ottawa, Canada: Minister of government Services, 1993.

Baker, Nancy C., *Baby Selling: the Scandal of Black Market Adoptions*, New York: The Vanguard Press, 1978.

Barnett, Randy, and Hagel, John, eds., *Assessing the Criminal*, Cambridge MA: Ballinger, 1977.

Barro, Robert J., "Don't Tinker with Social Security. Reinvent It," *Hoover Digest*, 1998, No. 4, pp. 9–11.

Becker, Gary, "It's Simple: Hike the Minimum Wage, and You Put People Out of Work," *Business Week Magazine*, 6 March 1995.

Becker, Gary, *The Economics of Discrimination*, Chicago: The University of Chicago Press, 1957.

W. E. Block, R. Whitehead, *Philosophy of Law*, Palgrave Studies in Classical Liberalism,
https://doi.org/10.1007/978-3-030-28360-5

Been, Vicki, "Locally Undesirable Land Uses in Minority Neighborhoods: Disproportionate Siting or Market Dynamics?" *Yale Law Journal* (April 1994), pp. 1383–1398.

Benson, Bruce L., 1989, Enforcement of Private Property Rights in Primitive Societies: Law Without Government, *The Journal of Libertarian Studies*, Vol. IX, No. 1, Winter, pp. 1–26.

Benson, Bruce L., 1992, "The Impetus for Recognizing Private Property and Adopting Ethical Behavior in a Market Economy: Natural Law Government Law or Evolving Self Interest," *Review of Austrian Economics*, Vol. 6, No. 2, pp. 43–80.

Benson, Bruce L., 1981, "Land Use Regulation: A Supply and Demand Analysis of Changing Property Rights," *The Journal of Libertarian Studies*, Vol. V, No. 4, Fall, pp. 435–451.

Block, Walter, "Voluntary Slavery," *The Libertarian Connection*, Vol. I, No. 3, April 1969, pp. 9–11.

Block, Walter, 1977, "Coase and Demsetz on Private Property Rights," *The Journal of Libertarian Studies*, Vol. 1, No. 2, Spring, pp. 111–116.

Block, Walter, "Abortion, Woman and Fetus: Rights in Conflict?" *Reason*, April 1978, pp. 18–25.

Block, Walter, ed., *Zoning: Its Costs and Relevance for the 1980s*, Vancouver: The Fraser Institute, 1980.

Block, Walter, "Zoning: A Tragic Public Policy," in *The Freeman*, August 1981, pp. 470–477.

Block, Walter, "Public Goods and Externalities: The Case of Roads," *The Journal of Libertarian Studies*, Vol. VII, No. 1, Spring 1983, pp. 1–34.

Block, Walter, "Neglect of the Marketplace: The Questionable Economics of America's Bishops," *Notre Dame Journal of Law. Ethics and Public Policy*, Vol. 2, No. 1, 1985, pp. 125–160.

Block, Walter, "Trading Money for Silence," *University of Hawaii Law Review*, Vol. 8, No. 1, Spring 1986a, pp. 57–73.

Block, Walter, *The U.S. Bishops and Their Critics: An Economic and Ethical Perspective*, Vancouver: The Fraser Institute, 1986b.

Block, Walter, "Population Growth: Is it a problem?" *Resolving Global Problems into the 21st century: How Can Science Help Proceedings of the Fourth National Conference of Canadian Pugwash*, Ottawa: CSP Publications, 1989, pp. 30–61.

Block, Walter, ed., *Economics and the Environment: A Reconciliation*, Vancouver: The Fraser Institute, 1990a.

Block, Walter, "Protection of property rights key to maintaining resources," *Environment Policy and Law*, Vol. 1, No. 3, June 1990b, p. 28.

Block, Walter, "Resource Misallocation, Externalities and Environmentalism in the U.S. and Canada," *Proceedings of the 24th Pacific Northwest Regional Economic Conference*, 1990c, pp. 91–94.

Block, Walter, "Earning Happiness Through Homesteading Unowned Land: a comment on 'Buying Misery with Federal Land' by Richard Stroup," *Journal of Social Political and Economic Studies*, Vol. 15, No. 2, Summer 1990d, pp. 237–253.

Block, Walter, "Ownership will save the environment," *New Environment*, First Quarter, 1991a, pp. 41–43.

Block, Walter, "Dumping on the Economy: Why Artificial Prices Encourage Waste," *Journal of Pricing Management*, Vol. 14, No. 2, Spring 1991b, pp. 21–26.

Block, Walter, "The Economics of Discrimination," *The Journal of Business Ethics*, Vol. 11, 1992, pp. 241–254.

Block, Walter, "Libertarianism vs. Libertinism," *The Journal of Libertarian Studies: An Interdisciplinary Review*, Vol. 11, No. 1, 1994, pp. 117–128.

Block, Walter, "Ethics, Efficiency, Coasean Property Rights and Psychic Income: A Reply to Demsetz," *Review of Austrian Economics*, Vol. 8, No. 2, 1995, pp. 61–125.

Block, Walter, "O.J.'s Defense: A Reductio Ad Absurdum of the Economics of Ronald Coase and Richard Posner," *European Journal of Law and Economics*, 1996, Vol. 3, pp. 265–286.

Block, Walter, "The Case for De-Criminalizing Blackmail: A Reply to Lindgren and Campbell," *Western State University Law Review*, Vol. 24, No. 2, Spring, 1997, pp. 225–246.

Block, Walter E. 2001. "Stem Cell Research: The Libertarian Compromise." September 3; http://archive.lewrockwell.com/block/block5.html.

DiLorenzo, Thomas J. and Walter E. Block. 2017. An Austro-Libertarian Critique of Public Choice; Addleton Academic Publishers; www.addletonacademicpublishers.com.

Block, Walter, and Gordon, David, "Extortion and the Exercise of Free Speech Rights: A Reply to Professors Posner, Epstein, Nozick and Lindgren," *Loyola of Los Angeles Law Review*, Vol. 19, No. 1, November 1985, pp. 37–54.

Boerner, Christopher, and Thomas Lambert, "Environmental Injustice," *The Public Interest* (Winter 1995), pp. 61–82.

Buchanan, James M., and Gordon Tullock, *The Calculus of Consent: Logical Foundations of Constitutional Democracy*, Ann Arbor: University of Michigan, 1971.

Bullard, Robert D., "Solid Waste Sites and the Black Houston Community," *Sociological Inquiry* (Spring 1983), pp. 273–288.

Card, Orson Scott, and Kidd, Kathryn H., *Lovelock*, New York: Tor Books, 1994.

Center For The Study Of American Business (April 1998), pp. 21–22.

Chester Residents v SIEF, U.S. Third Circuit Court of Appeals.

Coase, Ronald H., "The Problem of Social Cost," *Journal of Law and Economics*, October 1960, Vol. 3, pp. 1–44.

Commission for Racial Justice of the United Church of Christ, *Toxic Wastes and Race in the United States*, 1987.

Cordato, Roy E., "Subjective Value, Time Passage, and the Economics of Harmful Effects," *Hamline Law Review*, Vol. 12, No. 2, Spring 1989, pp. 229–244.

Cordato, Roy E., *Welfare Economics and Externalities in an Open-Ended Universe: A Modern Austrian Perspective*, Boston: Kluwer, 1992b.

Cordato, Roy, E., "Knowledge Problems and the Problem of Social Cost," *Journal of the History of Economic Thought*, 14 Fall 1992a.

Demsetz, Harold, "Ethics and Efficiency in Property Rights Systems," in *Time, Uncertainty and Disequilibrium: Explorations of Austrian Themes*, Mario Rizzo, ed., Lexington, MA: D.C. Heath and Co., 1979.

Detroit Daily News (September 18, 1998), at B1, col. 1.

DiLorenzo, Thomas, "Does Capitalism Cause Pollution?" St. Louis, Washington University: Center for the Study of American Business, Contemporary Issues Series 38, 1990.

Ehrlich, Paul, *The Population Bomb*, New York: Sierra Club- Ballantine, 1968.

Ely, John Hart, 1973, "The Wages of Crying Wolf: A Comment on *Roe v. Wade*," *The Yale Law Journal*, 82: 935.

Englehardt, Tristam H., Jr., "Viability and the Use of the Fetus," *Ethics and Public Policy*, Beauchamp, Tom L., and Pinkard, Terry P., eds., Englewood Cliffs, NJ: Prentice-Hall, 1980.

Environmental Protection Agency, "*Interim Guidance for Investigating Title VI Administrative Complaints Challenging Permits*," February 5, 1998.

Environmental Protection Agency, 1997, "About Environmental Justice," URL http://www/epa.gov/swerosps/ej/aboutej.htm (September 30, 1997).

EPA's Environmental Racism Rule Blamed For Job Losses In Poor Areas, *The Washington Times*, October 14, 1998, at A4, col. 4.

Epstein, Richard A., 1974, "substantive Due Process by Any Other Name: The Abortion Cases," in Phillip B. Kurland, et al., eds., *The Supreme Court Review 1973*, Chicago: University of Chicago Press.

Epstein, Richard A., *Forbidden Grounds: The Case Against Employment Discrimination Laws*, Cambridge: Harvard University Press, 1992.

Epstein, Richard A., *Simple Rules for a Complex World*, 1995.

Epstein, Richard A., *Takings: Private Property and the Power of Eminent Domain*, Harvard University Press, Cambridge, Massachusetts and London, England, 1985.

Evers, Williamson N., 1977a, "Toward a reformulation of the law of contracts," *The Journal of Libertarian Studies*, Vol. 1, No. 1, Winter, pp. 3–14.

Evers, Williamson N., 1977b, "Social contract: a critique " *The Journal of Libertarian Studies*, Vol. 1, Nc. 3, Sumner, pp. 185–194.

Fairley, Peter, "Shintech Siting Dispute Awakens a Sleeping Giant," Chemical Week (October 8, 1997), p. 45.

Feinberg, Joel, *Matters of Life and Death: New Introductory Essays in Moral Philosophy*, Regan, Tom, ed., New York: Random House, 1981.

Foreman, Christopher H., Jr., "A Winning Hand? The Uncertain Future of Environmental Justice," *The Brookings Review* (Spring 1996), pp. 22–25.

Freitas, Robert A., Jr., "Fetal Adoption: A Technological Solution to the Problem of Abortion Ethics," *The Humanist* (May/June 1980), pp. 22–23.

Friedman, Milton, "Say 'No' to Intolerance," *Liberty*, 1991.

Gordon, Doris, 1995, "Abortion and Rights: Applying Libertarian Principles Correctly," *Studies in Prolife Feminism*, Vol. 1, No. 2, spring, pp. 121–140.

Gore, Al, *Earth in the Balance: Ecology and the Human Spirit*, Boston: Houghton-Mifflin, 1992.

Hayek, F.A., *Capitalism and the Historians*, ed., (essays by T.S. Ashton, L.M. Hacker, W.H. Hutt, B. de Jouvenel), Chicago: The University of Chicago Press, 1954.

Herbenick, Raymond N., "Remarks on Abortion, Abandonment and Adoption Opportunities," *Philosophy and Public Affairs* 5 (1975), p. 98.

Hill, Peter J., and Meiners, Roger E., eds., *Who Owns the Environment?*, New York: Rowman and Littlefield, 1998.

Holmes, Andrew, and Lary B. Cowart, "Environmental Racism: The New Liability for Industrial Site Selection," *Real Estate Issues* (April 1996), pp. 1–3.

Hoppe, Hans-Hermann, *A Theory of Socialism and Capitalism: Economics, Politics and Ethics*, Boston: Dordrecht, 1989.

Hoppe, Hans-Hermann, *The Economics and Ethics of Private Property: Studies in Political Economy and Philosophy*, Boston: Kluwer, 1993.

Horwitz, Morton J., *The Transformation of American Law: 1780–1860*, Cambridge: Harvard University Press, 1977.

Huebner, Stephen, "Are Storm Clouds Brewing On The Environmental Justice Horizon?"

Krecke, Elisabeth, "Law and the Market Order: An Austrian Critique of the Economic Analysis of Law," paper presented at the Ludwig von Mises Institute's Austrian Scholar's Conference, New York City, October 9–11, 1992.

Lambert, Thomas, and Christopher Boerner, "Environmental Inequity: Economic Causes, Economic Solutions," *Yale Journal of Regulation* (Winter 1997), pp. 195–234.

Levin, Michael, "Comparable Worth: The Feminist Road to Socialism," *Commentary*, September 1984.

Levin, Michael, *Feminism and Freedom*, New York: Transaction Books, 1987.

Levin, Michael, *Why Race Matters*, Westport, CT: Praeger, 1977.

Luper, Steven, *Invulnerability: On Securing Happiness*, Chicago: Open Court, 1996.

Machan, Tibor R., 1983, "Social Contract as a Basis of Norms: A Critique," *The Journal of Libertarian Studies*, Vol. 7, No. 1, Spring, pp. 141–145.

Mack, Eric, "In Defense of Blackmail," 41 *Philosophical Studies* 274 (1982).

Margaret N. Maxey and Robert L. Kuhn, eds., *Regulatory Reform: New Vision or Old Curse*, New York: Praeger, 1985.

Mastio, David, "Revolt Brews Against EPA: Agencies Civil Rights Policies Squelch Plants," McElroy, Wendy.

McGee, Robert W., "Should Superfund Be Wasted? The Case to Trash the Comprehensive Environmental Response, Compensation and Liability Act of 1980 (CERCLA)," *Glendale Law Review*, Vol 11, Nos. 1–2, 1992, pp. 120–142.

McGee, Robert W., "Superfund: It' Time for Repeal After a Decade of Failure," *UCLA Journal of Environmental Law and Policy*, 12:1, 1993, pp. 165–182.

McGee, Robert, and Block, Walter, "Pollution Trading Permits as a Form of Market Socialism, and the Search for a Real Market Solution to Environmental Pollution," *Fordham University Law and Environmental Journal*, Vol. VI, No. 1, Fall 1994, pp. 51–77.

Moore, Thomas Gale, 1991, *Central Planning USA-Style: The Case Against Corporate Average Fuel Economy (CAFE) Standards*, Stanford: Hoover Institution.

Morreall, John, "Of Marsupials and Men: A Thought Experiment on Abortion," *Dialogos*, 37 (1981), p. 16.

Mulligan, James J., *Choose Life*, St. Louis, MO: The Pope John 51 Center, 1991.

Nicholson, Susan T., "The Roman Catholic Doctrine of Therapeutic Abortion," *Feminism and Philosophy*, Vetterling-Braggin, Nary, Elliston, Frederick A., and English, Jane, eds., Totowa, NJ: Littlefield, Adams, 1978, p. 392.

North, Gary, *The Coase Theorem*, Tyler, TX: The Institute for Christian Economics, 1992.

North, Gary, *Tools of Dominion: The Case Laws of Exodus*, Tyler, TX: Institute for Christian Economics, 1990.

Nozick, Robert, *Anarchy, State, and Utopia*, New York: Basic Books Inc., 1974.

Overall, Christine, *Ethics and Human Reproduction: A Feminist Analysis*, Winchester, MA: Allen and Unwin, 1987.

Paul, Ellen Frankel, and Paul, Jeffrey, "Self Ownership, Abortion and Infanticide," *Journal of Medical Ethics*, 5 (1979), p. 134.

Payne, Henry, "Environmental Justice Kills Jobs for the Poor," *The Wall Street Journal* (September 16, 1997), at A16, col. 4.

Posner, Richard A., "The Law and Economics Movement," *American Economic Review*, Vol. 77, No. 2, 1987, pp. 2–13.

Posner, Richard A., *Economic Analysis of Law*, 3rd ed., Boston: Little Brown, 1986.

Rathje, William L., "Rubbish!" *Atlantic Monthly*, Vol. 264, No. 6, December 1989, pp. 99–109.

Ray, Dixie Lee, 1990, *Trashing the Planet*, Washington, DC: Regnery Gateway.

Ross, Steven L., "Abortion and the Death of the Fetus," *Philosophy and Public Affairs*, 11 (1982), p. 232.

Rothbard, Murray N., "Law, Property Rights, and Air Pollution," *Economics and the Environment: A Reconciliation*, Walter Block, ed., Vancouver: The Fraser Institute, 1990.

Rothbard, Murray N., "Buchanan and Tullock's *The Calculus of Consent*," in *The Logic of Action: Applications and Criticism from the Austrian School*, Vol. II, Cheltenham, UK: Edward Elgar, 1997, pp. 269–274.

Rothbard, Murray N., *For a New Liberty*, Macmillan, New York, 1973.

Rothbard, Murray N., *Man, Economy and State*, Auburn AL: Mises Institute, 1993.

Rothbard, Murray N., *The Ethics of Liberty*, Humanities Press, Atlantic Highlands, NJ, 1982.

Rowland, Robyn, "Motherhood, Patriarchal Power, Alienation and the Issue of 'Choice in Sex Pre-Selection," Corea, Gena, et al., eds., *Man-Made Women*, Bloomington, IN: Indiana University Press, 1987.

Simon, Julian, *The Ultimate Resource*, Princeton: Princeton University Press, 1981.

Smith, George H., 1978, "William Wollaston on property rights," *The Journal of Libertarian Studies*, Vol. 2, No. 3, Fall, pp. 217–224.

Sowell, Thomas, "Preferential Policies," in *Thinking About America: The United States in the 1990*, Annelise Anderson and Dennis L. Bark, eds., San Francisco: The Hoover Institution Press, 1988.

Sowell, Thomas, "*Weber* and *Bakke* and the presuppositions of 'Affirmative Action,'" *Discrimination, Affirmative Action and Equal Opportunity*, Walter Block and Michael Walker, eds., Vancouver: The Fraser Institute, 1982.

Sowell, Thomas, *Civil Rights: Rhetoric or Reality*, New York: William Morrow, 1984.

Sowell, Thomas, *Ethnic America*, New York: Basic Books, 1981.

Sowell, Thomas, *Migrations and cultures: A World View*, New York: Basic Books, 1996.

Sowell, Thomas, *Race and Culture: A World View*, New York: Basic Books, 1994.

Sowell, Thomas, *Race and Economics*, New York: Longman, 1975.

Sowell, Thomas, *The Economics and Politics of Pace: An International Perspective*, New York, Morrow, 1983.

Sowell, Thomas, *The Vision of the Anointed*, New York: Basic Books, 1995.

Stroup, Richard L., and Baden, John A., "Endowment Areas: A Clearing in the Policy Wilderness," *Cato Journal*, 2 Winter 1982, pp. 691–708.

Stroup, Richard L., and John C. Goodman, et al., (1991) *Progressive Environmentalism: A Pro-Human, Pro-Science, Pro-Free Enterprise Agenda for Change*, Dallas, TX: National Center for Policy Analysis, Task Force Report.

Taylor, Joan Kennedy, *Reclaiming the Mainstream: Individualist Feminism Rediscovered*, Buffalo, NY: Prometheus, 1992.

Thompson, Judith Jarvis, *Rights. Restitution and Risk*, Cambridge: Harvard University Press, 1986.

Thompson, Judith Jarvis, *The Realm of Bights*, Cambridge: Harvard University Press, 1990.

Thomson, Judith Jarvis, 1971, "A Defense of Abortion," *Philosophy and Public Affairs*, Vol. 1, No. 1, pp. 47–66; Reprinted in *Moral Problems*, 2nd ed., Rachels, James, ed., New York: Harper and Row, 1975.

Tribe, Lawrence, 1990, *Abortion: The Clash of Absolutes*, New York: W.W. Norton.

The manufacturer's authorised representative in the EU is Springer Nature Customer Service Centre GmbH, Europaplatz 3, 69115 Heidelberg, Germany. If you have any concerns regarding our products, please contact ProductSafety@springernature.com

Printed and bound by CPI Group (UK) Ltd, Croydon, CR0 4YY
05/10/2026
02228143-0006